חומש קורן מקראות הדורות
THE KOREN MIKRAOT HADOROT

פרשת בשלח
PARASHAT BESHALAḤ

קורן ירושלים

THE ROHR FAMILY EDITION

חומש קורן מקראות הדורות
THE KOREN MIKRAOT HADOROT

THE ZAHAVA AND MOSHAEL STRAUS EDITION OF SEFER SHEMOT

פרשת בשלח עם רש״י
PARASHAT BESHALAḤ WITH RASHI

TORAH TRANSLATION BY
Rabbi Lord Jonathan Sacks שליט״א

RASHI'S COMMENTARY TRANSLATED BY
Rabbi Jonathan Mishkin

•

KOREN PUBLISHERS JERUSALEM

The Koren Mikraot HaDorot, The Rohr Edition
Volume 16: Parashat Beshalaḥ
First Edition, 2020

Koren Publishers Jerusalem Ltd.
POB 4044, Jerusalem 9104001, ISRAEL
POB 8531, New Milford, CT 06776, USA

www.korenpub.com

Torah Translation © 2019, Jonathan Sacks
Koren Tanakh Font © 1962, 2019 Koren Publishers Jerusalem Ltd.

Commentary © Koren Publishers Jerusalem Ltd., except as noted:
Commentaries of Philo, used with permission of Kodesh Press
Commentaries Rabbi Joseph B. Soloveitchik, used with permission of the OU Press
Commentaries of Nehama Leibowitz, used with permission of the World Zionist Organization

Considerable research and expense have gone into the creation of this publication.
Unauthorized copying may be considered *geneivat da'at* and breach of copyright law.
No part of this publication (content or design, including use of the Koren fonts) may
be reproduced, stored in a retrieval system or transmitted in any form or by any means
electronic, mechanical, photocopying or otherwise, without the prior written permission of
the publisher, except in the case of brief quotations embedded in critical articles or reviews.

The Tanakh translation is excerpted from the Magerman Edition of The Koren Tanakh.

The creation of this work was made possible with the generous support
of the Jewish Book Trust Inc.

Printed in ISRAEL

ISBN 978 965 7760 71 0

KMDBS01

The Rohr Family Edition of
The Koren Mikraot HaDorot
pays tribute to the memory of

Mr. Sami Rohr ז״ל
ר׳ שמואל ב״ר יהושע אליהו ז״ל

who served his Maker with joy
and whose far-reaching vision, warm open hand, love of Torah,
and love for every Jew were catalysts for the revival and growth of
vibrant Jewish life in the former Soviet Union
and in countless communities the world over

and to the memory of his beloved wife

Mrs. Charlotte Rohr (née Kastner) ע״ה
שרה בת ר׳ יקותיאל יהודה ע״ה

who survived the fires of the Shoah to become
the elegant and gracious matriarch,
first in Colombia and later in the United States,
of three generations of a family
nurtured by her love and unstinting devotion.
She found grace in the eyes of all those whose lives she touched.

Together they merited to see all their children
build lives enriched by faithful commitment
to the spreading of Torah and *Ahavat Yisrael*.

Dedicated with love by
The Rohr Family
NEW YORK, USA

Dedicated in memory of

Rabbi Dr. Norman Lamm, זצ"ל

President of Yeshiva University and Expositor of Centrist Orthodoxy
Torah Scholar, Philosopher, Leader, Orator and Rabbi
Beloved Husband, Father, Grandfather and Great Grandfather

תניא אמר רבי מאיר מניין לתחיית המתים מן התורה
שנאמר "אז ישיר משה ובני ישראל את השירה הזאת לה'"
שר לא נאמר אלא ישיר מכאן לתחיית המתים מן התורה

(Sanhedrin 91b)

Who made the words of Torah into a shira "that can heal the sick,
revive weary spirits, [and] elevate downtrodden hearts"
and taught that "Torah is eternity ensconced in music."

The Magerman Family

The Sinensky Family

CONTENTS

Publisher's Preface
xi

A Note on the Translation of Rashi
xv

PARASHAT BESHALAḤ WITH RASHI
1

HAFTARAT BESHALAḤ
57

FOR PARASHAT BESHALAḤ WITH COMMENTARIES AND THE BIBLICAL IMAGINATION
TURN TO THE OTHER END OF THIS VOLUME.

PUBLISHER'S PREFACE

The genius of Jewish commentary on the Torah is one of huge and critical import. Jewish life and law for millennia have been directed by our interpretations of the Torah, and each generation has looked to its rabbinic leadership for a deeper understanding of its teachings, its laws, its stories.

For centuries, *Mikraot Gedolot* have been a core part of understanding the Ḥumash; the words of Rashi, Ibn Ezra, Ramban, Rashbam, Ralbag, and other classic commentators illuminate and help us understand the Torah. But traditional editions of *Mikraot Gedolot* present only a slice in time and a small selection of the corpus of Jewish commentators. Almost every generation has produced rabbinic scholars who speak to their times, from Philo and Onkelos two thousand years ago, to Rabbi Joseph B. Soloveitchik, Rabbi Aharon Kotler, the Lubavitcher Rebbe, and Nehama Leibowitz in ours.

The Koren Mikraot HaDorot – Scriptures or Interpretations for the Generations – brings two millennia of Torah commentary into the hands and homes of Jews around the world. Readers will be able to encounter not only the classic commentators, but to gain a much broader sense of the issues that scholars grappled with in their time and the inspiration they drew from the ancient texts. We see, for example, how Philo speaks to an assimilating Greek Jewish audience in first-century Alexandria, and how similar yet different it is from Rabbi Samson Raphael Hirsch's approach to an equally assimilating nineteenth-century German readership; how the perspectives of Rabbi Soloveitchik and Rabbi Kotler differ in a post-Holocaust world; how Rav Se'adya Gaon interpreted the Torah for the Jews of Babylonia. It is an exciting journey through Jewish history via the unchanging words of the Torah.

◀

The text of the Torah features the exceptional new translation of Rabbi Lord Jonathan Sacks, together with the celebrated and meticulously accurate Koren Hebrew text. Of course, with the exception of Rashi – for whom we present an entirely new translation in full – the commentaries are selected. We offer this anthology not to limit our reader's exploration but rather as a gateway for further learning of Torah and its commentaries on a broader and deeper level than space here permits. We discuss below how to use this book.

We must thank **Pamela and George Rohr** of New York, who recognized the unique value of the *Koren Mikraot HaDorot* and its ability to communicate historical breadth and context to the reader. For my colleagues here at Koren, we thank you; for the many generations of users who will find this a continuing source of new learning, we are forever in your debt.

We also are indebted to **Zahava and Moshael Straus**, true leaders of this Jewish generation in so many fields, who have invested in the entire book of Shemot. Together, we were thus able to launch this innovative and unique project.

We are honored to acknowledge and thank **Debra and David Magerman**, whose support for the Koren Ḥumash with Rabbi Sacks's exemplary translation and commentary laid the foundation for the core English text of this work.

Finally, I must personally thank **Rabbi Marvin Hier**, with whom I had a special breakfast some years ago at the King David Hotel. During the meal, he raised the problem that so few people knew the writings of Rabbi Joseph B. Soloveitchik and Rabbi Aharon Kotler on the Torah; and I, who had just read some of Philo's work, had the same reaction. From that conversation came the seed for this project.

HOW TO USE *THE KOREN MIKRAOT HADOROT*

The Koren Mikraot HaDorot will be a fifty-five-volume edition of the Ḥumash (one for each *parasha* plus a companion volume). Each of the fifty-four volumes of the *parashot* can be read from right to left (Hebrew opening side), and left to right (English opening side).

Opening from the Hebrew side offers:
- the full Torah text, the translation of Rabbi Sacks, and the full commentary of Rashi in both Hebrew and the new English translation

- all *haftarot* associated with the *parasha* of the volume, including Rosh Ḥodesh and special readings, both in Hebrew and English

Opening from the English side presents four sections:
- **THE TIME OF THE SAGES** – includes commentaries from the Second Temple period and the talmudic period
- **THE CLASSIC COMMENTATORS** – quotes selected explanations by Rashi as well as most of the commentators found in traditional *Mikraot Gedolot*
- **CONFRONTING MODERNITY** – selects commentaries from the eighteenth century to the close of the twentieth century
- **THE BIBLICAL IMAGINATION** – features essays surveying some of the broader conceptual ideas as a supplement to the linear, text-based commentary

The first three of these sections each feature the relevant verses, in Hebrew and English, on the page alongside their respective commentaries, in chronological order, providing the reader with a single window onto the text without excessive page turning.

In addition to being a valuable resource in a Jewish home or synagogue library, we conceived of these volumes as a weekly accompaniment in the synagogue. There is scope for the reader to study each *parasha* on a weekly basis in preparation for the reading on Shabbat. One may select a particular group of commentators for study that week, or perhaps alternate between ancient and modern viewpoints. Some readers may choose to delve into the text through verse-by-verse interpretation, while others may prefer a conceptual perspective on the *parasha* as a whole. The broad array of options for learning means this is a series which can be returned to year after year, always presenting new insights and new approaches to understanding the text.

ACKNOWLEDGMENTS

The creation of this book was possible only thanks to the small but exceptional team here at Koren Jerusalem. We are grateful to:
- Rabbi Tzvi Hersh Weinreb, שליט״א, who conceptualized the structure of the project and provides both moral and halakhic leadership at Koren
- Rabbi Shai Finkelstein, whose encyclopedic knowledge of Torah and its interpreters is equaled only by his community leadership, formerly in Memphis and today in Jerusalem
- Rabbi Yedidya Naveh, whose knowledge, organizational skills, and superb leadership brought the disparate elements together

▸ Rabbi Jonathan Mishkin, the principal translator of the commentaries and all of the Rashi, who crafted a fluent, accurate, and eloquent English translation

Our design, editing, typesetting, and proofreading staff, including Tani Bayer, Esther Be'er, Debbie Ismailoff, Estie Dishon, and Carolyn Budow Ben David, enabled an attractive, user-friendly, and accurate edition of these works.

> "One silver basin" (Numbers 7:13) was brought as a symbol of the Torah, which has been likened to wine, as the verse states: "And drink of the wine which I have mingled" (Proverbs 9:5). Because it is customary to drink wine in a basin – as we see in the verse "that drink wine in basins" (Amos 6:6) – he therefore brought a basin. "Of seventy shekels, after the shekel of the sanctuary" (Numbers 7:13). Why? Because just as the numerical value of "wine" [*yayin*] is seventy, so there are seventy modes of expounding the Torah. (Bemidbar Rabba 13:16)

Each generation produces exceptional rabbinic, intellectual leadership. It has been our purpose to enable all Jews to taste the wine of those generations, in the hope of expanding the breadth and depth of their knowledge. Torah is our greatest treasure, and we need the wisdom of those generations to better understand this bountiful gift from God. We hope that we at Koren can deepen that understanding for all who seek it.

Matthew Miller, Publisher
Jerusalem, 5780 (2019)

A NOTE ON THE TRANSLATION OF RASHI

The translation of Rashi's commentary provided here is complete and unabridged, following the meticulously researched Hebrew version of the commentary published by Koren. This version omits some material published in other editions that was found likely to have been added later by Rashi's students and other authors. We have included all of Rashi's numerous grammatical and linguistic discussions, even though these tend to be of less interest to the English-speaking reader, for two reasons: First, we felt it important for the readership to be confident that they are holding a complete version of Rashi's commentary and to know that they are not missing any matter of potential interest it might contain. Second, we wished to impress upon the reader that the elegant Sacks translation of the Torah included in this volume represents only one reading among many possible interpretations. Rashi's inquiries into the meanings of individual words and phrases emphasize the ambiguity of the verses and the potential of any passage to be interpreted in several different ways. This multifaceted nature of the Torah is a central theme of *The Koren Mikraot HaDorot*.

The inclusion of these discussions – often technical and sometimes confusing – bears implications for the translation. Here the translator was often forced to insert himself into the discussion to clearly establish the grammatical difficulty or ambiguity in the Hebrew text that is troubling Rashi. Since these difficulties are not always conveyed in the Sacks verse translation, the reader will find bracketed editorial comments used more aggressively in these discussions. The editor's notes also serve to supply the English-speaking reader with relevant details regarding Hebrew grammar that Rashi assumes to be known to his audience, which are necessary to understanding his point.

Here at the outset, we will provide a very brief overview of the Hebrew system of *binyanim*, or Hebrew verb forms, which is central to so many of Rashi's grammatical arguments.

Hebrew verbs, which are always conjugated by number, person, gender, and tense, are also divided into seven categories of verbs called *binyanim*. Three of these are in the active voice, three passive, and one in a reflexive voice that is neither active nor passive. In theory, any three-letter root (*shoresh*) in Hebrew can be conjugated in any one of these forms, with slightly different meanings in each one, though few roots exist in all forms. Readers who encounter one of Rashi's discourses analyzing to which class a given verb belongs can refer to the following chart to orient themselves.

BINYAN NAME	EXAMPLE (PAST/FUTURE)	VOICE			
Paal (Kal) – פָּעַל (קל)	Katav/Yikhtov – write	Active			Simple
Hifil – הִפְעִיל	Hikdish/Yakdish – consecrate	Active		Causative	
Pi'el – פִּעֵל	Giddel/Yegaddel – promote or exalt	Active	Intensive		
Hitpael – הִתְפָּעֵל	Hitgaddel/Yitgaddel – become great	Reflexive			
Pual – פֻּעַל	Guddal/Yeguddal – be promoted or exalted	Passive			
Hufal – הֻפְעַל	Hukdash/Yukdash – be consecrated	Passive			
Nifal – נִפְעַל	Nikhtav/Yikkatev – be written	Passive			

Each of the three active conjugations pairs with one of the passive ones, as seen in the above chart, such that the seven *binyanim* can be simplified into three more basic forms. The simple form (*paal/nifal*) denotes simple actions. The causative form (*hifil/hufal*) is reserved for actions induced by the subject in the object, e.g., to cause something to become holy (consecrate). The intensive form (*pi'el/pual*) describes a special form of the action, usually more significant or intense. The reflexive form is considered a third subgroup of the intensive form and is used for actions done to oneself.

◀

Rashi's grammatical discussions also focus on the vocalization (*nikkud*, or vowel marks) of the Hebrew text. The reader can review the names of the vowel marks in the following chart, as well as see how these vowels are transliterated in this edition.

VOWEL MARK	NAME	TRANSLITERATION
בְּ	Sheva (*Ḥataf* when combined with a *segol, pataḥ,* or *kamatz*)	*e* or silent
בֶּ	Segol (in Rashi's language: *Pataḥ Katan*)	*e*
בַּ	Pataḥ	*a*
בָּ	Kamatz	*a* or *o*
בִּ	Ḥirik	*i*
בֵּ	Tzerei (in Rashi's language, also: *Kamatz Katan*)	*e* or *ei*
בֹ	Ḥolam (in Rashi's language: *Melafum*)	*o*
בֻּ	Kubbutz (in Rashi's language: *Shuruk*)	*u*
בוּ	Shuruk	*u*

For Rashi's terms in Old French, we have been guided by Yisrael Gukovitzky's dictionary *Targum HaLaaz* (1985).

Yedidya Naveh, Managing Editor
Jerusalem, 5780 (2019)

פרשת בשלח
PARASHAT BESHALAḤ

חומש עם רש"י
THE ḤUMASH WITH RASHI

13 **17** When Pharaoh let the people go, God did not lead them through the land of the Philistines, though it was the shorter way; "If the people face war," thought God, "they will change **18** their minds and go back to Egypt." So He led them on a roundabout course, by way of the wilderness, to the Sea of Reeds. **19** The Israelites left Egypt armed for battle. And Moshe took with him the remains of Yosef, who had bound the Israelites by oath: "When God comes to your aid, bring my remains

יג יז | וַיְהִי בְּשַׁלַּח פַּרְעֹה... וְלֹא־נָחָם. נְהָגָם, כְּמוֹ: "לֵךְ נְחֵה אֶת הָעָם" (להלן לב, לד), "בְּהִתְהַלֶּכְךָ תַּנְחֶה אֹתָךְ" (משלי ו, כב):

13:17 | וַיְהִי בְּשַׁלַּח פַּרְעֹה...וְלֹא־נָחָם – *When Pharaoh let...did not lead them*: The phrase means: "Did not lead them." The verb *naḥam* here is similar to its usage in the verse *Now go and lead [neḥei] the people* (32:34) and the verse *When you walk, it shall lead [tanḥeh] you* (Proverbs 6:22).

כִּי קָרוֹב הוּא. וְנוֹחַ לָשׁוּב בְּאוֹתוֹ הַדֶּרֶךְ לְמִצְרַיִם. וּמִדְרְשֵׁי אַגָּדָה יֵשׁ הַרְבֵּה:

כִּי קָרוֹב הוּא – *Though it was the shorter way*: Taking that route would have made it easy for Israel to return to Egypt. There are many midrashim that explain this clause.

בִּרְאוֹתָם מִלְחָמָה. כְּגוֹן מִלְחֶמֶת "וַיֵּרֶד הָעֲמָלֵקִי וְהַכְּנַעֲנִי" וְגוֹ' (במדבר יד, מה), אִם הָלְכוּ דֶּרֶךְ יָשָׁר הָיוּ חוֹזְרִים. מַה אִם כְּשֶׁהִקִּיפָם דֶּרֶךְ מְעֻקָּם אָמְרוּ: "נִתְּנָה רֹאשׁ וְנָשׁוּבָה מִצְרָיְמָה" (שם פסוק ד), אִם הוֹלִיכָם בִּפְשׁוּטָה עַל אַחַת כַּמָּה וְכַמָּה:

בִּרְאֹתָם מִלְחָמָה – *If the people face war*: Israel did eventually encounter battle, as the verse states: *Then the Amalekites came down, and the Canaanites who dwelled in that hill country* (Numbers 14:45). If the nation had followed the straight highway, they would have gone back to Egypt. We see that even though God led the people by a circuitous route, they still moaned: *Let us appoint a chief, and let us return to Egypt* (Numbers 14:4). So they surely would have attempted to return to that land had they been traveling on a direct road.

פֶּן יִנָּחֵם. יַחְשְׁבוּ מַחֲשָׁבָה עַל שֶׁיָּצְאוּ וְיִתְּנוּ לֵב לָשׁוּב:

פֶּן־יִנָּחֵם – *They will change their minds*: They will question the benefits of having left Egypt and set their minds to return.

יח | וַיַּסֵּב. הֱסִבָּם מִן הַדֶּרֶךְ הַפְּשׁוּטָה לַדֶּרֶךְ הָעֲקוּמָה:

18 | וַיַּסֵּב – *So He led them on a roundabout course*: He diverted them [*hesibbam*] from the direct route, toward an indirect one.

יַם־סוּף. כְּמוֹ לְיַם סוּף. וְסוּף הוּא לְשׁוֹן אֲגַם שֶׁגְּדֵלִים בּוֹ קָנִים, וְכֵן: "וַתָּשֶׂם בַּסּוּף" (לעיל ב, ג), "קָנֶה וָסוּף קָמֵלוּ" (ישעיה יט, ו):

יַם־סוּף – *The Sea of Reeds*: [Literally, simply "the Sea of Reeds," without the preposition "to."] The phrase should be read as if prefaced by a prepositional letter *lamed* – meaning, "to the Sea of Reeds." The term *suf* connotes a marshy area where reeds grow, as in the verse *She laid the child in it and placed it among the reeds [basuf] by the bank of the Nile* (2:3) and the verse *The rushes and reeds [suf] shall wither* (Isaiah 19:6).

שמות | פרק יג | בשלח

יז וַיְהִ֗י בְּשַׁלַּ֣ח פַּרְעֹה֮ אֶת־הָעָם֒ וְלֹא־נָחָ֣ם אֱלֹהִ֗ים דֶּ֚רֶךְ אֶ֣רֶץ פְּלִשְׁתִּ֔ים כִּ֥י קָר֖וֹב ה֑וּא כִּ֣י ׀ אָמַ֣ר אֱלֹהִ֗ים פֶּן־ יח יִנָּחֵ֥ם הָעָ֛ם בִּרְאֹתָ֥ם מִלְחָמָ֖ה וְשָׁ֥בוּ מִצְרָֽיְמָה: וַיַּסֵּ֨ב אֱלֹהִ֧ים ׀ אֶת־הָעָ֛ם דֶּ֥רֶךְ הַמִּדְבָּ֖ר יַם־ס֑וּף וַחֲמֻשִׁ֛ים יט עָל֥וּ בְנֵי־יִשְׂרָאֵ֖ל מֵאֶ֥רֶץ מִצְרָֽיִם: וַיִּקַּ֥ח מֹשֶׁ֛ה אֶת־ עַצְמ֥וֹת יוֹסֵ֖ף עִמּ֑וֹ כִּי֩ הַשְׁבֵּ֨עַ הִשְׁבִּ֜יעַ אֶת־בְּנֵ֤י יִשְׂרָאֵל֙ לֵאמֹ֔ר פָּקֹ֨ד יִפְקֹ֤ד אֱלֹהִים֙ אֶתְכֶ֔ם וְהַעֲלִיתֶ֧ם אֶת־

וַחֲמֻשִׁים. אֵין 'חֲמֻשִׁים' אֶלָּא מְזֻיָּנִים, וְכֵן הוּא אוֹמֵר: "וְאַתֶּם תַּעַבְרוּ חֲמֻשִׁים" (יהושע א, יד). וְכֵן תִּרְגֵּם אוּנְקְלוֹס "מְזָרְזִין", כְּמוֹ: "וַיָּרֶק אֶת חֲנִיכָיו" (בראשית יד, יד), "וְזָרֵיז". דָּבָר אַחֵר, "וַחֲמֻשִׁים", מְחֻמָּשִׁים, אֶחָד מֵחֲמִשָּׁה יָצְאוּ וְאַרְבָּעָה חֲלָקִים מֵתוּ בִּשְׁלֹשֶׁת יְמֵי אֲפֵלָה:

יט **הַשְׁבֵּעַ הִשְׁבִּיעַ.** הִשְׁבִּיעָם שֶׁיַּשְׁבִּיעוּ לִבְנֵיהֶם. וְלָמָּה לֹא הִשְׁבִּיעַ לְבָנָיו שֶׁיִּשָּׂאוּהוּ לְאֶרֶץ כְּנַעַן מִיָּד כְּמוֹ שֶׁהִשְׁבִּיעַ יַעֲקֹב? אָמַר יוֹסֵף: אֲנִי שַׁלִּיט הָיִיתִי בְּמִצְרַיִם וְהָיָה סֵפֶק בְּיָדִי לַעֲשׂוֹת, אֲבָל בָּנַי לֹא יַנִּיחוּם מִצְרִים לַעֲשׂוֹת, לְכָךְ הִשְׁבִּיעַ לְכְשֶׁיִּגָּאֲלוּ וְיֵצְאוּ מִשָּׁם שֶׁיִּשָּׂאוּהוּ:

וְהַעֲלִיתֶם אֶת עַצְמֹתַי מִזֶּה אִתְּכֶם. לְאֶחָיו הִשְׁבִּיעַ כֵּן, לָמַדְנוּ שֶׁאַף עַצְמוֹת כָּל הַשְּׁבָטִים הֶעֱלוּ עִמָּהֶם, שֶׁנֶּאֱמַר "אִתְּכֶם":

וַחֲמֻשִׁים – *Armed for battle*: The term *ḥamushim* always means "armed." We find a similar usage in the verse *But you shall pass before your brethren armed* (Joshua 1:14). The Targum renders the adjective as *mezarezin* ["armed"], the same verb he uses in translating the verse *He armed his trained servants* [Genesis 14:14; concerning a battle fought by Avraham] – *vezareiz*. An alternative interpretation for the word *ḥamushim* is to see it as a form of *ḥamisha* [meaning "five"]. According to this understanding, only a fifth of the Israelites survived to leave Egypt, while the other four fifths perished during the three days of darkness.

19 **הַשְׁבֵּעַ הִשְׁבִּיעַ** – *Who had bound by oath*: The doubled Hebrew verb connotes that Yosef had made the Israelites swear that they would in turn make their children swear to take his bones along when they departed Egypt. One might ask why Yosef did not ask his sons to bring his body to Canaan for burial immediately upon his death, as Yaakov had. Yosef understood that because he ruled Egypt, he had the privilege of burying his father wherever he wanted. However, he suspected that the Egyptians would not grant his own sons that same license. He therefore made the family swear to take his remains with them upon their eventual redemption.

וְהַעֲלִיתֶם אֶת־עַצְמֹתַי מִזֶּה אִתְּכֶם – *Bring my remains with you out of here*: Yosef made his brothers promise that they would demand that their own children take their bones to Canaan when they quit Egypt. The term "with you" [*ittekhem*] suggests that Yosef wanted his body to exit Egypt along with the bodies of his brothers.

EXODUS | CHAPTER 14 — THE ḤUMASH WITH RASHI | BESHALAḤ | 4

20 with you out of here." They set out from Sukkot and camped
21 at Etam, at the edge of the desert. The LORD went ahead of them by day in a column of cloud to guide them, and at night in a column of fire to give them light, so that they might travel
22 day and night. Neither the column of cloud by day nor that of fire by night once departed from the people.
14 1 ▸ Then the LORD said to Moshe, "Speak to the Israelites and
2 tell them to turn back and camp in front of Pi HaḤirot, between Migdol and the sea, before Baal Tzefon. Encamp fac-
3 ing it, by the sea. Pharaoh will think that the Israelites are

כ| וַיִּסְעוּ מִסֻּכֹּת. בַּיּוֹם הַשֵּׁנִי, שֶׁהֲרֵי בָּרִאשׁוֹן בָּאוּ מֵרַעְמְסֵס לְסֻכּוֹת (לעיל יב, לז):

כא| לַנְחֹתָם הַדֶּרֶךְ. נָקוּד פַּתָּח, שֶׁהוּא כְּמוֹ לְהַנְחוֹתָם, כְּמוֹ "לַרְאֹתְכֶם בַּדֶּרֶךְ אֲשֶׁר תֵּלְכוּ בָהּ" (דברים א, לג) שֶׁהוּא כְּמוֹ לְהַרְאוֹתְכֶם, אַף כָּאן לְהַנְחוֹתָם עַל יְדֵי שָׁלִיחַ. וּמִי הוּא הַשָּׁלִיחַ? עַמּוּד הֶעָנָן, וְהַקָּדוֹשׁ בָּרוּךְ הוּא בִּכְבוֹדוֹ מוֹלִיכוֹ לִפְנֵיהֶם, וּמִכָּל מָקוֹם אֶת עַמּוּד הֶעָנָן הֵכִין לְהַנְחוֹתָם עַל יָדוֹ, שֶׁהֲרֵי עַל יְדֵי עַמּוּד הֶעָנָן הֵם הוֹלְכִים. עַמּוּד הֶעָנָן אֵינוֹ לְאוֹרָה אֶלָּא לְהוֹרוֹתָם הַדֶּרֶךְ:

כב| לֹא־יָמִישׁ. הַקָּדוֹשׁ בָּרוּךְ הוּא אֶת "עַמּוּד הֶעָנָן יוֹמָם וְעַמּוּד הָאֵשׁ לָיְלָה", מַגִּיד שֶׁעַמּוּד הֶעָנָן מַשְׁלִים לְעַמּוּד הָאֵשׁ וְעַמּוּד הָאֵשׁ מַשְׁלִים לְעַמּוּד הֶעָנָן, שֶׁעַד שֶׁלֹּא יִשְׁקַע זֶה עוֹלֶה זֶה:

יד ב| וְיָשֻׁבוּ. לַאֲחוֹרֵיהֶם, לְצַד מִצְרַיִם הָיוּ מְקָרְבִין כָּל יוֹם הַשְּׁלִישִׁי, כְּדֵי לְהַטְעוֹת אֶת פַּרְעֹה שֶׁיֹּאמַר תּוֹעִים הֵם בַּדֶּרֶךְ, כְּמוֹ שֶׁנֶּאֱמַר: "וְאָמַר פַּרְעֹה לִבְנֵי יִשְׂרָאֵל" וְגוֹ' (להלן פסוק ג):

20| וַיִּסְעוּ מִסֻּכֹּת – *They set out from Sukkot*: Israel left Sukkot on the day after the exodus from Egypt, for on the first day they had traveled to Sukkot from Ramesses [see 12:37].

21| לַנְחֹתָם הַדֶּרֶךְ – *To guide them*: The letter *lamed* prefixed to the word *lanḥotam* is vocalized with a *pataḥ*. This is because the word is actually a contraction of *lehanḥotam*. We find a similar contraction in the verse *Fire by night to show you [larotekhem] by what way you should go* (Deuteronomy 1:33), a verb which should be understood as if it read *leharotekhem*. [And just as in that verse the "showing" was accomplished my means of an agent,] here too, the sense is that God was directing Israel by means of an emissary. This was the column of cloud that guided Israel through the desert, while God himself in turn directed the cloud before the nation. In any event, it was God who prepared the column of cloud to lead Israel, to show them the way to go. This phenomenon was not meant to provide light for the people, just to guide them.

22| לֹא־יָמִישׁ – *Neither departed*: God did not for a moment remove *the column of cloud by day nor that of fire by night*. This means that the two miraculous entities overlapped in their duties: the column of cloud appeared while the pillar of fire still hung in the sky, and at the end of its watch the fire waited for the cloud to rise before receding.

14 2| וְיָשֻׁבוּ – *Turn back*: On the third day, God instructed Israel to turn around and head back toward Egypt in order to deceive Pharaoh. When the king learns about Israel's meandering on the desert paths, he would say that the nation was disoriented and confused, as the verse states: *Pharaoh will think that the Israelites are lost across the land* (14:3).

◂

שמות | פרק יד | בשלח

כ עַצְמֹתַי מִזֶּה אִתְּכֶם: וַיִּסְעוּ מִסֻּכֹּת וַיַּחֲנוּ בְאֵתָם
כא בִּקְצֵה הַמִּדְבָּר: וַיהוָֹה הֹלֵךְ לִפְנֵיהֶם יוֹמָם בְּעַמּוּד
עָנָן לַנְחֹתָם הַדֶּרֶךְ וְלַיְלָה בְּעַמּוּד אֵשׁ לְהָאִיר לָהֶם
כב לָלֶכֶת יוֹמָם וָלָיְלָה: לֹא־יָמִישׁ עַמּוּד הֶעָנָן יוֹמָם
וְעַמּוּד הָאֵשׁ לָיְלָה לִפְנֵי הָעָם:

יד א וַיְדַבֵּר יְהוָֹה אֶל־מֹשֶׁה לֵּאמֹר: דַּבֵּר אֶל־בְּנֵי יִשְׂרָאֵל
ב וְיָשֻׁבוּ וְיַחֲנוּ לִפְנֵי פִּי הַחִירֹת בֵּין מִגְדֹּל וּבֵין הַיָּם לִפְנֵי
בַּעַל צְפֹן נִכְחוֹ תַחֲנוּ עַל־הַיָּם: וְאָמַר פַּרְעֹה לִבְנֵי
ג יִשְׂרָאֵל נְבֻכִים הֵם בָּאָרֶץ סָגַר עֲלֵיהֶם הַמִּדְבָּר:

וַיַּחֲנוּ לִפְנֵי פִּי הַחִירֹת. הִיא פִּיתוֹם, וְעַכְשָׁיו נִקְרֵאת "פִּי הַחִירֹת" עַל שֵׁם שֶׁנַּעֲשׂוּ שָׁם בְּנֵי חוֹרִין. וְהֵם שְׁנֵי סְלָעִים גְּבוֹהִים זְקוּפִים, וְהַגַּיְא שֶׁבֵּינֵיהֶם קָרוּי פִּי הַסְּלָעִים:

לִפְנֵי בַּעַל צְפֹן. הוּא נִשְׁאַר מִכָּל אֱלֹהֵי מִצְרַיִם כְּדֵי לְהַטְעוֹתָן שֶׁיֹּאמְרוּ: קָשָׁה יִרְאָתָן. וְעָלָיו פֵּרֵשׁ אִיּוֹב: "מַשְׂגִּיא לַגּוֹיִם וַיְאַבְּדֵם" (איוב יב, כג):

ג) **וְאָמַר פַּרְעֹה.** כְּשֶׁיִּשְׁמַע שֶׁהֵם שָׁבִים לַאֲחוֹרֵיהֶם:

לִבְנֵי יִשְׂרָאֵל. עַל בְּנֵי יִשְׂרָאֵל. וְכֵן: "ה' יִלָּחֵם לָכֶם" (להלן פסוק יד) – "עֲלֵיכֶם"; "וַיֹּאמְרוּ לוֹ אֵחִי הוּא" (בראשית כ, יג) – "חָמְרִי עָלַי:

נְבֻכִים הֵם. כְּלוּאִים וּמְשֻׁקָּעִים, וּבְלַעַז שירי״ר. כְּמוֹ: "נִבְכֵי יָם" (איוב לח, טז):

וְיַחֲנוּ לִפְנֵי פִּי הַחִירֹת – *And camp in front of Pi HaḤirot*: This location is synonymous with Pitom [mentioned in 1:11 as a city Israel was required to construct]. In our verse it is referred to as "Pi HaḤirot" because the people had been set free [*ḥorin*]. Two large rock outcrops stand at this spot, and the valley between them is called *Pi HaSela'im* [meaning "Mouth of the Rocks"].

לִפְנֵי בַּעַל צְפֹן – *Before Baal Tzefon*: Of all the Egyptian gods, this deity alone was not destroyed, in order to deceive its devotees into believing it remained powerful [and could still challenge God]. Hence the verse states: *He makes nations haughty and destroys them* (Job 12:23).

3 | **וְאָמַר פַּרְעֹה** – *Pharaoh will think*: Having heard that Israel turned back.

לִבְנֵי יִשְׂרָאֵל – *The Israelites*: [The literal translation of the first half of the verse is: "Pharaoh will say to the Israelites, 'They are lost etc.'" Rashi explains that the phrase *liVnei Yisrael* does not mean "to the Israelites," but] "about the Israelites." A similar use of the letter *lamed* appears in the verse *The Lord will fight for you [lakhem]* (14:14), where the word *lakhem* should be understood to mean "on your behalf," and in the verse *Say of me [li], 'He is my brother'* (Genesis 20:13).

נְבֻכִים הֵם – *They are lost*: [According to Rashi, the phrase *nevukhim hem* means] "They are trapped and stuck." The Old

4 lost across the land, that they are trapped in the desert. I will toughen Pharaoh's heart, and he will pursue them. I will be glorified over Pharaoh and all his force, and the Egyptians will
5 know that I am the Lord." And so they did. ▸ When the king of Egypt was told that the Israelites had escaped, he and his officials changed their minds about the people: "What have
6 we done, releasing the Israelites from serving us?" So the king

"בְּעֵמֶק הַבָּכָא" (תהלים פד, ז), "מִבְּכִי נְהָרוֹת" (איוב כח, יא). "נְבֻכִים הֵם" – כְּלוּאִים הֵם בַּמִּדְבָּר, שֶׁאֵינָן יוֹדְעִין לָצֵאת מִמֶּנּוּ וּלְהֵיכָן יֵלְכוּ:

French term for this verb is *serrer* [meaning "to lock away"]. Variations of the term appear in the verse *Have you entered into the straits [nivkhei] of the sea?* (Job 38:16), and in the verse, *passing through the narrow gorge [emek habakha]* (Psalms 84:7), and *He binds [mibbekhi] the floods so that they do not trickle* (Job 28:11). Pharaoh will suppose that Israel is imprisoned in the wilderness, unable to navigate its way out or to determine the path forward.

ד | **וְאִכָּבְדָה בְּפַרְעֹה.** כְּשֶׁהַקָּדוֹשׁ בָּרוּךְ הוּא מִתְנַקֵּם בָּרְשָׁעִים שְׁמוֹ מִתְגַּדֵּל וּמִתְכַּבֵּד. וְכֵן הוּא אוֹמֵר: "וְנִשְׁפַּטְתִּי אִתּוֹ" וְגוֹ' וְאַחַר כָּךְ: "וְהִתְגַּדִּלְתִּי וְהִתְקַדִּשְׁתִּי וְנוֹדַעְתִּי וְגוֹ'" (יחזקאל לח, כב-כג), וְאוֹמֵר: "שָׁמָּה שִׁבַּר רִשְׁפֵי קָשֶׁת" וְאַחַר כָּךְ: "נוֹדָע בִּיהוּדָה אֱלֹהִים" (תהלים עו, ב-ד), וְאוֹמֵר: "נוֹדָע ה' מִשְׁפָּט עָשָׂה" (שם ט, יז):

4 | **וְאִכָּבְדָה בְּפַרְעֹה** – *I will be glorified over Pharaoh*: When God exacts vengeance from the wicked, His name is exalted and honored. So states the verse *And I will contend with him.... Thus will I magnify Myself and sanctify Myself, and I will make Myself known in the eyes of many nations* (Ezekiel 38:22–23). And another verse states: *There He broke the flashing arrows.... In Yehuda is God known* (Psalms 76:4, 2), and *The Lord is known by the judgment which He executes* (Psalms 9:17).

בְּפַרְעֹה וּבְכָל־חֵילוֹ. הוּא הִתְחִיל בַּעֲבֵרָה וּמִמֶּנּוּ הִתְחִיל הַפֻּרְעָנוּת:

בְּפַרְעֹה וּבְכָל־חֵילוֹ – *Over Pharaoh and all his force*: Pharaoh will be drowned first, followed by his cavalry, because he initiated the oppression against Israel.

וַיַּעֲשׂוּ־כֵן. לְהַגִּיד שִׁבְחָן שֶׁשָּׁמְעוּ לְקוֹל מֹשֶׁה, וְלֹא אָמְרוּ: הֵיאַךְ נִתְקָרֵב אֶל רוֹדְפֵינוּ? אָנוּ צְרִיכִים לִבְרֹחַ! אֶלָּא אָמְרוּ: אֵין לָנוּ אֶלָּא דִּבְרֵי בֶן עַמְרָם:

וַיַּעֲשׂוּ־כֵן – *And so they did*: These words credit the Israelites for obeying Moshe and not protesting: "What sense does it make to approach our pursuers, when we should be fleeing from them?" Rather, they freely declared: "The will of the son of Amram is our command."

ה | **וַיֻּגַּד לְמֶלֶךְ מִצְרַיִם.** אִיקְטוֹרִין שָׁלַח עִמָּהֶם, וְכֵיוָן שֶׁהִגִּיעוּ לִשְׁלֹשֶׁת יָמִים שֶׁקָּבְעוּ לֵילֵךְ וְלָשׁוּב וְרָאוּ

5 | **וַיֻּגַּד לְמֶלֶךְ מִצְרַיִם** – *When the king of Egypt was told*: Pharaoh had sent army captains to accompany Israel and ensure that the people returned to Egypt after three days. On the fourth

ד וְחִזַּקְתִּ֞י אֶת־לֵֽב־פַּרְעֹה֙ וְרָדַ֣ף אַחֲרֵיהֶ֔ם וְאִכָּבְדָ֤ה בְּפַרְעֹה֙ וּבְכָל־חֵיל֔וֹ וְיָדְע֥וּ מִצְרַ֖יִם כִּֽי־אֲנִ֣י יְהוָ֑ה וַיַּֽעֲשׂוּ־
ה כֵֽן׃ וַיֻּגַּד֙ לְמֶ֣לֶךְ מִצְרַ֔יִם כִּ֥י בָרַ֖ח הָעָ֑ם וַ֠יֵּהָפֵ֠ךְ לְבַ֨ב פַּרְעֹ֤ה וַעֲבָדָיו֙ אֶל־הָעָ֔ם וַיֹּֽאמְרוּ֙ מַה־זֹּ֣את עָשִׂ֔ינוּ
ו כִּֽי־שִׁלַּ֥חְנוּ אֶת־יִשְׂרָאֵ֖ל מֵעָבְדֵֽנוּ׃ וַיֶּאְסֹ֖ר אֶת־רִכְבּ֑וֹ

שֶׁאֵינָן חוֹזְרִין לְמִצְרַיִם, בָּאוּ וְהִגִּידוּ לְפַרְעֹה בַּיּוֹם הָרְבִיעִי. וּבַחֲמִישִׁי וּבַשִּׁשִּׁי רָדְפוּ אַחֲרֵיהֶם, לֵיל שְׁבִיעִי יָרְדוּ לַיָּם, בְּשַׁחֲרִית אָמְרוּ שִׁירָה, וְהוּא יוֹם שְׁבִיעִי שֶׁל פֶּסַח. לְכָךְ אָנוּ קוֹרִין הַשִּׁירָה בַּיּוֹם הַשְּׁבִיעִי:

וַיֵּהָפֵךְ. נֶהְפַּךְ מִמַּה שֶׁהָיָה, שֶׁהֲרֵי אָמַר לָהֶם: "קוּמוּ צְּאוּ מִתּוֹךְ עַמִּי" (לעיל יב, לא), וְנֶהְפַּךְ לֵב עֲבָדָיו, שֶׁהֲרֵי לְשֶׁעָבַר הָיוּ אוֹמְרִים לוֹ: "עַד מָתַי יִהְיֶה זֶה לָנוּ לְמוֹקֵשׁ" (לעיל י, ז) וְעַכְשָׁיו נֶהְפְּכוּ לִרְדֹּף אַחֲרֵיהֶם בִּשְׁבִיל מָמוֹנָם שֶׁהִשְׁאִילוּם:

מֵעָבְדֵנוּ. מֵעֲבֹד אוֹתָנוּ:

ו| וַיֶּאְסֹר אֶת־רִכְבּוֹ. הוּא בְּעַצְמוֹ:

וְאֶת־עַמּוֹ לָקַח עִמּוֹ. מְשָׁכָם בִּדְבָרִים: לָקִינוּ וְנָטְלוּ מָמוֹנֵנוּ וְשִׁלַּחֲנוּם, בֹּאוּ עִמִּי וַאֲנִי לֹא אֶתְנַהֵג עִמָּכֶם כִּשְׁאָר מְלָכִים, דֶּרֶךְ מְלָכִים עֲבָדָיו קוֹדְמִין לוֹ בַּמִּלְחָמָה, וַאֲנִי אַקְדִּים לִפְנֵיכֶם, שֶׁנֶּאֱמַר: "וּפַרְעֹה הִקְרִיב" (להלן פסוק י), הִקְרִיב עַצְמוֹ וּמִהֵר לִפְנֵי חֲיָלוֹתָיו, דֶּרֶךְ מְלָכִים לִטֹּל בִּזָּה בָּרֹאשׁ כְּמוֹ שֶׁיִּבְחַר, אֲנִי אֶשְׁוֶה עִמָּכֶם בַּחֵלֶק, שֶׁנֶּאֱמַר: "אֲחַלֵּק שָׁלָל" (להלן טו, ט):

day, when the spies saw no indication that Israel meant to honor their promise, they reported the situation to Pharaoh. The fifth and sixth days were spent in pursuit of the former slaves. On the evening of the seventh day, Israel descended into the sea, and by morning they were singing God's praises for their salvation. That day was the seventh day of the Passover festival, which is why we read the Song at the Sea [Exodus 15, in the synagogue service] on that day of the holiday.

וַיֵּהָפֵךְ – *Changed*: Now Pharaoh regretted his command to Moshe, *Get up, get out from among my people* (12:31). And his officials too changed their minds, for they had previously argued: *How long must we leave this man to ensnare us?* (10:7). But now they yearned to chase after Israel to retrieve the valuables they had lent them.

מֵעָבְדֵנוּ – *From serving us*: [The word might be misunderstood to mean "from our slave." It actually means] "from serving us."

6 | וַיֶּאְסֹר אֶת־רִכְבּוֹ – *So the king harnessed his chariot*: In his eagerness, Pharaoh prepared his chariot himself.

וְאֶת־עַמּוֹ לָקַח עִמּוֹ – *And brought out his army*: Pharaoh persuaded his army to follow him by reminding them: "We were smitten by plagues, then they took our property, and then – we sent them away! If you come with me, I will not treat you the way that other kings behave. For other monarchs march behind their soldiers, but I will lead the way personally." Thus the verse states: *Pharaoh drew near* (14:10), meaning that the king put himself first and hurried ahead of his army. "Furthermore, while it is customary for other kings to claim first rights to the enemy's plunder, I will divide the bounty equally with you." Thus the verse states: *I will divide the spoils* (15:9).

7 harnessed his chariot and brought out his army. He took six hundred elite chariots and all the other chariots of Egypt,
8 with officers over them all. The Lord strengthened the heart of Pharaoh King of Egypt, and he pursued the Israelites, who
9 were leaving in defiance of them. ◂ The Egyptians, with all the king's horses and chariots, cavalry and infantry, chased and caught up with them as they were encamped by the sea
10 near Pi HaḤirot, before Baal Tzefon. Pharaoh drew near – the Israelites looked up: there were the Egyptians thundering after them. They were terrified and cried to the Lord for help.
11 "Were there no graves in Egypt?" they asked Moshe; "Is that

SHENI

ז| בָּחוּר. נִבְחָרִים. 'בָּחוּר' לְשׁוֹן יָחִיד, כָּל רֶכֶב וְרֶכֶב שֶׁבַּמִּנְיָן זֶה הָיָה בָחוּר:

7| בָּחוּר – *Elite*: [The term *baḥur* means] "chosen." It is a singular form, indicating that every single chariot was specially chosen.

וְכֹל רֶכֶב מִצְרָיִם. וְעִמָּהֶם כָּל שְׁאָר הָרֶכֶב. וּמֵהֵיכָן הָיוּ הַבְּהֵמוֹת הַלָּלוּ? אִם תֹּאמַר מִשֶּׁל מִצְרִים, הֲרֵי נֶאֱמַר: "וַיָּמָת כָּל מִקְנֵה מִצְרָיִם" (לעיל ט, ו)! וְאִם מִשֶּׁל יִשְׂרָאֵל, וַהֲלֹא נֶאֱמַר: "וְגַם מִקְנֵנוּ יֵלֵךְ עִמָּנוּ" (לעיל י, כו)! מִשֶּׁל מִי הָיוּ? מֵ"הַיָּרֵא אֶת דְּבַר ה'" (לעיל ט, כ). מִכָּאן הָיָה רַבִּי שִׁמְעוֹן אוֹמֵר: כָּשֵׁר שֶׁבַּגּוֹיִם הֲרֹג, טוֹב שֶׁבַּנְּחָשִׁים רְצֹץ אֶת מֹחוֹ:

וְכֹל רֶכֶב מִצְרָיִם – *And all the other chariots of Egypt*: The rest of the chariots in Egypt joined the 600 elite cavalry in the battle. Now one might ask where the army found horses to saddle for this mission. They could not have been the Egyptians' animals, since the text reports that *all the livestock of the Egyptians perished* [9:6, referring to the effects of the cattle plague]. And they could not have harnessed beasts belonging to the Israelites, since Moshe had insisted that *our livestock must go with us* (10:26). So whose animals were they? The horses belonged to *those of Pharaoh's officials who feared the Lord's word [and who] hurried to bring in their slaves and livestock* [9:20, thus saving them from the plagues]. This is why Rabbi Shimon used to say: Kill even the best of the gentiles; bash in the brains of even the most docile snakes. [For here even the God-fearing Egyptians were eventually enlisted to persecute Israel.]

וְשָׁלִשִׁם עַל־כֻּלּוֹ. שָׂרֵי צְבָאוֹת, כְּתַרְגּוּמוֹ:

וְשָׁלִשִׁם עַל־כֻּלּוֹ – *With officers over them all*: [The word *shalishim* is obscure. Rashi argues that it should be understood as referring to] army officers, as the Targum renders it.

ח| וַיְחַזֵּק יהוה אֶת־לֵב פַּרְעֹה. שֶׁהָיָה תוֹלֶה אִם לִרְדֹּף אִם לָאו, וְחִזֵּק אֶת לִבּוֹ לִרְדֹּף:

8| וַיְחַזֵּק יהוה אֶת־לֵב פַּרְעֹה – *The Lord strengthened the heart of Pharaoh*: Pharaoh could not decide whether to pursue Israel or not, and God strengthened his resolve so that he would.

בְּיָד רָמָה. בִּגְבוּרָה גְבוֹהָה וּמְפֻרְסָמֶת:

בְּיָד רָמָה – *In defiance of them*: Israel left with the upper hand over Egypt; their victory was universally understood.

שמות | פרק יד | בשלח

ז וְאֶת־עַמּוֹ לָקַח עִמּוֹ: וַיִּקַּח שֵׁשׁ־מֵאוֹת רֶכֶב בָּחוּר
ח וְכָל רֶכֶב מִצְרָיִם וְשָׁלִשִׁם עַל־כֻּלּוֹ: וַיְחַזֵּק יהוה אֶת־
לֵב פַּרְעֹה מֶלֶךְ מִצְרַיִם וַיִּרְדֹּף אַחֲרֵי בְּנֵי יִשְׂרָאֵל
ט וּבְנֵי יִשְׂרָאֵל יֹצְאִים בְּיָד רָמָה: וַיִּרְדְּפוּ מִצְרַיִם שני
אַחֲרֵיהֶם וַיַּשִּׂיגוּ אוֹתָם חֹנִים עַל־הַיָּם כָּל־סוּס רֶכֶב
פַּרְעֹה וּפָרָשָׁיו וְחֵילוֹ עַל־פִּי הַחִירֹת לִפְנֵי בַּעַל צְפֹן:
י וּפַרְעֹה הִקְרִיב וַיִּשְׂאוּ בְנֵי־יִשְׂרָאֵל אֶת־עֵינֵיהֶם וְהִנֵּה
מִצְרַיִם ׀ נֹסֵעַ אַחֲרֵיהֶם וַיִּירְאוּ מְאֹד וַיִּצְעֲקוּ בְנֵי־
יא יִשְׂרָאֵל אֶל־יהוה: וַיֹּאמְרוּ אֶל־מֹשֶׁה הַמִבְּלִי אֵין־

י| וּפַרְעֹה הִקְרִיב. הָיָה לוֹ לִכְתֹּב: 'וּפַרְעֹה קָרַב', מַהוּ "הִקְרִיב"? הִקְרִיב עַצְמוֹ וְנִתְאַמֵּץ לְקַדֵּם לִפְנֵיהֶם כְּמוֹ שֶׁהִתְנָה עִמָּהֶם:

נֹסֵעַ אַחֲרֵיהֶם. בְּלֵב אֶחָד כְּאִישׁ אֶחָד. דָּבָר אַחֵר, "וְהִנֵּה מִצְרַיִם נֹסֵעַ אַחֲרֵיהֶם", רָאוּ שַׂר שֶׁל מִצְרַיִם נוֹסֵעַ מִן הַשָּׁמַיִם לַעֲזוֹר לְמִצְרַיִם. תַּנְחוּמָא (יג):

וַיִּצְעָקוּ. תָּפְשׂוּ אֻמָּנוּת אֲבוֹתָם; בְּאַבְרָהָם הוּא אוֹמֵר: "אֶל הַמָּקוֹם אֲשֶׁר עָמַד שָׁם" (בראשית יט, כז), בְּיִצְחָק: "לָשׂוּחַ בַּשָּׂדֶה" (שם כד, סג), בְּיַעֲקֹב: "וַיִּפְגַּע בַּמָּקוֹם" (שם כח, יא):

יא| הַמִבְּלִי אֵין־קְבָרִים. וְכִי מֵחֲמַת חֶסְרוֹן קְבָרִים, שֶׁאֵין קְבָרִים

וּפַרְעֹה הִקְרִיב |10 – *Pharaoh drew near*: The more natural form of the verb here would have been *karav* [the simple, or *kal*, form], rather than *hikriv* [the *hifil* or causative construction, which suggests that Pharaoh drew others near]. What the term *hikriv* connotes is that the king pushed himself forward in an effort to lead his troops, just as he had promised he would.

נֹסֵעַ אַחֲרֵיהֶם – *Thundering after them*: The singular form of the verb *nosea* requires explication [since the hundreds of chariots and soldiers bearing down on Israel would seem to merit the plural *nose'im*]. The language suggests that the entire army was united in purpose and strategy to attack Israel. Another interpretation: This clause, which literally means "There was Egypt riding after them," signifies that the people saw Egypt's guardian angel streaking down from the heavens to assist his wards.

וַיִּצְעָקוּ – *And cried*: Israel adopted the practice of their ancestors, who had all prayed to God. For the Torah reports that *Avraham went early in the morning to the place where he had stood before the* Lord (Genesis 19:27); that *Yitzḥak went out to meditate in the field at the evening time* (Genesis 24:63); and that Yaakov *lighted on a certain place* [Genesis 28:11, also traditionally understood as a reference to prayer].

הַמִבְּלִי אֵין־קְבָרִים |11 – *Were there no graves in Egypt*: Did you take us out of Egypt due to the paucity of graves there; were

why you brought us here to die in the desert? What have you done to us, bringing us out of Egypt? Did we not tell you in Egypt: Leave us alone – let us serve the Egyptians. Better a life in servitude to Egypt than death in the desert." But Moshe told the people, "Fear not. Stand firm and see the deliverance the Lord will bring you today. The Egyptians you see today, you shall never see again. The Lord will fight for you. You stay silent."

15 The Lord said to Moshe, "Why are you crying out to Me? SHELISHI
16 Speak to the Israelites; have them move forward. Raise your staff, stretch out your hand over the sea and divide it, and the

בְּמִצְרַיִם לִקְבֹּר שָׁם, לְקַחְתָּנוּ מִשָּׁם? סִיפּוּ"ר פלינצ"א דינו"ן פוסי"ש בְּלַעַז:

you concerned there would be nowhere to bury us? This would be expressed in Old French as *si pour faillance de non fosses* [meaning "if for lack of no graves." In this case the double negative does not yield a positive expression, but serves to strengthen the objection].

יב| אֲשֶׁר דִּבַּרְנוּ אֵלֶיךָ בְמִצְרַיִם. וְהֵיכָן דִּבְּרוּ? "יֵרֶא ה' עֲלֵיכֶם וְיִשְׁפֹּט" (לעיל ה, כא):

12| אֲשֶׁר דִּבַּרְנוּ אֵלֶיךָ בְמִצְרַיִם – *Tell you in Egypt*: The people refer here to their earlier complaint, *May the Lord look on you and judge* (5:21).

מִמֻּתֵנוּ. מֵאֲשֶׁר נָמוּת. וְאִם הָיָה נָקוּד מְלֻאפוּם הָיָה נִבְאָר "מִמִּיתָתֵנוּ", עַכְשָׁיו שֶׁנָּקוּד בְּשׁוּרֶק נִבְאָר "מֵאֲשֶׁר נָמוּת". וְכֵן: "מִי יִתֵּן מוּתֵנוּ" (להלן טז, ג), שֶׁנָּמוּת, וְכֵן: "מִי יִתֵּן מוּתִי" דְּאַבְשָׁלוֹם (שמואל ב' יט, א), שֶׁאָמוּת, כְּמוֹ: "לְיוֹם קוּמִי לְעַד" (צפניה ג, ח), "עַד שׁוּבִי בְשָׁלוֹם" (דברי הימים ב' יח, כו), שֶׁאָקוּם, שֶׁאָשׁוּב:

מִמֻּתֵנוּ – *Than death*: The term means "than that we should die." [And not "than our death," a noun, as the translation here renders the word.] Had the word been vocalized with a *ḥolam* [making the word *mimoteinu*] its meaning would have been "than our death." However, since the vowel appearing in this word is a *kubbutz*, the word must be understood as a verb: "than that we should die." A similar instance of this word appears in the verse *If only we had died [mutenu] by the Lord's hand in Egypt* (16:3) and in David's lament: *Would I had died [muti] instead of you, Avshalom, my son, my son!* (II Samuel 19:1). See also similar constructions in the verses *Until the day that I rise up [kumi] to the prey* (Zephaniah 3:8), and *Until I return [shuvi] in peace* (II Chronicles 18:26).

יג| כִּי אֲשֶׁר רְאִיתֶם אֶת־מִצְרַיִם וְגוֹ'. מַה שֶּׁרְאִיתֶם אוֹתָם אֵינוֹ אֶלָּא הַיּוֹם, הַיּוֹם הוּא שֶׁרְאִיתֶם אוֹתָם וְלֹא תֹסִיפוּ עוֹד:

13| כִּי אֲשֶׁר רְאִיתֶם אֶת־מִצְרַיִם – *The Egyptians you see today*: [The construction of the verse is odd; it seems to literally mean: "That you see the Egyptians today, you will never see them again." Rashi explains that the verse means:] "That you see the Egyptians only for today; you will never see them again."

יד| יִלָּחֵם לָכֶם. בִּשְׁבִילְכֶם. וְכֵן: "כִּי ה' נִלְחָם לָהֶם" (להלן פסוק כה), וְכֵן:

14| יִלָּחֵם לָכֶם – *Will fight for you*: [The word *lakhem* does not only mean "to you" or "yours," but also] "on your behalf."

שמות | פרק יד

קְבָרִים֙ בְּמִצְרַ֔יִם לְקַחְתָּ֖נוּ לָמ֣וּת בַּמִּדְבָּ֑ר מַה־זֹּאת֙
יב עָשִׂ֣יתָ לָּ֔נוּ לְהוֹצִיאָ֖נוּ מִמִּצְרָֽיִם: הֲלֹא־זֶ֣ה הַדָּבָ֗ר
אֲשֶׁר֩ דִּבַּ֨רְנוּ אֵלֶ֤יךָ בְמִצְרַ֨יִם֙ לֵאמֹ֔ר חֲדַ֥ל מִמֶּ֖נּוּ
וְנַֽעַבְדָ֣ה אֶת־מִצְרָ֑יִם כִּ֣י ט֥וֹב לָ֨נוּ֙ עֲבֹ֣ד אֶת־מִצְרַ֔יִם
יג מִמֻּתֵ֖נוּ בַּמִּדְבָּֽר: וַיֹּ֨אמֶר מֹשֶׁ֣ה אֶל־הָעָם֮ אַל־תִּירָאוּ֒
הִֽתְיַצְּב֗וּ וּרְאוּ֙ אֶת־יְשׁוּעַ֣ת יְהֹוָ֔ה אֲשֶׁר־יַֽעֲשֶׂ֥ה לָכֶ֖ם
הַיּ֑וֹם כִּ֗י אֲשֶׁ֨ר רְאִיתֶ֤ם אֶת־מִצְרַ֨יִם֙ הַיּ֔וֹם לֹ֥א תֹסִ֛פוּ
יד לִרְאֹתָ֥ם ע֖וֹד עַד־עוֹלָֽם: יְהֹוָ֖ה יִלָּחֵ֣ם לָכֶ֑ם וְאַתֶּ֖ם
תַּֽחֲרִישֽׁוּן:

טו שלישי וַיֹּ֤אמֶר יְהֹוָה֙ אֶל־מֹשֶׁ֔ה מַה־תִּצְעַ֖ק אֵלָ֑י דַּבֵּ֥ר אֶל־
טז בְּנֵֽי־יִשְׂרָאֵ֖ל וְיִסָּֽעוּ: וְאַתָּ֞ה הָרֵ֣ם אֶֽת־מַטְּךָ֗ וּנְטֵ֧ה
אֶת־יָֽדְךָ֛ עַל־הַיָּ֖ם וּבְקָעֵ֑הוּ וְיָבֹ֧אוּ בְנֵֽי־יִשְׂרָאֵ֛ל בְּת֥וֹךְ

"חֵס לָאֵל תְּרִיבוּן" (איוב יג, ח), וְכֵן:
"וַֽאֲשֶׁר דִּבֶּר לִי" (בראשית כד, ז), וְכֵן:
"הַֽאַתֶּם תְּרִיבוּן לַבַּעַל" (שופטים ו, לא):

Similarly, the verse below states: *The LORD is fighting for them against Egypt* (14:25). And so does Job ask: *Will you contend on behalf of God?* (Job 13:8). We also find the verse *The LORD... who took me from my father's house, and from the land of my kindred, and who spoke for me* (Genesis 24:7). And likewise, *Will you plead on behalf of Baal?* (Judges 6:31).

טו מַה־תִּצְעַק אֵלָי. לָמַדְנוּ שֶׁהָיָה
מֹשֶׁה עוֹמֵד וּמִתְפַּלֵּל, אָמַר לוֹ
הַקָּדוֹשׁ בָּרוּךְ הוּא: לֹא עֵת עַתָּה
לְהַֽאֲרִיךְ שֶׁיִּשְׂרָאֵל נְתוּנִין בְּצָרָה.
דָּבָר אַחֵר, "מַה תִּצְעַק אֵלָי", עָלַי
הַדָּבָר וְלֹא עָלֶיךָ, כְּמוֹ שֶׁנֶּֽאֱמַר
לְהַלָּן: "עַל בָּנַי וְעַל פֹּעַל יָדַי תְּצַוֻּנִי"
(ישעיה מה, יא):

15 | מַה־תִּצְעַק אֵלָי – *Why are you crying out to Me*: We learn from God's statement that Moshe had been standing before Him and praying. Said the Holy One, blessed be He: "Now is not the time for extended prayer; at this moment Israel is in peril!" Another interpretation for this phrase: God said: "Why are you crying out?" It falls "to Me" to act now, not to you. We find a similar sentiment expressed in the verse *Concerning my sons, and concerning the work of My hands you command Me?* [Isaiah 45:11; i.e., God asks: Do you need to remind Me to take care of My own children?]

דַּבֵּר אֶל־בְּנֵֽי־יִשְׂרָאֵל וְיִסָּעוּ. אֵין
לָהֶם אֶלָּא לִסַּע, שֶׁאֵין הַיָּם עוֹמֵד
בִּפְנֵיהֶם, כְּדַאי זְכוּת אֲבוֹתֵיהֶם
וְהָאֱמָנָה שֶׁהֶאֱמִינוּ בִי וְיָֽצְאוּ, לִקְרֹעַ
לָהֶם אֶת הַיָּם:

דַּבֵּר אֶל־בְּנֵֽי־יִשְׂרָאֵל וְיִסָּעוּ – *Speak to the Israelites; have them move forward*: All they have to do is to move forward, for the sea will not stand in their way. The merits of their forefathers, together with the faith they put in Me when they left Egypt, will be sufficient to split the sea for them.

17 Israelites will walk through the sea on dry land. I will strengthen the Egyptians' hearts and they will go after them. Then will My glory bear down hard upon Pharaoh and his entire army, 18 his chariots and cavalry. And when My glory bears down upon Pharaoh, his chariots and cavalry, the Egyptians will 19 know that I am the Lord." Then the angel of God who had been traveling ahead of the Israelite camp moved and went behind them, and the column of cloud moved from in front of 20 them to their rear. It came between the Egyptian and Israelite camps, as cloud and darkness for one, but lighting the night 21 for the other, keeping the two apart all night. Then Moshe stretched out his hand over the sea, and the Lord drove the

---

יט-כ‎| וַיֵּלֶךְ מֵאַחֲרֵיהֶם. לְהַבְדִּיל בֵּין מַחֲנֵה מִצְרַיִם וּבֵין מַחֲנֵה יִשְׂרָאֵל וּלְקַבֵּל חִצִּים וּבַלִּיסְטְרָאוֹת שֶׁל מִצְרַיִם. בְּכָל מָקוֹם הוּא אוֹמֵר: "מַלְאַךְ ה'" וְכָאן: "מַלְאַךְ הָאֱלֹהִים", אֵין "אֱלֹהִים" בְּכָל מָקוֹם אֶלָּא דַּיָּן, מְלַמֵּד שֶׁהָיוּ יִשְׂרָאֵל נְתוּנִין בַּדִּין בְּאוֹתָהּ שָׁעָה אִם לְהִנָּגֵל אִם לְהֵאָבֵד עִם מִצְרַיִם:

מָשָׁל וַיָּבֹא בֵּין מַחֲנֵה מִצְרַיִם. לִמְהַלֵּךְ בַּדֶּרֶךְ וּבְנוֹ מְהַלֵּךְ לְפָנָיו. בָּאוּ לִסְטִים לִשְׁבּוֹתוֹ, נְטָלוֹ מִלְּפָנָיו וּנְתָנוֹ לְאַחֲרָיו. בָּא זְאֵב מֵאַחֲרָיו, נְתָנוֹ לְפָנָיו. בָּאוּ לִסְטִים לְפָנָיו וּזְאֵבִים מֵאַחֲרָיו, נְתָנוֹ עַל זְרוֹעוֹ וְנִלְחָם בָּהֶם. כָּךְ: "וְאָנֹכִי תִרְגַּלְתִּי לְאֶפְרַיִם קָחָם עַל זְרוֹעֹתָיו" (הושע יא, ג):

וַיִּסַּע עַמּוּד הֶעָנָן. כְּשֶׁחָשְׁכָה וְהִשְׁלִים עַמּוּד הֶעָנָן אֶת הַמַּחֲנֶה לְעַמּוּד הָאֵשׁ, לֹא נִסְתַּלֵּק הֶעָנָן כְּמוֹ שֶׁהָיָה רָגִיל לְהִסְתַּלֵּק עַרְבִית

וַיֵּלֶךְ מֵאַחֲרֵיהֶם |19–20 – *Moved and went behind them*: The column of cloud was positioned as a barrier between the Egyptian camp and the Israelite one. There it was able to absorb the arrows and catapulted rocks that the Egyptians hurled in Israel's direction. Now everywhere else in the Torah, emissaries of this type are referred to as "angels of the Lord," whereas in our verse the text uses the term "angel of God," this latter divine name [*Elohim*] signifies God acting in the role of judge. For at that moment, Israel themselves were being judged to determine whether they would be rescued or destroyed by the Egyptians.

וַיָּבֹא בֵּין מַחֲנֵה מִצְרַיִם – *It came between the Egyptian camp*: This may be compared to a man who is strolling along the road while his son skips ahead of him. Suddenly, bandits appear and attempt to snatch the lad, whereupon the father shoves his son behind him for protection. But then a wolf threatens the pair from behind, so the traveler again moves the boy in front of him. When the bandits approach from the front and the wolf from behind, the man has no choice but to hold the son in his arms and fight both dangers at once. This is the sense of the verse: *It was I was who guided Efrayim's first steps, carrying them in My arms*, (Hosea 11:3).

וַיִּסַּע עַמּוּד הֶעָנָן – *And the column of cloud moved*: The cloud only moved once it had become dark, and then it gave over Israel's protection to the pillar of fire. But the cloud did not dissipate completely like it usually did in the evenings; rather,

יי הַיָּם בַּיַּבָּשָׁה: וַאֲנִי הִנְנִי מְחַזֵּק אֶת־לֵב מִצְרַיִם וְיָבֹאוּ אַחֲרֵיהֶם וְאִכָּבְדָה בְּפַרְעֹה וּבְכָל־חֵילוֹ בְּרִכְבּוֹ
יח וּבְפָרָשָׁיו: וְיָדְעוּ מִצְרַיִם כִּי־אֲנִי יהוה בְּהִכָּבְדִי
יט בְּפַרְעֹה בְּרִכְבּוֹ וּבְפָרָשָׁיו: וַיִּסַּע מַלְאַךְ הָאֱלֹהִים הַהֹלֵךְ לִפְנֵי מַחֲנֵה יִשְׂרָאֵל וַיֵּלֶךְ מֵאַחֲרֵיהֶם וַיִּסַּע
כ עַמּוּד הֶעָנָן מִפְּנֵיהֶם וַיַּעֲמֹד מֵאַחֲרֵיהֶם: וַיָּבֹא בֵּין ׀ מַחֲנֵה מִצְרַיִם וּבֵין מַחֲנֵה יִשְׂרָאֵל וַיְהִי הֶעָנָן וְהַחֹשֶׁךְ וַיָּאֶר אֶת־הַלָּיְלָה וְלֹא־קָרַב זֶה אֶל־זֶה כָּל־הַלָּיְלָה:
כא וַיֵּט מֹשֶׁה אֶת־יָדוֹ עַל־הַיָּם וַיּוֹלֶךְ יהוה ׀ אֶת־הַיָּם

לְגַמְרֵי, חָלַף נָסַע וְהָלַךְ לוֹ מֵאַחֲרֵיהֶם לְהַחֲשִׁיךְ לְמִצְרִים:

וַיְהִי הֶעָנָן וְהַחֹשֶׁךְ. לְמִצְרִים:

וַיָּאֶר. עַמּוּד הָאֵשׁ "אֶת הַלַּיְלָה" לְיִשְׂרָאֵל, וְהוֹלֵךְ לִפְנֵיהֶם כְּדַרְכּוֹ לָלֶכֶת כָּל הַלַּיְלָה. וְהַחֹשֶׁךְ שֶׁל עֲרָפֶל לְצַד מִצְרִים:

וְלֹא־קָרַב זֶה אֶל־זֶה. מַחֲנֶה אֶל מַחֲנֶה:

כא | בְּרוּחַ קָדִים עַזָּה. בְּרוּחַ קָדִים שֶׁהִיא עַזָּה שֶׁבָּרוּחוֹת, הִיא הָרוּחַ שֶׁהַקָּדוֹשׁ בָּרוּךְ הוּא נִפְרָע בָּהּ מִן הָרְשָׁעִים, שֶׁנֶּאֱמַר: "כְּרוּחַ קָדִים אֲפִיצֵם" (ירמיה יח, יז), "יָבֹא קָדִים רוּחַ ה'" (הושע יג, טו), "רוּחַ הַקָּדִים שְׁבָרֵךְ בְּלֵב יַמִּים" (יחזקאל כז, כו), "הָגָה בְּרוּחוֹ הַקָּשָׁה בְּיוֹם קָדִים" (ישעיה כז, ח):

וַיִּבָּקְעוּ הַמָּיִם. כָּל מַיִם שֶׁבָּעוֹלָם:

it moved behind Israel in order to create darkness for the Egyptians.

וַיְהִי הֶעָנָן וְהַחֹשֶׁךְ – *As cloud and darkness for one*: [The phrase "for one" is absent from the Hebrew. Rashi explains that the darkness was intended solely] for the Egyptian army.

וַיָּאֶר – *But lighting*: The pillar of fire lit up the sky for Israel, and it stood before them providing light as it did every night. Meanwhile, on the Egyptian side, there was the thick fog of darkness.

וְלֹא־קָרַב זֶה אֶל־זֶה – *Keeping the two apart*: The pillar of cloud created a barrier between the two camps.

21 | בְּרוּחַ קָדִים עַזָּה – *By a strong east wind*: The east wind is the strongest of all winds. These are the gales that God uses to punish the wicked, as the verses state: *I will scatter them as with an east wind before the enemy* (Jeremiah 18:17), and *The east wind has broken you in the heart of the seas* (Ezekiel 27:26), and *He removed her by his rough blast on the day of the east wind* (Isaiah 27:8).

וַיִּבָּקְעוּ הַמַּיִם – *Dividing the waters*: All the water in the world was split [not just the Sea of Reeds].

◀

sea back by a strong east wind all night, turning it to dry land
22 and dividing the waters. So the Israelites walked through the
sea on dry land. To their right and left, the water was like a
23 wall. The Egyptians chased after them. All Pharaoh's horses,
24 chariots and cavalry followed them into the sea. During the
last watch of the night, the Lord looked down at the Egyptian
army from a column of fire and cloud and threw them into
25 a panic, clogging their chariot wheels so that it was hard for
them to move. The Egyptians said, "Let us flee from the Israelites. The Lord is fighting for them against Egypt."

כג| **כֹּל סוּס פַּרְעֹה**. וְכִי סוּס אֶחָד הָיָה?! מַגִּיד שֶׁאֵין כֻּלָּם חֲשׁוּבִין לִפְנֵי הַמָּקוֹם אֶלָּא כְּסוּס אֶחָד:

23| **כֹּל סוּס פַּרְעֹה** – *All Pharaoh's horses*: [The word "horses" – *sus* – is singular in the Hebrew.] Did Pharaoh have just one horse? Rather, the use of the singular conveys that from God's perspective, the entire cavalry may as well have been one animal.

כד| **בְּאַשְׁמֹרֶת הַבֹּקֶר**. שְׁלֹשֶׁת חֶלְקֵי הַלַּיְלָה קְרוּיִין "אַשְׁמֹרֶת", וְאוֹתָהּ שֶׁלִּפְנֵי הַיּוֹם קוֹרֵא "אַשְׁמֹרֶת הַבֹּקֶר". וְאוֹמֵר אֲנִי, שֶׁהוּא חָלוּק לְמִשְׁמְרוֹת שִׁיר מַלְאֲכֵי הַשָּׁרֵת, כַּת אַחַר כַּת לִשְׁלֹשָׁה חֲלָקִים, לְכָךְ קָרוּי "אַשְׁמֹרֶת", וְזֶהוּ שֶׁתִּרְגְּמוֹ אוּנְקְלוֹס: "מַטְּרַת":

24| **בְּאַשְׁמֹרֶת הַבֹּקֶר** – *During the last watch of the night*: The night is divided into three sections called "watches." The last watch, which precedes daybreak, is called "the morning watch." Now I say that the night is divided into three shifts to accommodate the three choirs of ministering angels who sing one after the other, and this is why they are called "watches." Indeed, Onkelos translates the Hebrew word *ashmoret* in the same way: *matterat* [meaning "watch"].

וַיַּשְׁקֵף. וַיַּבֵּט, כְּלוֹמַר פָּנָה חֲלָלֵיהֶם לְהַשְׁחִיתָם. וְתַרְגּוּמוֹ: "וְאִסְתְּכִי", אַף הוּא לְשׁוֹן הַבָּטָה, כְּמוֹ: "שְׂדֵה צֹפִים" (במדבר כג, יד), "חֲקַל סָכוּתָא":

וַיַּשְׁקֵף – *Looked down*: God gazed, He turned His attention to the Egyptians to destroy them. The Targum's translation of the verb is *ve'istakhi*, meaning "He gazed," just as it translates the phrase "field of vantage" (Numbers 23:14) as *ḥakal sakhuta*.

בְּעַמּוּד אֵשׁ וְעָנָן. עַמּוּד עָנָן יוֹרֵד וְעוֹשֶׂה אוֹתוֹ כְּטִיט, וְעַמּוּד אֵשׁ מַרְתִּיחוֹ, וְטַלְפֵי סוּסֵיהֶם מִשְׁתַּמְּטוֹת:

בְּעַמּוּד אֵשׁ וְעָנָן – *From a column of fire and cloud*: The column of cloud descended to the sea floor and turned it into clay, while the pillar of fire boiled the mud. This combination caused the horses' hoofs to become dislocated.

וַיָּהָם. לְשׁוֹן מְהוּמָה, אשטורדי"שון בְּלַעַ"ז. עִרְבְּבָם, נָטַל סִגְנִיּוֹת שֶׁלָּהֶם. וְשָׁנִינוּ בְּפִרְקֵי רַבִּי אֱלִיעֶזֶר בְּנוֹ שֶׁל

וַיָּהָם – *And threw them into a panic*: Confusion was sown among the Egyptians. This verb translates into Old French as *estordison* [meaning "dazed minds"]. God disoriented them,

שמות | פרק יד | בשלח

בְּרוּחַ קָדִים עַזָּה כָּל־הַלַּיְלָה וַיָּשֶׂם אֶת־הַיָּם לֶחָרָבָה
וַיִּבָּקְעוּ הַמָּיִם: וַיָּבֹאוּ בְנֵי־יִשְׂרָאֵל בְּתוֹךְ הַיָּם בַּיַּבָּשָׁה
וְהַמַּיִם לָהֶם חוֹמָה מִימִינָם וּמִשְּׂמֹאלָם: וַיִּרְדְּפוּ
מִצְרַיִם וַיָּבֹאוּ אַחֲרֵיהֶם כֹּל סוּס פַּרְעֹה רִכְבּוֹ וּפָרָשָׁיו
אֶל־תּוֹךְ הַיָּם: וַיְהִי בְּאַשְׁמֹרֶת הַבֹּקֶר וַיַּשְׁקֵף יְהוָה
אֶל־מַחֲנֵה מִצְרַיִם בְּעַמּוּד אֵשׁ וְעָנָן וַיָּהָם אֵת מַחֲנֵה
מִצְרָיִם: וַיָּסַר אֵת אֹפַן מַרְכְּבֹתָיו וַיְנַהֲגֵהוּ בִּכְבֵדֻת
וַיֹּאמֶר מִצְרַיִם אָנוּסָה מִפְּנֵי יִשְׂרָאֵל כִּי יְהוָה נִלְחָם
לָהֶם בְּמִצְרָיִם:

---

dulling their senses so that chaos ensued. We read in Pirkei DeRabbi Eliezer, authored by Rabbi Eliezer son of Rabbi Yosei the Galilean, that the term *mehuma* connotes a thunderous noise. The source for that interpretation is the verse: *But the* Lord *thundered with a great thunder on that day upon the Philistines and confused them [vayhummem]; and they were beaten before Israel* (I Samuel 7:10).

25 | וַיָּסַר אֵת אֹפַן מַרְכְּבֹתָיו – *Clogging their chariot wheels:* The fire was so strong that it burned the wheels, causing the chariots to be dragged along. The soldiers sitting in the vehicles were shaken and their limbs became disjointed.

וַיְנַהֲגֵהוּ בִּכְבֵדֻת – *It was hard for them to move:* The driving became heavy and difficult for them. Thus did God punish the Egyptians measure for measure, for an earlier verse states: *[Pharaoh] hardened his heart; his officials likewise* (9:34), and now, *It was hard from them to move.*

נִלְחָם לָהֶם בְּמִצְרָיִם – *Fighting for them against Egypt:* That is, against the Egyptians. Another interpretation takes the phrase literally: As God was striking the Egyptian cavalry at the sea, He simultaneously punished those citizens who had remained at home.

רַבִּי יוֹסֵי הַגְּלִילִי, כָּל מָקוֹם שֶׁנֶּאֱמַר "מְהוּמָה", הַרְעָשַׁת קוֹל הוּא, וְזֶה אָב לְכֻלָּן: "וַיַּרְעֵם ה' בְּקוֹל גָּדוֹל... עַל פְּלִשְׁתִּים וַיְהֻמֵּם" (שמואל א' ז, י):

כה] וַיָּסַר אֵת אֹפַן מַרְכְּבֹתָיו. מִכֹּחַ הָאֵשׁ נִשְׂרְפוּ הַגַּלְגַּלִּים, וְהַמֶּרְכָּבוֹת נִגְרָרוֹת, וְהַיּוֹשְׁבִים בָּהֶם נָעִים וְאֵבְרֵיהֶן מִתְפָּרְקִים:

וַיְנַהֲגֵהוּ בִּכְבֵדֻת. בְּהַנְהָגָה שֶׁהִיא כְּבֵדָה וְקָשָׁה לָהֶם. בְּמִדָּה שֶׁמָּדְדוּ, "וַיִּכְבַּד לֵב הוּא וַעֲבָדָיו" (לעיל ט, לד), אַף כָּאן, "וַיְנַהֲגֵהוּ בִּכְבֵדֻת":

נִלְחָם לָהֶם בְּמִצְרָיִם. בַּמִּצְרִים. דָּבָר אַחֵר "בְּמִצְרַיִם", בָּאָרֶץ מִצְרַיִם; שֶׁכְּשֵׁם שֶׁאֵלּוּ לוֹקִים עַל הַיָּם כָּךְ לוֹקִים אוֹתָם שֶׁנִּשְׁאֲרוּ בְּמִצְרַיִם:

26 Then the LORD said to Moshe, "Stretch out your hand over the sea. The waters will flow back over the Egyptians and their 27 chariots and cavalry." Moshe stretched out his hand over the sea, and at daybreak the water came back in full force. The Egyptians fled at its approach but the LORD swept them 28 into the sea. The waters returned, covering the chariots, the cavalry, and the whole Egyptian army that had followed the 29 Israelites into the sea. Not one of them remained. But the Israelites had walked through the sea on dry land, with a wall 30 of water to their right and left. That day, the LORD saved the Israelites from the Egyptians. And when the Israelites saw the 31 Egyptians dead on the seashore, and witnessed the wondrous power the LORD had unleashed against the Egyptians, the people were in awe of the LORD, and they believed in Him and in Moshe His servant.

REVI'I

כו| וְיָשֻׁבוּ הַמַּיִם. שֶׁזְּקוּפִים וְעוֹמְדִים כְּחוֹמָה, יָשׁוּבוּ לִמְקוֹמָם וִיכַסּוּ "עַל מִצְרָיִם":

וְיָשֻׁבוּ הַמַּיִם 26 – *The waters will flow back*: The waters, which have been standing erect like a wall, will return to their rightful place and thereby *flow back over the Egyptians*.

כז| לִפְנוֹת בֹּקֶר. לְעֵת שֶׁהַבֹּקֶר פּוֹנֶה לָבֹא:

לִפְנוֹת בֹּקֶר 27 – *At daybreak*: This is the moment that the morning turns [*poneh*] to come.

לְאֵיתָנוֹ. לְתָקְפּוֹ הָרִאשׁוֹן:

לְאֵיתָנוֹ – *In full force*: [The word *le'eitano* means,] "to its previous strength."

נָסִים לִקְרָאתוֹ. שֶׁהָיוּ מְהֻמָּמִים וּמְטֹרָפִים וְרָצִין לִקְרַאת הַמַּיִם:

נָסִים לִקְרָאתוֹ – *Fled at its approach*: [Literally, "fled toward it."] Because the Egyptians were discombobulated and crazed, they actually ran toward the approaching deluge.

וַיְנַעֵר יהוה. כְּאָדָם שֶׁמְּנַעֵר אֶת הַקְּדֵרָה, וְהוֹפֵךְ הָעֶלְיוֹן לְמַטָּה וְהַתַּחְתּוֹן לְמַעְלָה, כָּךְ הָיוּ עוֹלִין וְיוֹרְדִין וּמִשְׁתַּבְּרִין בַּיָּם. וְנָתַן הַקָּדוֹשׁ בָּרוּךְ הוּא בָּהֶם חַיּוּת לְקַבֵּל הַיִּסּוּרִין. "וְשַׁנִּיק", הוּא לְשׁוֹן טֵרוּף בְּלָשׁוֹן אֲרַמִּי, וְהַרְבֵּה יֵשׁ בְּמִדְרְשֵׁי אַגָּדָה:

וַיְנַעֵר יהוה – *The LORD swept them*: The action resembled the stirring of a pot, when the upper contents of a mix are turned downward and the ingredients on the bottom are moved to the top. So were the Egyptians churned up and whipped down, causing them to break apart in the sea. Meanwhile God kept them alive long enough to endure this thrashing. The Targum's translation for the verb is *veshaneik*, meaning "He mixed them." There are many descriptions of this moment is the aggadic midrashim.

כח| וַיְכַסּוּ אֶת הָרֶכֶב... לְכֹל חֵיל פַּרְעֹה. כֵּן דֶּרֶךְ הַמִּקְרָאוֹת לִכְתֹּב לָמֶ״ד יְתֵרָה, כְּמוֹ: "לְכָל כֵּלָיו

וַיְכַסּוּ אֶת הָרֶכֶב... לְכֹל חֵיל פַּרְעֹה 28 – *Covering the chariots...and the whole Egyptian army*: The letter *lamed* prefixed to the word *lekhol* seems to be superfluous. But such constructions are not

שמות | פרק יד | בשלח

רביעי

כו וַיֹּאמֶר יהוה אֶל־מֹשֶׁה נְטֵה אֶת־יָדְךָ עַל־הַיָּם וְיָשֻׁבוּ הַמַּיִם עַל־מִצְרַיִם עַל־רִכְבּוֹ וְעַל־פָּרָשָׁיו: כז וַיֵּט מֹשֶׁה אֶת־יָדוֹ עַל־הַיָּם וַיָּשָׁב הַיָּם לִפְנוֹת בֹּקֶר לְאֵיתָנוֹ וּמִצְרַיִם נָסִים לִקְרָאתוֹ וַיְנַעֵר יהוה אֶת־מִצְרַיִם בְּתוֹךְ הַיָּם: כח וַיָּשֻׁבוּ הַמַּיִם וַיְכַסּוּ אֶת־הָרֶכֶב וְאֶת־הַפָּרָשִׁים לְכֹל חֵיל פַּרְעֹה הַבָּאִים אַחֲרֵיהֶם בַּיָּם לֹא־נִשְׁאַר בָּהֶם עַד־אֶחָד: כט וּבְנֵי יִשְׂרָאֵל הָלְכוּ בַיַּבָּשָׁה בְּתוֹךְ הַיָּם וְהַמַּיִם לָהֶם חֹמָה מִימִינָם וּמִשְּׂמֹאלָם: ל וַיּוֹשַׁע יהוה בַּיּוֹם הַהוּא אֶת־יִשְׂרָאֵל מִיַּד מִצְרָיִם וַיַּרְא יִשְׂרָאֵל אֶת־מִצְרַיִם מֵת עַל־שְׂפַת הַיָּם: לא וַיַּרְא יִשְׂרָאֵל אֶת־הַיָּד הַגְּדֹלָה אֲשֶׁר עָשָׂה יהוה בְּמִצְרַיִם וַיִּירְאוּ הָעָם אֶת־יהוה וַיַּאֲמִינוּ בַּיהוָה וּבְמֹשֶׁה עַבְדּוֹ:

---

uncommon, for we read: *Make all [lekhol] of these of bronze* (27:3), as well as the verses, *All [lekhol] the Tabernacle utensils, for every use* (27:19), *And their sockets, and the pillars, and their cords all [lekhol] their instruments* (Numbers 4:32). This form is merely for stylistic embellishment.

30| וַיַּרְא יִשְׂרָאֵל אֶת־מִצְרַיִם מֵת – *The Israelites saw the Egyptians dead*: For the sea had expelled the Egyptian corpses onto the shore. This was done lest the Israelites worry that just as they had emerged safely on the opposite side of the sea, perhaps their enemies had also surfaced further down the coast and would continue their pursuit.

31| אֶת־הַיָּד הַגְּדֹלָה – *The wondrous power*: [Literally, "the great hand."] Israel witnessed the great strength that the hand of God had unleashed. The Torah employs the word "hand" to connote many different ideas, but all of them connote an actual hand on some level. Commentaries explain each case based on its context.

תֵּעָשֶׂה נְחֹשֶׁת" (להלן כז, ג), וְכֵן: "לְכֹל כְּלֵי הַמִּשְׁכָּן בְּכֹל עֲבֹדָתוֹ" (סוף פסוק יט), "וִיתֵדֹתָם וּמֵיתְרֵיהֶם לְכֹל כְּלֵיהֶם" (במדבר ד, לב), וְאֵינָהּ אֶלָּא תִּקּוּן לָשׁוֹן:

ל| וַיַּרְא יִשְׂרָאֵל אֶת־מִצְרַיִם מֵת. שֶׁפְּלָטָן הַיָּם עַל שְׂפָתוֹ, כְּדֵי שֶׁלֹּא יֹאמְרוּ יִשְׂרָאֵל: כְּשֵׁם שֶׁאָנוּ עוֹלִים מִצַּד זֶה כָּךְ הֵם עוֹלִים מִצַּד אַחֵר רָחוֹק מִמֶּנּוּ וְיִרְדְּפוּ אַחֲרֵינוּ:

לא| אֶת־הַיָּד הַגְּדֹלָה. אֶת הַגְּבוּרָה הַגְּדוֹלָה שֶׁעָשְׂתָה יָדוֹ שֶׁל הַקָּדוֹשׁ בָּרוּךְ הוּא. וְהַרְבֵּה לְשׁוֹנוֹת נוֹפְלִין עַל לְשׁוֹן "יָד", וְכֻלָּן לְשׁוֹן יָד מַמָּשׁ הֵן, וְהַמְפָרֵשׁ יְתַקֵּן הַלָּשׁוֹן אַחַר עִנְיַן הַדִּבּוּר:

15 **1** And then, Moshe and the Israelites sang this song to the Lord: I will sing to the Lord, for He has triumphed in glory; / **2** horse and horseman He hurled into the sea. / The Lord is my strength and song – / and now my salvation. / This is my

---

טו א] **אָז יָשִׁיר־מֹשֶׁה.** אָז כְּשֶׁרָאָה הַנֵּס עָלָה בְּלִבּוֹ שֶׁיָּשִׁיר שִׁירָה. וְכֵן: "אָז יְדַבֵּר יְהוֹשֻׁעַ" (יהושע י, יב), וְכֵן: "וּבַיִת יַעֲשֶׂה לְבַת פַּרְעֹה" (מלכים א' ז, ח), חָשַׁב בְּלִבּוֹ שֶׁיַּעֲשֶׂה לָהּ, אַף כָּאן, "יָשִׁיר", אָמַר לוֹ לִבּוֹ שֶׁיָּשִׁיר, וְכֵן עָשָׂה: "וַיֹּאמְרוּ לֵאמֹר אָשִׁירָה לַה'". וְכֵן בִּיהוֹשֻׁעַ כְּשֶׁרָאָה הַנֵּס אָמַר לוֹ לִבּוֹ שֶׁיְּדַבֵּר, וְכֵן עָשָׂה: "וַיֹּאמֶר לְעֵינֵי יִשְׂרָאֵל" (יהושע שם). וְכֵן שִׁירַת הַבְּאֵר שֶׁפָּתַח בָּהּ: "אָז יָשִׁיר יִשְׂרָאֵל", פֵּרֵשׁ אַחֲרָיו: "עֲלִי בְאֵר עֱנוּ לָהּ" (במדבר כא, יז). "אָז יִבְנֶה שְׁלֹמֹה בָּמָה" (מלכים א' יא, ז) פֵּרְשׁוּ בּוֹ חַכְמֵי יִשְׂרָאֵל שֶׁבִּקֵּשׁ לִבְנוֹת וְלֹא בָנָה. לָמַדְנוּ שֶׁהַיּוֹ"ד עַל שֵׁם הַמַּחֲשָׁבָה נֶאֶמְרָה. זֶהוּ לְיַשֵּׁב פְּשׁוּטוֹ. אֲבָל מִדְרָשׁוֹ, אָמְרוּ רַבּוֹתֵינוּ זִכְרוֹנָם לִבְרָכָה, מִכָּאן רֶמֶז לִתְחִיַּת הַמֵּתִים מִן הַתּוֹרָה, וְכֵן בְּכֻלָּן, חוּץ מִשֶּׁל שְׁלֹמֹה שֶׁפֵּרְשׁוּהוּ בִּקֵּשׁ לִבְנוֹת וְלֹא בָנָה. וְאֵין לוֹמַר וְלֵישֵׁב לָשׁוֹן הַזֶּה כִּשְׁאָר דְּבָרִים הַנִּכְתָּבִים בִּלְשׁוֹן עָתִיד וְהֵן מִיָּד, כְּגוֹן: "כָּכָה יַעֲשֶׂה אִיּוֹב" (איוב א, ה), "עַל פִּי ה' יַחֲנוּ" (במדבר ט, כ), "וְיֵשׁ אֲשֶׁר יִהְיֶה הֶעָנָן" (שם), לְפִי שֶׁהֵן דְּבַר הַהֹוֶה תָּמִיד וְנוֹפֵל בּוֹ בֵּין לְשׁוֹן עָתִיד בֵּין לְשׁוֹן עָבָר, אֲבָל זֶה שֶׁלֹּא הָיָה אֶלָּא לְשָׁעָה אֵינִי יָכוֹל לְיַשְּׁבוֹ בַּלָּשׁוֹן הַזֶּה.

---

15 | 1 | אָז יָשִׁיר־מֹשֶׁה – *And then Moshe sang*: [Literally, "will sing," in the future tense.] When Moshe saw the miracle, he formed the intention to sing a song. The Scripture similarly uses the future tense to express Yehoshua's reaction in the verse, *Then Yehoshua spoke [yedabber] to the* Lord *on the day when the* Lord *delivered up the Amorites before the children of Israel* (Joshua 10:12). Similarly we read, *Shlomo also made [yaaseh] a house for Pharaoh's daughter, whom he had taken as a wife* (I Kings 7:8), meaning that Shlomo determined that he would build her a home. So too here, when witnessing the splitting of the sea, he formed a plan to sing. And Moshe did indeed presently lead the nation in song, as the verse reports with the words *vayomeru lemor* etc. [here untranslated; literally, "and they said, saying:"]. Years later, during his battle with the Amorites, Yehoshua thought that he ought to respond by speaking words of praise to God. This he did, as the verse states: *And he said in the sight of Israel*. We find a parallel verse to ours in the Song of the Well in the book of Numbers, which states: *Then Israel sang [yashir] this song: Spring up, Well* (Numbers 21:17). On the other hand when the verse states: *Then Shlomo built [yivneh] a high place for Kemosh, the abomination of Moav* (I Kings 11:7), that has a slightly different connotation. For the Sages explain that the king planned to build such a monument to idolatry but that in the end he did not go through with it. We see that in all these cases the prefix letter *yod* indicates a person's intention. All this is the explanation of the verse's plain meaning. However, our Sages write in the Midrash that the future tense in our verse is the Torah's allusion to the resurrection of the dead. Furthermore, they hold that the other cases I have cited regarding Yehoshua and the Song of the Well also foreshadow future events. In any event the future construction we see in our verse is not like other such instances in Scripture that suggest a continuous action, such as *Thus Iyov would do [yaaseh]* (Job 1:5), or *According to the commandment of the* Lord *they would encamp [yahanu]* (Numbers 9:20), or subsequently *And at times it was, that the cloud would abide [yihyeh] from evening until morning* (Numbers 9:21). In these

▸

שמות | פרק טו

טו א אָז יָשִׁיר־מֹשֶׁה וּבְנֵי יִשְׂרָאֵל אֶת־הַשִּׁירָה הַזֹּאת לַיהוה וַיֹּאמְרוּ לֵאמֹר אָשִׁירָה לַיהוה כִּי־גָאֹה גָּאָה סוּס ב וְרֹכְבוֹ רָמָה בַיָּם: עָזִּי וְזִמְרָת יָהּ וַיְהִי־לִי

verses the future tense of the verbs connotes an action taking place repeatedly or continuously, which makes it appropriate to use either the future or past-tense form. However, in our case, because Moshe only sang once and not continually, we cannot explain *yashir* as representing a repeated action.

כִּי־גָאֹה גָּאָה — **For He has triumphed in glory**: This phrase should be taken as Targum translates it ["He is exalted above all proud things"]. Another interpretation: No matter how many songs I utter in praise of God, it would not sufficiently describe His greatness. This stands in contrast to mortal kings, whose subjects flatter them undeservedly.

כִּי־גָאֹה גָּאָה. כְּתַרְגּוּמוֹ. דָּבָר אַחֵר, "כִּי גָאֹה גָּאָה", עַל כָּל הַשִּׁירוֹת וְכָל מַה שֶׁאֲקַלֵּס בּוֹ עוֹד יֵשׁ נוֹסָפוֹת, וְלֹא כְּמִדַּת מֶלֶךְ בָּשָׂר וָדָם שֶׁמְּקַלְּסִין אוֹתוֹ וְאֵין בּוֹ:

סוּס וְרֹכְבוֹ — **Horse and horseman**: Horse and rider were fused together so that when the water raised them up to crests of the waves, and plunged them to the troughs of the sea, the pair was not separated.

סוּס וְרֹכְבוֹ. שְׁנֵיהֶם קְשׁוּרִים זֶה בָזֶה, וְהַמַּיִם מַעֲלִין אוֹתָן לָרוּם וְיוֹרְדִין לָעֹמֶק וְאֵינָן נִפְרָדִין:

רָמָה — **He hurled**: [The word *rama* means] "thrown." We find a similar usage in the verse, *they were cast [urmiv] into the midst of the burning fiery furnace* (Daniel 3:21). The Midrash contrasts the verb *rama* in this verse to the term appearing in verse 4, *Pharaoh's chariots and army He hurled [yara] into the sea,* explaining that the two terms connote that the cavalry were first raised to great heights by the waves but were then submerged in the depths of the ocean. This is similar to God's claim to Job: *Who cast [yara] its corner stone?* (Job 38:6), that is, who brought it down from above?

רָמָה. הִשְׁלִיךְ, וְכֵן: "וּרְמִיו לְגוֹא אַתּוּן נוּרָא" (דניאל ג, כא). וּמִדְרַשׁ אַגָּדָה, כָּתוּב אֶחָד אוֹמֵר "רָמָה" וְכָתוּב אֶחָד אוֹמֵר "יָרָה", מְלַמֵּד שֶׁהָיוּ עוֹלִין לָרוּם וְיוֹרְדִין לַתְּהוֹם, כְּמוֹ: "מִי יָרָה אֶבֶן פִּנָּתָהּ" (איוב לח, ו) מִלְמַעְלָה לְמַטָּה.

עָזִּי וְזִמְרָת יָהּ | 2 — **The Lord is my strength and song**: Onkelos translates this clause: "God is my strength and song," understanding *ozzi* as if it were written *uzzi* ["my strength"], and the word *vezimrat* as if it were *vezimrati* ["my song"]. But if Onkelos's interpretation is correct, why is it that the term *ozzi* appears in all of Scripture just three times with this vocalization, all of them in conjunction with the word *zimrat*? On all other occasions the *ayin* is vocalized with a *kubbutz*, such as in the verse *O Lord, my strength [uzzi] and my stronghold* (Jeremiah 16:19), and *Because of his strength [uzzo], will I wait*

עָזִּי וְזִמְרָת יָהּ. אוּנְקְלוֹס תִּרְגֵּם "עָזִּי" כְּמוֹ 'עֻזִּי', "וְזִמְרָת" כְּמוֹ 'זִמְרָתִי'. וַאֲנִי תָּמֵהַּ עַל לְשׁוֹן הַמִּקְרָא, שֶׁאֵין לְךָ כָּמוֹהוּ בִּנְקֻדָּתוֹ בַּמִּקְרָא אֶלָּא בִּשְׁלֹשָׁה מְקוֹמוֹת שֶׁהוּא סָמוּךְ אֵצֶל "וְזִמְרָת", וְכָל שְׁאָר מְקוֹמוֹת נָקוּד שׁוּרֻק, "ה' עָזִּי וּמָעֻזִּי" (ירמיה טז, יט), "עָזּוֹ אֵלֶיךָ אֶשְׁמֹרָה" (תהלים נט, י). וְכֵן

God, I will glorify Him, / my father's God, I will exalt Him. /

כָּל תֵּבָה בַּת שְׁתֵּי אוֹתִיּוֹת הַנְּקוּדָה מְלָאפוּם, כְּשֶׁהִיא מָאֳרֶכֶת בְּאוֹת שְׁלִישִׁית וְאֵין הַשְּׁנִיָּה בִּשְׁבָא חֲטוּפָה, הָרִאשׁוֹנָה נְקוּדָה בְּשׁוּרִיק, כְּגוֹן: עֹז עֻזִּי, דֹּק רֻקִּי, חֹק חֻקִּי, עֹל עֻלּוֹ, "יָסוּר... עֻלּוֹ" (ישעיה יד, כה), כֹּל כֻּלּוֹ, "וְשָׁלִשִׁים עַל כֻּלּוֹ" (לעיל יד, ז). וְאֵלּוּ שְׁלֹשָׁה "עָזִּי וְזִמְרָת" שֶׁל כָּאן וְשֶׁל יְשַׁעְיָה (יב, ב) וְשֶׁל תְּהִלִּים (קיח, יד) נְקוּדִים בַּחֲטָף קָמַץ; וְעוֹד, אֵין בְּאֶחָד מֵהֶם כָּתוּב "וְזִמְרָתִי" אֶלָּא "וְזִמְרָת", וְכֻלָּם סְמוּכִים לָהֶם: "וַיְהִי לִי לִישׁוּעָה". לְכָךְ אֲנִי אוֹמֵר לְיַשֵּׁב לְשׁוֹן הַמִּקְרָא, שֶׁאֵין "עָזִּי" כְּמוֹ "עֻזִּי" וְלֹא "וְזִמְרָת" כְּמוֹ "וְזִמְרָתִי", אֶלָּא "עָזִּי" שֵׁם דָּבָר הוּא, כְּמוֹ: "הַיֹּשְׁבִי בַּשָּׁמַיִם" (תה' קכג, א), "שֹׁכְנִי בְחַגְוֵי סָלַע" (עובדיה א, ג), "שֹׁכְנִי סְנֶה" (דברים לג, טז), וְזֶהוּ הַשֶּׁבַח: עָזִּי וְזִמְרָת יָהּ הוּא הָיָה לִי לִישׁוּעָה. וְ"זִמְרָת" דָּבוּק הוּא לְתֵבַת ה', כְּמוֹ "לְעֶזְרַת ה'" (שופטים ה, כג), "בְּעֶבְרַת ה'" (ישעיה ט, יח), "עַל דִּבְרַת בְּנֵי הָאָדָם" (קהלת ג, יח). וּלְשׁוֹן "וְזִמְרָת" לְשׁוֹן "לֹא תִזְמֹר" (ויקרא כה, ד), "זְמִיר עָרִיצִים" (ישעיה כה, ה), כְּסוּחַ וּכְרִיתָה, עֹז וּנְקָמָתוֹ שֶׁל אֱלֹהֵינוּ הָיָה לָנוּ לִישׁוּעָה. וְאַל תִּתְמַהּ עַל לְשׁוֹן "וַיְהִי", שֶׁלֹּא נֶאֱמַר "הָיָה", שֶׁיֵּשׁ לָנוּ מִקְרָאוֹת מְדַבְּרִים בְּלָשׁוֹן זֶה, וְזֶה דֻגְמָתוֹ: "אֶת קִירוֹת הַבַּיִת סָבִיב לַהֵיכָל וְלַדְּבִיר וַיַּעַשׂ צְלָעוֹת סָבִיב" (מלכים א' ו, ה), הָיָה לוֹ לוֹמַר: "עָשָׂה צְלָעוֹת סָבִיב"; וְכֵן בְּדִבְרֵי הַיָּמִים (ב' י, יז): "וּבְנֵי יִשְׂרָאֵל הַיֹּשְׁבִים בְּעָרֵי יְהוּדָה וַיִּמְלֹךְ עֲלֵיהֶם רְחַבְעָם", הָיָה לוֹ לוֹמַר: "מָלַךְ עֲלֵיהֶם רְחַבְעָם". "מִבִּלְתִּי יְכֹלֶת

(Psalms 59:10). Whenever a two letter word that is vocalized with a *ḥolam* [such as *oz* – "strength"] is subsequently lengthened to three letters [with the addition of a suffix], and the second letter of said word is not marked with a *sheva*, then the first letter's *ḥolam* becomes a *kubbutz*. Examples of this include, *oz* [meaning "strength"] which becomes *uzzi* ["my strength"], *rok* ["spittle"] which becomes *rukki*, *ḥok* ["statute"] which becomes *ḥukki*, and *ol* ["yoke"] which becomes *ulli*. Thus we find the word *ol* transformed into *ullo* in the verse *Then shall his yoke depart from off them* (Isaiah 14:25). And *kol* ["all"] becomes *kullo* in the verse *With officers over them all* (14:7). However, regarding the three instances of *ozzi vezimrat* – in our verse, in Isaiah (12:2) and in Psalms (118:14) – the vowel in question has become a *ḥataf kamatz* [in this edition a *kamatz katan*; in any event, the "o" sound in these verses is retained and not changed to "u," making them unique]. Furthermore, in all three cases the second term, *vezimrat*, does not appear in the as *vezimrati* [only with that suffix would it mean "my song"], and in all of them the phrase is followed by the words "was my salvation." Therefore, in order to explain properly the language of the verse, I must contend that the word *ozzi* is not synonymous with *uzzi*, nor is *vezimrat* the same as *vezimrati*. Rather the term *ozzi* is itself a noun [i.e., the suffixed *yod* does not signify "my"]. It is similar to the construction appearing in the verse *To you I lift my eyes, O You who dwells [hayoshevi] in the heavens* (Psalms 123:1); and in the verse *The pride of your heart has deceived you, you who dwell [shokheni] in the clefts of the rock* (Obadiah 1:3); and *For the good will of Him who dwelled [shokheni] in the bush* (Deuteronomy 33:16). The meaning of the praise offered is thus: "The strength and the vengeance [see further] of the Lord was my salvation." The word *vezimrat* is in the construct state, tying it to the word "Lord" as a possessed object. Similar cases appear in the verse *Because they did not come to the help of [ezrat] the Lord* (Judges 5:23), and in the verse *Through the wrath of [evrat] the Lord of Hosts is the land darkened* (Isaiah 9:18); and *After the speech of [divrat] the sons of men* (Ecclesiastes 3:18). As for the meaning of the word itself, it has a sense similar to that in the verses *You shall neither sow your field nor prune [tizmor] your vineyard* (Leviticus 25:4) and *So the cutting off [zemir] of the tyrants shall be brought low* (Isaiah 25:5). In all these cases the verb implies cutting down

◀

שמות | פרק טו

לִישׁוּעָה   זֶה אֵלִי וְאַנְוֵהוּ   אֱלֹהַי

ה׳ וְגו׳ וַיִּשְׁחָטֵם" (במדבר יד, טז), הָיָה לוֹ לוֹמַר: 'שְׁחָטָם'; "וְהָאֲנָשִׁים אֲשֶׁר שָׁלַח מֹשֶׁה... וַיָּמֻתוּ" (שם פסוקים לו-לז), 'מֵתוּ' הָיָה לוֹ לוֹמַר; "וַיַּחֲסֵף לֹא שָׂם לִבּוֹ אֶל דְּבַר ה׳ וַיַּעֲזֹב" (לעיל ט, כא), הָיָה לוֹ לוֹמַר: 'עָזַב':

or severing. Hence in our verse, Moshe's declaration means: "The strength and vengeance of our God was our salvation." Now you might argue that the verb *vayhi* ["was"] really should have been *haya*. [Verbs of this form, with a prefixed *vav*, usually introduce a new independent clause. According to Rashi's understanding, the whole sentence "the strength and vengeance of our God was our salvation" is a single independent clause, but the verb is situated in the middle rather than introducing it. This would seem to dictate that the verb should take the form *haya*, without a prefixed *vav*.] However, Scripture contains many similar instances. Examples include the verse *Around the outer wall of the House – the outer walls around the sanctuary and inner Sanctuary – he built [vayaas] a tiered structure* (I Kings 6:5), where the word ought to have been *asa* [since the whole quoted sentence is a single independent clause, and the verb is situated in the middle rather than introducing it]; and similarly, *But as for the children of Israel who dwelled in cities of Yehuda, Rehavam reigned [vayimlokh] over them* (II Chronicles 10:17) where the word should have been *malakh*. A third case is the verse *Because the LORD was not able to bring this people into the land which He swore to them, He has slain [vayishhatem] them in the wilderness* (Numbers 14:16), where the verse should have read *shehatam*. Additionally, in that same narrative, we read: *And the men, whom Moshe sent to spy out the land... died [vayamutu] by the plague before the LORD* (Numbers 14:36–37) where the word should have been *metu*. Finally, earlier in this book we read: *And those who set no stock in the LORD's word kept [vayaazov] their slaves and livestock where they were in the fields* (9:21) where the word should have been *azav*.

זֶה אֵלִי. בִּכְבוֹדוֹ נִגְלָה עֲלֵיהֶם וְהָיוּ מַרְאִין אוֹתוֹ בְּאֶצְבַּע, רָאֲתָה שִׁפְחָה עַל הַיָּם מַה שֶּׁלֹּא רָאוּ נְבִיאִים:

זֶה אֵלִי – *This is my God*: God revealed Himself in His glory to Israel such that they were able to point to Him with their fingers. The meanest Israelite maidservant witnessed at the sea a sight that even the later prophets were not privileged to see.

וְאַנְוֵהוּ. אוּנְקְלוֹס תִּרְגֵּם לְשׁוֹן נָוֶה, "נָוֶה שַׁאֲנָן" (ישעיה לג, כ), "לִנְוֵה צֹאן" (שם סה, י). דָּבָר אַחֵר, "וְאַנְוֵהוּ", לְשׁוֹן נוֹי, חֲסַפֵּר נוֹיוֹ וְשִׁבְחוֹ לְבָאֵי עוֹלָם, כְּגוֹן "מַה דּוֹדֵךְ מִדּוֹד" (שיר השירים ה, ט),

וְאַנְוֵהוּ – *I will glorify Him*: Onkelos translates the term *ve'anvehu* as related to the word *naveh* [meaning "dwelling"], as in the verse *Your eyes shall see Jerusalem a quiet habitation [naveh]* (Isaiah 33:20), or the verse *And Sharon shall be a fold [linvei] of flocks* (Isaiah 65:10). Another interpretation for the term *ve'anvehu* connects it to the root *noi* [meaning "beauty"], with

³⁄₄ The Lord is a Master of war; / the Lord is His name. / Pharaoh's chariots and army / He hurled into the sea; / the ₅ best of his officers / drowned in the Sea of Reeds. / The deep

"דּוֹדִי צַח וְאָדוֹם" (שם פסוק י) וְכָל הָעִנְיָן:

אֱלֹהֵי אָבִי. הוּא זֶה, "וַאֲרֹמְמֶנְהוּ":

אֱלֹהֵי אָבִי. לֹא אֲנִי תְּחִלַּת הַקְּדֻשָּׁה, מֻחְזֶקֶת וְעוֹמֶדֶת לִי הַקְּדֻשָּׁה וֶאֱלֹהוּתוֹ עָלַי מִימֵי אֲבוֹתַי:

ג| יהוה אִישׁ מִלְחָמָה. בַּעַל מִלְחָמוֹת, כְּמוֹ: "אִישׁ נָעֳמִי" (רות א, ג), וְכָל 'אִישׁ' וְ'אִישֵׁךְ' מְתַרְגְּמִין בַּעַל. וְכֵן: "וְחָזַקְתָּ וְהָיִיתָ לְאִישׁ" (מלכים א' ב, ב, ג), לְגִבּוֹר:

יהוה שְׁמוֹ. מִלְחֲמוֹתָיו לֹא בִּכְלֵי זַיִן חָלָם בִּשְׁמוֹ הוּא נִלְחָם, "וְחָלְכִי בָא חָלַךְ בְּשֵׁם ה' צְבָאוֹת" (שמואל א' יז, מה). דָּבָר אַחֵר, "ה' שְׁמוֹ", אַף בְּשָׁעָה שֶׁהוּא נִלְחָם וְנוֹקֵם מֵאוֹיְבָיו, חוֹזֵר הוּא בְּמִדָּתוֹ לְרַחֵם עַל קְרוּאָיו וְלָזוּן אֶת כָּל בָּאֵי עוֹלָם, וְלֹא כְמִדַּת מַלְכֵי אֲדָמָה כְּשֶׁהוּא עָסוּק בְּמִלְחָמָה פּוֹנֶה עַצְמוֹ מִכָּל עֲסָקִים וְאֵין בּוֹ כֹּחַ לַעֲשׂוֹת זוֹ וָזוֹ:

ד| יָרָה בַיָּם. "שָׂדֵי בְיַמָּא", "שָׂדֵי" לְשׁוֹן יְרִיָּה. וְכֵן הוּא אוֹמֵר: "אוֹ יָרֹה יִיָּרֶה" (להלן יט, יג), "אוֹ הִשְׁתַּדָּאָה יִשְׁתְּדֵי", וְהַתָּי"ו מְשַׁמֶּשֶׁת בְּחָלּוּ בִּמְקוֹם יִתְפָּעֵל:

the sense of: I will relate His beauty and His praise to everyone on earth. We find such sentiment in the verses: *What is your beloved more than another beloved!... My beloved is white and ruddy* (Song of Songs 5:9–10), and that whole passage.

אֱלֹהֵי אָבִי – *My father's God*: That is: He is my father's God; I will exalt him. [Rashi is explaining the apparent lack of a subject in this clause, arguing that "He" is the implied subject.]

אֱלֹהֵי אָבִי – *My father's God*: I am not the first one to experience His holiness. Rather, His sanctity and His divinity has been present at my side since the days of my ancestors.

3| יהוה אִישׁ מִלְחָמָה – *The Lord is Master of war*: The word *ish* here means "Master," as in the verse *And Elimelekh, Naomi's husband [ish] died* [Ruth 1:3; In Hebrew, "husband" and "master" are denoted by the same word, *baal*]. Every instance of the word *ish* in Scripture with the sense of "husband" is translated by the Targum as *baal*. And thus David, on his deathbed, advises his son Shlomo: *Be you strong, and show yourself a man [ish]* (I Kings 2:2).

יהוה שְׁמוֹ – *The Lord is His name*: [The connection between this phrase and the appellation "Master of war" is that] God does not fight wars with weapons but with the power of His name, as David declares to Golyat: *You come to me with a sword, and with a spear, and with a javelin. But I come to you in the name of the Lord of Hosts, the God of the armies of Israel* (I Samuel 17:45). Another interpretation: Even while God fights and wreaks vengeance upon His enemies, He still maintains His attribute of Mercy in dealing with those who call His name, sustaining all of creation. This stands in contrast to mortal kings, who have no interest in and are incapable of fulfilling their normal duties when they are engaged in war.

4| יָרָה בַיָּם – *He hurled into the sea*: Onkelos renders this phrase: *Shedi veyama* – "He cast them into the sea." We similarly find the verb *yara* used in the warning at Mount Sinai prior to revelation: *No hand shall touch him: he shall be stoned or shot with arrows [yaro yiyyareh]* (19:13), which Onkelos translates as *ishtedaa yishtedei* – "he will be shot." The letter *tav* in that case signals a passive construction of the verb.

◀

שמות | פרק טו

ג אָבִי וַאֲרֹמְמֶנְהוּ: יהוה אִישׁ מִלְחָמָה יהוה
ד שְׁמוֹ: מַרְכְּבֹת פַּרְעֹה וְחֵילוֹ יָרָה בַיָּם וּמִבְחַר
ה שָׁלִשָׁיו טֻבְּעוּ בְיַם־סוּף: תְּהֹמֹת יְכַסְיֻמוּ יָרְדוּ בִמְצוֹלֹת

וּמִבְחַר. שֵׁם דָּבָר, כְּמוֹ: "מֶרְכָּב" (ויקרא טו, ט), "מִשְׁכָּב" (שם פסוק ד), "מִקְרָא קֹדֶשׁ" (לעיל יב, טז):

טֻבְּעוּ. אֵין טְבִיעָה אֶלָּא בִּמְקוֹם טִיט, כְּמוֹ: "טָבַעְתִּי בִּיוֵן מְצוּלָה" (תהלים סט, ג), "וַיִּטְבַּע יִרְמְיָהוּ בַּטִּיט" (ירמיה לח, ו), מְלַמֵּד שֶׁנַּעֲשָׂה הַיָּם טִיט, לִגְמֹל לָהֶם כְּמִדָּתָם שֶׁשִּׁעְבְּדוּ אֶת יִשְׂרָאֵל בְּחֹמֶר וּבִלְבֵנִים:

ה | יְכַסְיֻמוּ. כְּמוֹ "יְכַסוּם". וְהַיּוּ"ד הָאֶמְצָעִית יְתֵרָה בּוֹ וְדֶרֶךְ מִקְרָאוֹת בְּכָךְ, כְּמוֹ: "וּבִקְרְךָ וְצֹאנְךָ יִרְבְּיֻן" (דברים ח, יג), "יִרְוְיֻן מִדֶּשֶׁן בֵּיתֶךָ" (תהלים לו, ט), וְהַיּוּ"ד רִאשׁוֹנָה שֶׁמַּשְׁמָעָהּ לְשׁוֹן עָתִיד, כָּךְ פֵּרְשֵׁהוּ: טֻבְּעוּ בְיַם סוּף כְּדֵי שֶׁיַּחְזְרוּ הַמַּיִם וִיכַסוּ אוֹתָן. "יְכַסְיֻמוּ" אֵין דּוֹמֶה לוֹ בַּמִּקְרָא בִּנְקֻדָּתוֹ, וְדַרְכּוֹ לִהְיוֹת נָקוּד "יְכַסְיֻמוֹ" מְלָאפוּם:

כְּמוֹ־אָבֶן. וּבְמָקוֹם אַחֵר "צָלְלוּ כַעוֹפֶרֶת" (להלן פסוק י), וּבְמָקוֹם אַחֵר "יֹאכְלֵמוֹ כַּקַּשׁ" (להלן פסוק ז). הָרְשָׁעִים כַּקַּשׁ הוֹלְכִים וּמִטָּרְפִין עוֹלִין וְיוֹרְדִין, בֵּינוֹנִים כָּאֶבֶן, וְהַכְּשֵׁרִים כַּעוֹפֶרֶת שֶׁנָּחוּ מִיָּד:

וּמִבְחַר – *The best*: The term *mivḥar* is a noun [meaning "a thing chosen." The initial *mem* prefixed to a verbal root creates a noun], similar in construction to the words *merkav* [chariot, i.e., "a thing ridden"], *mishkav* [couch, i.e., "a thing lain on"], and *mikra kodesh* [sacred assembly, i.e., "a thing called"].

טֻבְּעוּ – *Drowned*: The elite of Pharaoh's guard sank in the mud. We find similar language in the verse *I sink in deep mire* (Psalms 69:3) and the verse *Then they took Yirmeyahu and cast him into the pit… and Yirmeyahu sank in the mire* (Jeremiah 38:6). The sea had turned into mud in order to punish the Egyptians measure for measure. For the oppressors had compelled Israel to work with mortar and bricks.

5 | יְכַסְיֻמוּ – *Covered them*: The word in question is the same as *yekhasum* [the more usual spelling], meaning "covered them." The middle letter *yod* is superfluous, similar to the verbal forms in the verses *And when your herds and your flocks multiply [yirbiyun]* [Deuteronomy 8:13, the verb ought to have been *yirbun*] and *They are abundantly satisfied [yirveyun] with the fatness of your house* [Psalms 36:9, which could have read *yirvun*]. Meanwhile, the first letter *yod* of the word indicates the future tense [in contrast to the previous verb *tubbe'u*, which Rashi holds to mean "sank" in the mud – see above]. What this implies is that the cavalry became mired in the muck of the Sea of Reeds so that the water "would" return and cover them. The vocalization of the word *yekhasyumu* is unique; all other verbs of this form end with a *shuruk* rather than a *ḥolam*; so this word would ordinarily be *yekhasyumo*.

כְּמוֹ־אָבֶן – *Like a stone*: In verse 10 below, the soldiers are said to sink *like lead in mighty waters*, whereas in verse 7 the enemy is compared to straw: *It consumed them like stubble*. Each of these metaphors describes a different type of villain: The wicked were like straw which does not easily sink – they were tossed up and down in the sea until they died. The average characters sank slowly like a stone, and the most decent soldiers sank quickly like lead and suffered least of all.

waters covered them; / they sank to the depths like a stone. /
6 Your right hand, LORD, majestic in power,/ Your right hand,
7 LORD, shatters the enemy. / In the greatness of Your majesty,
You overthrew those who rose against You. / You sent forth
8 Your rage; it consumed them like stubble. / By the blast of
Your nostrils the waters heaped; / the surge stood upright as

ו| יְמִינְךָ... יְמִינְךָ. שְׁתֵּי פְעָמִים, כְּשֶׁיִּשְׂרָאֵל עוֹשִׂין רְצוֹנוֹ שֶׁל מָקוֹם הַשְּׂמֹאל נַעֲשֵׂית יָמִין:

יְמִינְךָ יהוה נֶאְדָּרִי בַּכֹּחַ. לְהַצִּיל אֶת יִשְׂרָאֵל, וִימִינְךָ הַשֵּׁנִית "תִּרְעַץ אוֹיֵב":

נֶאְדָּרִי. כְּמוֹ: "רַבָּתִי עָם" (איכה א, א), "שָׂרָתִי בַּמְּדִינוֹת" (שם), "גְּנֻבְתִי יוֹם" (בראשית לא, לט):

תִּרְעַץ אוֹיֵב. תָּמִיד הִיא רוֹעֶצֶת וּמְשַׁבֶּרֶת הָאוֹיֵב, וְדוֹמֶה לוֹ: "וַיִּרְעֲצוּ וַיְרֹצְצוּ אֶת בְּנֵי יִשְׂרָאֵל", בְּשׁוֹפְטִים (י, ח):

ז| תַּהֲרֹס קָמֶיךָ. תָּמִיד אַתָּה הוֹרֵס קָמֶיךָ הַקָּמִים נֶגְדְּךָ. וּמִי הֵם הַקָּמִים כְּנֶגְדּוֹ? אֵלּוּ הַקָּמִים עַל יִשְׂרָאֵל. וְכֵן הוּא אוֹמֵר: "כִּי הִנֵּה אוֹיְבֶיךָ יֶהֱמָיוּן" (תהלים פג, ג), וּמַה הִיא הַהֲמִיָּה? "עַל עַמְּךָ יַעֲרִימוּ סוֹד" (שם פסוק ד), וְעַל זֶה קוֹרֵא אוֹתָם אוֹיְבָיו:

ח| וּבְרוּחַ אַפֶּיךָ. הַיּוֹצֵא מִשְּׁנֵי נְחִירִים שֶׁל אַף. דִּבֵּר הַכָּתוּב כִּבְיָכוֹל בַּשְּׁכִינָה כִּדְמוּת מֶלֶךְ בָּשָׂר וָדָם, כְּדֵי לְהַשְׁמִיעַ אֹזֶן הַבְּרִיּוֹת כְּפִי הַהֹוֶה שֶׁיּוּכְלוּ לְהָבִין דָּבָר. כְּשָׁאָדָם

6| יְמִינְךָ... יְמִינְךָ – *Your right hand...Your right hand*: The phrase appears twice in the verse to imply that when Israel fulfills the will of God, then even His left hand [which signifies the attribute of Justice] behaves like His right hand [the attribute of Compassion].

יְמִינְךָ יהוה נֶאְדָּרִי בַּכֹּחַ – *Your right hand, LORD, majestic in power*: Your right hand engages in Israel's rescue, while Your other right hand "shatters the enemy."

נֶאְדָּרִי – *Majestic*: [The final *yod* of the word *nedari* is simply a poetic flourish with no added meaning. This is one of many such adjectives with an extra *yod*,] like *She that was great [rabati] among the nations and princess [sarati] among the provinces* (Lamentations 1:1) and *Whether stolen [genuveti] by day or stolen [genuveti] by night* (Genesis 31:39).

תִּרְעַץ אוֹיֵב – *Shatters the enemy*: The future tense of the verb *tiratz* teaches that God constantly smashes and breaks the enemy. We find the same root in the verse *And that year they crushed [vayiratzu] and oppressed the children of Israel* (Judges 10:8).

7| תַּהֲרֹס קָמֶיךָ – *You overthrew those who rose against You*: [This verb too is in the future tense, which can also be used in the sense of the present simple:] "You always overthrow those who rise up against You." And who are they? Those who strive to defeat Israel. So we see in the verse: *Your enemies make a tumult* (Psalms 83:3). What tumult do they cause? *They take crafty counsel against Your people* (Psalms 83:4). For this hostility to Israel, they are called Your enemies.

8| וּבְרוּחַ אַפֶּיךָ – *By the blast of Your nostrils*: [The word *af* means nose, but here the term *appekha* is plural. Thus the phrase must refer to] the wind that emerges from the nose's two nostrils. The text uses anthropomorphism, describing God as a king of flesh and blood, to make God's behavior more accessible to readers. God is therefore portrayed as a man who

שמות | פרק טו

א כְּמוֹ־אָבֶן: יְמִינְךָ יְהוָה נֶאְדָּרִי בַּכֹּחַ יְמִינְךָ
ו יְהוָה תִּרְעַץ אוֹיֵב: וּבְרֹב גְּאוֹנְךָ תַּהֲרֹס
ח קָמֶיךָ תְּשַׁלַּח חֲרֹנְךָ יֹאכְלֵמוֹ כַּקַּשׁ: וּבְרוּחַ
אַפֶּיךָ נֶעֶרְמוּ מַיִם נִצְּבוּ כְמוֹ־נֵד

כּוֹעֵס יוֹצֵא רוּחַ מִנְּחִירָיו, וְכֵן: "עָלָה עָשָׁן בְּאַפּוֹ" (תהלים יח, ט), וְכֵן: "וּמֵרוּחַ אַפּוֹ יִכְלוּ" (איוב ד, ט), וְזֶהוּ שֶׁאָמַר: "לְמַעַן שְׁמִי אַאֲרִיךְ אַפִּי" (ישעיה מח, ט), כְּשֶׁנַּעְפּוֹ נָחָה נְשִׁימָתוֹ אֲרֻכָּה וּכְשֶׁהוּא כּוֹעֵס נְשִׁימָתוֹ קְצָרָה. "וּתְהִלָּתִי אֶחֱטָם לָךְ" (שם), וּלְמַעַן תְּהִלָּתִי אָשִׂים חָטָם בְּאַפִּי לִסְתּוֹם נְחִירַי בִּפְנֵי הָאַף וְהָרוּחַ שֶׁלֹּא יֵצְאוּ "לָךְ", בִּשְׁבִילְךָ. "אֶחֱטָם" כְּמוֹ "נָאקָה הַחַטָּם" בְּמַסֶּכֶת שַׁבָּת (דף נא ע״ב), כָּךְ נִרְאָה בְּעֵינַי. וְכָל אַף וְחָרוֹן שֶׁבַּמִּקְרָא אֲנִי אוֹמֵר כֵּן: "חָרָה אַף" (ישעיה ה, כה) כְּמוֹ "וְעַצְמִי חָרָה מִנִּי חֹרֶב" (איוב ל, ל) לְשׁוֹן שְׂרֵפָה וּמוֹקֵד, שֶׁהַנְּחִירַיִם מִתְחַמְּמִים וְנֶחֱרִים בְּעֵת הַקֶּצֶף, וְחָרוֹן מִגִּזְרַת חָרָה כְּמוֹ רָצוֹן מִגִּזְרַת רָצָה, וְכֵן חֵמָה לְשׁוֹן חֲמִימוּת, עַל כֵּן הוּא אוֹמֵר: "וַחֲמָתוֹ בָּעֲרָה בוֹ" (אסתר א, יב), וּבְנוֹחַ הַחֵמָה אוֹמֵר: "נִתְקָרְרָה דַּעְתּוֹ" (יבמות סג ע״א).

נֶעֶרְמוּ מַיִם. אוּנְקְלוּס תִּרְגֵּם לְשׁוֹן עַרְמִימוּת. וּלְשׁוֹן צַחוּת הַמִּקְרָא כְּמוֹ: "עֲרֵמַת חִטִּים" (שיר השירים ז, ג), וְ"נִצְּבוּ כְמוֹ נֵד" יוֹכִיחַ.

---

snorts from his nostrils when angry. We find similar expressions in the verses *There went up a smoke out of His nostrils* (Psalms 18:9) and *By the breath of God they perish* (Job 4:9). Now when one is incensed, his breath becomes shorter, and when the person's anger abates, his breathing becomes slower and longer. Thus we read: *For My name's sake will I defer My anger* [Isaiah 48:9; literally, "lengthen my breath"]. And the same verse continues, *and for My praise will I refrain for you [ehetam lakh]* (Isaiah 48:9) – this literally means "I will hold my breath," blocking My nostrils to withhold the wind and wrath inside Me. Furthermore, the term *lakh* there means "on your behalf" [see commentary on 14:14]. We read in the Talmud (Shabbat 51b) that a camel may walk about on the Sabbath with a ring in its nose [*ḥatam*; this supports Rashi's claim that *eḥetam* means "I will block my nose"]. This seems to me correct. What's more, all instances of the term *ḥaron af* in Scripture connote this kind of human anger visible in the nose. Such is the case in the verse *Therefore the anger of the Lord burns [ḥara af] against His people* (Isaiah 5:25). The verb *ḥara* denotes burning and blazing, as in the verse *My bones are burned [ḥara] with heat* (Job 30:30). This is apparent in the nose because a person's nostrils become hot when he is angry. And the verbal noun *ḥaron* stems from the root *ḥara* just like the root *ratza* [meaning "to desire"] becomes *ratzon* ["will"]. Additionally, the word *ḥema*, also denoting anger, is derived from *ḥamimut* ["heat"], which explains the verse *And his anger [ḥamato] burned in him* (Esther 1:12). Conversely, when a person's anger dissipates, he is said to cool down [see Yevamot 63a].

נֶעֶרְמוּ מַיִם – *The waters heaped*: Onkelos connects the verb *ne'ermu* to *armimut* [meaning "wiliness" – the sea waters schemed to drown the Egyptians while sparing Israel]. But the clearest meaning for the term relates to the phrase "a heap [*aremat*] of wheat" (Song of Songs 7:3). The continuation of our verse confirms this understanding, as it states: *The surge stood upright*.

◀

9 a wall; / the deeps congealed at the heart of the sea. / The enemy said, "I will give chase, will overtake, / I will divide the spoils. / My desire shall gorge its fill of them. / I will draw my

נֶעֶרְמוּ מָיִם. מִמּוּקַד רוּחַ שֶׁיָּצָא מֵאַפְּךָ יָבְשׁוּ הַמַּיִם וְהֵם נַעֲשׂוּ כְּמִין גַּלִּים וּכְרִיּוֹת שֶׁל עֲרֵמָה שֶׁהֵם גְּבוֹהִים:

כְּמוֹ־נֵד. כְּתַרְגּוּמוֹ, "כְּשׁוּר", כְּחוֹמָה:

נֶעֶרְמוּ – *Heaped*: The burning blast from Your nostrils dried up the waters, which became like dunes and high piles of wheat.

כְּמוֹ־נֵד – *As a wall*: This should be understood as the Targum renders it: *shur* [meaning "wall"].

נֵד. לְשׁוֹן עִבּוּר וְכִנּוּס, כְּמוֹ: "נֵד קָצִיר בְּיוֹם נַחֲלָה" (ישעיה יז, יא), "כֹּנֵס כַּנֵּד" (תהלים לג, ז), לֹא כָּתַב 'כֹּנֵס כַּנּאד' אֶלָּא "כַּנֵּד", וְאִלּוּ הָיָה "כַּנּאד" כְּמוֹ 'בַּנּאדֹ' וְ'כֹנֵס' לְשׁוֹן הַכְנָסָה, הָיָה לוֹ לִכְתֹּב 'מַכְנִיס כְּבַנּאד מֵי הַיָּם'. אֶלָּא "כֹּנֵס" לְשׁוֹן אֹסֶף וְצוֹבֵר הוּא, וְכֵן: "קָמוּ נֵד אֶחָד" (יהושע ג, טז), "וַיַּעַמְדוּ נֵד אֶחָד" (שם פסוק יג), וְאֵין לְשׁוֹן קִימָה וַעֲמִידָה בְּנֹאדוֹת חֲלָא בְּחוֹמוֹת וְצִבּוּרִים. וְלֹא מָצִינוּ 'נֹאד' נָקוּד חָלֶם בְּמִלְחָמוֹת, כְּמוֹ: "שִׂימָה דִמְעָתִי בְנֹאדֶךָ" (תהלים נו, ט), "אֶת נֹאוד הֶחָלָב" (שופטים ד, יט):

נֵד – *A wall*: The term *ned* implies heaping and gathering together, as in the verse *Yet the harvest [ned] shall disappear in the day of grief* (Isaiah 17:11) and *He gathers the waters of the sea together like a heap [kaned]* (Psalms 33:7). Now note that this last verse does not read *kanod* [meaning "like a flask"]. If the term *kaned* were synonymous with *kanod*, and were the term "gathers" understood in the sense of the collecting of a liquid, the verse would be praising God for collecting the waters of the sea as into a flask. But the text actually means that God gathers the waters and heaps them up. The description of the Jordan splitting similarly reads: *The waters… rose up in a heap [ned]* (Joshua 3:16), and: *They shall stand in a single heap [ned]* (Joshua 3:13). It would not make sense to portray water as rising up and standing up in flasks, but the imagery is coherent when water is compared to walls and heaps. Furthermore, the word *nod* is always vocalized with a *holam* [and never with a *tzerei* as in *ned*]. Hence the verses *Put my tears into your bottle [nodekha]* (Psalms 56:9), and *She opened a bottle [nod] of milk* (Judges 4:19).

קָפְאוּ. כְּמוֹ: "וְכַגְּבִינָה תַּקְפִּיאֵנִי" (איוב י, י), שֶׁהִקְשׁוּ וְנַעֲשׂוּ כַּאֲבָנִים, וְהַמַּיִם זוֹרְקִים אֶת הַמִּצְרִים עַל הָאֶבֶן בְּכֹחַ וְנִלְחָמִים בָּם בְּכָל מִינֵי קֹשִׁי:

קָפְאוּ – *Congealed*: This verb makes a similar appearance in the verse *And curdled me [takpieni] like cheese* (Job 10:10), denoting a substance that has been solidified and made like stone. The sea thus cast the Egyptians forcefully against the rock-hard surface and fought them with all manner of harshness.

בְּלֶב־יָם. בְּחֹזֶק הַיָּם. וְדֶרֶךְ הַמִּקְרָאוֹת לְדַבֵּר כֵּן: "עַד לֵב הַשָּׁמַיִם" (דברים ד, יא), "בְּלֵב הָאֵלָה" (שמואל ב' יח, יד), לְשׁוֹן עִקָּרוֹ וְתָקְפּוֹ שֶׁל דָּבָר:

בְּלֶב־יָם – *At the heart of the sea*: The "heart" refers to the strength of the sea. For the term "heart" is often used in Scripture to refer to the strongest essence of an object. Hence we read: *And the mountain burned with fire to the heart of heaven* (Deuteronomy 4:11), and: *In the heart of the oak* (II Samuel 18:14).

ט נֹזְלִים ׃ קָפְאוּ תְהֹמֹת בְּלֶב־יָם אָמַר
אוֹיֵב אֶרְדֹּף אַשִּׂיג אֲחַלֵּק שָׁלָל תִּמְלָאֵמוֹ

9 אָמַר אוֹיֵב – *The enemy said:* In order to persuade his nation to follow him into battle, Pharaoh promised his army: *I will give chase, will overtake, I will divide the spoils* with my officers and my servants.

תִּמְלָאֵמוֹ – *Shall gorge:* The word *timla'emo* means "shall be filled with them" [*timmalei mehem*].

נַפְשִׁי – *My desire:* [Literally, "my soul," the word *nafshi* here means] "my spirit" or "my desire." Now, do not be surprised that a single word – *timla'emo* – represents a contraction of two words – *timmalei mehem*; such constructions are ubiquitous in Scripture. For example, when the verse states: *For you have given me [netattani] a Negev land* (Judges 1:15) the single word is a combination of *natatta li*. Similarly, the verse states: *They could not speak [dabbero] peaceably to him* (Genesis 37:4) as if the Torah was written: *dabber immo*. A further case appears in the verse *My children have gone out of me [yetza'uni]* (Jeremiah 10:20) which is the same as *yatze'u mimmenni*. Also: *I would declare to him [aggidennu] the number of my steps* (Job 31:37) where the text could have stated two words: *aggid lo*. In our verse as well, the verb *timla'emo* is likewise a substitute for the words *timmalei mehem*.

אָרִיק חַרְבִּי – *I will draw my sword:* The verb *arik* [literally, "empty"] in this phrase means "unsheathe." To remove a sword from its scabbard is to empty the case, which explains the use of this root. Similarly, in the narrative of Yosef's brothers we read: *And it came to pass as they emptied [merikim] their sacks* (Genesis 42:35), while a later verse states: *Will empty [yariku] his vessels* (Jeremiah 48:12). Now one might argue that while it makes sense to speak of a scabbard, vessel, or sack being emptied, one would not use such a verb in reference to the contents of these containers – the sword or the wine are not "emptied." Instead, this line of reasoning goes, the verb in question is the same as in the phrase *He armed [vayarek] his trained servants* (Genesis 14:14), and that here Pharaoh has boasted that he will arm himself with his sword. Nevertheless, we do indeed find the verb "to empty" [*haraka*] applied to the thing being taken out. Such is the sense of the verse *For your flowing [turak] oil*

ט | **אָמַר אוֹיֵב.** לְעַמּוֹ כְּשֶׁפִּתָּם בִּדְבָרִים, אֶרְדֹּף וְאַשִּׂיגֵם וַאֲחַלֵּק שָׁלָלָם עִם שָׂרַי וַעֲבָדַי:

תִּמְלָאֵמוֹ. תִּמָּלֵא מֵהֶם:

נַפְשִׁי. רוּחִי וּרְצוֹנִי. וְאַל תִּתְמַהּ עַל תֵּבָה הַמְדַבֶּרֶת בִּשְׁתַּיִם, "תִּמְלָאֵמוֹ" – תִּמָּלֵא מֵהֶם, יֵשׁ הַרְבֵּה בַּלָּשׁוֹן הַזֶּה: "כִּי אֶרֶץ הַנֶּגֶב נְתַתָּנִי" (שופטים א, טו) כְּמוֹ נָתַתָּ לִי, "וְלֹא יָכְלוּ דַּבְּרוֹ לְשָׁלֹם" (בראשית לז, ד) כְּמוֹ דַּבֵּר עִמּוֹ, "בָּנַי יְצָאֻנִי" (ירמיה י, כ) כְּמוֹ יָצְאוּ מִמֶּנִּי, "מִסְפַּר צְעָדַי אַגִּידֶנּוּ" (איוב לא, לז) כְּמוֹ אַגִּיד לוֹ, אַף כָּאן "תִּמְלָאֵמוֹ" תִּמָּלֵא נַפְשִׁי מֵהֶם:

אָרִיק חַרְבִּי. אֶשְׁלֹף. וְעַל שֵׁם שֶׁהוּא מֵרִיק אֶת הַתַּעַר בִּשְׁלִיפָתוֹ וְנִשְׁאָר רֵיק נוֹפֵל בּוֹ לְשׁוֹן הֲרָקָה, כְּמוֹ: "מְרִיקִים שַׂקֵּיהֶם" (בראשית מב, לה), "וְכֵלָיו יָרִיקוּ" (ירמיה מח, יב). וְאַל תֹּאמַר, אֵין לְשׁוֹן רִיקוּת נוֹפֵל עַל הַיּוֹצֵא אֶלָּא עַל הַתִּיק וְעַל הַשַּׂק וְעַל הַכְּלִי שֶׁיָּצָא מִמֶּנָּה, חֲבָל לֹא עַל הַחֶרֶב וְעַל הַיַּיִן, וְלִדְחֹק וּלְפָרֵשׁ "מֵרִיק חַרְבּוֹ" כִּלְשׁוֹן "וַיָּרֶק אֶת חֲנִיכָיו" (בראשית יד, יד), חָזֵין בְּחַרְבּוֹ – מַעֲנוּ הַלָּשׁוֹן מוּסָב אַף עַל הַיּוֹצֵא, "שֶׁמֶן תּוּרָק" (שיר השירים א, ג), "וְלֹא הוּרַק מִכְּלִי אֶל כֶּלִי" (ירמיה מח, יא), לֹא הוּרַק הַכְּלִי אֵין

10 sword, / and my hand destroy them." / You blew with Your wind; the sea covered over them. / They sank like lead in
11 mighty waters. / Who is like You, Lord, among the mighty? / Who is like You – majestic in holiness, / awesome in glory,
12 working wonders? / You reached out Your right hand – / the
13 earth swallowed them up. / In Your love, You guided out the people You redeemed. / In Your strength, You led them to
14 Your holy abode. / Nations heard and they trembled; / terror
15 seized the Philistines. / The chiefs of Edom were dismayed,

---

you are renowned (Song of Songs 1:3), as well as *He has not been emptied [hurak] from vessel to vessel* (Jeremiah 48:11). The subject of the verb in the latter verse in not the vessel but the wine. Thus the verb "to empty" can refer to contents being taken out. In conclusion, consider the verse *And they shall draw [veheriku] their swords against the beauty of your wisdom* (Ezekiel 28:7), regarding king Ḥiram.

תּוֹרִישֵׁמוֹ – *Shall destroy them*: The verb means that Pharaoh planned to despoil and impoverish Israel, as in the verse, *The Lord makes poor [morish] and makes rich* (I Samuel 2:7)

10 | **נָשַׁפְתָּ** – *You blew*: The term *nashafta* connotes blowing, as in the verse, *he merely blows [nashaf] upon them and they wither* (Isaiah 40:24).

צָלֲלוּ – *They sank*: They plunged, they descended into the deep. The word *tzalelu* is related to the term *metzula* ["depths," in verse 5].

כַּעוֹפָרֶת – *Like lead*: The Old French term for this material is *plomb*.

11 | **בָּאֵלִם** – *Among the mighty*: The term *elim* means "the mighty," as in the verse *He has also taken away the mighty [elei] of the land* (Ezekiel 17:13), and the verse *O my strength [eyaluti] hasten to help me* (Psalms 22:20).

נוֹרָא תְהִלֹּת – *Awesome in glory*: [Literally, "fearful of praises." This phrase means that] it is fearful to sing Your praises lest they fall short of adequate expression. Hence the Psalmist declares: *To You, silence is praise* (Psalms 65:2).

שמות | פרק טו

י נַפְשִׁ֔י אָרִ֣יק חַרְבִּ֔י תּוֹרִישֵׁ֖מוֹ יָדִ֑י׃
נָשַׁ֣פְתָּ בְרוּחֲךָ֖ כִּסָּ֣מוֹ יָ֑ם צָֽלֲלוּ֙ כַּֽעוֹפֶ֔רֶת בְּמַ֖יִם
יא אַדִּירִֽים׃ מִֽי־כָמֹ֤כָה בָּֽאֵלִם֙ יְהוָ֔ה מִ֥י
כָּמֹ֖כָה נֶאְדָּ֣ר בַּקֹּ֑דֶשׁ נוֹרָ֥א תְהִלֹּ֖ת עֹ֥שֵׂה
יב פֶֽלֶא׃ נָטִ֙יתָ֙ יְמִ֣ינְךָ֔ תִּבְלָעֵ֖מוֹ אָֽרֶץ׃ נָחִ֥יתָ
בְחַסְדְּךָ֖ עַם־ז֣וּ גָּאָ֑לְתָּ נֵהַ֥לְתָּ בְעָזְּךָ֖ אֶל־נְוֵ֥ה
יד קָדְשֶֽׁךָ׃ שָֽׁמְע֥וּ עַמִּ֖ים יִרְגָּז֑וּן חִ֣יל
טו אָחַ֔ז יֹשְׁבֵ֖י פְּלָֽשֶׁת׃ אָ֤ז נִבְהֲלוּ֙ אַלּוּפֵ֣י

12| נָטִיתָ יְמִינְךָ – *You reached out Your right hand*: When the Holy One, blessed be He, extends His hand, the wicked fall and perish, for all creatures lean on His arm and collapse when it is withdrawn. Thus the verse states: *When the Lord stretches out His hand, the helper shall stumble* (Isaiah 31:3). This may be compared to a man who holds a glass jar in his open palm. If he tilts his arm a bit, the vessel will tumble over and shatter.

תִּבְלָעֵמוֹ אָרֶץ – *The earth swallowed them up*: Burial was the Egyptians' reward for having once acknowledged that *The Lord is in the right* (9:27).

13| נֵהַלְתָּ – *You led*: The verb *nehalta* is related to the *menahel* [meaning "to direct"]. Onkelos translates the word as connoting "carrying" or "transporting," but it is unclear how he derives that from the Hebrew word *nehalta*.

14| יִרְגָּזוּן – *They trembled*: [The verb is in the present tense. It means:] "They tremble."

יֹשְׁבֵי פְּלָשֶׁת – *The Philistines*: The Philistines were terrified because they had previously killed members of the tribe of Efrayim when they had sought to force their way out of Egypt before the time had come, as is stated explicitly in the verse *The men of Gat...slew them* (I Chronicles 7:21).

15| אַלּוּפֵי אֱדוֹם...אֵילֵי מוֹאָב – *The chiefs of Edom...Moav's leaders*: Why were these nations at all afraid? Israel was not headed

---

יב| **נָטִיתָ יְמִינְךָ.** כְּשֶׁהַקָּדוֹשׁ בָּרוּךְ הוּא נוֹטֶה יָדוֹ הָרְשָׁעִים כָּלִים וְנוֹפְלִים, לְפִי שֶׁהַכֹּל נָתוּן בְּיָדוֹ וְנוֹפְלִים בִּנְטִיָּתָהּ, וְכֵן הוּא אוֹמֵר: "ה' יַטֶּה יָדוֹ וְכָשַׁל עוֹזֵר וְנָפַל עָזֻר" (ישעיה לא, ג). מָשָׁל לִכְלִי זְכוּכִית הַנְּתוּנִים בְּיַד אָדָם, מַטֶּה יָדוֹ מְעַט וְהֵם נוֹפְלִים וּמִשְׁתַּבְּרִים.

תִּבְלָעֵמוֹ אָרֶץ. מִכָּאן שֶׁזָּכוּ לִקְבוּרָה, בִּשְׂכַר שֶׁאָמְרוּ: "ה' הַצַּדִּיק" (לעיל ט, כז).

יג| **נֵהַלְתָּ.** לְשׁוֹן מְנַהֵל. וְאוּנְקְלוֹס תִּרְגֵּם לְשׁוֹן נוֹשֵׂא וְסוֹבֵל, וְלֹא דִקְדֵּק לְפָרֵשׁ אַחַר לְשׁוֹן הָעִבְרִית.

יד| **יִרְגָּזוּן.** מִתְרַגְּזִין.

יֹשְׁבֵי פְּלָשֶׁת. מִפְּנֵי שֶׁהָרְגוּ אֶת בְּנֵי אֶפְרַיִם שֶׁמִּהֲרוּ אֶת הַקֵּץ וְיָצְאוּ בְּחָזְקָה, כַּמְפוֹרָשׁ בְּדִבְרֵי הַיָּמִים (א' ז, כא): "וַהֲרָגוּם אַנְשֵׁי גַת".

טו| **אַלּוּפֵי אֱדוֹם... אֵילֵי מוֹאָב.** וַהֲלֹא לֹא הָיָה לָהֶם לִירֹא כְּלוּם, שֶׁהֲרֵי לֹא עֲלֵיהֶם הוֹלְכִים? אֶלָּא

then, / Moav's leaders were seized with trembling, / the people of Canaan melted away. / Dread, terror fell upon them; / by Your arm's power they were stilled as stone – / until Your people crossed, Lord, / until the people You acquired crossed over. / You will bring them, You will plant them on the mountain, Your heritage – / the place, Lord, that You made for Your dwelling, / the sanctuary, Lord, that Your hands established. / The Lord will reign for ever and all time. / This they sang when Pharaoh's horses, chariots, and cavalry had gone into the sea / and the Lord had brought the waters of the sea back over them / while the Israelites had walked on dry land through the sea.

¹⁶

¹⁷

¹⁸
¹⁹

מִפְּנֵי חֲנִיּוֹת שֶׁהָיוּ מִתְחוֹנְנִים וּמִתְעָרְדִים עַל כְּבוֹדָם שֶׁל יִשְׂרָאֵל:

in their direction. Rather, they were aggrieved and distressed that Israel had achieved such glory.

נָמֹגוּ. נָמַסּוּ, כְּמוֹ: "בִּרְבִיבִים תְּמֹגְגֶנָּה" (תהלים סה, יא), חָמְדוּ: עָלֵינוּ הֵם בָּאִים לְכַלּוֹתֵינוּ וְלִירַשׁ אֶת אַרְצֵנוּ:

נָמֹגוּ – *Melted away*: The word *namogu* means "melted." It appears in a different form in the verse, *You melted [temogegenna] with showers* (Psalms 65:11). The Canaanites were terrified that the Israelites were going to march on them, destroy them, and inherit their land.

טז | תִּפֹּל עֲלֵיהֶם אֵימָתָה. עַל הָרְחוֹקִים:

16 | **תִּפֹּל עֲלֵיהֶם אֵימָתָה** – *Dread fell upon them*: Dread fell upon distant peoples.

וָפַחַד. עַל הַקְּרוֹבִים, כְּעִנְיָן שֶׁנֶּאֱמַר: "כִּי שָׁמַעְנוּ אֵת אֲשֶׁר הוֹבִישׁ" וְגוֹ' (יהושע ב, י):

וָפַחַד – *Terror*: Terror beset those close by, as the verse attests [regarding the inhabitants of Yeriḥo], *For we have heard how the Lord dried up the waters of the Sea of Reeds* (Joshua 2:10).

עַד־יַעֲבֹר... עַד־יַעֲבֹר. כְּתַרְגּוּמוֹ:

עַד־יַעֲבֹר... עַד־יַעֲבֹר – *Until Your people crossed...crossed over*: The Targum's rendering of the verse is accurate. [It links the repeated phrase to Israel's crossing of the Jordan and Arnon rivers].

קָנִיתָ. חִבַּבְתָּ מִשְּׁאָר אֻמּוֹת, כְּחֵפֶץ הַקָּנוּי בְּדָמִים יְקָרִים שֶׁחָבִיב עַל הָאָדָם:

קָנִיתָ – *You acquired*: You adore Israel more than all the world's nations, as if it were an expensive object that a person purchases and cherishes.

יז-יח | תְּבִאֵמוֹ. נִתְנַבֵּא מֹשֶׁה שֶׁלֹּא יִכָּנֵס לָאָרֶץ, לְכָךְ לֹא נֶאֱמַר "תְּבִיאֵנוּ":

17–18 | **תְּבִאֵמוֹ** – *You will bring them*: Moshe prophesied that he would not accompany the nation into the land of Israel which is why he said "you will bring them" and not "you will bring us."

מָכוֹן לְשִׁבְתְּךָ. מִקְדָּשׁ שֶׁל מַטָּה מְכֻוָּן כְּנֶגֶד כִּסֵּא שֶׁל מַעְלָה אֲשֶׁר "פָּעַלְתָּ":

מָכוֹן לְשִׁבְתְּךָ – *The place...for Your dwelling*: The earthly Temple stands aligned with God's throne above, which He "made."

שמות | פרק טו

טז
אָז נִבְהֲלוּ אַלּוּפֵי אֱדוֹם אֵילֵי מוֹאָב יֹאחֲזֵמוֹ רָעַד נָמֹגוּ כֹּל יֹשְׁבֵי כְנָעַן: תִּפֹּל עֲלֵיהֶם אֵימָתָה וָפַחַד בִּגְדֹל זְרוֹעֲךָ יִדְּמוּ כָּאָבֶן עַד־יַעֲבֹר עַמְּךָ יהוה עַד־יַעֲבֹר עַם־זוּ קָנִיתָ:
יז תְּבִאֵמוֹ וְתִטָּעֵמוֹ בְּהַר נַחֲלָתְךָ מָכוֹן לְשִׁבְתְּךָ פָּעַלְתָּ יהוה מִקְּדָשׁ אֲדֹנָי כּוֹנְנוּ יָדֶיךָ:
יח יהוה ׀ יִמְלֹךְ לְעֹלָם וָעֶד: כִּי בָא סוּס פַּרְעֹה בְּרִכְבּוֹ וּבְפָרָשָׁיו בַּיָּם וַיָּשֶׁב יהוה עֲלֵהֶם אֶת־מֵי הַיָּם וּבְנֵי יִשְׂרָאֵל הָלְכוּ בַיַּבָּשָׁה בְּתוֹךְ הַיָּם:

מִקְּדָשׁ. הַטַּעַם עָלָיו זָקֵף גָּדוֹל לְהַפְרִידוֹ מִתֵּבַת הַשֵּׁם שֶׁלְּאַחֲרָיו, הַמִּקְדָּשׁ אֲשֶׁר כּוֹנְנוּ יָדֶיךָ ה'. חָבִיב בֵּית הַמִּקְדָּשׁ, שֶׁהָעוֹלָם נִבְרָא בְּיָד אַחַת, שֶׁנֶּאֱמַר "אַף יָדִי יָסְדָה אֶרֶץ" (ישעיה מח, יג), וּמִקְדָּשׁ בִּשְׁתֵּי יָדַיִם. וְאֵימָתַי יִבָּנֶה בִּשְׁתֵּי יָדָיִם? בִּזְמַן שֶׁ"ה' יִמְלֹךְ לְעֹלָם וָעֶד", לֶעָתִיד לָבֹא שֶׁכָּל הַמְּלוּכָה שֶׁלּוֹ, וּ"לְעֹלָם וָעֶד" לְשׁוֹן עוֹלָמִית הוּא וְהַוָּי"ו בּוֹ יְסוֹד, לְתֵיבָךְ הֵיא פְּתוּחָה, אֲבָל "וְאָנֹכִי הַיּוֹדֵעַ וָעֵד" (ירמיה כט, כג) שֶׁהַוָּי"ו בּוֹ שִׁמּוּשׁ, קְמוּצָה הִיא:

יט **כִּי בָא סוּס פַּרְעֹה.** כַּאֲשֶׁר בָּא סוּס פַּרְעֹה וְגוֹ':

מִקְּדָשׁ – *The sanctuary*: The cantillation symbol above this word, called a *zakef gadol*, signals the reader to pause and separate the word from the name of God which follows it. [Therefore, the phrase *mikdash Adonai* is not to be understood to mean "the Temple of God."] Rather, what the verse means is: *The sanctuary, Lord, that Your hands established*. We know that the Temple is beloved by God because, even though the world was created with one of God's hands – as the verse states: *My hand has also laid the foundation of the earth* (Isaiah 48:13) –the Temple was fashioned with both of His hands as our verse attests. And when will God use both of His hands to construct the Temple? When *the Lord will reign for ever and all time*. This expresses the hope for the future, when all fealty in the world will be directed to God alone. The phrase "for ever and all time" means "for all eternity." The letter *vav* represents a fundamental part of the word *va'ed* [and is not a conjunction]. The syllable is therefore vocalized with a *pataḥ*. In contrast, consider the verse *But I am He who knows and I am a witness [va'ed] says the Lord* (Jeremiah 29:23), where the *vav* that starts the word is a prefix, not part of the root. It is therefore vocalized with a *kamatz*.

19 **כִּי בָא סוּס פַּרְעֹה** – *When Pharaoh's horses had gone*: Israel recited this song as Pharaoh and the Egyptians were entering the sea.

20 Then Miriam, the prophetess, sister of Aharon, took a tambourine in her hand, and all the women followed her with
21 tambourines and dance. And Miriam led them in song: Sing to the LORD, for He has triumphed in glory; / horse and
22 horseman He hurled into the sea.   Moshe then led the Israelites from the Sea of Reeds out into the desert of Shur. For three days, they journeyed across the desert without find-
23 ing water. Eventually they came to Mara, but they could not drink the water there because it was bitter; because of this it

כ‎| מִרְיָם הַנְּבִיאָה. הֵיכָן נִתְנַבְּאָה? כְּשֶׁהִיא "אֲחוֹת אַהֲרֹן" קֹדֶם שֶׁנּוֹלַד מֹשֶׁה. אָמְרָה: עֲתִידָה אִמִּי שֶׁתֵּלֵד בֵּן וְכוּ' כִּדְאִיתָא בְּסוֹטָה (דף יב ע"ב). דָּבָר אַחֵר, "אֲחוֹת אַהֲרֹן", לְפִי שֶׁמָּסַר נַפְשׁוֹ עָלֶיהָ כְּשֶׁנִּצְטָרְעָה נִקְרֵאת עַל שְׁמוֹ:

אֶת־הַתֹּף. כְּלִי שֶׁל מִינֵי זֶמֶר:

בְּתֻפִּים וּבִמְחֹלֹת. מֻבְטָחוֹת הָיוּ צִדְקָנִיּוֹת שֶׁבַּדּוֹר שֶׁהַקָּדוֹשׁ בָּרוּךְ הוּא עוֹשֶׂה לָהֶם נִסִּים, וְהוֹצִיאוּ תֻּפִּים מִמִּצְרַיִם:

כא‎| וַתַּעַן לָהֶם מִרְיָם. מֹשֶׁה אָמַר שִׁירָה לָאֲנָשִׁים, הוּא אוֹמֵר וְהֵם עוֹנִין אַחֲרָיו, וּמִרְיָם אָמְרָה שִׁירָה לַנָּשִׁים:

כב‎| וַיַּסַּע מֹשֶׁה. הִסִּיעָן בְּעַל כָּרְחָם, שֶׁעִטְּרוּ מִצְרַיִם אֶת סוּסֵיהֶם בְּתַכְשִׁיטֵי זָהָב וָכֶסֶף וַאֲבָנִים טוֹבוֹת, וְהָיוּ יִשְׂרָאֵל מוֹצְאִין אוֹתָן בַּיָּם. וּגְדוֹלָה הָיְתָה בִּזַּת הַיָּם מִבִּזַּת מִצְרַיִם, שֶׁנֶּאֱמַר: "תּוֹרֵי זָהָב נַעֲשֶׂה לָּךְ עִם נְקֻדּוֹת הַכָּסֶף" (שיר השירים א, יא)‎, לְפִיכָךְ הֻצְרַךְ לְהַסִּיעָן בְּעַל כָּרְחָם:

20| **מִרְיָם הַנְּבִיאָה** – *Miriam, the prophetess*: When exactly did Miriam prophesy? When she was still just the "sister of Aharon." Before Moshe was born, Miriam predicted that her mother would bear a son who would become Israel's savior (Sota 12b). Another interpretation [for why the text refers to Miriam as the sister of Aharon and not that of Moshe]: Aharon took a risk for her by begging Moshe for compassion after Miriam was stricken with leprosy [in Numbers 12:10–12]. The Torah therefore refers to Miriam as Aharon's sister.

אֶת־הַתֹּף – *A tambourine*: The word *tof* refers to an instrument played with different types of music.

בְּתֻפִּים וּבִמְחֹלֹת – *With tambourines and dance*: So sure were the righteous Israelite women that God was going to perform miracles for them that they took tambourines with them out of Egypt in anticipation.

21| **וַתַּעַן לָהֶם מִרְיָם** – *And Miriam led them in song*: Moshe conducted the men in their praise of God by singing verses that they repeated after him. Meanwhile, Miriam led the women in song.

22| **וַיַּסַּע מֹשֶׁה** – *Moshe then led*: Moshe had to drag the Israelites away from the Sea of Reeds against their will. [Rashi is explaining why Moshe is the active force in the verse.] When the Egyptians set out in pursuit of their former slaves, they adorned the horses with gold and silver ornaments and festooned them with jewels. After the cavalry drowned, their valuables washed up upon the shore, enticing Israel into combing the beach for riches. Indeed, the value of the items the sea spat out exceeded the worth of what Israel plundered before the exodus. Thus the verse states: *We will make you*

שמות | פרק טו

כ וַתִּקַּח מִרְיָם הַנְּבִיאָה אֲחוֹת אַהֲרֹן אֶת־הַתֹּף בְּיָדָהּ
כא וַתֵּצֶאןָ כָל־הַנָּשִׁים אַחֲרֶיהָ בְּתֻפִּים וּבִמְחֹלֹת: וַתַּעַן
לָהֶם מִרְיָם שִׁירוּ לַיהוָה כִּי־גָאֹה גָּאָה סוּס וְרֹכְבוֹ
כב רָמָה בַיָּם: וַיַּסַּע מֹשֶׁה אֶת־יִשְׂרָאֵל מִיַּם־
סוּף וַיֵּצְאוּ אֶל־מִדְבַּר־שׁוּר וַיֵּלְכוּ שְׁלֹשֶׁת־יָמִים
כג בַּמִּדְבָּר וְלֹא־מָצְאוּ מָיִם: וַיָּבֹאוּ מָרָתָה וְלֹא יָכְלוּ
לִשְׁתֹּת מַיִם מִמָּרָה כִּי מָרִים הֵם עַל־כֵּן קָרָא־שְׁמָהּ

necklaces of gold studded with silver (Song of Songs 1:11). Because Israel was reluctant to abandon the treasure, Moshe had to force the people to move on.

23 | וַיָּבֹאוּ מָרָתָה – *They came to Mara*: The suffixed letter *heh* at the end of *Marata* is the equivalent of a prepositional prefix *lamed*, meaning "to." Hence *Marata* means the same as *leMara*. Nevertheless the word does not end with two *hehs* – one representing the third letter of the name *Mara* and a second indicating the nation had gone "to *Mara*" – because a *tav* replaces that first *heh*. When the word is in the construct form, [i.e., attached to following word to indicate possession, or in this case] attached to the following letter *heh* substituting for a *lamed*, the *heh* of the root is replaced by a *tav*. Similarly, whenever the letter *heh* stands as a member of the root word because it is feminine, it will be replaced by a *tav* in the construct form. Thus, although we read: *Fury [hema] is not in me* (Isaiah 27:4), we also find *And his anger [hamato] burned in him* (Esther 1:12), where the *heh* in the root is replaced by *tav* since the word is in the construct state, tied to the following letter *vav* [representing the pronoun "his"]. In another example, we find the verse *Of them you may buy bondmen and bondwomen [ama]* (Leviticus 25:44) where the noun *ama* ends with a *heh*. But when in the construct form, as in the verse, *Behold my maid [amati] Bilha* (Genesis 30:3), its *heh* is replaced with a *tav*. Other instances of this phenomenon appear with the verse *And man became a living [ḥayya] soul* (Genesis 2:7), which changes to *ḥayyat* in the verse *So that his life [ḥayyato] abhors bread* (Job 33:20). So too with *Between Rama and Beit El* (Judges 4:5), contrasted with *And his return was to Rama [Ramata]* (I Samuel 7:17).

כג: וַיָּבֹאוּ מָרָתָה. כְּמוֹ 'לְמָרָה', הֵ"א בְּסוֹף תֵּבָה בִּמְקוֹם לָמֶ"ד בִּתְחִלָּתָהּ, וְהַתָּי"ו הִיא בִּמְקוֹם הֵ"א הַנִּשְׁרֶשֶׁת בְּתֵבַת מָרָה, וּבִסְמִיכָתָהּ, כְּשֶׁהִיא נִדְבֶּקֶת לַהֵ"א שֶׁהוּא מוֹסִיף בִּמְקוֹם הַלָּמֶ"ד, תֵּהָפֵךְ הֵ"א שֶׁל שֹׁרֶשׁ לְתָי"ו. וְכֵן כָּל הֵ"א שֶׁהִיא שֹׁרֶשׁ בִּנְקֵבָה תֵּהָפֵךְ לְתָי"ו בִּסְמִיכָתָהּ. כְּמוֹ: "חֵמָה אֵין לִי" (ישעיה כז, ד), "וַחֲמַת הַמֶּלֶךְ בָּעֲרָה בּוֹ" (אסתר א, יב), הֲרֵי הֵ"א שֶׁל שֹׁרֶשׁ נֶהְפֶּכֶת לְתָי"ו מִפְּנֵי שֶׁנִּסְמְכָה עַל הַוָּי"ו הַנּוֹסֶפֶת. וְכֵן: "עֶבֶד וְאָמָה" (ויקרא כה, מד), "הִנֵּה אֲמָתִי בִלְהָה" (בראשית ל, ג), "לְנֶפֶשׁ חַיָּה" (שם ב, ז), "וְזִהֲמַתּוּ חַיָּתוֹ לָחֶם" (איוב לג, כ), "בֵּין הָרָמָה" (שופטים ד, ה), "וּתְשֻׁבָתוֹ הָרָמָתָה" (שמואל א' ז, יז):

▶

was named Mara. The people railed against Moshe – "What
are we to drink?" Moshe cried out to the Lord. And the
Lord showed him a piece of wood, which he threw into the
water – and the water became sweet. It was there that the
Lord gave His people decree and law; it was there that He
put them to the test. He said, "If you listen faithfully to the
voice of the Lord your God, doing what is right in His eyes,
heeding His commands and keeping His decrees, I will not
bring on you any of the sicknesses I brought on the Egyptians,
for I am the Lord – your Healer." And then they ar- HAMISHI
rived at Elim, where there were twelve springs and seventy

24 | וַיִּלֹּנוּ – *The people railed*: The word *vayilonu* is in the passive *nifal* form, and this is reflected in the Targum's rendering as well – *ve'itraamu*. It is common for Scripture to present complaints as an action done to oneself. Thus we find the reflexive terms *mitlonen* ["to complain"] and *mitro'em* ["to become angry"], rather than the active forms *lonen* and *ro'em*. The parallel in Old French would be the phrase *decomplesent se* [a reflexive form for complaining] where the addition *se* illustrates a reflection back onto the speaker.

25 | שָׁם שָׂם לוֹ – *It was there that the Lord gave*: God delivered some of His laws to Israel for them to study while they were encamped at Mara. The commandments regarding the Sabbath, the red heifer, and various laws of justice were issued at that time.

וְשָׁם נִסָּהוּ – *It was there that He put them to the test*: The nation's manners were tested at Mara, and that revealed their stubbornness. For rather than consulting with Moshe and politely asking for water, Israel complained about their situation.

26 | אִם־שָׁמוֹעַ תִּשְׁמַע – *If you listen faithfully*: If Israel accepts the laws upon themselves.

תַּעֲשֶׂה – *Doing*: If Israel acts properly.

וְהַאֲזַנְתָּ – *Heeding*: If Israel inclines its ears to hear the details of God's commandments.

כָּל־חֻקָּיו – *His decrees*: This refers to obligations that seem to have no rationale behind them and are merely the whims of

◂

כד מָרָה: וַיִּלֹּנוּ הָעָם עַל־מֹשֶׁה לֵּאמֹר מַה־נִּשְׁתֶּֽה:
כה וַיִּצְעַק אֶל־יְהוָה וַיּוֹרֵהוּ יְהוָה עֵץ וַיַּשְׁלֵךְ אֶל־הַמַּיִם
וַֽיִּמְתְּקוּ הַמָּיִם שָׁם שָׂם לוֹ חֹק וּמִשְׁפָּט וְשָׁם נִסָּֽהוּ:
כו וַיֹּאמֶר אִם־שָׁמוֹעַ תִּשְׁמַע לְקוֹל ׀ יְהוָה אֱלֹהֶיךָ
וְהַיָּשָׁר בְּעֵינָיו תַּעֲשֶׂה וְהַאֲזַנְתָּ לְמִצְוֹתָיו וְשָׁמַרְתָּ כָּל־
חֻקָּיו כָּל־הַֽמַּחֲלָה אֲשֶׁר־שַׂמְתִּי בְמִצְרַיִם לֹא־אָשִׂים
עָלֶיךָ כִּי אֲנִי יְהוָה רֹפְאֶֽךָ: חמישי וַיָּבֹאוּ אֵילִמָה
וְשָׁם שְׁתֵּים עֶשְׂרֵה עֵינֹת מַיִם וְשִׁבְעִים תְּמָרִים

---

the sovereign. One's evil inclination argues that such rules are silly prohibitions – what possible reason could there be for these things to be forbidden? Examples in this category include the statute outlawing the wearing of wool and linen woven into a single garment, the stricture against eating pig meat, the ritual of the red heifer [see Numbers 19], and others of this kind.

לֹא־אָשִׂים עָלֶיךָ – *I will not bring on you*: [If so, why does God need to be subsequently described as a "healer"? God is saying:] And if I do afflict you with such illnesses, you will be thoroughly cleansed from the disease as if you had never suffered, *for I am the Lord – your Healer*. [This represents the midrashic interpretation.] But the straightforward meaning of the text is that because *I am the Lord – your Healer*, I will prescribe the Torah and its commandments as prophylactics [and when you live well, *I will not [need to] bring on you any sicknesses*]. This may be compared to a doctor who tells his patient to avoid a certain food lest it make him sick. So do the verses state: *Fear the Lord and avoid evil. That will be a cure for your flesh* (Proverbs 3:7–8).

שְׁתֵּים עֶשְׂרֵה עֵינֹת מַיִם |27 – *Twelve springs*: God arranged one spring for each tribe.

וְשִׁבְעִים תְּמָרִים – *And seventy date palms*: The number of the fruit trees corresponded to the seventy elders of Israel [a figure introduced in Numbers 11:16].

מְקַנְטֵר עֲלֵיהֶם, מַה חִסּוּר בְּאֲכִילָתָן? לָמָּה נֶאֶסְרוּ? כְּגוֹן לְבִישַׁת כִּלְאַיִם וַאֲכִילַת חֲזִיר וּפָרָה אֲדֻמָּה וְכַיּוֹצֵא בָּהֶם:

לֹא־אָשִׂים עָלֶיךָ. וְאִם אָשִׂים הֲרֵי הִיא כְּלֹא הוּשְׂמָה, "כִּי אֲנִי ה' רֹפְאֶךָ". וּלְפִי פְשׁוּטוֹ, "כִּי אֲנִי ה' רֹפְאֶךָ", הַמְלַמֶּדְךָ תּוֹרָה וּמִצְוֹת לְמַעַן תִּנָּצֵל מֵהֶם, כְּרוֹפֵא הַזֶּה הָאוֹמֵר לָאָדָם: אַל תֹּאכַל דָּבָר זֶה פֶּן יְבִיאֲךָ לִידֵי חֳלִי זֶה. וְכֵן הוּא אוֹמֵר: "רִפְאוּת תְּהִי לְשָׁרֶּךָ" (משלי ג, ח):

כו שְׁתֵּים עֶשְׂרֵה עֵינֹת מַיִם. כְּנֶגֶד שְׁנֵים עָשָׂר שְׁבָטִים נִזְדַּמְּנוּ לָהֶם:

וְשִׁבְעִים תְּמָרִים. כְּנֶגֶד שִׁבְעִים זְקֵנִים:

EXODUS | CHAPTER 16 — THE ḤUMASH WITH RASHI | BESHALAḤ | 36

16 1 date palms. They encamped there by the water. They set out from Elim, and on the fifteenth day of the second month after leaving Egypt, the congregation of Israel all arrived at the 2 desert of Sin, between Elim and Sinai. In the desert, all the 3 community started railing against Moshe and Aharon. The Israelites said to them, "If only we had died by the LORD's hand in Egypt, when we sat by the fleshpots and ate our fill of bread. Instead, you have brought us out into this desert 4 to kill the entire assembly by starvation." Then the LORD said to Moshe, "I am going to rain down bread from heaven. Let the people go out and gather enough for each day; I will test them to see whether they will follow My law or not. 5 On the sixth day, they will have to prepare what they bring in. 6 It will be twice as much as they gather on all other days." So Moshe and Aharon told all the Israelites, "At evening you will

---

טז א| בַּחֲמִשָּׁה עָשָׂר יוֹם. נִתְפָּרֵשׁ הַיּוֹם שֶׁל חֲנִיָּה זוֹ לְפִי שֶׁבּוֹ בַיּוֹם כָּלְתָה הַחֲרָרָה שֶׁהוֹצִיאוּ מִמִּצְרַיִם וְהֻצְרְכוּ לַמָּן, לְלַמְּדֵנוּ שֶׁאָכְלוּ מִשְׁיָרֵי הַבָּצֵק שִׁשִּׁים וְאַחַת סְעֻדּוֹת, וְיָרַד לָהֶם מָן בְּשִׁשָּׁה עָשָׂר בְּאִיָּר, וְיוֹם אֶחָד בְּשַׁבָּת הָיָה, כִּדְאִיתָא בְּמַסֶּכֶת שַׁבָּת (דף פז ע״ב):

ב| וַיִּלּוֹנוּ. לְפִי שֶׁכָּלָה הַלֶּחֶם:

ג| מִי יִתֵּן מוּתֵנוּ. שֶׁנָּמוּת. וְאֵינוֹ שֵׁם דָּבָר כְּמוֹ 'מוֹתֵנוּ', אֶלָּא כְּמוֹ עֲשׂוֹתֵנוּ, חֲנוֹתֵנוּ, שׁוּבֵנוּ – לַעֲשׂוֹת אֲנַחְנוּ, לַחֲנוֹת אֲנַחְנוּ, לָמוּת אֲנַחְנוּ. "לְוַי דְּמִיתְנָא" – לוּ מָתַנוּ, הַלְוַאי וְהָיִינוּ מֵתִים:

ד| דְּבַר יוֹם בְּיוֹמוֹ. צֹרֶךְ אֲכִילַת יוֹם יִלְקְטוּ בְּיוֹמוֹ, וְלֹא יִלְקְטוּ הַיּוֹם לְצֹרֶךְ מָחָר:

16 1| בַּחֲמִשָּׁה עָשָׂר יוֹם — *On the fifteenth day*: The Torah mentions the date of Israel's encampment because on this day the people finished eating all the wafers they had taken with them from Egypt. Israel therefore needed the manna, whose advent is the subject of this chapter. We learn here that the remains of the dough they took on the exodus fed the people for sixty-one meals. [The figure assumes Israel ate two meals a day for thirty days, in addition to the evening meal of the fifteenth of Nisan, which they ate on the road.] The manna began to fall on the sixteenth of Iyar which was the first day of the week, as recorded in the Talmud (Shabbat 87b).

2| וַיִּלּוֹנוּ — *Started railing*: The nation complained to Moshe because their food had run out.

3| מִי יִתֵּן מוּתֵנוּ — *If only we had died*: The term *mutenu* is a verb meaning "that we should die." If the text had read *motenu*, that would have been a noun – "our deaths." *Mutenu* is similar to *asotenu* – "that we should make," *ḥanotenu* – "that we should encamp," *shuvenu* – "that we should return," and hence here: "that we should die." The Aramaic translation supports this, for it reads, *levei demeitena* – "if only we had died."

4| דְּבַר יוֹם בְּיוֹמוֹ — *Enough for each day*: The phrase *devar yom beyomo* means that on each day, Israel should collect just enough food for that day's consumption [a literal translation

שמות | פרק טז | בשלח

א וַיַּחֲנוּ־שָׁם עַל־הַמָּיִם: וַיִּסְעוּ מֵאֵילִם וַיָּבֹאוּ כָּל־עֲדַת בְּנֵי־יִשְׂרָאֵל אֶל־מִדְבַּר־סִין אֲשֶׁר בֵּין־אֵילִם וּבֵין סִינָי בַּחֲמִשָּׁה עָשָׂר יוֹם לַחֹדֶשׁ הַשֵּׁנִי לְצֵאתָם מֵאֶרֶץ מִצְרָיִם: ב וַיִּלּוֹנוּ כָּל־עֲדַת בְּנֵי־יִשְׂרָאֵל עַל־מֹשֶׁה וְעַל־אַהֲרֹן בַּמִּדְבָּר: ג וַיֹּאמְרוּ אֲלֵהֶם בְּנֵי יִשְׂרָאֵל מִי־יִתֵּן מוּתֵנוּ בְיַד־יהוה בְּאֶרֶץ מִצְרַיִם בְּשִׁבְתֵּנוּ עַל־סִיר הַבָּשָׂר בְּאָכְלֵנוּ לֶחֶם לָשֹׂבַע כִּי־הוֹצֵאתֶם אֹתָנוּ אֶל־הַמִּדְבָּר הַזֶּה לְהָמִית אֶת־כָּל־הַקָּהָל הַזֶּה בָּרָעָב: ד וַיֹּאמֶר יהוה אֶל־מֹשֶׁה הִנְנִי מַמְטִיר לָכֶם לֶחֶם מִן־הַשָּׁמָיִם וְיָצָא הָעָם וְלָקְטוּ דְּבַר־יוֹם בְּיוֹמוֹ לְמַעַן אֲנַסֶּנּוּ הֲיֵלֵךְ בְּתוֹרָתִי אִם־לֹא: ה וְהָיָה בַּיּוֹם הַשִּׁשִּׁי וְהֵכִינוּ אֵת אֲשֶׁר־יָבִיאוּ וְהָיָה מִשְׁנֶה עַל אֲשֶׁר־יִלְקְטוּ יוֹם | יוֹם: ו וַיֹּאמֶר מֹשֶׁה וְאַהֲרֹן אֶל־כָּל־בְּנֵי יִשְׂרָאֵל עֶרֶב

---

would be "each day's on that day"]; they should not take what they think they will need for the next day.

לְמַעַן אֲנַסֶּנּוּ – *I will test them*: I will test them every day *to see whether they will follow My law*, i.e., whether they will obey the rules governing the manna: the prohibitions on leaving leftover manna for the next day and on gathering food on the Sabbath.

5 | **וְהָיָה מִשְׁנֶה** – *It will be twice as much*: To satisfy the sixth day's and the Sabbath day's meals.

מִשְׁנֶה – *Twice*: The phrase means that the amount of manna available to the people would be twice what they would gather on the other days of the week.

6 | **עֶרֶב** – *At evening*: [Literally, "evening."] The preposition "at" is implied, and the term *erev* should be understood as *le'erev* – "at evening."

לְמַעַן אֲנַסֶּנּוּ. כִּי חֲנַנְּוּ "הֲיֵלֵךְ בְּתוֹרָתִי", אִם יִשְׁמְרוּ מִצְוֹת הַתְּלוּיוֹת בּוֹ, שֶׁלֹּא יוֹתִירוּ מִמֶּנּוּ וְלֹא יֵצְאוּ בְּשַׁבָּת לִלְקֹט:

(ה) וְהָיָה מִשְׁנֶה. לַיּוֹם וְלַמָּחֳרָת:

מִשְׁנֶה. עַל שֶׁהָיוּ רְגִילִים לִלְקֹט יוֹם יוֹם שֶׁל שְׁאָר יְמוֹת הַשָּׁבוּעַ:

(ו) עֶרֶב. כְּמוֹ לָעֶרֶב:

₇ know that it was the LORD who brought you out of Egypt, and by morning you shall see the LORD's glory, for He has heard you railing against Him. As for us, what are we that you rail ₈ against us?" Then Moshe said, "In the evening, the LORD will give you meat to eat, and in the morning bread to fill you, for He has heard you railing against Him. We – what are we? It

וִידַעְתֶּם כִּי יהוה הוֹצִיא אֶתְכֶם מֵאֶרֶץ מִצְרָיִם. לְפִי שֶׁאֲמַרְתֶּם לָנוּ: "כִּי הוֹצֵאתֶם אֹתָנוּ" (לעיל פסוק ג), תֵּדְעוּ כִּי לֹא אֲנַחְנוּ הַמּוֹצִיאִים אֶלָּא ה' הוֹצִיא אֶתְכֶם, שֶׁיָּגִיז לָכֶם אֶת הַשְּׂלָו:

וִידַעְתֶּם כִּי יהוה אֶתְכֶם מֵאֶרֶץ מִצְרָיִם – **You will know that it was the LORD who brought you out of Egypt:** Moshe and Aharon are rebuking the nation, who had complained: *You have brought us out into this desert to kill [us]* (16:3). The leaders are reminding Israel that it was not they who freed them from slavery, but God. It was He who would provide them with the quail.

ז| וּבֹקֶר וּרְאִיתֶם. לֹא עַל הַכָּבוֹד שֶׁנֶּאֱמַר: "וְהִנֵּה כְּבוֹד ה' נִרְאָה בֶּעָנָן" (להלן פסוק י) נֶאֱמַר, אֶלָּא כָּךְ אָמַר לָהֶם: עֶרֶב וִידַעְתֶּם כִּי הַיְכֹלֶת בְּיָדוֹ לָתֵן תַּאֲוַתְכֶם, וּבָשָׂר יִתֵּן, אַךְ לֹא בְּפָנִים מְאִירוֹת יִתְּנֶנָּה לָכֶם, כִּי שֶׁלֹּא כַּהֹגֶן שְׁאַלְתֶּם אוֹתוֹ, וּמִכֶּרֶס מְלֵאָה. וְהַלֶּחֶם שֶׁשְּׁאַלְתֶּם לְצֹרֶךְ, בִּירִידָתוֹ לַבֹּקֶר תִּרְאוּ אֶת כְּבוֹד אוֹר פָּנָיו, שֶׁיּוֹרִידֵהוּ לָכֶם דֶּרֶךְ חִבָּה בַּבֹּקֶר שֶׁיֵּשׁ שָׁהוּת לַהֲכִינוֹ, וְטַל מִלְמַעְלָה וְטַל מִלְּמַטָּה כְּמֻנָּח בִּקְפָסָא:

7| וּבֹקֶר וּרְאִיתֶם – **And by morning you shall see:** Moshe was not referring to the glory of God mentioned in the verse *And the glory of the LORD appeared in the midst of cloud* [16:10; that revelation appeared immediately rather than the next morning with the manna]. Rather, this is what he said to the nation: In the evening you will see proof of God's ability to feed your appetites, for He will lay out meat before you. However, God will not serve the meal with a glad countenance because you demanded the food improperly, while your bellies were still full. On the other hand, because the bread you requested represents a true need, when it descends to earth in the morning, you will witness the radiant manifestation of God. For the manna will be offered lovingly during the day, when there is time to prepare it, resting on a bed of dew and garnished with another layer of dew above, as if presented in a box.

אֶת־תְּלֻנֹּתֵיכֶם עַל־יהוה. כְּמוֹ אֲשֶׁר עַל ה':

אֶת־תְּלֻנֹּתֵיכֶם עַל־יהוה – **Your railing against the LORD:** [Even though the people's accusations were leveled at Moshe and Aharon] it was if they were complaining against God.

וְנַחְנוּ מָה. מָה אֲנַחְנוּ חֲשׁוּבִין:

וְנַחְנוּ מָה – **What are we:** Of what importance are we that you blame us for the situation?

כִּי תַלִּינוּ עָלֵינוּ. שֶׁתַּרְעִימוּ עָלֵינוּ אֶת הַכֹּל, אֶת בְּנֵיכֶם וּנְשֵׁיכֶם וּבְנוֹתֵיכֶם וְעֵרֶב רַב. וְעַל כָּרְחִי אֲנִי זָקוּק לְפָרֵשׁ "תַּלִּינוּ" בִּלְשׁוֹן תַּפְעִילוּ, מִפְּנֵי דִגְשׁוּתוֹ וּקְרִיאָתוֹ. שֶׁאִלּוּ הָיָה

כִּי תַלִּינוּ עָלֵינוּ – **That you rail against us:** The phrase means "You are leading everybody to complain against us" – your sons and daughters, your wives, and the mixed multitudes. I am forced to interpret the verb *tallinu* [translated here as "rail"] as being in the causative *hifil* form [and meaning rather: "to stir

שמות | פרק טז | בשלח

זּ וִידַעְתֶּ֕ם כִּ֧י יְהוָ֛ה הוֹצִ֥יא אֶתְכֶ֖ם מֵאֶ֥רֶץ מִצְרָֽיִם: וּבֹ֕קֶר
וּרְאִיתֶם֙ אֶת־כְּב֣וֹד יְהוָ֔ה בְּשָׁמְע֥וֹ אֶת־תְּלֻנֹּתֵיכֶ֖ם עַל־
ח יְהוָ֑ה וְנַ֣חְנוּ מָ֔ה כִּ֥י תַלֹּ֖ינוּ עָלֵֽינוּ: וַיֹּ֣אמֶר מֹשֶׁ֗ה בְּתֵ֣ת יְהוָ֩ה
לָכֶ֨ם בָּעֶ֜רֶב בָּשָׂ֣ר לֶאֱכֹ֗ל וְלֶ֤חֶם בַּבֹּ֙קֶר֙ לִשְׂבֹּ֔עַ
בִּשְׁמֹ֤עַ יְהוָה֙ אֶת־תְּלֻנֹּ֣תֵיכֶ֔ם אֲשֶׁר־אַתֶּ֥ם מַלִּינִ֖ם
עָלָ֑יו וְנַ֣חְנוּ מָ֔ה לֹא־עָלֵ֥ינוּ תְלֻנֹּתֵיכֶ֖ם כִּ֥י עַל־יְהוָֽה:

רָפָה הָיִיתִי מְפָרְשׁוֹ בִּלְשׁוֹן תִּפְעֲלוּ,
כְּמוֹ: "וַיָּלֶן הָעָם עַל מֹשֶׁה" (להלן יז, ג).
אוֹ חָם הָיָה דָּגוּשׁ וְאֵין בּוֹ יו"ד
וְנִקְרָא "תִּלּוֹנוּ", הָיִיתִי מְפָרְשׁוֹ לְשׁוֹן
תִּתְלוֹנְנוּ. עַכְשָׁיו הוּא מַשְׁמָע תַּלִּינוּ
אֶת אֲחֵרִים, כְּמוֹ בַּמְרַגְּלִים: "וַיַּלִּינוּ
עָלָיו אֶת כָּל הָעֵדָה" (במדבר יד, לו):

ח] בָּשָׂר לֶאֱכֹל. וְלֹא לִשְׂבֹּעַ, לִמְּדָה
תּוֹרָה דֶּרֶךְ אֶרֶץ שֶׁאֵין אוֹכְלִין בָּשָׂר
לָשֹׂבַע. וּמָה רָאָה לְהוֹרִיד לֶחֶם
בַּבֹּקֶר וּבָשָׂר בָּעֶרֶב? לְפִי שֶׁהַלֶּחֶם
שְׁאָלוּ כַּהֹגֶן, שֶׁאִי אֶפְשָׁר לוֹ לָאָדָם
בְּלֹא לֶחֶם, אֲבָל בָּשָׂר שָׁאֲלוּ שֶׁלֹּא
כַהֹגֶן, שֶׁהַרְבֵּה בְּהֵמוֹת הָיוּ לָהֶם,
וְעוֹד שֶׁהָיָה אֶפְשָׁר לָהֶם בְּלֹא בָּשָׂר,
לְפִיכָךְ נָתַן לָהֶם בִּשְׁעַת טֹרַח שֶׁלֹּא
כַהֹגֶן:

אֲשֶׁר־אַתֶּם מַלִּינִם עָלָיו. אֶת
הָאֲחֵרִים הַשּׁוֹמְעִים אֶתְכֶם
מִתְלוֹנְנִים:

---

up discontent in others"], because the *lamed* in the word is marked with a *dagesh*, and because of its vocalization. Both details suggest the *hifil* construction. For if the *lamed* lacked a *dagesh*, the verb would be categorized as a *kal* form – "you are railing," as in the verse *They railed [vayalen] against Moshe* (17:3). Conversely, had our word *tallinu* retained its *dagesh* but been pronounced *tillonu*, I would have interpreted it as a reflexive verb, as if it had read *titlonenu* [also meaning simply "to complain"; see commentary on 15:24]. However, the word as pronounced here means that the men were agitating others to rebel. We find a similar instance in the story of the spies who *made all the congregation murmur [vayallinu] against him* (Numbers 14:36).

8| בָּשָׂר לֶאֱכֹל – *Meat to eat:* You will be given meat to eat, but do not gorge yourselves. The Torah thereby teaches manners to its readers: One should not eat meat to satiety. Why did God provide the nation with bread in the morning and meat in the evening? The request for bread was appropriate because people cannot live without it. But the demand for meat was unnecessary for two reasons: Firstly, Israel owned plenty of animals which they could have slaughtered had they wanted to. Furthermore, people can endure very well without meat. As a rebuke, God sent them the quail in the evenings, which was an inconvenient time.

אֲשֶׁר־אַתֶּם מַלִּינִם עָלָיו – *Railing against Him:* [Here too, the verb *mallinim* is in the causative *hifil* construction; see commentary on the previous verse. Rashi explains that the phrase means:] "God has heard the people you have provoked to murmur against Him."

⁹ is not us you rail against, but the LORD." Then Moshe said to Aharon, "Tell all the community of Israel to come before the
¹⁰ LORD, because He has heard your railing." As soon as Aharon had spoken to the whole community of Israel, they looked toward the desert – and the glory of the LORD appeared in the midst of cloud.

¹¹/¹² The LORD spoke to Moshe and said, "I have heard the Israelites' railing. Tell them: At twilight you shall eat meat, and in the morning your fill of bread. Then you will know that I am
¹³ the LORD your God." That evening a flock of quail flew in and covered the camp; next morning a layer of dew surrounded
¹⁴ the camp. When the dew covering lifted, fine flakes covered

SHISHI

9 | קִרְבוּ – *Come:* To where the cloud will descend.

13 | הַשְּׂלָו – *Quail:* A type of bird that is very fat.

הָיְתָה שִׁכְבַת הַטָּל – *A layer of dew:* A covering of dew lay upon the manna. But later the Torah writes: *And when the dew fell upon the camp in the night, the manna fell upon it* (Numbers 11:9). How are these descriptions to be reconciled? First, one layer of dew fell to the ground. The manna descended upon that. Then an additional layer of dew coated the manna. Thus the food was presented to Israel like a gift wrapped in a box.

14 | וַתַּעַל שִׁכְבַת הַטָּל – *When the dew covering lifted:* When the sun rose, the dew that rested on top of the manna evaporated; it rose up to meet the sun. If you take an empty eggshell, fill it with dew and seal the opening, the egg will rise up when you put it in the sunlight. But our Sages interpret this phrase to mean that the dew came up out of the earth, and when the layer rose, it revealed the manna to the people on the desert floor. The substance was fine and *meḥuspas* – meaning "uncovered"; this is its only appearance of that word in Scripture. The word seems to be related to the mishnaic *ḥasifa udluskema* [meaning "a suitcase or a chest"]. When the dew lifted, the people saw that something thin was contained between two layers of moisture. Onkelos translates the term *meḥuspas* as *mekullaf* [meaning "peeled"] understanding it to be related

שמות | פרק טז | בשלח

ט וַיֹּ֤אמֶר מֹשֶׁה֙ אֶֽל־אַהֲרֹ֔ן אֱמֹ֗ר אֶֽל־כָּל־עֲדַת֙ בְּנֵ֣י יִשְׂרָאֵ֔ל קִרְב֖וּ לִפְנֵ֣י יְהוָ֑ה כִּ֣י שָׁמַ֔ע אֵ֖ת תְּלֻנֹּתֵיכֶֽם: וַיְהִ֗י כְּדַבֵּ֤ר אַֽהֲרֹן֙ אֶל־כָּל־עֲדַ֣ת בְּנֵֽי־יִשְׂרָאֵ֔ל וַיִּפְנ֖וּ אֶל־הַמִּדְבָּ֑ר וְהִנֵּה֙ כְּב֣וֹד יְהוָ֔ה נִרְאָ֖ה בֶּֽעָנָֽן:

ששי יא וַיְדַבֵּ֥ר יְהוָ֖ה אֶל־מֹשֶׁ֥ה לֵּאמֹֽר: יב שָׁמַ֗עְתִּי אֶת־תְּלוּנֹּת֮ בְּנֵ֣י יִשְׂרָאֵל֒ דַּבֵּ֨ר אֲלֵהֶ֜ם לֵאמֹ֗ר בֵּ֤ין הָֽעַרְבַּ֨יִם֙ תֹּֽאכְל֣וּ בָשָׂ֔ר וּבַבֹּ֖קֶר תִּשְׂבְּעוּ־לָ֑חֶם וִֽידַעְתֶּ֕ם כִּ֛י אֲנִ֥י יְהוָ֖ה אֱלֹֽהֵיכֶֽם: יג וַיְהִ֣י בָעֶ֔רֶב וַתַּ֣עַל הַשְּׂלָ֔ו וַתְּכַ֖ס אֶת־הַמַּֽחֲנֶ֑ה וּבַבֹּ֗קֶר הָֽיְתָה֙ שִׁכְבַ֣ת הַטַּ֔ל סָבִ֖יב לַֽמַּֽחֲנֶֽה: יד וַתַּ֖עַל שִׁכְבַ֣ת הַטָּ֑ל וְהִנֵּ֞ה עַל־פְּנֵ֤י הַמִּדְבָּר֙ דַּ֣ק מְחֻסְפָּ֔ס דַּ֥ק

---

to the phrase "peeling off [*maḥsof*] the white" (Genesis 30:37).

כַּכְּפֹר – *Like fine frost*: The parallel word in Old French is *gelide* ["frost"]. The word *gir* in Targum's phrase *dadak kegir* ["thin as *gir*"], can be found in the verse *When he makes all the stones of the altar as chalkstones [ke'avnei gir]* (Isaiah 27:9). Now this refers to a black color [while most chalk is white, dark-colored chalkstone can occur], and we mention it with regard to the commandment of covering up blood [introduced in Leviticus 17:13–14], that the rite may be performed with powdered chalkstone or orpiment [a mineral; see Ḥullin 88b]. Now when Targum translates our verse: "as thin as chalk like frost on the ground," it means that the manna was as thin as chalkstone and sat exposed on the ground like frost. The manna was scattered in thin patches joined together, just like frost lies unevenly on the ground. *Dak* translates as *tenves* ["thin"] in French – the manna had a thin flaky coating on top. The word *kegir* that the Targum includes is not actually represented in the verse.

לָחוּ שֶׁהָיָה דָּבָר דַּק מְחֻסְפָּס בְּתוֹכוֹ בֵּין שְׁתֵּי שִׁכְבוֹת הַטָּל. וְאוּנְקְלוֹס תִּרְגֵּם: "מְקֻלַּף", לְשׁוֹן "מַחְשֹׂף הַלָּבָן" (בראשית ל, לז):

כַּכְּפֹר. כְּפוֹר – גליד"א בְּלַעַז. "דַּעֲדַק כְּגִיר", "כְּאַבְנֵי גִר" (ישעיה כז, ט), וְהוּא מִין צֶבַע שָׁחוֹר כִּדְאָמְרִינַן גַּבֵּי כִּסּוּי הַדָּם: "הַגִּיר וְהַזַּרְנִיךְ" (חולין פח ע"ב). "דַּעֲדַק כְּגִיר כְּגִלְדָּא עַל אַרְעָא", דַּק הָיָה כְּגִיר וְשׁוֹכֵב מְגֻלֶּה כִּקְרַח עַל הָאָרֶץ, וְכֵן פֵּרוּשׁוֹ. "דַּק כַּכְּפֹר", שָׁטוּחַ קָלוּשׁ וּמְחֻבָּר כִּגְלִיד. "דַּק" טינבי"ש בְּלַעַז, שֶׁהָיָה מַגְלִיד גֶּלֶד דַּק מִלְמַעְלָה. וּ"כְגִיר" שֶׁתִּרְגְּמוֹ אוּנְקְלוֹס, תּוֹסֶפֶת הוּא עַל לְשׁוֹן הָעִבְרִית וְאֵין לוֹ תֵּבָה בַּפָּסוּק.

15 the floor of the desert like fine frost on the ground. When the Israelites saw it, they asked one another, "What is it?" for they did not recognize it. Moshe said to them, "This is the bread 16 the LORD has given you to eat. This is what the LORD has instructed: Each of you gather as much as you need, an omer for every person; each take enough for all the people in your tent."
17 The people of Israel did so. Some gathered more, others less.
18 But when they measured it with an omer measure, those who had gathered much had none left over, and those who gathered but little did not fall short. All had gathered as 19 much as they could eat. "Let no one leave any over for the 20 morning," said Moshe; but they did not listen to Moshe. Some of them left part of it till morning, and it became worm-infested and stank. Moshe was enraged with them.
21 Every morning they gathered it, all as much as they could

טו| מָן הוּא. הֲכָנַת מָזוֹן הוּא, כְּמוֹ: "וַיְמַן לָהֶם הַמֶּלֶךְ" (דניאל א, ה):

15| מָן הוּא – *What is it*: The term *man* refers to the preparation of food, as in the verse: *And the king appointed [vayman] them a daily provision* (Daniel 1:5). [According to this understanding, the people's exclamation would be more properly translated: "It is a ration."]

כִּי לֹא יָדְעוּ מַה־הוּא. שֶׁיִּקְרָאוּהוּ בִּשְׁמוֹ:

כִּי לֹא יָדְעוּ מַה־הוּא – *For they did not recognize it*: And hence could not call it by its proper name.

טז| עֹמֶר. שֵׁם מִדָּה:

16| עֹמֶר – *An omer*: Omer is the name of a measure.

מִסְפַּר נַפְשֹׁתֵיכֶם. כְּפִי מִנְיַן נְפָשׁוֹת שֶׁיֵּשׁ לְאִישׁ בְּאָהֳלוֹ תִּקְחוּ, עֹמֶר לְכָל גֻּלְגֹּלֶת:

מִסְפַּר נַפְשֹׁתֵיכֶם – *Each take enough*: [Literally, "the number of your souls."] Gather an amount of manna based on the number of souls in your household, where each person gets a single omer of food.

יז| הַמַּרְבֶּה וְהַמַּמְעִיט. יֵשׁ שֶׁלָּקְטוּ הַרְבֵּה וְיֵשׁ שֶׁלָּקְטוּ מְעַט, וּכְשֶׁבָּאוּ לְבֵיתָם מָדְדוּ בָעֹמֶר אִישׁ אִישׁ מַה שֶּׁלָּקְטוּ, וּמָצְאוּ שֶׁהַמַּרְבֶּה לִלְקֹט לֹא הֶעֱדִיף עַל עֹמֶר לַגֻּלְגֹּלֶת אֲשֶׁר בְּאָהֳלוֹ, וְהַמַּמְעִיט לִלְקֹט לֹא מָצָא חָסֵר מֵעֹמֶר לַגֻּלְגֹּלֶת, וְזֶהוּ נֵס גָּדוֹל שֶׁנַּעֲשָׂה בּוֹ:

17| הַמַּרְבֶּה וְהַמַּמְעִיט – *Some more, others less*: Some people gathered more, while others gathered less. But when all returned to their tents and measured what they had collected, they found that those who had brought home an excess amount now had exactly an omer of manna for each individual in his tent, whereas those who were more restrained, also managed to provide an omer for each family member. And this was a great miracle concerning the manna.

כ| וַיּוֹתִרוּ אֲנָשִׁים. דָּתָן וַאֲבִירָם:

20| וַיּוֹתִרוּ אֲנָשִׁים – *Some of them left it*: These individuals were Datan and Aviram [see Numbers 16].

שמות | פרק טז | בשלח

טו כִּפְפֹר עַל־הָאָרֶץ: וַיִּרְאוּ בְנֵי־יִשְׂרָאֵל וַיֹּאמְרוּ אִישׁ אֶל־אָחִיו מָן הוּא כִּי לֹא יָדְעוּ מַה־הוּא וַיֹּאמֶר מֹשֶׁה

טז אֲלֵהֶם הוּא הַלֶּחֶם אֲשֶׁר נָתַן יְהֹוָה לָכֶם לְאָכְלָה: זֶה הַדָּבָר אֲשֶׁר צִוָּה יְהֹוָה לִקְטוּ מִמֶּנּוּ אִישׁ לְפִי אָכְלוֹ עֹמֶר לַגֻּלְגֹּלֶת מִסְפַּר נַפְשֹׁתֵיכֶם אִישׁ לַאֲשֶׁר בְּאָהֳלוֹ

יז תִּקָּחוּ: וַיַּעֲשׂוּ־כֵן בְּנֵי יִשְׂרָאֵל וַיִּלְקְטוּ הַמַּרְבֶּה

יח וְהַמַּמְעִיט: וַיָּמֹדּוּ בָעֹמֶר וְלֹא הֶעְדִּיף הַמַּרְבֶּה

יט וְהַמַּמְעִיט לֹא הֶחְסִיר אִישׁ לְפִי־אָכְלוֹ לָקָטוּ: וַיֹּאמֶר מֹשֶׁה אֲלֵהֶם אִישׁ אַל־יוֹתֵר מִמֶּנּוּ עַד־בֹּקֶר: וְלֹא־

כ שָׁמְעוּ אֶל־מֹשֶׁה וַיּוֹתִרוּ אֲנָשִׁים מִמֶּנּוּ עַד־בֹּקֶר וַיָּרֻם

כא תּוֹלָעִים וַיִּבְאַשׁ וַיִּקְצֹף עֲלֵהֶם מֹשֶׁה: וַיִּלְקְטוּ אֹתוֹ בַּבֹּקֶר בַּבֹּקֶר אִישׁ כְּפִי אָכְלוֹ וְחַם הַשֶּׁמֶשׁ וְנָמָס:

וַיָּרֻם תּוֹלָעִים. לְשׁוֹן רִמָּה:

וַיִּבְאַשׁ. הֲרֵי זֶה מִקְרָא הָסוּף, שֶׁבַּתְּחִלָּה הִבְאִישׁ וּלְבַסּוֹף הִתְלִיעַ, כְּעִנְיָן שֶׁנֶּאֱמַר: "וְלֹא הִבְאִישׁ וְרִמָּה לֹא הָיְתָה בּוֹ" (להלן פסוק כד), וְכֵן דֶּרֶךְ כָּל הַמַּתְלִיעִים:

כא | וְחַם הַשֶּׁמֶשׁ וְנָמָס. הַנִּשְׁאָר בַּשָּׂדֶה נַעֲשֶׂה נְחָלִים וְשׁוֹתִין מִמֶּנּוּ אַיָּלִים וּצְבָאִים, וְאֻמּוֹת הָעוֹלָם צָדִין מֵהֶם וְטוֹעֲמִים בָּהֶם טַעַם מָן וְיוֹדְעִים מַה שִּׁבְחָן שֶׁל יִשְׂרָאֵל. **פָּשָׁר** (אונקלוס), לְשׁוֹן פּוֹשְׁרִין, עַל יְדֵי הַשֶּׁמֶשׁ מִתְחַמֵּם וּמַפְשִׁיר:

וְנָמָס. דישטמפרי"ר. וְדֻגְמָתוֹ בְּסַנְהֶדְרִין בְּסוֹף 'אַרְבַּע מִיתוֹת' (דף סז ע"ב).

וַיָּרֻם תּוֹלָעִים – *And it became worm-infested*: The verb *vayarum* derives from the word *rimma*, meaning "worms."

וַיִּבְאַשׁ – *And stank*: The clauses in this verse should be switched, for first the manna began to stink and then it became infested with worms. Therefore, when describing the opposite situation, the verse states: *It did not stink, nor did worms infest it* (16:24). Such is the normal process whenever food becomes wormy.

21 | וְחַם הַשֶּׁמֶשׁ וְנָמָס – *And when the sun grew hot, it melted away*: Any uncollected manna in the field melted into rivulets which the deer and the gazelles lapped up before being hunted by the nations of the world. Upon eating the animals' meat, the nations tasted the manna and understood how fortunate Israel was. The Targum's translation for *venamas – pashar* – is related to the Hebrew *posherin* [meaning "warm"], for the sun heated up the manna and thus melted it.

וְנָמָס – *It melted away*: The Old French equivalent for this verb is *destenperer* ["to make watery"]. The term *pashar* is similarly used in the Talmud (Sanhedrin 67b).

22 eat, and when the sun grew hot, it melted away. When the sixth day came, they gathered a double portion, two omers each. All the leaders of the community came and reported
23 this to Moshe. "This" he told them, "is what the Lord has said: Tomorrow is a day of rest, a holy Sabbath to the Lord. Bake now what you need to bake and cook what you need to cook. Whatever is left, keep carefully aside for the morning."
24 So they put it aside until the morning, as Moshe had instructed them, and it did not stink, nor did worms infest it.
25 And Moshe said, "Today, eat this, for today is a Sabbath to the
26 Lord; today you will not find it on the ground. Six days shall you gather it, but on the seventh day, the Sabbath, it will not
27 be there." Some people did go out to gather it on the seventh

כב| לָקְטוּ לֶחֶם מִשְׁנֶה. כְּשֶׁמָּדְדוּ אֶת לְקִיטָתָם בְּאָהֳלֵיהֶם מָצְאוּ כִפְלַיִם, "שְׁנֵי הָעֹמֶר לָאֶחָד". וּמִדְרַשׁ אַגָּדָה, "לֶחֶם מִשְׁנֶה" מִשֻׁנֶּה, אוֹתוֹ הַיּוֹם נִשְׁתַּנָּה לְשֶׁבַח בְּרֵיחוֹ וְטַעְמוֹ:

וַיַּגִּידוּ לְמֹשֶׁה. שְׁאָלוּהוּ מַה הַיּוֹם מִיָּמִים. וּמִכָּאן יֵשׁ לִלְמֹד שֶׁעֲדַיִן לֹא הִגִּיד לָהֶם מֹשֶׁה פָּרָשַׁת שַׁבָּת שֶׁנִּצְטַוָּה לוֹמַר לָהֶם: "וְהָיָה בַּיּוֹם הַשִּׁשִּׁי וְהֵכִינוּ" וְגוֹ' (לעיל פסוק ה), עַד שֶׁשָּׁאֲלוּ אֶת זֹאת. אָמַר לָהֶם: "הוּא אֲשֶׁר דִּבֶּר ה'" (כפסוק הבא), שֶׁנִּצְטַוֵּיתִי לוֹמַר לָכֶם. וּלְכָךְ עֲנָשׁוֹ הַכָּתוּב, שֶׁאָמַר לוֹ: "עַד אָנָה מֵאַנְתֶּם" (להלן פסוק כח) וְלֹא הוֹצִיאוֹ מִן הַכְּלָל:

כג| אֶת אֲשֶׁר תֹּאפוּ אֵפוּ. מַה שְּׁאַתֶּם רוֹצִים לֶאֱפוֹת בַּתַּנּוּר, "אֵפוּ" הַיּוֹם הַכֹּל לִשְׁנֵי יָמִים. וּמַה שֶּׁאַתֶּם צְרִיכִים לְבַשֵּׁל מִמֶּנּוּ בַּמַּיִם, "בַּשְּׁלוּ" הַיּוֹם. לְשׁוֹן אֲפִיָּה נוֹפֵל בְּלֶחֶם, וּלְשׁוֹן בִּשּׁוּל בְּתַבְשִׁיל:

22 | לָקְטוּ לֶחֶם מִשְׁנֶה – *They gathered a double portion*: When the Israelites measured their haul of manna in their tents, they found that the yield was twice as much as before – two omers per person. The aggadic interpretation for the term *mishneh* ["double"] is that the collection on the sixth day of the week was "different" [*meshuneh*], having a better scent and a richer taste.

וַיַּגִּידוּ לְמֹשֶׁה – *They reported this to Moshe*: The nation's elders asked their leader why this day was different than any other. The fact that the people inquired about the matter shows that Moshe had yet to describe the alternative protocol for the Sabbath described earlier in the text, *On the sixth day, they will have to prepare what they bring in* (16:5). The explanation was only provided once the people realized something had changed: *"This" he told them, "is what the Lord has said"* (16:23), that is, this is precisely the situation that God commanded me to clarify for you. Indeed, Moshe was himself punished for delaying this lesson, as God protested to him: *How long will you* [not "they"] *refuse to keep My commandments and laws?* (16:28), thereby including Moshe in the rebuke.

23 | אֶת אֲשֶׁר תֹּאפוּ אֵפוּ – *Bake what you need to bake*: Bake in the oven today whatever manna you wish to prepare for today and for tomorrow. Or boil today in water whatever you want to eat for these two days. The term *afiyya* refers to baked goods, while the verb *bishul* describes food that is cooked.

◀

שמות | פרק טז | בשלח

כב וַיְהִ֣י ׀ בַּיּ֣וֹם הַשִּׁשִּׁ֗י לָקְט֥וּ לֶ֙חֶם֙ מִשְׁנֶ֔ה שְׁנֵ֥י הָעֹ֖מֶר לָאֶחָ֑ד וַיָּבֹ֙אוּ֙ כָּל־נְשִׂיאֵ֣י הָעֵדָ֔ה וַיַּגִּ֖ידוּ לְמֹשֶֽׁה: כג וַיֹּ֣אמֶר אֲלֵהֶ֗ם ה֚וּא אֲשֶׁ֣ר דִּבֶּ֣ר יהו֔ה שַׁבָּת֧וֹן שַׁבַּת־קֹ֛דֶשׁ לַיהו֖ה מָחָ֑ר אֵ֣ת אֲשֶׁר־תֹּאפ֞וּ אֵפ֗וּ וְאֵ֤ת אֲשֶׁר־תְּבַשְּׁלוּ֙ בַּשֵּׁ֔לוּ וְאֵת֙ כָּל־הָ֣עֹדֵ֔ף הַנִּ֧יחוּ לָכֶ֛ם לְמִשְׁמֶ֖רֶת עַד־הַבֹּֽקֶר: כד וַיַּנִּ֤יחוּ אֹתוֹ֙ עַד־הַבֹּ֔קֶר כַּאֲשֶׁ֖ר צִוָּ֣ה מֹשֶׁ֑ה וְלֹ֣א הִבְאִ֔ישׁ וְרִמָּ֖ה לֹא־הָ֥יְתָה בּֽוֹ: כה וַיֹּ֤אמֶר מֹשֶׁה֙ אִכְלֻ֣הוּ הַיּ֔וֹם כִּֽי־שַׁבָּ֥ת הַיּ֖וֹם לַיהו֑ה הַיּ֕וֹם לֹ֥א תִמְצָאֻ֖הוּ בַּשָּׂדֶֽה: כו שֵׁ֥שֶׁת יָמִ֖ים תִּלְקְטֻ֑הוּ וּבַיּ֧וֹם הַשְּׁבִיעִ֛י שַׁבָּ֖ת לֹ֥א יִֽהְיֶה־בּֽוֹ: כז וַֽיְהִי֙ בַּיּ֣וֹם הַשְּׁבִיעִ֔י

לְמִשְׁמֶרֶת — Keep carefully: The word *mishmeret* means "storage."

25 | וַיֹּאמֶר מֹשֶׁה אִכְלֻהוּ הַיּוֹם — And Moshe said, "Today, eat this": The Israelites had been accustomed to going out in the mornings to collect the manna, and on the Sabbath they came to Moshe and asked whether they should venture out then as well. Said he: "Today you are to eat what you have already in your possession." At dinnertime they approached Moshe again and asked whether now it would be appropriate to look for fresh manna. Thereupon the leader confirmed: *Today is a Sabbath to the Lord.* But when Moshe saw they feared that the manna might have ceased falling forever, he continued: *Today you will not find it on the ground.* He emphasized that there would be no manna today, but that tomorrow the food would return.

26 | וּבַיּוֹם הַשְּׁבִיעִי שַׁבָּת — But on the seventh day, the Sabbath: Because the seventh day is the Sabbath, the manna will not be there. The purpose of this verse is to teach that in addition to the Sabbath, manna will not fall on Yom Kippur or on festival days [which are also referred to as "Sabbaths"].

לְמִשְׁמֶרֶת. לִגְנִיזָה.

כה] וַיֹּאמֶר מֹשֶׁה אִכְלֻהוּ הַיּוֹם. שַׁחֲרִית שֶׁהָיוּ רְגִילִים לָצֵאת וְלִלְקֹט, בָּאוּ לִשְׁאֹל אִם נֵצֵא אִם לָאו, אָמַר לָהֶם: אֶת שֶׁבְּיֶדְכֶם אִכְלוּ. לָעֶרֶב חָזְרוּ לְפָנָיו: מַהוּ לָצֵאת? אָמַר לָהֶם: "שַׁבָּת הַיּוֹם". רָאָה אוֹתָם דּוֹאֲגִים שֶׁמָּא פָּסַק הַמָּן וְלֹא יֵרֵד עוֹד, אָמַר לָהֶם: "הַיּוֹם לֹא תִמְצָאֻהוּ", מַה תַּלְמוּד לוֹמַר "הַיּוֹם"? הַיּוֹם לֹא תִמְצָאֻהוּ אֲבָל מָחָר תִּמְצָאֻהוּ:

כו] וּבַיּוֹם הַשְּׁבִיעִי שַׁבָּת. "שַׁבָּת" הוּא, הַמָּן "לֹא יִהְיֶה בּוֹ". וְלֹא בָּא הַכָּתוּב אֶלָּא לְרַבּוֹת יוֹם הַכִּפּוּרִים וְיָמִים טוֹבִים:

28 day; but they found none. Then the LORD said to Moshe, "How long will you refuse to keep My command-
29 ments and laws? Understand that the LORD has given you a Sabbath – that is why He gave you two days' bread on the sixth day. You shall each rest where you are: let no man depart
30 from where he is on the seventh day." So the people rested on
31 the seventh day. The house of Israel named it manna. It looked like white coriander seeds, and tasted like wafers made with
32 honey. Moshe said, "This is what the LORD commands: Let an omer of it be kept carefully aside for your descendants, that they may see the bread I fed you in the desert when I brought
33 you out of Egypt." Moshe said to Aharon, "Take an urn, put an

כח | עַד־אָנָה מֵאַנְתֶּם. מָשָׁל הֶדְיוֹט הוּא, בַּהֲדֵי הוּצָא לָקֵי כְּרַבָא, עַל יְדֵי הָרְשָׁעִים מִתְגַּנִּין הַכְּשֵׁרִים:

28| עַד־אָנָה מֵאַנְתֶּם – *How long will you refuse*: The verse illustrates the common proverb: Sometimes the cabbage is pulled out along with the weeds. That is, the virtuous might be accused when the wicked are rebuked. [Moshe was blameless, but God spoke of the nation as a collective.]

כט | רְאוּ. בְּעֵינֵיכֶם כִּי ה' בִּכְבוֹדוֹ מַזְהִיר אֶתְכֶם עַל הַשַּׁבָּת, שֶׁהֲרֵי נֵס נַעֲשֶׂה בְּכָל עֶרֶב שַׁבָּת לָתֵת לָכֶם לֶחֶם יוֹמָיִם:

29| רְאוּ – *Understand*: [Literally, "see."] You can see with your own eyes that it is God in His glory Who is commanding you to observe the Sabbath. Witness the miracle that occurs every Sabbath eve when two days' worth of bread appears on the desert floor.

שְׁבוּ אִישׁ תַּחְתָּיו. מִכַּאן סָמְכוּ חֲכָמִים אַרְבַּע אַמּוֹת לַיּוֹצֵא חוּץ לַתְּחוּם:

שְׁבוּ אִישׁ תַּחְתָּיו – *You shall each rest where you are*: According to the Sages, this verse supports the rule that should a person be in an isolated location on the Sabbath, he may walk no more than four cubits in any direction.

אַל־יֵצֵא אִישׁ מִמְּקֹמוֹ. אֵלּוּ אַלְפַּיִם אַמָּה, וְלֹא בִּמְפֹרָשׁ, שֶׁאֵין תְּחוּמִין אֶלָּא מִדִּבְרֵי סוֹפְרִים, וְעִקָּרוֹ שֶׁל מִקְרָא עַל לוֹקְטֵי הַמָּן נֶאֱמַר:

אַל־יֵצֵא אִישׁ מִמְּקֹמוֹ – *Let no man depart from where he is*: This verse alludes to the 2000-cubit boundary. [This border, called "the Sabbath limit" – *teḥum Shabbat* – surrounds a city, and one may not walk past this point on the Sabbath day.] The Torah does not state this law explicitly since such limits are rabbinic in nature. On its most basic level, the verse restricts the movement of manna gatherers specifically.

לא | וְהוּא כְּזֶרַע גַּד. עֵשֶׂב שְׁשְׁמוֹ אליינדר״י, וְזֶרַע שֶׁלּוֹ עָגֹל וְאֵינוֹ לָבָן, וְהַמָּן הָיָה לָבָן, וְאֵינוֹ נִמְשָׁל לְזֶרַע גַּד אֶלָּא לְעִנְיַן הָעִגּוּל, "כְּזֶרַע גַּד" הָיָה וְהוּא "לָבָן":

31| וְהוּא כְּזֶרַע גַּד – *It looked like white coriander seeds*: The verse compares manna to an herb known as *aillendre* [coriander]. This plant has seeds that are round but are not white like the manna. The verse means that the food was similar to coriander seeds in shape only but not in color: "It looked like coriander seeds," only "white."

◀

כח יָצְא֥וּ מִן־הָעָ֖ם לִלְקֹ֑ט וְלֹ֖א מָצָֽאוּ: וַיֹּ֥אמֶר יג
יהוה אֶל־מֹשֶׁ֑ה עַד־אָ֨נָה֙ מֵֽאַנְתֶּ֔ם לִשְׁמֹ֥ר מִצְוֺתַ֖י
וְתֽוֹרֹתָֽי: רְא֗וּ כִּֽי־יהוה֮ נָתַ֣ן לָכֶ֣ם הַשַּׁבָּת֒ עַל־כֵּ֠ן ה֣וּא
נֹתֵ֨ן לָכֶ֜ם בַּיּ֥וֹם הַשִּׁשִּׁ֛י לֶ֥חֶם יוֹמָ֑יִם שְׁב֣וּ ׀ אִ֣ישׁ תַּחְתָּ֗יו
ל אַל־יֵ֥צֵא אִ֛ישׁ מִמְּקֹמ֖וֹ בַּיּ֥וֹם הַשְּׁבִיעִֽי: וַיִּשְׁבְּת֥וּ הָעָ֖ם
לא בַּיּ֥וֹם הַשְּׁבִעִֽי: וַיִּקְרְא֧וּ בֵֽית־יִשְׂרָאֵ֛ל אֶת־שְׁמ֖וֹ מָ֑ן
לב וְה֗וּא כְּזֶ֤רַע גַּד֙ לָבָ֔ן וְטַעְמ֖וֹ כְּצַפִּיחִ֥ת בִּדְבָֽשׁ: וַיֹּ֣אמֶר
מֹשֶׁ֗ה זֶ֤ה הַדָּבָר֙ אֲשֶׁ֣ר צִוָּ֣ה יהו֔ה מְלֹ֤א הָעֹ֨מֶר֙ מִמֶּ֔נּוּ
לְמִשְׁמֶ֖רֶת לְדֹרֹתֵיכֶ֑ם לְמַ֣עַן ׀ יִרְא֣וּ אֶת־הַלֶּ֗חֶם אֲשֶׁ֨ר
הֶאֱכַ֤לְתִּי אֶתְכֶם֙ בַּמִּדְבָּ֔ר בְּהֽוֹצִיאִ֥י אֶתְכֶ֖ם מֵאֶ֥רֶץ
לג מִצְרָֽיִם: וַיֹּ֨אמֶר מֹשֶׁ֜ה אֶֽל־אַהֲרֹ֗ן קַ֚ח צִנְצֶ֣נֶת אַחַ֔ת

כְּצַפִּיחִת. בָּצֵק שֶׁמְּטַגְּנִין אוֹתוֹ בִּדְבַשׁ, וְקוֹרִין לוֹ 'אִסְקְרִיטִין' בִּלְשׁוֹן מִשְׁנָה (חלה א, ד; פסחים לז ע״א), וְהוּא תַּרְגּוּם שֶׁל אוּנְקְלוֹס:

לב | **לְמִשְׁמֶרֶת. לִגְנִיזָה:**

לְדֹרֹתֵיכֶם. בִּימֵי יִרְמְיָהוּ, כְּשֶׁהָיָה יִרְמְיָהוּ מוֹכִיחָם: לָמָּה אֵין אַתֶּם עוֹסְקִים בַּתּוֹרָה? וְהֵם אוֹמְרִים: נַנִּיחַ מְלַאכְתֵּנוּ וְנַעֲסֹק בַּתּוֹרָה, מֵהֵיכָן נִתְפַּרְנֵס? הוֹצִיא לָהֶם צִנְצֶנֶת הַמָּן, אָמַר לָהֶם: "הַדּוֹר אַתֶּם רְאוּ דְבַר ה׳" (ירמיה ב, לא), 'שִׁמְעוּ' לֹא נֶאֱמַר אֶלָּא "רְאוּ", בָּזֶה נִתְפַּרְנְסוּ אֲבוֹתֵיכֶם, הַרְבֵּה שְׁלוּחִין יֵשׁ לוֹ לַמָּקוֹם לְהָכִין מָזוֹן לִירֵאָיו:

לג | **צִנְצֶנֶת. צְלוֹחִית שֶׁל חֶרֶס,** כְּתַרְגּוּמוֹ:

וְהִנַּח אֹתוֹ לִפְנֵי יהוה. לִפְנֵי הָאָרוֹן, וְלֹא נֶאֱמַר מִקְרָא זֶה עַד שֶׁנִּבְנָה

כְּצַפִּיחִת – *Like wafers*: The manna tasted like dough fried in honey, a dish the Mishna refers to as *eskeritin* [a soft dumpling, see Ḥalla 1:4 and Pesaḥim 37a]. This is how Onkelos translates the term.

32 | **לְמִשְׁמֶרֶת** – *Be kept carefully aside*: *Lemishmeret* means "to be stored away."

לְדֹרֹתֵיכֶם – *For your descendants*: When the prophet Yirmeyahu rebuked the nation for their lack of Torah study, the people responded: If we quit our jobs and occupy ourselves with studying Torah, how will we live? Yirmeyahu took out the jar of manna and showed it to the Israelites, declaring: *O generation, see the word of the Lord* (Jeremiah 2:31). The prophet did not demand that his audience listen to God's message, but that they gaze upon His miraculous food. "Look," he said, "this is how your ancestors subsisted. The Lord has many agents He can dispatch to provide food for those who revere Him."

33 | **צִנְצֶנֶת** – *An urn*: The manna was placed in an earthenware jar, which is how the Targum renders the term [*tzelohit*].

וְהִנַּח אֹתוֹ לִפְנֵי יהוה – *And place it before the Lord*: The urn was to be placed before the Ark of the Covenant. Although this

omer of manna in it, and place it before the Lord to be kept
34 for future generations." As the Lord commanded Moshe, so
Aharon placed it before the Ark of Testimony to be kept with
35 care. The Israelites ate manna for forty years, until they came
to the land where they could settle down. They ate the manna
36 until they came to the border of Canaan. (An omer is a tenth
of an ephah.)

17 1 All the community of Israel moved on after that from the desert of Sin, traveling from place to place as the Lord guided them, and they camped at Refidim, but there was no water
2 there for the people to drink. The people started to wrangle with Moshe. "Give us water to drink," they raged. "Why do you wrangle with me?" asked Moshe. "Why are you testing
3 the Lord?" But the people were thirsty for water. They railed against Moshe, "Why did you bring us out of Egypt? Was it

SHEVI'I

אֹהֶל מוֹעֵד, חָלָא שֶׁנִּכְתַּב כָּאן בְּפָרָשַׁת הַמָּן:

לה] אַרְבָּעִים שָׁנָה. וַהֲלֹא חָסֵר שְׁלֹשִׁים יוֹם, שֶׁהֲרֵי בַּחֲמִשָּׁה עָשָׂר בְּאִיָּר יָרַד לָהֶם הַמָּן תְּחִלָּה וּבַחֲמִשָּׁה עָשָׂר בְּנִיסָן פָּסַק, שֶׁנֶּאֱמַר: "וַיִּשְׁבֹּת הַמָּן מִמָּחֳרָת" (יהושע ה, יב)? אֶלָּא מַגִּיד שֶׁהָעוּגוֹת שֶׁהוֹצִיאוּ יִשְׂרָאֵל מִמִּצְרַיִם טָעֲמוּ בָהֶם טַעַם מָן:

אֶל־אֶרֶץ נוֹשָׁבֶת. לְאַחַר שֶׁעָבְרוּ אֶת הַיַּרְדֵּן:

אֶל־קְצֵה אֶרֶץ כְּנָעַן. בִּתְחִלַּת הַגְּבוּל קֹדֶם שֶׁעָבְרוּ אֶת הַיַּרְדֵּן, וְהֵם עַרְבוֹת מוֹאָב. נִמְצְאוּ מַכְחִישִׁין זֶה אֶת זֶה! אֶלָּא בְּעַרְבוֹת מוֹאָב כְּשֶׁמֵּת מֹשֶׁה בְּשִׁבְעָה בַּאֲדָר פָּסַק הַמָּן מִלֵּרֵד, וְנִסְתַּפְּקוּ מִמָּן שֶׁלָּקְטוּ בּוֹ בַיּוֹם עַד שֶׁהִקְרִיבוּ הָעֹמֶר בְּשִׁשָּׁה

---

directive was only issued following construction of the Tabernacle, it is recorded here as part of the story of the manna.

35 | אַרְבָּעִים שָׁנָה – *For forty years*: In fact, Israel ate the manna for thirty days less than forty years, as follows: The food began to fall on the fifteenth of Iyar [the date is given at the start of the chapter]. And the manna stopped appearing on the fifteenth of Nisan [in the fortieth year], as the verse states: *And the manna ceased the next day, when they ate of the grain of the land* (Joshua 5:12). The Torah's figure of forty years here includes the thirty days that the people ate the cakes they had brought with them out of Egypt, which assumed the taste of the manna.

אֶל־אֶרֶץ נוֹשָׁבֶת – *To the land where they could settle down*: The manna disappeared after the nation crossed the Jordan River.

אֶל־קְצֵה אֶרֶץ כְּנָעַן – *To the border of Canaan*: According to this clause, Israel ate the manna throughout their desert travels before they crossed the Jordan River. The manna was available to them until they reached the border of Canaan in the region known as the Plains of Moav. But this verse contradicts itself [since it first states that Israel enjoyed the manna until they actually entered the land]. The difficulty can be reconciled as follows: The manna stopped falling on the seventh of Adar [the

שמות | פרק יז | בשלח

וְתֶן־שָׁמָּה מְלֹא־הָעֹמֶר מָן וְהַנַּח אֹתוֹ לִפְנֵי יהוה
לד לְמִשְׁמֶרֶת לְדֹרֹתֵיכֶם: כַּאֲשֶׁר צִוָּה יהוה אֶל־מֹשֶׁה
לה וַיַּנִּיחֵהוּ אַהֲרֹן לִפְנֵי הָעֵדֻת לְמִשְׁמָרֶת: וּבְנֵי יִשְׂרָאֵל
אָכְלוּ אֶת־הַמָּן אַרְבָּעִים שָׁנָה עַד־בֹּאָם אֶל־אֶרֶץ
נוֹשָׁבֶת אֶת־הַמָּן אָכְלוּ עַד־בֹּאָם אֶל־קְצֵה אֶרֶץ
לו כְּנָעַן: וְהָעֹמֶר עֲשִׂרִית הָאֵיפָה הוּא:

שביעי
יז א וַיִּסְעוּ כָּל־עֲדַת בְּנֵי־יִשְׂרָאֵל מִמִּדְבַּר־סִין לְמַסְעֵיהֶם
עַל־פִּי יהוה וַיַּחֲנוּ בִּרְפִידִים וְאֵין מַיִם לִשְׁתֹּת הָעָם:
ב וַיָּרֶב הָעָם עִם־מֹשֶׁה וַיֹּאמְרוּ תְּנוּ־לָנוּ מַיִם וְנִשְׁתֶּה
וַיֹּאמֶר לָהֶם מֹשֶׁה מַה־תְּרִיבוּן עִמָּדִי מַה־תְּנַסּוּן אֶת־
ג יהוה: וַיִּצְמָא שָׁם הָעָם לַמַּיִם וַיָּלֶן הָעָם עַל־מֹשֶׁה
וַיֹּאמֶר לָמָּה זֶּה הֶעֱלִיתָנוּ מִמִּצְרַיִם לְהָמִית אֹתִי וְאֶת־

---

month preceding Nisan] when Moshe passed away. At this point Israel was encamped on the Plains of Moav [outside the land of Canaan]. However, the manna that Israel collected on that day lasted through the sixteenth of Nisan when the nation brought their barley offering [the Omer offering brought on Passover inaugurated the new produce of every year; see Leviticus 23:9–14]. Hence the verse states: *And they ate of the grain of the land on the day after the Passover* (Joshua 5:11).

עֶשֶׂר בְּנֵיסָן, שֶׁנֶּאֱמַר: "וַיֹּאכְלוּ מֵעֲבוּר הָאָרֶץ מִמָּחֳרַת הַפֶּסַח" (יהושע ה, יא):

36 | עֲשִׂרִית הָאֵיפָה – *A tenth of an ephah*: There are three seah in an ephah, and six kav in a seah. There are four log in a kav, while a log holds the volume of six eggs. [These are all units of volume employed by the Talmud.] This means that a tenth of an ephah is equal to 43.2 egg-bulks. When dough measures at least one tenth of an ephah one is required to set aside ḥalla [a portion of the dough given to the priest; see Numbers 15:19–21]. It is also the minimum size for a meal offering.

לו| **עֲשִׂרִית הָאֵיפָה.** הָאֵיפָה שָׁלֹשׁ סְאִין, וְהַסְּאָה שֵׁשֶׁת קַבִּין, וְהַקַּב אַרְבָּעָה לֻגִּין, וְהַלֹּג שֵׁשׁ בֵּיצִים; נִמְצָא עֲשִׂירִית הָאֵיפָה אַרְבָּעִים וְשָׁלֹשׁ בֵּיצִים וְחֹמֶשׁ בֵּיצָה, וְהוּא שִׁעוּר לַחַלָּה וְלַמְּנָחוֹת:

17:2 | מַה־תְּנַסּוּן – *Why are you testing*: Saying: "Can he provide water for us in this desert wilderness?"

יז ב| **מַה־תְּנַסּוּן.** לוֹמַר, הֲיוּכַל לָתֵת מַיִם בְּאֶרֶץ צִיָּה:

4 to kill me, my children, and all my livestock by thirst?" "What shall I do with this people?" Moshe cried to the Lord – "an-
5 other moment and they will stone me." The Lord answered Moshe, "Walk out to face the people taking some of the elders of Israel with you. Take the staff with which you struck the Nile
6 in your hand, and go. I will be there before you by the rock at Ḥorev. Strike the rock, water will come out of it and the people will drink." And that is what Moshe did, before the eyes
7 of the elders of Israel. He named the place Masa and Meriva, because the people had quarreled and had tested the Lord, demanding, "Is the Lord among us or not?"
8/9 Then, at Refidim, Amalek came and attacked Israel. Moshe

ד| **עוֹד מְעָט.** אִם מַמְתִּין "עוֹד מְעָט", וּסְקָלֻנִי:

ה| **עֲבֹר לִפְנֵי הָעָם.** וּרְאֵה אִם יִסְקְלוּךָ, לָמָּה הוֹצֵאתָ לַעַז עַל בָּנַי?:

וְקַח אִתְּךָ מִזִּקְנֵי יִשְׂרָאֵל. לְעֵדוּת, שֶׁיִּרְאוּ שֶׁעַל יָדְךָ הַמַּיִם יוֹצְאִים מִן הַצּוּר, וְלֹא יֹאמְרוּ: מַעְיָנוֹת הָיוּ שָׁם מִימֵי קֶדֶם:

וּמַטְּךָ אֲשֶׁר הִכִּיתָ בּוֹ אֶת־הַיְאֹר. מַה תַּלְמוּד לוֹמַר: "אֲשֶׁר הִכִּיתָ בּוֹ אֶת הַיְאֹר"? אֶלָּא שֶׁהָיוּ יִשְׂרָאֵל אוֹמְרִים עַל הַמַּטֶּה שֶׁאֵינוֹ מוּכָן אֶלָּא לְפֻרְעָנוּת, בּוֹ לָקָה פַרְעֹה וּמִצְרַיִם כַּמָּה מַכּוֹת בְּמִצְרַיִם וְעַל הַיָּם, לְכָךְ נֶאֱמַר: "אֲשֶׁר הִכִּיתָ בּוֹ אֶת הַיְאֹר" וְהֵם אוֹמְרִים עָלָיו שֶׁאֵינוֹ אֶלָּא לְפֻרְעָנוּת, יִרְאוּ עַתָּה שֶׁאַף לְטוֹבָה הוּא מוּכָן:

ו| **וְהִכִּיתָ בַצּוּר.** עַל הַצּוּר לֹא נֶאֱמַר אֶלָּא "בַּצּוּר", מִכָּאן שֶׁהַמַּטֶּה הָיָה שֶׁל מִין דָּבָר חָזָק וּשְׁמוֹ

4| **עוֹד מְעָט** – *Another moment*: [Literally, "just another bit."] The verse means: If I wait "just another bit – they will stone me."

5| **עֲבֹר לִפְנֵי הָעָם** – *Walk out to face the people*: Let us see if they do in fact stone you. Moshe, why have you cast aspersions on My children?

וְקַח אִתְּךָ מִזִּקְנֵי יִשְׂרָאֵל – *Taking some of the elders of Israel with you*: The elders are to act as witnesses to verify that you have extracted water from the rock, lest the people argue that natural springs had always been there.

וּמַטְּךָ אֲשֶׁר הִכִּיתָ בּוֹ אֶת־הַיְאֹר – *The staff with which you struck the Nile*: Why was it significant that Moshe use the staff previously employed to effect the plague of blood? Because Moshe's staff had been used to strike Pharaoh and Egypt during the saga of the plagues, and was wielded to split the Sea of Reeds, the Israelites argued that the stick was only capable of inflicting punishment. Hence Moshe is now told to take hold of *the staff with which you struck the Nile,* thereby proving to the people that the instrument could also be used to call down blessing.

6| **וְהִכִּיתָ בַצּוּר** – *Strike the rock*: Moshe is not instructed to strike "upon the rock" [*al hatzur*], but to strike "in the rock" [*batzur*]. This teaches that the staff was composed of a hard material

שמות | פרק יז | בשלח

ד בָּנַי וְאֶת־מִקְנַי בַּצָּמָא: וַיִּצְעַק מֹשֶׁה אֶל־יְהֹוָה לֵאמֹר
ה מָה אֶעֱשֶׂה לָעָם הַזֶּה עוֹד מְעַט וּסְקָלֻנִי: וַיֹּאמֶר
יְהֹוָה אֶל־מֹשֶׁה עֲבֹר לִפְנֵי הָעָם וְקַח אִתְּךָ מִזִּקְנֵי
יִשְׂרָאֵל וּמַטְּךָ אֲשֶׁר הִכִּיתָ בּוֹ אֶת־הַיְאֹר קַח בְּיָדְךָ
ו וְהָלָכְתָּ: הִנְנִי עֹמֵד לְפָנֶיךָ שָּׁם ׀ עַל־הַצּוּר בְּחֹרֵב
וְהִכִּיתָ בַצּוּר וְיָצְאוּ מִמֶּנּוּ מַיִם וְשָׁתָה הָעָם וַיַּעַשׂ כֵּן
ז מֹשֶׁה לְעֵינֵי זִקְנֵי יִשְׂרָאֵל: וַיִּקְרָא שֵׁם הַמָּקוֹם מַסָּה
וּמְרִיבָה עַל־רִיב ׀ בְּנֵי יִשְׂרָאֵל וְעַל נַסֹּתָם אֶת־יְהֹוָה
לֵאמֹר הֲיֵשׁ יְהֹוָה בְּקִרְבֵּנוּ אִם־אָיִן:
ח וַיָּבֹא עֲמָלֵק וַיִּלָּחֶם עִם־יִשְׂרָאֵל בִּרְפִידִם: וַיֹּאמֶר

סַנְפִּירִינוֹן, וְהַצּוּר נִבְקַע מִפָּנָיו:

ח] וַיָּבֹא עֲמָלֵק. סָמַךְ פָּרָשָׁה זוֹ לְמִקְרָא זֶה, לוֹמַר, תָּמִיד אֲנִי בֵּינֵיכֶם וּמְזֻמָּן לְכָל צָרְכֵיכֶם, וְאַתֶּם אוֹמְרִים: "הֲיֵשׁ ה' בְּקִרְבֵּנוּ אִם אָיִן" (לעיל פסוק ז)?! חַיֵּיכֶם שֶׁהַכֶּלֶב בָּא וְנוֹשֵׁךְ אֶתְכֶם וְאַתֶּם צוֹעֲקִים לִי וְתֵדְעוּ הֵיכָן אֲנִי. מָשָׁל לְאָדָם שֶׁהִרְכִּיב בְּנוֹ עַל כְּתֵפוֹ וְיָצָא לַדֶּרֶךְ, הָיָה אוֹתוֹ הַבֵּן רוֹאֶה חֵפֶץ וְאוֹמֵר: אַבָּא, טֹל חֵפֶץ זֶה וְתֶן לִי! וְהוּא נוֹתֵן לוֹ, וְכֵן שְׁנִיָּה וְכֵן שְׁלִישִׁית. פָּגְעוּ בְּאָדָם אֶחָד, אָמַר לוֹ אוֹתוֹ הַבֵּן: רָאִיתָ אֶת אַבָּא? אָמַר לוֹ אָבִיו: אֵינְךָ יוֹדֵעַ הֵיכָן אֲנִי?! הִשְׁלִיכוֹ מֵעָלָיו, וּבָא הַכֶּלֶב וּנְשָׁכוֹ.

---

called *sanpirinon* [perhaps lapis lazuli] that was able to cleave the stone.

8| וַיָּבֹא עֲמָלֵק – **Then Amalek came:** The Torah juxtaposes the story of Amalek with Israel's demand for water in order to teach that one led to the other. For God chastised Israel: Are you unaware that I am with you always, that I am constantly ready to provide for you? How dare you ask: *Is the Lord among us or not* (17:7)? I swear on your lives that I will dispatch a dog to bite you [i.e., Amalek]. And when you cry for My assistance, then you will know where I am. The situation may be compared to a man who places his son on his shoulders and takes him for a walk. As they proceed, the boy sees some treat he desires and says: "Father! Get that for me!" And the father does. They continue on their way, and again the child asks for something, prompting the parent's indulgence. This keeps happening until, by and by, they meet an acquaintance, whereupon the boy turns to the man and says: "Have you seen my father anywhere?" The father explodes: "You ingrate! Don't you know where I am?" He immediately pulls the boy from his shoulders and throws him to the ground, whereupon a dog comes along and bites him.

said to Yehoshua, "Choose men for us, and go out and do battle against Amalek. Tomorrow I will stand on top of the hill
10 with the staff of God in my hand." Yehoshua fought the Amalekites as Moshe had directed him, while Moshe, Aharon, and
11 Hur climbed to the top of the hill. Whenever Moshe held his hand high, the Israelites prevailed, but whenever he let his
12 hand drop, the Amalekites prevailed. But Moshe's hands grew heavy. So they took a stone and placed it under him and he sat, while Aharon and Hur held up his hands, one on each side, so

9| בְּחַר־לָנוּ – *Choose for us*: Why does Moshe ask Yehoshua to choose men "for us" – as if to say "for me and for you"? He thereby equated his protégé to himself. Based on this statement, our Sages teach that a master should treat his student with the honor he himself deserves [see Avot 4:15]. Furthermore, how do we know that one should exercise the same respect toward one's fellow as one would to a teacher? We learn this rule from the verse *And Aharon said to Moshe, "Alas, my lord, I pray you"* (Numbers 12:11). Now was Aharon not older than Moshe by three years? And yet he treated his younger contemporary as his superior. Finally, we learn that one should fear one's teacher as one reveres God, as the verse states: *My lord Moshe restrain them [kela'em]* [Numbers 11:28, regarding those who prophesied without Moshe's permission]. Yehoshua advised Moshe to eradicate them [*kalem*] from the world. He felt that these men deserved to be destroyed for disrespecting his teacher Moshe, a crime as heinous as sinning against God.

וְצֵא הִלָּחֵם – *And go out and do battle*: Emerge from God's protective cloud and fight against Amalek.

מָחָר – *Tomorrow*: When the battle is fought, *I will stand on top of the hill*.

בְּחַר־לָנוּ אֲנָשִׁים – *Choose men for us*: [The term *anashim* denotes exceptional men.] Select mighty warriors who are also sin-fearing men, such that the merits they have accrued might assist us in victory. An alternative interpretation: Select men able to combat the witchcraft wielded by Amalek as a weapon.

10| וּמֹשֶׁה אַהֲרֹן וְחוּר – *Moshe, Aharon and Hur*: This episode teaches us rules for a fast day, for the nation of Israel were fasting as they were fighting Amalek. We learn that three people must advance together to pray before the Ark on a

שמות | פרק יז | בשלח

מֹשֶׁה אֶל־יְהוֹשֻׁעַ בְּחַר־לָנוּ אֲנָשִׁים וְצֵא הִלָּחֵם בַּעֲמָלֵק מָחָר אָנֹכִי נִצָּב עַל־רֹאשׁ הַגִּבְעָה וּמַטֵּה הָאֱלֹהִים בְּיָדִי: וַיַּעַשׂ יְהוֹשֻׁעַ כַּאֲשֶׁר אָמַר־לוֹ מֹשֶׁה לְהִלָּחֵם בַּעֲמָלֵק וּמֹשֶׁה אַהֲרֹן וְחוּר עָלוּ רֹאשׁ הַגִּבְעָה: וְהָיָה כַּאֲשֶׁר יָרִים מֹשֶׁה יָדוֹ וְגָבַר יִשְׂרָאֵל וְכַאֲשֶׁר יָנִיחַ יָדוֹ וְגָבַר עֲמָלֵק: וִידֵי מֹשֶׁה כְּבֵדִים וַיִּקְחוּ־אֶבֶן וַיָּשִׂימוּ תַחְתָּיו וַיֵּשֶׁב עָלֶיהָ וְאַהֲרֹן וְחוּר תָּמְכוּ בְיָדָיו מִזֶּה אֶחָד וּמִזֶּה אֶחָד

יא

יב

חוּר. בְּנָהּ שֶׁל מִרְיָם הָיָה:

כַּאֲשֶׁר יָרִים מֹשֶׁה יָדוֹ. וְכִי יָדָיו שֶׁל מֹשֶׁה נוֹצְחוֹת הָיוּ הַמִּלְחָמָה? וְכוּ', כִּדְאִיתָא בְּרֹאשׁ הַשָּׁנָה (דף כט ע"א):

וִידֵי מֹשֶׁה כְּבֵדִים. בִּשְׁבִיל שֶׁנִּתְעַצֵּל בַּמִּצְוָה וּמִנָּה אַחֵר תַּחְתָּיו, נִתְיַקְּרוּ יָדָיו:

וַיִּקְחוּ. אַהֲרֹן וְחוּר "וַיָּשִׂימוּ תַחְתָּיו", וְלֹא יָשַׁב לוֹ עַל כַּר וָכֶסֶת, אָמַר: יִשְׂרָאֵל שְׁרוּיִין בְּצַעַר, אַף אֲנִי אֶהְיֶה עִמָּהֶם בְּצַעַר:

וַיְהִי יָדָיו אֱמוּנָה. וַיְהִי מֹשֶׁה יָדָיו בֶּאֱמוּנָה פְרוּסוֹת הַשָּׁמַיִם בִּתְפִלָּה נֶאֱמָנָה וּנְכוֹנָה:

עַד־בֹּא הַשָּׁמֶשׁ. שֶׁהָיוּ עֲמָלֵקִים מְחַשְּׁבִין אֶת הַשָּׁעוֹת בְּאַסְטְרוֹלוֹגִיָּאה בְּאֵיזוֹ שָׁעָה הֵם נוֹצְחִים, וְהֶעֱמִיד לָהֶם מֹשֶׁה חַמָּה וְעִרְבֵּב אֶת הַשָּׁעוֹת:

fast day [to increase the community's chances of a successful hearing].

חוּר – *And Hur*: Ḥur was Miriam's son.

11 | כַּאֲשֶׁר יָרִים מֹשֶׁה יָדוֹ – *Whenever Moshe held his hand high*: Did Moshe's hands have the power to turn the battle in Israel's favor? See the Talmud's discussion on this matter (Rosh HaShana 29a). [According to that source, when Moshe raised his hands to the heavens, the people were encouraged to pray to God for assistance.]

12 | וִידֵי מֹשֶׁה כְּבֵדִים – *But Moshe's hands grew heavy*: Moshe's hands became heavy as a punishment for his laziness in passing on to Yehoshua the command to fight for Israel.

וַיִּקְחוּ – *So they took*: Moshe's companions Aharon and Ḥur procured a stone for him to sit on. Moshe refused to sit on a pillow or a blanket, for he argued: Since Israel is suffering the travails of war, I will join them in their discomfort.

וַיְהִי יָדָיו אֱמוּנָה – *So that his hands held true*: [Were the verb in this phrase actually referring to Moshe's hands, it would have been plural: *vayihyu*. Since the verb is singular – *vayhi* – its subject must be] Moshe, who faithfully held his hands spread out toward the sky in sincere and honest prayer.

עַד־בֹּא הַשָּׁמֶשׁ – *Until sunset*: The Amalekites used their knowledge of astrology to calculate the hour of their victory. But Moshe held the sun still in the sky and confused the hours for them.

13 that his hands held true until sunset. And Yehoshua overcame Amalek and his people by the sword.
14 Then the Lord said to Moshe, "Write this as a memorial on a scroll, and commit it to Yehoshua's ears: I will erase the memory of Amalek, utterly, from under the heavens." Moshe
15
16 built an altar and named it, "The Lord Is My Banner," saying, "There is a hand on the Lord's throne. The Lord will be at war with Amalek throughout the ages."

MAFTIR

יג| וַיַּחֲלֹשׁ יְהוֹשֻׁעַ. חָתַךְ רָאשֵׁי גִבּוֹרָיו, וְלֹא הִשְׁאִיר אֶלָּא חַלָּשִׁים שֶׁבָּהֶם, וְלֹא הֲרָגָם כֻּלָּם. מִכָּאן אָנוּ לְמֵדִים שֶׁעָשׂוּ עַל פִּי הַדִּבּוּר שֶׁל שְׁכִינָה:

יד| כְּתֹב זֹאת זִכָּרוֹן. שֶׁבָּא עֲמָלֵק לְהִזְדַּוֵּג לְיִשְׂרָאֵל קֹדֶם לְכָל הָאֻמּוֹת:

וְשִׂים בְּאָזְנֵי יְהוֹשֻׁעַ. הַמַּכְנִיס אֶת יִשְׂרָאֵל לָאָרֶץ, שֶׁיְּצַוֶּה אֶת יִשְׂרָאֵל לְשַׁלֵּם לוֹ אֶת גְּמוּלוֹ. כָּאן נִרְמַז לוֹ לְמֹשֶׁה שֶׁיְּהוֹשֻׁעַ מַכְנִיס אֶת יִשְׂרָאֵל לָאָרֶץ:

כִּי־מָחֹה אֶמְחֶה. לְכָךְ אֲנִי מַזְהִירְךָ כֵּן, כִּי חָפֵץ אֲנִי לִמְחוֹתוֹ:

טו| וַיִּקְרָא שְׁמוֹ. שֶׁל מִזְבֵּחַ ה' נִסִּי – הַקָּדוֹשׁ בָּרוּךְ הוּא עָשָׂה לָנוּ כָּאן נֵס. לֹא שֶׁהַמִּזְבֵּחַ קָרוּי ה', אֶלָּא הַמַּזְכִּיר שְׁמוֹ שֶׁל מִזְבֵּחַ

13| **וַיַּחֲלֹשׁ יְהוֹשֻׁעַ** – *And Yehoshua overcame*: [Literally, "And Yehoshua weakened."] Yehoshua decapitated Amalek's leading warriors, leaving alive only their weakest soldiers. He did not obliterate the entire enemy army. We learn from this that the Israelite battle plan must have been divinely ordained. [Yehoshua would not have exercised restraint unless commanded by God to do so.]

14| **כְּתֹב זֹאת זִכָּרוֹן** – *Write this as a memorial*: Record for posterity that Amalek was the first nation to contend with Israel.

וְשִׂים בְּאָזְנֵי יְהוֹשֻׁעַ – *And commit it to Yehoshua's ears*: Since Yehoshua will eventually lead the nation into the land of Israel, he will command the people to avenge Amalek's unprovoked aggression. Thus God hinted to Moshe that it would be his successor who would conduct Israel into their land.

כִּי־מָחֹה אֶמְחֶה – *I will erase*: I am directing you to remember the behavior of Amalek so that you will understand My plan to destroy them.

15| **וַיִּקְרָא שְׁמוֹ** – *And named it*: [The word *nes*, translated here as "banner," can also mean "miracle."] Moshe named the altar *Adonai Nisi*, meaning "the Holy One, blessed be He, performed a miracle for us here." This does not mean that Moshe gave

שמות | פרק יז

יג וַיְהִי יָדָיו אֱמוּנָה עַד־בֹּא הַשָּׁמֶשׁ: וַיַּחֲלֹשׁ יְהוֹשֻׁעַ אֶת־עֲמָלֵק וְאֶת־עַמּוֹ לְפִי־חָרֶב:
יד וַיֹּאמֶר יְהֹוָה אֶל־מֹשֶׁה כְּתֹב זֹאת זִכָּרוֹן בַּסֵּפֶר וְשִׂים בְּאָזְנֵי יְהוֹשֻׁעַ כִּי־מָחֹה אֶמְחֶה אֶת־זֵכֶר עֲמָלֵק מִתַּחַת הַשָּׁמָיִם: טו וַיִּבֶן מֹשֶׁה מִזְבֵּחַ וַיִּקְרָא שְׁמוֹ יְהֹוָה ׀ נִסִּי: טז וַיֹּאמֶר כִּי־יָד עַל־כֵּס יָהּ מִלְחָמָה לַיהֹוָה בַּעֲמָלֵק מִדֹּר דֹּר:

מפטיר

זוֹכֵר אֶת הַנֵּס שֶׁעָשָׂה הַמָּקוֹם, ה' הוּא נֵס שֶׁלָּנוּ:

טז| וַיֹּאמֶר. מֹשֶׁה. "כִּי יָד עַל כֵּס יָהּ" – יָדוֹ שֶׁל הַקָּדוֹשׁ בָּרוּךְ הוּא הוּרְמָה לִשָּׁבַע בְּכִסְאוֹ לִהְיוֹת לוֹ מִלְחָמָה וְאֵיבָה בַּעֲמָלֵק עוֹלָמִית. וּמַהוּ "כֵּס" וְלֹא נֶאֱמַר "כִּסֵּא", וְאַף הַשֵּׁם נֶחֱלַק לְחֶצְיוֹ? נִשְׁבַּע הַקָּדוֹשׁ בָּרוּךְ הוּא שֶׁאֵין שְׁמוֹ שָׁלֵם וְאֵין כִּסְאוֹ שָׁלֵם עַד שֶׁיִּמָּחֶה שְׁמוֹ שֶׁל עֲמָלֵק כֻּלּוֹ, וּכְשֶׁיִּמָּחֶה שְׁמוֹ יִהְיֶה הַשֵּׁם שָׁלֵם וְהַכִּסֵּא שָׁלֵם, שֶׁנֶּאֱמַר: "הָאוֹיֵב תַּמּוּ חֳרָבוֹת לָנֶצַח" (תהלים ט, ז) זֶהוּ עֵשָׂו שֶׁכָּתוּב בּוֹ: "וְעֶבְרָתוֹ שְׁמָרָה נֶצַח" (עמוס א, יא), "וְעָרִים נָתַשְׁתָּ אָבַד זִכְרָם הֵמָּה" (תהלים שם), מַהוּ אוֹמֵר אַחֲרָיו? "וַה' לְעוֹלָם יֵשֵׁב" (שם פסוק ח), הֲרֵי הַשֵּׁם שָׁלֵם, "כּוֹנֵן לַמִּשְׁפָּט כִּסְאוֹ" (שם), הֲרֵי הַכִּסֵּא שָׁלֵם.

---

the altar the name of God, but that people would recall God's miracle when they mentioned this altar, declaring: "The Lord is our Miracle."

16| וַיֹּאמֶר – *Saying*: Moshe said: *There is a hand on the Lord's throne*. The Holy One, blessed be He, raised His hand to swear by His throne, vowing to wage eternal war and to harbor perpetual enmity against Amalek. Why does the verse use the term *kes*, an abridged form of the word *kisei* [meaning "chair or throne"]? And why is the name of God halved [with just the first two letters – *yod-heh* – appearing]? Because God swore that his name would remain incomplete and his throne would also not be whole before the name of Esav [progenitor of Amalek; see Genesis 36:10–12] is blotted out from the world. However, when his name is erased, God's name and His throne will be complete. We see this as well in the verse which states: *The enemies have come to an end, in perpetual ruins* (Psalms 9:7). That verse evokes Esav – whom we know to have *kept his wrath perpetually* (Amos 1:11) – and it continues: *For you have destroyed the cities; their memorial is perished,* followed by the phrase *But the Lord shall endure forever* – indicating the wholeness of God's name – and *He has prepared His throne for judgment* (Psalms 9:8), showing that His throne will then be complete.

HAFTARAT BESHALAḤ

JUDGES
Ashkenazim begin here

4 Devora was a prophetess, the wife of Lapidot; she was judging
5 Israel at that time. She sat beneath Devora's palm between Rama and Beit El in the Efrayim hills; the Israelites would go up to her for judg-
6 ment. One day, she summoned Barak son of Avinoam from Kedesh Naftali and said to him, "The Lord, God of Israel, has commanded: Go, take ten thousand men of the people of Naftali and Zevulun
7 and lead them to Mount Tavor. And I shall lead to you at the Kishon Stream Sisera, Yavin's general, along with his chariots and his
8 hordes, and deliver him into your hands." Barak said to her, "If you
9 go with me, I will go; if not, I will not." "Then I shall go with you," she said, "but you will find no glory on the path you are taking, for the Lord will deliver Sisera into the hands of a woman." So Devora
10 arose and accompanied Barak to Kedesh. Barak mustered Zevulun and Naftali at Kedesh and advanced with ten thousand men behind
11 him, and Devora went up with him. Ḥever the Kenite had parted ways from the Kenites, who were descended from Ḥovav, Moshe's father-in-law. He had pitched his tent at Elon BeTzaananim, which
12 was by Kedesh. Sisera was informed that Barak son of Avinoam had
13 advanced to Mount Tavor. And Sisera mustered all his chariots – nine hundred iron chariots – and all his warriors from Ḥaroshet HaGoyim
14 to Kishon Stream. "Rise up!" Devora said to Barak. "For on this day, the Lord will deliver Sisera into your hands – the Lord marches before you!" Barak charged down Mount Tavor with ten thousand
15 men behind him. And the Lord threw Sisera, all his chariots, and his entire force into panic before Barak's swords. Sisera dismounted from
16 his chariot and fled on foot. Barak chased the chariots and warriors to Ḥaroshet HaGoyim, and all of Sisera's army fell by the sword; not
17 a single man survived. Now Sisera had fled on foot to the tent of Yael, the wife of Ḥever the Kenite, for there was peace between Yavin King
18 of Ḥatzor and Ḥever's family. Yael went out to meet Sisera. "Turn aside, my lord," she said to him, "turn aside to me – do not fear." He

הפטרת בשלח

וּדְבוֹרָה֙ אִשָּׁ֣ה נְבִיאָ֔ה אֵ֖שֶׁת לַפִּיד֑וֹת הִ֛יא שֹׁפְטָ֥ה אֶת־יִשְׂרָאֵ֖ל בָּעֵ֥ת הַהִֽיא׃ וְהִ֨יא יוֹשֶׁ֜בֶת תַּֽחַת־תֹּ֗מֶר דְּבוֹרָ֛ה בֵּ֥ין הָרָמָ֖ה וּבֵ֣ין בֵּֽית־אֵ֑ל בְּהַ֖ר אֶפְרָ֑יִם וַיַּעֲל֥וּ אֵלֶ֛יהָ בְּנֵ֥י יִשְׂרָאֵ֖ל לַמִּשְׁפָּֽט׃ וַתִּשְׁלַ֗ח וַתִּקְרָא֙ לְבָרָ֣ק בֶּן־אֲבִינֹ֔עַם מִקֶּ֖דֶשׁ נַפְתָּלִ֑י וַתֹּ֨אמֶר אֵלָ֜יו הֲלֹ֥א צִוָּ֣ה ׀ יְהֹוָ֣ה אֱלֹהֵֽי־יִשְׂרָאֵ֗ל לֵ֤ךְ וּמָֽשַׁכְתָּ֙ בְּהַ֣ר תָּב֔וֹר וְלָקַחְתָּ֣ עִמְּךָ֗ עֲשֶׂ֤רֶת אֲלָפִים֙ אִ֔ישׁ מִבְּנֵ֥י נַפְתָּלִ֖י וּמִבְּנֵ֥י זְבֻלֽוּן׃ וּמָשַׁכְתִּ֨י אֵלֶ֜יךָ אֶל־נַ֣חַל קִישׁ֗וֹן אֶת־סִֽיסְרָא֙ שַׂר־צְבָ֣א יָבִ֔ין וְאֶת־רִכְבּ֖וֹ וְאֶת־הֲמוֹנ֑וֹ וּנְתַתִּ֖יהוּ בְּיָדֶֽךָ׃ וַיֹּ֤אמֶר אֵלֶ֙יהָ֙ בָּרָ֔ק אִם־תֵּלְכִ֥י עִמִּ֖י וְהָלָ֑כְתִּי וְאִם־לֹ֥א תֵלְכִ֛י עִמִּ֖י לֹ֥א אֵלֵֽךְ׃ וַתֹּ֜אמֶר הָלֹ֧ךְ אֵלֵ֣ךְ עִמָּ֗ךְ אֶ֚פֶס כִּי֩ לֹ֨א תִֽהְיֶ֜ה תִּֽפְאַרְתְּךָ֗ עַל־הַדֶּ֙רֶךְ֙ אֲשֶׁ֣ר אַתָּ֣ה הוֹלֵ֔ךְ כִּ֣י בְיַד־אִשָּׁ֔ה יִמְכֹּ֥ר יְהוָ֖ה אֶת־סִֽיסְרָ֑א וַתָּ֧קָם דְּבוֹרָ֛ה וַתֵּ֥לֶךְ עִם־בָּרָ֖ק קֶֽדְשָׁה׃ וַיַּזְעֵ֨ק בָּרָ֜ק אֶת־זְבוּלֻ֤ן וְאֶת־נַפְתָּלִי֙ קֶ֔דְשָׁה וַיַּ֣עַל בְּרַגְלָ֔יו עֲשֶׂ֥רֶת אַלְפֵ֖י אִ֑ישׁ וַתַּ֥עַל עִמּ֖וֹ דְּבוֹרָֽה׃ וְחֶ֤בֶר הַקֵּינִי֙ נִפְרָ֣ד מִקַּ֔יִן מִבְּנֵ֥י חֹבָ֖ב חֹתֵ֣ן מֹשֶׁ֑ה וַיֵּ֣ט אׇהֳל֔וֹ עַד־אֵיל֥וֹן בְּצַעֲנַנִּ֖ים אֲשֶׁ֥ר אֶת־קֶֽדֶשׁ׃ וַיַּגִּ֖דוּ לְסִֽיסְרָ֑א כִּ֥י עָלָ֛ה בָּרָ֥ק בֶּן־אֲבִינֹ֖עַם הַ֥ר תָּבֽוֹר׃ וַיַּזְעֵ֨ק סִֽיסְרָ֜א אֶת־כׇּל־רִכְבּ֗וֹ תְּשַׁ֤ע מֵאוֹת֙ רֶ֣כֶב בַּרְזֶ֔ל וְאֶת־כׇּל־הָעָ֖ם אֲשֶׁ֣ר אִתּ֑וֹ מֵחֲרֹ֥שֶׁת הַגּוֹיִ֖ם אֶל־נַ֥חַל קִישֽׁוֹן׃ וַתֹּ֩אמֶר֩ דְּבֹרָ֨ה אֶל־בָּרָ֜ק ק֗וּם כִּ֣י זֶ֤ה הַיּוֹם֙ אֲשֶׁר֩ נָתַ֨ן יְהוָ֤ה אֶת־סִֽיסְרָא֙ בְּיָדֶ֔ךָ הֲלֹ֥א יְהוָ֖ה יָצָ֣א לְפָנֶ֑יךָ וַיֵּ֤רֶד בָּרָק֙ מֵהַ֣ר תָּב֔וֹר וַעֲשֶׂ֥רֶת אֲלָפִ֛ים אִ֖ישׁ אַחֲרָֽיו׃ וַיָּ֣הׇם יְהוָ֠ה אֶת־סִֽיסְרָ֨א וְאֶת־כׇּל־הָרֶ֧כֶב וְאֶת־כׇּל־הַֽמַּחֲנֶ֛ה לְפִי־חֶ֖רֶב לִפְנֵ֣י בָרָ֑ק וַיֵּ֨רֶד סִֽיסְרָ֜א מֵעַ֧ל הַמֶּרְכָּבָ֛ה וַיָּ֖נָס בְּרַגְלָֽיו׃ וּבָרָ֗ק רָדַ֛ף אַחֲרֵ֥י הָרֶ֖כֶב וְאַחֲרֵ֣י הַֽמַּחֲנֶ֑ה עַ֣ד חֲרֹ֣שֶׁת הַגּוֹיִ֗ם וַיִּפֹּ֞ל כׇּל־מַחֲנֵ֤ה סִֽיסְרָא֙ לְפִי־חֶ֔רֶב לֹ֥א נִשְׁאַ֖ר עַד־אֶחָֽד׃ וְסִֽיסְרָא֙ נָ֣ס בְּרַגְלָ֔יו אֶל־אֹ֖הֶל יָעֵ֑ל אֵ֖שֶׁת חֶ֣בֶר הַקֵּינִ֑י כִּ֣י שָׁל֗וֹם בֵּ֚ין יָבִ֣ין מֶֽלֶךְ־חָצ֔וֹר וּבֵ֕ין בֵּ֖ית חֶ֥בֶר הַקֵּינִֽי׃ וַתֵּצֵ֣א יָעֵל֮ לִקְרַ֣את סִֽיסְרָא֒ וַתֹּ֣אמֶר אֵלָ֗יו סוּרָ֧ה אֲדֹנִ֛י סוּרָ֥ה אֵלַ֖י אַל־תִּירָ֑א וַיָּ֤סַר אֵלֶ֙יהָ֙ הָאֹ֔הֱלָה וַתְּכַסֵּ֖הוּ בַּשְּׂמִיכָֽה׃

19 turned aside into her tent, and she covered him with a blanket. "Give me a little water, please," he asked her, "for I am thirsty." She opened a skin of
20 milk, gave him some to drink, and covered him once again. "Stand at the entrance to the tent," he told her, "and if anyone comes and asks you if
21 someone is here, say 'No.'" Then Yael, wife of Ḥever, picked up a tent-peg, grasped a mallet, crept up to him – he had fallen asleep, exhausted – and hammered the tent-peg through his temple until it sunk into the ground
22 and he died. Now Barak was chasing Sisera, and Yael went out to meet him. "Come," she said to him, "I will show you the man you seek." He came to her, and there was Sisera, sprawled out dead, with the tent-peg
23 through his temple. On that day, God subdued Yavin King of Canaan be- *Yemenites begin here*
24 fore the Israelites. And the hand of the Israelites grew harsher and harsher against Yavin King of Canaan until they had destroyed him.

1 And Devora sang – and Barak son of Avinoam with her – on that day: / *Sepharadim begin here*
2 "When locks were grown long in Israel, / when people offered themselves
3 willingly – / bless the Lord! / Hear, O kings, / give ear, O rulers, / I – to
4 the Lord I will sing, / I will chant to the Lord, God of Israel. / O Lord, when You left Se'ir, / when You marched from the fields of Edom, / the
5 earth shook, / the heavens poured – / rain poured from the clouds, / the mountains melted before the Lord, / Sinai itself before the Lord, God of
6 Israel! / In the days of Shamgar son of Anat, / in the days of Yael, / there were
7 no caravans; / wayfarers walked roundabout paths. / There were no unwalled cities in Israel, / none – / until you arose, Devora, / until you arose,
8 a mother in Israel! / When they chose new gods, / there was war at the gates – / but no shield or spear was seen / amid forty thousand of Israel! /
9 My heart is with Israel's leaders, / the people who offer themselves

הפטרת בשלח

יט וַיֹּ֣אמֶר אֵלֶ֗יהָ הַשְׁקִינִי־נָ֤א מְעַט־מַ֙יִם֙ כִּ֣י צָמֵ֔אתִי וַתִּפְתַּ֛ח אֶת־נֹ֥אוד
כ הֶחָלָ֖ב וַתַּשְׁקֵ֑הוּ וַתְּכַסֵּֽהוּ׃ וַיֹּ֣אמֶר אֵלֶ֔יהָ עֲמֹ֖ד פֶּ֣תַח הָאֹ֑הֶל וְהָיָ֣ה
כא אִם־אִ֞ישׁ יָב֤וֹא וּשְׁאֵלֵךְ֙ וְאָמַ֔ר הֲיֵֽשׁ־פֹּ֥ה אִ֖ישׁ וְאָמַ֥רְתְּ אָֽיִן׃ וַתִּקַּ֣ח
יָעֵ֣ל אֵֽשֶׁת־חֶ֠בֶר אֶת־יְתַ֨ד הָאֹ֜הֶל וַתָּ֧שֶׂם אֶת־הַמַּקֶּ֣בֶת בְּיָדָ֗הּ
וַתָּב֤וֹא אֵלָיו֙ בַּלָּ֔אט וַתִּתְקַ֤ע אֶת־הַיָּתֵד֙ בְּרַקָּת֔וֹ וַתִּצְנַ֖ח בָּאָ֑רֶץ
כב וְהֽוּא־נִרְדָּ֥ם וַיָּ֖עַף וַיָּמֹֽת׃ וְהִנֵּ֣ה בָרָק֮ רֹדֵ֣ף אֶת־סִֽיסְרָא֒ וַתֵּצֵ֤א יָעֵל֙
לִקְרָאת֔וֹ וַתֹּ֣אמֶר ל֔וֹ לֵ֣ךְ וְאַרְאֶ֔ךָּ אֶת־הָאִ֖ישׁ אֲשֶׁר־אַתָּ֣ה מְבַקֵּ֑שׁ
כג וַיָּבֹ֣א אֵלֶ֔יהָ וְהִנֵּ֤ה סִֽיסְרָא֙ נֹפֵ֣ל מֵ֔ת וְהַיָּתֵ֖ד בְּרַקָּתֽוֹ׃ וַיַּכְנַ֤ע אֱלֹהִים֙ תימנים מתחילים כאן
כד בַּיּ֣וֹם הַה֔וּא אֵ֖ת יָבִ֣ין מֶֽלֶךְ־כְּנָ֑עַן לִפְנֵ֖י בְּנֵ֥י יִשְׂרָאֵֽל׃ וַתֵּ֜לֶךְ יַ֤ד בְּנֵֽי־
יִשְׂרָאֵל֙ הָל֣וֹךְ וְקָשָׁ֔ה עַ֖ל יָבִ֣ין מֶֽלֶךְ־כְּנָ֑עַן עַ֚ד אֲשֶׁ֣ר הִכְרִ֔יתוּ אֵ֖ת
יָבִ֥ין מֶֽלֶךְ־כְּנָֽעַן׃

ה א וַתָּ֣שַׁר דְּבוֹרָ֔ה וּבָרָ֖ק בֶּן־אֲבִינֹ֑עַם בַּיּ֥וֹם הַה֖וּא ספרדים מתחילים כאן
ב לֵאמֹֽר׃ בִּפְרֹ֤עַ פְּרָעוֹת֙ בְּיִשְׂרָאֵ֔ל בְּהִתְנַדֵּ֖ב
ג עָ֑ם בָּרְכ֖וּ יְהוָֽה׃ שִׁמְע֣וּ מְלָכִ֔ים הַאֲזִ֖ינוּ
רֹֽזְנִ֑ים אָֽנֹכִ֗י לַֽיהוָה֙ אָנֹכִ֣י אָשִׁ֔ירָה אֲזַמֵּ֕ר
ד לַֽיהוָ֖ה אֱלֹהֵ֥י יִשְׂרָאֵֽל׃ יְהוָ֗ה בְּצֵאתְךָ֤
מִשֵּׂעִיר֙ בְּצַעְדְּךָ֙ מִשְּׂדֵ֣ה אֱד֔וֹם אֶ֣רֶץ
רָעָ֔שָׁה גַּם־שָׁמַ֖יִם נָטָ֑פוּ גַּם־עָבִ֖ים נָ֥טְפוּ
ה מָֽיִם׃ הָרִ֥ים נָזְל֖וּ מִפְּנֵ֣י יְהוָ֑ה זֶ֣ה
ו סִינַ֔י מִפְּנֵ֕י יְהוָ֖ה אֱלֹהֵ֥י יִשְׂרָאֵֽל׃ בִּימֵ֞י שַׁמְגַּ֤ר בֶּן־
עֲנָ֗ת בִּימֵ֣י יָעֵ֔ל חָדְל֖וּ אֳרָח֑וֹת וְהֹלְכֵ֣י
ז נְתִיב֔וֹת יֵלְכ֕וּ אֳרָח֖וֹת עֲקַלְקַלּֽוֹת׃ חָדְל֧וּ פְרָז֛וֹן בְּיִשְׂרָאֵ֖ל
חָדֵ֑לּוּ עַ֤ד שַׁקַּ֙מְתִּי֙ דְּבוֹרָ֔ה שַׁקַּ֖מְתִּי
ח אֵ֥ם בְּיִשְׂרָאֵֽל׃ יִבְחַר֙ אֱלֹהִ֣ים
חֲדָשִׁ֔ים אָ֖ז לָ֣חֶם שְׁעָרִ֑ים מָגֵ֤ן
אִם־יֵֽרָאֶה֙ וָרֹ֔מַח בְּאַרְבָּעִ֥ים אֶ֖לֶף
ט בְּיִשְׂרָאֵֽל׃ לִבִּי֙ לְחֽוֹקְקֵ֣י יִשְׂרָאֵ֔ל הַמִּתְנַדְּבִ֖ים

10 willingly – / bless the LORD! / O riders of white she-donkeys, /
11 mounted on fine saddles, / O wayfarers: / speak out – / louder than the sound of archers / by the watering places; / there they shall recount the LORD's graces, / how He graced the unwalled cities in Israel; / then, down to the gates / marched the people of the LORD! /
12 Awake, awake, Devora – / awake, awake, burst into song! / Arise,
13 Barak – / seize your captives, son of Avinoam; / then the remnant ruled over the mighty people, / the LORD ruled over the warriors
14 for me! / From Efrayim, rooted in Amalek: / 'After you, Binyamin, with your people!' / From Makhir marched down leaders, / from
15 Zevulun, wielders of the scribal staff. / Issachar's chiefs were with Devora, / Yissakhar, like Barak, charged into the valley, / while
16 amongst the clans of Reuven / was great soul-searching. / Why did you linger among the sheepfolds / to hear the whistling for the flocks? / Amongst the clans of Reuven / was great soul-searching. /
17 Gilad stayed put across the Jordan, / and why did Dan stay by the ships? / Asher lingered by the seashore, / staying put by its harbors. /
18 Zevulun, a people who risked their lives for death / with Naftali on
19 the open heights; / then came the kings to do battle, / then Canaan's kings did battle / at Tanakh, by the waters of Megido – / but they
20 took no spoil of silver! / From the heavens they fought; / the stars
21 from their courses fought against Sisera! / Kishon Stream swept them away, / the ancient stream, the Kishon Stream – / march on, my
22 soul, with might! / The hooves of horses hammered / with the gal-
23 lop, the gallop of the steeds! / 'Curse Meroz,' said the LORD's angel, /

בְּעָם בָּרְכוּ יְהוָֽה׃	רֹכְבֵי֙ אֲתֹנ֣וֹת י
צְחֹר֔וֹת יֹשְׁבֵ֥י עַל־מִדִּ֖ין וְהֹלְכֵ֥י
עַל־דֶּ֖רֶךְ שִֽׂיחוּ׃ מִקּ֣וֹל מְחַֽצְצִ֗ים בֵּ֚ין יא
מַשְׁאַבִּ֔ים שָׁ֤ם יְתַנּוּ֙ צִדְק֣וֹת יְהוָ֔ה צִדְקֹ֥ת
פִּרְזֹנ֖וֹ בְּיִשְׂרָאֵ֑ל אָ֛ז יָרְד֥וּ לַשְּׁעָרִ֖ים עַם־
יְהוָֽה׃ עוּרִ֤י עוּרִי֙ דְּבוֹרָ֔ה ע֥וּרִי יב
ע֖וּרִי דַּבְּרִי־שִׁ֑יר ק֥וּם בָּרָ֛ק וּֽשֲׁבֵ֥ה שֶׁבְיְךָ֖ בֶּן־
אֲבִינֹֽעַם׃ אָ֚ז יְרַ֣ד שָׂרִ֔יד לְאַדִּירִ֖ים עָ֑ם יְהוָ֕ה יג
יְרַד־לִ֖י בַּגִּבּוֹרִֽים׃ מִנִּ֣י אֶפְרַ֗יִם שָׁרְשָׁם֙ יד
בַּעֲמָלֵ֔ק אַחֲרֶ֥יךָ בִנְיָמִ֖ין בַּֽעֲמָמֶ֑יךָ מִנִּ֣י
מָכִ֗יר יָֽרְדוּ֙ מְחֹ֣קְקִ֔ים וּמִ֨זְּבוּלֻ֔ן מֹשְׁכִ֖ים בְּשֵׁ֥בֶט
סֹפֵֽר׃ וְשָׂרַ֤י בְּיִשָּׂשכָר֙ עִם־דְּבֹרָ֔ה וְיִ֨שָּׂשכָ֔ר טו
כֵּ֣ן בָּרָ֔ק בָּעֵ֖מֶק שֻׁלַּ֣ח
בְּרַגְלָ֑יו בִּפְלַגּ֣וֹת רְאוּבֵ֔ן גְּדֹלִ֖ים
חִקְקֵי־לֵֽב׃ לָ֣מָּה יָשַׁ֗בְתָּ בֵּ֚ין טז
הַֽמִּשְׁפְּתַ֔יִם לִשְׁמֹ֖עַ שְׁרִק֣וֹת עֲדָרִ֑ים לִפְלַגּ֣וֹת
רְאוּבֵ֔ן גְּדוֹלִ֖ים חִקְרֵי־לֵֽב׃ גִּלְעָ֗ד בְּעֵ֤בֶר הַיַּרְדֵּן֙ יז
שָׁכֵ֔ן וְדָ֕ן לָ֥מָּה יָג֖וּר אֳנִיּ֑וֹת אָשֵׁ֗ר
יָשַׁב֙ לְח֣וֹף יַמִּ֔ים וְעַ֥ל מִפְרָצָ֖יו
יִשְׁכּֽוֹן׃ זְבֻל֗וּן עַ֣ם חֵרֵ֥ף נַפְשׁ֛וֹ לָמ֖וּת וְנַפְתָּלִ֑י יח
עַ֖ל מְרוֹמֵ֥י שָׂדֶֽה׃ בָּ֤אוּ מְלָכִים֙ יט
נִלְחָ֔מוּ אָ֚ז נִלְחֲמ֣וּ מַלְכֵ֣י כְנַ֔עַן בְּתַעְנַ֖ךְ
עַל־מֵ֣י מְגִדּ֑וֹ בֶּ֥צַע כֶּ֖סֶף לֹ֥א
לָקָֽחוּ׃ מִן־שָׁמַ֖יִם נִלְחָ֑מוּ הַכּֽוֹכָבִים֙ כ
מִמְּסִלּוֹתָ֔ם נִלְחֲמ֖וּ עִם־סִֽיסְרָֽא׃ נַ֤חַל קִישׁוֹן֙ כא
גְּרָפָ֔ם נַ֧חַל קְדוּמִ֛ים נַ֥חַל קִישׁ֖וֹן תִּדְרְכִ֥י
נַפְשִׁ֖י עֹֽז׃ אָ֥ז הָלְמ֖וּ עִקְּבֵי־ כב
ס֑וּס מִֽדַּהֲר֖וֹת דַּהֲר֥וֹת אַבִּירָֽיו׃ א֣וֹרוּ כג

24 'curse its people harshly, / for they did not come to the aid of the LORD, / to the aid of the LORD amidst the warriors.' / Blessed beyond women be Yael, / wife of Hever the Kenite, / blessed beyond women in tents! /
25 Water he asked for, milk she gave; / in a princely bowl she offered
26 cream. / Her hand shot out for the tent-peg, / her right hand for the workman's hammer, / and hammered Sisera / and crushed his
27 head / and smashed and pierced his temple! / Between her legs he lay slumped, sprawled, / between her legs he slumped, sprawled, /
28 where he slumped, there he sprawled, slain! / Through the window she peered, / Sisera's mother wailed through the lattice, / 'Why does his chariot tarry so? / Why so late, the clank of his chariots?' /
29
30 The wisest of her ladies reply – / she even answers herself – / 'Why, they are dividing up the spoil they found, / a womb or two for every man, / a haul of colors for Sisera, / a haul of colors of embroidery, / colored embroidery, two apiece, for the spoilers' throats.' /
31 Thus may all Your enemies perish, O LORD, / and may His friends be like the risen sun!" / And the land was quiet for forty years.

מֵרֹ֣וז אָמַר֮ מַלְאַ֣ךְ יְהֹוָה֒ אֹ֣רוּ אָר֔וֹר
יֹשְׁבֶ֑יהָ כִּ֤י לֹא־בָ֙אוּ֙ לְעֶזְרַ֣ת יְהֹוָ֔ה לְעֶזְרַ֥ת
כד יְהֹוָ֖ה בַּגִּבּוֹרִֽים: תְּבֹרַךְ֙ מִנָּשִׁ֔ים
יָעֵ֕ל אֵ֖שֶׁת חֶ֣בֶר הַקֵּינִ֑י מִנָּשִׁ֥ים
כה בָּאֹ֖הֶל תְּבֹרָֽךְ: מַ֥יִם שָׁאַ֖ל חָלָ֣ב
כו נָתָ֑נָה בְּסֵ֥פֶל אַדִּירִ֖ים הִקְרִ֥יבָה חֶמְאָֽה: יָדָהּ֙
לַיָּתֵ֣ד תִּשְׁלַ֔חְנָה וִֽימִינָ֖הּ לְהַלְמ֣וּת
עֲמֵלִ֑ים וְהָלְמָ֤ה סִֽיסְרָא֙ מָחֲקָ֣ה רֹאשׁ֔וֹ וּמָחֲצָ֥ה
כז וְחָלְפָ֖ה רַקָּתֽוֹ: בֵּ֣ין רַגְלֶ֔יהָ כָּרַ֥ע נָפַ֖ל
שָׁכָ֑ב בֵּ֤ין רַגְלֶ֙יהָ֙ כָּרַ֣ע נָפָ֔ל בַּאֲשֶׁ֣ר
כח כָּרַ֔ע שָׁ֖ם נָפַ֥ל שָׁדֽוּד: בְּעַד֩ הַחַלּ֨וֹן נִשְׁקְפָ֧ה
וַתְּיַבֵּ֛ב אֵ֥ם סִֽיסְרָ֖א בְּעַ֣ד הָאֶשְׁנָ֑ב מַדּ֗וּעַ
בֹּשֵׁ֤שׁ רִכְבּוֹ֙ לָב֔וֹא מַדּ֣וּעַ אֶֽחֱר֔וּ פַּעֲמֵ֖י
כט מַרְכְּבוֹתָֽיו: חַכְמ֥וֹת שָׂרוֹתֶ֖יהָ תַּעֲנֶ֑ינָּה אַף־
ל הִ֕יא תָּשִׁ֥יב אֲמָרֶ֖יהָ לָֽהּ: הֲלֹ֨א יִמְצְא֜וּ יְחַלְּק֣וּ
שָׁלָ֗ל רַ֤חַם רַחֲמָתַ֙יִם֙ לְרֹ֣אשׁ גֶּ֔בֶר שְׁלַ֤ל
צְבָעִים֙ לְסִ֣יסְרָ֔א שְׁלַ֥ל צְבָעִ֖ים
לא רִקְמָ֑ה צֶ֥בַע רִקְמָתַ֖יִם לְצַוְּארֵ֥י שָׁלָֽל: כֵּ֣ן
יֹאבְד֤וּ כָל־אוֹיְבֶ֙יךָ֙ יְהֹוָ֔ה וְאֹ֣הֲבָ֔יו כְּצֵ֥את הַשֶּׁ֖מֶשׁ
בִּגְבֻרָת֑וֹ וַתִּשְׁקֹ֥ט הָאָ֖רֶץ אַרְבָּעִ֥ים שָׁנָֽה:

For the complete Rashi and haftara turn to the right side of this volume.

*For commentaries and the Biblical Imagination
turn to the left side of this volume.*

ture and significance of divine revelation, able to direct her compatriots toward heightened spiritual awareness.

Now we are left with the third of our questions: how did the women embarking on the exodus know that they ought to take musical instruments with them on their journey? Rashi cites a midrash: "So sure were the righteous Israelite women that God was going to perform miracles for them that they took tambourines with them out of Egypt in anticipation." Here we see the deep faith that the Hebrews bore within their hearts. For while the entire nation was familiar with Yosef's prophecy, "God will surely remember you and bring you out of this land to the land He promised to Avraham, Yitzhak, and Yaakov" (Genesis 50:24), it was the women who held onto this prediction with utter steadfastness, resisting cynicism and doubt. Because they were sure of the eventual advent of their salvation, they prepared for that time by formulating in advance the thanks they would express to God for their redemption. This refers us back the keystone of Miriam's prophecy that we articulated above: faith, even during the difficult and bitter slavery, that God would rescue Israel from their torment. It was at those most taxing moments that Miriam knew to stand by and wait, to risk her life for the chance to sing songs of gratitude to God.

rather an unshakeable faith in what she had been told, steadfast even in times of darkness and difficulty. Miriam was convinced that the light that had illuminated her home on the birth of her baby brother shone with an ultimate purpose. She was certain that the child would be saved. And since this inspiring quality inhered in Miriam even before Moshe's arrival on the scene, she could only be called "Aharon's sister."

In his discussion of our verse Rashi also refers to a later episode, which appears at the end of Parashat Behaalotekha. That tale finds Miriam and Aharon gossiping about the Moshe's marriage to a Kushite woman. When Miriam is stricken with leprosy as punishment for her disrespectful speech, Aharon begs Moshe to intervene, crying: "Please, my lord, do not hold against us the sin that we have foolishly committed! Let her not be like a stillborn child emerging from its mother's womb with half its flesh eaten away!" (Numbers 12:11–12). Moshe cedes to this request and prays successfully for Miriam's recovery. And so, because Aharon risked his life for Miriam, she is referred to as Aharon's sister. This description of Miriam is disconnected from her role as a prophet. Unlike the previous interpretation, according to which she is called "Aharon's sister" due to her circumstances when she prophesied, Rashi's second approach focuses on the close personal connection between Miriam and Aharon. Together, the two accounts highlight a complex and human family dynamic. Miriam is to some degree responsible for the birth of Moshe [see also Sota 12a], yet it is she who later levels criticism against him, and she in turn is saved by the intervention and self-sacrifice of their brother Aharon.

Taking a completely different tack, the *Keli Yakar* presents a novel understanding of why Miriam is called a prophetess in our verse.

> Miriam only became a prophetess at this point in the Torah's narrative. Indeed, all the Israelite women at that moment were privileged to see the Divine Presence – as our Sages claim, even the maidservants standing at the sea saw visions that the prophets of later eras were not granted [see Rashi on Exodus 15:2]. And so when our verse states that "all the women followed her with tambourines and dance," it means that Miriam was the first woman to be inspired with prophecy. All of the other women then followed in her footsteps, and they too merited this gift.

The *Keli Yakar* suggests that Miriam assumed the status of a prophetess only upon the splitting of the Sea of Reeds, and that her skill was no better or different than that of any of the other women of Israel. Still, Miriam was the first woman to perceive the vision and she immediately inspired the rest of the community. The Torah therefore presents her as a leader who understood the na-

Rashi, on the other hand, provides a different approach to our problem.

> When exactly did Miriam prophesy? When she was still just the "sister of Aharon." Before Moshe was born, Miriam predicted that her mother would bear a son who would become Israel's savior (Sota 12b). Another interpretation: Aharon took a risk for her by begging Moshe for compassion after Miriam was stricken with leprosy [in Numbers 12:10–12]. The Torah therefore refers to Miriam as Aharon's sister.

Rashi's explanation might seem forced. Would Miriam be termed a prophetess based solely on a single moment of divine inspiration? Furthermore, the classical elements that generally characterize prophetic episodes are found nowhere in Miriam's story. For example, the text of the Torah has not yet reported any specific communication that she ever received from God. To understand Rashi's comments therefore, we must examine the nature of Miriam's experience as described in detail by the talmudic passage that he cites. The passage in tractate Sota reads as follows:

> When Moshe was born, the entire house was filled with light. Her father Amram arose and kissed his daughter's head, saying to her: "My daughter, your prophecy has been fulfilled!" However, when they put the baby into the river, her father arose and hit her on her head, saying: "My daughter, where is your prophecy now?" And thus the verse states: "And his sister stood by at a distance to see what would happen to him" (Exodus 2:4). In other words, the sister remained close by to see whether her prophecy would endure.

The Talmud portrays Moshe's birth as the creation of a powerful light that sparked hope and joy within his household. But subsequently, when his son was placed in a basket and put in the river, Amram's dream of salvation dissolved into despair, and he abandoned all trust he had put in his daughter's prediction. Miriam, in contrast, was not so easily dissuaded, and stood by her brother in anticipation that her prophecy still had life in it. For the girl understood the depth of her inspiration and knew that a prophecy need not come true immediately or all at once. Usually one must wait for God's promises to be realized.

Prophecy is not magic. One must believe in God's communications even when the chances that they will come to fruition seem slim. We can only imagine how Miriam must have felt seeing her brother placed in the basket in the Nile. Every ripple of water, every lapping of the waves must have stopped the girl's heart and challenged her belief in God's word. Miriam was a prophetess, but that does not a connote a simple and reliable ability to foretell the future, but

THE PROPHECY OF MIRIAM

Having endured the excitement, and indeed the trauma, of the passage through the divided Sea of Reeds, Israel is overcome with emotion and breaks into song, led by their leader Moshe: "And then, Moshe and the Israelites sang this song to the LORD" (Exodus 15:1). The following poem gives voice to the hopes of a nation, and it has made such an impact on the Jewish imagination that we include its text in our daily morning services. However, it was not only Moshe who led the rescued masses in praising God for their salvation. The Torah relates that the prophet's sister Miriam also led the nation's women in reciting words of thanks: "Then Miriam, the prophetess, sister of Aharon, took a tambourine in her hand, and all the women followed her with tambourines and dance" (15:20).

In reading this verse, a few difficulties might occur to us:

1. When, and under what circumstances, had Miriam ever prophesied, such that the Torah labels her a "prophetess"?
2. Why is Miriam referred to here as the sister of Aharon? Was she not also the sister of Moshe?
3. How can we account for the tambourines that the women shook during their celebrations? Where did they get such instruments?

Commenting on Parashat Beshalaḥ, Rashbam addresses our second question: "Miriam is called Aharon's brother because he was the older of the two brothers." By this, perhaps Rashbam intends to convey that the significance of Aharon was in danger of being overshadowed by his younger brother, the larger-than-life leader of the nation. Therefore the Torah takes this opportunity to emphasize that Aharon remained important as the eldest in the family.

Ramban offers another suggestion:

> It seems to me that Miriam is linked here to Aharon in order to mention him by name, for his siblings Moshe and Miriam had already been mentioned in this passage while he had not. Calling Miriam the sister of Aharon was a sign of respect for him, for he was her older brother, a prophet, and a holy man of God.

In this telling, besides being the firstborn child in the family, Aharon stood out for his special relationship to God, which made him receptive to divine communication. This is why Miriam is called the "sister of Aharon."

It is therefore incumbent upon us to internalize the moral of this episode: Israel retains the power to split oceans and to cross treacherous passages safely to their opposite banks. We can overcome the barriers we encounter in our lives and survive to sing songs of thanks to God. When we proclaim our gratitude every morning with the words "You will bring them, You will plant them on the mountain, Your heritage – the place, Lord, that You made for Your dwelling, the sanctuary, Lord, that Your hands established" (Exodus 15:17), we are giving voice to our own desires and longings. For all our dreams can be realized even in the absence of a staff, even when our leaders walk behind us. Each of us can fulfill the command given to Moshe: "Speak to the Israelites; have them move forward."

of the Israelite camp moved and went behind them" (Exodus 14:19) it refers to Moshe, who was called the "angel of God". For we find that the term "angel" [*malakh*] can relate to people as well as to celestial entities, as in the verse "Then Ḥagai, messenger [*malakh*] of the LORD, sent by the LORD to the people, spoke" (Haggai 1:13).

According to the *Meshekh Ḥokhma*, God's command, "Speak to the Israelites; have them move forward" (Exodus 14:15), was in fact a directive for the people to advance toward the water while Moshe brought up the rear. In this reading, Moshe was the last Israelite to enter the sea – not to ensure that no one was being left behind, but to allow the nation to exhibit their faith in God by wading into the sea without any divine emissary to part the way before them. If so, the Sea of Reeds split open not due to the merit of Moshe, or of the people's ancestors, but thanks to the trust that Israel placed in God. These former slaves, who had only recently broken free from their shackles of slavery, were prepared to trust in God's command even if it meant endangering their lives. At this moment, Israel demonstrated its true character, the bravery of spirit first witnessed in Avraham when God commanded him to leave his home and set out toward an unknown, faraway land (Genesis 12:1). Avraham's descendants had to undergo an experience parallel to his in order to flourish as a free nation without the guiding hand of an intermediary between them and God.

Now, with this analysis in hand, we can resolve the difficulties we raised above. Firstly, Moshe called out to God because it was unclear to him at that point just how God planned to save Israel from the advancing Egyptians. God had warned Moshe that He would toughen Pharaoh's heart, and that the Egyptians would be finally defeated, but He had never explained precisely how this drama would play out. And as the threat of violence escalated, it became harder for Moshe to imagine that his charges could rise to the challenge of believing in God's salvation. And yet, here God was telling him to simply have the Israelites move forward. For God had faith in His people and knew that they possessed the fortitude necessary to place their lives in His hands. All they needed was the chance to prove it.

Thus the splitting of the Sea of Reeds represents not only a foundational moment in the Torah and in the nation's history; it serves as a lesson of faith for future generations of Jews. The story calls upon each man and woman to meet the challenge of faith when faced with a personal crisis. For example, the Talmud (Sota 2a) states that the ordeal of finding an appropriate spouse is as difficult as the test of splitting the sea. Another dictum claims that the perpetual chore of feeding one's family requires as much faith and stamina as that demanded of Israel on the shore of the Sea of Reeds (Pesaḥim 118a).

Rabbi Hirsch takes Rabbeinu Baḥya's conception of the miracle at the sea as an educational exercise one step further. In this reading, the people had to prove that they deserved to be rescued by believing God's promise to them, not only without the staff, but without any clear explanation for how they could possibly survive the ordeal. The strength of the nation's faith had to be tough enough to overcome their doubts and uncertainties. And hence the foundation for the nationhood of Israel was laid with their first independent steps to show their bravery and daring, absent any clear reassurances from others.

Now let us turn to Rabbi Joseph B. Soloveitchik's description of the scene at the sea prior to Israel's entry:

> At the splitting of the Sea of Reeds, the Creator offered the Israelites a role in their own redemption. He required a leap of faith: a jump into the water prior to the parting of the sea [see Sota 36–37]. The shock of cold water, the fear of drowning, became Israel's minute "contribution" to the miracle. At that moment they became partners with God, and as a result Moshe and the people sang the majestic Song of the Sea in gratitude.[2]

In Rabbi Soloveitchik's view, it was critical that the Israelites taste a bit of seawater in their mouths, feel the chill of the ocean splashing against their faces, and yet continue to wade forward, even as the sea drenched the clothes on their backs. By enduring this trial, the nation contributed in their own small way to the salvation of Israel. The people had to participate in their own rescue just as we as individuals must make a personal effort to raise ourselves from despair. In order to merit divine assistance, we must first demonstrate our willingness to act on our own behalf.

The concept of a trial of faith is emphasized by the *Meshekh Ḥokhma* on the same verse:

> We find the following idea in the Mekhilta: "Rabbi Yehuda taught: Said the Holy One, blessed be He, to His emissary: Moshe! All the people of Israel have to do is to move forward!" The midrash seems to mean that the nation had so far followed Moshe just as a flock of sheep ambles through a valley after their shepherd. But now as they progressed toward the sea, God ordered Moshe to reposition himself behind the people. It was their faith alone that was meant to guide Israel forward into the water, and it was in repayment of this trust that God would split the sea open for them. Hence when the verse states: "Then the angel of God who had been traveling ahead

---

2. *Chumash Mesoras Harav*, Exodus 14:15.

In this verse, Moshe is not being commanded to stretch his staff over the sea, for subsequently we find only that the prophet "stretched out his hand over the sea" (14:21). In fact, here God is instructing Moshe to lay down his staff and to not use it in effecting the miracle at the water. For there were some elements among the people who had little faith in their leader, claiming that he lacked the power to split open the sea without using his magic wand. Moshe was therefore instructed to dispense with the staff to teach that the implement itself bore no power.

Rabbeinu Bahya's understanding of our text reveals a new educational dimension to the miracle of the Sea of Reeds. The situation afforded an opportunity to transform the people's hour of need into a foundational experience in their national existence. It was at that precise point that the Israelites all realized that the authority of Moshe's leadership did not rely on his magic staff but solely on the will of God and His divine sanction. The staff was tossed aside and removed from center stage, allowing the nation to see clearly that they were being guided solely by the word of God. The message was clear: No tool is required to lead Israel toward liberty, only faith in divine providence. For on the rocky shores of the Sea of Reeds, finding itself faced with a crisis of belief, the nation of Israel passed its most difficult test and followed God's message into the unknown abyss. The absence of Moshe's staff from the episode compounded the internal struggle the people must have felt in a moment of crisis that had become a paramount test of faith.

The idea of this moment as a test has roots in God's directive to the Israelites, "Move forward," as if there were no sea in the way. This nuance is famously articulated by the Midrash[1], which describes the alacrity of Nahshon son of Aminadav, chief of the tribe of Yehuda, to plunge into the water before it had even been parted. The writings of Rabbi Samson Raphael Hirsch elaborate upon this idea.

> By insisting: "Why are you crying out to Me? Speak to the Israelites; have them move forward" (Exodus 14:15), God conveys that in truth, the people's salvation is dependent on them – they must make the first move. Furthermore, the Israelites must prove that they are worthy of deliverance by demonstrating their faith in God in practice. Such a bold step will in turn fortify the people's courage and spur them to act fearlessly. First let them descend to the sea without hesitation or trepidation. Only then will God pave a path toward their complete redemption.

---

1. Bemidbar Rabba, Naso 13:4

THE SPLITTING OF THE SEA OF REEDS –
A FOUNDATIONAL MOMENT

The splitting of the Sea of Reeds stands as one of Torah's most well-known and celebrated events, replete with inner meaning. Some thinkers hold up the miracle as a demonstration of how God can manipulate earth's natural forces. Other writers see the story as exemplifying God's justice toward humanity, wherein He metes out punishment measure for measure to those who have acted wickedly. Still another approach emphasizes the crossing of the sea as a turning point for Israel, when the nation attained a full sense of belief in Moshe as the servant of God. Still, I wish in this essay to focus on a different aspect of the splitting of the Sea of Reeds.

In our *parasha*, the Torah describes the situation immediately prior to the opening of the waters. The people stand on the beach, trembling in confusion and terror and unable to act or decide how to proceed. Some vocal individuals shout that the former slaves would all be better off returning to bondage in Egypt, while others insist that the men take up arms against the encroaching cavalry. Meanwhile, all are sure that their leader Moshe has been stricken impotent by the crisis. The Torah then presents God's reaction to Moshe's indecision: "The LORD said to Moshe, 'Why are you crying out to Me? Speak to the Israelites; have them move forward'" (Exodus 14:15). This verse poses the following three problems:

1. Why is Moshe pleading with God for succor? Has God not already told him: "I will toughen Pharaoh's heart, and he will pursue them. I will be glorified over Pharaoh and all his force, and the Egyptians will know that I am the LORD" (14:4)?
2. What exactly is implied by the verb "crying out" [*tze'aka*]? Does the verse imply that Moshe had been praying to God, or had he merely been expressing his anguish and despair?
3. How was Moshe supposed to instruct Israel to move forward if the sea was in the way? Surely the presence of this impassable barrier was the source of the problem to begin with – the difficulty in maneuvering around the water was the reason Moshe turned to God for aid!

Let us open our analysis with the assistance of Rabbeinu Baḥya. In that author's commentary to 14:16 – "Raise your staff, stretch out your hand over the sea and divide it" – Rabbeinu Baḥya writes as follows:

level onto our lifelong association with the Creator, another layer of holiness in an eternal quest to approach the divine.

As the Torah describes, the commandments surrounding the Sabbath were given to Israel well before the experience of revelation at Mount Sinai, where the rest of the Torah and its laws were delivered. The requirement to observe the seventh day stems from the intellectual acknowledgement of, and the emotional will to experience, the divine presence of God in our lives. Acceptance of the Sabbath brings the joyful recognition that God gave us the commandments out of love and the desire to enrich our existence. The Almighty does not issue decrees merely to exercise arbitrary power and authority over the world and its people.

In a certain sense, the Sabbath is a paradigm for the entire gamut of the Torah's commandments. We, the older generation, carry a responsibility to teach Israel's young people a new, creative approach to the Torah, one that forges a union between halakha and the Jewish experience. Our youth turn to us with open arms, ready to receive their parents' traditions tempered with modern sensitivities. Of course, we cannot resolve all difficulties that contemporary culture throws in our direction, and it is not our business to sell our children vacuous interpretations of religion. But it remains the obligation of the Jewish adult to bridge these real gaps as well as he or she can. By doing so, we fortify the observance of the Sabbath and protect the treasure that God so lovingly removed from His storehouse to bestow upon His nation Israel.

The Torah's statement "Understand that the Lord has given you a Sabbath" means that it should quickly become apparent to Israel that the Sabbath bestows divine blessings and munificence upon them. The nation will realize this when they consider the additional manna that falls on Friday and by the inner sense of satisfaction that they will inexplicably feel. And while it is true that the Sabbath is most basically a set of laws decreed by God, it should not be viewed as a burden or a regrettable cause of financial loss. Rather, the Sabbath is a gift to the Jewish people more precious than pearls. It is not for God's sake that we are called upon to observe this holy day of rest, but for our own benefit. For by keeping the Sabbath we are saturated with blessing and joy. Indeed, there exists not a single spiritual or ethical dimension that is not enhanced by Sabbath observance. The list of themes that the day enhances includes: the awareness of God and His relationship to the world, the individual's self-understanding, acknowledgement of one's obligations in this life, the consolation of the soul from its worries and concerns, and the joy of following the commandments. Any man or woman who seeks to build a connection to God by accepting the authority of heaven will find a rejuvenation of all these faculties on a weekly basis. Thus God withholds nothing good from the Jew who keeps the Sabbath. During the six preceding days God bestows His blessing upon that person, and that wealth in turn allows the family to observe the Sabbath properly and pleasantly.

In this excerpt, Rabbi Hirsch calls upon his readers to examine the character of the Sabbath and to discover the riches that come with honoring this day. The Sabbath was created for man, not for God; therefore we ought to fervently anticipate its arrival every week.

We now turn to Rabbi Joseph B. Soloveitchik for another insight regarding our conception of the Sabbath. He writes:

> The idea of the Sabbath is man's aloneness. And if man is alone, he is also with God. The charisma of the Sabbath expresses itself in the return of man to himself and to God, the source of holiness. Severance of the individual from working society establishes a permanent communion with God.[1]

According to Rabbi Soloveitchik, when we each make the effort to examine the laws of the Sabbath, including the prohibitions inherent in the day, we gain the ability to focus on building our relationship with God. We thereby add another

---

1. *Chumash Mesoras Harav,* Exodus 16:29.

their mission in life. What could be a more valuable gift than the ability to dwell freely in a state of sanctity and to thereby preserve one's own humanity?

Of course, it is not so easy to convince an average Jew that our definition represents the true conception of the Sabbath. Most of our community tends to view the holy day negatively, as a time stifled by suffocating regulations. How can we make the point that the Sabbath commandments conceal an invaluable gem?

Perhaps this can be achieved by realigning the meeting point between our observance of the law on the one hand, and our personal spiritual experiences on the other. There is a tendency for observant Jews to focus on the minutiae of the halakha, sometimes to the point of obsession, indulging their sense that every stringent detail must be adhered to. These attitudes surely have their place. And yet, such thinking poses the danger of creating a gulf between following the law and building a deeper appreciation of it. On the other hand, to be sure, deemphasizing the fine points of halakha risks skewing our attention toward the spiritual dimension of the Torah's practices at the expense of the law. This imbalance can open an equally wide chasm between the soul and the intellectual character of God's decrees, ultimately diluting the commandments until they are merely vague emotional themes.

When the Torah declares: "Understand that the LORD has given you a Sabbath" (16:29), it is signifying that the Sabbath demands weekly study in order to be followed properly. That attention to detail – understanding – is the only way that the institution of the Sabbath can be observed, preserved, and transmitted to subsequent generations. It is incumbent upon us to find the correct balance between the legal requirements of the day and the feelings that the Sabbath both elicits and encourages. Sitting around the Sabbath table, the Jewish family oscillates effortlessly and constantly between their awareness of the laws and their enjoyment of the atmosphere that imbues their time together. When this is done right, it becomes impossible to keep the Sabbath's halakhic particulars while ignoring the nature and quality of the hours during which those rules must be kept. One finds that the experience of one Sabbath differs in its flavor from that of the previous, and that it will in turn be surpassed by the next. This continuous development can be attributed to the focus that the family members devote to their Sabbaths. By truly living each of these days, the family grows together and its perceptions change. Thus our experience of subsequent holy days can constantly mature.

In his essay on Parashat Beshalaḥ (16:29), Rabbi Samson Raphael Hirsch presents a similar approach to what we have suggested. Rabbi Hirsch writes as follows:

observes the Sabbath incurs the penalty of death at the hands of heaven. The idea is echoed in the verse "The Israelites shall keep the Sabbath, making it a day of rest throughout their generations as a covenant forever" (Exodus 31:16). It is through Israel's observance of the seventh day that we will merit experiencing a day that is entirely Sabbath: the World to Come.

It is worth exploring Sforno's message in depth. At first glance, the Sabbath seems to comprise merely restrictions, limitations, and prohibitions. All activity during its twenty-five hours is restricted by the set of thirty-nine principal prohibited labors, their corollaries, and additional rabbinic decrees. All these rules hardly give one the impression that the Sabbath is a gift, surely not in the way that we normally consider the idea. And yet, Sforno encourages us to view the day as a treasure that God has reserved for His chosen nation. To address this tension, Sforno asks his readers not only to "see" but to "consider" the commandments bound up in the Sabbath, in order to uncover its true nature.

When we consider the Sabbath's commandments and its principal prohibition against performing work throughout the day, we realize that God intends for the Jewish people to fully halt their daily lives with the onset of the Sabbath. The cessation of labor affords us the opportunity to reflect on our routines, to evaluate our purpose and our direction on a weekly basis. This idea can explain why the Sabbath was presented to Israel so soon after their emergence from the Sea of Reeds and before the giving of the Torah. The ultimate goal of the salvation from physical slavery was to free the Israelites from their chained mentality, to break the bonds of apathy that had for so long defined their attitude toward existence. The perpetual toil in mortar and brick had stifled any consideration of what life really was about, or of what it could be. The Sabbath, which returns every seven days, bears the wondrous power to free the Hebrew mind from the troubles of our weekly duties and from the unrelenting burden of worry about earning a living. In the place of such anxieties, we are directed toward thoughts of spirituality and meaning. It thus becomes clear that the limitations that the law places on our activity during the Sabbath are no kind of punishment or attempt to restrict the community. On the contrary, these guidelines serve to enhance our opportunities for intellectual and religious development.

The Sabbath allows us the opportunity to gather with our families, to converse with one another, to debate spiritual matters, to analyze Torah passages and problems. In contrast, the bustle of the weekday is not as generous with its time; it is reluctant to yield its precious minutes, which should be used for working. It should therefore be clear why the Torah classifies the Sabbath as a gift – through it, God grants His chosen people a recurring chance to revitalize

THE SABBATH AS A MARK OF LOVE
BETWEEN GOD AND ISRAEL

The commandment of the Sabbath, God's gift to Israel, is presented in the Torah in a variety of contexts and circumstances. On occasion, the instruction to observe the Sabbath appears together with the underlying philosophy of creation, as in the verse "For in six days the LORD made heaven and earth, the sea, and all that they contain, and He rested on the seventh day" (Exodus 20:11). At other times, the holy day is defined in terms of historical memory: "Remember that you were slaves in Egypt…. That is why the LORD your God has commanded you to keep the Sabbath" (Deuteronomy 5:15). Still other passages associate the Sabbath with a social message: "For six days carry out your work, but on the seventh you must cease, so that your ox and donkey may rest, and even the children of maidservants and strangers be revived" (Exodus 23:12). Still, in Parashat Beshalaḥ, the Torah describes a different facet of the day when it states: "Understand [literally, 'see'] that the LORD has given you a Sabbath" (16:29). This short and enigmatic clause arouses the following three questions:

1. What exactly is Israel being asked to "understand" or "see" in this verse?
2. Why does the Torah argue that God has "given" the Sabbath to Israel, when what He has really done is ordered them to observe it?
3. Finally, why were the laws of the Sabbath communicated to the Israelites here in the desert of Sin, soon after the people's escape from Egypt, and weeks before the revelation at Mount Sinai (where the command to keep the Sabbath was repeated)?

Commenting on our text, Rabbi Ovadya Sforno addresses our first two questions simultaneously:

> Israel is here asked to consider that God's decrees governing the Sabbath are no mere set of laws. Rather, the day is a gift that no other nation on earth has been so fortunate as to receive. Thus our Sages boast (Shabbat 10b): "Said the LORD to Israel, 'Know that I hold a precious jewel in my treasury called "the Sabbath," and I wish to devote it to you.'" The idea that the Sabbath is an exclusively Jewish privilege also finds expression in the day's prayer service, which states: "You did not give it to the families of the earth," and the talmudic dictum (Shabbat 58b) that any gentile who fully

PARASHAT BESHALAḤ

THE **BIBLICAL** IMAGINATION

RABBI SHAI FINKELSTEIN

16 altar and named it, "The LORD Is My Banner," saying, "There is a hand on the LORD's throne. The LORD will be at war with Amalek throughout the ages."

MALBIM *(cont.)*

Israel's king Sha'ul, who would reign as God's representative [see "The Time of the Sages" on this verse]. In the end there will be an eternal war between God and Amalek – it will not be a fight between the "hand" [i.e., Moshe] and Amalek, nor between the "throne" [future monarchs] and Amalek, but one fought between God Himself and the enemy. This conflict will endure for many generations, as our Sages teach: The battle with Amalek will wage from the time of Moshe to the generation of Sha'ul, and after that it will resume during messianic times. The verse further implies that Amalek has raised its arm in defiance against the throne of God, in an attempt to revolt against God's authority. Therefore God has declared eternal war against them, similar to a human king who will stop at nothing to suppress a rebellion.

HAAMEK DAVAR

כִּי־יָד עַל־כֵּס יָהּ – *There is a hand on the LORD's throne:* We read in the Pesikta (12:9) that the phrase "there is a hand" actually refers to the hand of Amalek. The verse here speaks metaphorically, evoking a man who raises his hand in front of a king's face to deny his authority. This may be explained by citing the talmudic passage [Menaḥot 29b] which comments on the verse *For the LORD God [beYah Adonai] is an eternal rock [tzur olamim]* (Isaiah 26:4), as follows: Rav Yehuda son of Rabbi Ilai explains: The divine name *Yah* [spelled *yod-heh*] represents the two worlds that God created [this world and the World to Come]. He used a *yod* to fashion one and a *heh* to make the other. Thus God created [*yatzar*] worlds [*olamim*] through the first two letters of His name [the name *Yah* is an abbreviation of the four-letter name of God, spelled *yod-heh-vav-heh*]. He subsequently conducts matters in this world by dispatching the final letters *vav-heh*: the *vav* symbolizes God's attribute of glory, which sits above nature, whereas the final *heh* stands for God's dimension of sovereignty, by which He exercises His providence by natural means. Now when God attains dominion over the world, His name is complete, and the letters of creation – *yod-heh* – are united with the letters of control – *vav-heh*. But Amalek strove to separate God's authority from His creation, much like a person who puts his hand over the king's face to prevent him from governing his state. That is what Amalek tried to do by coming between the *yod-heh* and the *vav-heh*. מִדֹּר דֹּר – *Throughout the ages:* The verse uses the prepositional letter *mem* [literally, "from every generation"] instead of the expected letter *lamed* [which would yield "for every generation"]. This teaches that the struggle against Amalek did not begin at this moment, when they attacked Israel, but had already been raging for some time. For as early as the age of Avraham, the patriarch worked to draw the Divine Presence into this world. Hence for centuries there has been a tension between the providence of God and the power of nature [represented by *yod-heh* and *vav-heh*; this conflict is associated with Amalek, as mentioned above].

יט מֹשֶׁה מִזְבֵּחַ וַיִּקְרָא שְׁמוֹ יְהֹוָה ׀ נִסִּי: וַיֹּאמֶר כִּי־יָד עַל־כֵּס יָהּ מִלְחָמָה לַיהֹוָה בַּעֲמָלֵק מִדֹּר דֹּר:

RABBI SAMSON RAPHAEL HIRSCH *(cont.)*

built an altar to commemorate the episode, as the verse states: *And he erected there an altar, and called it El Elohei Yisrael* (Genesis 33:20). Similarly here, Moshe assembles an altar of remembrance after this first national victory over Amalek, having understood the spiritual significance of Israel's conquest. For Amalek's power is a destructive one, in contrast to Israel's mission which is constructive. That is, the Jews have been tasked with taking the mundane elements of the world and raising them up in peace to the service of God [as a sacrifice is offered up on an altar]. This altar therefore represents the hope that in messianic times the earth will become an exalted place, and the world as a whole will act as a Temple to God. This vision stands in contrast to Amalek's objective of wielding their sword in violence.

HAAMEK DAVAR

וַיִּבֶן מֹשֶׁה מִזְבֵּחַ – *Moshe built an altar:* Had the purpose of this altar been to commemorate the past – that is, to celebrate Israel's military success over Amalek, Moshe would have built it before God's pronouncement of the previous verse. We must therefore assert that the altar was in fact a statement of gratitude for God's promise to ultimately defeat Amalek [in the previous verse], which was good news to Israel.

VERSE 16

RABBI SAMSON RAPHAEL HIRSCH

כִּי־יָד עַל־כֵּס יָהּ – *There is a hand on the Lord's throne:* As long as humanity does not submit to God's will, as long as people view the apex of human achievement as embodied in acts of strength and heroism, rather than in living by the laws of ethics, God's authority will extend to nature alone. When the human race refuses to humble its heart before God, He does not rule over the world of men. At best, individuals will recognize the control that God exercises over the natural world, but they will not acknowledge that He has any business in their lives. Therefore, Moshe here declares his hope that one day the opposite will be true: Even though God's throne is at the moment incomplete [symbolized by the abbreviated form *kes*], and even though God's name and reputation are not universally accepted [signified by the shortened divine name *Yah*], nevertheless, the hand of God's providence that rules His throne is raised in oath to change that. In other words, the eternal battle against Amalek is meant to restore full reign of God's authority, and the war must go on forever until victory. This is God's goal for human history.

MALBIM

כִּי־יָד עַל־כֵּס יָהּ – *There is a hand on the Lord's throne:* The hand mentioned in this phrase refers to the war that Moshe fought, for he directed the people to battle, and *his hands held true until sunset* (17:12). Meanwhile, the term "the Lord's throne" anticipates the rule of

13 hands held true until sunset. And Yehoshua overcame Amalek and his people by the sword.
14 Then the Lord said to Moshe, "Write this as a memorial on a scroll, and commit it to Yehoshua's ears: I will erase the memory
15 of Amalek, utterly, from under the heavens." Moshe built an

MAFTIR

RABBI SAMSON RAPHAEL HIRSCH

כְּתֹב זֹאת זִכָּרוֹן בַּסֵּפֶר — *Write this as a memorial on a scroll:* [The term *basefer* literally means "on the scroll."] This refers to the known book – the Torah and its teachings. וְשִׂים בְּאָזְנֵי יְהוֹשֻׁעַ — *And commit it to Yehoshua's ears:* Once you have committed the general idea to writing, you must then explain the matter in elaborate detail to Yehoshua. This verse provides an excellent example of the relationship between Judaism's Written Torah and its Oral Law. אֶת־זֵכֶר עֲמָלֵק — *The memory of Amalek:* God does not threaten here to wipe out the actual Amalekite nation from the face of the earth, but to erase the memory and lionization of them – these are what damages the ethical standard of humanity. It is not uncommon for people to write paeans in honor of warriors they perceive as heroes. Murderers who suffocate societies' chances at happiness are immortalized for their bravery, their daring, and their brazen assertion of their individuality. But as long as this attitude survives, the younger generation will look up to their idols and long to emulate their acts of violence and brutality. The reign of Amalek will only ever end when divine morality becomes the lone standard for veneration. Then will adherence to the Torah's ethics serve to identify the true celebrities in this world. And as the demands for right behavior increase, so will the greatest of individuals be held accountable for their slightest indiscretion. For this is God's ultimate goal for human history, and this is why God vows that the credo for which Amalek stands must be eventually forgotten from the hearts of man.

RABBI JOSEPH B. SOLOVEITCHIK

כְּתֹב זֹאת זִכָּרוֹן בַּסֵּפֶר — *Write this as a memorial on a scroll:* The eternity of the Jewish nation is based upon continuity, and this continuity in turn is based mainly on memory. Here lies the fundamental difference between the non-Jewish world and the Jewish nation. The world etches its history on tablets, stones, statues, and pyramids, while our cultural history is based primarily on memory. At the same time that Moshe commanded Yehoshua to write, he also commanded him to remember. While the modern world suffers from memory deficit, our attaining the State of Israel is thanks to the eternal memory of the Jewish people.

VERSE 15

RABBI SAMSON RAPHAEL HIRSCH

וַיִּבֶן מֹשֶׁה מִזְבֵּחַ — *Moshe built an altar:* Recall that the patriarch Yaakov went through a nighttime encounter with the representative of Amalek [in Genesis 32:24–29; Yaakov's opponent, who is not identified in the story, is traditionally assumed to be an agent of Esav, Amalek's grandfather]. Afterward, he was assigned the new name "Yisrael," and he later

BESHALAH | CONFRONTING MODERNITY — SHEMOT | CHAPTER 17

יג אֱמוּנָה עַד־בֹּא הַשָּׁמֶשׁ: וַיַּחֲלֹשׁ יְהוֹשֻׁעַ אֶת־עֲמָלֵק וְאֶת־עַמּוֹ לְפִי־חָרֶב:

יד וַיֹּאמֶר יהוה אֶל־מֹשֶׁה כְּתֹב זֹאת זִכָּרוֹן בַּסֵּפֶר וְשִׂים בְּאָזְנֵי מפטיר

טו יְהוֹשֻׁעַ כִּי־מָחֹה אֶמְחֶה אֶת־זֵכֶר עֲמָלֵק מִתַּחַת הַשָּׁמָיִם: וַיִּבֶן

MALBIM (cont.)

the stone beneath him, that demonstrated how all of the people were prepared to submit to the rule of their leader. Hence the Torah describes Moshe's sovereignty as follows: *And He was king in Yeshurun, when the heads of the people and the tribes of Israel were gathered together* (Deuteronomy 33:5).

HAAMEK DAVAR

וִידֵי מֹשֶׁה כְּבֵדִים – *But Moshe's hands grew heavy:* Because Moshe was taller than both Aharon and Hur, as the Talmud states: Moshe was ten cubits tall [about eight feet, see Shabbat 92a], they found it difficult to support his arms while he stood. They therefore brought a stone for him to sit upon.

VERSE 13

RABBI SAMSON RAPHAEL HIRSCH

וַיַּחֲלֹשׁ יְהוֹשֻׁעַ אֶת־עֲמָלֵק – *And Yehoshua overcame Amalek:* [Literally, "weakened Amalek."] Yehoshua only managed to subdue Amalek, not destroy them. The enemy's complete downfall will only be achieved in messianic times. Because the Israelites had not yet reached the state of perfection that would have enabled a total victory, Amalek was kept alive to provide Israel with a foil. While Israel develops into the nation we are meant to be, Amalek serves as an educational contrast to what we should not become.

MALBIM

וַיַּחֲלֹשׁ יְהוֹשֻׁעַ אֶת־עֲמָלֵק – *And Yehoshua overcame Amalek:* [Literally, "weakened Amalek."] This battle was essentially fought by normal fighting means, with God providing some hidden assistance in the background. Because of this, Yehoshua was not able to obliterate Amalek, only to incapacitate them. God did not supply Israel with an explicit miracle that would have caused Amalek a decisive blow since Israel's merit was insufficient. Hence the war was waged by mere force of arms the way that most conflicts are.

VERSE 14

SHADAL

כְּתֹב זֹאת זִכָּרוֹן בַּסֵּפֶר – *Write this as a memorial on a scroll:* [The term *basefer* literally means "on the scroll."] This verse does not refer to the well-known book [i.e., the Torah]. Rather, God's statement simply means: Write this down on a scroll. We find a similar expression in the verse *Oh that my words were now written! Oh that they were inscribed in a book [basefer]!* (Job 19:23).

said to Yehoshua, "Choose men for us, and go out and do battle against Amalek. Tomorrow I will stand on top of the hill
10 with the staff of God in my hand." Yehoshua fought the Amalekites as Moshe had directed him, while Moshe, Aharon, and
11 Ḥur climbed to the top of the hill. Whenever Moshe held his hand high, the Israelites prevailed, but whenever he let his hand
12 drop, the Amalekites prevailed. But Moshe's hands grew heavy. So they took a stone and placed it under him and he sat, while Aharon and Ḥur held up his hands, one on each side, so that his

---

MALBIM (cont.)

weapon. This he did by taking Aharon and Ḥur to the top of the hill and praying to God for miraculous assistance. We find echoes of this arrangement in the practice of positioning two elders on either side of the cantor in the synagogue, as well as in the presence of a deputy to the right of the serving High Priest and the head of the priestly order on his left.

HAAMEK DAVAR

עָלוּ רֹאשׁ הַגִּבְעָה – *Climbed to the top of the hill:* The behavior of Moshe in this episode has served as the model for Jews throughout the generations. For even when the nation is certain of military success, they nevertheless turn to God in prayer. (Harḥev Davar)

VERSE 11

MALBIM

וְהָיָה כַּאֲשֶׁר יָרִים מֹשֶׁה יָדוֹ – *Whenever Moshe held his hand high:* Israel found success on the battlefield when they followed Moshe's lead and joined him in prayer. In those moments, they demonstrated their faith in God and in His servant. For when Moshe raised his arm, it was Israel's merits that allowed them to prevail. But when he lowered his hand, that signified that the nation's sins were too overwhelming and that the people lacked faith in God. It was at those times that the Amalekites prevailed.

VERSE 12

MALBIM

וִידֵי מֹשֶׁה כְּבֵדִים – *But Moshe's hands grew heavy:* Moshe's hands were weighted down by the plethora of nonbelievers in the nation. These people, who did not fully trust in God, made Moshe unable to lift his hands. This was a case of the material being stronger than the spiritual. The stone that Aharon and Ḥur placed beneath Moshe symbolized the unity of the Israelite nation, similar to the rock that crystallized when their ancestor Yaakov went to sleep during his journey. [According to that midrash, when Yaakov bedded down to sleep in Genesis 28:11, he arranged several stones as a pillow. During the night, these fused into one large rock to signify that his descendants would emerge as a nation with a single purpose.] Thus the verses refer to *the shepherd, the stone of Israel* (Genesis 49:24) – for just like a rock comprises many smaller grains which have been joined into a single piece, so too will the unity of Israel's believers overcome the force of its skeptics. When Moshe's aids placed

אֶל־יְהוֹשֻׁעַ בְּחַר־לָנוּ אֲנָשִׁים וְצֵא הִלָּחֵם בַּעֲמָלֵק מָחָר אָנֹכִי נִצָּב עַל־רֹאשׁ הַגִּבְעָה וּמַטֵּה הָאֱלֹהִים בְּיָדִי:
י וַיַּעַשׂ יְהוֹשֻׁעַ כַּאֲשֶׁר אָמַר־לוֹ מֹשֶׁה לְהִלָּחֵם בַּעֲמָלֵק
יא וּמֹשֶׁה אַהֲרֹן וְחוּר עָלוּ רֹאשׁ הַגִּבְעָה: וְהָיָה כַּאֲשֶׁר יָרִים מֹשֶׁה יָדוֹ וְגָבַר יִשְׂרָאֵל וְכַאֲשֶׁר יָנִיחַ יָדוֹ וְגָבַר עֲמָלֵק:
יב וִידֵי מֹשֶׁה כְּבֵדִים וַיִּקְחוּ־אֶבֶן וַיָּשִׂימוּ תַחְתָּיו וַיֵּשֶׁב עָלֶיהָ וְאַהֲרֹן וְחוּר תָּמְכוּ בְיָדָיו מִזֶּה אֶחָד וּמִזֶּה אֶחָד וַיְהִי יָדָיו

RABBI SAMSON RAPHAEL HIRSCH *(cont.)*

to the supernatural force that had defeated Pharaoh. Amalek alone did not fear God, before whom all the other nations trembled. For these people had inherited the national characteristic of their ancestors, who had chosen to determine their fortune through conquest, and who had adopted violence as their heritage. [Esav, the progenitor of Amalek, was blessed by his father Yitzhak with the words *By your sword shall you live* – Genesis 27:40.] Amalek sought praise and glory through garlands soaked in blood, and he strove to perpetuate the goal of self-aggrandizement inherent in the declaration *Let us make us a name* [Genesis 11:4, in connection with the Tower of Babel]. That was the motto with which that the elder Nimrod [the king associated with that hubristic project] inaugurated human history. And what had that effort been based on? The destruction of peace between nations and the obliteration of happiness among mankind.

VERSE 9

MALBIM

וַיֹּאמֶר מֹשֶׁה אֶל־יְהוֹשֻׁעַ – *Moshe said to Yehoshua:* During Israel's wars against Siḥon and Og, Moshe himself led the army's efforts, because in those instances God fought for Israel with open miracles. Thus the text states: *And the* Lord *said to me, Fear him not: for I will deliver him, and all his people, and his land, into your hand; and you shall do to him as you did to Siḥon king of the Amorites, who dwelt at Ḥeshbon* (Deuteronomy 3:2). At that point, Israel was deserving of revealed divine intervention, but in the current situation, God obscured His presence. This necessitated that Israel fight their war by natural means. To succeed in that effort, Moshe knew he would not be a capable general, for his proficiency was in working miracles provided by God. This is why Moshe assigned Yehoshua to lead the Israelite forces into battle – this leader would be the one eventually charged with conquering the land [and was actually a gifted military leader].

VERSE 10

MALBIM

לְהִלָּחֵם בַּעֲמָלֵק – *Fought the Amalekites:* Yehoshua's contribution was to direct the human forces on the ground, while at the same time Moshe deployed Israel's hidden

the staff with which you struck the Nile in your hand, and go.
6 I will be there before you by the rock at Ḥorev. Strike the rock, water will come out of it and the people will drink." And that
7 is what Moshe did, before the eyes of the elders of Israel. He named the place Masa and Meriva, because the people had quarreled and had tested the Lord, demanding, "Is the Lord among us or not?"
8/9 Then, at Refidim, Amalek came and attacked Israel. Moshe

RABBI SAMSON RAPHAEL HIRSCH (cont.)

omnipotent God. He remains in firm control of His creations, unfettered by any outside entities. God is master of the universe and completely free to act as He wishes; He is infinite, with no start or end. In contrast, humanity is a product of God's creativity. We have been endowed with free will of our own, which we are meant to exercise in order to fulfill our destiny as the chief servants of God in this world, and in order to rise above the forces of nature which operate blindly around us. This calling of human beings – to live as subordinates to the one God in conquering nature – is perhaps the most shocking reversal of ancient thinking that the Israelites would have encountered. And yet the Hebrews were required to adopt this philosophy in defiance of the teachings perpetuated in all the surrounding cultures. It is no wonder then that Israel only internalized this conception of reality incrementally. Each astonishing experience that the people witnessed, all the tests that they had to endure, served to develop the national understanding of how the world really works.

HAAMEK DAVAR

הֲיֵשׁ יהוה בְּקִרְבֵּנוּ אִם־אָיִן – *Is the Lord among us or not:* The people here wondered whether God directed their affairs outside of Moshe's involvement. They were uncertain whether God controlled all natural processes or not. It was this specific lack of faith that led to the attack of Amalek [in the next verse].

VERSE 8

OR HAḤAYYIM

וַיָּבֹא עֲמָלֵק וַיִּלָּחֶם – *Amalek came and attacked:* Israel was punished with this attack because they became lazy in their observance of the Torah, which is compared to both water and fire, as the verse states: *Is not My word like a fire?* [Jeremiah 23:29; the metaphor of water appears in the verse *Let everyone who thirsts, come to the water* – Isaiah 55:1]. For the Israelites did not fight the war of Torah [that is, they did not struggle to gain understanding]. In reaction, God punished them with a physical thirst corresponding to their neglect of their own spiritual drought, along with the hardship of battle for neglecting the intellectual fire of Torah study.

RABBI SAMSON RAPHAEL HIRSCH

וַיָּבֹא עֲמָלֵק וַיִּלָּחֶם – *Amalek came and attacked:* Amalek was the only nation to ever come and attack Israel without provocation. They viewed their mission as a challenge

מִזִּקְנֵי יִשְׂרָאֵל וּמַטְּךָ אֲשֶׁר הִכִּיתָ בּוֹ אֶת־הַיְאֹר קַח בְּיָדְךָ וְהָלָכְתָּ: הִנְנִי עֹמֵד לְפָנֶיךָ שָּׁם ׀ עַל־הַצּוּר בְּחֹרֵב וְהִכִּיתָ בַצּוּר וְיָצְאוּ מִמֶּנּוּ מַיִם וְשָׁתָה הָעָם וַיַּעַשׂ כֵּן מֹשֶׁה לְעֵינֵי זִקְנֵי יִשְׂרָאֵל: וַיִּקְרָא שֵׁם הַמָּקוֹם מַסָּה וּמְרִיבָה עַל־רִיב ׀ בְּנֵי יִשְׂרָאֵל וְעַל נַסֹּתָם אֶת־יהוה לֵאמֹר הֲיֵשׁ יהוה בְּקִרְבֵּנוּ אִם־אָיִן:

וַיָּבֹא עֲמָלֵק וַיִּלָּחֶם עִם־יִשְׂרָאֵל בִּרְפִידִם: וַיֹּאמֶר מֹשֶׁה

VERSE 6

SHADAL

הִנְנִי עֹמֵד לְפָנֶיךָ שָּׁם – *I will be there before you:* There you will see My glory, and that will indicate which rock I mean for you to strike.

MALBIM

הִנְנִי עֹמֵד לְפָנֶיךָ שָּׁם – *I will be there before you:* God informs Moshe that He will already be there at Ḥorev [i.e., Sinai], preparing and sanctifying the site for His revelation. For God planned to perform explicit miracles there during the delivery of the Torah, an event which would take place soon after the current episode. It was God's wish for Israel to draw water at the same place that they would drink in the message of the Torah. This is why God wanted to give Israel the water at Ḥorev rather than at Refidim [where they were encamped].

HAAMEK DAVAR

לְעֵינֵי זִקְנֵי יִשְׂרָאֵל – *Before the eyes of the elders of Israel:* It was Moshe's idea to include the elders as a mark of respect to them. Another reason why Moshe insisted that the elders witness the miracle was to obscure from them the fact that he had actually taken them along as protection from the angry people.

VERSE 7

RABBI SAMSON RAPHAEL HIRSCH

וַיִּקְרָא שֵׁם הַמָּקוֹם מַסָּה וּמְרִיבָה – *He named the place Masa and Meriva:* [The name of the place literally means "Test and Quarrel."] We should not be at all surprised at Israel's lack of faith and trust in God at this point. For what did they really know about the universe, God, and man, but what they had absorbed from the general cultural around them? And hence the Israelites still had to learn that the true nature of the world stood in direct contrast to what they believed. At that time the earth was thought to constitute a completely fixed system that was absolutely impervious to the influences of external forces; it followed a set of physical laws that were eternal and immutable. According to this ancient philosophy, the gods too were bound by this framework of nature, with man subservient to the powers of both nature and the gods. Thus Israel had to brace themselves to learn the truth about the world, which can be stated as follows: Nature was created intentionally by the one

2 the people to drink. The people started to wrangle with Moshe. "Give us water to drink," they raged. "Why do you wrangle with
3 me?" asked Moshe. "Why are you testing the Lord?" But the people were thirsty for water. They railed against Moshe, "Why did you bring us out of Egypt? Was it to kill me, my children,
4 and all my livestock by thirst?" "What shall I do with this people?" Moshe cried to the Lord – "another moment and they
5 will stone me." The Lord answered Moshe, "Walk out to face the people taking some of the elders of Israel with you. Take

---

OR HAḤAYYIM (cont.)

and terrible things in Egypt, they had seen astounding sights at the sea, and they had experienced unparalleled miracles in the wilderness. How could they commit such an error and not pray directly to God for water now? After all, this generation was well aware of the power of prayer and supplication to God. They know how He responded to their cries in Egypt, as the verse states: *God heard their groaning, and remembered His covenant with Avraham, with Yitzḥak, and with Yaakov* (2:24). And yet perhaps they believed that as long as God was in their midst, prayer was unnecessary. Since God had led the Israelites into the wilderness, He obviously planned on taking care of their needs, for otherwise they would all die. This is why the nation assumed that prayer was superfluous. However, when the people saw a dearth of water in their current circumstances, they inferred that God had abandoned them, in which case any petition would be futile. This explains the verse that quotes the people as having demanded: *Is the Lord among us nor not?* (17:7).

VERSE 4

MALBIM

וַיִּצְעַק מֹשֶׁה אֶל־יהוה – *Moshe cried to the Lord:* Once Moshe heard the people whining and testing God, he realized that the nation had lost all credit that would have provided them with water. Hence he asked God: *What shall I do with this people?*

VERSE 5

SHADAL

עֲבֹר לִפְנֵי הָעָם – *Walk out to face the people:* Do not be afraid that they might stone you.

MALBIM

וּמַטְּךָ אֲשֶׁר הִכִּיתָ בּוֹ אֶת־הַיְאֹר – *The staff with which you struck the Nile:* If Israel had accrued enough merit, Moshe would have had to merely speak to the earth to bring forth springs of water from the dry land. But since the Israelites were sorely lacking credit with God, Moshe required the use of a tool to draw forth the water. Moshe had previously employed this staff to miraculously transform the Nile into blood, and now he would use it to achieve the opposite effect – to create water from an unnatural source. In general, when a miraculous phenomenon is performed, it can also be undone in a reverse fashion.

פִּי יְהוָה וַיַּחֲנוּ בִּרְפִידִים וְאֵין מַיִם לִשְׁתֹּת הָעָם: וַיָּרֶב בּ
הָעָם עִם־מֹשֶׁה וַיֹּאמְרוּ תְּנוּ־לָנוּ מַיִם וְנִשְׁתֶּה וַיֹּאמֶר לָהֶם
מֹשֶׁה מַה־תְּרִיבוּן עִמָּדִי מַה־תְּנַסּוּן אֶת־יְהוָה: וַיִּצְמָא שָׁם ג
הָעָם לַמַּיִם וַיָּלֶן הָעָם עַל־מֹשֶׁה וַיֹּאמֶר לָמָּה זֶּה הֶעֱלִיתָנוּ
מִמִּצְרַיִם לְהָמִית אֹתִי וְאֶת־בָּנַי וְאֶת־מִקְנַי בַּצָּמָא: וַיִּצְעַק ד
מֹשֶׁה אֶל־יְהוָה לֵאמֹר מָה אֶעֱשֶׂה לָעָם הַזֶּה עוֹד מְעַט
וּסְקָלֻנִי: וַיֹּאמֶר יְהוָה אֶל־מֹשֶׁה עֲבֹר לִפְנֵי הָעָם וְקַח אִתְּךָ ה

VERSE 2

OR HAḤAYYIM

וַיָּרֶב הָעָם עִם־מֹשֶׁה – *The people started to wrangle with Moshe:* That the Israelites were "wrangling" is expressed in their demand of Moshe, "Give us water!" Did Moshe have any water to give them? They were merely looking to pick a fight. For if they had been genuinely asking Moshe to petition God on their behalf, they would have assumed the petitionary tone we see later on when God dispatches snakes and serpents to attack the Israelites [see the people's humble pleas in Numbers 21:7]. Perhaps Israel was coming to Moshe not as a supplicant but as a creditor, insisting on something he is owed. And although it seems that the nation was addressing Moshe alone, the verb "give" [*tenu*] is in the plural, because they were making demands of both God and Moshe.

MALBIM

וַיָּרֶב הָעָם עִם־מֹשֶׁה – *The people started to wrangle with Moshe:* There is a distinction between the term "community of Israel" [appearing in verse 1] and the simpler form "the people." The former label refers to the elders and important personages among the Israelites, people who did not quarrel with Moshe. It was the "people" – the masses – who were now starting a fight with their leader. Now the people were not experiencing a total lack of water – they were still carrying full flasks with them. This is why the text does not state at this early stage that *the people were thirsty for water* (17:3), and that that was the catalyst for their attack against Moshe. Rather, the nation instigated a dispute with Moshe in verse 2, even before they ran out of water and became thirsty. Thus Moshe responded: If your complaint is that I should give you water, *why do you wrangle with me?* Do I have water that I am keeping from you? I have no power to draw water out of the ground – that ability belongs exclusively to God. And if you are clamoring against God, *Why are you testing the* L<small>ORD</small>? Firstly, God is surely aware of your needs. Secondly, He is always willing and able to take care of you – but you must have a little patience.

VERSE 3

OR HAḤAYYIM

וַיִּצְמָא שָׁם הָעָם לַמַּיִם – *But the people were thirsty for water:* I have always wondered how the nation of Israel could have come to this. These people had witnessed amazing

33 of Egypt." Moshe said to Aharon, "Take an urn, put an omer of manna in it, and place it before the LORD to be kept for fu-
34 ture generations." As the LORD commanded Moshe, so Aharon placed it before the Ark of Testimony to be kept with care.
35 The Israelites ate manna for forty years, until they came to the land where they could settle down. They ate the manna until
36 they came to the border of Canaan. (An omer is a tenth of an ephah.)

17 1 All the community of Israel moved on after that from the desert of Sin, traveling from place to place as the LORD guided them, and they camped at Refidim, but there was no water there for

SHEVI'I

SHADAL (cont.)

their children ever have accepted such a tale in favor if they could have believed that their parents had been fed through natural means. To Rav Se'adya's arguments I would add that because the manna appeared regularly, the people would have had plenty of opportunity to examine the food and the process of its delivery to determine whether Moshe was perpetrating some trickery upon them. There was no thunder and lightning accompanying the daily breakfast that would have prevented the Israelites from getting a good look at how the manna appeared. Thus, because it is quite inconceivable that there was any deceit involved in the manna, it serves as the best proof that the Torah is of divine authorship.

VERSE 36

RABBI SAMSON RAPHAEL HIRSCH

וְהָעֹמֶר עֲשִׂרִית הָאֵיפָה הוּא – *An omer is a tenth of an ephah:* This measure subsequently became the standard gauge for all meal offerings and symbolized the usual amount of food one should present before God. Therefore, whenever a Jew brought an omer's worth of grain in the Temple, he recalled the graciousness of God in serving Israel that quantity of manna during the nation's youth.

CHAPTER 17, VERSE 1

RABBI SAMSON RAPHAEL HIRSCH

וְאֵין מַיִם לִשְׁתֹּת הָעָם – *But there was no water there for the people to drink:* Note that the verse does not state that the people had actually run out of water. Rather, they looked around at the terrain they had entered and guessed that it would not have enough drinkable water. Surely it held an insufficient amount to satisfy such a large nation. Hence the additional phrase "for the people to drink."

MALBIM

לְמַסְעֵיהֶם עַל־פִּי יהוה – *From place to place as the LORD guided them:* At each leg of the nation's journey, they shed an additional layer of Egyptian impurity and moved one step closer to God. And during each stage of the Israelites' travels God tested them and taught them various lessons, all as preparation for the receiving of the Torah.

לד אֶתְכֶם מֵאֶרֶץ מִצְרָיִם: וַיֹּאמֶר מֹשֶׁה אֶל־אַהֲרֹן קַח צִנְצֶנֶת אַחַת וְתֶן־שָׁמָּה מְלֹא־הָעֹמֶר מָן וְהַנַּח אֹתוֹ לִפְנֵי יהוה לְמִשְׁמֶרֶת לְדֹרֹתֵיכֶם: כַּאֲשֶׁר צִוָּה יהוה אֶל־מֹשֶׁה וַיַּנִּיחֵהוּ לה אַהֲרֹן לִפְנֵי הָעֵדֻת לְמִשְׁמָרֶת: וּבְנֵי יִשְׂרָאֵל אָכְלוּ אֶת־הַמָּן אַרְבָּעִים שָׁנָה עַד־בֹּאָם אֶל־אֶרֶץ נוֹשָׁבֶת אֶת־הַמָּן אָכְלוּ לו עַד־בֹּאָם אֶל־קְצֵה אֶרֶץ כְּנָעַן: וְהָעֹמֶר עֲשִׂרִית הָאֵיפָה הוּא:

יז א וַיִּסְעוּ כָּל־עֲדַת בְּנֵי־יִשְׂרָאֵל מִמִּדְבַּר־סִין לְמַסְעֵיהֶם עַל־ שביעי

VERSE 34

SHADAL

וְהַנַּח אֹתוֹ לִפְנֵי יהוה — *And place it before the* Lord: Moshe directed Aharon to do this only after the Tabernacle was constructed. [Since "before the Lord" generally refers to a place inside the Tabernacle.] Furthermore, Moshe recorded these three verses [33–35] at the end of the forty years.

MALBIM

לִפְנֵי הָעֵדֻת לְמִשְׁמָרֶת — *Before the Ark of Testimony to be kept with care:* The manna was placed in front of the Ark in order to associate the two objects: Israel only deserved to eat the manna by merit of their observance of the Torah, which was kept inside the Ark of the Covenant.

VERSE 35

SHADAL

וּבְנֵי יִשְׂרָאֵל אָכְלוּ אֶת־הַמָּן אַרְבָּעִים שָׁנָה — *The Israelites ate manna for forty years:* Some Bible critics argue that Moshe did not compose this verse [since the manna only ceased to fall after Moshe had died, in Joshua 5:12], but that is a spurious claim. For there is no reason why Moshe could not have written this text at the end of his life. After all, our passage does not declare that the manna ceased, as we read in the Book of Joshua, only that Israel enjoyed the food until they reached the border of Canaan, a milestone they had reached at the end of Moshe's life. Now how beautiful are the words of Rav Se'adya Gaon as he describes the manna as the most wondrous of all of God's miracles. Says he: A continuous phenomenon is much more impressive than a brief one. For it is impossible that close to a million souls were fed for forty years through some sort of trick or magic instead of with a novel food that the Creator fashioned out of thin air. If such an artifice had existed, ancient philosophers would have been able to reproduce that cunning, even to a small degree, in order to feed their students. It is also impossible that the nation of Israel contrived to fabricate a false story of the manna's existence and to lie to their children about it. Nor would

day. You shall each rest where you are: let no man depart from
30 where he is on the seventh day." So the people rested on the
31 seventh day. The house of Israel named it manna. It looked like
white coriander seeds, and tasted like wafers made with honey.
32 Moshe said, "This is what the LORD commands: Let an omer
of it be kept carefully aside for your descendants, that they may
see the bread I fed you in the desert when I brought you out

RABBI SAMSON RAPHAEL HIRSCH (cont.)

God's hand. Our Sages explained why the womenfolk were given the task of assigning a name to the bread. As we have said, the entire phenomenon of the manna was geared toward training the nation of Israel to accept the attribute of moderation. This, combined with faith in God and trust in His providence, were ideals which the women of the households were primarily responsible for inculcating in their families. It therefore made sense that it was they who recognized that the manna was a gift from God and that He granted each person just the right amount of food to cover his needs. The women named the food manna to give voice to these principles.

VERSE 32

MALBIM

מְלֹא הָעֹמֶר מִמֶּנּוּ לְמִשְׁמֶרֶת – *Let an omer of it be kept carefully:* The purpose of this command was to emphasize that the wonder of the manna was not restricted to the years Israel spent in the wilderness. For God's willingness to provide sustenance to those who devote their lives to the study of Torah and to the divine service continues in every generation. Such a person will find that God allows him to eat his bread without any toil or effort. He will in essence become an eater of manna.

MESHEKH ḤOKHMA

בְּמַעַן יִרְאוּ אֶת־הַלֶּחֶם אֲשֶׁר הֶאֱכַלְתִּי אֶתְכֶם – *That they may see the bread I fed you:* A person might think that divine providence only extends to him when he has fully adopted the ways of God. That is, only once he has conducted himself in a manner that overrides his natural inclinations will God show him His beneficence, but until he has reached that exalted level, he must fend for himself. But such is not the case. Observe: When exactly did God begin to present His gift of the manna to the Israelites? Was it after the people had received the Torah and begun to observe its commandments? No, the Israelites were graced with divine assistance long before that, for the verse refers to the manna as *the bread I fed you in the desert when I brought you out of Egypt*. Therefore, any Jew who is prepared to generally accept the obligations of God and His Torah need not worry about the source of his livelihood. For there is a stage when an individual has not yet fully subscribed to this way of life and has not completely abandoned the ways of the rest of the world. But if such a person is nevertheless committed to trying to serve God to the best of his abilities, the Almighty will support him and never leave him. Such a Jew can be assured that God will see to his sustenance.

לׄ אַל־יֵצֵא אִישׁ מִמְּקֹמ֖וֹ בַּיּ֥וֹם הַשְּׁבִיעִֽי: וַיִּשְׁבְּת֥וּ הָעָ֖ם בַּיּ֥וֹם
לאׄ הַשְּׁבִיעִֽי: וַיִּקְרְא֧וּ בֵֽית־יִשְׂרָאֵ֛ל אֶת־שְׁמ֖וֹ מָ֑ן וְה֗וּא כְּזֶ֤רַע גַּד֙
לבׄ לָבָ֔ן וְטַעְמ֖וֹ כְּצַפִּיחִ֥ת בִּדְבָֽשׁ: וַיֹּ֣אמֶר מֹשֶׁ֗ה זֶ֤ה הַדָּבָר֙ אֲשֶׁ֣ר
צִוָּ֣ה יְהֹוָ֗ה מְלֹ֤א הָעֹ֙מֶר֙ מִמֶּ֔נּוּ לְמִשְׁמֶ֖רֶת לְדֹרֹֽתֵיכֶ֑ם לְמַ֣עַן ׀
יִרְא֣וּ אֶת־הַלֶּ֗חֶם אֲשֶׁ֨ר הֶאֱכַ֤לְתִּי אֶתְכֶם֙ בַּמִּדְבָּ֔ר בְּהוֹצִיאִ֥י

RABBI JOSEPH B. SOLOVEITCHIK *(cont.)*

The idea of the Sabbath is man's aloneness. And if man is alone, he is also with God. The charisma of the Sabbath expresses itself in the return of man to himself and to God, the source of holiness. Severance of the individual from working society establishes a permanent communion with God.

VERSE 30

MALBIM

וַיִּשְׁבְּתוּ הָעָם – *So the people rested:* At this point, even the original dissenters listened to Moshe and rested on the seventh day.

MESHEKH ḤOKHMA

וַיִּשְׁבְּתוּ הָעָם בַּיּוֹם הַשְּׁבִיעִי – *So the people rested on the seventh day:* When one violates a negative commandment by merely being passive, it is easy to repent for the transgression. However, should a person actively violate a prohibition, negating the will of God, it becomes much more difficult to close the rift he has created. Thus the Talmud declares: How is one proved to be a repentant sinner? Rav Yehuda taught: If the temptation which caused the original transgression presents itself a second time, and the sinner refrains from indulging again, that is the mark of repentance. Rav Yehuda continued: Should one have the opportunity to sin with the same woman, at the same time, in the same place [and yet does not], he has demonstrated his reform]. Now when the Israelites kept their food overnight during the week, their transgression was a passive one [they did not have to do anything to violate the command – they just let the food be]. Hence the sinners could easily effect repentance for their behavior. On the other hand, when some went out to the fields to seek manna, they were engaged in an active violation of God's commandment, so these people had to make more of an effort to return to God's good favor. Their repentance was not accepted until they had actually "rested on the seventh day."

VERSE 31

RABBI SAMSON RAPHAEL HIRSCH

וַיִּקְרְאוּ בֵית־יִשְׂרָאֵל אֶת־שְׁמוֹ מָן – *The house of Israel named it manna:* [The word "house" – *bayit* – is traditionally associated with the nation's women.] It was the Israelite women who named the manna, for it was they who were in charge of family life and feeding their households. They called the food manna – the *manot* ["portions"] that were distributed by

27 not be there." Some people did go out to gather it on the sev-
28 enth day; but they found none.   Then the LORD said to Moshe, "How long will you refuse to keep My command-
29 ments and laws? Understand that the LORD has given you a Sabbath – that is why He gave you two days' bread on the sixth

VERSE 29

RABBI SAMSON RAPHAEL HIRSCH

רְאוּ – *Understand:* [Literally, "see."] You Israelites can see for yourselves and verify through the changes in the manna's distribution and the feelings that the Sabbath stirs within you that the holy day is a divine blessing. The Sabbath is a statute instituted by God and given as a precious gift to the Jewish nation. It should not be a burden, a mere set of restrictions that cause loss to the individual. And God has given the Sabbath is to and for you, not for His own sake; recognize the happiness and fulfillment that it provides. Indeed, there is not a single spiritual or ethical concept which is not enhanced by recognition of the Sabbath: awareness of God and the world, knowledge of oneself, the sense of human obligation, consolation of the soul from life's travails, the joy at fulfilling commandments, feelings of contentedness, and the satisfaction of accomplishment. All of these are brought into sharp relief by the shift in temperament and atmosphere that the Sabbath offers. All of these are refreshed every week for the individual who seeks his livelihood under the laws of God. For God's aim is not to deprive His people of anything by his demand to observe the Sabbath. On the contrary, the blessings He sends you during the first six days of the week will enable you to keep the Sabbath on the seventh.

RABBI JOSEPH B. SOLOVEITCHIK

אַל־יֵצֵא אִישׁ מִמְּקֹמוֹ – *Let no man depart from where he is:* Working man is always in the public domain. He is manufacturing, trading, exchanging goods and services, talking, arguing, fighting, or helping – always with somebody. No wonder Eve was created the very instant Adam was charged with the task of working and keeping the Garden of Eden. He was placed there, charged with work, and, as a working being, he needed help. People who retire from business or from a profession quickly discover that they are unneeded, lonely, and abandoned by society; the world passes them by. If a man stops working, there is no need for him to maintain lines of communication with his community. Without work and responsibility, communal ties gradually disappear. Yet on the Sabbath, God told man to stop working, to leave off in the middle, to retreat and rest. In other words, man is supposed to withdraw from society on the Sabbath. Man retreats from the "thou" into privacy and aloneness. On the Sabbath, the individual gains supremacy over the community. He withdraws from conquest and acquisition, from his coworkers, partners, and associates, into the mysterious abode of a lonely "I" existence. Man remains alone, and he should experience the Sabbath as a lone being. On the Sabbath God tolerates no competition; He does not want to share man with anybody else. Hence, He told man to retreat from society: *The seventh [day] is a Sabbath to the LORD, your God* (20:10). Everything belongs to Him. Cease to be a slave to your work; cease being a servant to society; be exclusively Mine.

כז יְהְיֶה־בּוֹ: וַיְהִי בַּיּוֹם הַשְּׁבִיעִי יָצְאוּ מִן־הָעָם לִלְקֹט וְלֹא
כח מָצָאוּ: וַיֹּאמֶר יְהוָה אֶל־מֹשֶׁה עַד־אָנָה מֵאַנְתֶּם
כט לִשְׁמֹר מִצְוֹתַי וְתוֹרֹתָי: רְאוּ כִּי־יְהוָה נָתַן לָכֶם הַשַּׁבָּת עַל־
כֵּן הוּא נֹתֵן לָכֶם בַּיּוֹם הַשִּׁשִּׁי לֶחֶם יוֹמָיִם שְׁבוּ ׀ אִישׁ תַּחְתָּיו

VERSE 27

OR HAHAYYIM

וְלֹא מָצָאוּ – *But they found none:* Had the people located any manna in the desert, they would have gathered it. [Thus they are rebuked for even looking.]

MALBIM

יָצְאוּ מִן־הָעָם לִלְקֹט – *Some people did go out to gather it:* There were some individuals who refused to accept the restriction forbidding them from working one day of the week. For they believed that they would thereby suffer a loss of one seventh of their sustenance. Every day of the week, their efforts provided the nation with food to eat that day, and these people feared they would starve on the day they were forced to be idle.

VERSE 28

RABBI SAMSON RAPHAEL HIRSCH

מִצְוֹתַי וְתוֹרֹתָי – *My commandments and laws:* When a person insists on running his business on the Sabbath in violation of God's will, he betrays his belief that God does not actively feed and sustain him throughout his life. Such a person boasts that he does not need God's assistance or approval to succeed, and that his survival does not depend on divine grace, but on the force and measure of his own personal efforts. If he can only take advantage of the natural laws of the universe and exploit the world in his favor, he will meet with triumph. All he must do is try, and he will succeed; and when he has succeeded he will be happy. At no point does he rely on God, but on his faculties alone. The Jew who continues advancing his financial interests on the Sabbath turns his back on God, in clear neglect of His will. Such a person thinks that he has no master in the world save himself. And thus it is as if this vile creature has rejected the entire Torah.

MALBIM

עַד־אָנָה מֵאַנְתֶּם – *How long will you refuse:* "To refuse" [*me'en*] is not the same thing as "not to want" [*lo ava*]. The latter is an emotion, whereas "refusal" is a verbal statement that might be uttered even when the speaker, deep down, really does want to comply. Every person wants in his heart to fulfill God's decrees, but some might say that they do not because of the effort involved in doing so. Now in this verse God rebukes Israel, arguing that even if they were convinced that they would suffer financial loss by working on the Sabbath, they should have been prepared to observe the day as one of God's "commandments and laws." The Sabbath does not only represent one of God's statutes; it comprises great teachings, testifying to the creation of the world, to the phenomenon of providence, and God's performance of miracles for the service of man.

cook. Whatever is left, keep carefully aside for the morning."
24 So they put it aside until the morning, as Moshe had instructed them, and it did not stink, nor did worms infest it.
25 And Moshe said, "Today, eat this, for today is a Sabbath to
26 the Lord; today you will not find it on the ground. Six days shall you gather it, but on the seventh day, the Sabbath, it will

---

OR HAḤAYYIM (cont.)

eat this (16:25); that is, the Sabbath was the only day of the week when eating day-old manna was permitted. And lest the people err and think that it was only on that first Sabbath that leftover manna was allowed, Moshe stressed: *For today is a Sabbath to the Lord.* Thus the language of the command was only meant to exclude similar consumption on weekdays, not on other Sabbaths.

RABBI SAMSON RAPHAEL HIRSCH

אָכְלֻהוּ הַיּוֹם — *Today, eat this:* During the week, Israel was able to eat only that which they collected on any given day; their toil provided the families with food for immediate consumption. However, the Sabbath meals were served without any prior labor. Now Israel's inactivity on the Sabbath did not betray any sort of objectionable laziness, but represented the will of the Almighty; it was idleness dedicated to God. The positive value of not exerting oneself in forbidden labor is as great as any of God's commandments. At the same time, enjoying one's meals on the Sabbath became a sacred rite that Jews perform in the presence of God.

VERSE 26

HAAMEK DAVAR

שֵׁשֶׁת יָמִים תִּלְקְטֻהוּ — *Six days shall you gather it:* This entire sentence seems superfluous until we realize that it relates back to the warning issued above. In verse 23, Israel was told to prepare their meals on the sixth day to be able to eat on the Sabbath. This meant that food that was not specially prepared for the Sabbath would rot. Our verse now clarifies that this consequence was only with regard to the first Sabbath, when Israel was not fully informed about the nature of the day. [That is, since the people did not know when they were collecting the manna on the first Friday that they were assembling food to be eaten on the next day, all of their gathering was done with the sixth day in mind. Hence, the Israelites still had to somehow demonstrate that the excess food was special for the Sabbath by specially preparing it.] However, regarding future weeks, the people were told, *Six days shall you gather it, but on the seventh day, the Sabbath, it will not be there.* Hence, when the food would be collected on subsequent Fridays, the people would know that they were gathering it for the Sabbath, and there is no greater preparation than that. [Therefore, in the future, even if Israel did not cook or bake the manna on the sixth day, preferring to eat it raw on the Sabbath, the food would remain wholesome and edible the next day.]

כד לָכֶם לְמִשְׁמֶרֶת עַד־הַבֹּקֶר: וַיַּנִּיחוּ אֹתוֹ עַד־הַבֹּקֶר כַּאֲשֶׁר
כה צִוָּה מֹשֶׁה וְלֹא הִבְאִישׁ וְרִמָּה לֹא־הָיְתָה בּוֹ: וַיֹּאמֶר מֹשֶׁה
אִכְלֻהוּ הַיּוֹם כִּי־שַׁבָּת הַיּוֹם לַיהוָה הַיּוֹם לֹא תִמְצָאֻהוּ
כו בַּשָּׂדֶה: שֵׁשֶׁת יָמִים תִּלְקְטֻהוּ וּבַיּוֹם הַשְּׁבִיעִי שַׁבָּת לֹא

MALBIM (cont.)

would cease His work on that day. Therefore, twice as much manna was provided on the sixth day, and the surplus was evident even in its raw state. When God told Moshe: *On the sixth day, they will have to prepare what they bring in* (16:5), He did not mean that the food would only be blessed and augmented once it had been baked or cooked. Rather, the point of that instruction was that some of the excess manna that Israel collected on the sixth day should be readied for meals on the Sabbath day. Whoever wanted to eat baked manna on the Sabbath should bake it on Friday; whoever preferred cooked manna should take care of that before the Sabbath began as well. For just like His people, God performed all of His necessary labor – i.e., providing the manna – on the sixth day, in preparation for tomorrow.

VERSE 24

MALBIM

וַיַּנִּיחוּ אֹתוֹ עַד־הַבֹּקֶר – *So they put it aside until the morning:* Because Israel set aside the manna both as a testament to God and to fulfill His command, it did not stink by the next day. Neither did worms infest it, for the worms usually preceded the stench.

VERSE 25

OR HAḤAYYIM

אִכְלֻהוּ הַיּוֹם – *Today, eat this:* Moshe's statement appears curious: Why does he have to tell the people to eat the manna on the Sabbath? Why wouldn't they? Perhaps he was concerned that the Israelites had misunderstood his previous instruction, *Whatever is left, keep carefully aside for the morning* (16:23), and believed that they were only supposed to carefully keep yesterday's manna, not that they were permitted to eat it as well. After all, while the text never explicitly states that during the week the people were forbidden from eating manna that they left overnight, still, since our verse grants permission to the people to eat day-old manna, that implies that during the week such a meal was not only repugnant [since the food had decomposed] but prohibited. The Israelites might even have already been taught at this early stage the prohibition *You shall not eat any abominable thing* (Deuteronomy 14:3), in which case it was clearly wrong for them to indulge in the worm-infested leftovers. This in turn might have led the Israelites to suspect that even though on the Sabbath morning the leftover manna was not at all deteriorated, they were still prohibited from eating it. Hence Moshe had to specify that now Israel was in fact allowed to partake of yesterday's manna. The leader was also careful to emphasize: *Today,*

22 When the sixth day came, they gathered a double portion, two omers each. All the leaders of the community came and report-
23 ed this to Moshe. "This" he told them, "is what the LORD has said: Tomorrow is a day of rest, a holy Sabbath to the LORD. Bake now what you need to bake and cook what you need to

─────────────── OR HAḤAYYIM *(cont.)* ───────────────

issuing to honor the seventh day, physical proof that God forbade them to labor on the Sabbath. This would necessarily convince the Hebrews of the supreme importance of the day that commemorates creation and frighten them against transgressing its sanctity. For this impression to be made upon Israel, Moshe understood that the matter of the extra food had to be kept secret. Had the nation known that they were meant to gather more than their usual amount, they would not have been surprised to learn that behind the scenes, God was working a miracle to provide the people's Sabbath meals.

VERSE 23

─────────────── RABBI SAMSON RAPHAEL HIRSCH ───────────────

אֶת אֲשֶׁר־תֹּאפוּ אֵפוּ – *Bake now what you need to bake:* In order to educate the nation in the right values for pursuing a livelihood, God trained Israel to accept that He would distribute sufficient manna to them every day. This was intended to teach them not only about the ills of laziness and greed and the benefits of hard work, but chiefly that he who has true faith in the Creator does not worry about where his next meal is coming from. For the miser and the hoarder practically deny that God is committed to feeding all His creations. In a similar fashion, God used the manna as a hands-on method to educate the Israelites as to the particulars of the Sabbath laws. The first lesson was to explain to the budding nation the relationship between the Sabbath and the previous six days of the week. While during the week man is best served by performing his labors as he ought to, without undo concern for tomorrow, in this verse the Hebrews are told that the Sabbath is different: One must plan ahead on the sixth day in order to eat on the seventh. Furthermore, not only must the Jew plan regarding his physical survival on the Sabbath, but he must consider the spiritual continuity of the nation. When it comes to preparation for mitzvot, any advance arrangements will always stand us in good stead – the surplus will never be destroyed by worms but will be divinely protected by God's blessing.

─────────────── MALBIM ───────────────

אֶת אֲשֶׁר־תֹּאפוּ אֵפוּ – *Bake now what you need to bake:* The purpose of this statement – that there would be double the amount of manna in the nation's pots even before they began to cook it – was to dispel the Israelites' misunderstanding of the Sabbath arrangements. Initially, the tribal leaders who approached Moshe [with the extra manna in the previous verse], believed that it was the process of cooking the manna which would increase its mass. Therefore, they thought, the purpose of the Sabbath was to provide a day of rest only for the human beings – they were forbidden to go out to the fields to collect the manna. But the food would still appear on the desert floor – God would not be taking a day off. Thus a correction was in order: Tomorrow was to be "a holy Sabbath to the LORD" and He too

כב וַיְהִי ׀ בַּיּוֹם הַשִּׁשִּׁי לָקְטוּ לֶחֶם מִשְׁנֶה שְׁנֵי הָעֹמֶר לָאֶחָד
כג וַיָּבֹאוּ כָּל־נְשִׂיאֵי הָעֵדָה וַיַּגִּידוּ לְמֹשֶׁה: וַיֹּאמֶר אֲלֵהֶם הוּא אֲשֶׁר דִּבֶּר יהוה שַׁבָּתוֹן שַׁבַּת־קֹדֶשׁ לַיהוָה מָחָר אֵת אֲשֶׁר־תֹּאפוּ אֵפוּ וְאֵת אֲשֶׁר־תְּבַשְּׁלוּ בַּשֵּׁלוּ וְאֵת כָּל־הָעֹדֵף הַנִּיחוּ

VERSE 22

---OR HAḤAYYIM---

וַיָּבֹאוּ כָּל־נְשִׂיאֵי הָעֵדָה – *All the leaders of the community came:* Since Israel's leaders felt the need to inform Moshe of this new development, Moshe must not have previously told the people about God's scheme to provide double the amount of manna on the sixth day. But this surely represents a difficulty: How could Moshe have withheld his prophecy from the audience for whom it was intended? After all, Moshe himself taught us that a prophet is forbidden to suppress the word of God [see Deuteronomy 18:19]. And heaven forbid that Moshe merely forgot to repeat what God had told him, only remembering the message once the leaders appeared with an abundance of manna. For once we entertain that possibility, who is to say how many other laws God related to Moshe that he subsequently neglected to teach the Jewish people! That material would still be unknown even today. Rather, we must interpret this passage in Moshe's favor, for note: When Moshe explains the situation to his people in the verse *"This" he told them, "is what the Lord has said"* (16:23) he does not imply the word *lemor* [meaning "saying," or "to say"; this word commonly prefaces commandments issued to Moshe]. This means that although God had previously explained to Moshe what the sixth day's manna crop would look like, He did not direct Moshe "to say" this detail to the people in advance. Moshe inferred correctly that he was not initially supposed to pass along this information to the Israelites. Support for this interpretation appears in verse 5, when God explains: *On the sixth day, they will have to prepare what they bring in. It will be twice as much as they gather on all other days.* That announcement is not prefaced by any statement such as "Speak to the people of Israel and tell them etc." Hence when the leaders ask for an explanation for the surplus food, Moshe tells them: *This is what the Lord has said: Tomorrow is a day of rest* (16:23). What he meant was: Yes, in fact God revealed this secret to me, but I was under instructions not to repeat His explanation to you. Of course, this reading raises the following difficulty: After the people questioned the sixth day's yield, Moshe elaborated on its significance [in verse 23]. And yet, who gave him permission to now reveal what God had previously told him to withhold? It is evident that Moshe understood what God's plan had been all along. God wanted to plant the seed of faith in the people's hearts, to demonstrate to them the great significance of the Sabbath. To do this, God wanted Israel to experience the message of the holy day conveyed directly from Him, rather than hearing about it beforehand from a human agent. Therefore, the Israelites were to go to the fields on the morning of the sixth day with the assumption that the food collection would be the same as it had been all week. Suddenly, they would discover an abundance of manna when they returned to their tents, finding that their kitchens were overflowing with twice the usual amount of the food. They would thus see a tangible manifestation of the command that God was

18 But when they measured it with an omer measure, those who had gathered much had none left over, and those who gathered but little did not fall short. All had gathered as much as they could
19 eat. "Let no one leave any over for the morning," said Moshe;
20 but they did not listen to Moshe. Some of them left part of it till morning, and it became worm-infested and stank. Moshe was
21 enraged with them. Every morning they gathered it, all as much as they could eat, and when the sun grew hot, it melted away.

VERSE 20

OR HAḤAYYIM

וַיָּרֻם תּוֹלָעִים וַיִּבְאַשׁ – *And it became worm-infested and stank:* When the Israelites left the manna overnight the food assumed a nasty character because the people had contravened the Torah's command. On the other hand, when Moshe assured the people that the extra manna that they collected on the sixth day could be kept for consumption on the Sabbath, the text reports: *They put it aside until the morning, as Moshe had instructed them, and it did not stink, nor did worms infest it* (16:24). This means that the manna was not overcome by foulness [because of the Israelites' foul behavior], and it therefore was saved from the worms. Similarly we find that when righteous people are buried, they are not consumed by worms, since during their lifetimes they engaged in no sin and therefore were in no way disgusting when they died.

SHADAL

וַיָּרֻם תּוֹלָעִים וַיִּבְאַשׁ – *And it became worm-infested and stank:* God arranged for the leftover manna to become wormy in order to train Israel to rely on His miracles. For the manna did not naturally attract worms – as we see, the food remained maggot-free on the Sabbath.

RABBI SAMSON RAPHAEL HIRSCH

וְלֹא־שָׁמְעוּ אֶל־מֹשֶׁה – *But they did not listen to Moshe:* The people were put to the test during the six days of the week in an exercise that would train them in the fundamentals of the Jewish conception of survival. In the process, a valuable lesson was imparted to all future generations as well. Our culture finds repulsive the attribute of laziness, but no less so the unrelenting pursuit of wealth; miserliness is scorned along with dependency on others. Judaism praises diligence – we admire the individual who is satisfied with the minimum he needs, for that exemplifies faith in God. Such a person possesses confidence that God will always support him.

VERSE 21

SHADAL

וְחַם הַשֶּׁמֶשׁ וְנָמָס – *And when the sun grew hot, it melted away:* The manna did not dissolve as soon as the sun rose, but later in the day when its heat was felt. As the atmosphere heated up, the manna would slowly melt into liquid.

יח וַיָּמֹדּוּ בָעֹמֶר וְלֹא הֶעְדִּיף הַמַּרְבֶּה וְהַמַּמְעִיט לֹא הֶחְסִיר
יט אִישׁ לְפִי־אָכְלוֹ לָקָטוּ: וַיֹּאמֶר מֹשֶׁה אֲלֵהֶם אִישׁ אַל־יוֹתֵר
כ מִמֶּנּוּ עַד־בֹּקֶר: וְלֹא־שָׁמְעוּ אֶל־מֹשֶׁה וַיּוֹתִרוּ אֲנָשִׁים מִמֶּנּוּ
כא עַד־בֹּקֶר וַיָּרֻם תּוֹלָעִים וַיִּבְאַשׁ וַיִּקְצֹף עֲלֵהֶם מֹשֶׁה: וַיִּלְקְטוּ
אֹתוֹ בַּבֹּקֶר בַּבֹּקֶר אִישׁ כְּפִי אָכְלוֹ וְחַם הַשֶּׁמֶשׁ וְנָמָס:

VERSE 19

OR HAHAYYIM

אִישׁ אַל־יוֹתֵר מִמֶּנּוּ עַד־בֹּקֶר – *Let no one leave any over for the morning:* [We see no explicit command by God to this effect.] Perhaps it was Moshe's idea to command Israel not to leave any manna overnight, having understood that God would be providing food for the nation on a daily basis. Israel was therefore not to prepare food on one day to be eaten on the next. This suggestion helps explain why the Torah relates that *they did not listen to Moshe* (16:20) — a phrase which is superfluous considering how continuation of the verse details their disobedience. What's more, that verse could have simply stated: "But they did not listen and left part of it till morning" [omitting specific reference to Moshe]. Rather, according to my understanding, the people felt free to ignore an instruction that had not originally been decreed by God, but which Moshe had invented. Note as well that regarding the command that the Israelites collect just as much food as they need, Moshe prefaces the instruction with the words *This is what the* LORD *has instructed* (16:16), a clause which is absent in this verse, supporting the contention that God had not authored this rule. Nevertheless, once Moshe devised this restriction regarding leaving the manna over, God agreed that it was a good idea, which explains why the leftover food subsequently *became worm-infested and stank* (16:20). This proves the truth of the adage that the independent reasoning of a wise man is preferable to the words of a prophet. On the other hand, it is also possible that God had initially told Moshe to forbid Israel from keeping the food for the next day. According to this reading, the introductory statement *This is what the* LORD *has instructed* (16:16) referred to this later detail as well as all of the other particulars governing the gathering and storing of the manna. The text then emphasizes that the people violated Moshe's command because they believed it to have been his own creation, and thought that on the contrary, the teaching of a prophet always outweighs the logic of a wise man.

MALBIM

אִישׁ אַל־יוֹתֵר מִמֶּנּוּ עַד־בֹּקֶר – *Let no one leave any over for the morning:* This verse contains a relevant message for all times: An individual must always trust that God will provide him with sustenance. And any person who has enough to eat today but worries how he will survive tomorrow is surely a creature of little faith. And so comment our Sages, regarding the verse *Your life shall hang in doubt before you; and you shall fear day and night and have no assurance of your life* (Deuteronomy 28:66): This curse describes the person who feels he must stock up on wheat for an entire year, rather than letting nature take its course. For one who relies on the providence of God fears not what tomorrow will bring.

covered the camp; next morning a layer of dew surrounded
14 the camp. When the dew covering lifted, fine flakes covered
15 the floor of the desert like fine frost on the ground. When the Israelites saw it, they asked one another, "What is it?" for they did not recognize it. Moshe said to them, "This is the bread
16 the Lord has given you to eat. This is what the Lord has instructed: Each of you gather as much as you need, an omer for every person; each take enough for all the people in your tent."
17 The people of Israel did so. Some gathered more, others less.

MALBIM *(cont.)*

restrictions would apply to all future generations' behavior when seeking their livelihoods in this world. The first of these rules is a warning to the Israelites not to collect more food than they need. No hoarding of extra supplies was permitted so there would be no sale of or trade in the miraculous food. The message for later communities is that one should never strive to amass more wealth than one needs – such an attitude reflects a lack of faith that God will provide. Furthermore, when we engage in the excessive pursuit of money, God will not allow us to really enjoy it. And thus states the verse *For you shall eat the labor of your hands: happy shall you be, and it shall be well with you* (Psalms 128:2), meaning that a person will be happy if he strives to gain only sufficient means to live and no more. He shall then be happy in this world, and it will be well with him in the next world. The second message to emerge from this passage is that a person should never eat more than his fill, nor should he starve himself. Rather, one should consume enough to satisfy his hunger, represented in the verse by the phrase "an omer for every person." This was enough for each Israelite. And thirdly, our text teaches that a man is responsible for feeding his wife and children, as the people were directed to *each take enough for all the people in your tent*. One may never cavalierly demand that one's family members fend for themselves – the Israelites were not to send the women and children to gather the manna from the fields. For it is best for a woman to remain home, modestly keeping the tent for her family, while her children learn from her.

VERSE 17

MALBIM

וַיַּעֲשׂוּ־כֵן בְּנֵי יִשְׂרָאֵל – *The people of Israel did so:* When the Israelites went out to reap the manna from the desert floor, some of them brought home more than others. Nevertheless, when everyone returned to their tents and measured their haul with an omer measure, they found that each person had exactly that amount for each family member. This was a rebuke to those of little faith who had feared that God would not provide for them in the future. For those individuals had wasted their time gathering food that had disappeared, time that could have been better spent in prayer. Meanwhile, those who gathered less than they should have taken, ended up with more. This confirmed the lesson that in the face of God's providence, additional effort is unnecessary.

יד שִׁכְבַת הַטָּל סָבִיב לַמַּחֲנֶה: וַתַּעַל שִׁכְבַת הַטָּל וְהִנֵּה עַל־
טו פְּנֵי הַמִּדְבָּר דַּק מְחֻסְפָּס דַּק כַּכְּפֹר עַל־הָאָרֶץ: וַיִּרְאוּ בְנֵי־
יִשְׂרָאֵל וַיֹּאמְרוּ אִישׁ אֶל־אָחִיו מָן הוּא כִּי לֹא יָדְעוּ מַה־
הוּא וַיֹּאמֶר מֹשֶׁה אֲלֵהֶם הוּא הַלֶּחֶם אֲשֶׁר נָתַן יהוה לָכֶם
טז לְאָכְלָה: זֶה הַדָּבָר אֲשֶׁר צִוָּה יהוה לִקְטוּ מִמֶּנּוּ אִישׁ לְפִי
אָכְלוֹ עֹמֶר לַגֻּלְגֹּלֶת מִסְפַּר נַפְשֹׁתֵיכֶם אִישׁ לַאֲשֶׁר בְּאָהֳלוֹ
יז תִּקָּחוּ: וַיַּעֲשׂוּ־כֵן בְּנֵי יִשְׂרָאֵל וַיִּלְקְטוּ הַמַּרְבֶּה וְהַמַּמְעִיט:

SHADAL *(cont.)*

---

fly between countries, appearing in Arabia from the Red Sea in numbers so large as to defy calculation. Quails fly close to the ground which makes their capture by hand easy. God directed the birds to arrive on the very day of Israel's complaints of hunger.

RABBI SAMSON RAPHAEL HIRSCH

וַיְהִי בָעֶרֶב וַתַּעַל הַשְּׂלָו – *That evening a flock of quail flew in:* God did not provide Israel with quail as a blessing, but in order to teach them that He Himself had heard their complaints. This was why the people were able to collect the birds effortlessly when the quail landed right at their feet. On the other hand, when God served the nation the manna, the Israelites had to go out to the fields to collect their breakfast. For that food was provided as a sign of God's graciousness and love, and therefore required human participation to bring it home.

VERSE 15

MALBIM

מָן הוּא – *What is it:* This was the Israelites' reaction when they first encountered the manna. Moshe had promised them that in the morning they would find food on the ground, so the people had no doubt that this new substance, which they had never seen before, was the bread that Moshe had alluded to. However, the people initially believed the manna to be akin to the grains they were familiar with – wheat and barley – which have to be winnowed and sorted from the chaff before they can be ground up and baked. Hence when the people said *man hu* they were stating that the material required processing to make it edible. For the term *man* suggests preparation, as in the verse *Who has appointed [minna] your food and your drink* (Daniel 1:10). Thereupon Moshe corrected Israel's impression of the food, saying: *This is the bread that the Lord has given you to eat.* The food is ready for consumption; all you have to do is collect the bread and eat it, with no preparation required.

VERSE 16

MALBIM

זֶה הַדָּבָר אֲשֶׁר צִוָּה יהוה – *This is what the Lord has instructed:* Israel should be aware that there are certain rules governing their appreciation of the new food. And these

10 Lord, because He has heard your railing." As soon as Aharon had spoken to the whole community of Israel, they looked toward the desert – and the glory of the Lord appeared in the midst of cloud.
11,12 The Lord spoke to Moshe and said, "I have heard the Israelites' railing. Tell them: At twilight you shall eat meat, and in the morning your fill of bread. Then you will know that I am
13 the Lord your God." That evening a flock of quail flew in and

SHISHI

VERSE 10

OR HAḤAYYIM

וַיְהִי כְּדַבֵּר אַהֲרֹן – *As soon as Aharon had spoken:* It was as if God was sitting and waiting for the people to turn and look toward Him.

RABBI SAMSON RAPHAEL HIRSCH

וַיְהִי כְּדַבֵּר אַהֲרֹן – *As soon as Aharon had spoken:* Whatever Moshe and Aharon had said to the nation until this point was all just preparation for the following speech of God. The point was to lay the groundwork for God's oration so that people would understand what He was about to tell them and learn the relevant lessons.

MALBIM

וַיְהִי כְּדַבֵּר אַהֲרֹן – *As soon as Aharon had spoken:* The speech that Aharon gave Israel was much longer than the brief statement he was instructed to convey to them. Aharon took the opportunity to deliver a lengthy rebuke, a castigation to which the people responded. Following that exchange, the nation *looked toward the desert.* For while the people were expressing their discontent regarding their condition in the wilderness, they had turned their backs to the offending environment in a physical demonstration of their desire to return to Egypt. Now however they redirected their attention to the place they found so distasteful and agreed to follow God wherever He may lead. That their repentance was accepted was visible through the symbol of God's manifestation *in the midst of cloud.* This was a sign that God was satisfied with Israel's contrition, similar to the divine response described in the verse *And Moshe said, This is the thing which the Lord commanded you to do: and the glory of the Lord shall appear to you* (Leviticus 9:6).

VERSE 12

HAAMEK DAVAR

וִידַעְתֶּם – *Then you will know:* Israel would no longer harbor any misconceptions about who their true savior was. Moshe had not independently effected the entire nation's release from slavery, against God's will. Rather, it was God Himself who took them out, and He was the One who would now satisfy their hunger.

VERSE 13

SHADAL

וַיְהִי בָעֶרֶב וַתַּעַל הַשְּׂלָו – *That evening a flock of quail flew in:* Selav is the Arabic term for the bird known in Latin as *coturnix,* and in Italian as *quaglia* [i.e., quail]. These birds commonly

י בְּנֵי יִשְׂרָאֵל קִרְבוּ לִפְנֵי יהוה כִּי שָׁמַע אֵת תְּלֻנֹּתֵיכֶם: וַיְהִי
כְּדַבֵּר אַהֲרֹן אֶל־כָּל־עֲדַת בְּנֵי־יִשְׂרָאֵל וַיִּפְנוּ אֶל־הַמִּדְבָּר
וְהִנֵּה כְּבוֹד יהוה נִרְאָה בֶּעָנָן:
יא ששי וַיְדַבֵּר יהוה אֶל־מֹשֶׁה לֵּאמֹר: שָׁמַעְתִּי אֶת־תְּלוּנֹּת בְּנֵי
יִשְׂרָאֵל דַּבֵּר אֲלֵהֶם לֵאמֹר בֵּין הָעַרְבַּיִם תֹּאכְלוּ בָשָׂר
וּבַבֹּקֶר תִּשְׂבְּעוּ־לָחֶם וִידַעְתֶּם כִּי אֲנִי יהוה אֱלֹהֵיכֶם:
יג וַיְהִי בָעֶרֶב וַתַּעַל הַשְּׂלָו וַתְּכַס אֶת־הַמַּחֲנֶה וּבַבֹּקֶר הָיְתָה

SHADAL

כִּי שָׁמַע אֵת תְּלֻנֹּתֵיכֶם — *Because He has heard your railing:* [This passage seems to repeat the substance of the passage immediately preceding. Shadal explains:] It seems that at first, when Moshe and Aharon told Israel: *At evening you will know that it was the Lord etc.* (16:6), the people refused to listen or cease their complaining. However, now that the Israelites witnessed the cloud appearing in the desert [in verse 10], they paid attention to what their leaders were promising them. It was then that Moshe assured them that God had *heard the Israelites railing.... At twilight you shall eat meat, and in the morning you fill of bread* (16:12). Even though the Torah nowhere reports that Moshe repeated this statement to his charges [only God's message to Moshe is recorded], the fact that God instructed His agent: *Tell them etc.* (16:12), leaves little doubt that Moshe proceeded to follow God's directions.

RABBI SAMSON RAPHAEL HIRSCH

כִּי שָׁמַע אֵת תְּלֻנֹּתֵיכֶם — *Because He has heard your railing:* God has already heard your complaints; he has no need for me to report our conversation to Him.

MALBIM

קִרְבוּ — *Come:* Moshe told the people to approach God, to return to a state of closeness to Him, since He comes close to those who seek Him. Since God had heard the people's complaints, they had to make the effort to come to Him and avoid creating a rift out of their discontent.

MESHEKH ḤOKHMA

וַיֹּאמֶר מֹשֶׁה אֶל־אַהֲרֹן — *Then Moshe said to Aharon:* It is certainly shocking that Moshe did not tell the people this himself. It is possible however that while Aharon addressed Israel, Moshe was busy preparing himself to commune with God. Had Moshe taken the time to speak with the nation, he would not have been ready to immediately converse with the Almighty. It is true that Moshe was in general able to receive divine communication on the spur of the moment, as the verse states: *And Moshe said to them, "Stand still, and I will hear what the Lord will command concerning you"* (Numbers 9:8). Nevertheless, according to the Rambam, writing in *Hilkhot Yesodei HaTorah* (7:6), Moshe only achieved this level of prophecy following the giving of the Torah. It was then that he separated from his wife in order to be constantly alert and available to receive God's message.

you railing against Him. As for us, what are we that you rail
8 against us?" Then Moshe said, "In the evening, the LORD will give you meat to eat, and in the morning bread to fill you, for He has heard you railing against Him. We – what are we? It
9 is not us you rail against, but the LORD." Then Moshe said to Aharon, "Tell all the community of Israel to come before the

---

RABBI SAMSON RAPHAEL HIRSCH (cont.)

way through the wilderness? Israel received bread from the sky daily! Any other person, indeed anyone slightly less impressive than Moshe, would have undoubtedly been unable to resist the temptation to self-aggrandizement over such a feat – but not Moshe. Our leader unequivocally and instinctively recoiled from such celebrity. Here, not only does he deflect the nation's complaints against him and his brother, telling the people that in truth, their quarrel is with God, for he and Aharon are but mere instruments in His hand; but he then takes his modesty one step further. By informing Israel: *In the evening, the LORD will give you meat to eat, and in the morning bread to fill you, for He has heard you railing against Him,* Moshe emphasizes that God is aware of Israel's complaints even without having conversed with Him. Moshe thereby teaches the people not only about the honor and the greatness of God, but that they are direct beneficiaries of his providence. This represents a confession by Moshe that as God's agent he is wholly dispensable, and that the nation could get along well enough without him and Aharon standing at their head. Indeed, Moshe would always measure the success of his mission by his ability to persuade the people that everything they experience should be credited to God directly, and that no human representative ever plays any part in the miracles or successes described in these stories.

MALBIM

וְנַחְנוּ מָה – *What are we:* This verse shows Moshe attempting to soften the bite of Israel's complaint by arguing that the nation was not really finding any fault with him or with Aharon. Instead, they were merely complaining about the dearth of food. As for the earlier statement in which the people are indeed said to attack the leaders [see 16:2], that was only Israel's attempt to persuade the men who were closest to God to petition Him on their behalf.

VERSE 9

OR HAḤAYYIM

וַיֹּאמֶר מֹשֶׁה אֶל־אַהֲרֹן – *Then Moshe said to Aharon:* It is possible that Moshe spoke these words to Aharon on the first day [i.e., the day before the manna first appeared], when Israel complained. On the other hand, it is also possible that the conversation took place on the following day. If that is the case, then the previous statement in verse 6, *At evening you will know that it was the LORD who brought you out of Egypt,* does not refer to the evening of the first day when the nation lodged their complaint [since, according to this understanding, the meat did not begin to appear on that day] but to evenings in general. For in contrast to the mornings when Israel would eat bread, meat would be served for dinner.

כְּבוֹד יהוה בְּשָׁמְעוֹ אֶת־תְּלֻנֹּתֵיכֶם עַל־יהוה וְנַחְנוּ מָה כִּי
תַלִּינוּ עָלֵינוּ: וַיֹּאמֶר מֹשֶׁה בְּתֵת יהוה לָכֶם בָּעֶרֶב בָּשָׂר תַלִּינוּ ח
לֶאֱכֹל וְלֶחֶם בַּבֹּקֶר לִשְׂבֹּעַ בִּשְׁמֹעַ יהוה אֶת־תְּלֻנֹּתֵיכֶם
אֲשֶׁר־אַתֶּם מַלִּינִם עָלָיו וְנַחְנוּ מָה לֹא־עָלֵינוּ תְלֻנֹּתֵיכֶם
כִּי עַל־יהוה: וַיֹּאמֶר מֹשֶׁה אֶל־אַהֲרֹן אֱמֹר אֶל־כָּל־עֲדַת ט

MALBIM *(cont.)*

14:31). The meaning of this verse starts with the assumption that God deserves our respect for providing food for every living being. For one could not imagine that God would put into this world some creature that He would then neglect to feed, creating a being that would know only suffering. That would hardly be honorable for God. Instead, whenever God impoverishes the destitute of this world, He empowers the wealthy to sustain them by instilling in them feelings of compassion and sympathy that move them to provide charity to the poor. For all rich people require servants and employees, and by filling these roles, the needy eagerly find their livelihoods. However, should a comfortable person mock the pauper by refusing to hire him or grant him a donation, that constitutes an affront of blasphemy against the Creator, tantamount to implying that He made the poor man go hungry. Conversely, should those who have been graced with sufficient money share their good fortune with the less secure, those philanthropists honor God, for it is to God's credit that He feeds all of His creations. Now this is why Moshe told the people that God had *heard you railing against Him,* for even though God would have been justified in ignoring such a rude assault – the people should have politely requested food – nevertheless, He acknowledged that it was His duty to feed the nation. From this perspective, Israel was correct to point out that God had not prepared meals for them in the wilderness, a neglect which appeared to dishonor Him.

VERSE 8

RABBI SAMSON RAPHAEL HIRSCH

וְנַחְנוּ מָה – *What are we:* This statement perfectly demonstrates the characterization of Moshe as the most humble man ever to walk the face of the earth [see Numbers 12:3]. Here was a man who requested nothing for himself, who sought not the slightest recognition for the job he did. Time and again, he excused the attacks hurled his way and ignored the ill treatment he received from the nation. For Moshe was only ever interested in being a loyal servant of God. Now imagine how any other prophet would react if a comparable statement to the following was said about him: *That caused His glorious arm to go to the right hand of Moshe, dividing the water before them, to make Himself an everlasting name* (Isaiah 63:12). Picture the monument such a man would construct to himself! At the very least, we would have expected Moshe to absorb a little of the blinding light that emanated from the miracle of the splitting of the sea. In other religions, men of faith are credited with performing miracles to provide bread for their people. But how can such a claim compare to the ongoing feeding of two and a half million souls for forty years as the nation trudged its

5 On the sixth day, they will have to prepare what they bring in.
6 It will be twice as much as they gather on all other days." So Moshe and Aharon told all the Israelites, "At evening you will
7 know that it was the LORD who brought you out of Egypt, and by morning you shall see the LORD's glory, for He has heard

VERSE 6

OR HAHAYYIM

עֶרֶב וִידַעְתֶּם – *At evening you will know:* Moshe predicted that Israel would gain this awareness following the evening's miracle [of meat], and not due to the morning's wonder [of the manna]. This was because in Israel's eyes, it seemed like a far greater challenge for God to provide them with meat than with bread.

MALBIM

עֶרֶב וִידַעְתֶּם – *At evening you will know:* The message in this verse may be explained with a metaphor. Consider a man who sets out to rescue his friend from mortal danger and takes along with him a gold crown to give him as a gift following the ordeal. Surely, the benefactor will first save his friend from peril, and only then bestow the present upon him. But if the liberator first tosses the crown to the victim, the latter can be assured that his savior has already seen to his deliverance. The same can be said here, when Israel lacked bread and believed they were at risk of starvation. God planned on providing them with the staple of bread, but also wanted to treat His nation with meat as an added delicacy. It would therefore have made sense for God to first deliver the necessary bread to the people, thereby staving off their hunger, and only then supply the meat as a luxury. And yet we see that God gave Israel meat in the evening, and followed it with manna only the next morning. This proved that really, the nation was never in any actual danger of dying. For God had planned well in advance of the exodus how exactly He would sustain Israel in the wilderness. God knew He was removing the Hebrews from the midst of a civilization where food was readily available and leading them into the desert where it was not. And if He had arranged for His people to eat bread and meat while they were still in Egypt, certainly He would continue to assure such necessities and luxuries in the wilderness. Hence God determined to serve Israel meat first, to show them that He had prepared everything for them, just as if they had still been in their original homes. And once they saw that meat had been given to them, they would have no doubt that bread was sure to come. This is what Moshe meant when he said: *At evening you will know that it was the LORD who brought you out of Egypt,* a statement that emphasized that it was not Moshe and Aharon who had effected Israel's release, but God Himself. He is the only being who can lay out a meal in the middle of the desert to rival any fare one might find in the city. The people would realize this when they received their first course of meat in the evening.

VERSE 7

MALBIM

בְּשָׁמְעוֹ אֶת־תְּלֻנֹּתֵיכֶם – *For He has heard you railing:* The wise man wrote: *He that oppresses the poor blasphemes his Maker: but he that honors Him is gracious to the poor* (Proverbs

ה לְמַעַן אֲנַסֶּנּוּ הֲיֵלֵךְ בְּתוֹרָתִי אִם־לֹא: וְהָיָה בַּיּוֹם הַשִּׁשִּׁי
וְהֵכִינוּ אֵת אֲשֶׁר־יָבִיאוּ וְהָיָה מִשְׁנֶה עַל אֲשֶׁר־יִלְקְטוּ יוֹם ׀
ו יוֹם: וַיֹּאמֶר מֹשֶׁה וְאַהֲרֹן אֶל־כָּל־בְּנֵי יִשְׂרָאֵל עֶרֶב וִידַעְתֶּם
ז כִּי יְהֹוָה הוֹצִיא אֶתְכֶם מֵאֶרֶץ מִצְרָיִם: וּבֹקֶר וּרְאִיתֶם אֶת־

MALBIM (cont.)
---

a population of manna-eaters. Furthermore, just as the manna that God served Israel had no inedible parts, nor any undigestible content features, similarly were the people who ate it devoid of material concerns and ugly physical desires. Rather, they were immersed in spirituality, and the passions of their souls always trumped the needs of their bodies. Thus God declared that the food He would provide would descend from heaven and be given them as long as they followed His laws and put their faith in His providence.

HAAMEK DAVAR

הִנְנִי מַמְטִיר לָכֶם – *I am going to rain down:* At this stage in the narrative, God does not yet state that He has *heard the Israelites' railing* (16:12), nor does He even reject the nation's complaint. This was because initially, the protest that the people were lodging was directed only at Moshe and Aharon, based on the people's perception of the leaders' mismanagement. To a certain degree, Israel could be forgiven their outburst, for one cannot blame a person for what he says in the heat of emotion, and people are driven to distraction by a hungry belly. Furthermore, the Hebrews' comment about the fleshpots was merely something that they imagined. Although here God did not want to rebuke Israel for asking for meat, it was nevertheless not the right time to give it to them, since their hearts were not really in it. If they had been sincere in their complaint, as the nation later was [see Numbers 11], they would have been accused of being ungrateful.

NEHAMA LEIBOWITZ

לְמַעַן אֲנַסֶּנּוּ – *I will test them:* The test of the manna exemplified the struggle of everyday life, the uncertainty of where one's next meal will come from. Such is the existence of an individual who lives hand to mouth. On the other hand, some commentators understand the desert era as one of leisure, when the Israelites did not have to strain themselves for a living or break a sweat to feed their families. During that period, the Israelites' meals were served to them on a silver platter, and they led carefree lives. But why would such circumstances be referred to as a test? Apparently, it really is difficult to go through one's days with no challenges.

VERSE 5

OR HAHAYYIM

וְהֵכִינוּ אֵת אֲשֶׁר־יָבִיאוּ – *They will have to prepare what they bring in:* [Wouldn't the Israelites always have to prepare what they brought in? Rather,] "bringing in" the manna back to their tents was itself part of the "preparations" the Israelites had to make before eating. On the sixth day, the nation would have to "prepare" [that is, bring in] excess manna, since they would not be able to collect any on the Sabbath.

of Israel all arrived at the desert of Sin, between Elim and Sinai. 2 In the desert, all the community started railing against Moshe 3 and Aharon. The Israelites said to them, "If only we had died by the LORD's hand in Egypt, when we sat by the fleshpots and ate our fill of bread. Instead, you have brought us out into this desert to kill the entire assembly by starvation." 4 Then the LORD said to Moshe, "I am going to rain down bread from heaven. Let the people go out and gather enough for each day; I will test them to see whether they will follow My law or not.

OR HAḤAYYIM (cont.)

The people who had "sat by the fleshpots" were the nation's elite, who disdained mere bread and who were accustomed to eating meat. Our verse mentions these people first because in any description of sinful groups, the smaller party is criticized before the larger. The text continues to quote those who claimed to have eaten their fill of bread during the oppression. They now saw themselves as having to trek through an uninhabited wilderness where bread would be impossible to procure. These people betrayed their lack of patience; they should have been able to wait for their Master to serve them food.

SHADAL

בְּשִׁבְתֵּנוּ עַל־סִיר הַבָּשָׂר – *When we sat by the fleshpots:* Elsewhere, the Torah describes the diet that Israel remembers as comprising *the fish, which we did eat in Egypt for nothing; the cucumbers, and the melons, and the leeks, and the onions, and the garlic* (Numbers 11:5) with no mention of meat whatsoever. According to Avraham Ḥai Mainster [one of Luzzatto's students] the menu mentioned in Numbers represents the foods that the Egyptians provided the Hebrews for free. But if an individual slave had owned herds of sheep and cattle, his wife would have brought him his own meat, which he would then cook at the worksite.

VERSE 4

RABBI SAMSON RAPHAEL HIRSCH

הֲיֵלֵךְ בְּתוֹרָתִי – *Whether they will follow My law:* True followers of the Torah must be content to provide themselves and their families with the daily minima of sustenance. They work as much as is required to eat for today, and do not overly concern themselves with tomorrow's meals, allowing God to worry about how they will feed their families the next day. These are people who trust that He who created today and the livelihood to see them through it will similarly fashion tomorrow and the provisions it requires. Only those who possess unconditional faith in God will be assured of not violating the Torah's laws out of fear — justified or imagined — for their physical needs.

MALBIM

וְלָקְטוּ דְּבַר־יוֹם בְּיוֹמוֹ – *Gather enough for each day:* The bread that would appear on the desert floor would require the minimal effort of being collected on a daily basis. And because no strenuous labor would be needed to feed their families, the Israelites would have plenty of available time to study Torah. Thus our Sages claim: The Torah was really only given for

בַּחֲמִשָּׁה עָשָׂר יוֹם לַחֹדֶשׁ הַשֵּׁנִי לְצֵאתָם מֵאֶרֶץ מִצְרָיִם:
ג וַיִּלּוֹנוּ כָּל־עֲדַת בְּנֵי־יִשְׂרָאֵל עַל־מֹשֶׁה וְעַל־אַהֲרֹן בַּמִּדְבָּר: וַיִּלּוֹנוּ
ג וַיֹּאמְרוּ אֲלֵהֶם בְּנֵי יִשְׂרָאֵל מִי־יִתֵּן מוּתֵנוּ בְיַד־יהוה בְּאֶרֶץ
מִצְרַיִם בְּשִׁבְתֵּנוּ עַל־סִיר הַבָּשָׂר בְּאָכְלֵנוּ לֶחֶם לָשֹׂבַע כִּי־
הוֹצֵאתֶם אֹתָנוּ אֶל־הַמִּדְבָּר הַזֶּה לְהָמִית אֶת־כָּל־הַקָּהָל
הַזֶּה בָּרָעָב: וַיֹּאמֶר יהוה אֶל־מֹשֶׁה הִנְנִי מַמְטִיר יב
לָכֶם לֶחֶם מִן־הַשָּׁמָיִם וְיָצָא הָעָם וְלָקְטוּ דְּבַר־יוֹם בְּיוֹמוֹ

VERSE 2

─── OR HAḤAYYIM ───

בַּמִּדְבָּר – *In the desert:* The verse emphasizes that Israel issued their complaints in the desert to point out that it was their arrival in the wilderness that provoked their dissatisfaction. For the people understood that they had bypassed a shorter route that would have led them to the land of Canaan, and that they were instead taking a detour into the desert. Now God had important motives in directing the nation's travels this way, but the people believed that it was Moshe's idea to take the circuitous path, for reasons known only to him.

─── MESHEKH ḤOKHMA ───

כָּל־עֲדַת בְּנֵי־יִשְׂרָאֵל – *All the community:* It was the mixed multitudes and the outside nations who had joined Israel in their escape from Egypt who instigated these complaints against Moshe and Aharon. This is clearly described later in Parashat Behaalotekha, where the verse states: *And the mixed multitude that was among them felt a lusting: and the children of Israel also wept again, and said, Who shall give us meat to eat?* (Numbers 11:4).

VERSE 3

─── OR HAḤAYYIM ───

בְּשִׁבְתֵּנוּ עַל־סִיר הַבָּשָׂר – *When we sat by the fleshpots:* This makes it clear that the people who were lodging their complaints against Moshe and Aharon had not themselves suffered beneath the lash in Egypt. Rather, they were the Israelite foremen who had been exempt from the actual labors of slavery. Meanwhile, the unfortunates who had had to endure the true burden of the exile had subsisted on the "bread of affliction" – they would not have reminisced about missing the fleshpots of Egypt. Alternatively, the speakers in this verse might have been the infamous wicked men Datan and Aviram [see Numbers

בְּאָכְלֵנוּ לֶחֶם לָשֹׂבַע – *And ate our fill of bread:* The verse mentions two different foods that the Israelites had apparently enjoyed in Egypt: meat and an abundance of bread to go with it. For the people would dip their bread in the stew and eat it that way. Alternatively, the phrase could be viewed as representing the demands of two different groups of people. When the text states that *all the community started railing against Moshe and Aharon* it does not suggest that the nation in its entirety began protesting against God and His prophet. Rather, one faction of malcontents desired meat while another pined for bread.

water became sweet. It was there that the Lord gave His people decree and law; it was there that He put them to the test. 26 He said, "If you listen faithfully to the voice of the Lord your God, doing what is right in His eyes, heeding His commands and keeping His decrees, I will not bring on you any of the sicknesses I brought on the Egyptians, for I am the Lord – your 27 Healer." And then they arrived at Elim, where there were twelve springs and seventy date palms. They encamped 16 1 there by the water. They set out from Elim, and on the fifteenth day of the second month after leaving Egypt, the congregation

ḤAMISHI

HAAMEK DAVAR *(cont.)*

to show the people the progression of their fortunes and the relationship between living a life of Torah and one's material wellbeing. For at Mara, Moshe introduced to his people the notion that a life devoted to the Torah implies being satisfied with limited luxuries. Still, such a circumstance of want is only necessary at the start of one's career in Torah learning. Once a person achieves success in this area, he is likely to warrant a richer lifestyle. Thus we read in the first chapter of tractate Avoda Zara (19b): When an individual occupies himself with the Torah, his possessions prosper. Hence, at Mara, Israel was introduced to the Torah in an environment of deprivation and minimal amenities. But subsequently, after having spent time studying the Torah at Elim, they enjoyed the wealth of water and fruit that that location provided. Dates symbolize the richness of Torah, as the Talmud states: Ulla happened to be in Babylonia. Seeing that a basket of dates sold for a *zuz*, he exclaimed:

These Babylonian Jews can buy a basket of honey for a *zuz* and yet they do not occupy themselves with Torah! [That is, even though food is cheap, the community does not take advantage of its good fortune to spend time studying.] Such a correlation is also apparent in the secular working world. For when a person's livelihood depends on toiling the ground, he will never achieve the honor and stature that he can if he works his way up through the ranks of the army. Consider the cadet who begins his life in the military: The common soldier begins with a meager stipend, and as he is promoted he garners greater salary and respect. Likewise, an individual who gains knowledge of the Torah receives prestige and wealth corresponding to his accomplishments. This is what God demonstrated to Israel as they began their commitment to living by the Torah. This message would inform all future generations of Jews.

CHAPTER **16**, VERSE 1
RABBI SAMSON RAPHAEL HIRSCH

עֲדַת בְּנֵי־יִשְׂרָאֵל – *The congregation of Israel:* The term "congregation," used to describe the nation in this verse, is meant to portray Israel at its most exalted level – a people united in a common purpose. This goal was to fulfill their destiny as a community of God worthy of being called a "congregation." The fact that the Torah employs this term so early in Israel's national history alerts us to the importance of upcoming events in establishing the foundation for the burgeoning people of Israel.

שָׁם לוֹ חֹק וּמִשְׁפָּט וְשָׁם נִסָּהוּ: וַיֹּאמֶר אִם־שָׁמוֹעַ תִּשְׁמַע כּוּ
לְקוֹל ׀ יְהֹוָה אֱלֹהֶיךָ וְהַיָּשָׁר בְּעֵינָיו תַּעֲשֶׂה וְהַאֲזַנְתָּ לְמִצְוֺתָיו
וְשָׁמַרְתָּ כָּל־חֻקָּיו כָּל־הַמַּחֲלָה אֲשֶׁר־שַׂמְתִּי בְמִצְרַיִם
לֹא־אָשִׂים עָלֶיךָ כִּי אֲנִי יְהֹוָה רֹפְאֶךָ: וַיָּבֹאוּ כּוּ חמישי
אֵילִמָה וְשָׁם שְׁתֵּים עֶשְׂרֵה עֵינֹת מַיִם וְשִׁבְעִים תְּמָרִים
וַיַּחֲנוּ־שָׁם עַל־הַמָּיִם: וַיִּסְעוּ מֵאֵילִם וַיָּבֹאוּ כָּל־עֲדַת טז א
בְּנֵי־יִשְׂרָאֵל אֶל־מִדְבַּר־סִין אֲשֶׁר בֵּין־אֵילִם וּבֵין סִינָי

VERSE 26

OR HAḤAYYIM

רֹפְאֶךָ — *Your Healer:* [If, as the verse claims, God would not inflict any sickness on the Israelites, why would He need to "heal" them? In fact,] this offer relates to illnesses that the Israelites might contract through natural means, not those sent from heaven. Thus do our Sages, of blessed memory teach: Everything is within the hands of heaven save [illness caused by] cold and heat. Hence God guarantees Israel that even if they fall prey to some malady that He has not inflicted upon them, He will heal that too.

RABBI SAMSON RAPHAEL HIRSCH

וְשָׁמַרְתָּ כָּל־חֻקָּיו — *Keeping His decrees:* There is a dual significance to the Torah's usage of the verb "keeping" [*shimmur*] in connection with God's laws. God has given us His laws and instructed us to guard them like a treasure, and such a guardianship has two facets: First, Israel must spread the word of the Torah by studying its particulars. For if laws remain unfamiliar to the people who are meant to observe them, they will quickly be forgotten and abandoned, like a pledge which cannot be returned to its owner. Second, if the nation is to be attentive in observing the laws in its daily life, it will construct measures to protect the system and prevent violation of the statutes. These man-made restrictions are meant as precautions to "keep" God's Torah safe from infractions. The laws whose observance most requires such precautions are those rules which govern our physical desires and passions of the heart. These are the rules most in danger of neglect.

VERSE 27

HAAMEK DAVAR

וְשָׁם שְׁתֵּים עֶשְׂרֵה עֵינֹת מַיִם — *Where there were twelve springs:* The Torah informs us that God prepared the site in advance of Israel's arrival. This we learn in the Mekhilta, cited by the Ramban: Rabbi Elazar HaModa'i taught: When the Holy One, blessed be He, created His world, He dug twelve springs on behalf of the twelve tribes of Israel and planted seventy date palms corresponding to the seventy elders in the nation. What does the Torah mean by stating that Israel "encamped there by the water"? It implies that at that campsite, the people were engaged in studying the Torah that they were given at Mara. Now there is no doubt that Israel traveled to Elim immediately following the ordeal at Mara in order

22 He hurled into the sea. Moshe then led the Israelites from the Sea of Reeds out into the desert of Shur. For three days, they journeyed across the desert without finding water.
23 Eventually they came to Mara, but they could not drink the water there because it was bitter; because of this it was named
24 Mara. The people railed against Moshe – "What are we to
25 drink?" Moshe cried out to the Lord. And the Lord showed him a piece of wood, which he threw into the water – and the

---
VERSE 24
OR HAHAYYIM

וַיִּלֹּנוּ הָעָם – *The people railed:* The choice of verb here implies that Israel's statement was not merely a question of information – "What shall we drink?" – it was an attack against Moshe. Had the people simply asked their leader how they were to proceed, God would not have held them to account.

MALBIM

וַיִּלֹּנוּ הָעָם – *The people railed:* The appropriate response to the Israelites' predicament would have been for the people to pray to God to provide them with water. Instead, the nation converged on Moshe, a sign that they were still immature.

VERSE 25
RABBI SAMSON RAPHAEL HIRSCH

וְשָׁם נִסָּהוּ – *It was there that He put them to the test:* The exodus from Egypt and the splitting of the sea proved to Israel then and for all time that God brings Himself close to Israel during times of exceptional necessity. And yet, during the nation's travels through the wilderness, they should have learned to trust in God under all conditions, including for the satisfaction of their ordinary daily needs. For certainly, the regular and unexceptional tasks of daily living are not too small to be excluded from God's providence. Know that God is constantly aware of His creatures' conditions and requirements. Every breath we take is monitored by God's eternal watchfulness.

HAAMEK DAVAR

וְשָׁם נִסָּהוּ – *It was there that He put them to the test:* The lesson of this episode was geared toward all future generations. God wanted to condition Israel to learn not to panic should they ever experience want in their households. A later verse refers to this process as a test: *That He might afflict you, and that he might test you, to do you good at your latter end* (Deuteronomy 8:16). Now the first generation of Israelites did not need to be taught about God's direct providence, as they saw His helping hand constantly. However, future eras of Jews would not benefit from such open displays of God's involvement in their lives. Hence they would have to be taught to trust that in the last moment God will always save them from starvation or dying of thirst. This was demonstrated at Mara, where God saved the people by introducing Moshe to a certain piece of wood which sweetened the waters and saved the Israelites' lives.

כב לַיהוָה כִּי־גָאֹה גָּאָה סוּס וְרֹכְבוֹ רָמָה בַיָּם: וַיַּסַּ֤ע
מֹשֶׁ֨ה אֶת־יִשְׂרָאֵל֙ מִיַּם־ס֔וּף וַיֵּצְא֖וּ אֶל־מִדְבַּר־שׁ֑וּר וַיֵּלְכ֧וּ
כג שְׁלֹ֣שֶׁת־יָמִ֛ים בַּמִּדְבָּ֖ר וְלֹא־מָ֥צְאוּ מָֽיִם: וַיָּבֹ֣אוּ מָרָ֔תָה וְלֹ֣א
יָֽכְלוּ֙ לִשְׁתֹּ֤ת מַ֨יִם֙ מִמָּרָ֔ה כִּ֥י מָרִ֖ים הֵ֑ם עַל־כֵּ֥ן קָרָֽא־שְׁמָ֖הּ
כד מָרָֽה: וַיִּלֹּ֧נוּ הָעָ֛ם עַל־מֹשֶׁ֖ה לֵּאמֹ֑ר מַה־נִּשְׁתֶּֽה: וַיִּצְעַ֣ק אֶל־
כה יְהוָ֗ה וַיּוֹרֵ֤הוּ יְהוָה֙ עֵ֔ץ וַיַּשְׁלֵךְ֙ אֶל־הַמַּ֔יִם וַֽיִּמְתְּק֖וּ הַמָּ֑יִם שָׁ֣ם

VERSE 22

MALBIM

וְלֹא־מָצְאוּ מָיִם — *Without finding water:* The Israelites expected to find a miraculous source of drinking water just like during the crossing of the sea when God provided the people with sweet water from the depths of the ocean to sustain them. Although they thought that such a wonder would surely be repeated in the wilderness, no miracle made itself apparent. This was because when God divided the sea on Israel's behalf, He opened His trove of wonders and miracles in the process, thereby facilitating the additional service of potable water. However, once the waves had closed, the storehouse of miracles was also shut, and Israel unfortunately lacked the merits that would warrant new wonders. Additionally, preparations for the giving of the Torah had already begun, and it was crucial that in advance of the revelation Israel be tested and taught that they are always dependent on God. Therefore God initially allowed Israel to experience the hardship of the desert, where water is nearly impossible to locate.

VERSE 23

HAKETAV VEHAKABBALA

עַל־כֵּן קָרָא־שְׁמָהּ מָרָה — *Because of this it was named Mara:* The reader might have thought that the name *Mara* [meaning "bitter," but also "rebelled"] was chosen to reflect Israel's rebellion against God, as in the verse *It was the man of God who was disobedient [mara] to the word of the Lord* (I Kings 13:26). For here the Israelites revolted against Moshe and angered him with their criticisms. After all, we find a subsequent location called *Masa* ["Test"] and *Meriva* ["Quarrel"] *because the people had quarreled and had tested the Lord* (17:7), in a seeming parallel to the current circumstance. Hence the text emphasizes that the site's name refers in fact to the bitterness of its water. It would have been inappropriate to immortalize Israel's complaint by naming the place after their displeasure, since the people immediately repented for their ingratitude and prayed to God.

HAAMEK DAVAR

וְלֹא יָכְלוּ לִשְׁתֹּת מַיִם — *But they could not drink the water:* As soon as the Israelites saw the abundance of water at this place, they wanted to drink their fill and enjoy themselves. But once they found that the water was undrinkable, they were unable to control their disappointment.

for Your dwelling, / the sanctuary, Lord, that Your hands established. / The Lord will reign for ever and all time. / This ¹⁸ ¹⁹ they sang when Pharaoh's horses, chariots, and cavalry had gone into the sea / and the Lord had brought the waters of the sea back over them / while the Israelites had walked on dry land through the sea.

²⁰ Then Miriam, the prophetess, sister of Aharon, took a tambourine in her hand, and all the women followed her with tambourines and dance. And Miriam led them in song: Sing to the ²¹ Lord, for He has triumphed in glory; / horse and horseman

VERSE 20

SHADAL

וּבִמְחֹלֹת – *And dance:* Most gentile Bible scholars, including Rosenmueller and Gesenius, believe that the word *meḥola* denotes a dance, and Mendelssohn agrees with them. However, several scriptural verses prove that this is the name of a musical instrument, just like the term *tof*.

RABBI SAMSON RAPHAEL HIRSCH

אֲחוֹת אַהֲרֹן – *Sister of Aharon:* The Torah compares Miriam's standing among the Israelite women to Aharon's reputation among the nation's men. For just as it was Aharon's responsibility to convey Moshe's pronouncements to the menfolk, so was Miriam tasked with spreading the word of the prophet to the women.

MALBIM

אֲחוֹת אַהֲרֹן – *Sister of Aharon:* Miriam is referred to here as the sister of Aharon [and not that of her more famous brother, Moshe], because she had begun prophesying when she was still just the sister of Aharon, before Moshe was born. It was then that the young girl predicted that her pregnant mother would give birth to Israel's savior and redeemer. Now that the words of the prophetess Miriam had finally come true [for Moshe the deliverer had now completely freed the Israelites], she *took a tambourine in her hand*.

VERSE 21

RABBI SAMSON RAPHAEL HIRSCH

וַתַּעַן לָהֶם מִרְיָם – *And Miriam led them in song:* Why is the objective pronoun *lahem* ["them"] in the masculine form, considering that Miriam was leading the nation's women? Perhaps the text teaches that although the women's participation in the song of gratitude followed that of the men, they stood as equals in their appreciation of God and in their ability to express the exalted national mission that is the substance of the poem.

MALBIM

וַתַּעַן לָהֶם מִרְיָם – *And Miriam led them in song:* The women knew that the salvation of Israel had been effected due to their merit, and so they formed their own special chorus.

יָדֶיךָ: יְהוָה ׀ יִמְלֹךְ לְעֹלָם וָעֶד: כִּי
בָא סוּס פַּרְעֹה בְּרִכְבּוֹ וּבְפָרָשָׁיו בַּיָּם וַיָּשֶׁב יְהוָה עֲלֵהֶם אֶת־מֵי
הַיָּם וּבְנֵי יִשְׂרָאֵל הָלְכוּ בַיַּבָּשָׁה בְּתוֹךְ הַיָּם:

וַתִּקַּח מִרְיָם הַנְּבִיאָה אֲחוֹת אַהֲרֹן אֶת־הַתֹּף בְּיָדָהּ וַתֵּצֶאןָ
כָל־הַנָּשִׁים אַחֲרֶיהָ בְּתֻפִּים וּבִמְחֹלֹת: וַתַּעַן לָהֶם מִרְיָם שִׁירוּ

VERSE 18

SHADAL

לְעֹלָם וָעֶד – *For ever and all time:* God will be Israel's king; they will serve Him, follow His statutes, and accept Him as their monarch in place of a human king. Indeed, the Torah essentially does not support the institution of monarchy for the nation of Israel [see e.g., I Samuel 10:18-19]. Additionally, this verse alludes to the ideal future when God will be recognized as the true ruler over the entire universe. At that time the Lord will be one and His name one.

RABBI SAMSON RAPHAEL HIRSCH

לְעֹלָם וָעֶד – *For ever and all time:* This verse holds two possible interpretations. On the one hand, the text might be promising that God's rule in this world will be eternally apparent. Just as the might of God was revealed in an indisputable manner at the sea, so would He continue to dominate the world from now on. Alternatively, the verse might refer to the distant future, meaning that there will come a time when all of humanity will accept God's undeniable supremacy.

MALBIM

לְעֹלָם וָעֶד – *For ever and all time:* God's reign over the world will be characterized by supernatural providential involvement. The rules of nature have no limiting power over God's will. For He will direct His actions from within the Temple – it is from there that He will rule over His creations.

VERSE 19

HAAMEK DAVAR

כִּי בָא סוּס פַּרְעֹה – *When Pharaoh's horses had gone:* [The phrase "this they sang" is absent from the original Hebrew. Hence] the nature of this verse is unclear: Does it represent the last statement of the song, or is it a return to the narrative telling of the story? If the latter, the verse serves to summarize the event and to explain what led Israel to compose the song of praise to God. In truth, our verse relates back to the previous sentence, *The Lord will reign for ever and all time* (15:18), a prophecy of messianic times. It is well known that when that era begins, the widescale justice that will be administered will reach Israel as well. The anticipation of such a reckoning made the Sages so anxious that Ulla and other Sages declared: Let the Messiah come, but let me not be there to see it! Hence, because the judgment described in the previous verse foreshadows the ultimate reign of God, this verse reassures Israel that they will not be washed away by God's judgment as the Egyptians were.

16 the people of Canaan melted away. / Dread, terror fell upon them; / by Your arm's power they were stilled as stone – / until Your people crossed, LORD, / until the people You acquired
17 crossed over. / You will bring them, You will plant them on the mountain, Your heritage – / the place, LORD, that You made

---
MALBIM (cont.)

Your heritage. This will take place during the seven years of conquest and the seven years of settlement in the land of Israel. The metaphor in this verse might be elaborated to describe a man who wishes to plant a precious and spry sapling. He chooses to root his tree on a hill of fertile soil, hoping that the location will yield rich and delicious fruit. So did God decide to plant His vine on the mountain of His heritage, a place conducive to holiness, prophecy, and divine inspiration. מָכוֹן לְשִׁבְתְּךָ – *The place for your dwelling:* Are not the heavens usually referred to as the place where God lives? We find such a label several times in King Shlomo's prayer, e.g., *Then hear their prayer and their supplication in heaven, Your dwelling place* (I Kings 8:49). The Temple too is considered a place where God dwells, but there is a difference between the two domains. For the heavens is where God is situated, and it is from there that He controls nature and the laws of the universe that He first formed during the six days of creation. Meanwhile, the Temple represents the source of the supernatural miracles and wonders that God performs. Now allow me to explain the difference between the verbs *maaseh* and *peula* [both meaning "make" or "do"; the latter verb appears in this verse]. The term *maaseh* represents a complete task, whereas a *peula* signifies a continuous or occasional activity. The fixed laws of nature fall within the category of *maaseh* because God completed them during the six days of creation. This is the sort of job that God directs from His abode in the heavens. On the other hand, the divine intervention that God performs through miracles is a *peula* because these wonders are not an established fixture of the world – they are executed only when the need for them arises. Hence, we can understand the relevance of *peula* to the "dwelling place" mentioned in this verse. For until this point, God had only the heavenly abode which is the source of His *maasim*. But now He would have a dwelling from which to perform His *peulot* as well – the miracles that God plans for the world, which would be unfettered by the laws of nature. Our verse continues to identify the Temple as a "sanctuary of the Lord" [*mikdash Adonai*] meaning a structure erected in God's name. The message conveyed from this site would be that God is the master of the universe and can bend it to His will. It is a sanctuary *that Your hands established,* in contrast to His celestial dwelling, where God rules with a single hand [since nature has been programmed to run in an orderly, regular way]. The actions that emanate from the Temple would be performed by both of God's hands because their character would be somewhat dependent on the behavior of mankind. Since human beings exercise their free will with both their right and left hand, representing wise choices and foolish decisions, God too employs both of His hands in response to what humanity does. Regarding this point, our Sages write: The actions of the righteous are greater than the creation of heaven and earth. For God fashioned the world with one hand, whereas here the verse states: *The sanctuary, Lord, that Your hands established.*

טז כָּל־יֹשְׁבֵי כְנָעַן: תִּפֹּל עֲלֵיהֶם אֵימָתָה
וָפַחַד בִּגְדֹל זְרוֹעֲךָ יִדְּמוּ כָּאָבֶן עַד־
יַעֲבֹר עַמְּךָ יהוה עַד־יַעֲבֹר עַם־זוּ
יז קָנִיתָ: תְּבִאֵמוֹ וְתִטָּעֵמוֹ בְּהַר נַחֲלָתְךָ מָכוֹן
לְשִׁבְתְּךָ פָּעַלְתָּ יהוה מִקְּדָשׁ אֲדֹנָי כּוֹנְנוּ

SHADAL

אַלּוּפֵי אֱדוֹם – *The chiefs of Edom:* [This seems to clash with Edom's defiance of Israel in Numbers 20:14–21.] It seems to me that the chieftains mentioned here were not subservient to the reigning king of Edom and had rebelled against him. Or perhaps these warlords had never all accepted the rule of a single monarch, and some of them ruled smaller states alongside the king who controlled the broader realm of Edom. And so, while the powerful king of Edom was not at all intimidated by Israel's appearance on the political landscape and met them at his border with an extensive army, the "children of Esav" were afraid of their distant Israelite cousins [see Deuteronomy 2:4].

RABBI SAMSON RAPHAEL HIRSCH

אֵילֵי מוֹאָב – *Moav's leaders:* The rulers of Moav are referred to as *elim*, which denotes powerful and rich men. The Moabites were most proud of their land for the wealth it produced on their behalf. In addition, they were infrequently bothered by the travails of war. But now the upper class of this state began to fear that their comfortable life was in jeopardy, that their riches might be seized by the menace arising from the south.

VERSE 16

RABBI SAMSON RAPHAEL HIRSCH

אֵימָתָה וָפַחַד – *Dread, terror:* The term *eima* denotes the dread that a person feels when in the presence of an overwhelmingly powerful force. *Pahad*, on the other hand, implies the fear of imminent danger. All of the neighboring peoples acknowledged the might and the greatness of God that had suddenly appeared in their midst; they thus experienced *eima*. But they also were terrified of the implications of God's revelation and what they expected might happen to them [hence *pahad*].

VERSE 17

RABBI SAMSON RAPHAEL HIRSCH

בְּהַר נַחֲלָתְךָ – *The mountain, Your heritage:* God was not bringing Israel to a land that belonged to them, but to a territory that was essentially His. Hence when they arrived there, the Israelites' goal in settling and developing that country would be solely for the glorification of God.

MALBIM

תְּבִאֵמוֹ – *You will bring them:* "Your arm's power" will cause the Canaanites' hearts to be "stilled as stone" (15:16) when You bring Israel to the land and *plant them on the mountain,*

12 / awesome in glory, working wonders? / You reached out Your
13 right hand – / the earth swallowed them up. / In Your love, You guided out the people You redeemed. / In Your strength, You
14 led them to Your holy abode. / Nations heard and they trem-
15 bled; / terror seized the Philistines. / The chiefs of Edom were dismayed, then, / Moav's leaders were seized with trembling, /

MALBIM

אֶל־נְוֵה קָדְשֶׁךָ – *To Your holy abode:* You directed the nation to the land that would serve as Your holy abode. That is where Your holiness dwells, where your providential guidance is seen most clearly, and the location from which sanctity will emanate.

VERSE 14

SHADAL

שָׁמְעוּ עַמִּים יִרְגָּזוּן – *Nations heard and they trembled:* Moshe's song initially mentions those countries whom Israel would first encounter on their travels on their way to Canaan. Subsequently, it describes the inhabitants of Canaan itself, who would be forced out of their homes by the invading Israelites. A successful invasion of the promised land would require first that the neighboring states be swiftly dispatched. For if the people of Philistia, Edom, and Moav were suitably terrified of the encroaching Hebrews, they would not inhibit their progress with unnecessary battles. After that, it would make Israel's task easier if the Canaanites too were afraid of them, for that lack of morale would facilitate their defeat. It is with respect to the first three peoples [the Philistines, Edom, and Moav] that the text states: *They were stilled as stone – until Your people crossed* [15:16; i.e., before Israel crossed the Jordan]. In defiance of the Canaanites themselves, the verse states: *You will bring them [Israel], You will plant them on the mountain* (15:17).

MALBIM

שָׁמְעוּ עַמִּים יִרְגָּזוּן – *Nations heard and they trembled:* The surrounding nations were sure to hear of God's mighty actions at the sea, and this would cause them to tremble with fear. These states would then be terrified to confront Israel. *Terror seized the Philistines* and the chiefs of Edom and Moav *were seized with trembling* (15:15), for their territories bordered the land of Israel. Similarly, that verse continues, all the courage of *the people of Canaan melted away.*

VERSE 15

OR HAHAYYIM

אָז נִבְהֲלוּ אַלּוּפֵי אֱדוֹם – *The chiefs of Edom were dismayed, then:* The word "then" suggests that the Edomites' fear was not of an Israelite invasion into their homeland at that time [which was forbidden by God; see Deuteronomy 2:4–5], but rather relates to a different, future era. In fact, the Edomites' terror is reserved for the arrival of the Messiah. A later verse similarly states [as part of Bilam's prophecies]: *And Edom shall be his possession* [Numbers 24:18, referring to a future conquest of Edom by Israel]. In that future time, Israel will also be allowed to conquer the lands of Moav and Amon [which were currently proscribed; see Deuteronomy 2:9–10, 19].

יג פֶּלֶא: נָטִיתָ יְמִינְךָ תִּבְלָעֵמוֹ אָרֶץ: נָחִיתָ
בְחַסְדְּךָ עַם־זוּ גָּאָלְתָּ נֵהַלְתָּ בְעָזְּךָ אֶל־נְוֵה
יד קָדְשֶׁךָ: שָׁמְעוּ עַמִּים יִרְגָּזוּן חִיל
טו אָחַז יֹשְׁבֵי פְּלָשֶׁת: אָז נִבְהֲלוּ אַלּוּפֵי
אֱדוֹם אֵילֵי מוֹאָב יֹאחֲזֵמוֹ רָעַד נָמֹגוּ

MALBIM (cont.)

universe; rather, He fashioned the world and then left it to its own devices. But we say to the nations of the world: *Let them give glory to the* LORD *and declare His praise on the islands* (Isaiah 42:12). God is responsible for conducting the world unceasingly; it is He who sustains us all. God acts with righteousness, compassion, and justice. And not only does He deserve all our gratitude and praise for this, but He is "awesome in glory" – capable of creating wonders that overrule the laws of nature. It is those miracles which most obviously demonstrate God's glory, for not only did He create the entire world, not only does he see to its normal functioning, but He can manipulate His works for His own purposes.

VERSE 12

SHADAL

נָטִיתָ יְמִינְךָ – *You reached out Your right hand:* God waved His hand like a master beckoning his servants. Thus did the earth rush to do God's bidding, just as a faithful servant would, and "swallowed up" His enemies.

RABBI SAMSON RAPHAEL HIRSCH

נָטִיתָ יְמִינְךָ – *You reached out Your right hand:* God stretched out His right hand to assist us, and the earth swallowed up the Egyptians. In a single sentence, the text summarizes the miracle the world witnessed upon the revelation of God's providence. For at one and the same time He effected our salvation and their destruction – both were achieved with the same act.

VERSE 13

SHADAL

אֶל־נְוֵה קָדְשֶׁךָ – *To Your holy abode:* According to Rashbam, this term refers to the land of Canaan. It is called God's "abode" because it is the place where He is to be worshipped. Traditionally, God is said to dwell in any location where people serve Him.

RABBI SAMSON RAPHAEL HIRSCH

נָחִיתָ בְחַסְדְּךָ – *In Your love, You guided:* God's redemption of Israel from slavery and torment was primarily an act of justice, but His continued guidance of the people toward their goal was an expression of love, i.e., caring for another out of sheer empathy. Israel's purpose was not simply to take possession of a fruitful land, but to settle and create a country that was a "holy abode" for God; a place which promoted His absolute rule.

9 heart of the sea. / The enemy said, "I will give chase, will overtake, / I will divide the spoils. / My desire shall gorge its fill of them. / I will draw my sword, / and my hand destroy them." /
10 You blew with Your wind; the sea covered over them. / They
11 sank like lead in mighty waters. / Who is like You, Lord, among the mighty? / Who is like You – majestic in holiness,

VERSE 10

SHADAL

צָלֲלוּ כַּעוֹפֶרֶת – *They sank like lead:* Lead falls rapidly through water because of its density and quickly sinks out of sight.

HAAMEK DAVAR

נָשַׁפְתָּ בְרוּחֲךָ – *You blew with Your wind:* [The term "Your wind" – *ruḥakha* – is singular.] God employed a single wind to cover the Egyptians with the sea, thereby upending all their boasts and plans. צָלֲלוּ כַּעוֹפֶרֶת – *They sank like lead:* God did not require very much effort to send the Egyptians to their doom as one would when trying to sink something light.

VERSE 11

RABBI SAMSON RAPHAEL HIRSCH

נֶאְדָּר בַּקֹּדֶשׁ – *Majestic in holiness:* The concept of holiness denotes a state whereby something enjoys a completely free existence. Such an entity is not dependent on any external force; it is totally independent in will and action. In essence, true holiness can only be ascribed to God, whereas people or things that are said to be "holy to the Lord" possess only a relative degree of independence. Such a person or object is severed from all things except God, before whom he or it stands ready to serve. It may be said that the term "holiness," when applied to a human being, refers to his highest possible state of moral freedom. It is in such a state that the person is not bound to any desires or passions which might prevent him from fulfilling God's will.

MALBIM

בָּאֵלִם – *Among the mighty:* The term *elim* refers to powerful natural forces, as in the verse *Ascribe to the Lord, O you mighty [benei elim], ascribe to the Lord glory and strength* (Psalms 29:1). Thus our verse proclaims that no one can compare to God among all the world's mighty powers. *Who is like You – majestic in holiness?* The concept of holiness signifies God's distinction and transcendence of the laws of nature that govern the world – a vast gulf separates Him from all spheres of the physical. Nevertheless, He remains "awesome in glory." Now philosophers too argue that God is above and beyond the entire world, but according to those thinkers, this results in God being alienated from His creations. Therefore, they say, human obligation is limited to acknowledging God's role in fashioning the world, but not to praising Him for continued involvement in human or natural affairs. For there is no divine providence and no hand of God intervening in the running of the

אוֹיֵב אָרְדֹּף אַשִּׂיג אֲחַלֵּק שָׁלָל תִּמְלָאֵמוֹ נַפְשִׁי אָרִיק חַרְבִּי תּוֹרִישֵׁמוֹ יָדִי: נָשַׁפְתָּ בְרוּחֲךָ כִּסָּמוֹ יָם צָלֲלוּ כַּעוֹפֶרֶת בְּמַיִם אַדִּירִים: מִי־כָמֹכָה בָּאֵלִם יהוה מִי כָּמֹכָה נֶאְדָּר בַּקֹּדֶשׁ נוֹרָא תְהִלֹּת עֹשֵׂה

VERSE 9

OR HAḤAYYIM

אֲחַלֵּק שָׁלָל — *I will divide the spoils:* The enemy planned to abuse Israel in three ways upon overtaking them. First, they would claim Israel's possessions and divide the spoils equally amongst themselves. Then they would return their former slaves to bondage, as expressed in the phrase *My desire shall gorge its fill of them,* i.e., they wanted to take the people themselves and not just their property. This clause betrays their desire to bring their oppression of the Israelites down to depths not previously reached. The third goal of this pursuit was to put Moshe, Aharon, and all of Israel's elders and leaders to the sword. Thus they stated: *I will draw my sword.* Regarding Moshe himself, the Egyptian army vowed: *And my hand destroy them,* echoing the sentiment first expressed in the verse *Word reached Pharaoh and he sought to kill Moshe* (2:15). Early on, the king had attempted to have Moshe killed, but his neck proved impervious to the executioner's sword, as Moshe proclaimed: *My father's God has helped me, saving me from Pharaoh's sword* (18:4). Hence the Egyptians were eager for another attempt to defeat Moshe by unsheathing their swords and attacking the neck that had eluded them earlier.

RABBI SAMSON RAPHAEL HIRSCH

אָרְדֹּף אַשִּׂיג אֲחַלֵּק שָׁלָל — *I will give chase, will overtake, I will divide the spoils:* The song as a whole seems to describe the story of the Egyptians' destruction backward. The poem presents the most dramatic and significant stage of the narrative first, even though it happened last. Thus the passage opens with the verse *Horse and horseman He hurled into the sea* (15:1). After recounting that achievement, the text praises God as *a Master of war* (15:3), who humbles all enemies before Him. After all, Pharaoh's army was drowned in the depths of the sea because they declared themselves to be enemies of God and opponents of humanity. Thus did the Almighty command the very depths to pile themselves up to create a passageway for Israel's salvation. When they glimpsed this new road, the enemy sought to use it for himself to charge toward victory and fulfill his dastardly plans. For the pursuer viewed this sudden appearance of a route through the sea as a natural phenomenon that could serve him just as well as his quarry. Note that the Egyptians are referred to in this verse as *oyev* without the definite article *ha* [literally, the phrase should be translated: "An enemy said, etc."]. This teaches us that it was not just this particular foe who doubted God's ability to control nature and bend it to His will — all detractors of God deny His power to use the world's forces in the pursuit of justice.

5 drowned in the Sea of Reeds. / The deep waters covered them; /
6 they sank to the depths like a stone. / Your right hand, Lord, majestic in power,/ Your right hand, Lord, shatters the ene-
7 my. / In the greatness of Your majesty, You overthrew those who rose against You. / You sent forth Your rage; it consumed them
8 like stubble. / By the blast of Your nostrils the waters heaped; / the surge stood upright as a wall; / the deeps congealed at the

---

MALBIM

תַּהֲרֹס קָמֶיךָ – *You overthrew those who rose against You:* [The verb *taharos* is typically used in the sense of demolishing structures.] This phrase refers to those who delude themselves into challenging God in war. When an army forms its battle lines, it sets its soldiers up like a brick wall with the components pressed close together. Should the line not hold – if its men break formation and begin to flee – that is akin to a building being overthrown and demolished. This is the sense of the verse *You overthrew those who rose against You.* This occurred when the soldiers turned tail and ran, crying: *Let us flee from the Israelites. The Lord is fighting for them against Egypt* (14:25). It was at that moment that their military edifice began to crumble, and the Egyptians lost all ability to rise again to threaten Israel. Still, it was too late for them because the Egyptians had enraged God with their continuous wickedness, casting babies into the river and so on, so that God was compelled to "send forth His rage." This divine wrath was the fire that burned up the Egyptians, who are here compared to stubble.

MESHEKH ḤOKHMA

וּבְרֹב גְּאוֹנְךָ – *In the greatness of Your majesty:* Certainly God does not require many [*rov*] means of force to crush lowly human beings. God overthrew those who rose against Him without any real act, just by releasing His anger. That is, the power of His rage and the withdrawal of His providence from the Egyptians alone "consumed them like stubble."

VERSE 8

MALBIM

נֶעֶרְמוּ מַיִם – *The waters heaped:* God's plan was to first pile up the waters so that they stood on either side of the path like walls, and then to melt them back into liquid form. As soon as the Israelites passed a given point on the route, the frozen water that surrounded them melted and that portion of the wall dissolved. In addition to these walls of water, the depths of the sea had hardened and risen across the width of the ocean like a land bridge or an elongated island. When the Egyptians encountered the causeway it did not occur to them that they were riding across the surface of the sea.

HAAMEK DAVAR

קָפְאוּ תְהֹמֹת בְּלֶב־יָם – *The deeps congealed at the heart of the sea:* The waters froze into a solid mass. This circumstance caused the Egyptians much suffering, for the soldiers were hurled against the surface before they died. All of this was caused by "the blast of God's nostrils."

BESHALAH | CONFRONTING MODERNITY — SHEMOT | CHAPTER 15

שָׁלִשָׁיו טֻבְּעוּ בְיַם־סוּף: תְּהֹמֹת יְכַסְיֻמוּ יָרְדוּ בִמְצוֹלֹת ה
כְּמוֹ־אָבֶן: יְמִינְךָ יְהוָה נֶאְדָּרִי בַּכֹּחַ יְמִינְךָ ו
יְהוָה תִּרְעַץ אוֹיֵב: וּבְרֹב גְּאוֹנְךָ תַּהֲרֹס ז
קָמֶיךָ תְּשַׁלַּח חֲרֹנְךָ יֹאכְלֵמוֹ כַּקַּשׁ: וּבְרוּחַ ח
אַפֶּיךָ נֶעֶרְמוּ מַיִם נִצְּבוּ כְמוֹ־נֵד

VERSE 5

OR HAHAYYIM

תְּהֹמֹת יְכַסְיֻמוּ — *The deep waters covered them:* The plural form of the term *tehomot* ["waters," rather than "water"] corroborates my theory proposed earlier, wherein the lower half of the sea was transformed into dry land, while the upper half was split down its middle. Each part of the ocean is referred to as a separate "deep water" — each deep because of the great volume of water each contained. To drown the Egyptians, God combined the waters of both deeps to cover up the army.

MALBIM

תְּהֹמֹת יְכַסְיֻמוּ — *The deep waters covered them:* I have previously written that the depths of the water that had first been lifted up burst into icicles and came crashing down upon the Egyptians' heads. This prevented the soldiers from swimming for their lives, for even the horses, which are normally quite capable swimmers, were weighted down by the blocks of ice. Thus our verse means that the depths of the water, which were formerly the lower reaches of the sea, covered up the cavalry by falling on them from above and pushing them down. Hence the soldiers *sank to the depths like a stone,* which cannot float or swim upon the surface of the sea.

VERSE 6

MALBIM

יְמִינְךָ — *Your right hand:* God's right hand represents His exalted side, the dimension that is occasionally "majestic in power." The term "power" in this verse refers to God's potential energy, His strength as it is before it is expressed His actions. This strength of God is most powerfully illustrated in His patience and tolerance, a power which is greater than any outward exercise of might. Thus the verse states: *He who is slow to anger is better than the mighty* (Proverbs 16:32), for such a person controls his passions. And so does Moshe plead: *And now, I pray You, let the power of my Lord be great, according as You have spoken, saying, The Lord is longsuffering, and great in love, forgiving iniquity and transgression* (Numbers 14:17–18). It is this internal might that *shatters the enemy,* for God waits quietly for the sinner to surpass all limits before completely destroying him.

VERSE 7

OR HAHAYYIM

וּבְרֹב גְּאוֹנְךָ — *In the greatness of Your majesty:* Needless to say, God does not require all [*rov*] of the weapons in His arsenal in order to overthrow those who rebel against Him. One bolt of His rage is sufficient to consume His enemies like a fire burns stubble.

I will sing to the Lord, for He has triumphed in glory; / horse
2 and horseman He hurled into the sea. / The Lord is my strength
and song – / and now my salvation. / This is my God, I will
3 glorify Him, / my father's God, I will exalt Him. / The Lord is
4 a Master of war; / the Lord is His name. / Pharaoh's chariots
and army / He hurled into the sea; / the best of his officers /

HAAMEK DAVAR (cont.)

know only that He transcends our intelligence and intellect. Another verse similarly states: *You are my God, and I will praise You; my God, I will exalt You* (Psalms 118:28). That verse means that at times, when God acts compassionately toward me, I happily thank Him; but when He executes justice against me, I can only offer statements of exaltation. For I recognize that God's understanding is so far removed from my own that His judgements must be correct, although their reasoning is beyond me.

VERSE 3

SHADAL

אִישׁ מִלְחָמָה – *A Master of war:* More than any other general or soldier, Gods deserve to be called the Master of war, for no one can stand up to Him.

MALBIM

אִישׁ מִלְחָמָה – *A Master of war:* Because God is a clever warrior, Pharaoh's chariots and army entered the sea and met their end there. The verse labels God a *Master of war* because He plots and strategizes to position the enemy just where He wants them. Furthermore, the weapons of war that God employed to defeat the Egyptians were not the simple elements of nature. When He acts thus, He is termed *Elohim, Shaddai,* or *Tzevaot*. Rather, *the Lord is His name* – symbolizing how He performed explicit miracles and wonders never seen before.

VERSE 4

RABBI SAMSON RAPHAEL HIRSCH

וּמִבְחַר שָׁלִשָׁיו – *The best of his officers:* These men were the leaders of their army, and they should have been able to organize a counterattack or at least some reasonable response to the circumstance in which they found themselves. Instead, they lost all means to act; a higher power seized them, bound them, and held them fast in the place where they sank. Now this all did not take place in a sea that was unfamiliar to Pharaoh's military, but in the Sea of Reeds, whose contours had been navigated numerous times by the professional and elite soldiers. They should have known this territory inside and out, and under normal conditions should have been able to escape their predicament. One receives the impression that the Torah emphasizes this easy and utter defeat of Pharaoh's experienced men in order to discredit those who claim that this all was a regular phenomenon. For those who surmise that the splitting of the sea was a normal event caused by extreme tidal shifts must explain why the Egyptian officers, who must have known about this atmospheric feature, were unable to avoid being swept away.

אָשִׁירָה לַיהוה כִּי־גָאֹה גָּאָה סוּס
וְרֹכְבוֹ רָמָה בַיָּם: עָזִּי וְזִמְרָת יָהּ וַיְהִי־לִי
לִישׁוּעָה זֶה אֵלִי וְאַנְוֵהוּ אֱלֹהֵי
אָבִי וַאֲרֹמְמֶנְהוּ: יהוה אִישׁ מִלְחָמָה יהוה
שְׁמוֹ: מַרְכְּבֹת פַּרְעֹה וְחֵילוֹ יָרָה בַיָּם וּמִבְחַר

MALBIM (cont.)

successful warrior understands the mechanisms and strategies of war. For battles are won by those who can outwit the enemy and lure the opposing armies into traps that will defeat them. Thus the verse states: *The Lord shall go forth as a mighty man, He shall stir up ardor like a man of war* (Isaiah 42:13). For we see that by tricking the Egyptians into entering the sea toward their own deaths, God behaved like a warrior.

VERSE 2

OR HAHAYYIM

עָזִּי וְזִמְרָת יָהּ – *The Lord is my strength and my song*: [The author is about to comment on the order of the clauses in this verse.] When people stand before God to praise and exalt Him, it is reasonable for them to begin by mentioning how God benefits them directly, and only then to refer to God's relationship with his ancestors. The men of the Great Assembly [a body of 120 scholars formed at the end of the Biblical era and credited by the Talmud with the composition of many Jewish prayers] employed just such a dual construction when they wrote the first benediction of the silent *Amida*. That text opens with the line: "Our God and God of our fathers." The first statement in our verse, *The Lord is my strength and song – and now my salvation*, refers to how God redeemed the Israelites even before the set time [of four hundred years] had come, demonstrating God's compassion for His people.

RABBI SAMSON RAPHAEL HIRSCH

וְאַנְוֵהוּ – *I will glorify Him*: I will dedicate myself to being a place and a home [*naveh*] for Him. My entire existence and life is a Temple for God's glorification and exaltation. My whole purpose is to act as a conduit for revelation of the Divine Presence in this world. **אֱלֹהֵי אָבִי וַאֲרֹמְמֶנְהוּ** – *My father's God, I will exalt Him*: God has maintained the covenant He established with my ancestors. This good faith is what characterized God for my fathers, and that is how they described Him to me. However, I will praise Him even higher to publicize awareness of God and His authority throughout the world. This then is the mission thrust upon each subsequent generation of Israel: To carry the message of God's existence, to extol Him to the nations, and to elevate step by step the Creator's standing among mankind.

HAAMEK DAVAR

וַאֲרֹמְמֶנְהוּ – *I will exalt Him*: The verb here derives from the term *romemut* [meaning "loftiness"]. Human beings may not grasp how God's actions in this world benefit us; we

30 right and left. That day, the Lord saved the Israelites from the Egyptians. And when the Israelites saw the Egyptians dead
31 on the seashore, and witnessed the wondrous power the Lord had unleashed against the Egyptians, the people were in awe of the Lord, and they believed in Him and in Moshe His servant.

15 1 And then, Moshe and the Israelites sang this song to the Lord:

RABBI SAMSON RAPHAEL HIRSCH (cont.)

God. There is only one being in the world whom we must simultaneously revere and trust, and that is God, who is singular and unique. God's attribute of love is equal to His dimension of righteousness, and his attribute of Justice is matched by His attribute of Compassion. There are no limits to the might of God's strength when He exercises His attribute of mercy or executes divine justice. The salvation that Israel witnessed at the sea was an eternal one, unparalleled in its greatness. For the miracles at the sea incorporated three of God's dimensions: His readiness to judge humanity, such that all people should fear Him forever; His unbounded compassion, such that Israel might faithfully anticipate His assistance at all times; and His unlimited power, such that His creations will submit freely to His commandments.

MALBIM

וַיִּירְאוּ... וַיַּאֲמִינוּ – *Were in awe...and they believed:* Until this point, Israel's awe of God had been limited to a fear of recompense and punishment. When identifying this feeling, the Torah employs the prepositional letter *mem* ["from" or "of"], meaning "to be afraid of" something. At this point in the narrative, Israel began to revere the exalted nature of God, an attitude often expressed with the word *et* [used here; this term precedes a definite direct object]. Now, as for the verb "to believe," when this term appears with a prepositional letter *lamed*, that signifies that the individual believes what he is being told. But if a *bet* follows the verb instead, that means that the subject has faith "in" the object himself and its lasting power. Such is the sense of the verse *Then the Lord said to Moshe, "I will come to you in a dense cloud, that the people may hear Me speaking to you. They will then believe you [bekha] forever"* (19:9). And so, until this point Israel still had some pockets of individuals who did not yet recognize the greatness of God, and who imagined that Moshe himself was orchestrating the wonders they were witnessing using magic tricks. This meant that the nation believed in Moshe but not in God. Still, there were other Hebrews who trusted in God but not in His human representative; they felt that Moshe was inventing his negotiating tactics from whole cloth. These are the people who had complained to Moshe: *What have you done to us, bringing us of Egypt?* (14:11). But now, following the successful crossing of the Sea of Reeds, the entire nation would be in awe in the exalted nature of God, and would believe both in Him and that Moshe was His loyal servant.

CHAPTER 15, VERSE 1

MALBIM

כִּי־גָאֹה גָּאָה – *For He has triumphed in glory:* Some soldiers are heroic, and others are "masters of war" [see verse 3]. The hero triumphs through his raw might, but the

ל וַיּוֹשַׁע יְהוָה בַּיּוֹם הַהוּא אֶת־יִשְׂרָאֵל מִיַּד מִצְרָיִם וַיַּרְא
לא יִשְׂרָאֵל אֶת־מִצְרַיִם מֵת עַל־שְׂפַת הַיָּם: וַיַּרְא יִשְׂרָאֵל אֶת־
הַיָּד הַגְּדֹלָה אֲשֶׁר עָשָׂה יְהוָה בְּמִצְרַיִם וַיִּירְאוּ הָעָם אֶת־
יְהוָה וַיַּאֲמִינוּ בַּיהוָה וּבְמֹשֶׁה עַבְדּוֹ:

טו א אָז יָשִׁיר־מֹשֶׁה וּבְנֵי יִשְׂרָאֵל אֶת־הַשִּׁירָה הַזֹּאת לַיהוָה וַיֹּאמְרוּ

─── MESHEKH ḤOKHMA *(cont.)* ───

over how to respond to the imminent arrival of the Egyptian army. Some people even suggested that the nation turn and go back to slavery. That disunity fractured the people and made them susceptible to collective punishment, for the bonds of love that had protected them were now dissolved. This allowed Samael to demand of God: "Rightfully You must judge the Israelites as individuals [since they show no solidarity], and since they have worshipped idols, How then can you perform miracles on their behalf?"

VERSE 30

─── OR HAḤAYYIM ───

בַּיּוֹם הַהוּא — *That day:* The verse emphasizes that Israel's redemption was effected on the day that the Egyptians were drowned in the sea. Even though the nation had left Egypt some days before, they had remained fearful of their former masters and dreaded being hunted down and seized. וַיַּרְא יִשְׂרָאֵל אֶת־מִצְרַיִם — *And when the Israelites saw the Egyptians:* Why does the Torah have to tell us that the Israelites viewed the dead bodies of the Egyptians? Surely the soldiers had expired when they disappeared into the sea. Our Sages address this question, explaining that the Israelites actually saw their foes suffering their death throes, for the oppressors were cast upon the shore still living, and gasped their last breaths on the beach. The purpose of this was to have the Egyptians experience the shame of facing their victims just before they died, knowing that their punishment was just recompense for their behavior. Thus the verse should be understood to mean "The Israelites saw the Egyptians dying on the seashore."

─── MALBIM ───

בַּיּוֹם הַהוּא — *That day:* This verse testifies that complete emancipation from the Egyptian state was only achieved on that day. The plagues that the Egyptians had been forced to endure only caused them temporary setbacks, as is seen from the continued fortitude of the oppressors and their desire to chase Israel down now. But the victory at the sea was final. the Egyptians were thereby sapped of any will to provoke Israel until the time of Shishak [see I Kings 11, 14], when God delivered Israel into that ruler's hands as punishment for their sins.

VERSE 31

─── RABBI SAMSON RAPHAEL HIRSCH ───

וַיִּירְאוּ... וַיַּאֲמִינוּ — *Were in awe...and they believed:* Awe and belief represent the two most fundamental conditions of faith, which are present in the heart of every Jew who stands before

Egyptians fled at its approach but the LORD swept them into
28 the sea. The waters returned, covering the chariots, the cavalry, and the whole Egyptian army that had followed the Israelites
29 into the sea. Not one of them remained. But the Israelites had walked through the sea on dry land, with a wall of water to their

---

HAAMEK DAVAR (cont.)

Israelites were not fully protective barriers with the task of shielding them from the Egyptians. For the latter, who were behind Israel, were fleeing and drowning and posed no threat. The sense of this verse is that the waters had merely solidified like a wall and were prevented from flowing back to their place.

MESHEKH ḤOKHMA

וְהַמַּיִם לָהֶם חֹמָה – *With a wall of water:* When one examines the ways of the Torah, one discovers that its commandments can be divided into two categories: Laws whose meaning is obscure, such as prohibitions of idolatry and illicit sexual unions, might be punishable with lashes, excision, stoning, or other forms of execution. However, such consequences are not imposed for rules with social utility, such as the prohibitions on talebearing, gossip, and theft. Lashes are not administered for such infractions, which either can be resolved through monetary payments, or involve no real action. [Crimes of speech and thought are generally not considered judicable.] Now these qualifications are restricted to the crimes of individuals, but when a community becomes corrupt, quite the opposite holds true, as stated in the Talmud Yerushalmi (Pe'ah 1:1): In the era of King David, the generation of Israel was almost entirely righteous, but the nation was defeated in its wars due to the activities of talebearers among them. Conversely, the during the reign of King Aḥav, idolatry was widely practiced by the nation. But since the people did not inform on each other, Israel met only success on the battlefield. For when the congregation of Israel is awash in idolatry and licentiousness, the Divine Presence can still abide among them, but when disputes and talebearing are rife in the nation, the Divine Presence abandons the people. With this in mind, we can understand the midrash appearing in Yalkut Shimoni (paragraph 234): What transpired when the Sea of Reeds stood upright as walls on either side of the escaping Israelites? Samael [an angel known in rabbinic lore as an accuser or angel of death] addressed God saying: "Master of the Universe! Surely, You are aware that the Israelites worshipped idols when they were imprisoned in Egypt! Why then do You perform these wonders on their behalf?" This complaint was overheard by the guardian angel of the sea, who became enraged and attempted to drown the Israelites. This is alluded to by the spelling of the word *ḥoma* without a *vav* [as if it were *ḥema*, meaning "anger"]. And why did Samael not level this charge regarding the miracles that God executed when the nation was still in Egypt? For even though the Israelites engaged in idolatry then and neglected the practice of circumcision, they treated each other properly, refusing to inform on fellow Hebrews and showing genuine love for their compatriots. And that is why God delivered plagues against His people's oppressors. However, when the Israelites were encamped at the beach, they split into four different factions, squabbling

כח לִקְרָאתוֹ וַיְנַעֵר יְהֹוָה אֶת־מִצְרַיִם בְּתוֹךְ הַיָּם: וַיָּשֻׁבוּ הַמַּיִם וַיְכַסּוּ אֶת־הָרֶכֶב וְאֶת־הַפָּרָשִׁים לְכֹל חֵיל פַּרְעֹה הַבָּאִים כט אַחֲרֵיהֶם בַּיָּם לֹא־נִשְׁאַר בָּהֶם עַד־אֶחָד: וּבְנֵי יִשְׂרָאֵל הָלְכוּ בַיַּבָּשָׁה בְּתוֹךְ הַיָּם וְהַמַּיִם לָהֶם חֹמָה מִימִינָם וּמִשְּׂמֹאלָם:

OR HAḤAYYIM *(cont.)*

Himself. This explains those instances where the sky and the earth, the stars and the sun, are ordered about by the virtuous. Now we are equipped to explain the dispute between Moshe and the sea at that critical moment of Israel's birth. Because Israel arrived at the seashore unarmed with the might of the Torah — having not yet experienced revelation at Mount Sinai — they lacked the influence to command nature to do their bidding. This is why the sea balked at Moshe's request to open itself up for the people. And when the ocean scoffed that humanity was only as old as the sixth day, whereas the seas were created on the third day, it was really hinting that Moshe himself was not a Torah scholar. For if the prophet had mastered the Torah — which was older than even creation, having been composed by God before He made the world — then Moshe would have been able to harness its potency and demand the sea's compliance. In response to this assertion, God joined the dispute and extended His "right arm" to Moshe. That is, He assured Moshe that he was a Torah scholar, for the term "right" often refers to the Torah, as the verse states: *from His right hand went a fiery law for them* (Deuteronomy 33:2). As soon as the sea saw this expression of God's right hand, it understood the allusion and immediately withdrew, as per its built-in condition. And from then onward, every intensely righteous individual who stands empowered with the strength of the Torah's message will be able to demand that water divide upon his command.

VERSE 28

RABBI SAMSON RAPHAEL HIRSCH

וַיָּשֻׁבוּ הַמַּיִם – *The waters returned:* It seems to be that both of these events happened simultaneously: While the Israelites were completing their crossing of the sea on the eastern shore, the waves were washing away the Egyptians behind them on the western side. Thus was the mighty hand of God revealed during this event, for it became patently clear how the entire natural world bends to the will of God, He who judges all the world.

MALBIM

וַיָּשֻׁבוּ הַמַּיִם – *The waters returned:* After God "swept" the Egyptians into the sea's abyss [in the previous verse] and the soldiers' heads were smashed against the rocky depths, the waters returned to cover them up along with their chariots.

VERSE 29

HAAMEK DAVAR

וְהַמַּיִם לָהֶם חֹמָה – *With a wall of water:* The term "wall" [*ḥoma*] is written defectively here [i.e., without the letter *vav*]. This indicates that the walls forming on either side of the

24 the sea. During the last watch of the night, the LORD looked down at the Egyptian army from a column of fire and cloud
25 and threw them into a panic, clogging their chariot wheels so that it was hard for them to move. The Egyptians said, "Let us flee from the Israelites. The LORD is fighting for them against Egypt."
26 Then the LORD said to Moshe, "Stretch out your hand over the sea. The waters will flow back over the Egyptians and their
27 chariots and cavalry." Moshe stretched out his hand over the sea, and at daybreak the water came back in full force. The

REVI'I

VERSE 27
OR HAḤAYYIM

וַיָּשָׁב הַיָּם לִפְנוֹת בֹּקֶר לְאֵיתָנוֹ – *At daybreak the water came back in full force:* Our Sages interpret the word *le'eitano* as an allusion to the term *tenai* [meaning "condition"], teaching that when God created the oceans at the dawn of the world, He stipulated that the Sea of Reeds must later agree to split open to rescue Israel. And yet it seems out of place for the Torah to mention this feature of the water at the point when Israel had already made their crossing; the text should have alluded to this idea earlier, as the sea was being divided. One possible explanation for this is that only after the waters had returned to their proper place did the sea realize what was really going on. For the body of water at first believed that when it was asked to divide down its middle, that transformation would be its last, that God had decreed that its time had come to be destroyed from the world. However, when the walls of water fell, the sea understood that it had merely been called upon to fulfill its ancient promise, and that its deformation was merely temporary.... Let us now examine the nature of this condition that God stipulated when He first fashioned the seas. If, on the one hand, it had been made clear that the splitting would be required to save the Israelites from the charging Egyptian cavalry, why was the sea agitated and confused when it was called upon to assist the nation? We know that it was reluctant to comply with Moshe's demand to open up, as our Sages write: The sea defied Moshe and refused to split itself saying: "No, I will not divide my waves for you, human! I was created on the third day [of creation], whereas you [human beings] were not formed until the sixth day!" And thus the standoff remained, until God stepped in and reached out His right arm toward Moshe's, as the verse states: *That caused His glorious arm to go at the right hand of Moshe, dividing the water before them* (Isaiah 63:12). Furthermore, we have reports that water does split, against its will, for the very worthy, as the Talmud relates with respect to Rabbi Pinḥas ben Yair [see Ḥullin 7a, where that rabbi demanded that a river split open to enable him to proceed on a mission]. And if the original condition was restricted to the event of the exodus, how could Rabbi Pinḥas ben Yair possibly wield any power to counteract laws of nature embedded in the oceans from the start of time? In truth, we must clarify what the Sages meant by God having worked a condition into nature. Upon fashioning all His creations, God ensured that they would always be subservient to the Torah and to its adherents. Nature was to obey the commands issued to it by the righteous, whose authority is as binding as that of the Creator

כד פַּרְעֹה רִכְבּוֹ וּפָרָשָׁיו אֶל־תּוֹךְ הַיָּם: וַיְהִי בְּאַשְׁמֹרֶת הַבֹּקֶר וַיַּשְׁקֵף יהוה אֶל־מַחֲנֵה מִצְרַיִם בְּעַמּוּד אֵשׁ וְעָנָן וַיָּהָם אֵת

כה מַחֲנֵה מִצְרָיִם: וַיָּסַר אֵת אֹפַן מַרְכְּבֹתָיו וַיְנַהֲגֵהוּ בִּכְבֵדֻת וַיֹּאמֶר מִצְרַיִם אָנוּסָה מִפְּנֵי יִשְׂרָאֵל כִּי יהוה נִלְחָם לָהֶם בְּמִצְרָיִם:

כו וַיֹּאמֶר יהוה אֶל־מֹשֶׁה נְטֵה אֶת־יָדְךָ עַל־הַיָּם וְיָשֻׁבוּ הַמַּיִם   רביעי עַל־מִצְרַיִם עַל־רִכְבּוֹ וְעַל־פָּרָשָׁיו: וַיֵּט מֹשֶׁה אֶת־יָדוֹ

כז עַל־הַיָּם וַיָּשָׁב הַיָּם לִפְנוֹת בֹּקֶר לְאֵיתָנוֹ וּמִצְרַיִם נָסִים

VERSE 24

MALBIM

וַיְהִי בְּאַשְׁמֹרֶת הַבֹּקֶר – *During the last watch of the night:* It was at that time that the column of cloud was scheduled to return to its rightful position in front of Israel and for the pillar of fire to dissipate. But now the fire moved from hovering behind Israel to enter the Egyptian camp, intermixed with the column of cloud. God meanwhile peered down at the Egyptians as one looks through a window. All this caused the Egyptian camp to erupt into a confused panic. For they suddenly realized that God had entered their midst to fight them.

VERSE 25

MALBIM

וַיָּסַר אֵת אֹפַן מַרְכְּבֹתָיו – *Clogging their chariot wheels:* The pillar of fire set to work burning the wheels of the chariots, which were made of wood. But the fire had an additional task as well: to melt the frozen ground and turn it into miry clay. Naturally, this caused the cavalry to become stuck, and the entire army became clogged and unable to move. For when Israel first entered the sea, the job of the pillar of fire was merely to melt the ice walls bordering the nation's path as soon as the people passed. But now the fire turned its attention to the seabed, which had been made dry and solid, and melted it back into its original state of sludge. It was because of that that the Egyptians were convinced that God was fighting against them on Israel's behalf, and they attempted to flee back to the shore.

VERSE 26

OR HAḤAYYIM

נְטֵה אֶת־יָדְךָ עַל־הַיָּם – *Stretch out your hand over the sea:* Why did Moshe have to act to return the waters to their place? After all, the water was not standing still and upright all on its own, and it would not continue to do so once Israel had clambered onto the far shore and the last of the Egyptians had entered the sea. Now it is possible that the seabed would have remained exposed of its own volition even after Israel had passed through the breach, for the sea reasoned that it was God's intention to allow the cavalry to cross just as Israel had. Therefore God issued Moshe a direct command after the soldiers were well within, to let the sea know that its service was complete and that it was time to revert to normal.

22 all night, turning it to dry land and dividing the waters. So the Israelites walked through the sea on dry land. To their right and
23 left, the water was like a wall. The Egyptians chased after them. All Pharaoh's horses, chariots and cavalry followed them into

HAKETAV VEHAKABBALA

וַיָּבֹאוּ בְנֵי־יִשְׂרָאֵל בְּתוֹךְ הַיָּם – *So the Israelites walked through the sea:* [Literally, "came through the sea."] It is usual to refer to seafarers as having "gone down to sea" [*yoredei hayam,* see, e.g., Psalms 107:23]. Thus, we might have expected our verse to state that Israel "descended" into the Sea of Reeds instead of using the verb "came". However, the author Rabbi Naftali Hertz Viesel, explains that in fact, the usual perception of how the Sea of Reeds was split is inaccurate. Rather in order to provide a dry causeway for Israel to cross on, God lifted up the seabed from the bottom of the ocean and raised it to sit at sea level. The Israelites were thereby provided with a ready-made path for them to walk on [and never for a moment "descended"]. Now in order for the ocean floor to be raised as a flat surface with no dips or rises in it, the displaced water had to fall away to enable the creation of a new land mass. Still, the tendency of water is to flow downward, as gravity dictates, and had God allowed the water to act naturally, it would have drained off the rising land to the left and to the right areas of the sea, or ahead and back toward the beaches. This then was the additional miracle that God performed at that moment: He did not permit the water that was pushed aside by the rising land to behave normally, but divided these waters and piled them up in the air on either side of the new highway. God achieved this by causing a strong east wind to blow against the sea throughout the night. This pushed the water off the elevated sea floor as it rose, freezing it into a wall on either side of the land bridge. What emerges from this description is that the primary miracle in this chapter was not God's splitting of the ocean down the middle, but His miraculous lifting of the sea bed. A secondary wonder was that the water that was being pushed aside did not run off in all directions, which would have been normal, but was held in place by the wind and formed into guardrails for the crossing Israelites.

VERSE 23

MALBIM

וַיִּרְדְּפוּ מִצְרַיִם – *The Egyptians chased:* The Egyptians believed they were pursuing the Israelites across dry land, for the space that God had cleared was so wide they could not glimpse the sea that remained beyond the thoroughfare on either side. First to lead the charge after Israel was Pharaoh himself, with his horse-driven chariot guard. They were followed by all the cavalry until the entire army had entered the breach and the ocean's depths.

HAAMEK DAVAR

וַיִּרְדְּפוּ מִצְרַיִם וַיָּבֹאוּ אַחֲרֵיהֶם – *The Egyptians chased after them:* The entire population followed Israel, but only the "horses, chariots, and cavalry" went as far as the exposed sea floor. Some of the citizens continued the pursuit, but most had not proceeded that far before the waters returned.

כב כָּל־הַלַּיְלָה וַיָּשֶׂם אֶת־הַיָּם לֶחָרָבָה וַיִּבָּקְעוּ הַמָּיִם: וַיָּבֹאוּ
בְנֵי־יִשְׂרָאֵל בְּתוֹךְ הַיָּם בַּיַּבָּשָׁה וְהַמַּיִם לָהֶם חֹמָה מִימִינָם
כג וּמִשְּׂמֹאלָם: וַיִּרְדְּפוּ מִצְרַיִם וַיָּבֹאוּ אַחֲרֵיהֶם כֹּל סוּס

SHADAL *(cont.)*

why did He employ a strong east wind to dry and solidify the sea waters?... [The 17th century Genevan Bible scholar Johannes] Clericus posited that Israel crossed the Sea of Reeds at its northern end toward Suez and Pi Hahirot. Many others who followed Clericus accepted his approach, and the Arabs share this tradition as well. Now according to this understanding, the Israelites crossed the sea as the waters were receding at low tide. But then Moshe stretched out his hand prompting the Lord to deliver a fierce wind blowing from north to south, thereby delaying the waters' return. What this meant is that the low tide lasted many more hours than usual. This interpretation was necessary because the scholars could not understand how the wind alone could dry up the sea without blowing away the very people who were trying to cross it. Indeed, Clericus cites a similar event that took place in Holland in the year 1672 during a sea battle between the English and the Dutch. In the pitch of the action a powerful wind kept the tide at bay for an abnormally long twelve hours, thereby preventing the English ships from approaching the Dutch shore. This resulted in a fantastic victory for the people of Holland. However, [the writer] Isaak Markus Jost takes exception to this approach and denies that the manipulation of the tides was the key to Israel's survival. Rather, the entire event was governed by powerful storm winds. And as for the question of how the Israelites were able to cross the water with such a tempest raging all around them, Jost explains that in fact, the atmospheric anomaly took place on the previous day and night. This meant that by the time Moshe was ready to lead his people forward, the sea had sufficiently dried up, allowing for Israel's escape before the waters came flooding back. However it really happened, one thing is clear: This episode combined the miraculous with the normal movement of natural elements.... I should mention as well that peoples in the surrounding lands maintain a memory of the Sea of Reeds having been once dried up. Diodorus Siculus, for example, writes that a civilization of fishermen situated by the sea held a tradition from their ancestors that one time the entire sea was turned into land.

VERSE 22

OR HAHAYYIM

בְּתוֹךְ הַיָּם בַּיַּבָּשָׁה – *Through the sea on dry land:* The people did not actually wade through the water, but crossed in the space where the water had previously been. Additionally, by using the phrase "dry land," the Torah emphasizes that the exposed surface was not muddy and mucky as the sea bottom usually is, but dry and suitable for travel.

וְהַמַּיִם לָהֶם חֹמָה – *The water was like a wall:* The water that was pushed aside to expose the sea floor did not merge with the outside areas but stayed where it was. Furthermore, the water did not form a box around the Israelites but stood just on either side of them, thereby allowing them to move forward and the Egyptians to follow.

16 Speak to the Israelites; have them move forward. Raise your staff, stretch out your hand over the sea and divide it, and the
17 Israelites will walk through the sea on dry land. I will strengthen the Egyptians' hearts and they will go after them. Then will My glory bear down hard upon Pharaoh and his entire army,
18 his chariots and cavalry. And when My glory bears down upon Pharaoh, his chariots and cavalry, the Egyptians will know that
19 I am the Lord." Then the angel of God who had been traveling ahead of the Israelite camp moved and went behind them, and the column of cloud moved from in front of them to their rear.
20 It came between the Egyptian and Israelite camps, as cloud and darkness for one, but lighting the night for the other, keeping
21 the two apart all night. Then Moshe stretched out his hand over the sea, and the Lord drove the sea back by a strong east wind

---

VERSE 19

HAAMEK DAVAR

וַיִּסַּע מַלְאַךְ הָאֱלֹהִים – *Then the angel of God moved:* This refers to the angel who is a constant companion of the Divine Presence.

VERSE 20

MALBIM

וַיָּבֹא בֵּין מַחֲנֵה מִצְרַיִם וּבֵין מַחֲנֵה יִשְׂרָאֵל – *It came between the Egyptian and Israelite camps:* The column of cloud positioned itself between the Egyptian and the Israelite camps, darkening the sky for the Egyptian army and blocking their view of the pillar of fire and the Israelites. For if the soldiers had seen fire hovering in sky in front of them, that would have frightened them into retreating and they never would have pursued Israel into the sea. Thus does a later verse describe the situation: *And when they cried to the Lord, He put darkness between you and Egypt, and brought the sea upon them and covered them* (Joshua 24:7). It was the combination of the natural nocturnal darkness and the enveloping cloud that obscured all sight of the fire's brightness. Meanwhile, the pillar of fire lit up the night for the Israelites more than it usually did, such that the entire camp was bathed in light. And thus the two camps stood opposite each other all through the night, with neither one approaching the other. Now the pillar of fire moved behind Israel as well, for an entirely different purpose: It would eventually serve to melt the walls of ice that the sea water had formed on either side of the fleeing Israelites.

VERSE 21

SHADAL

וַיָּשֶׂם אֶת־הַיָּם לֶחָרָבָה – *Turning it into dry land:* From the Torah's description of this monumental event, it is clear that God orchestrated the miracle by merging natural elements with the supernatural. After all, if God was interested merely in suspending the rules of nature,

יִשְׂרָאֵל וְיִסָּעוּ: וְאַתָּה הָרֵם אֶת־מַטְּךָ וּנְטֵה אֶת־יָדְךָ עַל־ טז
הַיָּם וּבְקָעֵהוּ וְיָבֹאוּ בְנֵי־יִשְׂרָאֵל בְּתוֹךְ הַיָּם בַּיַּבָּשָׁה: וַאֲנִי יז
הִנְנִי מְחַזֵּק אֶת־לֵב מִצְרַיִם וְיָבֹאוּ אַחֲרֵיהֶם וְאִכָּבְדָה
בְּפַרְעֹה וּבְכָל־חֵילוֹ בְּרִכְבּוֹ וּבְפָרָשָׁיו: וְיָדְעוּ מִצְרַיִם כִּי־ יח
אֲנִי יְהוָה בְּהִכָּבְדִי בְּפַרְעֹה בְּרִכְבּוֹ וּבְפָרָשָׁיו: וַיִּסַּע מַלְאַךְ יט
הָאֱלֹהִים הַהֹלֵךְ לִפְנֵי מַחֲנֵה יִשְׂרָאֵל וַיֵּלֶךְ מֵאַחֲרֵיהֶם
וַיִּסַּע עַמּוּד הֶעָנָן מִפְּנֵיהֶם וַיַּעֲמֹד מֵאַחֲרֵיהֶם: וַיָּבֹא בֵּין ׀ כ
מַחֲנֵה מִצְרַיִם וּבֵין מַחֲנֵה יִשְׂרָאֵל וַיְהִי הֶעָנָן וְהַחֹשֶׁךְ וַיָּאֶר
אֶת־הַלָּיְלָה וְלֹא־קָרַב זֶה אֶל־זֶה כָּל־הַלָּיְלָה: וַיֵּט מֹשֶׁה כא
אֶת־יָדוֹ עַל־הַיָּם וַיּוֹלֶךְ יְהוָה ׀ אֶת־הַיָּם בְּרוּחַ קָדִים עַזָּה

VERSE 17

OR HAḤAYYIM

וַאֲנִי הִנְנִי מְחַזֵּק אֶת־לֵב מִצְרַיִם — *I will strengthen the Egyptians' hearts:* In this verse, God demonstrates compassion and consideration for Israel by telling them in advance that the Egyptian army will follow on their heels. This was meant to relieve Israel of their stress and fear. For once they saw the dry path of land forming on the seabed and remaining while the Egyptians set out toward them through the sea, they would quite likely panic and lose faith that their salvation was at hand. "Look!" they would cry, "they are following us through the sea! Soon they will be upon us!" Thus God assured Israel from the outset that the Egyptians' move was all part of His plan to wreak His final vengeance against them. In order to *be glorified over Pharaoh and all his force* (14:4), He laid a trap for the charging cavalry.

MALBIM

וַאֲנִי הִנְנִי מְחַזֵּק אֶת־לֵב מִצְרַיִם — *I will strengthen the Egyptians' hearts:* God performed other wonders to lure the Egyptians into the depths of the sea without realizing exactly where they were going. The army was deceived into thinking that they were merely marching on dry land, and that their pursuit of Israel was a routine mission. In this way God would *be glorified over Pharaoh and all his force* (14:4), for the soldiers would soon understand that they were being punished measure for measure for how they treated Israel [when they cast the infants into the Nile].

VERSE 18

RABBI SAMSON RAPHAEL HIRSCH

בְּהִכָּבְדִי בְּפַרְעֹה — *When My glory bears down upon Pharaoh:* This massive revelation of My glory will teach Egyptian civilization a powerful lesson. The demonstration of My might will serve as a warning to other kings like Pharaoh who boast of their own greatness, their wealth, and their military victories with no thought for ethical principles.

14 Egyptians you see today, you shall never see again. The Lord will fight for you. You stay silent."
15 The Lord said to Moshe, "Why are you crying out to Me? SHELISHI

OR HAḤAYYIM (cont.)

and embolden their faith; encourage them to have complete confidence as they stride toward the sea, even before it splits open. I will provide a miracle for them in repayment of the trust they place in Me. And because of their positive attitude, My attribute of Compassion will overcome that of Justice.

RABBI SAMSON RAPHAEL HIRSCH

וַיִּסָּעוּ – *Have them move forward:* At this moment of truth, the people's salvation is dependent on them – they must make the first move. Furthermore, the Israelites must prove that they are worthy of deliverance by demonstrating their faith in God in practice. Such a bold step will in turn fortify the people's courage and spur them to act fearlessly. First let them descend to the sea without hesitation or trepidation. Only then will God pave a path toward their complete redemption.

MESHEKH ḤOKHMA

וַיִּסָּעוּ – *Have them move forward:* The Mekhilta cites the following interpretation for this verse: Rabbi Yehuda teaches: Said the Holy One, blessed be He, to Moshe: "Moshe! All the people of Israel must do is to move forward!" What this statement seems to convey is an instruction both to Moshe and Israel about how to proceed. Until this point, Israel had walked after Moshe in the wilderness like sheep who follow their shepherd through a valley. However, at the sea, the Holy One, blessed be He, commanded Moshe to allow the people to inch toward the water in front of him. The Israelites were to demonstrate their trust in God, and on the merit of the faith leading them into the sea, the waters would divide before them. Thus when the verse states: *Then the angel of God who had been traveling ahead of the Israelite camp moved and went behind them* (14:19), it refers to Moshe, who is here called "the angel [*malakh*] of God." We find a similar expression in the verse *Then Ḥagai, messenger [malakh] of the Lord, sent by the Lord to the people, spoke.* (Haggai 1:13). As a reward for Israel leading the way into the sea, and for Moshe picking up the rear, God divided the water for the nation's ultimate escape. Thus the Mekhilta informs us that while Israel was deliberating about how to proceed, Naḥshon son of Aminadav leaped and dove into the sea. This then is what the verse means when it states: *Speak to the Israelites; have them move forward* – you, Moshe, are to hang back and let Israel earn its own salvation.

RABBI JOSEPH B. SOLOVEITCHIK

וַיִּסָּעוּ – *Have them move forward:* At the splitting of the Sea of Reeds, the Creator offered the Israelites a role in their own redemption. He required a leap of faith: a jump into the water prior to the parting of the sea [see Sota 36–37]. The shock of cold water, the fear of drowning, became Israel's minute "contribution" to the miracle. At that moment they became partners with God, and as a result Moshe and the people sang the majestic Song of the Sea in gratitude.

יַעֲשֶׂה לָכֶם הַיּוֹם כִּי אֲשֶׁר רְאִיתֶם אֶת־מִצְרַיִם הַיּוֹם לֹא
יד תֹסִפוּ לִרְאֹתָם עוֹד עַד־עוֹלָם: יהוה יִלָּחֵם לָכֶם וְאַתֶּם
תַּחֲרִשׁוּן:
טו וַיֹּאמֶר יהוה אֶל־מֹשֶׁה מַה־תִּצְעַק אֵלָי דַּבֵּר אֶל־בְּנֵי־ יא שלישי

MALBIM (cont.)

apprehending Israel. The Hebrews, for their part, several times expressed their willingness to return to Egypt. But once the Egyptian cavalry had been wiped out, the oppressors gave up their mission of retrieving their slaves, and Israel took their final and eternal leave of them.

VERSE 14

OR HAHAYYIM

וְאַתֶּם תַּחֲרִשׁוּן – *You stay silent:* We can explain this clause through the following statement of our Sages: Four different personalities adopted various approaches in seeking God's assistance, with the best approach taken by Ḥizkiya. That king of Yehuda understood that he lacked the ability either to defeat or to expel the invading Assyrians; he did not even possess the strength to petition God to rescue the state. Instead, he determined merely to lie on his bed, and leave the defense of the land in God's hands. And indeed God picked up the mantle, as the verse states: *And it came to pass that night, that the angel of the Lord went out and smote in the camp of Assyria a hundred and eighty five thousand: and when they arose early in the morning, behold, they were all dead corpses* (II Kings 19:35). This was what Moshe meant when he told the Israelites, *you stay silent* – If you cannot even compose yourselves enough to verbalize a request to God, as Ḥizkiya could not, then just be quiet while He fights your battle for you.

MESHEKH ḤOKHMA

וְאַתֶּם תַּחֲרִשׁוּן – *You stay silent:* Moshe assured Israel that this would not be the only time when God would fight on Israel's behalf. Rather, from then on, the nation could expect God to vanquish its enemies. Now on this occasion, the people lodged a penetrating complaint against God: Why did the Holy One, blessed be He, rescue Israel from Egypt if He would immediately thereafter be required to fight the Egyptians to protect their lives? To this lament, Moshe answered: Recognize that God plans on supporting Israel even in situations when you have no such legitimate claims against Him. Such was the case in the times of Sisera's invasion [see Judges 4] and that of Zeraḥ, king of Kush [see II Chronicles 14], and in all future circumstances when the nation found itself embarrassed by its own behavior. This is what Moshe meant when he pronounced: *The Lord will fight for you* even when *you stay silent*, that is even when you are unable to level any accusation against God, and are ashamed to speak, you will be able to rely on God to defend you against your enemies.

VERSE 15

OR HAHAYYIM

דַּבֵּר אֶל־בְּנֵי־יִשְׂרָאֵל – *Speak to the Israelites:* This statement was meant as advice for the people and was spoken in tones of kindness and compassion: Speak to the people

11 to the LORD for help. "Were there no graves in Egypt?" they asked Moshe; "Is that why you brought us here to die in the desert? What have you done to us, bringing us out of Egypt?
12 Did we not tell you in Egypt: Leave us alone – let us serve the Egyptians. Better a life in servitude to Egypt than death in
13 the desert." But Moshe told the people, "Fear not. Stand firm and see the deliverance the LORD will bring you today. The

---
SHADAL (cont.)

enemy army in battle did not occur to them at all. Instead, they envisioned themselves running for their lives. But since the only two avenues open to them were the desert and the sea, they imagined that they would soon be dead [of starvation and thirst]. Moshe understood what they were thinking and responded, *Fear not…for the LORD will fight for you* (14:13–14) against the Egyptians.

HAAMEK DAVAR

וְנַעַבְדָה אֶת־מִצְרָיִם – *Let us serve the Egyptians:* Israel had only ever complained about the undue suffering they had to endure and the pain that was inflicted upon them. They had never protested their lot of having to serve the monarchy per se.

VERSE 13

OR HAḤAYYIM

הִתְיַצְּבוּ וּרְאוּ – *Stand firm and see:* Perhaps what Moshe meant was that the Israelites should stand confidently before God in prayer, thereby affirming that their earlier effort – *They cried to the LORD for help* (14:10) – had been the correct strategy. We find similar references to prayer as "standing" in the verse *I am the woman who stood by you here, praying to the LORD* (I Samuel 1:26).

SHADAL

לֹא תֹסִפוּ לִרְאֹתָם עוֹד עַד־עוֹלָם – *You shall never see again:* Moshe's statement in this verse is both a promise and a commandment. On the one hand, God was guaranteeing Israel that the Egyptian threat was about to end once and for all – they would never have to see their foes again. But in addition to that, God was instructing the Israelites that it would be inappropriate for them ever to return willingly to the scene of their oppression.

MALBIM

וַיֹּאמֶר מֹשֶׁה אֶל־הָעָם – *But Moshe told the people:* Moshe spoke of a deliverance that would effect several necessary results. Firstly, the wonders that were about to be performed at the sea would serve to sanctify God's name. This is what Moshe referred to when he said: *Stand firm and see the deliverance the LORD will bring you today* – for the miraculous salvation about to be worked would outshine all of the previous marvels and signs that the world had witnessed. Naturally, this would expand God's reputation among the surrounding nations. Secondly, the imminent rescue of God's nation and the defeat of their enemy would be the reason that *the Egyptians you see today, you shall never see again.* Absent the miracle at the Sea of Reeds and the obliteration of Pharaoh's army, the Egyptians would have relentlessly pursued their goal of

יא בְּנֵי־יִשְׂרָאֵל אֶל־יְהוָה: וַיֹּאמְרוּ אֶל־מֹשֶׁה הֲמִבְּלִי אֵין־קְבָרִים בְּמִצְרַיִם לְקַחְתָּנוּ לָמוּת בַּמִּדְבָּר מַה־זֹּאת עָשִׂיתָ לָּנוּ לְהוֹצִיאָנוּ מִמִּצְרָיִם: יב הֲלֹא־זֶה הַדָּבָר אֲשֶׁר דִּבַּרְנוּ אֵלֶיךָ בְמִצְרַיִם לֵאמֹר חֲדַל מִמֶּנּוּ וְנַעַבְדָה אֶת־מִצְרָיִם כִּי טוֹב לָנוּ עֲבֹד אֶת־מִצְרַיִם מִמֻּתֵנוּ בַּמִּדְבָּר: יג וַיֹּאמֶר מֹשֶׁה אֶל־הָעָם אַל־תִּירָאוּ הִתְיַצְּבוּ וּרְאוּ אֶת־יְשׁוּעַת יְהוָה אֲשֶׁר

VERSE 11

RABBI SAMSON RAPHAEL HIRSCH

הַמִבְּלִי אֵין־קְבָרִים בְּמִצְרַיִם – *Were there no graves in Egypt:* The doubts that Israel expresses time and again actually illustrate a positive dimension of our heritage. According to Rabbi Yehuda HaLevi in *The Kuzari* [part I, chapters 49, 51 and 87], Israel's struggles with faith prove the veracity of Moshe's mission. This prophet was forced to lead a nation comprising clearheaded and intelligent people, a community that was not easily persuaded by grandiloquent speeches and fantastic promises. These Hebrews were quick to challenge any potential savior by questioning his methods and his motives. And so, if in the end this group of skeptics was convinced to follow Moshe's Torah and stand against the world in doing so, if we have been willing to sacrifice our lives for our religion, that shows that the mission of the man Moshe stood the test of Israel's examinations. The force of Moshe's actions and behavior satisfied Israel as to the truth of his message. They, and we, were convinced for all time. The cutting sarcasm that Israel expresses in this verse, even in the most trying and unparalleled moment of fear and desperation, demonstrates the characteristic sense of humor that the Jews are known for, in all its insight and honesty.

MALBIM

וַיֹּאמְרוּ אֶל־מֹשֶׁה – *They asked Moshe:* Some nations love their freedom so much that they would rather die than submit to the hardships of slavery. Other groups think of life as the ultimate value and given the option would choose an existence of degradation and servitude over death. Hence, when made to confront their mortality, the people of Israel express this protest to their leader: Were you really of the opinion that we are the type of people who prefer death to bondage? Why did you need to take us out of Egypt to have us lose our lives in battle in the sands of this wilderness? Why, we could have rebelled against our oppressors at home, and been cut down in a familiar setting, thereby skipping this pretense of escape. *Were there no graves in Egypt* that you brought us out here, where there is plenty of available land to hold our corpses? There were sufficient graves in Egypt where we could have died and been buried.

VERSE 12

SHADAL

מִמֻּתֵנוּ בַּמִּדְבָּר – *Than death in the desert:* Note that the Israelites do not complain that they will be slaughtered by the Egyptians' swords, since the possibility of actually engaging the

6 the Israelites from serving us?" So the king harnessed his chari-
7 ot and brought out his army. He took six hundred elite chariots and all the other chariots of Egypt, with officers over them all.
8 The LORD strengthened the heart of Pharaoh King of Egypt, and he pursued the Israelites, who were leaving in defiance of
9 them. The Egyptians, with all the king's horses and chariots, cavalry and infantry, chased and caught up with them as they were encamped by the sea near Pi HaḤirot, before Baal Tzefon. SHENI
10 Pharaoh drew near – the Israelites looked up: there were the Egyptians thundering after them. They were terrified and cried

---

MALBIM

וַיִּרְדְּפוּ מִצְרַיִם אַחֲרֵיהֶם – *The Egyptians chased after them:* This verse describes the behavior of the Egyptian home front after their king set out to recapture Israel in the wilderness. After Pharaoh left the state with his small militia, and the people received word that their representatives were riding out to war, the entire Egyptian populace assembled themselves to join the fray. However, by the time Pharaoh, with his horses and chariots, arrived at Israel's previous location, the latter had already moved on from Pi HaḤirot and had camped closer to the sea. The king's forces rested at Pi HaḤirot, while the Egyptian populace who had arrived in waves to join him, went straight down to the sea where Israel had stopped. Therefore, those who *caught up with* Israel were the citizen army, for the professionals had not yet arrived.

VERSE 10

RABBI SAMSON RAPHAEL HIRSCH

וַיִּצְעֲקוּ בְנֵי־יִשְׂרָאֵל – *And cried for help:* [Literally, "and the Israelites cried for help"] Our verse repeats the subject *Benei Yisrael* [the Israelites, despite already having mentioned them at the start of the sentence] to emphasize that their fear and cries to God were completely natural and normal. The people still deserved the name "Israel" despite their panic, an emotion which in no way detracted from their national character.

MALBIM

וּפַרְעֹה הִקְרִיב – *Pharaoh drew near:* The current verse expresses two stages of Israel's reaction to the Egyptians' arrival. At first, when *Pharaoh drew near,* the Israelites were unafraid, for they saw just a small force rolling toward them; they thought that Pharaoh was uninterested in fighting a war against them. But then the people *looked up: there were the Egyptians thundering after them,* meaning the entire Egyptian populace, who was trailing the national guard. These people were streaming forward in great numbers and they were armed to the teeth. It was at this point that the Israelites became *terrified and cried to the LORD for help.* Initially, Israel had faith in God and petitioned Him to force Pharaoh to retreat. But when the nation saw that instead the king was advancing, they feared that God would not provide them with any miraculous salvation. They suddenly thought poorly of Moshe, believing that God had never instructed him to lead them out of Egypt, and that his mandate had been merely to alleviate their slavery, not to abandon them in the wilderness.

BESHALAH | CONFRONTING MODERNITY — SHEMOT | CHAPTER 14

י עָשִׂינוּ כִּי־שִׁלַּחְנוּ אֶת־יִשְׂרָאֵל מֵעָבְדֵנוּ: וַיֶּאְסֹר אֶת־רִכְבּוֹ
וְאֶת־עַמּוֹ לָקַח עִמּוֹ: וַיִּקַּח שֵׁשׁ־מֵאוֹת רֶכֶב בָּחוּר וְכֹל
ח רֶכֶב מִצְרָיִם וְשָׁלִשִׁם עַל־כֻּלּוֹ: וַיְחַזֵּק יהוה אֶת־לֵב פַּרְעֹה
מֶלֶךְ מִצְרַיִם וַיִּרְדֹּף אַחֲרֵי בְּנֵי יִשְׂרָאֵל וּבְנֵי יִשְׂרָאֵל יֹצְאִים
ט בְּיָד רָמָה: וַיִּרְדְּפוּ מִצְרַיִם אַחֲרֵיהֶם וַיַּשִּׂיגוּ אוֹתָם חֹנִים שני
עַל־הַיָּם כָּל־סוּס רֶכֶב פַּרְעֹה וּפָרָשָׁיו וְחֵילוֹ עַל־פִּי הַחִירֹת
י לִפְנֵי בַּעַל צְפֹן: וּפַרְעֹה הִקְרִיב וַיִּשְׂאוּ בְנֵי־יִשְׂרָאֵל אֶת־
עֵינֵיהֶם וְהִנֵּה מִצְרַיִם ׀ נֹסֵעַ אַחֲרֵיהֶם וַיִּירְאוּ מְאֹד וַיִּצְעֲקוּ

VERSE 6
MALBIM

וַיֶּאְסֹר אֶת־רִכְבּוֹ — *So the king harnessed his chariot:* Because Pharaoh believed that Israel was desperately fleeing from him, that they were lost and terrified in the wilderness, he suspected that they were also entertaining the possibility of returning to the familiarity of Egypt. This is why Pharaoh did not enlist a huge contingent of soldiers to force Israel's return. Instead, he merely harnessed his own chariot and, taking along his personal bodyguard, set out to reclaim his slaves. And although Pharaoh was accompanied by *six hundred elite chariots and all the other chariots of Egypt*, that was not actually so large a number, for most of the horses in Egypt had perished during the cattle plague.

VERSE 7
HAAMEK DAVAR

וְכֹל רֶכֶב מִצְרָיִם — *And all the other chariots of Egypt:* This clause identifies chariots which did not belong to Egypt's standing army. These were privately owned vehicles whose drivers were not battle-ready. To chase after his quarry, Pharaoh commandeered all his citizens' chariots. And since these were irregular forces, the army needed to appoint officers to direct them, which explains the end of this verse — *with officers over them all.*

VERSE 9
RABBI SAMSON RAPHAEL HIRSCH

כָּל־סוּס רֶכֶב פַּרְעֹה — *All the king's horses and chariots:* Pharaoh's army is never discussed without the text mentioning its horses. It was these beasts that posed the greatest danger to Israel, and the nation so feared them that they believed there was no way they could escape into the wilderness. Meanwhile, the Israelites possessed only cows, sheep, and donkeys to carry them, peaceful animals that were hardly the engines of war that the Egyptian cavalry represented. War horses were not a feature of Israel's battle experience, nor did they ever play an important role in Israel's national achievements.

column of cloud to guide them, and at night in a column of fire to give them light, so that they might travel day and night. Neither the column of cloud by day nor that of fire by night once departed from the people.

14 ¹ Then the Lord said to Moshe, "Speak to the Israelites and tell them to turn back and camp in front of Pi HaḤirot, between Migdol and the sea, before Baal Tzefon. Encamp facing it, by ³ the sea. Pharaoh will think that the Israelites are lost across the ⁴ land, that they are trapped in the desert. I will toughen Pharaoh's heart, and he will pursue them. I will be glorified over Pharaoh and all his force, and the Egyptians will know that I ⁵ am the Lord." And so they did. When the king of Egypt was told that the Israelites had escaped, he and his officials changed their minds about the people: "What have we done, releasing

---
HAAMEK DAVAR (cont.)

God would perform at the sea, they would see and acknowledge that *I am the Lord*, who formerly executed all the miracles in the Egyptian homeland. Previously, Moshe had only mentioned that God's deeds would educate and convince Pharaoh himself. That is, the leader's statements to this effect were all expressed in the singular [see for example 8:18 and 9:29]. This was because the miracles of the plagues were produced only in front of Pharaoh, and he was the only person to see Moshe pray for the torments' removal. Thus the king learned very well that God keeps His word and follows through on his threats. But while this was happening, the rest of the Egyptian nation was oblivious to the interplay between God's pronouncements and His actions; all they saw was the steady stream of plagues that came and went. Now however, God announces that all of the Egyptians will observe His power and *will know that I am the Lord*.

VERSE 5
HAAMEK DAVAR

מַה־זֹּאת עָשִׂינוּ – *What have we done:* This statement does not reflect the Egyptians' astonishment at having released Israel from bondage – they recognized that they had little choice in the matter. Rather, they could not believe how negligent they were in not insisting that Israel's leaders solemnly swear to return to Egypt following the celebration of their festival in the wilderness. This point explains why our verse states: *What have we done, releasing the Israelites* [*Yisrael*, instead of the more common term *Benei Yisrael*, or the generic noun *am* – "nation"], referring to the leadership. The Egyptians now regretted not having made the Hebrews' release conditional on their elders' agreement to return. If these men had returned after their holiday, the nation would have surely followed them back to servitude.

עָנָ֞ן לַנְחֹתָ֤ם הַדֶּ֙רֶךְ֙ וְלַ֣יְלָה בְּעַמּ֤וּד אֵשׁ֙ לְהָאִ֣יר לָהֶ֔ם לָלֶ֖כֶת
כב יוֹמָ֥ם וָלָֽיְלָה׃ לֹֽא־יָמִ֞ישׁ עַמּ֤וּד הֶֽעָנָן֙ יוֹמָ֔ם וְעַמּ֥וּד הָאֵ֖שׁ לָ֑יְלָה
לִפְנֵ֖י הָעָֽם׃

יד א וַיְדַבֵּ֥ר יְהֹוָ֖ה אֶל־מֹשֶׁ֥ה לֵּאמֹֽר׃ דַּבֵּר֮ אֶל־בְּנֵ֣י יִשְׂרָאֵל֒ וְיָשֻׁ֗בוּ
וְיַחֲנוּ֙ לִפְנֵי֙ פִּ֣י הַחִירֹ֔ת בֵּ֥ין מִגְדֹּ֖ל וּבֵ֣ין הַיָּ֑ם לִפְנֵי֙ בַּ֣עַל צְפֹ֔ן
ג נִכְח֥וֹ תַחֲנ֖וּ עַל־הַיָּֽם׃ וְאָמַ֤ר פַּרְעֹה֙ לִבְנֵ֣י יִשְׂרָאֵ֔ל נְבֻכִ֥ים
ד הֵ֖ם בָּאָ֑רֶץ סָגַ֥ר עֲלֵיהֶ֖ם הַמִּדְבָּֽר׃ וְחִזַּקְתִּ֣י אֶת־לֵב־פַּרְעֹה֮
וְרָדַ֣ף אַחֲרֵיהֶם֒ וְאִכָּבְדָ֤ה בְּפַרְעֹה֙ וּבְכָל־חֵיל֔וֹ וְיָדְע֥וּ מִצְרַ֖יִם
ה כִּֽי־אֲנִ֣י יְהֹוָ֑ה וַיַּֽעֲשׂוּ־כֵֽן׃ וַיֻּגַּד֙ לְמֶ֣לֶךְ מִצְרַ֔יִם כִּ֥י בָרַ֖ח הָעָ֑ם
וַיֵּ֠הָפֵ֠ךְ לְבַ֨ב פַּרְעֹ֤ה וַעֲבָדָיו֙ אֶל־הָעָ֔ם וַיֹּֽאמְר֖וּ מַה־זֹּ֣את

CHAPTER 14, VERSE 2
SHADAL

לִפְנֵי בַּעַל צְפֹן – *Before Baal Tzefon:* The term *Baal Tzefon* is apparently the Torah's rendition of the word "Typhon," which was the name of a wicked Egyptian angel. The Egyptians had the practice of assigning this name to wastelands between the Nile and the Sea of Reeds. God led the Israelites to this area to deceive their erstwhile overlords into thinking that God had been no match for their angel (as Rashi explains). For they suspected that once the Israelites entered the domain of this evil god, it was he who caused them to begin wandering aimlessly through the desert. In addition, once the Egyptians saw where Israel had camped, they realized that it was not their intention to celebrate a festival to their God, since the location where they had stopped was dominated by their nasty deity and therefore not conducive to such an assembly.

VERSE 3
HAAMEK DAVAR

נְבֻכִים הֵם בָּאָרֶץ – *They are lost across the land:* Pharaoh will believe that Israel has taken a wrong turn through the desert dunes. **סָגַר עֲלֵיהֶם הַמִּדְבָּר** – *They are trapped in the desert:* Alternatively, the king might conclude that Israel's intention was not to cross the desert, even though they knew the proper route through it, and that this is why they had retreated from the wilderness.

VERSE 4
HAAMEK DAVAR

וְיָדְעוּ מִצְרַיִם – *And the Egyptians will know:* This prediction relates to the Egyptian population left behind on the seashore. When these people witnessed the wonders

19 The Israelites left Egypt armed for battle. And Moshe took with him the remains of Yosef, who had bound the Israelites by oath: "When God comes to your aid, bring my remains with you out
20 of here." They set out from Sukkot and camped at Etam, at the
21 edge of the desert. The LORD went ahead of them by day in a

---

RABBI JOSEPH B. SOLOVEITCHIK *(cont.)*

that one could identify as a Jew and act in accordance with Jewish precepts, both in poverty as a slave and in royal grandeur as the ruler of Egypt. Without his example as a precedent, Jews could not have endured the centuries of enslavement in Egypt. And why was Moshe so dedicated to this task? The commentators suggest it was because he was a grandson of Levi, Yosef's greatest antagonist. *Shimon and Levi are brothers... at their whim they hamstrung oxen* (Genesis 49:5–6). Levi was among the greatest of scoffers as Yosef recounted his dreams. But through his great descendant Moshe, Levi vicariously acknowledged his mistake. The Talmud (Sota 20b) comments on the phrase *Moshe took with him the remains of Yosef* as "with him in his abode." Moshe both physically carried Yosef's coffin and internalized Yosef's legacy. Moshe acknowledged that the entire nation owed their everlasting gratitude to Yosef, not only for their physical wellbeing (which had already been acknowledged as foretold in Yosef's first dream), but also, and perhaps mainly, for his spiritual leadership and example as represented in his second dream. This belated recognition constituted the complete fulfillment of the vision *The sun, moon, and eleven stars were bowing down to me* (Genesis 37:9). Could there be a more beautiful example of such obeisance than Moshe carrying Yosef's coffin on his shoulders? Yosef's spiritual mission on earth was now validated, his second dream fulfilled in its entirety.

VERSE 21
OR HAḤAYYIM

לַנְחֹתָם – *To guide them:* [Properly spelled, this word would be *lehanḥotam*. The contraction *lanḥotam*] suggests that the column of cloud traveled ahead of the people to make the route comfortable [*noaḥ*] for the nation. For the exodus took place at the start of the hot season, and God spread a protective cloud above Israel to shield them from the unpleasantness of the sun. This is why the cloud was only present during daylight hours. This screen was distinct from a separate cloud that traveled ahead of Israel to direct them through the wilderness. The role of that second cloud was to pave the path ahead of the people's feet – it leveled mounds and obstacles and filled in pits, indicating which way the nation should walk.

MALBIM

הֹלֵךְ לִפְנֵיהֶם – *Went ahead of them:* God's column of cloud and pillar of fire led Israel through the wilderness on an unceasing trek. The nation was pressured to travel day and night without resting. Pharaoh interpreted this forced march as meaning that the Hebrews were terrified that he would reclaim them and were running for their lives. When the king further saw that Israel was retracing their steps, he was convinced that his former slaves were lost and that God had abandoned them.

מִצְרָיִם: וַיִּקַּח מֹשֶׁה אֶת־עַצְמוֹת יוֹסֵף עִמּוֹ כִּי הַשְׁבֵּעַ
הִשְׁבִּיעַ אֶת־בְּנֵי יִשְׂרָאֵל לֵאמֹר פָּקֹד יִפְקֹד אֱלֹהִים אֶתְכֶם
וְהַעֲלִיתֶם אֶת־עַצְמֹתַי מִזֶּה אִתְּכֶם: וַיִּסְעוּ מִסֻּכֹּת וַיַּחֲנוּ
בְאֵתָם בִּקְצֵה הַמִּדְבָּר: וַיהֹוָה הֹלֵךְ לִפְנֵיהֶם יוֹמָם בְּעַמּוּד

MALBIM (cont.)

Reeds; rather, He had them wander around the desert for a time to deceive Pharaoh into thinking they were lost there. Still, our verse informs us that *the Israelites left Egypt armed for battle.* They thus prepared for the time when the Canaanites would be sufficiently frightened and readied themselves to receive divine assistance in conquering them.

VERSE 19

OR HAḤAYYIM

וְהַעֲלִיתֶם אֶת־עַצְמֹתַי מִזֶּה אִתְּכֶם – *Bring my remains with you out of here:* When Yosef's brothers agreed to take his body with them upon their eventual departure from Egypt, they were repairing the rift that they had caused by selling him into slavery decades earlier. It was that gesture of transporting his body to Canaan that would reunite the family. Thus Yosef emphasizes that they should take his remains with them – that would symbolize that he had once again joined the group of his father's sons.

RABBI SAMSON RAPHAEL HIRSCH

אֶת־עַצְמוֹת יוֹסֵף – *The remains of Yosef:* Why is this matter mentioned here and not earlier when Israel actually left Ramesses [in 12:37]? Perhaps the Torah is illustrating a contrast between the confidence of one individual and the doubt of an entire nation. For 600,000 armed men found it difficult to trust that God would grant them victory in their wars of conquest in Canaan [hence God's reservations in 13:17]. But while Israel lacked faith in God's promise to bequeath the land to them, one true Jew – Yosef the righteous – remained steadfast in his belief that God would return His people to the land. Yosef knew this would happen even though he did not see it in his lifetime; he trusted it would occur after his death. And of course, his faith was eventually rewarded.

MALBIM

אֶת־עַצְמוֹת יוֹסֵף – *The remains of Yosef:* It certainly would have been more convenient for Israel to wait until they reached their homeland and to then send messengers back to Egypt to retrieve Yosef's coffin. However, the nation felt obliged to honor the promise that Yosef had made his brothers swear, namely that they would take his bones with them when they left the country. Since Yosef had insisted that they take his remains "with you," he indicated his preference to leave along with the entire people rather than to be fetched later.

RABBI JOSEPH B. SOLOVEITCHIK

אֶת־עַצְמוֹת יוֹסֵף – *The remains of Yosef:* Moshe acknowledged the importance of Yosef and his spiritual mission as the paragon of Jewish commitment in exile. Yosef had demonstrated

13 17 When Pharaoh let the people go, God did not lead them through the land of the Philistines, though it was the shorter way; "If the people face war," thought God, "they will change 18 their minds and go back to Egypt." So He led them on a roundabout course, by way of the wilderness, to the Sea of Reeds.

RABBI SAMSON RAPHAEL HIRSCH *(cont.)*

willingness to protect them. This meant that they were missing that element which affords the soldier the courage to rely on Him under all circumstances. For the truly faithful know that everything rests in the hands of God.

MALBIM

וַיְהִי בְּשַׁלַּח פַּרְעֹה – *When Pharaoh let the people go:* The story that the exodus narrative tells is one of Pharaoh being forced to set Israel free of his own volition. God did not forcibly emancipate His nation from Egypt by crushing the Egyptian army in battle. Furthermore, even though God repeatedly warned the king and threatened to strike him with plagues and wonders for the sake of sanctifying and publicizing His name, He did not cause Israel to leave by having them rise in rebellion. There were two reasons why God managed Israel's departure in this way: Firstly, the redemption was being conducted some time before the completion of the decreed four hundred years of slavery. This meant that God could not take Israel out of the land without Pharaoh's permission [since the Egyptians were rightfully owed four full centuries]. Secondly, the intensity of divine assistance that God bestows upon anyone depends on their level of preparation to receive such aid. And so, for Israel to have a chance at defeating the Canaanite nations, who were physically stronger and better trained than they were, they needed to boost their courage and their confidence. It is only once they had reached that state of mind that God could provide them with strength and the power beyond their natural faculties. This is why the Israelites would have been unable to field a worthy army at the outset of their emancipation, and why God did not assign them the task of overrunning the Egyptian state. Instead, He manipulated events so that Pharaoh would cast Israel out willingly.

VERSE 18

MALBIM

דֶּרֶךְ הַמִּדְבָּר יַם-סוּף – *By way of the wilderness, to the Sea of Reeds:* God helped Israel to prepare for their future confrontations, partially by leading them through the desert to the Sea of Reeds. For the episode that happened there had several results [in addition to disposing of the Egyptian enemy]. Firstly, the splitting of the sea struck fear in the hearts of the Canaanites, as the verse states: *Nations heard and they trembled* (15:14). Secondly, following their rescue, Israel *believed in the* LORD *and in Moshe His servant* (14:31). It was for these reasons that God took Israel to the Sea of Reeds. And after they had spent a year in the desert and had acquired faith and courage, they were then ready to march on the land of Canaan, which they would have conquered immediately had it not been for the sin of the spies. Nevertheless, God did not lead the Israelites straight to the Sea of

יג ויְהִי בְּשַׁלַּח פַּרְעֹה אֶת־הָעָם וְלֹא־נָחָם אֱלֹהִים דֶּרֶךְ אֶרֶץ
פְּלִשְׁתִּים כִּי קָרוֹב הוּא כִּי ׀ אָמַר אֱלֹהִים פֶּן־יִנָּחֵם הָעָם
יח בִּרְאֹתָם מִלְחָמָה וְשָׁבוּ מִצְרָיְמָה: וַיַּסֵּב אֱלֹהִים ׀ אֶת־הָעָם
דֶּרֶךְ הַמִּדְבָּר יַם־סוּף וַחֲמֻשִׁים עָלוּ בְנֵי־יִשְׂרָאֵל מֵאֶרֶץ

CHAPTER 13, VERSE 17

OR HAHAYYIM

וַיְהִי בְּשַׁלַּח פַּרְעֹה אֶת־הָעָם — *When Pharaoh let the people go:* Why does this passage begin with the word *vayhi* [literally, "and it was"], a term that usually foreshadows anguish and ill fortune? Also, why does the text seem to attribute Israel's emancipation to Pharaoh instead of identifying the Creator as the true author of the exodus? In truth, these two details of Israel's redemption are intertwined. The term *vayhi* hints at the impending terror that the nation would experience when they saw Pharaoh and his army bearing down upon them. And Pharaoh's pursuit was in turn influenced by how God chose not to have Israel leave Egypt against Pharaoh's will [by just pushing the king and his guards aside]. For Pharaoh was livid that God had compelled him to do His bidding and willingly release his Hebrew slaves. Pharaoh resented how his own arm had been twisted until he himself uttered the words *Get up, get out from among my people, you and the Israelites* (12:31). Of course, this plan also led Pharaoh into his own destruction and that of his nation. And from God's perspective, that was not a joyous outcome but a tragic one. For the Holy One, blessed be He, is never pleased when His creations are destroyed.

SHADAL

וְלֹא־נָחָם אֱלֹהִים — *God did not lead them:* God was reluctant to lead Israel straight to their homeland, where they would immediately have to engage in wars of conquest. For He knew that their fearful hearts would prefer to return to the Egyptian slavery than to plunge into the horrors of battle. God therefore led the people into the wilderness where they could slowly undergo the training and acquire the temperament necessary to govern themselves in their own land. There was also an additional reason behind this delay in reaching the land of Israel. For while the entire nation sojourned together in the desert, they were able to receive the Torah and its commandments and be taught the proper reverence of God required to walk in His ways. Before they settled down to a permanent existence in the land, Israel had to be guided in the right philosophy of trusting in God and His servant, Moshe. On the other hand, had the Israelites been brought directly to their land, the tribes would soon have dispersed to their respective territories and it would have become impossible to teach them as a single nation under God.

RABBI SAMSON RAPHAEL HIRSCH

וְלֹא־נָחָם אֱלֹהִים — *God did not lead them:* Of course Israel did not lack the armaments necessary to confront the Philistines. What they were missing was bravery and the fighting spirit required to engage in war. Furthermore, they still had not fully developed trust in God's

פרשת בשלח
PARASHAT BESHALAḤ

CONFRONTING
MODERNITY

18TH CENTURY

RABBI ḤAYYIM IBN ATTAR – *OR HAḤAYYIM*,
1696, MOROCCO – 1743, ISRAEL

19TH CENTURY

RABBI YAAKOV TZVI MECKLENBURG –
***HAKETAV VEHAKABBALA*,**
1785 – 1865, GERMANY

SHADAL, 1800 – 1865, ITALY

RABBI SAMSON RAPHAEL HIRSCH,
1808 – 1888, GERMANY

MALBIM, 1809 – 1879, UKRAINE

RABBI NAFTALI TZVI YEHUDA BERLIN –
***HAAMEK DAVAR*,** 1816, BELARUS – 1893, POLAND

20TH CENTURY

RABBI MEIR SIMḤA OF DVINSK – *MESHEKH HOKHMA*, 1843, LITHUANIA – 1926, LATVIA

RABBI JOSEPH B. SOLOVEITCHIK,
1903, LITHUANIA – 1993, USA

NEHAMA LEIBOWITZ,
1905, LATVIA – 1997, ISRAEL

15 of Amalek, utterly, from under the heavens." Moshe built an
16 altar and named it, "The LORD Is My Banner," saying, "There is a hand on the LORD's throne. The LORD will be at war with Amalek throughout the ages."

―――― RASHI *(cont.)* ――――

have come to an end, in perpetual ruins (Psalms 9:7). That verse evokes Esav – whom we know to have *kept his wrath perpetually* (Amos 1:11) – and it continues: *For you have destroyed the cities; their memorial is perished,* followed by the phrase *But the LORD shall endure forever* – indicating the wholeness of God's name – and *He has prepared His throne for judgment* (Psalms 9:8), showing that His throne will then be complete.

―――― RASHBAM ――――

כִּי־יָד עַל־כֵּס יָהּ – *There is a hand on the LORD's throne:* Said Moshe: I have called the altar "The LORD is My Banner" much in the same way that a person might be named *Eliezer* [meaning "God is my aid"] or *Emmanuel* ["God is with us"]. For the Holy One, blessed be He, has raised His hand to His throne and sworn that *The LORD will be at war with Amalek throughout the ages.* The imagery here is similar to that in the verse *For I lift up my hand to heaven* [Deuteronomy 32:40, where the gesture denotes an oath]. That is the straightforward meaning of the text. Other commentators explain that there will be a war against Amalek when a mighty hand rules on the secure throne of God, that is, once an able king rules over Israel. But this reading seems incorrect to me, for if the verse meant that, it should have stated: "a hand will be on the LORD's throne" – in the future tense. Rather, the sense of the verse is I have explained it above: God swears now on His existing throne.

―――― IBN EZRA ――――

כִּי־יָד עַל־כֵּס יָהּ – *There is a hand on the LORD's throne:* We find a similar imagery in the verse *For I lift up my hand to heaven* (Deuteronomy 32:40). The text portrays God as placing His hand on His throne to swear an oath. Rabbi Yehoshua interprets it to mean that the first king to occupy Israel's throne will wield a mighty hand. This refers to Sha'ul [who fought Amalek upon assuming the monarchy, see I Samuel 15]. And so states the verse: *Then Shlomo sat on the throne of the LORD as king instead of David his father* [I Chronicles 29:23; the cited verse supports the idea that the human king of Israel is said to sit upon God's throne].

―――― ABARBANEL ――――

מִדֹּר דֹּר – *Throughout the ages:* The reason God is locked in an eternal conflict with Amalek is because they attempted to belittle Him and to diminish the glory of God in this world. Even after the wonders that God had performed in Egypt, Amalek struck out at the divine throne, displaying its insolence and lack of reverence. And because Amalek's goal was to challenge God's authority, He is determined to avenge His honor – to destroy that nation and repair the blasphemy that they intended. Furthermore, Amalek must pay for their despicable tactic of attacking from the rear [as described in Deuteronomy 25:17–18]. Hence both God and the nation of Israel must seek their vengeance against this people. The LORD, may He be blessed, will erase the memory of Amalek from the world, while Israel remembers their heinous behavior.

וַיִּ֤בֶן מֹשֶׁה֙ מִזְבֵּ֔חַ וַיִּקְרָ֥א שְׁמ֖וֹ יְהוָ֥ה ׀ נִסִּֽי׃ וַיֹּ֗אמֶר כִּי־יָד֙ עַל־כֵּ֣ס יָ֔הּ מִלְחָמָ֥ה לַיהוָ֖ה בַּֽעֲמָלֵ֑ק מִדֹּ֖ר דֹּֽר׃

RABBI AVRAHAM BEN HARAMBAM

כְּתֹב זֹאת זִכָּרוֹן בַּסֵּפֶר – *Write this as a memorial on a scroll:* According to our Sages, even before Moshe wrote the Torah at the end of Israel's forty year sojourn, he recorded the events in the desert as they transpired. Moshe would present these short texts to the people as distinct passages. Eventually all of these records were collected and arranged, other material was added to them as dictated by God to produce the entire Torah from the first letter *bet* of Genesis to the final *lamed* of Deuteronomy. Support for this theory can be found in the statement at the end of Parashat Mishpatim: *And Moshe wrote down all the Lord's words.... And he took the book of the covenant; and read it aloud to the people* (24:4, 7). The text referred to there is not the Torah as we know it, which at that time was incomplete. It seems to me that our current verse describes the recording of just such a limited nature. Now Rav Se'adya Gaon argues that the command here alludes to the parallel passage, *Remember what Amalek did to you* [Deuteronomy 25:17; i.e., that is the account that Yehoshua was commanded to write].

VERSE 15

RASHI

וַיִּקְרָא שְׁמוֹ – *And named it:* [The word *nes*, translated here as "banner," can also mean "miracle."] Moshe named the altar *Adonai Nisi*, meaning "the Holy One, blessed be He, performed a miracle for us here." This does not mean that Moshe gave the altar the name of God, but that people would recall God's miracle when they mentioned this altar, declaring: "The Lord is our Miracle."

RASHBAM

יהוה נִסִּי – *The Lord is my banner:* The staff of God was held aloft like a banner on the hilltop. And in the future, God will raise that same symbol when Amalek is ultimately defeated on the battlefield, as God promises: *I will erase the memory of Amalek, utterly* (17:14).

SFORNO

וַיִּקְרָא שְׁמוֹ – *And named it:* "It" refers [not to the altar but] to God, whom Moshe named in his prayer, as in the verse *I called upon Your name, O Lord* (Lamentations 3:55).

VERSE 16

RASHI

וַיֹּאמֶר – *Saying:* Moshe said: *There is a hand on the Lord's throne.* The Holy One, blessed be He, raised His hand to swear by His throne, vowing to wage eternal war and to harbor perpetual enmity against Amalek. Why does the verse use the term *kes*, an abridged form of the word *kisei* [meaning "chair or throne"]? And why is the name of God halved [with just the first two letters – *yod-heh* – appearing]? Because God swore that his name would remain incomplete and his throne would also not be whole before the name of Esav [progenitor of Amalek; see Genesis 36:10–12] is blotted out from the world. However, when his name is erased, God's name and His throne will be complete. We see this as well in the verse which states: *The enemies*

12 drop, the Amalekites prevailed. But Moshe's hands grew heavy. So they took a stone and placed it under him and he sat, while Aharon and Ḥur held up his hands, one on each side, so that his
13 hands held true until sunset. And Yehoshua overcame Amalek and his people by the sword.
14 Then the LORD said to Moshe, "Write this as a memorial on a scroll, and commit it to Yehoshua's ears: I will erase the memory

MAFTIR

RASHBAM

וַיַּחֲלֹשׁ יְהוֹשֻׁעַ – *And Yehoshua overcame:* [Literally, "And Yehoshua weakened."] He defeated the enemy. We find a similar usage of this verb in the verse, *But Moshe said, "It is neither the sound of triumph nor the wailing of defeat [ḥalusha]. What I hear is the sound of revelry"* (32:18).

SFORNO

אֶת־עֲמָלֵק וְאֶת־עַמּוֹ – *Amalek and his people:* This refers to mercenaries whom Amalek had enlisted from other nations.

VERSE 14

RASHI

כְּתֹב זֹאת זִכָּרוֹן – *Write this as a memorial:* Record for posterity that Amalek was the first nation to contend with Israel. וְשִׂים בְּאָזְנֵי יְהוֹשֻׁעַ – *And commit it to Yehoshua's ears:* Since Yehoshua will eventually lead the nation into the land of Israel, he will command the people to avenge Amalek's unprovoked aggression. Thus God hinted to Moshe that it would be his successor who would conduct Israel into their land. כִּי־מָחֹה אֶמְחֶה – *I will erase:* I am directing you to remember the behavior of Amalek so that you will understand My plan to destroy them.

IBN EZRA

בַּסֵּפֶר – *On a scroll:* [Literally, "on the scroll."] This passage was stated during Israel's fortieth year in the desert. Proof for this lies in how the word *basefer* is vocalized with a *pataḥ* [rendering it "on the scroll"]. This means that the account of the conflict was to be recorded in a well-known scroll, which can only refer to the Torah. Still, it is possible that God refers to a different scroll that Israel possessed, subsequently called "The Book of the Wars of the LORD" [see Numbers 21:14]. That work has been lost to history along with other texts mentioned in Scripture: The Book of the Upright [see Joshua:10:13], The Tales of the Prophet Ido [see II Chronicles 13:22], The History of the Kings of Israel [I Kings 14:19], and additional writings of King Shlomo [alluded to in I Kings 5:12]. כִּי־מָחֹה אֶמְחֶה – *I will erase:* The reason Amalek must be obliterated is that they angered God. At a time when *terror seized the Philistines* (15:14), when *the chiefs of Edom were dismayed* and *Moav's leaders were seized with trembling* (15:15), Amalek learned of the signs and wonders God had performed in Egypt and remained unimpressed. Even as they knew about the might God exercised on behalf of His nation Israel, they traveled from a distant land to fight the people *with no fear of God* (Deuteronomy 25:18).

יב וִידֵי מֹשֶׁה כְּבֵדִים וַיִּקְחוּ־אֶבֶן וַיָּשִׂימוּ תַחְתָּיו וַיֵּשֶׁב עָלֶיהָ וְאַהֲרֹן וְחוּר תָּמְכוּ בְיָדָיו מִזֶּה אֶחָד וּמִזֶּה אֶחָד וַיְהִי יָדָיו אֱמוּנָה עַד־בֹּא הַשָּׁמֶשׁ: יג וַיַּחֲלֹשׁ יְהוֹשֻׁעַ אֶת־עֲמָלֵק וְאֶת־עַמּוֹ לְפִי־חָרֶב:

מפטיר יד וַיֹּאמֶר יְהוָה אֶל־מֹשֶׁה כְּתֹב זֹאת זִכָּרוֹן בַּסֵּפֶר וְשִׂים בְּאָזְנֵי יְהוֹשֻׁעַ כִּי־מָחֹה אֶמְחֶה אֶת־זֵכֶר עֲמָלֵק מִתַּחַת הַשָּׁמָיִם:

VERSE 12

RASHI

וִידֵי מֹשֶׁה כְּבֵדִים – **But Moshe's hands grew heavy:** Moshe's hands became heavy as a punishment for his laziness in passing on to Yehoshua the command to fight for Israel. וַיִּקְחוּ – **So they took:** Moshe's companions Aharon and Hur procured a stone for him to sit on. Moshe refused to sit on a pillow or a blanket, for he argued: Since Israel is suffering the travails of war, I will join them in their discomfort. וַיְהִי יָדָיו אֱמוּנָה – **So that his hands held true:** [Were the verb in this phrase actually referring to Moshe's hands, it would have been plural: *vayihyu*. Since the verb is singular – *vayhi* – its subject must be] Moshe, who faithfully held his hands spread out toward the sky in sincere and honest prayer. עַד־בֹּא הַשָּׁמֶשׁ – **Until sunset:** The Amalekites used their knowledge of astrology to calculate the hour of their victory. But Moshe held the sun still in the sky and confused the hours for them.

RASHBAM

וַיְהִי יָדָיו אֱמוּנָה – **So that his hands held true:** [Literally, "his hands were faith."] The phrase means that Moshe's arms maintained their strength.

HIZKUNI

וַיְהִי יָדָיו אֱמוּנָה – **So that his hands held true:** [Literally, "his hands were faith."] The text mentions the term *emuna* [meaning "faith"] to recall the faith that Avraham possessed, as the verse states: *And he believed [he'emin] in the* LORD (Genesis 15:6). The verse also suggests the merit accrued by Yitzhak, as the verse states: *And Yitzhak came [ba] from the way of Be'er Lahai Ro'i* (Genesis 24:62), and that of Yaakov about whom the verse states: *And as he passed over Penuel the sun [hashemesh] rose upon him* [Genesis 32:32; combined, these two words form the phrase *bo hashemesh* – meaning "sunset" – which appears in this verse].

VERSE 13

RASHI

וַיַּחֲלֹשׁ יְהוֹשֻׁעַ – **And Yehoshua overcame:** [Literally, "And Yehoshua weakened."] Yehoshua decapitated Amalek's leading warriors, leaving alive only their weakest soldiers. He did not obliterate the entire enemy army. We learn from this that the Israelite battle plan must have been divinely ordained. [Yehoshua would not have exercised restraint unless commanded by God to do so.]

against Amalek. Tomorrow I will stand on top of the hill with
10 the staff of God in my hand." Yehoshua fought the Amalekites
as Moshe had directed him, while Moshe, Aharon, and Hur
11 climbed to the top of the hill. Whenever Moshe held his hand
high, the Israelites prevailed, but whenever he let his hand

ABARBANEL

אָנֹכִי נִצָּב עַל־רֹאשׁ הַגִּבְעָה – *I will stand on top of the hill:* It is possible that Moshe had no desire to personally join in the fighting so as not to lower himself to the level of Amalek. Had Moshe too taken up arms, Amalek would have been able to boast that they contended with Moshe himself and with all of Israel. Moshe disparaged Amalek by sending his deputy Yehoshua to fight them in his stead. He also avoided sending the entire Israelite army to fight off the menace, telling Yehoshua to take just a few men to handle the problem. All of this was to preserve the honor of Moshe and the nation.

VERSE 10

RASHI

וּמֹשֶׁה אַהֲרֹן וְחוּר – *Moshe, Aharon, and Hur:* This episode teaches us rules for a fast day, for the nation of Israel were fasting as they were fighting Amalek. We learn that three people must advance together to pray before the Ark on a fast day [to increase the community's chances of a successful hearing]. וְחוּר – *And Hur:* Hur was Miriam's son.

BEKHOR SHOR

וּמֹשֶׁה אַהֲרֹן וְחוּר – *Moshe, Aharon, and Hur:* The two men accompanied Moshe up the hill in order to support his arms. For Moshe knew that if he lowered his arms, his soldiers would flinch and Amalek would dominate them.

GUR ARYEH

וְחוּר – *And Hur:* According to Rashi, Hur was Miriam's son. He thus explains why this man was chosen to assist Moshe instead of the leader's other nephews, Nadav and Avihu [Aharon's sons]. Since Hur was Miriam's son, all three siblings were represented on the mountain. Their combined merits would secure victory for Israel's fighting forces. For Moshe, Aharon and Miriam served as Israel's shepherds, and Hur added Miriam's value to the effort.

VERSE 11

RASHI

כַּאֲשֶׁר יָרִים מֹשֶׁה יָדוֹ – *Whenever Moshe held his hand high:* Did Moshe's hands have the power to turn the battle in Israel's favor? See the Talmud's discussion on this matter (Rosh HaShana 29a). [According to that source, when Moshe raised his hands to the heavens, the people were encouraged to pray to God for assistance.]

RASHBAM

כַּאֲשֶׁר יָרִים מֹשֶׁה יָדוֹ – *Whenever Moshe held his hand high:* Along with the staff.

אָנֹכִי נִצָּב עַל־רֹאשׁ הַגִּבְעָה וּמַטֵּה הָאֱלֹהִים בְּיָדִי:
יא וַיַּעַשׂ יְהוֹשֻׁעַ כַּאֲשֶׁר אָמַר־לוֹ מֹשֶׁה לְהִלָּחֵם בַּעֲמָלֵק
וּמֹשֶׁה אַהֲרֹן וְחוּר עָלוּ רֹאשׁ הַגִּבְעָה: וְהָיָה כַּאֲשֶׁר יָרִים
מֹשֶׁה יָדוֹ וְגָבַר יִשְׂרָאֵל וְכַאֲשֶׁר יָנִיחַ יָדוֹ וְגָבַר עֲמָלֵק:

RAMBAN

וַיֹּאמֶר מֹשֶׁה אֶל־יְהוֹשֻׁעַ – *Moshe said to Yehoshua:* It seems from this text that as long as Moshe had known his aide, he called him Yehoshua. We similarly read later: *Yehoshua heard the noise of the people shouting* (32:17). And so when we encounter the verse *And Moshe called Hoshea son of Nun Yehoshua* (Numbers 13:16), we must understand that this refers to a change of name Moshe instituted early on [not during the story of the spies where that verse occurs]. That verse informs us that the Hoshea bin Nun is the same man whom Moshe called Yehoshua.... Moshe perhaps feared that Amalek would overpower Israel with their skilled swordsmanship, for Yitzḥak had blessed their ancestor Esav: *By your sword shall you live* (Genesis 27:40). Know that the first and last wars that Israel fights will be against this family, for Amalek descends from Esav [see Genesis 36:12]. These people are the mightiest of nations, and they were the first to attack us. Furthermore, Esav's descendants were responsible for destroying our Temple and for the current exile, as our Sages have stated: Today we are in the exile of Edom [Avoda Zara 2b; Rome is traditionally associated with Esav and Edom]. And when these people are ultimately defeated, and they and their allies are weakened, we will enjoy eternal salvation. Thus the verse states: *And liberators shall ascend upon Mount Zion to judge the mountain of Esav, and the kingdom shall be the Lord's* (Obadiah 1:21). Recognize that the battle that Moshe and Yehoshua fought against Amalek will be repeated by Eliyahu and the Messiah son of Yosef when they confront Esav's future descendants. This is why Moshe made such a concerted effort to defeat this enemy.

ḤIZKUNI

אָנֹכִי נִצָּב עַל־רֹאשׁ הַגִּבְעָה – *I will stand on top of the hill:* I will position myself there so that our soldiers will be able to see me. The sight of me will encourage the men as they face battle. This effort is similar to the gesture in the verse *For Yehoshua did not withdraw his hand, with which he stretched out the spear, until he had utterly destroyed all the inhabitants of Ai* (Joshua 8:26). For it is the universal custom for armies to appoint one of their soldiers to hold aloft the regiment's or country's colors when the enemy is engaged. This flag bearer stands on an elevated spot so that his compatriots can glimpse him as they charge into battle. The figure remains a motivating sign throughout the conflict. Of course, should the banner be lowered or fall, that would suggest to the troops that their national symbol had been toppled, and with it their morale. In the current episode, the staff in Moshe's hands served the role of Israel's standard and a sign for the people's victory.

7 is what Moshe did, before the eyes of the elders of Israel. He named the place Masa and Meriva, because the people had quarreled and had tested the LORD, demanding, "Is the LORD among us or not?"

8
9 Then, at Refidim, Amalek came and attacked Israel. Moshe said to Yehoshua, "Choose men for us, and go out and do battle

---

ABARBANEL *(cont.)*

no such courtesy, preferring instead to strike suddenly like bandits in the night.... When reviewing this episode later, the Torah characterizes Amalek's assault: *He met you by the way, and smote the hindmost of you, all that were feeble in your rear, when you were faint and weary* (Deuteronomy 25:18). They were comparable to thieves who come to steal and then lash out when they are discovered. Some authors argue that Amalek had not set out from their home to confront Israel but were merely traveling to another land when they chanced upon the Israelites camping at Refidim. They observed the Hebrews lying hungry and thirsty in their tents, and instead of aiding them, decided to fight them.

VERSE 9

RASHI

בְּחַר־לָנוּ – *Choose for us:* Why does Moshe ask Yehoshua to choose men "for us" – as if to say "for me and for you"? He thereby equated his protégé to himself. Based on this statement, our Sages teach that a master should treat his student with the honor he himself deserves [see Avot 4:15]. Furthermore, how do we know that one should exercise the same respect toward one's fellow as one would to a teacher? We learn this rule from the verse *And Aharon said to Moshe, "Alas, my lord, I pray you"* (Numbers 12:11). Now was Aharon not older than Moshe by three years? And yet he treated his younger contemporary as his superior. Finally, we learn that one should fear one's teacher as one reveres God, as the verse states: *My lord Moshe restrain them [kela'em]* [Numbers 11:28, regarding those who prophesied without Moshe's permission]. Yehoshua advised Moshe to eradicate them [*kalem*] from the world. He felt that these men deserved to be destroyed for disrespecting his teacher Moshe, a crime as heinous as a sinning against God. וְצֵא הִלָּחֵם – *And go out and do battle:* Emerge from God's protective cloud and fight against Amalek. מָחָר – *Tomorrow:* When the battle is fought, *I will stand on top of the hill.* בְּחַר־לָנוּ אֲנָשִׁים – *Choose men for us:* [The term *anashim* denotes exceptional men.] Select mighty warriors who are also sin-fearing men, such that the merits they have accrued might assist us in victory. An alternative interpretation: Select men able to combat the witchcraft wielded by Amalek as a weapon.

IBN EZRA

וַיֹּאמֶר מֹשֶׁה אֶל־יְהוֹשֻׁעַ – *Moshe said to Yehoshua:* Yehoshua was the grandson of Elishama son of Amihud, chief of the tribe of Efrayim [see Numbers 1:10]. He is referred to here as Yehoshua since that is the name Moshe gave him on account of the spies. [Before that his name had been Hoshea; see Numbers 13:8, 16.] וּמַטֵּה הָאֱלֹהִים בְּיָדִי – *With the staff of God in my hand:* I will raise the staff when I pray to God.

BESHALAḤ | THE CLASSIC COMMENTATORS — SHEMOT | CHAPTER 17

זִקְנֵי יִשְׂרָאֵל: וַיִּקְרָא שֵׁם הַמָּקוֹם מַסָּה וּמְרִיבָה עַל־רִיב ׀ בְּנֵי יִשְׂרָאֵל וְעַל נַסֹּתָם אֶת־יהוה לֵאמֹר הֲיֵשׁ יהוה בְּקִרְבֵּנוּ אִם־אָיִן:

ח וַיָּבֹא עֲמָלֵק וַיִּלָּחֶם עִם־יִשְׂרָאֵל בִּרְפִידִם: וַיֹּאמֶר מֹשֶׁה אֶל־יְהוֹשֻׁעַ בְּחַר־לָנוּ אֲנָשִׁים וְצֵא הִלָּחֵם בַּעֲמָלֵק מָחָר

VERSE 8

RASHI

וַיָּבֹא עֲמָלֵק — *Then Amalek came:* The Torah juxtaposes the story of Amalek with Israel's demand for water in order to teach that one led to the other. For God chastised Israel: Are you unaware that I am with you always, that I am constantly ready to provide for you? How dare you ask: *Is the Lord among us or not* (17:7)? I swear on your lives that I will dispatch a dog to bite you [i.e., Amalek]. And when you cry for My assistance, then you will know where I am. The situation may be compared to a man who places his son on his shoulders and takes him for a walk. As they proceed, the boy sees some treat he desires and says: "Father! Get that for me!" And the father does. They continue on their way, and again the child asks for something, prompting the parent's indulgence. This keeps happening until, by and by, they meet an acquaintance, whereupon the boy turns to the man and says: "Have you seen my father anywhere?" The father explodes: "You ingrate! Don't you know where I am?" He immediately pulls the boy from his shoulders and throws him to the ground, whereupon a dog comes along and bites him.

IBN EZRA

וַיָּבֹא עֲמָלֵק — *Then Amalek came:* The nation of Amalek arrived, they who dwelled in the land of the Negev [see Numbers 13:29].

ḤIZKUNI

וַיָּבֹא עֲמָלֵק — *Then Amalek came:* Where exactly did Amalek arrive from? Our verse hearkens back to an earlier text, *And Esav took his wives, and his sons...and went into another country away from his brother Yaakov* (Genesis 36:6). Commenting on that verse, Rashi writes that Esav settled there to escape the decree imposed on Yitzḥak's descendants in the verse *Your seed shall be a stranger in a land that is not theirs* (Genesis 15:13). Said Esav: I am leaving — I want no part in this gift of land or in the price I would have to pay to get it. Another reason Esav put distance between himself and his brother was that he was ashamed for having sold his birthright to Yaakov. Because of this, Esav's grandson Amalek [see Genesis 36:12] waited for Israel to leave Egypt and finish suffering their four-hundred-year affliction. [Once the curse had been satisfied, they were happy to fight to regain the blessing.]

ABARBANEL

וַיָּבֹא עֲמָלֵק — *Then Amalek came:* The Torah describes Amalek's depravity and wickedness in flouting the chivalry of kings who determine to attack their enemies. The usual protocol is to issue a declaration of war, announcing one's intention to do battle. But Amalek showed

3 me?" asked Moshe. "Why are you testing the Lord?" But the people were thirsty for water. They railed against Moshe, "Why did you bring us out of Egypt? Was it to kill me, my children,
4 and all my livestock by thirst?" "What shall I do with this people?" Moshe cried to the Lord – "another moment and they
5 will stone me." The Lord answered Moshe, "Walk out to face the people taking some of the elders of Israel with you. Take
6 the staff with which you struck the Nile in your hand, and go. I will be there before you by the rock at Ḥorev. Strike the rock, water will come out of it and the people will drink." And that

─────────── RASHI *(cont.)* ───────────

of inflicting punishment. Hence Moshe is now told to take hold of *the staff with which you struck the Nile,* thereby proving to the people that the instrument could also be used to call down blessing.

─────────── IBN EZRA ───────────

וַיֹּאמֶר יהוה אֶל־מֹשֶׁה – *The Lord answered Moshe:* Because God heard Moshe tell Him: *Another moment and they will stone me* (17:4), He instructed His emissary to face the people who had been fighting with him and to tell them that he would now give them water.

─────────── RAMBAN ───────────

וּמַטְּךָ אֲשֶׁר הִכִּיתָ בּוֹ אֶת־הַיְאֹר – *The staff with which you struck the Nile:* That is, the staff that Aharon used to strike the Nile upon your command [see 7:19] The rod here is mentioned as effecting the plague of blood – note that God does not declare: "Take the staff that was turned into a snake," or: "Take the staff that you used to perform the signs." The association that God does make here emphasizes how at the Nile the waters were turned to blood and their inherent nature was transformed. Now that same rod would be used to extract water from a rock, a miracle that similarly overturns the natural order of things.

VERSE 6

─────────── RASHI ───────────

וְהִכִּיתָ בַצּוּר – *Strike the rock:* Moshe is not instructed to strike "upon the rock" [*al hatzur*], but to strike "in the rock" [*batzur*]. This teaches that the staff was composed of a hard material called *sanpirinon* [perhaps lapis lazuli] that was able to cleave the stone.

─────────── RAMBAN ───────────

הִנְנִי עֹמֵד לְפָנֶיךָ שָּׁם – *I will be there before you:* According to our Sages, from this moment onward the location became a permanent source of water, perpetuating the wonder as long as Israel remained in the desert. For this reason, the Divine Presence revealed itself at this spot. The same sort of divine revelation occurred when the manna was first delivered, as the verse states: *And by morning you shall see the Lord's glory* (16:7), since that miracle too was constantly repeated.

מֹשֶׁה מַה־תְּרִיבוּן עִמָּדִי מַה־תְּנַסּוּן אֶת־יְהוָה: וַיִּצְמָא שָׁם הָעָם לַמַּיִם וַיָּלֶן הָעָם עַל־מֹשֶׁה וַיֹּאמֶר לָמָּה זֶּה הֶעֱלִיתָנוּ מִמִּצְרַיִם לְהָמִית אֹתִי וְאֶת־בָּנַי וְאֶת־מִקְנַי בַּצָּמָא: וַיִּצְעַק מֹשֶׁה אֶל־יְהוָה לֵאמֹר מָה אֶעֱשֶׂה לָעָם הַזֶּה עוֹד מְעַט וּסְקָלֻנִי: וַיֹּאמֶר יְהוָה אֶל־מֹשֶׁה עֲבֹר לִפְנֵי הָעָם וְקַח אִתְּךָ מִזִּקְנֵי יִשְׂרָאֵל וּמַטְּךָ אֲשֶׁר הִכִּיתָ בּוֹ אֶת־הַיְאֹר קַח בְּיָדְךָ וְהָלָכְתָּ: הִנְנִי עֹמֵד לְפָנֶיךָ שָּׁם ׀ עַל־הַצּוּר בְּחֹרֵב וְהִכִּיתָ בַצּוּר וְיָצְאוּ מִמֶּנּוּ מַיִם וְשָׁתָה הָעָם וַיַּעַשׂ כֵּן מֹשֶׁה לְעֵינֵי

VERSE 3

IBN EZRA

וַיִּצְמָא שָׁם הָעָם – *But the people were thirsty:* When the people became overwhelmed with thirst, they became angry with Moshe. They accused him of harming them by taking them out of Egypt.

ABARBANEL

לָמָּה זֶּה הֶעֱלִיתָנוּ מִמִּצְרַיִם – *Why did you bring us out of Egypt?:* With this comment, the Israelites let show their belief that Moshe himself was responsible for removing the nation from Egypt, and that he had not simply been following God's instructions. Since they denied God's providence in their emancipation, the Israelites now felt that they would all die in the wilderness. And even if the men were somehow able to endure, the feeble children would most likely not survive the desert thirst. And all the cattle would surely perish under such conditions.

VERSE 4

IBN EZRA

וַיִּצְעַק מֹשֶׁה – *Moshe cried:* Moshe's fear of being stoned was a figure of speech [he knew he was in no danger]. For the people had quarreled often with Moshe and criticized him. Now he complains that they would stone him to death if they could.

VERSE 5

RASHI

עֲבֹר לִפְנֵי הָעָם – *Walk out to face the people:* Let us see if they do in fact stone you. Moshe, why have you cast aspersions on My children? **וְקַח אִתְּךָ מִזִּקְנֵי יִשְׂרָאֵל** – *Taking some of the elders of Israel with you:* The elders are to act as witnesses to verify that you have extracted water from the rock, lest the people argue that natural springs had always been there.

וּמַטְּךָ אֲשֶׁר הִכִּיתָ בּוֹ אֶת־הַיְאֹר – *The staff with which you struck the Nile:* Why was it significant that Moshe use the staff previously employed to effect the plague of blood? Because Moshe's staff had been used to strike Pharaoh and Egypt during the saga of the plagues, and was wielded to split the Sea of Reeds, the Israelites argued that the stick was only capable

down. They ate the manna until they came to the border of Canaan. (An omer is a tenth of an ephah.) 17:1 All the community of Israel moved on after that from the desert of Sin, traveling from place to place as the LORD guided them, and they camped at Refidim, but there was no water there for 2 the people to drink. The people started to wrangle with Moshe. "Give us water to drink," they raged. "Why do you wrangle with

SHEVI'I

RAMBAN (cont.)

your brother Aharon — give us water! It's your job to serve us, and our blood will be on your heads if we die." To this provocation, Moshe responds: *Why do you wrangle with me? Why are you testing the LORD?* (17:2) You people are picking a fight with God to test whether He is able to provide you with water. It would be a better strategy to back off me and pray to God for assistance — perhaps He will answer you. Indeed, all along the nation was motivated by their desire to test God, as the verse subsequently states: *He named the place Masa and Meriva, because the people had quarreled and had tested the LORD, demanding, "Is the LORD among us or not?"* (17:7) Israel's anger against Moshe then abated, as the people managed to survive for a day or two with water from their waterskins. But then, when they became parched and "thirsty for water," they began to complain — *vayalen* [rather than to fight] — using the standard arguments: *Why did you bring us out of Egypt?* (17:3). When Moshe saw that they were truly thirsty, he petitioned God and reported to Him the anxiety that the people had caused him earlier when they fought with him.

VERSE 2

RASHI

מַה־תְּנַסּוּן — *Why are you testing:* Saying: "Can he provide water for us in this desert wilderness?"

IBN EZRA

וַיָּרֶב הָעָם — *The people started to wrangle:* Note that the text states merely "the people" without the adjective "all" that we find in the previous chapter when the people hungered for food: *In the desert, all the community started railing against Moshe and Aharon* (16:2). The language in this verse therefore indicates that the nation comprised two groups. The first one had no water and hence wrangled with Moshe [who responded "why do you wrangle with me?"]. But the second half of the nation still had water that they had saved from their stay at Alush [see Numbers 33:13]. This group simply wanted to test the LORD to see if He would provide them with water [hence Moshe's response: "Why are you testing the LORD?"].

SFORNO

מַה־תְּנַסּוּן — *Why are you testing:* If you are fighting with me in order to test the One who has sent me, that is certainly an unwise tactic. You will only bring evil upon yourselves, since this challenge you put to God courts danger. If God gets angry at you, He will act to destroy you. Thus the verse states, *when your fathers tempted Moshe, they saw My deeds* (Psalms 95:9), i.e., how I harmed them.

אַרְבָּעִ֣ים שָׁנָ֔ה עַד־בֹּאָ֖ם אֶל־אֶ֣רֶץ נוֹשָׁ֑בֶת אֶת־הַמָּן֙ אָֽכְל֔וּ עַד־בֹּאָ֕ם אֶל־קְצֵ֖ה אֶ֥רֶץ כְּנָֽעַן: וְהָעֹ֕מֶר עֲשִׂרִ֥ית הָאֵיפָ֖ה הֽוּא:

יז א וַ֠יִּסְע֠וּ כָּל־עֲדַ֨ת בְּנֵֽי־יִשְׂרָאֵ֧ל מִמִּדְבַּר־סִ֛ין לְמַסְעֵיהֶ֖ם עַל־פִּ֣י יְהוָ֑ה וַֽיַּחֲנוּ֙ בִּרְפִידִ֔ים וְאֵ֥ין מַ֖יִם לִשְׁתֹּ֥ת הָעָֽם: וַיָּ֤רֶב הָעָם֙ עִם־מֹשֶׁ֔ה וַיֹּ֣אמְר֔וּ תְּנוּ־לָ֥נוּ מַ֖יִם וְנִשְׁתֶּ֑ה וַיֹּ֤אמֶר לָהֶם֙ שביעי

RASHI (cont.)

The difficulty can be reconciled as follows: The manna stopped falling on the seventh of Adar [the month preceding Nisan] when Moshe passed away. At this point Israel was encamped on the Plains of Moav [outside the land of Canaan]. However, the manna that Israel collected on that day lasted through the sixteenth of Nisan when the nation brought their barley offering [the Omer offering brought on Passover inaugurated the new produce of every year; see Leviticus 23:9–14]. Hence the verse states: *And they ate of the grain of the land on the day after the Passover* (Joshua 5:11).

IBN EZRA

וּבְנֵי יִשְׂרָאֵל אָכְלוּ אֶת־הַמָּן – *The Israelites ate manna:* The miracle of this food was superior to all the other wonders that Moshe performed, for there were many additional minor miracles associated with the manna. Furthermore, the marvel of the manna endured for forty years, in contrast to the other events, which were fleeting.

VERSE 36

RASHI

עֲשִׂרִית הָאֵיפָה – *A tenth of an ephah:* There are three seah in an ephah, and six kav in a seah. There are four log in a kav, while a log holds the volume of six eggs. [These are all units of volume employed by the Talmud.] This means that a tenth of an ephah is equal to 43.2 egg-bulks. When dough measures at least one tenth of an ephah one is required to set aside halla [a portion of the dough given to the priest; see Numbers 15:19–21]. It is also the minimum size for a meal offering.

CHAPTER 17, VERSE 1

RAMBAN

וְאֵין מַיִם לִשְׁתֹּת הָעָם – *But there was no water there for the people to drink:* When Israel arrived at Refidim and found that the place lacked springs of water, they immediately began to quarrel with the prophet, as the verse states: *The people started to wrangle with Moshe* (17:2). Now there is a distinction between the Torah's usage of the verbs *vayillonu* ["rail" in 16:2] and *vayarev* ["wrangle" in 17:2]. For when the text features the former term, it connotes that the people are grumbling about their circumstances, asking: "What shall we do? What will we eat? Where will we find water?" On the other hand, the term *vayarev* shows that the Israelites were picking a fight with their leaders. They were making demands like: "You and

tasted like wafers made with honey. Moshe said, "This is what the LORD commands: Let an omer of it be kept carefully aside for your descendants, that they may see the bread I fed you in 33 the desert when I brought you out of Egypt." Moshe said to Aharon, "Take an urn, put an omer of manna in it, and place 34 it before the LORD to be kept for future generations." As the LORD commanded Moshe, so Aharon placed it before the Ark 35 of Testimony to be kept with care. The Israelites ate manna for forty years, until they came to the land where they could settle

VERSE 33

RASHI

צִנְצֶנֶת – *An urn:* The manna was placed in an earthenware jar, which is how the Targum renders the term [*tzelohit*]. וְהַנַּח אֹתוֹ לִפְנֵי יהוה – *And place it before the LORD:* The urn was to be placed before the Ark of the Covenant. Although this directive was only issued following construction of the Tabernacle, it is recorded here as part of the story of the manna.

IBN EZRA

וְהַנַּח אֹתוֹ לִפְנֵי יהוה – *And place it before the LORD:* The combination of this verse and the next teaches us that "before the LORD" is synonymous with "before the Testimony," i.e., the Ark of the Covenant. The latter is referred to as the Ark of Testimony because it held the tablets of the covenant [which in turn are called the "tablets of testimony," for example in Exodus 31:18 and 32:15].

BEKHOR SHOR

וְהַנַּח אֹתוֹ לִפְנֵי יהוה – *And place it before the LORD:* Before the Tabernacle was constructed, the urn of manna sat in front of the platform used to offer sacrifices.

VERSE 35

RASHI

אַרְבָּעִים שָׁנָה – *For forty years:* In fact, Israel ate the manna for thirty days less than forty years, as follows: The food began to fall on the fifteenth of Iyar [the date is given at the start of the chapter]. And the manna stopped appearing on the fifteenth of Nisan [in the fortieth year], as the verse states: *And the manna ceased the next day, when they ate of the grain of the land* (Joshua 5:12). The Torah's figure of forty years here includes the thirty days that the people ate the cakes they had brought with them out of Egypt, which assumed the taste of the manna. אֶל־אֶרֶץ נוֹשָׁבֶת – *To the land where they could settle down:* The manna disappeared after the nation crossed the Jordan River. אֶל־קְצֵה אֶרֶץ כְּנָעַן – *To the border of Canaan:* According to this clause, Israel ate the manna throughout their desert travels before they crossed the Jordan River. The manna was available to them until they reached the border of Canaan in the region known as the Plains of Moav. But this verse contradicts itself [since it first states that Israel enjoyed the manna until they actually entered the land].

לְבָן וְטַעְמוֹ כְּצַפִּיחִת בִּדְבָשׁ: וַיֹּאמֶר מֹשֶׁה זֶה הַדָּבָר אֲשֶׁר לּג
צִוָּה יהוה מְלֹא הָעֹמֶר מִמֶּנּוּ לְמִשְׁמֶרֶת לְדֹרֹתֵיכֶם לְמַעַן ׀
יִרְאוּ אֶת־הַלֶּחֶם אֲשֶׁר הֶאֱכַלְתִּי אֶתְכֶם בַּמִּדְבָּר בְּהוֹצִיאִי
אֶתְכֶם מֵאֶרֶץ מִצְרָיִם: וַיֹּאמֶר מֹשֶׁה אֶל־אַהֲרֹן קַח צִנְצֶנֶת לּד
אַחַת וְתֶן־שָׁמָּה מְלֹא־הָעֹמֶר מָן וְהַנַּח אֹתוֹ לִפְנֵי יהוה
לְמִשְׁמֶרֶת לְדֹרֹתֵיכֶם: כַּאֲשֶׁר צִוָּה יהוה אֶל־מֹשֶׁה וַיַּנִּיחֵהוּ לּה
אַהֲרֹן לִפְנֵי הָעֵדֻת לְמִשְׁמָרֶת: וּבְנֵי יִשְׂרָאֵל אָכְלוּ אֶת־הַמָּן

RASHBAM

וְטַעְמוֹ כְּצַפִּיחִת בִּדְבָשׁ – *It tasted like wafers made with honey:* Elsewhere, the text offers another description: *The taste of it was like the taste of oil cake* (Numbers 11:8). How are these contrasting comparisons to be reconciled? Our Sages have explained that while the food tasted like honey to the children, it reminded their elders of oil. But in my opinion, the straightforward meaning of the text is that when the manna was eaten as found, without being ground up, it was like wafers made with honey, just like nuts are sweet if eaten whole but their taste changes when pounded into a paste. Indeed, that later text states: *And the people went about and gathered it and ground it in mills, or beat it in a mortar, and boiled it in a pot, and made cakes of it* (Numbers 11:8), which is why *the taste of it was like the taste of oil cake*. It was just like nuts or olives which can be transformed into oils when crushed. Hence the word used here is *veta'mo* [literally, "its taste was"], but there *vehaya ta'mo* ["its taste became"]. That is, the sweet natural flavor of the manna was replaced with an oily consistency. **כְּזֶרַע גַּד** – *Coriander seeds:* This is a type of round legume.

VERSE 32

RASHI

לְדֹרֹתֵיכֶם – *For your descendants:* When the prophet Yirmeyahu rebuked the nation for their lack of Torah study, the people responded: If we quit our jobs and occupy ourselves with studying Torah, how will we live? Yirmeyahu took out the jar of manna and showed it to the Israelites, declaring: O generation, see the word of the LORD (Jeremiah 2:31). The prophet did not demand that his audience listen to God's message, but that they gaze upon His miraculous food. "Look," he said, "this is how your ancestors subsisted. The LORD has many agents He can dispatch to provide food for those who revere Him."

IBN EZRA

וַיֹּאמֶר מֹשֶׁה – *Moshe said:* The rightful place of this passage is later in the book, after the Torah describes the construction of the Tabernacle. However, the placement of the manna in an urn to be viewed by future generations was recorded here, in conjunction with the manna's introduction, to teach about an additional miracle – namely that the food survived intact for many years. Finally, it is because Moshe is citing God in this verse that he uses the first person in stating: *That they may see the bread I fed you in the desert.*

²⁸ none. Then the Lord said to Moshe, "How long will
²⁹ you refuse to keep My commandments and laws? Understand that the Lord has given you a Sabbath – that is why He gave you two days' bread on the sixth day. You shall each rest where you are: let no man depart from where he is on the seventh
³⁰ day." So the people rested on the seventh day. The house of Is-
³¹ rael named it manna. It looked like white coriander seeds, and

---

IBN EZRA (cont.)

His creation of the world. This is why God provided you with twice as much manna on the sixth day as He usually gives you. שְׁבוּ אִישׁ תַּחְתָּיו – *You shall each rest where you are:* Everyone must stay in their tents. אַל יֵצֵא אִישׁ מִמְּקֹמוֹ – *Let no man depart from where he is:* Nobody should venture outside in order to collect manna, as some people did.

BEKHOR SHOR

רְאוּ – *Understand:* [Literally, "see."] You can see with your own eyes that it is God who has commanded you to observe the Sabbath, for He gave you twice as much manna on the sixth day as usual, and none appears on the ground on the holy day. These phenomena can only be orchestrated by God Himself. Hence, *let no man depart from where he is* – in honor of the Sabbath.

SFORNO

רְאוּ – *Understand:* Think about how *the Lord has given you a Sabbath.* The Sabbath is not only a set of commandments to obey; it is also a gift that no other people has been privileged to receive. Hence our Sages quote God as declaring: "I have a wonderful gift in My storehouse called the Sabbath, and I wish to bestow it upon the people of Israel" (Shabbat 10b). Similarly the traditional Sabbath prayers include the statement: "You did not give it to the nations of the world, and no uncircumcised people shall relish in its peacefulness." But *the Israelites shall keep the Sabbath, making it a day of rest throughout their generations as a covenant forever* (31:16). And by commemorating the Sabbath day, they will merit an era that is entirely Sabbath and rest for everlasting life [Tamid 33b; referring to messianic times].

VERSE 30

RASHBAM

וַיִּשְׁבְּתוּ הָעָם – *So the people rested:* Israel observed the Sabbath on that day, and at the end of every subsequent week.

VERSE 31

RASHI

כְּצַפִּיחִת – *Like wafers:* The manna tasted like dough fried in honey, a dish the Mishna refers to as *eskeritin* [a soft dumpling, see Ḥalla 1:4 and Pesaḥim 37a]. This is how Onkelos translates the term.

כח וַיֹּאמֶר יהוה אֶל־מֹשֶׁה עַד־אָנָה מֵאַנְתֶּם מָצָאוּ:
כט לִשְׁמֹר מִצְוֺתַי וְתוֹרֹתָי: רְאוּ כִּי־יהוה נָתַן לָכֶם הַשַּׁבָּת עַל־
כֵּן הוּא נֹתֵן לָכֶם בַּיּוֹם הַשִּׁשִּׁי לֶחֶם יוֹמָיִם שְׁבוּ ׀ אִישׁ תַּחְתָּיו
ל אַל־יֵצֵא אִישׁ מִמְּקֹמוֹ בַּיּוֹם הַשְּׁבִיעִי: וַיִּשְׁבְּתוּ הָעָם בַּיּוֹם
לא הַשְּׁבִיעִי: וַיִּקְרְאוּ בֵית־יִשְׂרָאֵל אֶת־שְׁמוֹ מָן וְהוּא כְּזֶרַע גַּד

VERSE 28

RASHI

עַד־אָנָה מֵאַנְתֶּם – *How long will you refuse:* The verse illustrates the common proverb: Sometimes the cabbage is pulled out along with the weeds. That is, the virtuous might be accused when the wicked are rebuked. [Moshe was blameless, but God spoke of the nation as a collective.]

SFORNO

עַד־אָנָה מֵאַנְתֶּם לִשְׁמֹר – *How long will you refuse to keep:* All of you are responsible for not observing the Sabbath. Even you, Moshe, are guilty, even though you stayed home, for by neglecting to teach the people the laws of the Sabbath and their proper applications, you caused them to desecrate the day. What you said to them was that they could collect the manna for six days and not on the seventh, a rule which they violated. Then you explained that there would be no manna to be found on the Sabbath, and they refused to believe that claim. But what you failed to do was to teach them My commandments, including the point that any food collection on the holy day would transgress the prohibition of labor on the Sabbath. For the act of gathering manna constitutes the labor of plucking [*tolesh*, like picking fruit from a tree], and of carrying objects from one domain to the other [since the food would have to be brought into the camp from outside].

VERSE 29

RASHI

רְאוּ – *Understand:* [Literally, "see."] You can see with your own eyes that it is God in His glory Who is commanding you to observe the Sabbath. Witness the miracle that occurs every Sabbath eve when two days' worth of bread appears on the desert floor. שְׁבוּ אִישׁ תַּחְתָּיו – *You shall each rest where you are:* According to the Sages, this verse supports the rule that should a person be in an isolated location on the Sabbath, he may walk no more than four cubits in any direction. אַל־יֵצֵא אִישׁ מִמְּקֹמוֹ – *Let no man depart from where he is:* This verse alludes to the 2000-cubit boundary. [This border, called "the Sabbath limit" – *tehum Shabbat* – surrounds a city, and one may not walk past this point on the Sabbath day.] The Torah does not state this law explicitly since such limits are rabbinic in nature. On its most basic level, the verse restricts the movement of manna gatherers specifically.

IBN EZRA

רְאוּ – *Understand:* [Literally, "see."] See the wonder that God will perform on your behalf to convey that you should avoid labor on the Sabbath just as God rested following

said: Tomorrow is a day of rest, a holy Sabbath to the Lord. Bake now what you need to bake and cook what you need to cook. Whatever is left, keep carefully aside for the morning."
24 So they put it aside until the morning, as Moshe had instructed
25 them, and it did not stink, nor did worms infest it. And Moshe said, "Today, eat this, for today is a Sabbath to the Lord; today
26 you will not find it on the ground. Six days shall you gather it,
27 but on the seventh day, the Sabbath, it will not be there." Some people did go out to gather it on the seventh day; but they found

VERSE 26

RASHI

וּבַיּוֹם הַשְּׁבִיעִי שַׁבָּת – *But on the seventh day, the Sabbath:* Because the seventh day is the Sabbath, the manna will not be there. The purpose of this verse is to teach that in addition to the Sabbath, manna will not fall on Yom Kippur or on festival days [which are also referred to as "Sabbaths"].

ḤIZKUNI

וּבַיּוֹם הַשְּׁבִיעִי שַׁבָּת – *But on the seventh day, the Sabbath:* There are people whose faith in tradition is weak. These individuals use our text to prove that the Sabbath begins in the morning and comprises the day and its following night, for Moshe told the people: *Today is a Sabbath to the Lord.* They tell us to note that Moshe did not claim that the upcoming night would be defined as the Sabbath. Furthermore, Moshe declared that *tomorrow is a day of rest* (16:23) which also implies that the Sabbath need not be observed until the morning. But such an approach ignores such statements as *From the fourteenth day of the first month in the evening until the twenty-first day of the month in the evening, you may eat only unleavened bread* (12:18) and *On the ninth day of the month at evening, from evening to evening shall you celebrate your Sabbath* (Leviticus 23:32).

VERSE 27

IBN EZRA

יָצְאוּ מִן־הָעָם לִלְקֹט – *Some people did go out to gather it:* These skeptics went out to the fields only to see if Moshe had spoken the truth.

ḤIZKUNI

יָצְאוּ מִן־הָעָם לִלְקֹט – *Some people did go out to gather it:* Not only did these individuals demonstrate a lack of faith by going out to the fields, but they also violated the Sabbath by carrying their utensils with them. For Moshe had already declared: *Tomorrow is a day of rest, a holy Sabbath to the Lord* (16:23). [That is, the people had already been warned not to perform work such as carrying items outside the camp on the holy day.]

דִּבֶּר יְהוָה שַׁבָּתוֹן שַׁבַּת־קֹדֶשׁ לַיהוָה מָחָר אֵת אֲשֶׁר־
תֹּאפוּ אֵפוּ וְאֵת אֲשֶׁר־תְּבַשְּׁלוּ בַּשֵּׁלוּ וְאֵת כָּל־הָעֹדֵף הַנִּיחוּ
כד לָכֶם לְמִשְׁמֶרֶת עַד־הַבֹּקֶר: וַיַּנִּיחוּ אֹתוֹ עַד־הַבֹּקֶר כַּאֲשֶׁר
כה צִוָּה מֹשֶׁה וְלֹא הִבְאִישׁ וְרִמָּה לֹא־הָיְתָה בּוֹ: וַיֹּאמֶר מֹשֶׁה
אִכְלֻהוּ הַיּוֹם כִּי־שַׁבָּת הַיּוֹם לַיהוָה הַיּוֹם לֹא תִמְצָאֻהוּ
כו בַּשָּׂדֶה: שֵׁשֶׁת יָמִים תִּלְקְטֻהוּ וּבַיּוֹם הַשְּׁבִיעִי שַׁבָּת לֹא
כז יִהְיֶה־בּוֹ: וַיְהִי בַּיּוֹם הַשְּׁבִיעִי יָצְאוּ מִן־הָעָם לִלְקֹט וְלֹא

IBN EZRA

הַנִּיחוּ לָכֶם לְמִשְׁמֶרֶת עַד־הַבֹּקֶר — *Keep carefully aside for the morning:* Put the extra manna aside until the morning, and I will tell you what to do with it. Moshe refrained from explaining to the people on Friday that there would be no manna in the fields the following morning. He only revealed the secret of the Sabbath day to them on the day itself.

ABARBANEL

שַׁבָּתוֹן שַׁבַּת־קֹדֶשׁ לַיהוָה — *A day of rest, a holy Sabbath to the Lord:* The verse includes two terms for the Sabbath to teach that the day bears two layers of significance. It is both "a day of rest" for the people, during which they are to perform no labor, and it is "a holy day to the Lord," commemorating God's completion of creation.

VERSE 24

RALBAG

וְלֹא הִבְאִישׁ — *And it did not stink:* It seems that when the people reported to Moshe that the leftover manna *did not stink, nor did worms infest it,* that was when he told them to eat on the Sabbath the food they had saved. "Furthermore," he said, "do not go out to collect manna from the desert, for you will find none there today." The purpose of this arrangement was to teach Israel to believe in the Sabbath and its importance.

VERSE 25

RASHI

אִכְלֻהוּ הַיּוֹם — *Today, eat this:* The Israelites had been accustomed to going out in the mornings to collect the manna, and on the Sabbath they came to Moshe and asked whether they should venture out then as well. Said he: "Today you are to eat what you have already in your possession." At dinnertime they approached Moshe again and asked whether now it would be appropriate to look for fresh manna. Thereupon the leader confirmed: *Today is a Sabbath to the Lord.* But when Moshe saw they feared that the manna might have ceased falling forever, he continued: *Today you will not find it on the ground.* He emphasized that there would be no manna today, but that tomorrow the food would return.

21 enraged with them. Every morning they gathered it, all as much as they could eat, and when the sun grew hot, it melted away.
22 When the sixth day came, they gathered a double portion, two omers each. All the leaders of the community came and report-
23 ed this to Moshe. "This" he told them, "is what the Lord has

---

RASHI (cont.)

leader why this day was different than any other. The fact that the people inquired about the matter shows that Moshe had yet to describe the alternative protocol for the Sabbath described earlier in the text, *On the sixth day, they will have to prepare what they bring in* (16:5). The explanation was only provided once the people realized something had changed:

"This" he told them, "is what the Lord has said" (16:23), that is, this is precisely the situation that God commanded me to clarify for you. Indeed, Moshe was himself punished for delaying this lesson, as God protested to him: *How long will you* [not "they"] *refuse to keep My commandments and laws?* (16:28), thereby including Moshe in the rebuke.

IBN EZRA

לָקְטוּ לֶחֶם מִשְׁנֶה – *They gathered a double portion:* On this day, Moshe expressly commanded Israel to collect twice as much food as before, but he did not explain why they should do this. Furthermore, the verse states that *they gathered a double portion,* not that they found they had twice as much as usual [contrast with Rashi's explanation]. Meanwhile, *the leaders of the community came and reported this to Moshe* that the people had done as they were told. The point of their mission was to ask why the nation had been instructed to double their collection efforts, and how the people could possibly consume so much food in one day.

BEKHOR SHOR

וַיָּבֹאוּ כָּל־נְשִׂיאֵי הָעֵדָה – *All the leaders of the community came:* After the people discovered how much food they had, they were tempted – but afraid – to leave the uneaten victuals for the next day. For they had seen Moshe's displeasure when some individuals had previously left manna overnight.

VERSE 23

RASHI

אֵת אֲשֶׁר־תֹּאפוּ אֵפוּ – *Bake what you need to bake:* Bake in the oven today whatever manna you wish to prepare for today and for tomorrow. Or boil today in water whatever you want to eat for these two days. The term *afiyya* refers to baked goods, while the verb *bishul* describes food that is cooked.

RASHBAM

הוּא אֲשֶׁר דִּבֶּר יהוה – *This is what the Lord has said:* "In fact," said Moshe, "God told me about this development on the first day of the manna, but I did not share this information with you." For Moshe had wanted the people to be surprised when they discovered double the normal amount of food, in order to then teach them how the Sabbath should be honored.

כא עַד־בֹּקֶר וַיָּרֻם תּוֹלָעִים וַיִּבְאַשׁ וַיִּקְצֹף עֲלֵהֶם מֹשֶׁה: וַיִּלְקְטוּ
כב אֹתוֹ בַּבֹּקֶר בַּבֹּקֶר אִישׁ כְּפִי אָכְלוֹ וְחַם הַשֶּׁמֶשׁ וְנָמָס: וַיְהִי ׀
בַּיּוֹם הַשִּׁשִּׁי לָקְטוּ לֶחֶם מִשְׁנֶה שְׁנֵי הָעֹמֶר לָאֶחָד וַיָּבֹאוּ
כג כָּל־נְשִׂיאֵי הָעֵדָה וַיַּגִּידוּ לְמֹשֶׁה: וַיֹּאמֶר אֲלֵהֶם הוּא אֲשֶׁר

RAMBAN (cont.)

manna kept overnight on the Sabbath, the Torah states that *it did not stink, nor did worms infest it* (16:24). If the manna had followed the natural order of things and began to stink before becoming infested with worms, then it would have been sufficient to state: "It did not stink." That would have necessarily implied that it never reached the point of infestation. Now even when things become wormy in the natural world, they only smell in cases when the object is warm and damp; dry things that attract worms do not stink at all. For example, one can find worms on wood or fruits that are still growing or that have recently been cut down. It follows that the Torah is informing us here that the manna that some individuals kept in their tents for the next day was made to smell bad miraculously.

SFORNO

וַיִּקְצֹף עֲלֵהֶם מֹשֶׁה – *Moshe was enraged with them:* These people had not left over food because it was more than they could eat. Rather, the recalcitrant individuals had done it deliberately to test God.

VERSE 21

RASHI

וְחַם הַשֶּׁמֶשׁ וְנָמָס – *And when the sun grew hot, it melted away:* Any uncollected manna in the field melted into rivulets which the deer and the gazelles lapped up before being hunted by the nations of the world. Upon eating the animals' meat, the nations tasted the manna and understood how fortunate Israel was. The Targum's translation for *venamas – pashar –* is related to the Hebrew *posherin* [meaning "warm"], for the sun heated up the manna and thus melted it.

SFORNO

וְחַם הַשֶּׁמֶשׁ וְנָמָס – *And when the sun grew hot, it melted away:* Hence the people set out in the morning to collect the manna before the heat of the sun managed to dissolve it.

VERSE 22

RASHI

לָקְטוּ לֶחֶם מִשְׁנֶה – *They gathered a double portion:* When the Israelites measured their haul of manna in their tents, they found that the yield was twice as much as before – two omers per person. The aggadic interpretation for the term *mishneh* ["double"] is that the collection on the sixth day of the week was "different" [*meshuneh*], having a better scent and a richer taste. וַיַּגִּידוּ לְמֹשֶׁה – *They reported this to Moshe:* The nation's elders asked their

17
18 The people of Israel did so. Some gathered more, others less. But when they measured it with an omer measure, those who had gathered much had none left over, and those who gathered but little did not fall short. All had gathered as much as they could
19 eat. "Let no one leave any over for the morning," said Moshe;
20 but they did not listen to Moshe. Some of them left part of it till morning, and it became worm-infested and stank. Moshe was

VERSE 18

IBN EZRA

וַיָּמֹדּוּ בָעֹמֶר – *But when they measured it with an omer:* When the Israelites gathered their manna in the fields, they estimated an omer's worth for each person in their household. But when they returned home and accurately measured their yield, they found that their estimations had been precise.

BEKHOR SHOR

וְלֹא הֶעְדִּיף הַמַּרְבֶּה – *Those who had gathered much had none left over:* According to the simple understanding of the text, people who had taken too much disposed of their leftovers. Those whose collection had been found wanting went back outside and took enough to reach the standard measurement.

VERSE 19

IBN EZRA

אִישׁ אַל־יוֹתֵר מִמֶּנּוּ עַד־בֹּקֶר – *Let no one leave any over for the morning:* The reason Israel was told not to save any of their manna overnight was to train them to trust that God would provide for them the next day as well. The Israelites were not commanded to consume all the collected food, but to get rid of any food that they had no appetite to finish by throwing it away outside of their tents.

BEKHOR SHOR

אִישׁ אַל־יוֹתֵר מִמֶּנּוּ – *Let no one leave any over:* Anyone who held on to his manna overnight would betray a lack of faith in God.

VERSE 20

RASHI

וַיּוֹתִרוּ אֲנָשִׁים – *Some of them left it:* These individuals were Datan and Aviram [see Numbers 16]. וַיָּבְאַשׁ – *And stank:* The clauses in this verse should be switched, for first the manna began to stink and then it became infested with worms. Therefore, when describing the opposite situation, the verse states: *It did not stink, nor did worms infest it* (16:24). Such is the normal process whenever food becomes wormy.

RAMBAN

וַיָּרֻם תּוֹלָעִים וַיִּבְאַשׁ – *And it became worm-infested and stank:* According to the straightforward meaning of the text, the leftover manna became worm-infested before it started to stink [contrary to the laws of nature]. For note, that when describing the converse state of

יז תִּקָּחוּ: וַיַּעֲשׂוּ־כֵן בְּנֵי יִשְׂרָאֵל וַיִּלְקְטוּ הַמַּרְבֶּה וְהַמַּמְעִיט:
יח וַיָּמֹדּוּ בָעֹמֶר וְלֹא הֶעְדִּיף הַמַּרְבֶּה וְהַמַּמְעִיט לֹא הֶחְסִיר
יט אִישׁ לְפִי־אָכְלוֹ לָקָטוּ: וַיֹּאמֶר מֹשֶׁה אֲלֵהֶם אִישׁ אַל־יוֹתֵר
כ מִמֶּנּוּ עַד־בֹּקֶר: וְלֹא־שָׁמְעוּ אֶל־מֹשֶׁה וַיּוֹתִרוּ אֲנָשִׁים מִמֶּנּוּ

BEKHOR SHOR

אִישׁ לְפִי אָכְלוֹ – *As much as you need:* Each individual should collect the manna based on his own appetite – some people require more, others less. מִסְפַּר נַפְשֹׁתֵיכֶם – *Each take enough:* [Literally, "the number of your souls."] Gather food according to the number of individuals you have been blessed with. Take enough to provide for your household – neither more nor less.

RABBI AVRAHAM BEN HARAMBAM

אִישׁ לְפִי אָכְלוֹ – *As much as you need:* Such was the wonder of the manna and the sign that it descended from God – the same amount of food satisfied both a large person and his smaller neighbor; the strong and the weak both consumed the same portion of manna.

VERSE 17

RASHI

הַמַּרְבֶּה וְהַמַּמְעִיט – *Some more, others less:* Some people gathered more, while others gathered less. But when all returned to their tents and measured what they had collected, they found that those who had brought home an excess amount now had exactly an omer of manna for each individual in his tent, whereas those who were more restrained, also managed to provide an omer for each family member. And this was a great miracle concerning the manna.

BEKHOR SHOR

הַמַּרְבֶּה וְהַמַּמְעִיט – *Some more, others less:* When the Israelites went out to the fields, some Hebrews collected a great deal of manna, while other people took home less. And yet, miraculously, all the portions evened out – if a person took an insufficient quantity it subsequently turned into more, while he who had filled his arms with manna found that his serving had become smaller. In the end everyone had exactly the same amount.

ABARBANEL

הַמַּרְבֶּה וְהַמַּמְעִיט – *Some more, others less:* If a person collected a great deal of manna, since he had many mouths to feed at home, he still ended up with exactly an omer of food per person. If somebody else had a small family for whom he sought provisions, he too would find himself with no less than an omer to serve each of his dependents. It was as if God was aware of every family's needs and doled out the food commensurate with that. There is a valuable lesson here for our times as well: Every person receives exactly what he needs in this world, and upon our deaths we find that no one has actually been better off. For when we die, we take nothing with us; our wealth does not follow us into the next world. And those whose possessions are paltry still have enough, for the Lord provides bread for all creatures and sustains all people.

13 the LORD your God." That evening a flock of quail flew in and covered the camp; next morning a layer of dew surrounded
14 the camp. When the dew covering lifted, fine flakes covered
15 the floor of the desert like fine frost on the ground. When the Israelites saw it, they asked one another, "What is it?" for they did not recognize it. Moshe said to them, "This is the bread
16 the LORD has given you to eat. This is what the LORD has instructed: Each of you gather as much as you need, an omer for every person; each take enough for all the people in your tent."

RASHI (cont.)

fill it with dew and seal the opening, the egg will rise up when you put it in the sunlight. But our Sages interpret this phrase to mean that the dew came up out of the earth, and when the layer rose, it revealed the manna to the people on the desert floor. The substance was fine and *meḥuspas* – meaning "uncovered"; this is its only appearance of that word in Scripture.

VERSE 15

RASHI

מָן הוּא – *What is it:* The term *man* refers to the preparation of food, as in the verse: *And the king appointed [vayman] them a daily provision* (Daniel 1:5). [According to this understanding, the people's exclamation would be more properly translated: "It is a ration."] כִּי לֹא יָדְעוּ מַה־הוּא – *For they did not recognize it:* And hence could not call it by its proper name.

RASHBAM

מָן הוּא – *What is it:* In my opinion, the term *man* is an Egyptian translation of the Hebrew word *ma* [meaning "what"]. Naturally, the Israelites were fluent in the language of their former home country, and that is what they spoke when they first encountered the strange food, asking: *What is it?* Moshe recorded the words he heard from the people in order to explain why they called the miraculous food "manna."

IBN EZRA

מָן הוּא – *What is it:* Rabbeinu Shlomo writes that the words *man hu* are Arabic for "what is it?" But he was ill-informed, because the Arabic for that question is in fact *ma huwi*, whereas the correct meaning of *man hu* in Arabic would be "who is it?"

VERSE 16

RASHI

עֹמֶר – *An omer:* Omer is the name of a measure. מִסְפַּר נַפְשֹׁתֵיכֶם – *Each take enough:* [Literally, "the number of your souls."] Gather an amount of manna based on the number of souls in your household, where each person gets a single omer of food.

יג וַיְהִי בָעֶרֶב וַתַּעַל הַשְּׂלָו וַתְּכַס אֶת־הַמַּחֲנֶה וּבַבֹּקֶר הָיְתָה
שִׁכְבַת הַטָּל סָבִיב לַמַּחֲנֶה: וַתַּעַל שִׁכְבַת הַטָּל וְהִנֵּה עַל־ יד
פְּנֵי הַמִּדְבָּר דַּק מְחֻסְפָּס דַּק כַּכְּפֹר עַל־הָאָרֶץ: וַיִּרְאוּ בְנֵי־ טו
יִשְׂרָאֵל וַיֹּאמְרוּ אִישׁ אֶל־אָחִיו מָן הוּא כִּי לֹא יָדְעוּ מַה־
הוּא וַיֹּאמֶר מֹשֶׁה אֲלֵהֶם הוּא הַלֶּחֶם אֲשֶׁר נָתַן יהוה לָכֶם
לְאָכְלָה: זֶה הַדָּבָר אֲשֶׁר צִוָּה יהוה לִקְטוּ מִמֶּנּוּ אִישׁ לְפִי טז
אָכְלוֹ עֹמֶר לַגֻּלְגֹּלֶת מִסְפַּר נַפְשֹׁתֵיכֶם אִישׁ לַאֲשֶׁר בְּאָהֳלוֹ

VERSE 13

RASHI

הַשְּׂלָו – *Quail:* A type of bird that is very fat.
הָיְתָה שִׁכְבַת הַטָּל – *A layer of dew:* A covering of dew lay upon the manna. But later the Torah writes: *And when the dew fell upon the camp in the night, the manna fell upon it* (Numbers 11:9). How are these descriptions to be reconciled? First, one layer of dew fell to the ground. The manna descended upon that. Then an additional layer of dew coated the manna. Thus the food was presented to Israel like a gift wrapped in a box.

BEKHOR SHOR

וַתַּעַל הַשְּׂלָו – *A flock of quail flew in:* It seems to me that this is the same quail that is described in Parashat Behaalotekha [see Numbers 11:31–32]. The birds are first mentioned now [even though they were provided to Israel much later] since the Torah now describes the advent of the manna. It is clear that Israel did not receive quail at this early stage, because if they had, and Moshe had seen that God was able to adequately feed the entire nation with this fowl, he would not have later questioned God saying: *Shall flocks and herds be slain for them, to suffice them? Or shall all the fish of the sea be gathered together for them, to suffice them?* (Numbers 11:22).

ḤIZKUNI

וַתַּעַל הַשְּׂלָו – *A flock of quail flew in:* Israel was only fed quail this one time [and not every day], which is why we read in Parashat Behaalotekha: *And the mixed multitude that was among them fell a lusting; and the children of Israel also wept again, and said, "Who shall give us meat to eat?"* (Numbers 11:4). Following that demand, God provided them with the birds a second time. Only the manna fell on a regular, daily basis all during the forty years that the nation spent in the desert.

VERSE 14

RASHI

וַתַּעַל שִׁכְבַת הַטָּל – *When the dew covering lifted:* When the sun rose, the dew that rested on top of the manna evaporated; it rose up to meet the sun. If you take an empty eggshell,

8 against us?" Then Moshe said, "In the evening, the Lord will give you meat to eat, and in the morning bread to fill you, for He has heard you railing against Him. We – what are we? It
9 is not us you rail against, but the Lord." Then Moshe said to Aharon, "Tell all the community of Israel to come before the
10 Lord, because He has heard your railing." As soon as Aharon had spoken to the whole community of Israel, they looked toward the desert – and the glory of the Lord appeared in the midst of cloud.
11/12 The Lord spoke to Moshe and said, "I have heard the Israelites' railing. Tell them: At twilight you shall eat meat, and in the morning your fill of bread. Then you will know that I am

SHISHI

VERSE 10

IBN EZRA

וַיְהִי כְּדַבֵּר אַהֲרֹן – *As soon as Aharon had spoken:* It immediately became clear to the people, just as Aharon was telling them to come, that the cloud had appeared, and within it the glory of God was seen.

VERSE 11

IBN EZRA

וַיְדַבֵּר יהוה אֶל־מֹשֶׁה – *The Lord spoke to Moshe:* The nation watched as Moshe approached the glory of God and spoke with Him.

VERSE 12

RAMBAN

בֵּין הָעַרְבַּיִם תֹּאכְלוּ בָשָׂר – *At twilight you shall eat meat:* This information had already been passed along to Israel [in verse 8], but it is repeated here because God declares that He has *heard the Israelites' railing*. Now at first God had offered to *rain down bread from heaven* (16:4) an act that would have been done out divine kindness for Israel, or because they deserved such treatment. Now however, God announces that He considers the nation's complaints to be sinful. Nevertheless, He will still provide food for them so that they *will know that I am the Lord your God*. For even until now, the people did not believe in God, which is why they attacked His prophets. It is possible that at first, God did not promise Israel that He would supply them with manna for the duration of their stay in the wilderness. The nation might have imagined that the miracle food would appear for a day or two, as long as they remained in that enchanted spot, but that when they moved to the next location that site would have naturally available food for them. However, the current statement, *At twilight you shall eat meat*, means that every evening they will enjoy a meat dinner, whereas they would receive *in the morning your fill of bread* – for as long as they traveled through the wilderness.

ח תְלֻנֹּתֵיכֶם עָלֵינוּ: וַיֹּאמֶר מֹשֶׁה בְּתֵת יהוה לָכֶם בָּעֶרֶב בָּשָׂר לֶאֱכֹל וְלֶחֶם בַּבֹּקֶר לִשְׂבֹּעַ בִּשְׁמֹעַ יהוה אֶת־תְּלֻנֹּתֵיכֶם אֲשֶׁר־אַתֶּם מַלִּינִם עָלָיו וְנַחְנוּ מָה לֹא־עָלֵינוּ תְלֻנֹּתֵיכֶם כִּי עַל־יהוה: ט וַיֹּאמֶר מֹשֶׁה אֶל־אַהֲרֹן אֱמֹר אֶל־כָּל־עֲדַת בְּנֵי יִשְׂרָאֵל קִרְבוּ לִפְנֵי יהוה כִּי שָׁמַע אֵת תְּלֻנֹּתֵיכֶם: י וַיְהִי כְּדַבֵּר אַהֲרֹן אֶל־כָּל־עֲדַת בְּנֵי־יִשְׂרָאֵל וַיִּפְנוּ אֶל־הַמִּדְבָּר וְהִנֵּה כְּבוֹד יהוה נִרְאָה בֶּעָנָן: יא וַיְדַבֵּר יהוה אֶל־מֹשֶׁה לֵּאמֹר: שָׁמַעְתִּי אֶת־תְּלוּנֹּת בְּנֵי ששי יִשְׂרָאֵל דַּבֵּר אֲלֵהֶם לֵאמֹר בֵּין הָעַרְבַּיִם תֹּאכְלוּ בָשָׂר וּבַבֹּקֶר תִּשְׂבְּעוּ־לָחֶם וִידַעְתֶּם כִּי אֲנִי יהוה אֱלֹהֵיכֶם:

VERSE 8

RASHI

בָּשָׂר לֶאֱכֹל — *Meat to eat:* You will be given meat to eat, but do not gorge yourselves. The Torah thereby teaches manners to its readers: One should not eat meat to satiety. Why did God provide the nation with bread in the morning and meat in the evening? The request for bread was appropriate because people cannot live without it. But the demand for meat was unnecessary for two reasons: Firstly, Israel owned plenty of animals which they could have slaughtered had they wanted to. Furthermore, people can endure very well without meat. As a rebuke, God sent them the quail in the evenings, which was an inconvenient time. אֲשֶׁר־אַתֶּם מַלִּינִם עָלָיו — *Railing against Him:* [Here too, the verb *mallinim* is in the causative *hifil* construction; see commentary on the previous verse. Rashi explains that the phrase means:] "God has heard the people you have provoked to murmur against Him."

VERSE 9

RASHI

קִרְבוּ — *Come:* To where the cloud will descend.

IBN EZRA

קִרְבוּ — *Come:* Turn toward the desert [see next verse].

RABBI AVRAHAM BEN HARAMBAM

קִרְבוּ לִפְנֵי יהוה — *Come before the Lord:* This statement is somewhat vague since the Tabernacle had not yet been constructed, and there was nowhere specific where Israel could approach God. Hence it seems to me that Moshe commanded Aharon to instruct Israel to prepare themselves spiritually, and to mentally attune themselves by clearing their minds and directing their thoughts. Thus they would be ready to see what was to transpire.

6 It will be twice as much as they gather on all other days." So Moshe and Aharon told all the Israelites, "At evening you will
7 know that it was the LORD who brought you out of Egypt, and by morning you shall see the LORD's glory, for He has heard you railing against Him. As for us, what are we that you rail

---

SFORNO

עֶרֶב וִידַעְתֶּם – *At evening you will know:* [Moshe was praying:] May it be God's will that when God promises to provide you with food, He does so in a timely fashion, such that you will receive what you need each evening. When that happens, you will surely know *that it was the LORD who brought you out of Egypt,* for not only did He fully remove you from that country, He is also keen to remove the hardships that you suffered there. When you were in Egypt you sat at the fleshpots, but they were empty as you waited, not knowing when you would be fed – like animals who have no fixed mealtimes. So write our Sages: At first the Israelites survived like chickens who peck at the trash heaps to find food. But when Moshe arrived, he arranged for the people to eat at set times [see Yoma 75b].

VERSE 7

RASHI

וּבֹקֶר וּרְאִיתֶם – *And by morning you shall see:* Moshe was not referring to the glory of God mentioned in the verse *And the glory of the LORD appeared in the midst of cloud* [16:10; that revelation appeared immediately rather than the next morning with the manna]. Rather, this is what he said to the nation: In the evening you will see proof of God's ability to feed your appetites, for He will lay out meat before you. However, God will not serve the meal with a glad countenance because you demanded the food improperly, while your bellies were still full. On the other hand, because the bread you requested represents a true need, when it descends to earth in the morning, you will witness the radiant manifestation of God. For the manna will be offered lovingly during the day, when there is time to prepare it, resting on a bed of dew and garnished with another layer of dew above, as if presented in a box.

אֶת־תְּלֻנֹּתֵיכֶם עַל־יהוה – *Your railing against the LORD:* [Even though the people's accusations were leveled at Moshe and Aharon] it was if they were complaining against God.

וְנַחְנוּ מָה – *What are we:* Of what importance are we that you blame us for the situation?

כִּי תַלִּינוּ עָלֵינוּ – *That you rail against us:* The phrase means "You are leading everybody to complain against us" – your sons and daughters, your wives, and the mixed multitudes. I am forced to interpret the verb *tallinu* [translated here as "rail"] as being in the causative *hifil* form [and meaning rather: "to stir up discontent in others"].

RAMBAN

וְנַחְנוּ מָה – *What are we:* Moshe and Aharon are showing their modesty in this verse, for they argue: Why do you credit us with having taken you out of the land of Egypt [in verse 3], why, we are nothing and our actions are meaningless. *It is not us you rail against, but the LORD.* He is the one who rescued you from slavery; we merely watched.

וְהֵכִינוּ אֵת אֲשֶׁר־יָבִיאוּ וְהָיָה מִשְׁנֶה עַל אֲשֶׁר־יִלְקְטוּ יוֹם ׀ יוֹם:
1 וַיֹּאמֶר מֹשֶׁה וְאַהֲרֹן אֶל־כָּל־בְּנֵי יִשְׂרָאֵל עֶרֶב וִידַעְתֶּם
2 כִּי יהוה הוֹצִיא אֶתְכֶם מֵאֶרֶץ מִצְרָיִם: וּבֹקֶר וּרְאִיתֶם אֶת־
כְּבוֹד יהוה בְּשָׁמְעוֹ אֶת־תְּלֻנֹּתֵיכֶם עַל־יהוה וְנַחְנוּ מָה כִּי

SFORNO

וְהֵכִינוּ אֵת אֲשֶׁר־יָבִיאוּ — *They will have to prepare what they bring in:* Israel was thereby encouraged to prepare the Sabbath delicacies, and to start that activity on the sixth day, well in advance of the holy day.

VERSE 6

RASHI

הוֹצִיא אֶתְכֶם מֵאֶרֶץ מִצְרָיִם — *Brought you out of Egypt:* Moshe and Aharon are rebuking the nation, who had complained: *You have brought us out into this desert to kill [us]* (16:3). The leaders are reminding Israel that it was not they who freed them from slavery, but God. It was He who would provide them with the quail.

IBN EZRA

וַיֹּאמֶר מֹשֶׁה וְאַהֲרֹן — *So Moshe and Aharon told:* Israel's leaders told the people that they were about to provide two signs that would prove *that it was the* LORD *who brought you out of Egypt* — one in the evening [when the quail arrived], and the other the next morning [with the appearance of the manna]. Actually, our verse should have read: "At evening and by morning you will know that it was the LORD who brought you out of Egypt." But that would have made for an awkward transition to the next verse, *And by morning you shall see the* LORD's *glory,* since the nation would only see God's glory during the day, as will become clear.

RAMBAN

עֶרֶב וִידַעְתֶּם — *At evening you will know:* It seems to me that the manna represented a far greater miracle than the quail. For to provide Israel with these birds, God merely had to blow a wind to carry them in from the sea, which was well within the laws of nature. However, the manna was a novel substance that God fashioned specifically for Israel out of the air, similar to the wonders He worked during the original six days of creation. This is what our Sages meant when they claimed that the manna was formed at dusk on the world's sixth day [see Avot 5:6]. Hence the text states: *At evening you will know that it was the* LORD *who brought you out of Egypt,* when He sets the table to serve you meat in the wilderness. But with the truly great miracle that God will perform for you starting tomorrow, you will witness the glory of His kingship. *For what god is there in heaven or in earth, that can do according to Your works, and according to Your might?* (Deuteronomy 3:24). The great and wondrous acts that God performs demonstrate His glory to the world.

3 and Aharon. The Israelites said to them, "If only we had died by the Lord's hand in Egypt, when we sat by the fleshpots and ate our fill of bread. Instead, you have brought us out into this
4 desert to kill the entire assembly by starvation." Then the Lord said to Moshe, "I am going to rain down bread from heaven. Let the people go out and gather enough for each day; I will test them to see whether they will follow My law or not.
5 On the sixth day, they will have to prepare what they bring in.

RASHBAM

דְּבַר־יוֹם בְּיוֹמוֹ – *Enough for each day:* Even if some people attempted to gather more than what they needed, when they got home they would find that they had collected just enough for each day. Thus the verse states: *But when they measured it with an omer measure, those who had gathered much had none left over, and those who gathered but little did not fall short* (16:18). לְמַעַן אֲנַסֶּנּוּ – *I will test them:* For every day their eyes will turn to Me, relying on Me to feed them. Because of this dependence, Israel will have trust in Me and will follow My laws. So does a later description read in Parashat Ekev: *And He humbled you and suffered you to hunger…that He might test you, to do you good at your latter end* (Deuteronomy 8:3–16).

RAMBAN

לְמַעַן אֲנַסֶּנּוּ – *I will test them:* The test lay in the paucity of food in the wilderness and the impossibility of procuring sustenance in any way other than collecting the manna. This was bread that their fathers had never known nor described to them, and it became something that the people looked forward to daily, while listening to God and following Him…. For after all, God could have led the Hebrews toward populated regions that surrounded the desert, but instead He took them into a barrenness of serpents and scorpions. He did this to cultivate a regular dependency upon Him, to test Israel and to ultimately benefit them, so that they would believe in Him forever.

RABBEINU BAḤYA

לֶחֶם מִן־הַשָּׁמַיִם – *Bread from heaven:* The Torah refers to the manna as bread because the Israelites made it so [this refers to the midrash according to which the manna tasted however the Israelites desired]. God did not actually rain loaves of bread down to the desert floor…. Understand that the manna comprised fine seeds that the people could gather, an activity which is mentioned throughout this narrative. The manna resembled round, peeled grains.

VERSE 5

RASHI

וְהָיָה מִשְׁנֶה – *It will be twice as much:* To satisfy the sixth day's and the Sabbath day's meals.

מִשְׁנֶה – *Twice:* The phrase means that the amount of manna available to the people would be twice what they would gather on the other days of the week.

וַיֹּאמְר֨וּ אֲלֵהֶ֜ם בְּנֵ֣י יִשְׂרָאֵ֗ל מִֽי־יִתֵּ֨ן מוּתֵ֤נוּ בְיַד־יְהוָה֙ בְּאֶ֣רֶץ מִצְרַ֔יִם בְּשִׁבְתֵּ֨נוּ֙ עַל־סִ֣יר הַבָּשָׂ֔ר בְּאָכְלֵ֥נוּ לֶ֖חֶם לָשֹׂ֑בַע כִּֽי־הוֹצֵאתֶ֤ם אֹתָ֨נוּ֙ אֶל־הַמִּדְבָּ֣ר הַזֶּ֔ה לְהָמִ֛ית אֶת־כָּל־הַקָּהָ֥ל הַזֶּ֖ה בָּרָעָֽב׃ ד וַיֹּ֤אמֶר יְהוָה֙ אֶל־מֹשֶׁ֔ה הִנְנִ֨י מַמְטִ֥יר לָכֶ֛ם לֶ֖חֶם מִן־הַשָּׁמָ֑יִם וְיָצָ֨א הָעָ֤ם וְלָֽקְטוּ֙ דְּבַר־י֣וֹם בְּיוֹמ֔וֹ לְמַ֧עַן אֲנַסֶּ֛נּוּ הֲיֵלֵ֥ךְ בְּתוֹרָתִ֖י אִם־לֹֽא׃ ה וְהָיָה֙ בַּיּ֣וֹם הַשִּׁשִּׁ֔י יב

RAMBAN (cont.)

all perish in the great wilderness they had entered. Hence the verse emphasizes: *In the desert, all the community started railing against Moshe and Aharon* — it was because of the desert that the nation had become anxious for their welfare. Similarly, the subsequent verse states: *You have brought us out into this desert to kill the entire assembly by starvation* (16:3). That complaint mentions two critical elements: the desert and the great size of the assembly, in order to impose upon Moshe that the former could not possibly provide for the latter, and that hunger would surely be the death of them all. God heard the people's criticism and began to prepare provisions for them in the wilderness, to take care of them until they arrived in their homeland.

VERSE 3

RASHBAM

בְּיַד־יְהוָה — *By the Lord's hand:* They would rather enter the grave in ripe old age [in Egypt] and not due to starvation in the wilderness.

RABBEINU BAḤYA

בְּיַד־יְהוָה — *By the Lord's hand:* It would have been better for us if we had died during the three days of darkness. While the Egyptians were suffering through that plague, Israel's wicked were silently put to death. Such is the interpretation of Rabbeinu Ḥananel.

SFORNO

בְּיַד־יְהוָה — *By the Lord's hand:* We would have preferred to have died while sitting around the fleshpots of Egypt. If God desired to kill us, He might have done us the service of doing so while we were satiated with Egypt's plenty. So does the verse state: *Those slain with the sword are better than those slain with hunger* (Lamentations 4:9).

VERSE 4

RASHI

דְּבַר־יוֹם בְּיוֹמוֹ — *Enough for each day:* The phrase *devar yom beyomo* means that on each day, Israel should collect just enough food for that day's consumption [a literal translation would be "each day's on that day"]; they should not take what they think they will need for the next day. לְמַעַן אֲנַסֶּנּוּ — *I will test them:* I will test them every day *to see whether they will follow My law*, i.e., whether they will obey the rules governing the manna: the prohibitions on leaving leftover manna for the next day and on gathering food on the Sabbath.

16 1 there by the water. They set out from Elim, and on the fifteenth day of the second month after leaving Egypt, the congregation of Israel all arrived at the desert of Sin, between Elim and Sinai. 2 In the desert, all the community started railing against Moshe

---
RAMBAN (cont.)

verse states: *and they removed from Etzion Gever, and pitched in the wilderness of Tzin, which is Kadesh* (Numbers 33:36), to distinguish that place from the current one.

VERSE 2

RASHI

וַיִּלּוֹנוּ – *Started railing:* The nation complained to Moshe because their food had run out.

IBN EZRA

וַיִּלּוֹנוּ – *Started railing:* When Israel found bitter water at Mara, they blamed Moshe alone for their condition because he alone had led them [to that place, in 15:23]. Furthermore, it was only a part of the nation who complained to Moshe then, which is why the verse states: *The people railed against Moshe* [15:24; the word "all" – *kol* – is absent from that passage]. But now, in the desert of Sin, the verse states that *all the community started railing against Moshe and Aharon*, since it was the two of them who had taken Israel out of Egypt altogether. An additional difference between the two instances is that in the former, the people thirsted for water, while now the Israelites were desperate for meat and bread. For by this point, thirty days after the exodus, the people had eaten most of the cattle they had brought with them. Buying food from neighboring nations presented a difficulty because it was so expensive to procure food for such a large nation.

RABBI AVRAHAM BEN HARAMBAM

בַּמִּדְבָּר – *In the desert:* It is obvious that the people's grievance in the current chapter was more powerful than their complaint for water in the previous episode. For although Israel was thirsty earlier, they supposed that water would be delivered to them through rain or from some spring they would discover. Hence they asked Moshe: *What are we to drink?* (15:24), a question which does not express the same level of desperation that we see in the accusation *You have brought us out into this desert to kill the entire assembly by starvation* (16:3). Israel recognized the paucity of vegetation in the desert and understood that they were quite distant from the land of Israel and the gardens which flourished there. This then was the nature of their attack against Moshe.

RAMBAN

בַּמִּדְבָּר – *In the desert:* In my opinion, the text informs us of Israel's geographic position to explain why they were complaining against Moshe. For by the time they reached the desert of Sin they were quite a distance from the familiar land of Egypt. Looking around them, they panicked: What will we find to eat in this barren wasteland that we have entered? Indeed, Israel might have imagined that after a few days of travel they were to arrive at some of the surrounding populated cities. But now a full month had gone by since their departure and they had not encountered any civilization. This is why they feared that they would

א וַיִּחֲנוּ־שָׁם עַל־הַמָּיִם: וַיִּסְעוּ מֵאֵילִם וַיָּבֹאוּ כָּל־עֲדַת טז
בְּנֵי־יִשְׂרָאֵל אֶל־מִדְבַּר־סִין אֲשֶׁר בֵּין־אֵילִם וּבֵין סִינָי
בַּחֲמִשָּׁה עָשָׂר יוֹם לַחֹדֶשׁ הַשֵּׁנִי לְצֵאתָם מֵאֶרֶץ מִצְרָיִם:
ב וַיִּלּוֹנוּ כָּל־עֲדַת בְּנֵי־יִשְׂרָאֵל עַל־מֹשֶׁה וְעַל־אַהֲרֹן בַּמִּדְבָּר: וַיִּלּוֹנוּ

CHAPTER 16, VERSE 1

RASHI

בַּחֲמִשָּׁה עָשָׂר יוֹם — *On the fifteenth day:* The Torah mentions the date of Israel's encampment because on this day the people finished eating all the wafers they had taken with them from Egypt. Israel therefore needed the manna, whose advent is the subject of this chapter. We learn here that the remains of the dough they took on the exodus fed the people for sixty-one meals. [The figure assumes Israel ate two meals a day for thirty days, in addition to the evening meal of the fifteenth of Nisan, which they ate on the road.] The manna began to fall on the sixteenth of Iyar which was the first day of the week, as recorded in the Talmud (Shabbat 87b).

IBN EZRA

וַיִּסְעוּ מֵאֵילִם — *They set out from Elim:* According to Rav Se'adya Gaon, the Torah mentions that Israel's departure from Elim took place on the fifteenth of Iyar in order to tell us that the exodus from Egypt took place on a Thursday. Now if we assume that Israel left Egypt on Thursday [the fifteenth of Nisan], then the first day of that Nisan was also a Thursday, and the beginning of the month of Iyar fell on Friday and the Sabbath [where the second day of the New Moon is the first of the month]. Now our verse teaches that Israel arrived in the desert of Sin on the fifteenth and upon setting up their camp complained about their hunger. In response Moshe informed them that they would be given meat that evening and manna the next morning. We can reason that the first day of the manna was a Sunday because the verse states: *On the sixth day, they will have to prepare what they bring in* (16:5) — a statement that was made on the sixth day of the week, which was also the sixth day in a row that Israel had eaten manna. We should accept the Gaon's claim [that the redemption took place on Thursday] because it is corroborated by our tradition [see Shabbat 87b], and not merely because that author made the point — for how does he know that the manna started falling on the day following Israel's arrival in the desert of Sin? Perhaps the nation had lived there for four or more days before the miraculous food began to arrive. But certainly the manna first appeared on Sunday, and Israel counted six days from that point, for all nations of the world depend on Israel's counting to establish the days of the week.

RAMBAN

בֵּין־אֵילִם וּבֵין סִינָי — *Between Elim and Sinai:* The text describes Israel's location here in order to distinguish their position in the desert of Sin from a similar sounding place — the wilderness of Tzin, spelled with a *tzadi* rather than a *samekh*. Israel arrived in the desert of Tzin in the fortieth year, and there Miriam died [as reported in Numbers 20:1]. Hence the later

27 Healer." And then they arrived at Elim, where there HAMISHI
were twelve springs and seventy date palms. They encamped

IBN EZRA

וְשִׁבְעִים תְּמָרִים – *And seventy date palms:* According to Rav Se'adya Gaon, when Israel arrived at Elim they found there seventy different types of palm trees [seventy individual plants would be far too few to satisfy such a large population]. Other authors suggest that each tribe enjoyed the fruits of seventy trees, while still others write that every individual Israelite had use of seventy date palms. But all of these approaches are unnecessary, for the twelve springs and the seventy trees that Israel encountered were not created just then for the benefit of Israel. Furthermore, dates do not ripen in the month of Iyar [when the episode occurred, and the amount of available fruit is hence irrelevant]. In my opinion, Israel camped at Mara for just one day, but tarried in Elim for around twenty days. Thus the end of the verse that states that *they encamped there by the water* emphasizes that Israel stayed for a period at that place. In the next verse we read that Israel *set out from Elim on the fifteenth day of the second month* [16:1; again to stress that that site hosted Israel for a significant amount of time]. During the fifteen days afterward, Israel camped at four locations: the Sin desert, Dofka, Alush and Refidim [see Numbers 33:11–14], arriving in the Sinai desert at the start of the third month [see 19:1]. The Torah mentions the date palms only to teach us that the water at Elim was potable, for palm trees need fresh water in order to thrive.

RABBI AVRAHAM BEN HARAMBAM

וַיָּבֹאוּ אֵילִמָה – *And then they arrived at Elim:* The sojourn at Elim was intended to provide therapy, some rest, and relaxation for the nation, which had recently undergone the trauma of the exodus. They were therefore brought to Elim, with its fresh springs. We know the water was healthy because it was able to produce the seventy date palms mentioned in the same verse. **וַיַּחֲנוּ־שָׁם** – *They encamped there:* The phrase suggests Israel's contentment to stay at Elim for a time in order to recover.

HIZKUNI

וַיַּחֲנוּ־שָׁם – *They encamped there:* Israel settled down in Elim in order to learn the Torah that God had commanded them, as the verse states: *It was there that the Lord gave His people decree and law* (15:25).

GUR ARYEH

שְׁתֵּים עֶשְׂרֵה עֵינֹת מַיִם – *Twelve springs:* According to Rashi, God dug one spring for each tribe. Rashi feels compelled to interpret the verse this way since the text cannot be telling us that these springs provided enough drinking water for the entire nation. For there were only twelve springs, and as with the seventy date palms, which could not possibly have produced enough fruit for a community boasting 600,000 adult men, this figure too must hold some other significance. Thus Rashi explains that God directed Israel to a site which He had prepared for their arrival by arranging twelve springs in honor of their twelve tribes, and seventy trees corresponding to the number of the people's elders. Indeed, the Mekhilta states that these natural features had been waiting for Israel's arrival since the six days of creation.

כב לֹא־אָשִׂים עָלֶיךָ כִּי אֲנִי יהוה רֹפְאֶךָ: וַיָּבֹאוּ חמישי
אֵילִמָה וְשָׁם שְׁתֵּים עֶשְׂרֵה עֵינֹת מַיִם וְשִׁבְעִים תְּמָרִים

IBN EZRA (cont.)

practices of the gentiles. **כָּל־הַמַּחֲלָה** – *Any of the sicknesses:* Always remember what you saw in Egypt: how I afflicted that nation's populace with illnesses, torments and plagues because they rebelled against Me. And if you keep that in mind and observe My statutes you will avoid all of that, for I will have no need to punish you as I did them. Not only that, but you will never need medical assistance, for I, the Lord, will be your physician who heals you from all of earth's ills. Observe how I cured the bitter waters in a way that no human doctor could achieve. Note that what you witnessed at Mara was the opposite of what the Egyptians suffered during their first plague. For initially, the Nile waters were fresh and healthy, but I subsequently made them undrinkable. But here, the water you found at Mara started off bitter and unpalatable, and I cured it for you. Thus is God capable of performing an act and its inverse. And so you would be wise to not rebel against God but to love Him so that He will do good for you.

SFORNO

רֹפְאֶךָ – *Your Healer:* All of My commandments serve to cure the individual's soul from the diseases of passion and false ideas. This in turn elevates the person, making one holy to God. Similarly, the verse states: *And you shall be holy to Me, for I the Lord am holy, and have separated you from the peoples, that you should be mine* (Leviticus 20:26). However, if you betray Me, your soul will become sick and profane, and those who desecrate the name of the Lord deserve punishment.

KELI YAKAR

רֹפְאֶךָ – *Your Healer:* Just as your eyes have witnessed that I have the power to remedy bitterness by adding another bitter ingredient, so ought you now to accept the responsibility of listening *to the voice of the Lord, your God doing what is right in His eyes.* For even though at first glance the Torah and its commandments appear to be difficult, and their observance to be fraught with bitterness, one eventually learns that Judaism's ways are sweet. They act as a cure for the bones and medicine for the body. God's laws save the individual from all of the illnesses that God visited upon the Egyptians, both the physical torments and spiritual afflictions that result from the nation's stubbornness. And should a person not realize the treasured benefits that the Torah holds for him and the healing powers it possesses, that is no matter, for *I am the Lord – your Healer.* Only the physician really needs to know how His remedies work. All the patient must do is trust the doctor's knowledge and good intentions and know that he has his charges' best interests at heart.

VERSE 27

RASHI

שְׁתֵּים עֶשְׂרֵה עֵינֹת מַיִם – *Twelve springs:* God arranged one spring for each tribe. **וְשִׁבְעִים תְּמָרִים** – *And seventy date palms:* The number of the fruit trees corresponded to the seventy elders of Israel [a figure introduced in Numbers 11:16].

water became sweet. It was there that the LORD gave His people decree and law; it was there that He put them to the test. 26 He said, "If you listen faithfully to the voice of the LORD your God, doing what is right in His eyes, heeding His commands and keeping His decrees, I will not bring on you any of the sicknesses I brought on the Egyptians, for I am the LORD – your

---

RASHI *(cont.)*

to hear the details of God's commandments. כָּל־חֻקָּיו – *His decrees:* This refers to obligations that seem to have no rationale behind them and are merely the whims of the sovereign. One's evil inclination argues that such rules are silly prohibitions – what possible reason could there be for these things to be forbidden? Examples in this category include the statute outlawing the wearing of wool and linen woven into a single garment, the stricture against eating pig meat, the ritual of the red heifer [see Numbers 19], and others of this kind. לֹא־אָשִׂים עָלֶיךָ – *I will not bring on you:* [If so, why does God need to be subsequently described as a "healer"? God is saying:] And if I do afflict you with such illnesses, you will be thoroughly cleansed from the disease as if you had never suffered, *for I am the LORD – your Healer.* [This represents the midrashic interpretation.] But the straightforward meaning of the text is that because *I am the LORD – your Healer,* I will prescribe the Torah and its commandments as prophylactics [and when you live well, *I will not [need to] bring on you the sicknesses*]. This may be compared to a doctor who tells his patient to avoid a certain food lest it make him sick. So do the verses state: *Fear the LORD and avoid evil. That will be a cure for your flesh* (Proverbs 3:7–8).

RASHBAM

כָּל־הַמַּחֲלָה אֲשֶׁר־שַׂמְתִּי בְמִצְרַיִם – *The sicknesses I brought on the Egyptians:* This refers to God's transformation of the Egyptians' water into blood, leaving the population with nothing to drink. רֹפְאֶךָ – *Your Healer:* See, I have cured your water. We find similar language used when the prophet Elisha remedies the undrinkable water at Yeriḥo [see II Kings 2:19–22]. The sicknesses mentioned in this verse refer to water-borne diseases, as the verse states, *Serve the LORD your God, and He will bless your bread, your water. I will banish all sickness from your midst* (Exodus 23:25).

IBN EZRA

אִם־שָׁמוֹעַ תִּשְׁמַע – *If you listen faithfully:* I have already written that when the verb "to listen" is followed by either the prepositional letters *lamed* or *bet* [as opposed to taking a direct object], it does not connote listening to the specific words being spoken, but to understanding the overall message being expressed. Thus in our verse, the point is that Israel must accept generally what God is commanding them to do. וְהַיָּשָׁר בְּעֵינָיו תַּעֲשֶׂה – *Doing what is right in His eyes:* This refers to the positive commandments [which must be actively "done"]. וְהַאֲזַנְתָּ לְמִצְוֺתָיו – *Heeding His commands:* Israel must understand what the negative commandments consist of. וְשָׁמַרְתָּ כָּל־חֻקָּיו – *And keeping His decrees:* If Israel is cautious not to violate these laws, similar to the verse *And you shall not walk in the practices [ḥukkot] of the nation which I cast out before you* (Leviticus 20:23). It is God's mandate that Israel not mimic the

כא שָׁם לוֹ חֹק וּמִשְׁפָּט וְשָׁם נִסָּהוּ: וַיֹּאמֶר אִם־שָׁמוֹעַ תִּשְׁמַע לְקוֹל ׀ יהוה אֱלֹהֶיךָ וְהַיָּשָׁר בְּעֵינָיו תַּעֲשֶׂה וְהַאֲזַנְתָּ לְמִצְוֹתָיו וְשָׁמַרְתָּ כָּל־חֻקָּיו כָּל־הַמַּחֲלָה אֲשֶׁר־שַׂמְתִּי בְמִצְרַיִם

RAMBAN (cont.)

the regular laws of nature]. Customs are also referred to as *mishpat*, since they are regular and measured. Thus we find: *This was his practice [mishpato] all the time he dwelt in the country* (I Samuel 27:11).... The verse here therefore suggests that Moshe trained Israel to endure the hardships of the wilderness, an ordeal which meant suffering from hunger and thirst and calling to God for assistance, rather than complaining. The leader exposed his people to customs they would need to construct a healthy society such as loving one another, following the advice of the nation's elders, behaving modestly within their tents regarding women and children, and treating traveling salesmen who entered the Israelite camp properly and respectfully. Moshe guided Israel by teaching them to not behave like savages who unabashedly partake in all manner of licentiousness. Thus we read: *When you go out to encamp against your enemies, then keep you from every evil thing* (Deuteronomy 23:10). Similarly did Yehoshua try to shape his own generation, as the verse states: *So Yehoshua made a covenant with the people that day and set them a statute [hok] and an ordinance [mishpat] in Shekhem* (Joshua 24:25). As with Moshe, the terms *hok* and *mishpat* in that verse do not refer to the Torah's rules and regulations, but to the civilized etiquette every society demands. Thus the Talmud explains that Yehoshua conditioned Israel's inheritance of the land upon their acceptance of ten fundamental principles [which went beyond the Torah's strictures; see Bava Kamma 80b]. Our verse continues to state that *it was there that He put them to the test*. This means that Israel were led along a route that offered no water and were then brought to a place whose water was bitter, all in order to test their reactions to those difficulties. Therefore the verse states: *And He humbled you, and suffered you to hunger... that He might test you, to do you good at your latter end* (Deuteronomy 8:3–16).

RABBEINU BAHYA

חֹק וּמִשְׁפָּט – *Decree and law:* According to some authors, the verse describes how God taught Israel survival skills in the desert by showing them the beneficial properties of certain plants and warning them off other dangerous or harmful shrubs. For some vegetation present medicinal effects while other weeds can be poisonous. Indeed, there are plants that can turn bitter water sweet, and others whose admixture to drinkable water will putrefy it. All of these attributes are either perfectly reasonable or mysterious. Thus our verse uses the phrase *hok umishpat* to indicate that some elements in nature are within our understanding [*mishpat*], while other features of the natural world operate beyond our ken [*hok*. Traditionally, the former term is held to refer to laws that are accessible by reason and the latter to statutes whose logic is hidden].

VERSE 26

RASHI

אִם־שָׁמוֹעַ תִּשְׁמַע – *If you listen faithfully:* If Israel accepts the laws upon themselves.

תַּעֲשֶׂה – *Doing:* If Israel acts properly.

וְהַאֲזַנְתָּ – *Heeding:* If Israel inclines its ears

days, they journeyed across the desert without finding water.
23 Eventually they came to Mara, but they could not drink the water there because it was bitter; because of this it was named
24 Mara. The people railed against Moshe – "What are we to
25 drink?" Moshe cried out to the Lord. And the Lord showed him a piece of wood, which he threw into the water – and the

---

IBN EZRA

קָרָא שְׁמָהּ מָרָה – *It was named Mara:* [Literally, "He named it Mara," where the word *mara* literally means "bitter." Ibn Ezra explains that "he" refers generally to] whoever named the place.

VERSE 24

RABBI AVRAHAM BEN HARAMBAM

וַיִּלֹּנוּ – *Railed:* Even though the content of Israel's request was legitimate, the tone of their complaint was disrespectful. Hence our Sages write: All of Israel's demands were fair, but they expressed them in a quarrelsome manner.

VERSE 25

RASHI

שָׁם שָׂם לוֹ – *It was there that the Lord gave:* God delivered some of His laws to Israel for them to study while they were encamped at Mara. The commandments regarding the Sabbath, the red heifer, and various laws of justice were issued at that time. וְשָׁם נִסָּהוּ – *It was there that He put them to the test:* The nation's manners were tested at Mara, and that revealed their stubbornness. For rather than consulting with Moshe and politely asking for water, Israel complained about their situation.

RASHBAM

וַיּוֹרֵהוּ – *Showed him:* [This verb can mean both "show" and "teach."] Use of the verb is similar to the verse *They shall teach [yoru] Yaakov Your judgments, and Israel Your Torah* [Deuteronomy 33:10, that is, God instructed Moshe how to improve the water]. שָׁם שָׂם לוֹ – *It was there that the Lord gave:* At Mara, God orchestrated a plan to test Israel. First He arranged matters so that the people thirsted for water, following which He cured the undrinkable pool that they encountered. At that point God disciplined the nation, instructing them if they accepted the laws and statutes that He taught them, He would provide them with all their needs. This is reflected in the following verse, *If you listen faithfully to the voice of the Lord your God…heeding His commands and keeping His decrees.*

RAMBAN

חֹק וּמִשְׁפָּט – *Decree and law:* The straightforward meaning of this clause is as follows: When Israel began their travels through the great and terrible wilderness, Moshe established practices for the nation in order to take care of their food and other needs, protocols that the people observed until they arrived in the land where they would settle. The term *hok* connotes a custom or a convention, as in the verse *Feed me with my allotted [hukki] portion* (Proverbs 30:8), and the verse *Thus says the Lord: If I have not appointed My covenant with day and night, the ordinances [hukkot] of heaven and earth* [Jeremiah 33:25, referring to

כג שְׁלֹשֶׁת־יָמִים בַּמִּדְבָּר וְלֹא־מָצְאוּ מָיִם: וַיָּבֹאוּ מָרָתָה וְלֹא
יָכְלוּ לִשְׁתֹּת מַיִם מִמָּרָה כִּי מָרִים הֵם עַל־כֵּן קָרָא־שְׁמָהּ
כה מָרָה: וַיִּלֹּנוּ הָעָם עַל־מֹשֶׁה לֵּאמֹר מַה־נִּשְׁתֶּה: וַיִּצְעַק אֶל־
יְהוָה וַיּוֹרֵהוּ יְהוָה עֵץ וַיַּשְׁלֵךְ אֶל־הַמַּיִם וַיִּמְתְּקוּ הַמָּיִם שָׁם

RASHI (cont.)

before the exodus. Thus the verse states: *We will make you necklaces of gold studded with silver* (Song of Songs 1:11). Because Israel was reluctant to abandon the treasure, Moshe had to force the people to move on.

IBN EZRA

וַיַּסַּע מֹשֶׁה – *Moshe then led:* Moshe now led the people. The column of cloud and the pillar of fire had previously gone before Israel to show them the way out of Egypt, while the nation traveled during the day as well as at night. However, after Pharaoh drowned, Israel no longer feared recapture or attack, and they felt no urgency to journey at night.

RABBI AVRAHAM BEN HARAMBAM

וְלֹא־מָצְאוּ מָיִם – *Without finding water:* The verse does not suggest that Israel went three days without drinking water, but that they found no natural source to replenish the remaining water that they carried with them.

ABARBANEL

וַיַּסַּע מֹשֶׁה – *Moshe then led:* Perhaps the Israelites were afraid of striding into the terrible unknown desert, and as such they procrastinated on the seashore as long as they could. This is why Moshe was forced to drag the people away from the beach against their will [see Rashi]. An alternative explanation for this verse's opening is that Moshe personally directed the nation on the march forward because the tribes had not yet organized themselves with the system of banners, princes, and trumpet blasts to steer their movements. None of these institutions were put into place until Israel reached Mount Sinai [see Numbers 10]. Furthermore, the column of cloud only traveled in front of the people from the start of the exodus until Israel traversed the Sea of Reeds and the Egyptians drowned. After that event, the Hebrews no longer relied on the guidance of the cloud to escort them, but followed their human leader Moshe into the wilderness. However, when Israel was unable to find potable water at Mara [in the following passage], the people believed that Moshe's ignorance of the desert landscape was at fault. After all, he should have been able to identify an appropriate encampment that could provide them with fresh water. Once Israel lost faith in Moshe's navigational abilities, they refused to depart from Mara until the cloud appeared once again, which the Torah refers to as "traveling as the Lord guided them" (17:1).

VERSE 23

RASHI

וַיָּבֹאוּ מָרָתָה – *They came to Mara:* The suffixed letter *heh* at the end of *Marata* is the equivalent of a prepositional prefix *lamed*, meaning "to." Hence *Marata* means the same as *leMara*.

20 Then Miriam, the prophetess, sister of Aharon, took a tambourine in her hand, and all the women followed her with tam-
21 bourines and dance. And Miriam led them in song: Sing to the Lord, for He has triumphed in glory; / horse and horseman
22 He hurled into the sea.   Moshe then led the Israelites from the Sea of Reeds out into the desert of Shur. For three

---

RAMBAN (cont.)

this passage while he had not. Calling Miriam the sister of Aharon was a sign of respect for him, for he was her older brother, a prophet, and a holy man of God.

KELI YAKAR

וַתִּקַּח מִרְיָם הַנְּבִיאָה – *Then Miriam, the prophetess, took:* Miriam became a prophetess at this point. Indeed, all the women of that time were privileged to see the Divine Presence, a fact that explains the statement *This is my God, I will glorify Him* (15:2). Thus do our Sages claim: Even the maidservants standing at the sea saw visions that the prophets [of later eras] were not granted. And when our verse states that *all the women followed her with tambourines and dance*, it means that while Miriam was the first woman to be inspired with prophecy, subsequently all of the other women followed in her footsteps, and they too merited this gift. Now in general, the Divine Presence only visits a person through joy. This presents a difficulty for women, who suffer the pain of childbirth. Therefore, to ensure that her fellow women would also receive the prophetic spirit, Miriam led the community in song and dance to raise their emotions to the level of ecstasy. Meanwhile, Miriam is referred to as Aharon's sister because she was equal to him in prophecy; she did not, however, reach the degree achieved by her other brother Moshe.

VERSE 21

RASHI

וַתַּעַן לָהֶם מִרְיָם – *And Miriam led them in song:* Moshe conducted the men in their praise of God by singing verses that they repeated after him. Meanwhile, Miriam led the women in song.

HIZKUNI

שִׁירוּ לַיהוה – *Sing to the Lord:* In fact Miriam and the women repeated the Song at the Sea in its entirety. However, since the Torah has just recorded the full text of the poem, it now suffices with the opening verse.

VERSE 22

RASHI

וַיַּסַּע מֹשֶׁה – *Moshe then led:* Moshe had to drag the Israelites away from the Sea of Reeds against their will. [Rashi is explaining why Moshe is the active force in the verse.] When the Egyptians set out in pursuit of their former slaves, they adorned the horses with gold and silver ornaments and festooned them with jewels. After the cavalry drowned, their valuables washed up upon the shore, enticing Israel into combing the beach for riches. Indeed, the value of the items the sea spat out exceeded the worth of what Israel plundered

וַתִּקַּח֩ מִרְיָ֨ם הַנְּבִיאָ֜ה אֲח֧וֹת אַהֲרֹ֛ן אֶת־הַתֹּ֖ף בְּיָדָ֑הּ וַתֵּצֶ֤אןָ כ
כָֽל־הַנָּשִׁים֙ אַחֲרֶ֔יהָ בְּתֻפִּ֖ים וּבִמְחֹלֹֽת: וַתַּ֥עַן לָהֶ֖ם מִרְיָ֑ם שִׁ֤ירוּ כא
לַֽיהוָֹה֙ כִּֽי־גָאֹ֣ה גָּאָ֔ה ס֥וּס וְרֹכְב֖וֹ רָמָ֥ה בַיָּֽם: וַיַּסַּ֨ע כב
מֹשֶׁ֤ה אֶת־יִשְׂרָאֵל֙ מִיַּם־ס֔וּף וַיֵּצְא֖וּ אֶל־מִדְבַּר־שׁ֑וּר וַיֵּלְכ֧וּ

RAMBAN

כִּי בָא סוּס פַּרְעֹה – *When Pharaoh's horses had gone:* The style of this verse follows neither poetic language nor that of prophecies. Rather, the purpose of this sentence is to establish when exactly Moshe offered his song of praise to God [and is not part of the song itself]. *This they sang when Pharaoh's horses...had gone into the sea,* means that immediately afterward – on that very day – Israel expressed its gratitude to the Lord. Not the next day or sometime after that, but right then. Alternatively, the sense of the verse is that *When Pharaoh's horses, chariots, and cavalry had gone into the sea and the Lord had brought the waters of the sea back over them, the Israelites sang this song* while they were still walking on dry land through the sea. In other words, the people broke into song when they were still in the middle of the sea, even before they had reached the opposite shore.

VERSE 20

RASHI

מִרְיָם הַנְּבִיאָה – *Miriam, the prophetess:* When exactly did Miriam prophesy? When she was still just the "sister of Aharon." Before Moshe was born, Miriam predicted that her mother would bear a son who would become Israel's savior (Sota 12b). Another interpretation [for why the text refers to Miriam as the sister of Aharon and not that of Moshe]: Aharon took a risk for her by begging Moshe for compassion after Miriam was stricken with leprosy [in Numbers 12:10–12]. The Torah therefore refers to Miriam as Aharon's sister. **אֶת־הַתֹּף** – *A tambourine:* The word *tof* refers to an instrument played with different types of music. **בְּתֻפִּים וּבִמְחֹלֹת** – *With tambourines and dance:* So sure were the righteous Israelite women that God was going to perform miracles for them that they took tambourines with them out of Egypt in anticipation.

RASHBAM

אֲחוֹת אַהֲרֹן – *Sister of Aharon:* Miriam is called Aharon's brother [and not Moshe's] because he was the older brother.

IBN EZRA

מִרְיָם הַנְּבִיאָה אֲחוֹת אַהֲרֹן – *Miriam, the prophetess, sister of Aharon:* Some authors explain that Miriam was Aharon's sister [i.e., his equal] in prophetic power. Perhaps she was thus called in Egypt to distinguish her abilities from somebody like Moshe. Nevertheless, as I have written elsewhere, Aharon's skills in this area were on a relatively high level before the arrival of Moshe.

RAMBAN

אֲחוֹת אַהֲרֹן – *Sister of Aharon:* It seems to me that Miriam is linked here to Aharon in order to mention him by name, for his siblings Moshe and Miriam had already been mentioned in

17 crossed over. / You will bring them, You will plant them on the mountain, Your heritage – / the place, Lord, that You made for Your dwelling, / the sanctuary, Lord, that Your hands established. / 18 The Lord will reign for ever and all time. / 19 This they sang when Pharaoh's horses, chariots, and cavalry had gone into the sea / and the Lord had brought the waters of the sea back over them / while the Israelites had walked on dry land through the sea.

RASHBAM

יהוה יִמְלֹךְ – *The Lord will reign:* After Israel settles in their land, the kingship of the Holy One, blessed be He, will become known to all nations.

IBN EZRA

יהוה יִמְלֹךְ – *The Lord will reign:* When Israel constructs the Temple in God's name, His kingship will become known throughout the land.

RAMBAN

יהוה יִמְלֹךְ לְעֹלָם וָעֶד – *The Lord will reign for ever and all time:* Here Moshe makes the following point: God has now convincingly demonstrated that He is king and ruler over the universe by saving His servants and vanquishing those who rebelled against Him. So may it remain God's will to maintain these practices across the generations, never averting His eyes from the righteous, nor ignoring the villainy perpetrated by the wicked.

RALBAG

יהוה יִמְלֹךְ לְעֹלָם וָעֶד – *The Lord will reign for ever and all time:* In this way God's reign over the world will become complete, when all of humanity adopts the language of fealty to His rulership, when every person declares the name of the Lord, and when all people stand shoulder to shoulder to perform His service. It is then that no one will deny the true faith.

VERSE 19

RASHI

כִּי בָא סוּס פַּרְעֹה – *When Pharaoh's horses had gone:* Israel recited this song as Pharaoh and the Egyptians were entering the sea.

IBN EZRA

כִּי בָא סוּס פַּרְעֹה – *When Pharaoh's horses had gone:* [The phrase "This they sang" is an addition of the translator. The Hebrew begins: "When Pharaoh's horses…"] In my opinion, this verse represents the last sentence in Israel's song. Its function is to summarize the miracle within the miracle [of God drowning one nation while rescuing the other]. וַיָּשֶׁב יהוה עֲלֵהֶם – *The Lord had brought back over them:* The term "them" refers back to Pharaoh's horses, his chariots and cavalry, but also to the king himself. For when the verse states: *The enemy said, "I will give chase" etc.* (15:9), it is quoting Pharaoh. The text then continues: *The earth swallowed them up* [15:12; showing that the same man who had threatened Israel was subsequently killed]. Furthermore, a later verse clearly states: *He overthrew Pharaoh and his host in the Sea of Reeds* (Psalms 136:15).

יֹ קָנִיתָ: תְּבִאֵמוֹ וְתִטָּעֵמוֹ בְּהַר נַחֲלָתְךָ מָכוֹן לְשִׁבְתְּךָ פָּעַלְתָּ יהוה מִקְּדָשׁ אֲדֹנָי כּוֹנְנוּ יה יָדֶיךָ: יהוה ׀ יִמְלֹךְ לְעֹלָם וָעֶד: כִּי בָא סוּס פַּרְעֹה בְּרִכְבּוֹ וּבְפָרָשָׁיו בַּיָּם וַיָּשֶׁב יהוה עֲלֵהֶם אֶת־מֵי הַיָּם וּבְנֵי יִשְׂרָאֵל הָלְכוּ בַיַּבָּשָׁה בְּתוֹךְ הַיָּם:

IBN EZRA

תִּפֹּל עֲלֵיהֶם אֵימָתָה — *Dread fell upon them:* The dread here is felt by the Edomites and Moabites listed in verse 15, even though the Canaanites are mentioned more recently. This interpretation is necessary because the sentence continues: *Until Your people crossed, Lord,* meaning the first clause must refer to the people who were passed by on Israel's journey toward the land of Canaan [before they crossed the Jordan River]. Furthermore, the text twice states *until Your people crossed,* because Israel went around Mount Se'ir [Edom's domain] "for a long time" (Deuteronomy 2:1). God is said to have "acquired" Israel because the people were first slaves to Egypt, whereupon God secured them to be His own servants.

VERSE 17

RASHI

תְּבִאֵמוֹ — *You will bring them:* Moshe prophesied that he would not accompany the nation into the land of Israel which is why he said "you will bring them" and not "you will bring us." **מָכוֹן לְשִׁבְתְּךָ** — *The place for Your dwelling:* The earthly Temple stands aligned with God's throne above, which He "made."

IBN EZRA

תְּבִאֵמוֹ וְתִטָּעֵמוֹ — *You will bring them, You will plant them:* This statement represents Moshe's prayer that Israel remain in their land for a long time and not be exiled [for some time must pass for a tree to firmly take root]. Similarly we read: *In the mountain of the height of Israel will I plant it* (Ezekiel 17:23). **בְּהַר נַחֲלָתְךָ** — *On the mountain, Your heritage:* This is an allusion to Mount Moria [the Temple Mount in Jerusalem]. Hence the verse continues: *The place, Lord, that You made for Your dwelling.* **פָּעַלְתָּ** — *That you made:* You have prepared the mountain as a site for Your sanctuary. The place in question stands opposite its heavenly counterpart. The nature of earthly locations depends on the quality of the star that hovers above them. Those who are expert in astrology understand this.

RABBI AVRAHAM BEN HARAMBAM

מִקְּדָשׁ אֲדֹנָי — *The sanctuary, Lord:* Moshe here alludes to how Israel's desire to reach the land of Israel was not due to the place's promise of material pleasures. Rather, the nation was eager to engage in the service of God in the Temple.

VERSE 18

RASHI

לְעֹלָם וָעֶד — *For ever and all time:* The phrase means "for all eternity."

guided out the people You redeemed. / In Your strength, You
14 led them to Your holy abode. / Nations heard and they trem-
15 bled; / terror seized the Philistines. / The chiefs of Edom were
dismayed, then, / Moav's leaders were seized with trembling, /
16 the people of Canaan melted away. / Dread, terror fell upon
them; / by Your arm's power they were stilled as stone – / until Your people crossed, LORD, / until the people You acquired

---
RAMBAN (cont.)

seized the Philistines" here and "Dread, terror will fall upon them" in verse 16. Ramban explains:] Perhaps the surrounding nations had already "heard" news of God's activities in Egypt. They now "tremble" constantly from the terror that "has seized" them. Moshe now prays that "dread, terror will fall upon them," preventing them from challenging Israel in battle.

VERSE 15

RASHI

אַלּוּפֵי אֱדוֹם אֵילֵי מוֹאָב – *The chiefs of Edom...Moav's leaders:* Why were these nations at all afraid? Israel was not headed in their direction. Rather, they were aggrieved and distressed that Israel had achieved such glory. נָמֹגוּ – *Melted away:* The word *namogu* means "melted." It appears in a different form in the verse, *You melted [temogegenna] with showers* (Psalms 65:11). The Canaanites were terrified that the Israelites were going to march on them, destroy them, and inherit their land.

SFORNO

אָז נִבְהֲלוּ אַלּוּפֵי אֱדוֹם – *The chiefs of Edom were dismayed, then:* The Edomite leaders became unsettled when they witnessed God's miracles, even though they knew that Israel would not wage war against them. [see Deuteronomy 2:4–5]. Nevertheless, the sight put the fear of God in them. יֹאחֲזֵמוֹ רָעַד – *Were seized with trembling:* [The verb is expressed in the future tense to express Moshe's prayer:] May it be God's will that these peoples be seized with trembling, and will shrink from rising against us. נָמֹגוּ כֹּל יֹשְׁבֵי כְנָעַן – *The people of Canaan melted away:* The inhabitants of Canaan would lose all hope upon hearing of these events, for they knew that Israel was headed their way to expel them from their land. This is why Raḥav stated: *As soon as we heard these things, our hearts melted* (Joshua 2:11).

VERSE 16

RASHI

תִּפֹּל עֲלֵיהֶם אֵימָתָה – *Dread fell upon them:* Dread fell upon distant peoples. וָפַחַד – *Terror:* Terror beset those who close by, as the verse attests [regarding the inhabitants of Yeriḥo], *For we have heard how the* LORD *dried up the waters of the Sea of Reeds* (Joshua 2:10). עַד־יַעֲבֹר... עַד־יַעֲבֹר – *Until Your people crossed...crossed over:* The Targum's rendering of the verse is accurate. [It links the repeated phrase to Israel's crossing of the Jordan and Arnon rivers].

בְּחַסְדְּךָ עַם־זוּ גָּאָלְתָּ   נֵהַלְתָּ בְעָזְּךָ אֶל־נְוֵה
קָדְשֶׁךָ: יד

שָׁמְעוּ עַמִּים יִרְגָּזוּן   חִיל
אָחַז יֹשְׁבֵי פְּלָשֶׁת: טו

אָז נִבְהֲלוּ אַלּוּפֵי אֱדוֹם   אֵילֵי מוֹאָב יֹאחֲזֵמוֹ רָעַד   נָמֹגוּ
כֹּל יֹשְׁבֵי כְנָעַן: טז

תִּפֹּל עֲלֵיהֶם אֵימָתָה וָפַחַד   בִּגְדֹל זְרוֹעֲךָ יִדְּמוּ כָּאָבֶן   עַד־
יַעֲבֹר עַמְּךָ יהוה   עַד־יַעֲבֹר עַם־זוּ

RAMBAN

תִּבְלָעֵמוֹ אָרֶץ — *The earth swallowed them up:* After the soldiers drowned in the sea, the waves washed the bodies ashore, as the verse states: *The Israelites saw the Egyptians dead on the seashore* (14:30). As the corpses lay on the beach, they decomposed and returned to the dust of the earth. Thus were they swallowed up and destroyed by the land.

VERSE 13

RASHBAM

נֵהַלְתָּ — *You led:* You lead Israel now in order to eventually bring them into the land of Canaan, which You will bequeath to them. That country is "Your holy abode."

IBN EZRA

אֶל־נְוֵה קָדְשֶׁךָ — *To Your holy abode:* The allusion is to Mount Sinai, the dwelling place of God's glory.

RAMBAN

אֶל־נְוֵה קָדְשֶׁךָ — *To Your holy abode:* Moshe refers here to the Temple, as he states below: *Your dwelling, the sanctuary, Lord, that Your hands established* (15:17).

VERSE 14

RASHI

יֹשְׁבֵי פְּלָשֶׁת — *The Philistines:* The Philistines were terrified because they had previously killed members of the tribe of Efrayim when they had sought to force their way out of Egypt before the time had come, as is stated explicitly in the verse *The men of Gat…slew them* (I Chronicles 7:21).

RASHBAM

יֹשְׁבֵי פְּלָשֶׁת — *The Philistines:* The inhabitants of Philistia and the chiefs of Edom and Moav all belong to nations neighboring the land of Israel.

RAMBAN

שָׁמְעוּ עַמִּים יִרְגָּזוּן — *Nations heard and they trembled:* [The tense of these verses in Hebrew shifts several times. Literally, they seem to mean: "Nations heard and they tremble, terror

10 them." / You blew with Your wind; the sea covered over them. /
11 They sank like lead in mighty waters. / Who is like You, Lord, among the mighty? / Who is like You – majestic in holiness, /
12 awesome in glory, working wonders? / You reached out Your
13 right hand – / the earth swallowed them up. / In Your love, You

---

RASHBAM

נוֹרָא תְהִלֹּת – *Awesome in glory:* [Literally, "fearful of praises."] The people's songs of praise present you as revered and as threatening, as in the verse *The people were in awe of the Lord* (14:31).

IBN EZRA

בָּאֵלִם – *Among the mighty:* The term *elim* refers to holy angels of the celestial realm, while the phrase *benei elim* [in Psalms 29:1] describes the stars. **נֶאְדָּר בַּקֹּדֶשׁ** – *Majestic in holiness:* This phrase is a reference to God's throne of glory.

RAMBAN

נוֹרָא תְהִלֹּת – *Awesome in glory:* [Literally, "fearful of praises."] This phrase means that God performs awesome acts for which He is then lauded. For example, He wreaks vengeance against people who defy His will, but in the process saves His loyal servants. Hence, He is terrifying and praiseworthy simultaneously. And while earthly kings are feared for their tyranny and their perverseness, the Lord is feared for those things which garner Him praise.

SFORNO

עֹשֵׂה פֶלֶא – *Working wonders:* God performs miracles that are supernatural such as creating columns of cloud and pillars of fire.

VERSE 12

RASHI

נָטִיתָ יְמִינְךָ – *You reached out Your right hand:* When the Holy One, blessed be He, extends His hand, the wicked fall and perish, for all creatures lean on His arm and collapse when it is withdrawn. Thus the verse states: *When the Lord stretches out His hand, the helper shall stumble* (Isaiah 31:3). This may be compared to a man who holds a glass jar in his open palm. If he tilts his arm a bit, the vessel will tumble over and shatter. **תִּבְלָעֵמוֹ אָרֶץ** – *The earth swallowed them up:* Burial was the Egyptians' reward for having once acknowledged that *The Lord is in the right* (9:27).

IBN EZRA

נָטִיתָ יְמִינְךָ – *You reached out Your right hand:* The world saw evidence of Your wonders when Your exalted name reached out from the highest heavens and caused the lowly earth to swallow up the enemy. In a single moment, Your right hand, which rests on the supreme heights beyond the heavens, stretched to the depths of the seas. **יְמִינְךָ** – *Your right hand:* That is, Your power.

נַפְשִׁ֔י אָרִ֥יק חַרְבִּ֖י תּוֹרִישֵׁ֣מוֹ יָדִֽי: נָשַׁ֥פְתָּ
בְרוּחֲךָ֖ כִּסָּ֣מוֹ יָ֑ם צָֽלֲלוּ֙ כַּֽעוֹפֶ֔רֶת בְּמַ֖יִם
יא אַדִּירִֽים: מִֽי־כָמֹ֤כָה בָּֽאֵלִם֙ יְהֹוָ֔ה מִ֥י
כָּמֹ֖כָה נֶאְדָּ֣ר בַּקֹּ֑דֶשׁ נוֹרָ֥א תְהִלֹּ֖ת עֹ֥שֵׂה
יב פֶ֑לֶא: נָטִ֨יתָ֙ יְמִ֣ינְךָ֔ תִּבְלָעֵ֖מוֹ אָֽרֶץ: נָחִ֥יתָ

RAMBAN *(cont.)*

congealed. When the enemy saw that the waters had parted, *they said, "I will give chase, will overtake"* Israel in the midst of the sea, *I will divide the spoils. My desire shall gorge its fill of them.* However, *You blew with Your wind; the sea covered over them.* Moshe found it appropriate to mention the Egyptians' scheme to draw attention to God's wonders. For it was He who strengthened the oppressors' resolve and turned their wisdom to the foolishness, luring them into the water, as I have explained above [in comments to 14:21]. Hence Moshe follows this verse with the statement *Who is like You, LORD, among the mighty* (15:11). Only God can simultaneously perform wonders that are opposites of each other [that is, rescuing the Israelites and destroying the Egyptians at the same time].

VERSE 10

BEKHOR SHOR

צָֽלֲלוּ כַּֽעוֹפֶרֶת בְּמַיִם אַדִּירִים – *They sank like lead in mighty waters:* According to the Sages, the Egyptians sank like lead in waters that were mighty. But perhaps the verse should be interpreted: The mighty sank like lead in the waters.

RAMBAN

צָֽלֲלוּ כַּֽעוֹפֶרֶת בְּמַיִם אַדִּירִים – *They sank like lead in mighty waters:* They plummeted through the water like falling lead. Moshe mentions the sinking of the army twice in this song to emphasize God's role in drowning the Egyptians – singing in verse 5 that *they sank to the depths like a stone,* and in verse 10 that *they sank like lead.* For surely some of the Egyptian soldiers must have known how to swim, and they were not far from the shore. Furthermore, those men who were riding horses should have been saved, since horses are capable of swimming, while those who carried shields could have used them as flotation devices. And yet, not a single Egyptian survived the experience. This is the meaning of the verse *The LORD swept them into the sea* (14:27). God used a fierce wind to lift them up and plunge them into the ocean.

VERSE 11

RASHI

בָּאֵלִם – *Among the mighty:* The term *elim* means "the mighty." **נוֹרָא תְהִלֹּת** – *Awesome in glory:* [Literally, "fearful of praises." This phrase means that] it is fearful to sing Your praises lest they fall short of adequate expression. Hence the Psalmist declares: *To You, silence is praise* (Psalms 65:2).

7 enemy. / In the greatness of Your majesty, You overthrew those who rose against You. / You sent forth Your rage; it consumed
8 them like stubble. / By the blast of Your nostrils the waters heaped; / the surge stood upright as a wall; / the deeps con-
9 gealed at the heart of the sea. / The enemy said, "I will give chase, will overtake, / I will divide the spoils. / My desire shall gorge its fill of them. / I will draw my sword, / and my hand destroy

---

RASHI (cont.)

refers to the strength of the sea. For the term "heart" is often used in Scripture to refer to the strongest essence of an object. Hence we read: *And the mountain burned with fire to the heart of heaven* (Deuteronomy 4:11), and: *In the heart of the oak* (II Samuel 18:14).

RASHBAM

וּבְרוּחַ אַפֶּיךָ – *By the blast of Your nostrils:* This refers to the *strong east wind [that blew] all night* (14:21).

VERSE 9

RASHI

אָמַר אוֹיֵב – *The enemy said:* In order to persuade his nation to follow him into battle, Pharaoh promised his army: *I will give chase, will overtake, I will divide the spoils* with my officers and my servants. נַפְשִׁי – *My desire:* [Literally, "my soul," the word *nafshi* here means] "my spirit" or "my desire." תּוֹרִישֵׁמוֹ – *Destroy them:* The verb means that Pharaoh planned to despoil and impoverish Israel, as in the verse, *The Lord makes poor [morish] and makes rich* (I Samuel 2:7).

RASHBAM

אָמַר אוֹיֵב – *The enemy said:* When they saw that the sea had been transformed to dry land, *the enemy said, "I will give chase".*

RAMBAN

אָמַר אוֹיֵב אֶרְדֹּף אַשִּׂיג – *The enemy said, "I will give chase, will overtake":* In the work *Midrash Ḥazit*, I have read the following idea. Rabbi Yishmael taught: It would have made more sense for the verse *The enemy said, "I will give chase, will overtake"* to have been placed at the start of this song. Rather, we must conclude that events in the Torah are not always recorded in chronological order. Onkelos too accepts this approach, for he translates our verse: "The enemy had said," thereby explaining that although the Egyptians' statement of purpose appears here in verse 9, it refers to their earlier plan to pursue the Israelites. However, in my opinion, the position of this verse is correct, and its content should be understood in connection with the preceding text. First the passage describes that the army drowned in the sea and descended to its depths. This happened when the waters rushed back and swallowed up the chariots and their horsemen. The following verses (8–10) describe how the Egyptians found themselves in that horrible position: *By the blast of [God's] nostrils* – that is, the strong east wind – *the waters heaped...the deeps*

ז יְהוה תִּרְעַץ אוֹיֵב: וּבְרֹב גְּאוֹנְךָ תַּהֲרֹס
ח קָמֶיךָ תְּשַׁלַּח חֲרֹנְךָ יֹאכְלֵמוֹ כַּקַּשׁ: וּבְרוּחַ
אַפֶּיךָ נֶעֶרְמוּ מַיִם נִצְּבוּ כְמוֹ־נֵד
ט נֹזְלִים קָפְאוּ תְהֹמֹת בְּלֶב־יָם: אָמַר
אוֹיֵב אֶרְדֹּף אַשִּׂיג אֲחַלֵּק שָׁלָל תִּמְלָאֵמוֹ

SFORNO

יְמִינְךָ יהוה נֶאְדָּרִי בַּכֹּחַ – *Your right hand, Lᴏʀᴅ, majestic in power:* It is God's right hand which is successful in battle, not the right hand of Pharaoh's army or the best of his officers, for they rely on arms of flesh and blood.

VERSE 7

RASHI

תַּהֲרֹס קָמֶיךָ – *You overthrew those who rose against You:* [This verb too is in the future tense, which can also be used in the sense of the present simple:] "You always overthrow those who rise up against You." And who are they? Those who strive to defeat Israel. So we see in the verse: *Your enemies make a tumult* (Psalms 83:3). What tumult do they cause? *They take crafty counsel against Your people* (Psalms 83:4). For this hostility to Israel, they are called Your enemies.

RASHBAM

תַּהֲרֹס קָמֶיךָ – *You overthrew those who rose against You:* The term *taharos* derives from the verb *hasara*, which signifies the taking down or overthrow of a thing.

IBN EZRA

תְּשַׁלַּח חֲרֹנְךָ יֹאכְלֵמוֹ כַּקַּשׁ – *You sent forth your rage; it consumed them like stubble:* God requires no iron weapons to destroy those who challenge Him. Simply by unleashing His rage He can consume these enemies like stubble burns in a fire. For God's anger burns with a blazing heat.

VERSE 8

RASHI

וּבְרוּחַ אַפֶּיךָ – *By the blast of Your nostrils:* [The word *af* means nose, but here the term *appekha* is plural. Thus the phrase must refer to] the wind that emerges from the nose's two nostrils. The text uses anthropomorphism, describing God as a king of flesh and blood, to make God's behavior more accessible to readers. God is therefore portrayed as a man who snorts from his nostrils when angry. **נֶעֶרְמוּ** – *Heaped:* The burning blast from Your nostrils dried up the waters, which became like dunes and high piles of wheat. **קָפְאוּ** – *Congealed:* This verb makes a similar appearance in the verse *And curdled me [takpi'eni] like cheese* (Job 10:10), denoting a substance that has been solidified and made like stone. The sea thus cast the Egyptians forcefully against the rock-hard surface and fought them with all manner of harshness. **בְּלֶב־יָם** – *At the heart of the sea:* The "heart"

4 LORD is a Master of war; / the LORD is His name. / Pharaoh's chariots and army / He hurled into the sea; / the best of his offi-
5 cers / drowned in the Sea of Reeds. / The deep waters covered
6 them; / they sank to the depths like a stone. / Your right hand, LORD, majestic in power, / Your right hand, LORD, shatters the

---

KELI YAKAR (cont.)

to the beach where plant life still grows. The bottom of the sea at that point is covered with mud and clay, which is where the officers met their demise, sinking in the mire where the reeds grow, even though the water there was not particularly deep. Meanwhile, out in the ocean, Pharaoh was being hurled into the depths. It would have been inaccurate to say that the king sank in the muck, there because no clay or mud is to be found where he was.

VERSE 5

RASHI

כְּמוֹ־אָבֶן – *Like a stone:* In verse 10 below, the soldiers are said to sink *like lead in mighty waters,* whereas in verse 7 the enemy is compared to straw: *It consumed them like stubble.* Each of these metaphors describes a different type of villain: The wicked were like straw which does not easily sink – they were tossed up and down in the sea until they died. The average characters sank slowly like a stone, and the most decent soldiers sank quickly like lead and suffered least of all.

RABBI AVRAHAM BEN HARAMBAM

תְּהֹמֹת יְכַסְיֻמוּ יָרְדוּ בִמְצוֹלֹת – *The deep waters covered them; they sank to the depths:* It is common for songs and poems written with imagery and metaphor to repeat the same idea using alternative language. Hence it is unnecessary to attempt to distinguish between the terms *tehomot* and *metzulot.* Similarly, the word *tubbe'u* [they drowned, in 15:4] is synonymous with *yaredu* [they sank, in our verse], and the verb *tzalelu* [they sank, in 15:10]. Similarly, the stone in verse 5 is no different than the lead in verse 10 – in poetry, the author merely finds descriptive ways to say the same thing.

VERSE 6

RASHI

יְמִינְךָ... יְמִינְךָ – *Your right hand…Your right hand:* The phrase appears twice in the verse to imply that when Israel fulfills the will of God, then even His left hand [which signifies the attribute of Justice] behaves like His right hand [the attribute of Compassion]. יְמִינְךָ יהוה נֶאְדָּרִי בַּכֹּחַ – *Your right hand, LORD, majestic in power:* Your right hand is majestic in power as it engages in Israel's rescue, while Your other right hand "shatters the enemy."

RASHBAM

יְמִינְךָ יהוה – *Your right hand, LORD:* The phrase means: "Your right hand – LORD, majestic in power – shatters the enemy." The term "right hand" is feminine [and therefore "majestic," which is masculine, refers to God, not to His hand].

מַרְכְּבֹת פַּרְעֹה וְחֵילוֹ יָרָה בַיָּם וּמִבְחַר שָׁלִשָׁיו טֻבְּעוּ בְיַם־סוּף: ⁵ תְּהֹמֹת יְכַסְיֻמוּ יָרְדוּ בִמְצוֹלֹת כְּמוֹ־אָבֶן: ⁶ יְמִינְךָ יְהוָה נֶאְדָּרִי בַּכֹּחַ יְמִינְךָ ⁴ שְׁמוֹ:

RASHBAM

יהוה שְׁמוֹ — *The Lord is His name: The Lord is known by the judgment which He executes* (Psalms 9:17).

ABARBANEL

אִישׁ מִלְחָמָה — *A Master of war:* [Literally, "Man of war."] Since I find it distasteful to describe God using the term "man," I would prefer to offer two other interpretations for this verse. Firstly, Moshe here might be asking rhetorically: Is God really a man of war? Nonsense! God does not behave like people do in waging war with others. On the contrary, *the Lord is His name,* and that name represents a benevolent God defined by compassion; He is not a "man of war" or violence. And the suffering that the Egyptians endured as they drowned in the sea was punishment for their own nasty behavior; they brought it upon themselves. Alternatively, the verse might be a response to Pharaoh's claim upon Moshe's arrival in Egypt: *Who is this Lord that I should obey Him and send Israel forth? I do not know the Lord* (5:2). Now, standing on the seashore, Moshe mocks Pharaoh, saying: Do you not know who the Lord is? Why, He is a Man of war; the Lord is His name! For Pharaoh, you fancied yourself a capable warrior, seeking to pursue Israel and destroy them. But now look who has outmatched you — the Lord, whom you claimed not to recognize.

VERSE 4

RASHI

טֻבְּעוּ — *Drowned:* The elite of Pharaoh's guard sank in the mud. We find similar language in the verse *I sink in deep mire* (Psalms 69:3) and the verse *Then they took Yirmeyahu and cast him into the pit... and Yirmeyahu sank in the mire* (Jeremiah 38:6). The sea had turned into mud in order to punish the Egyptians measure for measure. For the oppressors had compelled Israel to work with mortar and bricks.

RASHBAM

יָרָה בַיָּם — *He hurled into the sea:* The verb *yara* here is the same as that in the verse *And the shooters shot [vayoru] from wall upon your servants* (II Samuel 11:24). It means to hurl or to cast.

KELI YAKAR

יָרָה בַיָּם — *He hurled into the sea:* We must explain why our verse first states that *Pharaoh's chariots and army He hurled into the sea,* and then states that *the best of his officers drowned* [or "were mired"; see Rashi] *in the Sea of Reeds.* It seems to me that Pharaoh rode in front of his armed forces, leading his soldiers in the attack. When Pharaoh and the enlisted men who were near his chariot found themselves in the middle of the sea, well beyond the vegetation of the shoreline, the king's advisors and officers were much farther back, close

2 horse and horseman He hurled into the sea. / The Lord is my strength and song – / and now my salvation. / This is my God,
3 I will glorify Him, / my father's God, I will exalt Him. / The

---

BEKHOR SHOR

עָזִּי וְזִמְרָת יָהּ – *The Lord is my strength and song:* God is strength for me, but a pruning blade for my enemies, pruning [*zomer*] and cutting them.

ABARBANEL

עָזִּי וְזִמְרָת יָהּ – *The Lord is my strength and song:* Both my strength exercised in battle and my songs of praise are due only to God, Rock of Ages [The abbreviated divine name *Yah* appears in conjunction with the appellation "Rock of Ages" in Isaiah 26:4]. For the wonder that was the splitting of the Sea of Reeds is a reminder that God created the world to begin with [and hence is capable of manipulating nature], an idea encapsulated in this divine name [which can also be understood to mean "Rock of Worlds"]. Moshe's song and celebration were not predicated by the drowning of the Egyptians, for God derives no pleasure from the death of the wicked. Rather, our joy stemmed from the "salvation" God granted Israel; that is the reason we praised and exalted His name. Furthermore, quite apart from that gracious act of deliverance, God would still deserve our song, for He is our God who conducts our lives and fights our wars in Egypt. Hence, *I will glorify Him [ve'anvehu]* and pay tribute to Him in song. Alternatively, the term *ve'anvehu* suggests: I will build a home [*naveh*] or temple in His honor, a place where He will be venerated.

SFORNO

אֱלֹהֵי אָבִי – *My father's God:* He is the God of [*Elohei*] Yaakov, who *erected there an altar and called it El Elohei Yisrael* (Genesis 33:20), thereby declaring that God is tremendous in His greatness and providence – two characteristics signifying God's fundamental attributes of Compassion and Justice. וַאֲרֹמְמֶנְהוּ – *And I will exalt Him:* I will bow down to Him, I will humble myself and proclaim to all of humanity that the purpose of creation is to perform the will of God. That is our highest calling, since it represents the greatest blessing and praise toward God. This is similarly expressed in the verse *Teach me to do Your will, for you are my God* (Psalms 143:10).

VERSE 3

RASHI

יהוה שְׁמוֹ – *The Lord is His name:* [The connection between this phrase and the appellation "Master of war" is that] God does not fight wars with weapons but with the power of His name, as David declares to Golyat: *You come to me with a sword, and with a spear, and with a javelin. But I come to you in the name of the Lord of hosts, the God of the armies of Israel* (I Samuel 17:45). Another interpretation: Even while God fights and wreaks vengeance upon His enemies, He still maintains His attribute of Mercy in dealing with those who call His name, sustaining all of creation. This stands in contrast to mortal kings, who are have no interest in and are incapable of fulfilling their normal duties when they are engaged in war.

ג וְרִכְבּוֹ יָרָה בַיָּם: עָזִּי וְזִמְרָת יָהּ וַיְהִי־לִי
לִישׁוּעָה זֶה אֵלִי וְאַנְוֵהוּ אֱלֹהֵי
ד אָבִי וַאֲרֹמְמֶנְהוּ: יהוה אִישׁ מִלְחָמָה יהוה

GUR ARYEH

אָז יָשִׁיר־מֹשֶׁה — *And then Moshe sang:* [The Hebrew verb *yashir* is in the future tense.] In his commentary to this verse, Rashi interprets the phrase as indicating that when Moshe witnessed the miracle at the sea, he conceived the idea to sing a song of praise to celebrate the occasion. Thus Rashi explains why the verb is expressed in the future tense — Moshe was planning what he was going to do. However, there is a difficulty with this approach: Why would the text only tell us what Moshe intended to do, when it is quite clear that he did sing in practice? We might answer by explaining that singing is fundamentally an act of the heart, for when a righteous person is roused to joy, a song bursts from his soul. And there is no doubt that at that moment the Israelites were overwhelmed with emotion and joyfully expressed their feelings through this poem. This is what Rashi means when he writes that the people were determined in their hearts to sing to God — the experience of the miracle affected them on a visceral level. This was not an intellectual response, like when a person forces himself to recite some prepared speech. Such a declamation would hardly reflect the spontaneous ecstasy that the people were feeling. Here the text conveys the exhilaration that swelled in the Israelites' hearts, which aroused a need to shout their gratitude and happiness to their Savior. It therefore makes sense for the verse to describe the process whereby Israel came to pronounce their song — their feelings determined that they would sing [*yashir*].

VERSE 2

RASHI

זֶה אֵלִי — *This is my God:* God revealed Himself in His glory to Israel such that they were able to point to Him with their fingers. The meanest Israelite maidservant witnessed at the sea a sight that even the later prophets were not privileged to see. **וְאַנְוֵהוּ** — *I will glorify Him:* Onkelos translates the term *ve'anvehu* as related to the word *naveh* [meaning "dwelling"], as in the verse *Your eyes shall see Jerusalem a quiet habitation [naveh]* (Isaiah 33:20), or the verse *And Sharon shall be a fold [linvei] of flocks* (Isaiah 65:10). Another interpretation for the term *ve'anvehu* connects it to the root *noi* [meaning "beauty"], with the sense of: I will relate His beauty and His praise to everyone on earth. We find such sentiment in the verses: *What is your beloved more than another beloved!... My beloved is white and ruddy* (Song of Songs 5:9–10), and that whole passage. **אֱלֹהֵי אָבִי** — *My father's God:* I am not the first one to experience His holiness. Rather, His sanctity and His divinity has been present at my side since the days of my ancestors.

RASHBAM

עָזִּי וְזִמְרָת יָהּ — *The Lord is my strength and song:* The phrase means that God is Israel's strength and song, and He is my salvation.

31 the seashore, and witnessed the wondrous power the LORD had unleashed against the Egyptians, the people were in awe of the LORD, and they believed in Him and in Moshe His servant.

15 1 And then, Moshe and the Israelites sang this song to the LORD: I will sing to the LORD, for He has triumphed in glory; /

RABBI AVRAHAM BEN HARAMBAM

וַיַּאֲמִינוּ בַּיהוה – *And they believed in the* LORD: The miracle of the sea added to and strengthened the faith the Israelites already possessed. Lest you argue that the text already attests: *And the people believed. When they heard that the* LORD *was watching over [them]...they bowed their heads and prostrated themselves* (4:31), recognize that this additional wonder deepened that belief.

CHAPTER 15, VERSE 1

RASHI

אָז יָשִׁיר־מֹשֶׁה – *And then Moshe sang:* [Literally, "will sing," in the future tense.] When Moshe saw the miracle, he formed the intention to sing a song. The prefix letter *yod* indicates a person's intention. This is the explanation of the verse's plain meaning. However, our Sages write in the Midrash that the future tense in our verse is the Torah's allusion to the resurrection of the dead. **כִּי־גָאֹה גָּאָה** – *For He has triumphed in glory:* This phrase should be taken as Targum translates it ["He is exalted above all proud things"]. Another interpretation: No matter how many songs I utter in praise of God, it would not sufficiently describe His greatness. This stands in contrast to mortal kings, whose subjects flatter them undeservedly. **סוּס וְרֹכְבוֹ** – *Horse and horseman:* Horse and rider were fused together so that when the water raised them up to the crests of the waves, and plunged them to the troughs of the sea, the pair was not separated.

IBN EZRA

וַיֹּאמְרוּ לֵאמֹר – *They said, saying:* [This phrase is absent from the translation here. It can also be understood to mean "they said to say."] Every one of the Israelites was to recite each of the following praises of the song. Alternatively, the phrase means that future generations should recite this song of thanks. **כִּי־גָאֹה גָּאָה** – *For He has triumphed in glory:* God demonstrated His glory by vanquishing both horse and rider. The horse exudes power and status, and his warrior master dominates the battlefield. But God cast them both into the sea like one would shoot an arrow.

ABARBANEL

אָז יָשִׁיר־מֹשֶׁה – *And then Moshe sang:* Moshe and the nation did not sing this song simultaneously. Rather, Moshe would first utter a verse, whereupon Israel would proclaim: *I will sing to the* LORD, *for He has triumphed in glory; horse and horseman He hurled into the sea.* In other words, Moshe composed each verse on his own, and upon declaring each separate idea, the people would issue the same response: *I will sing to the* LORD, *etc.* That was the only verse the nation sang throughout this series of praises, and this is what the phrase *vayomeru lemor* [untranslated here; literally, "they said, saying"] implies.

אֶת־מִצְרַיִם מֵת עַל־שְׂפַת הַיָּם: וַיַּרְא יִשְׂרָאֵל אֶת־הַיָּד הַגְּדֹלָה אֲשֶׁר עָשָׂה יהוה בְּמִצְרַיִם וַיִּירְאוּ הָעָם אֶת־יהוה וַיַּאֲמִינוּ בַּיהוה וּבְמֹשֶׁה עַבְדּוֹ: לֹא

טו א אָז יָשִׁיר־מֹשֶׁה וּבְנֵי יִשְׂרָאֵל אֶת־הַשִּׁירָה הַזֹּאת לַיהוה וַיֹּאמְרוּ לֵאמֹר אָשִׁירָה לַיהוה כִּי־גָאֹה גָּאָה סוּס

---- RASHBAM (cont.) ----

the voice of the Lord God walking in the garden in the breeze of the day [Genesis 3:8; that is, it was the man and woman who were walking through the garden, not God].

---- IBN EZRA ----

בַּיּוֹם הַהוּא – *That day:* It was at that moment that Israel was fully redeemed from Egypt. Although they had been released from bondage some days earlier, the people walked through Pharaoh's land with the specter of re-enslavement hanging over their heads. Now when the Egyptian soldiers drowned, their bodies did not wash up on the beach, since a later verse states: *The earth swallowed them up* [15:12; suggesting that they were buried in the ocean floor]. When our verse states that *the Israelites saw the Egyptians dead on the seashore*, it means that the Hebrews stood on the beach and watched while their foes sank beneath the waves.

---- RALBAG ----

מֵת עַל־שְׂפַת הַיָּם – *Dead on the seashore:* As the first Israelites clambered out of the seabed, they witnessed the Egyptians drowning in the waves. Alternatively, perhaps the sea spat out the dying soldiers from its midst for them to expire on the beach in view of the Israelites. Still, the first interpretation seems more likely to me.

---- SFORNO ----

בַּיּוֹם הַהוּא – *That day:* Only when the Israelites watched their former oppressors dying did they feel they were truly free. Beforehand, they had seen themselves merely as escaping slaves.

---- VERSE 31 ----

---- RASHI ----

אֶת־הַיָּד הַגְּדֹלָה – *The wondrous power:* [Literally, "the great hand."] Israel witnessed the great strength that the hand of God had unleashed.

---- RASHBAM ----

וַיַּאֲמִינוּ בַּיהוה – *And they believed in the Lord:* The people now had faith that they would not even perish of hunger in the wilderness.

---- IBN EZRA ----

וַיַּאֲמִינוּ בַּיהוה – *And they believed in the Lord:* Israel believed that God was true, and they trusted that Moshe was his loyal servant who did only what God commanded him to do.

27 chariots and cavalry." Moshe stretched out his hand over the sea, and at daybreak the water came back in full force. The Egyptians fled at its approach but the LORD swept them into
28 the sea. The waters returned, covering the chariots, the cavalry, and the whole Egyptian army that had followed the Israelites
29 into the sea. Not one of them remained. But the Israelites had walked through the sea on dry land, with a wall of water to their
30 right and left. That day, the LORD saved the Israelites from the Egyptians. And when the Israelites saw the Egyptians dead on

VERSE 29

IBN EZRA

הָלְכוּ בַיַּבָּשָׁה – *Walked through on dry land:* God at that time performed a miracle within a miracle. For at the point where the Israelites were crossing the sea, the east wind dried up the water before their feet. Simultaneously, a second wind blew at Pharaoh's position, melting the water that had frozen into walls surrounding the Egyptian army. What this means is that there were two winds blowing at the same time – one howling and the other murmuring – not very far from each other. Thus the Song at the Sea speaks of two winds: First it states: *By the blast of Your nostrils the waters heaped* (15:8) referring to the gusts that saved Israel; and then a second verse claims: *You blew with your wind; the sea covered them* (15:10) thanking God for sinking the Egyptians…. Now do not wonder how all of Israel could manage to cross the sea over the course of a single night. Could such a feat be accomplished when the number 600,000 comprised not even a quarter of the Israelite camp? [The figure, which appears in 12:37, comprises just the armed men and does not include their wives, children, and the elderly.] There are several possible ways to resolve this difficulty. Firstly, perhaps it was only the men who lured the army into the sea, while the rest of the population continued traveling on land elsewhere. Alternatively, there might have been twelve different crossing points, as our Sages, of blessed memory, claim. Now Israel did not traverse the width of the sea, but walked along its length to the Shur desert, emerging close to where they entered.

VERSE 30

RASHI

וַיַּרְא יִשְׂרָאֵל אֶת־מִצְרַיִם מֵת – *The Israelites saw the Egyptians dead:* For the sea had expelled the Egyptian corpses onto the shore. This was done lest the Israelites worry that just as they had emerged safely on the opposite side of the sea, perhaps their enemies had also surfaced further down the coast and would continue their pursuit.

RASHBAM

מֵת עַל־שְׂפַת הַיָּם – *Dead on the seashore:* From their vantage point on the beach, the Israelites were able to watch the sea returning to its normal condition and swallowing up the Egyptian army. This is the straightforward meaning of the text. [According to this understanding, the verse should properly be translated: "And when, on the seashore, the Israelites saw the Egyptians dying…"] I have similarly explained the verse *And they heard*

כז עַל־מִצְרַיִם עַל־רִכְבּוֹ וְעַל־פָּרָשָׁיו: וַיֵּט מֹשֶׁה אֶת־יָדוֹ עַל־
הַיָּם וַיָּשָׁב הַיָּם לִפְנוֹת בֹּקֶר לְאֵיתָנוֹ וּמִצְרַיִם נָסִים לִקְרָאתוֹ
כח וַיְנַעֵר יְהוָה אֶת־מִצְרַיִם בְּתוֹךְ הַיָּם: וַיָּשֻׁבוּ הַמַּיִם וַיְכַסּוּ
אֶת־הָרֶכֶב וְאֶת־הַפָּרָשִׁים לְכֹל חֵיל פַּרְעֹה הַבָּאִים אַחֲרֵיהֶם
כט בַּיָּם לֹא־נִשְׁאַר בָּהֶם עַד־אֶחָד: וּבְנֵי יִשְׂרָאֵל הָלְכוּ בַיַּבָּשָׁה
ל בְּתוֹךְ הַיָּם וְהַמַּיִם לָהֶם חֹמָה מִימִינָם וּמִשְּׂמֹאלָם: וַיּוֹשַׁע
יְהוָה בַּיּוֹם הַהוּא אֶת־יִשְׂרָאֵל מִיַּד מִצְרָיִם וַיַּרְא יִשְׂרָאֵל

IBN EZRA

וַיָּשֻׁבוּ הַמַּיִם – *The waters will flow back:* The walls of water will disintegrate as the solid sea reverts to a liquid state.

VERSE 27

RASHI

נָסִים לִקְרָאתוֹ – *Fled at its approach:* [Literally, "fled toward it."] Because the Egyptians were discombobulated and crazed, they actually ran toward the approaching deluge.

וַיְנַעֵר יְהוָה – *The Lord swept them:* The action resembled the stirring of a pot, when the upper contents of a mix are turned downward and the ingredients on the bottom are moved to the top. So were the Egyptians churned up and whipped down, causing them to break apart in the sea. Meanwhile God kept them alive long enough to endure this thrashing.

RASHBAM

וּמִצְרַיִם נָסִים לִקְרָאתוֹ – *The Egyptians fled at its approach:* [Literally, "fled toward it."] While they were attempting to maneuver their chariots to withdraw, before they were able to turn around completely, the crashing sea swept them away.

IBN EZRA

וּמִצְרַיִם נָסִים לִקְרָאתוֹ – *The Egyptians fled at its approach:* May the bones of the dog Ḥivi be pulverized! [Ibn Ezra refers to the heretical ninth-century Persian writer Ḥivi Al-Balkhi, whose interpretation he is about to contest. By transposing the letters *bet* and *kaf* in the name Balakh, our author creates the insult HaKalbi – "the dog-like".] For he claims that Moshe knew the schedule of the tides and purposely led Israel into the water at its regular time of low tide. But Pharaoh was ignorant of changing sea levels and entered the sea at high tide. Of course, this approach is sheer folly. The sea does not dry up even at low tide, nor does this natural phenomenon ever create a "wall of water" to the right and left (14:22). What's more, the shift from low to high water occurs gradually over many hours [not suddenly as the narrative suggests; the Egyptians would surely have managed to escape a slowly rising sea]. Finally, the entire Israelite nation had not yet finished crossing the sea when Pharaoh and his army started to drown [thus, according to Al-Balkhi, low tide and high tide must have been happening at the same time, which is of course impossible].

All Pharaoh's horses, chariots and cavalry followed them into
24 the sea. During the last watch of the night, the LORD looked
down at the Egyptian army from a column of fire and cloud
25 and threw them into a panic, clogging their chariot wheels so
that it was hard for them to move. The Egyptians said, "Let us
flee from the Israelites. The LORD is fighting for them against
Egypt."
26 Then the LORD said to Moshe, "Stretch out your hand over   REVI'I
the sea. The waters will flow back over the Egyptians and their

VERSE 25

RASHI

וַיָּסַר אֵת אֹפַן מַרְכְּבֹתָיו – *Clogging their chariot wheels:* The fire was so strong that it burned the wheels, causing the chariots to be dragged along. The soldiers sitting in the vehicles were shaken and their limbs became disjointed. וַיְנַהֲגֵהוּ בִּכְבֵדֻת – *It was hard for them to move:* The driving became heavy and difficult for them. Thus did God punish the Egyptians measure for measure, for an earlier verse states: *[Pharaoh] hardened his heart; his officials likewise* (9:34), and now, *It was hard for them to move.* נִלְחָם לָהֶם בְּמִצְרָיִם – *Fighting for them against Egypt:* That is, against the Egyptians. Another interpretation takes the phrase literally: As God was striking the Egyptian cavalry at the sea, He simultaneously punished those citizens who had remained at home.

RASHBAM

וַיָּסַר אֵת אֹפַן מַרְכְּבֹתָיו – *Clogging their chariot wheels:* When the Egyptians realized they were descending into chaos, they struggled to turn the chariots around to retreat from the impending deluge. But they were unable to properly direct their vehicles, since those who turned around ran into other soldiers who were still facing forward. Why did they try to go back? Because they said: *Let us flee from the Israelites. The LORD is fighting for them against Egypt.*

SFORNO

וַיָּסַר אֵת אֹפַן מַרְכְּבֹתָיו – *Clogging their chariot wheels:* God burned the wheels off their chariots with His pillar of fire. וַיְנַהֲגֵהוּ בִּכְבֵדֻת – *It was hard for them to move:* The chariots were stuck in the mud. נִלְחָם לָהֶם – *Fighting for them:* If we flee, He will stop fighting us.

VERSE 26

RASHI

וְיָשֻׁבוּ הַמַּיִם – *The waters will flow back:* The waters, which have been standing erect like a wall, will return to their rightful place and thereby *flow back over the Egyptians.*

RASHBAM

נְטֵה אֶת־יָדְךָ – *Stretch out your hand:* Once Israel has crossed to the far seashore.

כד פַּרְעֹה רִכְבּוֹ וּפָרָשָׁיו אֶל־תּוֹךְ הַיָּם: וַיְהִי בְּאַשְׁמֹרֶת הַבֹּקֶר וַיַּשְׁקֵף יהוה אֶל־מַחֲנֵה מִצְרַיִם בְּעַמּוּד אֵשׁ וְעָנָן וַיָּהָם אֵת כה מַחֲנֵה מִצְרָיִם: וַיָּסַר אֵת אֹפַן מַרְכְּבֹתָיו וַיְנַהֲגֵהוּ בִּכְבֵדֻת וַיֹּאמֶר מִצְרַיִם אָנוּסָה מִפְּנֵי יִשְׂרָאֵל כִּי יהוה נִלְחָם לָהֶם בְּמִצְרָיִם: כו וַיֹּאמֶר יהוה אֶל־מֹשֶׁה נְטֵה אֶת־יָדְךָ עַל־הַיָּם וְיָשֻׁבוּ הַמַּיִם רביעי

VERSE 24

RASHI

בְּאַשְׁמֹרֶת הַבֹּקֶר – *During the last watch of the night:* The night is divided into three sections called "watches." The last watch, which precedes daybreak, is called "the morning watch." Now I say that the night is divided into three shifts to accommodate the three choirs of ministering angels who sing one after the other, and this is why they are called "watches." Indeed, Onkelos translates the Hebrew word *ashmoret* in the same way: *matterat* [meaning "watch"]. **וַיַּשְׁקֵף** – *Looked down:* God gazed, He turned His attention to the Egyptians to destroy them. **וַיָּהָם** – *And threw them into a panic:* Confusion was sown among the Egyptians. This verb translates into Old French as *estordison* [meaning "dazed minds"]. God disoriented them, dulling their senses so that chaos ensued. We read in Pirkei DeRabbi Eliezer, authored by Rabbi Eliezer son of Rabbi Yosei the Galilean, that the term *mehuma* connotes a thunderous noise. The source for that interpretation is the verse: *But the Lord thundered with a great thunder on that day upon the Philistines and confused them [vayhummem]; and they were beaten before Israel* (I Samuel 7:10).

RABBI AVRAHAM BEN HARAMBAM

בְּעַמּוּד אֵשׁ וְעָנָן – *From a column of fire and cloud:* According to my grandfather, of blessed memory, God looked down at the Egyptian army from a whirlwind of fire and cloud. Indeed, at that same time, light was swirled together with darkness creating a terrifying atmosphere for the Egyptians. This analysis seems correct to me. Suddenly, when *the Lord looked down at the Egyptian army*, they realized they were standing between two solid walls of water. The shock of this sight, combined with the soldiers' exhaustion after days of travel and the appearance of the pillar of fire within a column of cloud, paralyzed the army with fear. Furthermore, the position of the celestial fiery cloud – hovering in the air above the soldiers' heads, and not spinning along the ground as it was perceived by the Israelites –contributed to their anxiety. This is the sense of the phrase: *The Lord looked down at the Egyptian army.*

SFORNO

וַיָּהָם – *And threw them into a panic:* God afflicted the Egyptians with many illnesses, similar to His punishment of the Philistines, as the verse states: *The hand of the Lord was against the city with a very great panic [mehuma]: and He smote the men of the city, both small and great, and they were inwardly struck with swellings* (I Samuel 5:9).

21 the two apart all night. Then Moshe stretched out his hand over the sea, and the Lord drove the sea back by a strong east wind
22 all night, turning it to dry land and dividing the waters. So the Israelites walked through the sea on dry land. To their right and
23 left, the water was like a wall. The Egyptians chased after them.

RAMBAN (cont.)

God to destroy them. For the soldiers believed that it was the wind that had driven back the sea and not the hand of God acting on Israel's behalf. And even though winds do not usually split bodies of water, the enemy ignored that detail. They were thus enticed to follow Israel into the breach to satisfy their lust for violence against them.

VERSE 22

IBN EZRA

וְהַמַּיִם לָהֶם חוֹמָה – *The water was like a wall:* This indicates that the water congealed into a solid, as the verse states: *The surge stood upright as a wall* (15:8). After most of the Israelites had crossed the sea, the water, which had frozen in place, began to melt. As the dissolving mass of water pooled on the ocean floor, it formed a barrier between the army and the Israelites, who stood on dry land. Hence the soldiers fled toward the advancing water [the literal meaning of verse 27], because they believed they could get through it and advance to the land they saw Israel standing on. But the walls of water continued to revert to their former state, thereby keeping the cavalry from reaching the opposite shore.

ḤIZKUNI

וַיָּבֹאוּ בְנֵי־יִשְׂרָאֵל בְּתוֹךְ הַיָּם – *So the Israelites walked through the sea:* Israel did not cross the entire width of the Sea of Reeds, because it is well known that the body of water does not sit between the land of Egypt and the land of Canaan. Rather, Israel only had to enter part way into the water to lure the army in after them; the latter would be drowned; and Israel would circle back and emerge on the same side of the sea. This is evident from how Israel entered the sea from the Etam desert and returned to the Etam desert after going through the water. [See a later description of Israel's journey in Numbers 33:6–8.]

בְּתוֹךְ הַיָּם – *Through the sea:* Even though the nation simply entered, turned around, and came out, the Torah describes this as walking *through the sea.*

VERSE 23

RASHI

כָּל סוּס פַּרְעֹה – *All Pharaoh's horses:* [The word "horses" – *sus* – is singular in the Hebrew.] Did Pharaoh have just one horse? Rather, the use of the singular conveys that from God's perspective, the entire cavalry may as well have been one animal.

BEKHOR SHOR

וַיָּבֹאוּ אַחֲרֵיהֶם – *They chased after them:* Because of the darkness of the night, the army followed Israel blindly. Then the Egyptians did not realize they had walked into a trap until they were already in the middle of the sea.

כא אֶת־הַלַּ֗יְלָה וְלֹא־קָרַ֥ב זֶ֛ה אֶל־זֶ֖ה כָּל־הַלָּֽיְלָה: וַיֵּ֨ט מֹשֶׁ֣ה
אֶת־יָדוֹ֮ עַל־הַיָּם֒ וַיּ֣וֹלֶךְ יְהוָ֣ה ׀ אֶת־הַ֠יָּ֠ם בְּר֨וּחַ קָדִ֤ים עַזָּה֙
כב כָּל־הַלַּ֔יְלָה וַיָּ֥שֶׂם אֶת־הַיָּ֖ם לֶחָרָבָ֑ה וַיִּבָּקְע֖וּ הַמָּֽיִם: וַיָּבֹ֧אוּ
בְנֵֽי־יִשְׂרָאֵ֛ל בְּת֥וֹךְ הַיָּ֖ם בַּיַּבָּשָׁ֑ה וְהַמַּ֤יִם לָהֶם֙ חוֹמָ֔ה מִֽימִינָ֖ם
כג וּמִשְּׂמֹאלָֽם: וַיִּרְדְּפ֤וּ מִצְרַ֙יִם֙ וַיָּבֹ֣אוּ אַחֲרֵיהֶ֔ם כֹּ֚ל ס֣וּס

RASHI (cont.)

from the Hebrew. Rashi explains that the darkness was intended solely] for the Egyptian army. **וַיָּאֶר** – *But lighting:* The pillar of fire lit up the sky for Israel, and it stood before them providing light as it did every night. Meanwhile, on the Egyptian side, there was the thick fog of darkness. **וְלֹא־קָרַב זֶה אֶל־זֶה** – *Keeping the two apart:* The pillar of cloud created a barrier between the two camps.

BEKHOR SHOR

וַיָּאֶר אֶת־הַלַּיְלָה – *Lighting the night:* Here the word *vaya'er* actually means that the cloud "darkened" the night, as in the verse, *the cloud casts darkness [oro]* (Job 37:11). This is the understanding of Menahem ben Saruq. But Onkelos understands the phrase to mean that the pillar of fire stood in front of the Israelite camp as it normally did, lighting the sky for the people's benefit. While the Hebrews enjoyed the light, the Egyptian camp suffered in the dark.

VERSE 21

RASHI

בְּרוּחַ קָדִים עַזָּה – *By a strong east wind:* The east wind is the strongest of all winds. These are the gales that God uses to punish the wicked, as the verses state: *I will scatter them as with an east wind before the enemy* (Jeremiah 18:17). **וַיִּבָּקְעוּ הַמָּיִם** – *Dividing the waters:* All the water in the world was split [not just the Sea of Reeds].

RASHBAM

בְּרוּחַ קָדִים עַזָּה – *By a strong east wind:* God performed this miracle using the normal laws of nature, sending a wind to dry up the water and to freeze the rivers.

IBN EZRA

כָּל־הַלַּיְלָה – *All night:* The wind continued blowing throughout the night, never pausing even while the people of Israel were crossing the sea.

RAMBAN

בְּרוּחַ קָדִים עַזָּה – *By a strong east wind:* It was God's plan to divide the sea by employing a strong, dry wind from the east, thereby giving the impression that the wind was actually drying up the ocean. This is how another verse describes the event: *An east wind shall come, the wind of the L*ORD *shall come up from the wilderness, and his spring shall become dry, and his fountain shall be dried up* (Hosea 13:15). This phenomenon misled the Egyptians, allowing

17 Israelites will walk through the sea on dry land. I will strengthen the Egyptians' hearts and they will go after them. Then will My glory bear down hard upon Pharaoh and his entire army,
18 his chariots and cavalry. And when My glory bears down upon Pharaoh, his chariots and cavalry, the Egyptians will know that
19 I am the LORD." Then the angel of God who had been traveling ahead of the Israelite camp moved and went behind them, and the column of cloud moved from in front of them to their rear.
20 It came between the Egyptian and Israelite camps, as cloud and darkness for one, but lighting the night for the other, keeping

---

RASHBAM (cont.)

Consequently, the cloud too ceased hovering before the people and moved to stand behind them. The angel repositioned the cloud so that it interposed between the Egyptian camp and the Israelite one, creating a curtain of darkness between the two foes, as reported in the Book of Joshua (24:7). This barrier had the effect of *keeping the two apart all night* (14:20).

IBN EZRA

וַיִּסַּע מַלְאַךְ הָאֱלֹהִים – *Then the angel of God moved:* This angel of God is the "Great Prince" [the angel Mikhael referred to in Daniel 12:1 as the *great chief angel who stands for the children of Your people*]. This is the figure about whom the verse states: *The LORD went ahead of them by day in a column of cloud to guide them* (13:21). When this guardian angel subsequently relocated to protect Israel from behind, the cloud accompanying him moved as well. As for those commentaries who claim that the cloud itself is the angel referred to in this verse, I challenge them to find any verse which refers to the cloud as an angel of God. For if indeed the angel and the cloud are identical, why would this verse first state that the angel of God *moved and went behind* the nation, and then that the cloud *moved from in front of them to their rear*? And should proponents of that approach respond that the text merely repeats the same idea in two ways, I would answer that it is only Scripture's prophecies and remonstrances which exhibit this tendency. When describing historical details, the text does not employ that literary technique.

VERSE 20

RASHI

וַיָּבֹא בֵּין מַחֲנֵה מִצְרַיִם – *It came between the Egyptian camp:* This may be compared to a man who is strolling along the road while his son skips ahead of him. Suddenly, bandits appear and attempt to snatch the lad, whereupon the father shoves his son behind him for protection. But then a wolf threatens the pair from behind, so the traveler again moves the boy in front of him. When the bandits approach from the front and the wolf from behind, the man has no choice but to hold the son in his arms and fight both dangers at once. This is the sense of the verse: *It was I was who guided Efrayim's first steps, carrying them in My arms*, (Hosea 11:3). וַיְהִי הֶעָנָן וְהַחֹשֶׁךְ – *As cloud and darkness for one:* [The phrase "for one" is absent

יז הַיָּם וּבְקָעֵהוּ וְיָבֹאוּ בְנֵי־יִשְׂרָאֵל בְּתוֹךְ הַיָּם בַּיַּבָּשָׁה: וַאֲנִי
הִנְנִי מְחַזֵּק אֶת־לֵב מִצְרַיִם וְיָבֹאוּ אַחֲרֵיהֶם וְאִכָּבְדָה
יח בְּפַרְעֹה וּבְכָל־חֵילוֹ בְּרִכְבּוֹ וּבְפָרָשָׁיו: וְיָדְעוּ מִצְרַיִם כִּי־
אֲנִי יְהוָה בְּהִכָּבְדִי בְּפַרְעֹה בְּרִכְבּוֹ וּבְפָרָשָׁיו: וַיִּסַּע מַלְאַךְ
יט הָאֱלֹהִים הַהֹלֵךְ לִפְנֵי מַחֲנֵה יִשְׂרָאֵל וַיֵּלֶךְ מֵאַחֲרֵיהֶם
כ וַיִּסַּע עַמּוּד הֶעָנָן מִפְּנֵיהֶם וַיַּעֲמֹד מֵאַחֲרֵיהֶם: וַיָּבֹא בֵּין ׀
מַחֲנֵה מִצְרַיִם וּבֵין מַחֲנֵה יִשְׂרָאֵל וַיְהִי הֶעָנָן וְהַחֹשֶׁךְ וַיָּאֶר

KELI YAKAR *(cont.)*

draw water from the rock, the verse states: *And Moshe lifted up his hand, and with his rod he smote the rock twice* (Numbers 20:11). There, Moshe set aside his hand and did not use it to effect the miracle, using the staff instead. This misstep brought Israel back to their original belief that the power of the miracle lay in the rod. Thus Moshe caused the people's faith in God to backslide, as the verse states: *Because you did not believe in Me, to sanctify Me in the eyes of the children of Israel, therefore you shall not bring the congregation in to the land which I have given them* (Numbers 20:12).

VERSE 18
SFORNO

וְיָדְעוּ מִצְרַיִם – *The Egyptians will know:* Those citizens left behind in Egypt will repent and revere Me, since after all, *I have no pleasure in the death of him that dies, says the* Lord *God; therefore repent, and live* (Ezekiel 18:32).

VERSE 19
RASHI

וַיֵּלֶךְ מֵאַחֲרֵיהֶם – *Moved and went behind them:* The column of cloud was positioned as a barrier between the Egyptian camp and the Israelite one. There it was able to absorb the arrows and catapulted rocks that the Egyptians hurled in Israel's direction. Now everywhere else in the Torah, emissaries of this type are referred to as "angels of the Lord," whereas in our verse the text uses the term "angel of God," this latter divine name [*Elohim*] signifies God acting in the role of judge. For at that moment, Israel themselves were being judged to determine whether they would be rescued or destroyed by the Egyptians. **וַיִּסַּע עַמּוּד הֶעָנָן** – *And the column of cloud moved:* The cloud only moved once it had become dark, and then it gave over Israel's protection to the pillar of fire. But the cloud did not dissipate completely like it usually did in the evenings; rather, it moved behind Israel in order to create darkness for the Egyptians.

RASHBAM

וַיִּסַּע מַלְאַךְ הָאֱלֹהִים – *Then the angel of God moved:* The angel of God who had been leading the column of cloud in front of Israel's camp now moved behind the nation.

14 Egyptians you see today, you shall never see again. The LORD will fight for you. You stay silent."
15 The LORD said to Moshe, "Why are you crying out to Me? SHELISHI
16 Speak to the Israelites; have them move forward. Raise your staff, stretch out your hand over the sea and divide it, and the

---------- RAMBAN (cont.) ----------

what measures you should take; there is really no need to cry. For I have already informed you that *I will be glorified over Pharaoh*. The text does not record Moshe's actual plea to God because it was included in the general complaint of the nation expressed in verse 10.

---------- SFORNO ----------

מַה־תִּצְעַק אֵלָי – *Why are you crying out to Me*: Moshe's distress was not caused by fear of the situation, but by his displeasure at Israel's leaders' temerity in stating: *Were there no graves in Egypt?* (14:11). Moshe subsequently feared that out of sheer audacity the people would refuse to enter the ocean. God responded to this concern by saying: *Why are you crying out to Me?* Your suspicions concerning the people are unfounded. Simply "speak to the Israelites"; they will comply and "move forward."

VERSE 16

---------- IBN EZRA ----------

וְאַתָּה הָרֵם אֶת־מַטְּךָ – *Raise your staff*: At this point, God instructed Moshe to raise his staff and divide the sea before Israel ventured forward. Note that Moshe is not told to strike the water, just that he should reach out his staff in the direction of the sea. This is similar to Moshe's gesture in the verse *Moshe raised his staff toward the sky: the LORD sent thunderclaps and hail* (9:23). We know that it was not the staff which caused the sea to open up; rather, from the moment Moshe stretched his hand toward the water, *the LORD drove the sea back by a strong east wind...dividing the waters* (14:21).

---------- RABBEINU BAḤYA ----------

וְאַתָּה הָרֵם אֶת־מַטְּךָ – *Raise your staff*: In this verse, Moshe is not being commanded to stretch his staff over the sea, for subsequently we find only that the prophet *stretched out his hand over the sea* (14:21). In fact, here God is instructing Moshe to lay down his staff and to not use it in effecting the miracle at the water. For there were some elements among the people who had little faith in their leader, claiming that he lacked the power to split open the sea without using his magic wand. Hence God told Moshe: "Raise your staff," meaning that he was to put it aside.

---------- KELI YAKAR ----------

וְאַתָּה הָרֵם אֶת־מַטְּךָ – *Raise your staff*: The current episode helps explain just what Moshe's sin was at the waters of Meriva [see Numbers 20:7–13]. Moshe's behavior in that instance is described as exactly the opposite of what we see here. In our text the leader is told: *Raise your staff* – meaning "put aside your staff" – and *stretch out your hand over the sea*. The effect of this was to instill faith in the people. But when Moshe was called upon to

יד תֹּסִפוּ לִרְאֹתָם עוֹד עַד־עוֹלָם: יהוה יִלָּחֵם לָכֶם וְאַתֶּם תַּחֲרִשׁוּן:
טו וַיֹּאמֶר יהוה אֶל־מֹשֶׁה מַה־תִּצְעַק אֵלָי דַּבֵּר אֶל־בְּנֵי־ יא שלישי
טז יִשְׂרָאֵל וְיִסָּעוּ: וְאַתָּה הָרֵם אֶת־מַטְּךָ וּנְטֵה אֶת־יָדְךָ עַל־

VERSE 14

RALBAG

וְאַתֶּם תַּחֲרִשׁוּן – *You stay silent:* It is possible that Moshe directed the people to be quiet – not to cry out nor talk amongst themselves – in order to mislead the Egyptians. For if the army heard the nation, they would be able to gauge their distance from them and would begin firing arrows or other missiles in their direction. This was why God situated His pillar of cloud between Israel and the Egyptians [in verse 19]: to prevent the soldiers from seeing their quarry and harming them.

VERSE 15

RASHI

מַה־תִּצְעַק אֵלָי – *Why are you crying out to Me:* We learn from God's statement that Moshe had been standing before Him and praying. Said the Holy One, blessed be He: "Now is not the time for extended prayer; at this moment Israel is in peril!" Another interpretation for this phrase: God said: "Why are you crying out?" It falls "to Me" to act now, not to you. We find a similar sentiment expressed in the verse *Concerning my sons, and concerning the work of My hands you command Me?* [Isaiah 45:11; i.e., God asks: Do you need to remind Me to take care of My own children?]

דַּבֵּר אֶל־בְּנֵי־יִשְׂרָאֵל וְיִסָּעוּ – *Speak to the Israelites; have them move forward:* All they have to do is to move forward, for the sea will not stand in their way. The merits of their forefathers, together with the faith they put in Me when they left Egypt, will be sufficient to split the sea for them.

IBN EZRA

מַה־תִּצְעַק אֵלָי – *Why are you crying out to Me:* According to some opinions, Moshe was crying out to God. But I must dismiss this interpretation, because God had already informed His agent: *I will be glorified over Pharaoh* [14:4]; that is, Moshe knew that the Egyptians were about to be destroyed and would not have panicked]. Rather, these words were spoken to Moshe as Israel's representative, for the people had screamed to God for help. **וְיִסָּעוּ** – *Have them move forward:* The people should inch forward until they reach the seashore.

RAMBAN

מַה־תִּצְעַק אֵלָי – *Why are you crying out to Me:* Our Sages have explained correctly that Moshe stood on the beach in prayer and petition, for he was at a loss as to how to proceed. And even though God had told him *I will be glorified over Pharaoh* (14:4), he still had no idea what he was meant to do at that moment with the sea raging in front of him and the enemy rampaging behind. He therefore begged God to show him the correct course of action. Hence God reproached Moshe saying: *Why are you crying out to Me?* Moshe, you could just ask

Egyptians thundering after them. They were terrified and cried
11 to the Lord for help. "Were there no graves in Egypt?" they asked Moshe; "Is that why you brought us here to die in the desert? What have you done to us, bringing us out of Egypt?
12 Did we not tell you in Egypt: Leave us alone – let us serve the Egyptians. Better a life in servitude to Egypt than death in
13 the desert." But Moshe told the people, "Fear not. Stand firm and see the deliverance the Lord will bring you today. The

---
IBN EZRA

הֲלֹא־זֶה הַדָּבָר – *Did we not:* Nowhere in the previous chapters do we find Israel making such an objection. And yet, such a conversation must have transpired, since Israel would not have blatantly lied to Moshe's face. The complaint cited here must have been part of the people's response in the verse *In the brokenness of their spirit and the brutal labor they did not listen to him* (6:9).

VERSE 13
IBN EZRA

הִתְיַצְּבוּ – *Stand firm:* It is quite surprising that a community boasting 600,000 able men were so terrified of the army pursuing them. Why did they not merely form ranks and fight for their lives and those of their children? The explanation is clear: The Egyptians were the Israelites' erstwhile masters, and the Hebrews who left Egypt had been trained to suffer under their taskmasters' whips and to cringe at their presence. For Israel to now turn on their former oppressors was mentally too difficult for them. Furthermore, the Israelites were lazy and untrained in the art of battle.... God subsequently arranged matters such that all those weak men who left Egypt died in the wilderness, for they lacked the fortitude to combat the Canaanite peoples. It was only the second generation, which possessed the confidence to fight for their land, and which had not known the bitterness of the slavery, that was able to challenge the Canaanites.

RAMBAN

לֹא תֹסִפוּ לִרְאֹתָם עוֹד עַד־עוֹלָם – *You shall never see again:* According to our Sages, this verse represents a negative commandment binding upon all future generations. Based on that understanding, this verse comprises two parts. Firstly, Moshe assures his people: *Fear not. Stand firm and see the deliverance the Lord will bring you today,* never will you return to serve them. And as for *the Egyptians you see today,* God commands you to never willingly see them again. Thus, in the second half of the verse, Moshe instructs Israel never to visit Egypt, even though the text does not report God Himself ever expressing such a law. Our text is similar to the verse *But he shall not multiply horses to himself, nor cause the people to return to Egypt, so that he should multiply horses: since the Lord has said to you, You shall never return that way again* [Deuteronomy 17:16; concerning the future king of Israel], which is also a commandment, not just a promise.

עֵינֵיהֶם וְהִנֵּה מִצְרַיִם ׀ נֹסֵעַ אַחֲרֵיהֶם וַיִּירְאוּ מְאֹד וַיִּצְעֲקוּ
בְנֵי־יִשְׂרָאֵל אֶל־יהוה: וַיֹּאמְרוּ אֶל־מֹשֶׁה הֲמִבְּלִי אֵין־ יא
קְבָרִים בְּמִצְרַיִם לְקַחְתָּנוּ לָמוּת בַּמִּדְבָּר מַה־זֹּאת עָשִׂיתָ
לָּנוּ לְהוֹצִיאָנוּ מִמִּצְרָיִם: הֲלֹא־זֶה הַדָּבָר אֲשֶׁר דִּבַּרְנוּ אֵלֶיךָ יב
בְמִצְרַיִם לֵאמֹר חֲדַל מִמֶּנּוּ וְנַעַבְדָה אֶת־מִצְרָיִם כִּי טוֹב
לָנוּ עֲבֹד אֶת־מִצְרַיִם מִמֻּתֵנוּ בַּמִּדְבָּר: וַיֹּאמֶר מֹשֶׁה אֶל־ יג
הָעָם אַל־תִּירָאוּ הִתְיַצְּבוּ וּרְאוּ אֶת־יְשׁוּעַת יהוה אֲשֶׁר־
יַעֲשֶׂה לָכֶם הַיּוֹם כִּי אֲשֶׁר רְאִיתֶם אֶת־מִצְרַיִם הַיּוֹם לֹא

VERSE 11

RASHBAM

לָמוּת בַּמִּדְבָּר – *To die in the desert:* This wilderness holds no bread and offers no water. Even in the absence of murderous pursuers, we would surely perish from hunger.

RABBI AVRAHAM BEN HARAMBAM

וַיֹּאמְרוּ אֶל־מֹשֶׁה – *They asked Moshe:* This complaint was lodged by only some of the people, not the entire nation. The current episode is an excellent illustration of the dictum "A man should not be held responsible for what he says when under duress." According to our Sages, the individuals offering this sarcastic remark were Datan and Aviram [see Numbers 16:1]. This is an example of the rabbinic practice of attributing all possible sins to those wicked men. [The value in identifying anonymous sinners with known criminals is that it limits the number of evildoers in Israel.]

ABARBANEL

הֲמִבְּלִי אֵין־קְבָרִים – *Were there no graves in Egypt:* In most large and populous countries, the state ensures that there are sufficient graves to serve its citizens. This is because the people insist on keeping their environment clean. However, in a wilderness devoid of people, dead bodies are tossed aside like refuse and left unburied. This then is Israel's complaint to Moshe: You seem to have rejected the natural fate our bodies would have received had you let us remain in Egypt. Upon our eventual deaths there, or even our murders, the Egyptians would have afforded us proper burials, because like every society they would not want their land littered with human carcasses. But instead of allowing us that privilege, you have removed us to the wilderness where we can never be buried. Why do you wish death upon us? What reason could you have to deprive our bones of the decent grave they might have had?

VERSE 12

RASHI

אֲשֶׁר דִּבַּרְנוּ אֵלֶיךָ בְּמִצְרַיִם – *Tell you in Egypt:* The people refer here to their earlier complaint, *May the Lord look on you and judge* (5:21).

8 The Lord strengthened the heart of Pharaoh King of Egypt, and he pursued the Israelites, who were leaving in defiance of
9 them. The Egyptians, with all the king's horses and chariots, SHENI cavalry and infantry, chased and caught up with them as they were encamped by the sea near Pi HaHirot, before Baal Tzefon.
10 Pharaoh drew near – the Israelites looked up: there were the

---

IBN EZRA

וּפַרְעֹה הִקְרִיב – *Pharaoh drew near:* [The verb *hikriv* is in the causative *hifil* form, indicating that] Pharaoh caused his camp to draw near to Israel. [That is, Ibn Ezra understands the word as a transitive verb, with the army as the implied object.]

BEKHOR SHOR

וַיִּירְאוּ מְאֹד – *They were terrified:* Israel had long been conditioned to fear the Egyptians, for the latter had enslaved and tormented them for years.

RAMBAN

וַיִּצְעֲקוּ בְנֵי־יִשְׂרָאֵל אֶל־יהוה – *And called to the Lord for help:* It seems incongruous that people who are calling out to God for salvation should simultaneously complain about their previous redemption [in the following verse], arguing that they would have been better off had God never rescued them from Egypt. The truth of the matter is that standing on the seashore, Israel was divided into different factions, and our text reports the attitudes of each group. The first approach to the crisis was that of the faithful, who cried out to God for assistance. Next to those people were others who denied the agency of God's prophet and refused to acknowledge the deliverance they had been granted. Those were the individuals who complained: *Better a life in servitude to Egypt than death in the desert* (14:12). This explains the later verse which reads: *The people were in awe of the Lord, and they believed in Him and in Moshe His servant* (14:31), intentionally using the term "people" [*am*] instead of the name "Israel." For the latter is used to identify individuals of standing, whereas the word "*am*" refers to the masses. The Sages teach that whenever a verse uses the term *am* it is meant disparagingly; whereas the name "Israel" is a mark of approval. Still, there is an alternative way to understand this passage. It is possible that the nation as a whole did trust in God and prayed to Him to rescue them from the Egyptians, but they suspected Moshe of having taken them out of Egypt in order to rule over them. And even though Israel had seen the signs and wonders that Moshe had performed, they thought that he might have done so by some trickery, or that God had only punished the Egyptians because of their wickedness [and not out of any love of Israel]. After all, they thought, were God truly intent on redeeming them, why would Pharaoh still be giving chase?

ABARBANEL

וַיִּירְאוּ מְאֹד – *They were terrified:* Why was Israel so terrified at the sight of the approaching Egyptians? They knew that many of the soldiers charging them with spears raised had vengeance on their minds after suffering the loss of their firstborn sons. The Israelites also understood that the advancing foe was incensed over the theft Israel had perpetrated before their departure [in 12:35–36].

רֶכֶב מִצְרַיִם וְשָׁלִשִׁם עַל־כֻּלּוֹ: וַיְחַזֵּק יהוה אֶת־לֵב פַּרְעֹה ח
מֶלֶךְ מִצְרַיִם וַיִּרְדֹּף אַחֲרֵי בְּנֵי יִשְׂרָאֵל וּבְנֵי יִשְׂרָאֵל יֹצְאִים
בְּיָד רָמָה: וַיִּרְדְּפוּ מִצְרַיִם אַחֲרֵיהֶם וַיַּשִּׂיגוּ אוֹתָם חֹנִים ט שני
עַל־הַיָּם כָּל־סוּס רֶכֶב פַּרְעֹה וּפָרָשָׁיו וְחֵילוֹ עַל־פִּי הַחִירֹת
לִפְנֵי בַּעַל צְפֹן: וּפַרְעֹה הִקְרִיב וַיִּשְׂאוּ בְנֵי־יִשְׂרָאֵל אֶת־ י

VERSE 8

RASHI

וַיְחַזֵּק יהוה אֶת־לֵב פַּרְעֹה – *The Lord strengthened the heart of Pharaoh:* Pharaoh could not decide whether to pursue Israel or not, and God strengthened his resolve so that he would. בְּיָד רָמָה – *In defiance of them:* Israel left with the upper hand over Egypt; their victory was universally understood.

RASHBAM

יֹצְאִים בְּיָד רָמָה – *Were leaving in defiance of them:* At first, the Israelites marched out of Egypt with no worries on their minds. But then, when they saw Pharaoh and his people chasing after them [as reported in the upcoming verses], they were terrified.

VERSE 9

IBN EZRA

כָּל־סוּס רֶכֶב פַּרְעֹה – *All the king's horses:* [The word "horses" – *sus* – is singular in the Hebrew.] Rather than charging Israel in a haphazard way, the cavalry arrived in formation, moving like a single animal.

VERSE 10

RASHI

וּפַרְעֹה הִקְרִיב – *Pharaoh drew near:* The more natural form of the verb here would have been *karav* [the simple, or *kal*, form], rather than *hikriv* [the *hifil* or causative construction, which suggests that Pharaoh drew others near]. What the term *hikriv* connotes is that the king pushed himself forward in an effort to lead his troops, just as he had promised he would. נֹסֵעַ אַחֲרֵיהֶם – *Thundering after them:* The singular form of the verb *nosea* requires explication [since the hundreds of chariots and soldiers bearing down on Israel would seem to merit the plural *nose'im*]. The language suggests that the entire army was united in purpose and strategy to attack Israel. Another interpretation: This clause, which literally means "There was Egypt riding after them," signifies that the people saw Egypt's guardian angel streaking down from the heavens to assist his wards. וַיִּצְעֲקוּ – *And cried:* Israel adopted the practice of their ancestors, who had all prayed to God. For the Torah reports that *Avraham went early in the morning to the place where he had stood before the Lord* (Genesis 19:27); that *Yitzhak went out to meditate in the field at the evening time* (Genesis 24:63); and that Yaakov *lighted on a certain place* [Genesis 28:11, also traditionally understood as a reference to prayer].

their minds about the people: "What have we done, releasing
6 the Israelites from serving us?" So the king harnessed his chari-
7 ot and brought out his army. He took six hundred elite chariots and all the other chariots of Egypt, with officers over them all.

RASHI (cont.)

army to follow him by reminding them: "We were smitten by plagues, then they took our property, and then — we sent them away! If you come with me, I will not treat you the way that other kings behave. For other monarchs march behind their soldiers, but I will lead the way personally." Thus the verse states: *Pharaoh drew near* (14:10), meaning that the king put himself first and hurried ahead of his army. "Furthermore, while it is customary for other kings to claim first rights to the enemy's plunder, I will divide the bounty equally with you." Thus the verse states: *I will divide the spoils* (15:9).

IBN EZRA

וַיֶּאְסֹר אֶת־רִכְבּוֹ — *So the king harnessed his chariot:* He commanded his servants to do so. The sense here is similar to the verse *So Shlomo built the house, and finished it* [I Kings 6:14; i.e., Pharaoh no more harnessed his own chariot than King Shlomo built the Temple with his own hands.]

RALBAG

וְאֶת־עַמּוֹ לָקַח עִמּוֹ — *And brought out his army:* Pharaoh likely had to persuade or incite the populace to chase after Israel. For the Egyptians had already witnessed the wonders that God had performed on the nation's behalf, and they would have been unwilling and afraid to provoke Him again. Or perhaps Pharaoh used force to compel his army to set out after the slaves.

VERSE 7

RASHI

רֶכֶב בָּחוּר — *Elite chariots:* [The term *baḥur* means] "chosen." It is a singular form, indicating that every single chariot was specially chosen. וְכֹל רֶכֶב מִצְרָיִם — *And all the other chariots of Egypt:* The rest of the chariots in Egypt joined the 600 elite cavalry in the battle. Now one might ask where the army found horses to saddle for this mission. They could not have been the Egyptians' animals, since the text reports that *all the livestock of the Egyptians perished* [9:6, referring to the effects of the cattle plague]. And they could not have harnessed beasts belonging to the Israelites, since Moshe had insisted that *our livestock must go with us* (10:26). So whose animals were they? The horses belonged to *those of Pharaoh's officials who feared the* LORD's *word [and who] hurried to bring in their slaves and livestock* [9:20, thus saving them from the plagues]. This is why Rabbi Shimon used to say: Kill even the best of the gentiles; bash in the brains of even the most docile snakes. [For here even the God-fearing Egyptians were eventually enlisted to persecute Israel.]

עָשִׂינוּ כִּי־שִׁלַּחְנוּ אֶת־יִשְׂרָאֵל מֵעָבְדֵנוּ: וַיֶּאְסֹר אֶת־רִכְבּוֹ
וְאֶת־עַמּוֹ לָקַח עִמּוֹ: וַיִּקַּח שֵׁשׁ־מֵאוֹת רֶכֶב בָּחוּר וְכֹל

RAMBAN

וַיֻּגַּד לְמֶלֶךְ מִצְרַיִם — *When the king of Egypt was told:* After Israel turned and camped in front of Pi HaHirot, before Baal Tzefon, *the king of Egypt was told that the Israelites had escaped*. Pharaoh believed that the Israelites were *lost across the land* (14:3) for they were clearly not headed toward a campground suitable for sacrifice and worship. This is what the verse means when it states: *The Israelites, who were leaving in defiance of them* (14:8) — they waved flags and banners in triumph, and generally conducted themselves like the freed people they were, dancing joyously with songs and musical instruments. They were in no way behaving like slaves destined to return to the grind of their former labors. All this was reported back to Pharaoh.

SFORNO

מַה־זֹּאת עָשִׂינוּ — *What have we done:* We have not sought the assistance of our god Baal Tzefon. Surely he would have helped us to keep our slaves chained in Egypt.

KELI YAKAR

כִּי בָרַח הָעָם — *That the Israelites had escaped:* [Literally, "that the nation had escaped."] Whenever the text uses the term *am*, it refers [not to the Israelites generally, but] to the "great variety of other people" (12:38) — gentiles who latched onto Israel during the exodus after recognizing the Hebrews' exalted status. Now Pharaoh hoped that this population could serve as his allies for the following reason: Once the outsiders saw that the Israelites were lost in the wilderness, they would suspect that God had abandoned His charges. As such, these non-Israelites would decide to abandon their hosts and return home to Egypt. They would be eager to do so, inhibited only by their Israelite companions who were detaining them. But when the mixed multitude of gentiles saw the Egyptian cavalry riding to their rescue, they would certainly rebel against Israel and head back toward Egypt. This is why Pharaoh pursued Israel with a relatively small army — he expected to be assisted by his countrymen. This then is how we should understand the verse *When the king of Egypt was told that the [nation] had escaped:* The text does not suggest that Pharaoh sent soldiers to shadow Israel's movements [as Rashi explains] — there is no evidence of such a presence in the verses. Instead, the term *am* refers to Egyptians who had grabbed at the chance to run away with Israel. Initially the king despised these people for wanting to leave their homeland. But then *he and his officials changed their minds about the people* — that is, Pharaoh and his ministers realized that they could use these opportunists to their advantage.

VERSE 6

RASHI

וַיֶּאְסֹר אֶת־רִכְבּוֹ — *So the king harnessed his chariot:* In his eagerness, Pharaoh prepared his chariot himself. **וְאֶת־עַמּוֹ לָקַח עִמּוֹ** — *And brought out his army:* Pharaoh persuaded his

3 the sea. Pharaoh will think that the Israelites are lost across the
4 land, that they are trapped in the desert. I will toughen Pharaoh's heart, and he will pursue them. I will be glorified over Pharaoh and all his force, and the Egyptians will know that I
5 am the Lord." And so they did. When the king of Egypt was told that the Israelites had escaped, he and his officials changed

---

RAMBAN (cont.)

Israel, even if he learned that they meant to escape completely. At that point he was prepared to let Moshe do what he wanted with his people. Hence it was necessary to explain that God would enable the king to pursue them by strengthening his resolve. God therefore restates His plan to *strengthen the Egyptians' hearts and they will go after them* (14:17). Once they reached the sea, the Egyptians would certainly require some external inducement to chase after the Israelites. For once the army saw that God had split open the water for His people and led them across on dry land, would they have any courage of their own to continue hunting this charmed nation? They had just witnessed the most amazing sight ever seen by human eyes! To think that they would still be able to defeat Israel would have been madness. Hence God turned their wisdom into folly and emboldened them to enter the sea.

RALBAG

וְיָדְעוּ מִצְרַיִם כִּי־אֲנִי יהוה — *The Egyptians will know that I am the Lord:* Israel will not have to fear further pursuit by the Egyptians, because once I am through with them they will have been persuaded that I am the Lord. The oppressors will realize the futility of attempting to recapture or kill the Israelites. Thus the goal in cowing Egypt was not to convert them to the Hebrew faith [as the clause *the Egyptians will known that I am the Lord* might suggest], but to assure Israel that their foes were no longer a threat. The Egyptians would understand that God had been fighting for His nation and that they stood no chance in the face of His extraordinary power.

VERSE 5

RASHI

וַיֻּגַּד לְמֶלֶךְ מִצְרַיִם — *When the king of Egypt was told:* Pharaoh had sent army captains to accompany Israel and ensure that the people returned to Egypt after three days. On the fourth day, when the spies saw no indication that Israel meant to honor their promise, they reported the situation to Pharaoh. The fifth and sixth days were spent in pursuit of the former slaves. On the evening of the seventh day, Israel descended into the sea, and by morning they were singing God's praises for their salvation. That day was the seventh day of the Passover festival, which is why we read the Song at the Sea [Exodus 15, in the synagogue service] on that day of the holiday. וַיֵּהָפֵךְ — *Changed:* Now Pharaoh regretted his command to Moshe, *Get up, get out from among my people* (12:31). And his officials too changed their minds, for they had previously argued: *How long must we leave this man to ensnare us?* (10:7). But now they yearned to chase after Israel to retrieve the valuables they had lent them.

נְכֹחוֹ תַחֲנוּ עַל־הַיָּם: וְאָמַר פַּרְעֹה לִבְנֵי יִשְׂרָאֵל נְבֻכִים
הֵם בָּאָרֶץ סָגַר עֲלֵיהֶם הַמִּדְבָּר: וְחִזַּקְתִּי אֶת־לֵב־פַּרְעֹה
וְרָדַף אַחֲרֵיהֶם וְאִכָּבְדָה בְּפַרְעֹה וּבְכָל־חֵילוֹ וְיָדְעוּ מִצְרַיִם
כִּי־אֲנִי יְהוָה וַיַּעֲשׂוּ־כֵן: וַיֻּגַּד לְמֶלֶךְ מִצְרַיִם כִּי בָרַח הָעָם
וַיֵּהָפֵךְ לְבַב פַּרְעֹה וַעֲבָדָיו אֶל־הָעָם וַיֹּאמְרוּ מַה־זֹּאת

VERSE 3

RASHI

נְבֻכִים הֵם – *They are lost:* [According to Rashi, the phrase *nevukhim hem* means] "They are trapped and stuck." Pharaoh will suppose that Israel is imprisoned in the wilderness, unable to navigate its way out or to determine the path forward.

SFORNO

סָגַר עֲלֵיהֶם הַמִּדְבָּר – *They are trapped in the desert:* Pharaoh will believe that Baal Tzefon has closed the wilderness upon Israel.

VERSE 4

RASHI

וְאִכָּבְדָה בְּפַרְעֹה – *I will be glorified over Pharaoh:* When God exacts vengeance from the wicked, His name is exalted and honored. So states the verse *And I will contend with him.... Thus will I magnify Myself and sanctify Myself, and I will make Myself known in the eyes of many nations* (Ezekiel 38:22–23). And another verse states: *There He broke the flashing arrows.... In Yehuda is God known* (Psalms 76:4, 2), and *The Lord is known by the judgment which He executes* (Psalms 9:17).

בְּפַרְעֹה וּבְכָל־חֵילוֹ – *Over Pharaoh and all his force:* Pharaoh will be drowned first, followed by his cavalry, because he initiated the oppression against Israel. **וַיַּעֲשׂוּ־כֵן** – *And so they did:* These words credit the Israelites for obeying Moshe and not protesting: "What sense does it make to approach our pursuers, when we should be fleeing from them?" Rather, they freely declared: "The will of the son of Amram is our command."

IBN EZRA

וְחִזַּקְתִּי אֶת־לֵב־פַּרְעֹה – *I will toughen Pharaoh's heart:* I will make him act as if he has completely forgotten the devastation of the plagues that I visited upon him. **וְאִכָּבְדָה בְּפַרְעֹה** – *I will be glorified over Pharaoh:* When I drown Pharaoh and his army, My glory [*kevodi*] shall be known throughout the world. **וְיָדְעוּ מִצְרַיִם** – *The Egyptians will know:* The survivors will recognize that God is the Lord, as will the victims just before they drown.

RAMBAN

וְחִזַּקְתִּי אֶת־לֵב־פַּרְעֹה וְרָדַף אַחֲרֵיהֶם – *I will toughen Pharaoh's heart, and he will pursue them:* Because Pharaoh was mortally afraid of the plague of the firstborn – going so far as to plead with Moshe: *But bless me too* (12:32) – he lacked the courage to pursue

22 to give them light, so that they might travel day and night. Neither the column of cloud by day nor that of fire by night once departed from the people.

14:1 Then the LORD said to Moshe, "Speak to the Israelites and tell them to turn back and camp in front of Pi HaHirot, between Migdol and the sea, before Baal Tzefon. Encamp facing it, by

---

RASHI (cont.)

as the verse states: *Pharaoh will think that the Israelites are lost across the land* (14:3). וְיָחֲנוּ לִפְנֵי פִּי הַחִירֹת – *And camp in front of Pi HaHirot:* This location is synonymous with Pitom [mentioned in 1:11 as a city Israel was required to construct]. In our verse it is referred to as "Pi HaHirot" because the people had been set free [*horin*]. Two large rock outcrops stand at this spot, and the valley between them is called *Pi HaSela'im* [meaning "Mouth of the Rocks"]. לִפְנֵי בַּעַל צְפֹן – *Before Baal Tzefon:* Of all the Egyptian gods, this deity alone was not destroyed, in order to deceive its devotees into believing it remained powerful [and could still challenge God]. Hence the verse states: *He makes nations haughty and destroys them* (Job 12:23).

BEKHOR SHOR

וַיָּשֻׁבוּ וְיַחֲנוּ – *Turn back and camp:* Said God to Moshe: I do not want you to seem like liars, for you told Pharaoh that you would embark on a three-day journey and return. Furthermore, you borrowed items from the Egyptians on condition that you would give them back. Therefore, turn back in order to stay true to your word.

RABBI AVRAHAM BEN HARAMBAM

דַּבֵּר אֶל־בְּנֵי יִשְׂרָאֵל וְיָשֻׁבוּ – *Speak to the Israelites and tell them to turn back:* These instructions seem unnecessary, since the people were already walking and encamping exactly where the column of cloud directed them. Rather, the point of this communication [including the rationale in the following verses that the maneuver was meant to bait the Egyptians] was to explain to the people that they were going the right way, despite being led off the main road. Our Sages argue that Moshe was the only one to receive this message from God, and he did not share God's reasoning with the people [who remained unaware that Pharaoh would give chase]. Nevertheless, my initial interpretation seems correct to me.

KELI YAKAR

לִפְנֵי בַּעַל צְפֹן – *Before Baal Tzefon:* Baal Tzefon was an Egyptian god whom the people believed provided them with gold and jewels, as it was thought that *gold comes out of the north [tzafon]* (Job 37:22). Meanwhile, God had intentionally destroyed all the false gods save Baal Tzefon in order to trick the Egyptians. For when they realized that their deity was still standing, they reasoned that that god would correct the injustice done to them by the Israelites, who had robbed them [in 12:35–36], and force the former slaves to return their valuables.

יוֹמָם וָלָיְלָה: לֹא־יָמִישׁ עַמּוּד הֶעָנָן יוֹמָם וְעַמּוּד הָאֵשׁ לָיְלָה לִפְנֵי הָעָם:

יד א וַיְדַבֵּר יהוה אֶל־מֹשֶׁה לֵּאמֹר: דַּבֵּר אֶל־בְּנֵי יִשְׂרָאֵל וְיָשֻׁבוּ וְיַחֲנוּ לִפְנֵי פִּי הַחִירֹת בֵּין מִגְדֹּל וּבֵין הַיָּם לִפְנֵי בַּעַל צְפֹן

IBN EZRA

הָלַךְ לִפְנֵיהֶם — *Went ahead of them:* [This verse seems strange in light of God's transcendent nature, as expressed in the verses:] *The lofty One that inhabits eternity — His name is holy* (Isaiah 57:15) and *He is enthroned from ancient times* (Psalms 55:20). Know that Scripture expresses itself in language that people will readily understand. Hence, because God's power accompanied Israel, this verse is written as if God Himself traveled alongside them. We find a similarly anthropomorphic verse that states: *That caused His glorious arm to go at the right hand of Moshe* (Isaiah 63:12).

RAMBAN

וַיהוה — *The Lord:* [Literally, "and the Lord."] Our Sages expounded the principle that when the Torah uses the phrase "and the Lord," it includes both God and His celestial retinue. Thus God guided Israel during the day, whereas His angels guarded them at night. What this means is that God dwelled in the midst of the cloud that hovered above Israel and traveled before them by day, while the divine court dwelled within the pillar of fire at night, lighting the sky for the nation.

RABBEINU BAḤYA

לָלֶכֶת יוֹמָם וָלָיְלָה — *So that they might travel day and night:* The Israelites were so eager to receive the Torah on the fiftieth day [following the exodus] that they drove themselves ceaselessly, traveling both during the day and the night. This was abnormal behavior for wayfarers, who are generally exhausted from their daytime progress and must rest at night.

VERSE 22

RASHI

לֹא־יָמִישׁ — *Neither departed:* God did not for a moment remove *the column of cloud by day nor that of fire by night.* This means that the two miraculous entities overlapped in their duties: the column of cloud appeared while the pillar of fire still hung in the sky, and at the end of its watch the fire waited for the cloud to rise before receding.

CHAPTER 14, VERSE 2

RASHI

וְיָשֻׁבוּ — *Turn back:* On the third day, God instructed Israel to turn around and head back toward Egypt in order to deceive Pharaoh. When the king learns about Israel's meandering on the desert paths, he would say that the nation was disoriented and confused,

19 The Israelites left Egypt armed for battle. And Moshe took with him the remains of Yosef, who had bound the Israelites by oath: "When God comes to your aid, bring my remains with you out 20 of here." They set out from Sukkot and camped at Etam, at the 21 edge of the desert. The Lord went ahead of them by day in a column of cloud to guide them, and at night in a column of fire

VERSE 19

RASHI

הַשְׁבֵּעַ הִשְׁבִּיעַ – *Who had bound by oath:* The doubled Hebrew verb connotes that Yosef had made the Israelites swear that they would in turn make their children swear to take his bones along when they departed Egypt. One might ask why Yosef did not ask his sons to bring his body to Canaan for burial immediately upon his death, as Yaakov had. Yosef understood that because he ruled Egypt, he had the privilege of burying his father wherever he wanted. However, he suspected that the Egyptians would not grant his own sons that same license. He therefore made the family swear to take his remains with them upon their eventual redemption.

וְהַעֲלִיתֶם אֶת־עַצְמֹתַי מִזֶּה אִתְּכֶם – *Bring my remains with you out of here:* Yosef made his brothers promise that they would demand that their own children take their bones to Canaan when they quit Egypt. The term "with you" [*ittekhem*] suggests that Yosef wanted his body to exit Egypt along with the bodies of his brothers.

SFORNO

כִּי הַשְׁבֵּעַ הִשְׁבִּיעַ אֶת־בְּנֵי יִשְׂרָאֵל – *Who had bound the Israelites by oath:* As leader of that generation, is was Moshe's responsibility to fulfill the communal oath.

VERSE 20

RASHI

וַיִּסְעוּ מִסֻּכֹּת – *They set out from Sukkot:* Israel left Sukkot on the day after the exodus from Egypt, for on the first day they had traveled to Sukkot from Ramesses [see 12:37].

VERSE 21

RASHI

לַנְחֹתָם הַדֶּרֶךְ – *To guide them:* Here the sense is that God was directing Israel by means of an emissary. This was the column of cloud that guided Israel through the desert, while God himself in turn directed the cloud before the nation. In any event, it was God who prepared the column of cloud to lead Israel, to show them the way to go. This phenomenon was not meant to provide light for the people, just to guide them.

RASHBAM

וַיהוה הֹלֵךְ לִפְנֵיהֶם – *The Lord went ahead of them:* This refers to God's emissaries who showed Israel the path: the pillar of fire and the column of cloud. יוֹמָם וָלַיְלָה – *Day and night:* When Pharaoh hears that Israel is traveling through the night, he will understand that the nation is escaping and set out in pursuit.

יט מִצְרָיִם: וַיִּקַּח מֹשֶׁה אֶת־עַצְמוֹת יוֹסֵף עִמּוֹ כִּי הַשְׁבֵּעַ
הִשְׁבִּיעַ אֶת־בְּנֵי יִשְׂרָאֵל לֵאמֹר פָּקֹד יִפְקֹד אֱלֹהִים אֶתְכֶם
כ וְהַעֲלִיתֶם אֶת־עַצְמֹתַי מִזֶּה אִתְּכֶם: וַיִּסְעוּ מִסֻּכֹּת וַיַּחֲנוּ
כא בְאֵתָם בִּקְצֵה הַמִּדְבָּר: וַיהוָה הֹלֵךְ לִפְנֵיהֶם יוֹמָם בְּעַמּוּד
עָנָן לַנְחֹתָם הַדֶּרֶךְ וְלַיְלָה בְּעַמּוּד אֵשׁ לְהָאִיר לָהֶם לָלֶכֶת

IBN EZRA

וַחֲמֻשִׁים – *Armed for battle:* The text mentions that Israel was armed in contrast with the previous verse, which stated: *If the people face war, they will change their minds and go back to Egypt*. In fact, the people had left Egypt carrying weapons of war; they did not scurry out of Egypt like escaping slaves but "in defiance of" the Egyptians (14:8).

BEKHOR SHOR

וַחֲמֻשִׁים – *Armed for battle:* The term *ḥamushim* is used here in a sense similar to that of the verse *Stock up [veḥimmesh] the land of Egypt* [Genesis 41:34, part of Yosef's directives in advance of the seven years of famine]. That is, Israel left Egypt stocked with provisions for a lengthy journey. Evidence for this is that the people managed to survive for a full month until the manna began to fall on the fifteenth of Iyar [as described at the start of chapter 16].

RAMBAN

וַחֲמֻשִׁים – *Armed for battle:* Even though God protected Israel from war by leading them into the wilderness, the nation was still afraid that the Philistines who lived in nearby settlements would attack them. They were therefore armed just in case they had to engage the enemy.

RABBEINU BAḤYA

וַחֲמֻשִׁים – *Armed for battle:* Israel is not like other nations, who must arm themselves with weapons before confronting an enemy [for it has God to fight for it]. Still, it is prudent to anticipate having to act by natural means. Miracles might later follow.

RALBAG

וַחֲמֻשִׁים – *Armed for battle:* [Ralbag interprets the Hebrew term to mean that] every Israelite was equipped with whatever supplies he might need. It was if God anticipated every circumstance Israel might encounter and made sure that the people could manage. He thereby prevented any desire to return to Egypt.

SFORNO

וַיַּסֵּב – *He led them on a roundabout course:* The alternative route that Israel followed would not be traveled by informers from Egypt, and hence Israel would be unaware of Pharaoh's approach until he was right upon them. Therefore the verse states: *The Israelites looked up: there were the Egyptians thundering after them* (14:10). At that point it was impossible for Israel to return to Egypt, for Pharaoh and his army would not have accepted them.

13 **17** When Pharaoh let the people go, God did not lead them through the land of the Philistines, though it was the shorter way; "If the people face war," thought God, "they will change **18** their minds and go back to Egypt." So He led them on a roundabout course, by way of the wilderness, to the Sea of Reeds.

ḤIZKUNI (cont.)

a right that Moshe had fought to secure: *Let us take a three-day journey into the wilderness and sacrifice to the Lord our God* (5:3). Had God instead led Israel into an area populated by the Philistines, Pharaoh would have accused Moshe of deceit.... Secondly, God feared that the Philistines would not permit Israel to pass through their territory and would instead wage war against them. Israel of course was not trained in battle and would have difficulty repelling an Egyptian attack. Because such an encounter would take place close to Egypt, the people would choose to return to Pharaoh to be resold as slaves.... The third motive underlying God's plan was a practical consideration: No body of water stands in Philistia, and God was intent on splitting a sea for Israel and using the water to drown the cavalry. Hence God directed the nation into the wilderness and toward the planned miracle at the Sea of Reeds.

VERSE 18

RASHI

יַם־סוּף – *The Sea of Reeds:* [Literally, simply "the Sea of Reeds," without the preposition "to."] The phrase should be read as if prefaced by a prepositional letter *lamed* – meaning, "to the Sea of Reeds." The term *suf* connotes a marshy area where reeds grow, as in the verse *She laid the child in it and placed it among the reeds [basuf] by the bank of the Nile* (2:3) and the verse *The rushes and reeds [suf] shall wither* (Isaiah 19:6). וַחֲמֻשִׁים – *Armed for battle:* The term *ḥamushim* always means "armed." We find a similar usage in the verse *But you shall pass before your brethren armed* (Joshua 1:14). The Targum renders the adjective as *mezarezin* ["armed"], the same verb he uses in translating the verse *He armed his trained servants* [Genesis 14:14 concerning a battle fought by Avraham] – *vezareiz*. An alternative interpretation for the word *ḥamushim* is to see it as a form of *ḥamisha* [meaning "five"]. According to this understanding, only a fifth of the Israelites survived to leave Egypt, while the other four fifths perished during the three days of darkness.

RASHBAM

דֶּרֶךְ הַמִּדְבָּר – *By way of the wilderness:* God led Israel to a distant land, as the verse states: *It is eleven days' journey from Ḥorev by the way of Mount Se'ir* (Deuteronomy 1:2). That the Philistines stood directly in between Egypt and Canaan is evident from Yitzḥak's experience. Due to the famine raging in Canaan, the patriarch passed through the land of the Philistines intending to reach Egypt. He would have continued to that southern country had God not told him: *Do not go down into Egypt; dwell in the land which I shall tell you of... And Yitzḥak dwelled in Gerar* (Genesis 26:2–6).

יג ‏וַיְהִ֗י בְּשַׁלַּ֣ח פַּרְעֹה֮ אֶת־הָעָם֒ וְלֹא־נָחָ֣ם אֱלֹהִ֗ים דֶּ֚רֶךְ אֶ֣רֶץ פְּלִשְׁתִּ֔ים כִּ֥י קָר֖וֹב ה֑וּא כִּ֣י ׀ אָמַ֣ר אֱלֹהִ֗ים פֶּֽן־יִנָּחֵ֥ם הָעָ֛ם בִּרְאֹתָ֥ם מִלְחָמָ֖ה וְשָׁ֥בוּ מִצְרָֽיְמָה: יח וַיַּסֵּ֨ב אֱלֹהִ֧ים ׀ אֶת־הָעָ֛ם דֶּ֥רֶךְ הַמִּדְבָּ֖ר יַם־ס֑וּף וַחֲמֻשִׁ֛ים עָל֥וּ בְנֵֽי־יִשְׂרָאֵ֖ל מֵאֶ֥רֶץ

CHAPTER 13, VERSE 17

RASHI

כִּי קָרוֹב הוּא – *Though it was the shorter way:* Taking that route would have made it easy for Israel to return to Egypt. There are many midrashim that explain this clause. **בִּרְאֹתָם מִלְחָמָה** – *If the people face war:* Israel did eventually encounter battle, as the verse states: *Then the Amalekites came down, and the Canaanites who dwelled in that hill country* (Numbers 14:45). If the nation had followed the straight highway, they would have gone back to Egypt. We see that even though God led the people by a circuitous route, they still moaned: *Let us appoint a chief, and let us return to Egypt* (Numbers 14:4). So they surely would have attempted to return to that land had they been traveling on a direct road. **פֶּן־יִנָּחֵם** – *They will change their minds:* They will question the benefits of having left Egypt and set their minds to return.

BEKHOR SHOR

בִּרְאֹתָם מִלְחָמָה – *If the people face war:* The war in question was a potential defensive stand against Pharaoh. Consider that if Israel had not crossed through the Sea of Reeds, the Egyptian cavalry would not have drowned there. The army would have chased after Israel into the wilderness and the Hebrews would have had to fight them on dry land. In that case, the Philistines would have joined the fray and Israel would have ended up battling the Egyptians from the rear and the Philistines from the fore. **וְשָׁבוּ מִצְרָיְמָה** – *Go back to Egypt:* Even though God could easily have stricken the Egyptians on the spot, He desired to perform many miracles and wonders on His nation's behalf: to dry up the sea, to lead Israel through it, and to drown the Egyptian army.

HIZKUNI

דֶּרֶךְ אֶרֶץ פְּלִשְׁתִּים – *Through the land of the Philistines:* God did not wish to lead Israel into conflict with the Philistines since the treaty that Avraham had contracted to with that people was still in effect. God remembered the statement that the patriarch agreed to, *Now therefore swear to me here by God that you will not deal falsely with me, nor with my son, nor with my son's son* (Genesis 21:23). This is why God led Avraham's descendants away from the Philistines.

ABARBANEL

דֶּרֶךְ אֶרֶץ פְּלִשְׁתִּים – *Through the land of the Philistines:* God had three reasons to divert Israel from the Philistine route to Canaan. Firstly, the Israelites had been released from Egypt by Pharaoh and given permission to enter the desert for the purpose of serving God,

פרשת בשלח
PARASHAT BESHALAḤ

THE **CLASSIC** COMMENTATORS

10TH CENTURY

11TH CENTURY

12TH CENTURY
- **RASHI**, 1040 – 1105, FRANCE
- **RASHBAM**, 1080 – 1160, FRANCE
- **RABBI AVRAHAM IBN EZRA**, 1089, SPAIN – 1164, ENGLAND
- **RABBI YOSEF BEKHOR SHOR**, 12TH CENTURY, FRANCE

13TH CENTURY
- **RABBI AVRAHAM BEN HARAMBAM**, 1186 – 1237, EGYPT
- **RAMBAN**, 1194, SPAIN – 1270, ISRAEL
- **RABBI ḤIZKIYA BEN MANOAḤ – ḤIZKUNI**, 13TH CENTURY, FRANCE

14TH CENTURY
- **RABBEINU BAḤYA BEN ASHER**, 1255 – 1340, SPAIN
- **RALBAG**, 1288 – 1344, PROVENCE

15TH CENTURY

16TH CENTURY
- **RABBI YITZḤAK ABARBANEL**, 1437, PORTUGAL – 1508, ITALY
- **RABBI OVADYA SFORNO**, 1475 – 1550, ITALY
- **MAHARAL – *GUR ARYEH***, 1512 POLAND – 1609, BOHEMIA

17TH CENTURY
- **RABBI SHLOMO EFRAYIM LUNTSCHITZ – *KELI YAKAR***, 1550, POLAND – 1619, BOHEMIA

15–16 of Amalek, utterly, from under the heavens." Moshe built an altar and named it, "The LORD Is My Banner," saying, "There is a hand on the LORD's throne. The LORD will be at war with Amalek throughout the ages."

TALMUD BAVLI

כִּי־יָד עַל־כֵּס יָהּ – *There is a hand on the* LORD's *throne:* It is taught in a *baraita*: Rabbi Yosei says: Three commandments were imparted to the Israelites upon their entrance into the land of Israel: to establish a king for themselves, to annihilate the seed of Amalek in war, and to build themselves a temple. I would not know which they were obligated to perform first, but for the verse that states: *There is a hand on the* LORD's *throne. The* LORD *will be at war with Amalek.* This must mean they were obligated to establish a king for themselves first, before waging war with Amalek, for this "throne" is an allusion to kingship, as the verse states: *Then Shlomo sat on the throne of the* LORD *as king* (I Chronicles 29:23). And still I would not know whether building the Temple takes priority over destroying Amalek, but for the verse that states: *When He gives you rest from all your enemies round about, so that you dwell in safety; then there shall be a place which the* LORD *your God shall choose to cause His name to dwell there* (Deuteronomy 12:10–11). We therefore conclude that Israel must first obliterate Amalek. (Sanhedrin 20b)

LEKAḤ TOV

כִּי־יָד עַל־כֵּס יָהּ – *There is a hand on the* LORD's *throne:* As long as wicked people exist in the world, it is as if God's authority is incomplete, and His name is deficient. [Both words of the phrase "the LORD's throne" – *kes yah* – are truncated.] But when the villains have been excised from the earth, God's throne will be complete and His name will be perfect.... Rabbi Eliezer taught: The Holy One, blessed be He, vowed that whenever a potential convert wishes to join Israel from one of the other nations, he should be accepted, but no descendant of Amalek can ever be welcomed into the Jewish people.

MIDRASH AGGADA

כִּי־יָד עַל־כֵּס יָהּ – *There is a hand on the* LORD's *throne:* Moshe declared: When Israel establishes a king to rule over them – a "hand" who represents the throne of God – then there shall be a war with Amalek. מִדֹּר דֹּר – *Throughout the ages:* This refers to two generations: that of King Sha'ul [who defeated Agag the Amalekite king; see I Samuel 15], and the era of Mordekhai the righteous [who vanquished Haman, the descendant of Agag].

טו וַיִּבֶן מֹשֶׁה מִזְבֵּחַ וַיִּקְרָא שְׁמוֹ יהוה ׀ נִסִּי: וַיֹּאמֶר כִּי־יָד עַל־כֵּס יָהּ מִלְחָמָה לַיהוה בַּעֲמָלֵק מִדֹּר דֹּר:

ESTHER RABBA (cont.)

was told a clue, but it made no impression upon him. On the other hand, both David and Mordekhai recognized when something was being implied. The Holy One, blessed be He, said to Yaakov: *Behold, I am with you, and will keep you in all places to which you go* (Genesis 28:15). And yet, immediately the text reports: *And he was afraid* (Genesis 28:17). How could an individual who receives direct assurances from God ever be afraid? For he reasoned: Perhaps I contracted some impurity while living in Lavan's impure house [and no longer deserve God's providence]. When God told Moshe, *commit it to Yehoshua's ears,* He implied that Moshe would die and Yehoshua would be the one to lead Israel into the promised land. But Moshe missed the message, as later verse states: *And I besought the LORD at that time, saying…. I pray you, let me go over, and see the good land that is beyond the Jordan* [Deuteronomy 3:23, 25; Moshe still believed he had some chance to enter the land of Israel]. (6:6)

VERSE 15

MEKHILTA DERABBI SHIMON

יהוה נִסִּי – *The LORD is My Banner:* [The phrase can also be translated: "The LORD is My Miracle."] Rabbi Yehoshua taught: Moshe called the altar he built "My Miracle," telling Israel: It was because of me that God performed His miraculous salvation for you. Rabbi Elazar HaModa'i said: It was God who named the altar "My Miracle" [the whole second half of the verse can also be translated "…and the LORD named it 'My Miracle'"], teaching that whenever miracles are performed for Israel, it is as if God himself shares in the experience. Conversely, whenever Israel endures some sort of trouble, it is as if God is suffering as well. And when Israel enjoys times of happiness, God is pleased too, as the verse states: *I rejoice in Your salvation* (I Samuel 2:1).

VERSE 16

PHILO

מִלְחָמָה לַיהוה בַּעֲמָלֵק – *The LORD will be at war with Amalek:* Amalek seeks to devour the whole soul and licks it up, leaving no seed behind, nor anything that can excite virtue.

12 drop, the Amalekites prevailed. But Moshe's hands grew heavy. So they took a stone and placed it under him and he sat, while Aharon and Ḥur held up his hands, one on each side, so that his
13 hands held true until sunset. And Yehoshua overcame Amalek and his people by the sword.
14 Then the Lord said to Moshe, "Write this as a memorial on a scroll, and commit it to Yehoshua's ears: I will erase the memory

MAFTIR

MEKHILTA DERABBI SHIMON *(cont.)*

did he capture them to torture or humiliate them, but dispatched them swiftly. Rabbi Elazar HaModa'i taught: The phrasing of this verse teaches that the war was not waged according to God's instructions [the soldiers were victorious "by the sword" alone].

VERSE 14

MEKHILTA DERABBI SHIMON

כִּי־מָחֹה אֶמְחֶה – *I will erase utterly:* The doubling of the Hebrew verb indicates that all remembrance of Amalek would be wiped out from this world as well as from the next world. Rabbi Yehoshua taught: The first word, *maḥo*, indicates that Amalek himself would be killed, while the second verb, *emḥeh*, means that God would destroy the man's family. Rabbi Elazar HaModa'i taught: When God vows to obliterate Amalek, this refers to Agag [the Amalekite king mentioned in I Samuel 15]. With the term "memory" [*zekher*], God threatens to finish off Haman [a descendant of Agag]. The term *maḥo* suggests a war against the person of Amalek and his entire family, while *emḥeh* means that the whole generation to attack Israel would perish. מִתַּחַת הַשָּׁמָיִם – *From under the heavens:* Rabbi Yehoshua taught: This means that not a single grandson nor great-grandson of Amalek would remain alive in the world. Nobody would be able to point to a camel and say: "See that beast? It belonged to Amalek. That sheep there? An Amalekite used to own it. That tree too was planted by an Amalekite." Rabbi Eliezer taught: Said Moshe to the Holy One, blessed be He: Master of the Universe! In the future You will scatter your children to the four directions of the world, as the verse states: *For I have spread you abroad as the four winds of the heaven, says the Lord* (Zechariah 2:10). What is to prevent Amalek from chasing them down and killing them? And if that happens, what will become of the Torah that you have given them? Who will read it? [This is why God agreed to annihilate Amalek utterly.] Rabbi Eliezer taught: Said Moshe to God: Let the name of these people be exterminated and forgotten from the world. Furthermore, let all idolatry be abolished along with those who worship it. If that happens, God will remain as the lone recognized deity in the world. So states the verse: *And liberators shall ascend upon Mount Zion to judge the mountain of Esav* (Obadiah 1:21), while a further verse proclaims: *And the Lord shall be king over all the earth* (Zechariah 14:9).

ESTHER RABBA

וְשִׂים בְּאָזְנֵי יְהוֹשֻׁעַ – *Commit it to Yehoshua's ears:* There were four righteous men who were given hints. Two of the individuals understood what was being intimated, while the other two failed to realize the point. Moshe received a hint but did not understand it. Yaakov too

יב וִידֵי מֹשֶׁה כְּבֵדִים וַיִּקְחוּ־אֶבֶן וַיָּשִׂימוּ תַחְתָּיו וַיֵּשֶׁב עָלֶיהָ וְאַהֲרֹן וְחוּר תָּמְכוּ בְיָדָיו מִזֶּה אֶחָד וּמִזֶּה אֶחָד וַיְהִי יָדָיו אֱמוּנָה עַד־בֹּא הַשָּׁמֶשׁ: יג וַיַּחֲלֹשׁ יְהוֹשֻׁעַ אֶת־עֲמָלֵק וְאֶת־עַמּוֹ לְפִי־חָרֶב:

יד וַיֹּאמֶר יהוה אֶל־מֹשֶׁה כְּתֹב זֹאת זִכָּרוֹן בַּסֵּפֶר וְשִׂים בְּאָזְנֵי יְהוֹשֻׁעַ כִּי־מָחֹה אֶמְחֶה אֶת־זֵכֶר עֲמָלֵק מִתַּחַת הַשָּׁמָיִם: מפטיר

MEKHILTA DERABBI SHIMON

כַּאֲשֶׁר יָרִים מֹשֶׁה יָדוֹ — *Whenever Moshe held his hand high:* Rabbi Eliezer taught: Were the hands of Moshe capable of ensuring victory or defeat? Rather, so long as Israel fulfilled the will of God and believed in Moshe, God performed miracles and wonders for them.

VERSE 12

TALMUD BAVLI

וַיִּקְחוּ־אֶבֶן וַיָּשִׂימוּ תַחְתָּיו — *They took a stone and placed it under him:* Did Moshe not own a pillow or a blanket that he could have sat on? Moshe said to himself: "While Israel suffers the pain and anxiety of war, shall I sit in comfort? No, I too will endure pain and anxiety." Indeed, whoever is prepared to share in the hardship of the community will live to see the nation consoled. (Taanit 11a)

SEKHEL TOV

וִידֵי מֹשֶׁה כְּבֵדִים — *But Moshe's hands grew heavy:* In the previous verse mentions Moshe's hand [in the singular], but now Aharon and Ḥur had to hold up both his hands. This should be understood as follows: Initially Moshe held only one hand aloft and switched hands when the first one got tired. But eventually both of his hands grew heavy. And why so? Moshe was punished for delaying Israel's salvation by one day [he told Yehoshua that he would ascend the hill only "tomorrow" in verse 9]. Hence his arms became exhausted like those of a man who must transport two full buckets of water with a shoulder pole. The episode teaches that one should never put off the fulfillment of a mitzva.

VERSE 13

MEKHILTA DERABBI SHIMON

וַיַּחֲלֹשׁ יְהוֹשֻׁעַ — *And Yehoshua overcame:* Rabbi Yehoshua taught: How did Yehoshua defeat Amalek? He cut off the heads of the toughest warriors manning the enemy's front line. Rabbi Elazar HaModa'i said: The word *vayaḥalosh* should be seen as an acronym for three verbs: Yehoshua prayed [*vayḥal*], he seized [*vayoḥaz*] the enemy, and he smashed [*vayishbor*] them. **עֲמָלֵק** — *Amalek:* This refers to the person himself [i.e., the original Amalek, son of Elifaz son of Esav, listed in Genesis 36:12]. **וְאֶת־עַמּוֹ** — *And his people:* This refers to the man's descendants. Meanwhile, the [apparently superfluous] term *"et"* refers to that nation's allies who had joined in the fight. Such is the interpretation of Rabbi Yehoshua. **לְפִי־חָרֶב** — *By the sword:* Rabbi Yehoshua taught: Israel did not mutilate the enemy, nor

said to Yehoshua, "Choose men for us, and go out and do battle against Amalek. Tomorrow I will stand on top of the hill
10 with the staff of God in my hand." Yehoshua fought the Amalekites as Moshe had directed him, while Moshe, Aharon, and
11 Ḥur climbed to the top of the hill. Whenever Moshe held his hand high, the Israelites prevailed, but whenever he let his hand

--- **AVOT DERABBI NATAN** *(cont.)* ---

no less than the fear of heaven. How do we know that the honor of one's student should be as important to the teacher as his own? We learn that lesson from Moshe our teacher, who said to Yehoshua: *Choose men for us, and go out and do battle against Amalek.* Note that Moshe did not say to his aide: Choose men for "me" but for "us." The teacher thereby equated his student to himself. (27)

--- **SHEMOT RABBA** ---

וַיֹּאמֶר מֹשֶׁה אֶל־יְהוֹשֻׁעַ – *Moshe said to Yehoshua:* Why did Moshe choose Yehoshua to lead the counterattack against Amalek? The main reason is that Moshe wanted Yehoshua to gain battle experience, since he would be the one to lead Israel in conquering the land. Another interpretation for Yehoshua's selection: Moshe said to him: It was due to your ancestor [Yosef] that Israel descended to Egypt, so you must engage the enemy who attacks us upon our escape from there. Another interpretation: Why did Moshe choose Yehoshua to defend Israel? Said he to him: Your ancestor declared: *This do, and live: I fear God* (Genesis 32:18), whereas Amalek is criticized for how *he feared not God* (Deuteronomy 25:18). Let the descendant of he who proudly announced his fear of God come and vanquish the one who lacks reverence. (Beshalaḥ 26:3)

--- **LEKAḤ TOV** ---

וַיֹּאמֶר מֹשֶׁה אֶל־יְהוֹשֻׁעַ – *Moshe said to Yehoshua:* Moshe's emissary was not yet named Yehoshua, since his name was only altered in the second year, before the mission of the spies, as the verse there states: *And Moshe called Hoshea son of Nun Yehoshua* (Numbers 13:16). The man is referred to here as Yehoshua since that is how he would eventually be known.

VERSE 10

--- **PESIKTA DERAV KAHANA** ---

וּמֹשֶׁה אַהֲרֹן וְחוּר – *Moshe, Aharon, and Ḥur:* We learn from this episode that it is appropriate for three people to join together when leading the community in prayer: The leader should always be accompanied by two assistants. (3)

VERSE 11

--- **MISHNA** ---

כַּאֲשֶׁר יָרִים מֹשֶׁה יָדוֹ – *Whenever Moshe held his hand high:* Is it the hands of Moshe that win a battle or lose it? Rather, the episode teaches that when [the Israelites followed his gesture and] looked upward, they directed their hearts to their Father in heaven. That in turn helped them to prevail against the enemy. But when they did not submit to the authority of God, they would fall. (Rosh HaShana 3:8)

אֶל־יְהוֹשֻׁעַ בְּחַר־לָנוּ אֲנָשִׁים וְצֵא הִלָּחֵם בַּעֲמָלֵק מָחָר
אָנֹכִי נִצָּב עַל־רֹאשׁ הַגִּבְעָה וּמַטֵּה הָאֱלֹהִים בְּיָדִי:
י וַיַּעַשׂ יְהוֹשֻׁעַ כַּאֲשֶׁר אָמַר־לוֹ מֹשֶׁה לְהִלָּחֵם בַּעֲמָלֵק
יא וּמֹשֶׁה אַהֲרֹן וְחוּר עָלוּ רֹאשׁ הַגִּבְעָה: וְהָיָה כַּאֲשֶׁר יָרִים
מֹשֶׁה יָדוֹ וְגָבַר יִשְׂרָאֵל וְכַאֲשֶׁר יָנִיחַ יָדוֹ וְגָבַר עֲמָלֵק:

———————————— ESTHER RABBA ————————————

וַיָּבֹא עֲמָלֵק – *Amalek came:* Where did Amalek come from when they attacked Israel? Rabbi Kruspedai said in the name of Rabbi Yoḥanan: The enemy had previously gone to consult with the wicked Bilam. Said they to the sorcerer: "We know that you are a clever advisor whose advice never fails. Look at what the Israelite people did to the Egyptians, who had, after all, treated them well in their hour of need. Now if Israel had no compunction decimating Egypt, to whom they owed a debt of gratitude, how much more so will they have little trouble destroying the rest of us. Bilam, how should we protect ourselves?" Said he to them: "Go and attack them preemptively." (7:13)

VERSE 9

———————————— MEKHILTA DERABBI SHIMON ————————————

וַיֹּאמֶר מֹשֶׁה אֶל־יְהוֹשֻׁעַ – *Moshe said to Yehoshua:* Rabbi Yehoshua taught: Moshe said to Yehoshua: Step out from behind God's protective cloud to engage Amalek. Rabbi Elazar HaModa'i taught: Said the Holy One, blessed be He, to Moshe: Go tell Yehoshua: Are you saving your head to be fitted for a crown? Your task is to go out and fight Amalek.

———————————— PESIKTA DERAV KAHANA ————————————

וַיֹּאמֶר מֹשֶׁה אֶל־יְהוֹשֻׁעַ – *Moshe said to Yehoshua:* Why did Moshe pick Yehoshua to lead Israel's army? Yehoshua was descended from Yosef, about whom the prophet states: *And the house of Yaakov shall be fire, and the house of Yosef flame, the house of Esav, straw* (Obadiah 1:18). Let the fire rage from the house of Yosef and consume the stubble that is the people of Esav. [Amalek was descended from Esav.] And sure enough, *Yehoshua overcame Amalek and his people by the sword* (17:13). **אָנֹכִי נִצָּב עַל־רֹאשׁ הַגִּבְעָה** – *I will stand on top of the hill:* This phrase illustrates how righteous people agree to preside over communal needs. **אָנֹכִי נִצָּב** – *I will stand:* That is, I will stand in prayer. The connotation is similar in the verse *The Lord descended in a cloud and stood with him there* (34:5). **עַל־רֹאשׁ הַגִּבְעָה** – *On top of the hill:* When I petition God for assistance, I will invoke the merits of the patriarchs, symbolized by the verse *From the top of the rocks I see him* [Numbers 23:9; for the symbolism, see Isaiah 51:1–2]. And I will also mention the deeds of the matriarchs, as that verse continues: *And from the hills I behold him.* (3)

———————————— AVOT DERABBI NATAN ————————————

בְּחַר־לָנוּ אֲנָשִׁים – *Choose men for us:* Rabbi Eliezer ben Shamua taught: The honor of one's student should be as important to the teacher as his own, the honor of one's friend as dear to the student as the reverence for his rabbi, and the fear one feels of his rabbi should be

water will come out of it and the people will drink." And that
is what Moshe did, before the eyes of the elders of Israel. He named the place Masa and Meriva, because the people had quarreled and had tested the LORD, demanding, "Is the LORD among us or not?"

Then, at Refidim, Amalek came and attacked Israel. Moshe

SHEMOT RABBA

מַסָּה וּמְרִיבָה – *Massa and Meriva:* What arguments did Israel posit at Massa and Meriva? Rabbi Yehuda, Rabbi Neḥemya, and the Rabbis disagreed about how to interpret the incident. Rabbi Yehuda explained: The Israelites declared: "If indeed God is master over all the world [and can miraculously provide us with water] like He is master over us, then we will serve Him; otherwise, we will rebel and go our own way." According to Rabbi Neḥemya, the people whined: "God should provide us with sufficient food like a monarch is supposed to when he dwells among his citizens, who can appeal directly to him. If He does so, we will serve Him; otherwise we will rebel and reject His authority." The Rabbis provided a third approach to Israel's attitude: The nation formulated a test of God's power saying: "If God can read our thoughts and know that we doubt His abilities, we will serve Him; otherwise we will lose faith in Him." (Beshalaḥ 26:2)

VERSE 8

MEKHILTA DERABBI SHIMON

וַיָּבֹא עֲמָלֵק – *Amalek came:* Rabbi Yehoshua taught: The Amalekites managed to infiltrate Israel's camp by finding openings between the clouds of glory. Once inside, they kidnapped Israelites and killed them…. Rabbi Eliezer taught: Amalek attacked Israel brazenly. For in the past, Amalek had confronted Israel with trepidation, as the verse states: *Remember what Amalek did to you by the way, when you came out of Egypt, how he met you by the way* [Deuteronomy 25:17–18; these later verses suggest that there had been an earlier encounter that was coincidental rather than deliberate]. But now Amalek assaulted the nation boldly, which is what the verse connotes when it states: *Amalek came and attacked Israel.* Rabbi Yosei ben Ḥalafta taught: Their battle plan was carefully planned before they set out. First Amalek assembled thousands of soldiers from other nations to commit this outrage. Said the allies: "Pharaoh opposed these people, and he ended up at the bottom of the ocean thanks to their God; how can we possibly defeat them?" But Amalek volunteered to lead the charge. Said they: "Let us be the first to challenge Israel. If they defeat us, the rest of you can run away. But if we rout them, you all can join in." … Rabbi Yehuda HaNasi taught: Amalek traveled from their homeland in the Mountains of Se'ir, a distance of four hundred parasangs [about 1600 kilometers] to wage war against Israel. Other commentators claim: The ingrates came along and attacked the ingrates. [Amalek was ungrateful for the immunity granted them from Israelite conquest in Deuteronomy 2:4–5. Israel was ungrateful to God for all the benefits He was bestowing upon them.]

בַּצּוּר וְיָצְאוּ מִמֶּנּוּ מַיִם וְשָׁתָה הָעָם וַיַּעַשׂ כֵּן מֹשֶׁה לְעֵינֵי זִקְנֵי יִשְׂרָאֵל: וַיִּקְרָא שֵׁם הַמָּקוֹם מַסָּה וּמְרִיבָה עַל־רִיב ׀ בְּנֵי יִשְׂרָאֵל וְעַל נַסֹּתָם אֶת־יהוה לֵאמֹר הֲיֵשׁ יהוה בְּקִרְבֵּנוּ אִם־אָיִן:

וַיָּבֹא עֲמָלֵק וַיִּלָּחֶם עִם־יִשְׂרָאֵל בִּרְפִידִם: וַיֹּאמֶר מֹשֶׁה

SHEMOT RABBA *(cont.)*

providing Israel with water, as the verse states: *I will be there before you by the rock.* [Although God was present, He instructed Moshe to draw the water from the stone rather than doing it Himself.] (Beshalaḥ 25:5)

VERSE 7

SIFREI BEMIDBAR

מַסָּה וּמְרִיבָה – *Masa and Meriva:* Do not imagine that the site was called Masa and Meriva before Israel's arrival. Rather, it was so named because of the incident that occurred there. Lest you think that that it was the place's original name, the verse clarifies that it was called that because of the people's quarrel. [*Masa* and *Meriva* mean "test" and "quarrel" respectively.] (Behaalotekha 86)

PESIKTA DERAV KAHANA

הֲיֵשׁ יהוה בְּקִרְבֵּנוּ אִם־אָיִן – *Is the Lord among us or not:* Rabbi Levi taught: To what may Israel be compared? To a man who carries his son on his shoulders and takes him out for a walk in the market. Soon enough, some delight catches the boy's fancy, and he asks his father to buy it for him. The father happily indulges the child. They continue their stroll, and again the child sees some object that he desires, and the man agrees to get it for him. And so they proceed down the street until they chance upon an acquaintance, whereupon the child shouts down from his perch: "Have you seen my father anywhere?" Peeved, the man rebukes his child: "You ingrate! You have been riding on my shoulders all morning and I've fulfilled every wish of yours. And now you have the impudence to ask where I am?" In disgust, the man casts his son to the ground, where a dog comes along and bites him. This is how Israel treated the Holy One, blessed be He, after He freed the nation from Egypt. For God surrounded the people with seven clouds of glory to protect them, as the verse states: *He led him about [or "enveloped him"], He instructed him, He kept him as the apple of his eye* (Deuteronomy 32:10); He provided manna for the Israelites every day, and quail to satisfy their desire for meat. But even though God had met all of their needs, the people began to doubt whether He was indeed committed to their welfare, arguing: *Is the Lord among us or not?* Annoyed, the Holy One, blessed be He, chastised His children: "Ungrateful people! I will let you know exactly where I am. Here, the dog will come to bite you." Thus the narrative continues: *Then, at Refidim, Amalek came and attacked Israel* (17:8). (3)

3 me?" asked Moshe. "Why are you testing the LORD?" But the people were thirsty for water. They railed against Moshe, "Why did you bring us out of Egypt? Was it to kill me, my children,
4 and all my livestock by thirst?" "What shall I do with this people?" Moshe cried to the LORD – "another moment and they
5 will stone me." The LORD answered Moshe, "Walk out to face the people taking some of the elders of Israel with you. Take
6 the staff with which you struck the Nile in your hand, and go. I will be there before you by the rock at Ḥorev. Strike the rock,

---

MEKHILTA DERABBI SHIMON (cont.)

and ran into the midst of the congregation and behold, the plague had begun among the people. And he put on incense and made atonement for the people (Numbers 17:12). Secondly, the Ark of the Covenant was feared as an agent of destruction when it was seen to kill Uza [see II Samuel 6] and the Philistines in Beit Shemesh [see I Samuel 5]. But with this object too, the people came to understand that its presence could be a force for good, as the verse states: And it was told to King David saying, the LORD has blessed the house of Oved Edom, and all that he has, because of the ark of God (II Samuel 6:12) Finally, when Israel saw the power that the staff exercised in effecting the ten plagues in Egypt, they viewed it as an artifact of doom. However, Moshe was subsequently told to take the staff with which you struck the Nile [to provide the thirsty people with water].

TALMUD BAVLI

אֲשֶׁר הִכִּיתָ בּוֹ אֶת־הַיְאֹר – With which you struck the Nile: Rabbi Abbahu says: When a person causes another to perform a mitzva, the verse ascribes him credit as though he fulfilled it himself, as the verse states: The LORD answered Moshe "…Take the staff with which you struck the Nile in your hand." Now was it really Moshe who had struck the Nile [in 7:19–20]? Was it not Aharon who struck it? Rather, the current verse teaches the stated principle: When a person causes another to perform a mitzva [as Moshe encouraged Aharon to effect the plague], the verse ascribes him credit as though he fulfilled it himself. (Sanhedrin 99b)

LEKAḤ TOV

עֲבֹר לִפְנֵי הָעָם – Walk out to the face the people: [Literally, "pass before the people."] God instructed Moshe to give the sinful Israelites a free pass. וְקַח אִתְּךָ מִזִּקְנֵי יִשְׂרָאֵל – Taking some of the elders of Israel with you: Moshe was directed to take some elders with him who could later testify that he drew water miraculously from the rock, and did not merely expose springs that had long flowed there.

VERSE 6

SHEMOT RABBA

הִנְנִי עֹמֵד לְפָנֶיךָ – I will be there before you: All the favors Avraham had once performed on behalf of the ministering angels were later mirrored by God's treatment of Avraham's children in the wilderness. When Avraham offered water to his visitors – as the verse states, let a little water, I pray you, be fetched, and wash your feet (Genesis 18:4) – he employed a servant to attend to the angels. That is why the Holy One, blessed be He, also used an emissary when

גמֹשֶׁה מַה־תְּרִיבוּן עִמָּדִי מַה־תְּנַסּוּן אֶת־יְהֹוָה: וַיִּצְמָא שָׁם הָעָם לַמַּיִם וַיָּלֶן הָעָם עַל־מֹשֶׁה וַיֹּאמֶר לָמָּה זֶּה הֶעֱלִיתָנוּ מִמִּצְרַיִם לְהָמִית אֹתִי וְאֶת־בָּנַי וְאֶת־מִקְנַי בַּצָּמָא: וַיִּצְעַק מֹשֶׁה אֶל־יְהֹוָה לֵאמֹר מָה אֶעֱשֶׂה לָעָם הַזֶּה עוֹד מְעַט וּסְקָלֻנִי: וַיֹּאמֶר יְהֹוָה אֶל־מֹשֶׁה עֲבֹר לִפְנֵי הָעָם וְקַח אִתְּךָ מִזִּקְנֵי יִשְׂרָאֵל וּמַטְּךָ אֲשֶׁר הִכִּיתָ בּוֹ אֶת־הַיְאֹר קַח בְּיָדְךָ וְהָלָכְתָּ: הִנְנִי עֹמֵד לְפָנֶיךָ שָּׁם ׀ עַל־הַצּוּר בְּחֹרֵב וְהִכִּיתָ

VERSE 3

LEKAH TOV

וַיָּלֶן הָעָם עַל־מֹשֶׁה – *They railed against Moshe:* [The word "railed" – *vayalen* – appears in the singular.] The entire nation united to inveigh against Moshe. **אֹתִי וְאֶת־בָּנַי וְאֶת־מִקְנַי** – *Me, my children, and all my livestock:* With this statement Israel equated their cattle to themselves. This was because a person's life depends on his livelihood. When one travels without his beasts of burden, he suffers.

VERSE 4

MEKHILTA DERABBI SHIMON

וַיִּצְעַק מֹשֶׁה אֶל־יְהֹוָה לֵאמֹר – *Moshe cried to the* Lord: Moshe could have said: Since Israel is criticizing me, I refuse to petition God to show them compassion. But Moshe was better than that. Instead he beseeched God: What can I do for this people, who are suffering from thirst? [Another interpretation: Moshe complained:] Master of the Universe! Between You and them, I am caught between a rock and hard place. For you have insisted that I not lose patience with Israel, as the verse states: *Carry them in your bosom as a nursing father carries the sucking child* [Numbers 11:12; and so my options for disciplining them are limited]. In this episode, God's temper toward Israel was easy while Moshe's was harsh. However, during the sin of the golden calf, God's anger flared while Moshe attempted to assuage His ire.

SIFREI BEMIDBAR

מָה אֶעֱשֶׂה לָעָם הַזֶּה – *What shall I do with this people:* When the Torah employs the term "people" [*am*], it connotes the wicked element within the nation, as the verse states: *What shall I do with this people?* (Behaalotekha 85)

VERSE 5

MEKHILTA DERABBI SHIMON

וּמַטְּךָ אֲשֶׁר הִכִּיתָ בּוֹ אֶת־הַיְאֹר – *The staff with which you struck the Nile:* The staff is one of three items which initially made Israel anxious, since they believed these to be objects of punishment. They were: the staff, the Ark of the Covenant, and the incense. Israel learned to fear the incense when they witnessed the deaths of Nadav and Avihu, which they associated with the burning of that substance [in Leviticus 10]. Later, the people learned that incense could serve as a blessing, as the verse states: *And Aharon took as Moshe commanded,*

it, and place it before the Lord to be kept for future genera-
34 tions." As the Lord commanded Moshe, so Aharon placed it
35 before the Ark of Testimony to be kept with care. The Israelites
ate manna for forty years, until they came to the land where
they could settle down. They ate the manna until they came to
36 the border of Canaan. (An omer is a tenth of an ephah.)
17 1 All the community of Israel moved on after that from the desert shevi'i
of Sin, traveling from place to place as the Lord guided them,
and they camped at Refidim, but there was no water there for
2 the people to drink. The people started to wrangle with Moshe.
"Give us water to drink," they raged. "Why do you wrangle with

---

TALMUD BAVLI (cont.)

before entering the land of Israel]. How can these clauses be reconciled? Moshe died [before entering the land] on the seventh of Adar, which is when the manna ceased. Israel continued to eat the collected manna that they kept in their vessels until the sixteenth of Nisan [after they entered the land of Israel]. It is taught in another *baraita*, regarding the verse *The Israelites ate manna for forty years:* Did they really eat the miracle food for forty years? Did they not eat it for forty years less thirty days? [They had traveled for thirty days before reaching this point.] Rather, this verse comes to tell you that they enjoyed the taste of manna in the unleavened cakes that they took out with them from Egypt [in 12:39]. (Kiddushin 38a)

CHAPTER 17, VERSE 1

MEKHILTA DERABBI SHIMON

מִמִּדְבַּר־סִין – *From the desert of Sin:* In our tradition, acrimony [*sina*] between Israel and God only arises when the people sin or transgress His commandments. [This connects the acrimonious dispute in this chapter to Israel's sins in the previous episode.]

LEKAḤ TOV

וַיַּחֲנוּ בִּרְפִידִים – *And they camped at Refidim:* Why was the place called Refidim? It was so named because it was there that the Israelites relaxed [*rafu*] their observance of the commandments. In punishment for that, the Amalekite enemy attacked [in 17:8]. For Israel only ever suffers external assault because of sin.

VERSE 2

MEKHILTA DERABBI SHIMON

וַיָּרֶב הָעָם עִם־מֹשֶׁה – *The people started to wrangle with Moshe:* It was at this point that Israel crossed all boundaries by criticizing Moshe personally. מַה־תְּנַסּוּן אֶת־יהוה – *Why are you testing the Lord:* Whenever you quarrel with me, it is tantamount to challenging God. Another interpretation [for the word "testing" – *tenassun*]: Even though you rebel against me, God will continue to provide miracles [*nissim*] and wonders on your behalf, and he will thereby promote His name in the world.

אַחַ֗ת וְתֶן־שָׁ֤מָּה מְלֹֽא־הָעֹ֙מֶר֙ מָ֔ן וְהַנַּ֥ח אֹת֖וֹ לִפְנֵ֣י יְהֹוָ֑ה
לְמִשְׁמֶ֖רֶת לְדֹרֹתֵיכֶֽם: כַּאֲשֶׁ֛ר צִוָּ֥ה יְהֹוָ֖ה אֶל־מֹשֶׁ֑ה וַיַּנִּיחֵ֧הוּ לה
אַהֲרֹ֛ן לִפְנֵ֥י הָעֵדֻ֖ת לְמִשְׁמָֽרֶת: וּבְנֵ֣י יִשְׂרָאֵ֗ל אָֽכְל֤וּ אֶת־הַמָּן֙ לה
אַרְבָּעִ֣ים שָׁנָ֔ה עַד־בֹּאָ֖ם אֶל־אֶ֣רֶץ נוֹשָׁ֑בֶת אֶת־הַמָּן֙ אָֽכְל֔וּ
עַד־בֹּאָ֕ם אֶל־קְצֵ֖ה אֶ֥רֶץ כְּנָֽעַן: וְהָעֹ֕מֶר עֲשִׂרִ֥ית הָאֵיפָ֖ה לו
הֽוּא:

יז א וַ֠יִּסְע֠וּ כָּל־עֲדַ֨ת בְּנֵֽי־יִשְׂרָאֵ֧ל מִמִּדְבַּר־סִ֛ין לְמַסְעֵיהֶ֖ם עַל־ שביעי
פִּ֣י יְהֹוָ֑ה וַֽיַּחֲנוּ֙ בִּרְפִידִ֔ים וְאֵ֥ין מַ֖יִם לִשְׁתֹּ֥ת הָעָֽם: וַיָּ֤רֶב
הָעָם֙ עִם־מֹשֶׁ֔ה וַיֹּ֣אמְר֔וּ תְּנוּ־לָ֥נוּ מַ֖יִם וְנִשְׁתֶּ֑ה וַיֹּ֤אמֶר לָהֶם֙

MEKHILTA DERABBI SHIMON (cont.)

lead. However, we can infer that the term *an urn* [*tzintzenet*] implies a vessel with the property of keeping its contents cool [*tzonen*]. That can only mean that the urn was earthenware. **וְהַנַּח אֹתוֹ לִפְנֵי יְהֹוָה** – *And place it before the* LORD: Rabbi Yehoshua taught: For the sake of the ancestors. Rabbi Elazar HaModa'i taught: For the benefit of the descendants [who will not have seen it fall]. Rabbi Yosei taught: The manna was kept for use by Yirmeyahu the prophet. For in rebuking the nation of his times, that agent of God pleaded with Israel to study the Torah. Said they: "If we engage in Torah study, how will we have time to earn a living?" But Yirmeyahu held aloft the jar of manna and said: "Your ancestors occupied themselves with the study of Torah and this was how they fed their families. So too are you guaranteed divine support if you make study a priority." The jar of manna discussed in this chapter is one of three items that Eliyahu the prophet is destined to display before the people of Israel. The other two are a jar of water containing the ashes of the red heifer [see Numbers 19] and a jar of anointing oil [used to dedicate the Tabernacle and its accoutrements, see Exodus 30:22–33].

LEKAH TOV

וַיֹּאמֶר מֹשֶׁה אֶל־אַהֲרֹן – *Moshe said to Aharon*: Why did Moshe instruct Aharon to set aside the urn [rather than doing it himself]? Because Aharon was the man who would in the future sanctify the Holy of Holies. He would one day serve in the Tabernacle before the Ark of the Testimony, and it would be his own staff that would be kept in perpetuity as a sign to rebellious traitors [see Numbers 17:25].

VERSE 35

TALMUD BAVLI

עַד־בֹּאָם אֶל־אֶרֶץ נוֹשָׁבֶת – *Until they came to the land where they could settle down:* Now it is difficult to say that the Israelites really ate the manna *until they came to the land where they could settle down*, since the verse continues: *Until they came to the border of Canaan* [suggesting that the people already stopped eating manna while on the plains of Moav,

29 laws? Understand that the LORD has given you a Sabbath – that is why He gave you two days' bread on the sixth day. You shall each rest where you are: let no man depart from where he is 30 on the seventh day." So the people rested on the seventh day. 31 The house of Israel named it manna. It looked like white co- 32 riander seeds, and tasted like wafers made with honey. Moshe said, "This is what the LORD commands: Let an omer of it be kept carefully aside for your descendants, that they may see the bread I fed you in the desert when I brought you out of Egypt." 33 Moshe said to Aharon, "Take an urn, put an omer of manna in

VERSE 31

TALMUD BAVLI

וְהוּא כְּזֶרַע גַּד לָבָן – *It looked like white coriander seeds:* Rabbi Asi taught: It was round like a coriander seed and white like a pearl. This was also taught in a *baraita*: Coriander [*gad*] is so named because it is similar to flax seeds on their stalks [which are bound – *agud* – in a bundle]. Others say: It was called coriander [*gad*] because it was similar to a tale [*haggada*], which draws a person's heart toward it, just like life is drawn to water. It was taught in another *baraita*: Why is it called *gad*? Because it told [*maggid*] the Jewish people [secrets such as the paternity of a baby. If a woman remarried and gave birth eight months afterward, it might be unclear who the father was. The manna would reveal] whether the baby was born after nine months and belongs to the first husband or if it was born after seven months and belongs to the second husband. [Since the manna was collected by each family based on the number of its biological members, the amount of manna given to each house could resolve the mystery.] The manna was called "white" because it cleansed Israel's sins. [The people feared that if they sinned the manna would not continue to fall, so they constantly devoted themselves to introspection and repentance.] (Yoma 75a)

VERSE 32

LEKAḤ TOV

לְמִשְׁמֶרֶת לְדֹרֹתֵיכֶם – *Kept carefully aside for your descendants:* The manna placed in the urn did not rot, nor did worms infest it, nor did it melt. Corresponding to these three miracles, we find three instances of the term *mishmeret* [denoting "a thing carefully kept"] in this passage, in verses 32, 33 and 34. Another interpretation [for why the term is used three times]: The manna is to be kept on hand as a testimony for the people in the wilderness, for the nation's era in the land of Israel [when the manna no longer fell], and for future generations. For the urn of manna was hidden away along with Aharon's staff in its full bloom, the Ark of the Testimony, and all the other Tabernacle utensils in tunnels beneath the Temple. Who stored these objects to protect them from theft and sacrilege? King Yoshiyahu.

VERSE 33

MEKHILTA DERABBI SHIMON

קַח צִנְצֶנֶת אַחַת – *Take an urn:* The text does not specify what material the urn was made of. We do not know if the plan called for a vessel of gold, or of silver, copper, iron, tin, or even

כט לִשְׁמֹר מִצְוֺתַי וְתוֹרֹתָי: רְאוּ כִּי־יהוה נָתַן לָכֶם הַשַּׁבָּת עַל־
כֵּן הוּא נֹתֵן לָכֶם בַּיּוֹם הַשִּׁשִּׁי לֶחֶם יוֹמָיִם שְׁבוּ ׀ אִישׁ תַּחְתָּיו
אַל־יֵצֵא אִישׁ מִמְּקֹמוֹ בַּיּוֹם הַשְּׁבִיעִי: ל וַיִּשְׁבְּתוּ הָעָם בַּיּוֹם
הַשְּׁבִעִי: לא וַיִּקְרְאוּ בֵית־יִשְׂרָאֵל אֶת־שְׁמוֹ מָן וְהוּא כְּזֶרַע גַּד
לָבָן וְטַעְמוֹ כְּצַפִּיחִת בִּדְבָשׁ: לב וַיֹּאמֶר מֹשֶׁה זֶה הַדָּבָר אֲשֶׁר
צִוָּה יהוה מְלֹא הָעֹמֶר מִמֶּנּוּ לְמִשְׁמֶרֶת לְדֹרֹתֵיכֶם לְמַעַן ׀
יִרְאוּ אֶת־הַלֶּחֶם אֲשֶׁר הֶאֱכַלְתִּי אֶתְכֶם בַּמִּדְבָּר בְּהוֹצִיאִי
אֶתְכֶם מֵאֶרֶץ מִצְרָיִם: לג וַיֹּאמֶר מֹשֶׁה אֶל־אַהֲרֹן קַח צִנְצֶנֶת

VERSE 29

MEKHILTA DERABBI SHIMON

אַל־יֵצֵא אִישׁ מִמְּקֹמוֹ – *Let no man depart from where he is:* On the Sabbath, a Jew is forbidden to travel more than two thousand cubits beyond the city limits. (21:13)

TANHUMA

רְאוּ – *Understand:* What did Moshe mean by "understand"? Rabbi Yitzḥak taught: What Moshe tried to convey to the people was this: Understand how to respond to the nations of the world when they ask why you bother to observe the Sabbath, and what miracles were performed for you in this connection. You tell them that God miraculously gave you twice as much manna as usual in order to prepare for the Sabbath day. Hence, *on the sixth day, they will have to prepare what they bring in. It will be twice as much as they gather on all other days* (16:5). (Buber, Beshalaḥ 24)

LEKAḤ TOV

רְאוּ – *Understand:* [Literally, "see."] The term "seeing" connotes "understanding".… Said the Holy One, blessed be He, to Moshe: Moshe! I have a precious gift tucked away in My treasury, an institution called "the Sabbath," and I wish to bestow it to the people of Israel. Go and inform them what they are about to receive. נָתַן לָכֶם – *Has given to you:* Moshe thereby emphasized in this verse that the Torah was being given to Israel, as opposed to the nations of the world, who would not enjoy that gift. Thus the verse states: *He has not dealt so with any other nation; and as for His ordinances – they have not known them, Halleluya!* (Psalms 147:20). הַשַּׁבָּת – *A Sabbath:* [Literally, "the Sabbath."] The definite article identifies this day with the Sabbath that followed the six days of creation [in Genesis 2:1–3].

VERSE 30

SIFREI ZUTA

בַּיּוֹם הַשְּׁבִיעִי – *On the seventh day:* Rabbi Eliezer son of Rabbi Shimon taught: When the verse states that *the people rested on the seventh day,* it teaches that Israel only observed the Sabbath of that first week. However, the nation did not continue to do so during their subsequent forty years in the wilderness. (9:4)

24 So they put it aside until the morning, as Moshe had instructed them, and it did not stink, nor did worms infest it. 25 And Moshe said, "Today, eat this, for today is a Sabbath to the 26 LORD; today you will not find it on the ground. Six days shall you gather it, but on the seventh day, the Sabbath, it will not be 27 there." Some people did go out to gather it on the seventh day; 28 but they found none.   Then the LORD said to Moshe, "How long will you refuse to keep My commandments and

VERSE 26
MEKHILTA DERABBI SHIMON

שֵׁשֶׁת יָמִים תִּלְקְטֻהוּ – *Six days shall you gather it:* Rabbi Yehoshua taught: From this verse we only learn that no manna fell on the Sabbath. How do we know that the ground was bare on festival days as well? The final words of the verse: *It will not be there* [the word "there" seems superfluous] teach this point.

VERSE 27
TALMUD BAVLI

יָצְאוּ מִן־הָעָם – *Some people did go out:* Rav Yehuda taught in the name of Rav: If only Israel had fully observed that first Sabbath, they would have been impervious to attack from any nation or state. Instead, we find that *some people did go out to gather it on the seventh day.* And this disobedience was soon followed by the arrival of Amalek [in 17:8]. (Shabbat 118b)

PESIKTA DERAV KAHANA

וְלֹא מָצָאוּ – *But they found none:* Rabbi Yehuda son of Rabbi Simon taught: The Holy One, blessed be He, said to Israel: Your ancestors found no fault in me; have you found some fault? For I told Israel: *Six days shall you gather it, but on the seventh day, the Sabbath, it will not be there* (16:26). Yet they disobeyed me, and *some people did go out to gather it on the seventh day; but they found none.* Had they found manna they would have indeed gathered it. (14)

VERSE 28
TALMUD YERUSHALMI

מִצְוֹתַי וְתוֹרֹתָי – *My commandments and laws:* Observance of the Sabbath is as important as all the Torah's other commandments combined, as the verse states [here in specific reference to the Sabbath]: *How long will you refuse to keep My commandments and laws?* (Nedarim 3:9)

MIDRASH AGGADA

עַד־אָנָה מֵאַנְתֶּם – *How long will you refuse:* The Holy One, blessed be He, was rebuking Moshe as well, because the prophet had neglected to properly warn Israel about how to observe the Sabbath. So Moshe subsequently taught them: *Understand that the LORD has given you a Sabbath* (16:29).

כד לָכֶ֔ם לְמִשְׁמֶ֖רֶת עַד־הַבֹּֽקֶר׃ וַיַּנִּ֤יחוּ אֹתוֹ֙ עַד־הַבֹּ֔קֶר כַּאֲשֶׁ֖ר
כה צִוָּ֣ה מֹשֶׁ֑ה וְלֹ֣א הִבְאִ֔ישׁ וְרִמָּ֖ה לֹא־הָ֥יְתָה בּֽוֹ׃ וַיֹּ֤אמֶר מֹשֶׁה֙
אִכְלֻ֣הוּ הַיּ֔וֹם כִּֽי־שַׁבָּ֥ת הַיּ֖וֹם לַיהוָ֑ה הַיּ֕וֹם לֹ֥א תִמְצָאֻ֖הוּ
כו בַּשָּׂדֶֽה׃ שֵׁ֥שֶׁת יָמִ֖ים תִּלְקְטֻ֑הוּ וּבַיּ֧וֹם הַשְּׁבִיעִ֛י שַׁבָּ֖ת לֹ֥א
כז יִֽהְיֶה־בּֽוֹ׃ וַֽיְהִי֙ בַּיּ֣וֹם הַשְּׁבִיעִ֔י יָצְא֥וּ מִן־הָעָ֖ם לִלְקֹ֑ט וְלֹ֖א
כח מָצָֽאוּ׃ וַיֹּ֥אמֶר יְהוָ֖ה אֶל־מֹשֶׁ֑ה עַד־אָ֨נָה֙ מֵֽאַנְתֶּ֔ם יג

VERSE 24

LEKAḤ TOV

כַּאֲשֶׁר צִוָּה מֹשֶׁה – **As Moshe had instructed them:** Because Moshe had previously been angry when Israel left over manna during the week, the verse now emphasizes that the people had the leader's permission to keep food for the Sabbath day.

VERSE 25

TALMUD YERUSHALMI

הַיּוֹם – **Today:** Rabbi Levi said: If the nation of Israel had only observed one Sabbath perfectly, the son of David [i.e., the Messiah] would have arrived. What is the source for this claim? The verse which states: *And Moshe said, "Today, eat this, for today is a Sabbath to the* LORD" [emphasizing that only one day would be sufficient to fulfill the commandment], while a later verse promises: *In ease and rest shall you be saved* [Isaiah 30:15, implying that observance of the Sabbath hastens the redemption]. (Taanit 1:5)

TALMUD BAVLI

הַיּוֹם – **Today:** Our Sages taught that a person must eat three meals on the Sabbath, whereas Rabbi Ḥidka said there must be four meals. Rabbi Yoḥanan taught: Both approaches are based on the same verse, which states: *Today, eat this, for today is a Sabbath to the* LORD; *today you will not find it on the ground.* The word "today" appears three times in the verse. The Sages understand this to hint at the total number of Sabbath meals, including supper [of Friday night]; Rabbi Ḥidka holds that there must be three meals during the Sabbath day itself, and an additional meal the previous evening. (Shabbat 117b)

YALKUT SHIMONI

הַיּוֹם לֹא תִמְצָאֻהוּ בַּשָּׂדֶה – **Today you will not find it on the ground:** At that moment the hearts of our ancestors were broken. Said they: "Perhaps if there is no manna today, we will not find any tomorrow either." But Moshe appeased them saying: "Only *today you will not find it on the ground;* however, be assured that it will be there tomorrow." Rabbi Elazar ben Ḥasma taught: Moshe is contrasting the current world with the next: In this world you will not find the manna, but it will be there for you in the next world. (Beshalaḥ 261)

20 but they did not listen to Moshe. Some of them left part of it till morning, and it became worm-infested and stank. Moshe was 21 enraged with them. Every morning they gathered it, all as much as they could eat, and when the sun grew hot, it melted away. 22 When the sixth day came, they gathered a double portion, two omers each. All the leaders of the community came and report- 23 ed this to Moshe. "This" he told them, "is what the LORD has said: Tomorrow is a day of rest, a holy Sabbath to the LORD. Bake now what you need to bake and cook what you need to cook. Whatever is left, keep carefully aside for the morning."

YALKUT SHIMONI

וְחַם הַשֶּׁמֶשׁ וְנָמָס – *And when the sun grew hot, it melted away:* The manna dissolved each day so that Israel would not be burdened with it along their travels. Another interpretation: It was preferable for Israel to eat fresh manna every day than to eat food that had become stale. Another interpretation: Each day, the Israelites were required to turn their eyes to their Father in heaven to request more food to feed their families. (Beshalaḥ 258)

VERSE 22

MIDRASH AGGADA

וַיָּבֹאוּ כָּל־נְשִׂיאֵי הָעֵדָה – *All the leaders of the community came:* The people were surprised, for on the previous days, when they had measured the amount of manna they collected, they had found just the sufficient amount for each person's appetite. On the sixth day, however, the Israelites found twice as much manna in their possession. Moshe explained the matter to them saying: *Tomorrow is a day of rest, a holy Sabbath to the LORD. Bake now what you need to bake and cook what you need to cook* (16:23). The Sages associate this verse with the practice of *eruv tavshilin*, showing that it is hinted at in the Torah. [*Eruv tavshilin* is a ritual performed on a Thursday when a festival falls on Friday. By preparing a nominal amount of food in advance, it becomes permitted to cook on the festival for the Sabbath.]

VERSE 23

TALMUD BAVLI

אֲשֶׁר־תֹּאפוּ אֵפוּ – *Bake now what you need to bake:* According to Rabbi Elazar, this verse teaches that when one prepares food on the festival [that falls on a Friday] for the following Sabbath day, he may only bake if one has already baked something the previous day [Thursday, thus beginning the preparations for the Sabbath before the festival]. Similarly, one may only cook if one has already cooked. Hence we find scriptural evidence for the [rabbinic] institution of *eruv tavshilin* [see also commentary on verse 22]. (Beitza 15b)

LEKAḤ TOV

אֲשֶׁר־תֹּאפוּ אֵפוּ – *Bake now what you need to bake:* When Israel ate the manna, they tasted whatever they desired. The food tasted baked to those who wanted it so or boiled for those who preferred that sort of preparation.

כ מִמֶּנּוּ עַד־בֹּקֶר: וְלֹא־שָׁמְעוּ אֶל־מֹשֶׁה וַיּוֹתִרוּ אֲנָשִׁים מִמֶּנּוּ
כא עַד־בֹּקֶר וַיָּרֻם תּוֹלָעִים וַיִּבְאַשׁ וַיִּקְצֹף עֲלֵהֶם מֹשֶׁה: וַיִּלְקְטוּ
כב אֹתוֹ בַּבֹּקֶר בַּבֹּקֶר אִישׁ כְּפִי אָכְלוֹ וְחַם הַשֶּׁמֶשׁ וְנָמָס: וַיְהִי ׀
בַּיּוֹם הַשִּׁשִּׁי לָקְטוּ לֶחֶם מִשְׁנֶה שְׁנֵי הָעֹמֶר לָאֶחָד וַיָּבֹאוּ
כג כָּל־נְשִׂיאֵי הָעֵדָה וַיַּגִּידוּ לְמֹשֶׁה: וַיֹּאמֶר אֲלֵהֶם הוּא אֲשֶׁר
דִּבֶּר יְהוָה שַׁבָּתוֹן שַׁבַּת־קֹדֶשׁ לַיהוָה מָחָר אֵת אֲשֶׁר־
תֹּאפוּ אֵפוּ וְאֵת אֲשֶׁר־תְּבַשְּׁלוּ בַּשֵּׁלוּ וְאֵת כָּל־הָעֹדֵף הַנִּיחוּ

VERSE 20

TANHUMA

וַיּוֹתִרוּ אֲנָשִׁים מִמֶּנּוּ עַד־בֹּקֶר — *Some of them left part of it till morning:* Who were the disobedient Israelites? Datan and Aviram [mentioned by name in Numbers 16:1]. Rabbi Yehoshua of Sikhnin said in the name of Rabbi Levi: When the defiant Hebrews left their manna overnight, causing it to rot, the worms left the sinners' tents and crawled into their neighbors' dwellings. The Holy One, blessed be He, denounced them and declared: Did you think that your neglect of My command would remain concealed from Me? No person can hide his behavior from My sight. (Buber, Beshalaḥ 24)

VAYIKRA RABBA

וַיִּקְצֹף עֲלֵהֶם מֹשֶׁה — *Moshe was enraged with them:* Rav Huna taught: On three occasions Moshe lost his temper and consequently forgot a law relevant to the situation. This happened regarding the Sabbath, metal utensils, and a bereaved individual. The first case took place when the manna was first given to Israel and some of the people *left part of it till morning.* Because Moshe became angry, he forgot to teach the nation about the special provisions for the Sabbath. Hence he would be required to explain later: *This is what the Lord has said.... Today, eat this, for today is a Sabbath to the Lord; today you will not find it on the ground* (16:23–25). (Shemini 13:1)

VERSE 21

MEKHILTA DERABBI SHIMON

וְחַם הַשֶּׁמֶשׁ וְנָמָס — *And when the sun grew hot, it melted away:* The manna on the desert floor began to melt at the fourth hour of the day. [Based on the language of the verse here,] one might have thought that it would make more sense to put the melting point at midday [when the sun is at its highest position in the sky]. But, an earlier verse states: *And the Lord appeared to him by the terebinths of Mamre, as he sat in the tent door in the heat of the day* (Genesis 18:1). Thus the Torah refers to the hottest part of the day as "the heat of the day," whereas "when the sun grows hot" denotes only the fourth hour of the day. **וְנָמָס** — *It melted away:* When the sun hit the manna it melted and dissolved, then flowed into local streams. These in turn carried the substance to the sea. Meanwhile, deer and gazelles that had lapped up the diluted manna were later hunted and eaten by the surrounding nations. As a result, even the gentiles were given a taste of the wondrous food that God had served the Israelites.

15 the floor of the desert like fine frost on the ground. When the Israelites saw it, they asked one another, "What is it?" for they did not recognize it. Moshe said to them, "This is the bread the
16 LORD has given you to eat. This is what the LORD has instructed: Each of you gather as much as you need, an omer for every
17 person; each take enough for all the people in your tent." The
18 people of Israel did so. Some gathered more, others less. But when they measured it with an omer measure, those who had gathered much had none left over, and those who gathered but little did not fall short. All had gathered as much as they could
19 eat. "Let no one leave any over for the morning," said Moshe;

--- LEKAḤ TOV ---

עֹמֶר לַגֻּלְגֹּלֶת – *An omer for every person:* Why were the Israelites given an omer's worth of manna each? That was the most nutritious serving of that food. If they had eaten less, it would have caused a stomachache; if they had been given more, the people would have descended into gluttony.

VERSE 17

--- LEKAḤ TOV ---

וַיִּלְקְטוּ הַמַּרְבֶּה וְהַמַּמְעִיט – *Some gathered more, others less:* The following circumstance describes how the Israelites used the manna's miraculous nature to their advantage. Consider a slave who escaped his master and was sheltered in the neighbor's house. The latter claimed to have bought the slave himself, while the original owner argued that his fellow was holding his property unlawfully. A simple test could determine the truth, as the parties examined which household possessed an extra omer's worth of manna. If the plaintiff's pantry had enough omers to serve the slave, then clearly the slave belonged there. But if the neighbor's total included a sufficient amount for the slave, that proved that the man had indeed been sold. Such a method could also be employed to resolve disputes when a woman ran away from her husband's home.

VERSE 19

--- LEKAḤ TOV ---

וַיֹּאמֶר מֹשֶׁה – *Said Moshe:* Moshe instructed the nation's elders, who passed the message along to the people. אִישׁ אַל־יוֹתֵר מִמֶּנּוּ עַד־בֹּקֶר – *Let no one leave any over for the morning:* The reason Israel was told to dispose of any leftover manna was to train them to become reliant on their Father in heaven. For if a woman had five children or more, she constantly worried that the manna would not fall tomorrow and that her family would starve. Hence the mother would become accustomed to praying to God for His continued support.

טו פְּנֵי הַמִּדְבָּר דַּק מְחֻסְפָּס דַּק כַּכְּפֹר עַל־הָאָרֶץ: וַיִּרְאוּ בְנֵי־יִשְׂרָאֵל וַיֹּאמְרוּ אִישׁ אֶל־אָחִיו מָן הוּא כִּי לֹא יָדְעוּ מַה־הוּא וַיֹּאמֶר מֹשֶׁה אֲלֵהֶם הוּא הַלֶּחֶם אֲשֶׁר נָתַן יְהוָה לָכֶם לְאָכְלָה: טז זֶה הַדָּבָר אֲשֶׁר צִוָּה יְהוָה לִקְטוּ מִמֶּנּוּ אִישׁ לְפִי אָכְלוֹ עֹמֶר לַגֻּלְגֹּלֶת מִסְפַּר נַפְשֹׁתֵיכֶם אִישׁ לַאֲשֶׁר בְּאָהֳלוֹ תִּקָּחוּ: יז וַיַּעֲשׂוּ־כֵן בְּנֵי יִשְׂרָאֵל וַיִּלְקְטוּ הַמַּרְבֶּה וְהַמַּמְעִיט: יח וַיָּמֹדּוּ בָעֹמֶר וְלֹא הֶעְדִּיף הַמַּרְבֶּה וְהַמַּמְעִיט לֹא הֶחְסִיר אִישׁ לְפִי־אָכְלוֹ לָקָטוּ: יט וַיֹּאמֶר מֹשֶׁה אֲלֵהֶם אִישׁ אַל־יוֹתֵר

TANHUMA

וַתַּעַל שִׁכְבַת הַטָּל — *When the dew covering lifted:* The verse states: *Whatever the Lord wishes, He has done in heaven and in earth, in the seas, and all deep places* (Psalms 135:6). When He so desired, He divided the sea on Israel's behalf and turned it into dry land. And then, when it suited Him, He made it back into water. Now it is usual for the skies to emit rain and dew and for the land to produce bread, as the verse confirms: *As for the earth, out of it comes bread* (Job 28:5). But by God's decree, food fell from the sky, as the verse states: *I am going to rain down bread from heaven* (16:4), and dew was lifted out of the ground, as we read: *When the dew covering lifted.* (Buber, Beshalah 20)

VERSE 15

LEKAH TOV

מָן הוּא — *What is it:* The Israelites used the term *man*, which is the Egyptian equivalent of the Hebrew *ma* [meaning "what"].

VERSE 16

TANHUMA

לַאֲשֶׁר בְּאָהֳלוֹ — *For all the people in your tent:* Rabbi Hama son of Rabbi Hanina taught: Israel was encamped at Alush [mentioned in Numbers 33:13] when they began to receive the manna. What was the significance of that location? For the nation was rewarded the manna due to the merit of our matriarch Sara, who was instructed by Avraham: *Make ready quickly three measures of fine meal, knead it [lushi], and make cakes* (Genesis 18:6). And therefore the manna was served to her descendants at Alush. **עֹמֶר לַגֻּלְגֹּלֶת** — *An omer for every person:* The Holy One, blessed be He, said to Israel: Consider the difference between Me and you. You offer before Me just a single omer throughout the entire year, as the verse states: *Then you shall bring an omer of the first fruits of your harvest to the priest; and he shall wave the omer before the Lord* (Leviticus 23:10), whereas I provide an omer's worth of food to every single Israelite, as the verse states: *An omer for every person.* Furthermore, I serve the manna to you every single day, as the verse states: *Let the people go out and gather enough for each day* (16:4). (Buber, Beshalah 23)

He has heard you railing against Him. We – what are we? It is not us you rail against, but the LORD." Then Moshe said to Aharon, "Tell all the community of Israel to come before the LORD, because He has heard your railing." As soon as Aharon had spoken to the whole community of Israel, they looked toward the desert – and the glory of the LORD appeared in the midst of cloud.

The LORD spoke to Moshe and said, "I have heard the Israelites' railing. Tell them: At twilight you shall eat meat, and in the morning your fill of bread. Then you will know that I am the LORD your God." That evening a flock of quail flew in and covered the camp; next morning a layer of dew surrounded the camp. When the dew covering lifted, fine flakes covered

SHISHI

LEKAḤ TOV *(cont.)*

with as much equanimity as if they had been a single complaint. [Hence, the word is spelled as if it were singular.] This is why the Torah employs the phrase *the Israelites' railing* – to show that even when they criticize God they are still Israel, they remain God's children, God's beloved, descendants of Avraham His favored one, the progeny of Yitzḥak who was bound in God's name, and the scions of Yaakov His firstborn son.

VERSE 13

MEKHILTA DERABBI SHIMON

וַתְּכַס אֶת־הַמַּחֲנֶה – *And covered the camp:* It is unclear from this text how high the quails stacked up in the Israelite camp. However, a later verse states: *And a wind went out from the LORD and brought quails from the sea… round about the camp, and about two cubits high upon the face of the earth* (Numbers 11:31). The quails were piled up to exactly the height of a person's heart, such that one did not even have to bend down or reach up to collect them.

MIDRASH AGGADA

שִׁכְבַת הַטָּל – *A layer of dew:* In preparation for the manna, dew descended and washed clean the desert floor, whereupon the manna fell upon the dew. Then a second layer of dew covered the manna. This kept the manna from becoming dirty or dusty.

VERSE 14

TALMUD BAVLI

דַּק מְחֻסְפָּס – *Fine flakes:* Rabbi Yosei bar Rabbi Ḥanina taught: There was dew above the manna and dew below it such that it resembled a gift wrapped in a box. The manna is described as "fine flakes" [*meḥuspas*]. Reish Lakish taught: This means that the food melted [*nimmoaḥ*] in the palm [*pissat*] of the hand. Rabbi Yoḥanan offered an alternative interpretation for the term: The substance of the manna was absorbed into the body's two hundred and forty-eight limbs [the numerical value of *meḥuspas*]. (Yoma 75b)

3 and Aharon. The Israelites said to them, "If only we had died by the Lord's hand in Egypt, when we sat by the fleshpots and ate our fill of bread. Instead, you have brought us out into this
4 desert to kill the entire assembly by starvation." Then the Lord said to Moshe, "I am going to rain down bread from heaven. Let the people go out and gather enough for each day; I will test them to see whether they will follow My law or not.

TALMUD BAVLI *(cont.)*
---

the sea (Numbers 11:31). Similarly, the text reports that Avraham *took butter and milk* (Genesis 18:8), while later God promised, *I am going to rain down bread from heaven.* (Bava Metzia 86b) וַיֵּצֵא הָעָם וְלָקְטוּ – *Let the people go out and gather:* A later verse describes Israel's activity as follows: *And the people went about and gathered it* [Numbers 11:8, which suggests that the manna had to be sought; our verse seems to imply it was more readily available]. How do we reconcile the two accounts? If an individual was righteous, the manna fell just in front of his tent. If he was an average sort of character, he had merely to *go out and gather.* But if the person was wicked, he had to "go about" to find the manna. (Yoma 75a)

BERESHIT RABBA

הִנְנִי מַמְטִיר לָכֶם לֶחֶם – *I am going to rain down bread:* When Yitzhak blessed Yaakov by promising him: *Therefore God give you of the dew of heaven* (Genesis 27:28) that was an allusion to the manna, about which God said: *I am going to rain down bread from heaven.* (Toledot 66:3)

SHEMOT RABBA

הִנְנִי מַמְטִיר לָכֶם לֶחֶם – *I am going to rain down bread:* The manna which fell for Israel tasted different to each person according to his character. When people in their prime ate it, it tasted like bread, as the verse states: *I am going to rain down bread from heaven.* When old people chewed it, it reminded them of honey-soaked wafers, as the verse states, *It tasted like wafers made with honey* (16:31). To a child it recalled milk from his mother's breast [shad], as the verse states: *And the taste of it was like the taste of oil cake [leshad hashamen]* (Numbers 11:8). If the manna was fed to the sick, it was like flour mixed with honey, as the verse states: *My bread also which I gave you, fine flour, and oil, and honey, with which I fed you* (Ezekiel 16:19). But if an idolater ate the manna, it tasted bitter as a coriander seed, as the verse states: *And the manna was like coriander seed* (Numbers 11:7). (Shemot 5:9) דְּבַר־יוֹם בְּיוֹמוֹ – *Enough for each day:* The Holy One, blessed be He, said to Israel: With the measure that a man uses, so shall it be meted out to him. I gave you the Torah with the hope that you would study it "daily," as the verses state: *Happy is the man who hearkens to Me, watching daily at My gates* (Proverbs 8:34), and *They seek Me daily, and desire to know My ways* (Isaiah 58:2). And if you do so, I will provide you with your "daily" bread from the heaven, as the verse states: *Let the people go out and gather enough for each day; I will test them to see whether they will follow My law or not.* Furthermore, those who engage in regular Torah study will be blessed, as the verse states: *Blessed be the Lord who day by day bears our burden* (Psalms 68:20). (Beshalah 26:9)

ה לְמַעַן אֲנַסֶּנּוּ הֲיֵלֵךְ בְּתוֹרָתִי אִם־לֹא: וְהָיָה בַּיּוֹם הַשִּׁשִּׁי וְהֵכִינוּ אֵת אֲשֶׁר־יָבִיאוּ וְהָיָה מִשְׁנֶה עַל אֲשֶׁר־יִלְקְטוּ יוֹם ׀
ו יוֹם: וַיֹּאמֶר מֹשֶׁה וְאַהֲרֹן אֶל־כָּל־בְּנֵי יִשְׂרָאֵל עֶרֶב וִידַעְתֶּם
ז כִּי יְהֹוָה הוֹצִיא אֶתְכֶם מֵאֶרֶץ מִצְרָיִם: וּבֹקֶר וּרְאִיתֶם אֶת־ כְּבוֹד יְהֹוָה בְּשָׁמְעוֹ אֶת־תְּלֻנֹּתֵיכֶם עַל־יְהֹוָה וְנַחְנוּ מָה כִּי
ח תלינו עָלֵינוּ: וַיֹּאמֶר מֹשֶׁה בְּתֵת יְהֹוָה לָכֶם בָּעֶרֶב בָּשָׂר תַלִּינוּ לֶאֱכֹל וְלֶחֶם בַּבֹּקֶר לִשְׂבֹּעַ בִּשְׁמֹעַ יְהֹוָה אֶת־תְּלֻנֹּתֵיכֶם

VERSE 5

MEKHILTA DERABBI SHIMON

וְהָיָה מִשְׁנֶה – *It will be twice as much:* The manna that descended to earth on the sixth day was different [*meshuneh*, evoking *mishneh* here]. Each day of the week the Israelites were provided with a single omer's worth of food, but in honor of the Sabbath they received two omers of the substance. On each day, the smell of the manna wafted through the camp, but on the Sabbath the scent was even stronger. The regular manna glistened like gold, but it shone even more on the Sabbath.

TALMUD BAVLI

וְהָיָה בַּיּוֹם הַשִּׁשִּׁי וְהֵכִינוּ – *On the sixth day, they will have to prepare:* We learn from this verse that one can prepare food for the Sabbath during the week, and food for festivals during the week. However, one may not prepare food on a festival for a subsequent Sabbath, nor can one prepare food on the Sabbath for an upcoming festival day. (Eruvin 38b) וְהֵכִינוּ אֵת אֲשֶׁר־יָבִיאוּ – *They will have to prepare what they bring in:* Rav Ḥisda taught: A person should always rise early the day before the Sabbath in order to make preparations for the Sabbath, like the verse states: *On the sixth day, they will have to prepare what they bring in* – implying that the Israelites began preparing the food for the Sabbath immediately upon collecting the manna in the morning. Rabbi Abba said: At a Sabbath meal, a person is obligated to break two loaves of bread, for the verse states: *When the sixth day came, they gathered a double portion, two omers each* (16:22). Rav Ashi said: I saw that Rav Kahana held two loaves in his hand, but only broke one, since the verse states, *they gathered* [that is, twice as much must be "gathered," but not consumed]. (Shabbat 117b)

TANHUMA

מִשְׁנֶה – *Twice as much:* What does the word *mishneh* mean? If we suggest it reflects how Israel collected twice as much manna on the sixth day as they did during the week, [wouldn't the statement be superfluous? After all,] does the text not state later: *When the sixth day came, they gathered a double portion, two omers each* (16:22)? Rabbi Ḥizkiya bar Ḥiyya explained: The word *mishneh* actually teaches that the manna that fell on the sixth day was different [*meshuneh*] in its taste, smell, and appearance from that of the rest of the week. What's more, usually, leftover manna that was held overnight

5 On the sixth day, they will have to prepare what they bring in.
6 It will be twice as much as they gather on all other days." So Moshe and Aharon told all the Israelites, "At evening you will
7 know that it was the LORD who brought you out of Egypt, and by morning you shall see the LORD's glory, for He has heard you railing against Him. As for us, what are we that you rail
8 against us?" Then Moshe said, "In the evening, the LORD will give you meat to eat, and in the morning bread to fill you, for

─────────── TANHUMA *(cont.)* ───────────

became rotten by morning. But manna that was reserved for the Sabbath meals *did not stink, nor did worms infest it* (16:24). (Buber, Beshalah 24)

─────────── YALKUT SHIMONI ───────────

וְהָיָה בַּיּוֹם הַשִּׁשִּׁי וְהֵכִינוּ – *On the sixth day, they will have to prepare:* Rav Ḥisda taught: A Jew should start preparing for the Sabbath as soon as possible, as the verse states: *On the sixth day, they will have to prepare what they bring in* – Israel began to get ready for the Sabbath immediately upon collecting their manna on the sixth day. (Beshalaḥ 258)

VERSE 6

─────────── MEKHILTA DERABBI SHIMON ───────────

עֶרֶב וִידַעְתֶּם – *At evening you will know:* While you sleep secure in your beds, God will be busying Himself with your sustenance. After all, *it was the LORD who brought you out of Egypt.* Because the verse juxtaposes these two acts, our Sages argue that the greatness of the exodus was equal to that of all the subsequent miracles and wonders that God performed in providing for Israel in the wilderness.

VERSE 7

─────────── TALMUD BAVLI ───────────

וְנַחְנוּ מָה – *What are we:* Said the Holy One, blessed be He, to Israel: The reason I love you so is that even when I grant you great honor, you bear it humbly. For example, when I bestowed greatness upon Avraham, he responded by saying: *I am but dust and ashes* (Genesis 18:27). Similarly, though I raised Moshe and Aharon to the nation's leadership, they protested: *What are we that you rail against us?* (Ḥullin 89a)

─────────── LEKAḤ TOV ───────────

וּרְאִיתֶם אֶת כְּבוֹד יהוה – *You shall see the LORD's glory:* This verse teaches that God gave the manna to Israel with a radiant countenance.

VERSE 8

─────────── BEMIDBAR RABBA ───────────

לֹא־עָלֵינוּ תְלֻנֹּתֵיכֶם – *It is not us you rail against:* Rabbi Ḥanina taught: Whenever a person complains about a teacher, it is as if he has found fault in God Himself, as the verse states: *It is not us you rail against, but the LORD.* (Koraḥ 18:20)

אֲשֶׁר־אַתֶּם מַלִּינִם עָלָיו וְנַחְנוּ מָה לֹא־עָלֵינוּ תְלֻנֹּתֵיכֶם
כִּי עַל־יְהוָה: וַיֹּאמֶר מֹשֶׁה אֶל־אַהֲרֹן אֱמֹר אֶל־כָּל־עֲדַת
בְּנֵי יִשְׂרָאֵל קִרְבוּ לִפְנֵי יְהוָה כִּי שָׁמַע אֵת תְּלֻנֹּתֵיכֶם: וַיְהִי
כְּדַבֵּר אַהֲרֹן אֶל־כָּל־עֲדַת בְּנֵי־יִשְׂרָאֵל וַיִּפְנוּ אֶל־הַמִּדְבָּר
וְהִנֵּה כְּבוֹד יְהוָה נִרְאָה בֶּעָנָן:

ששי יא וַיְדַבֵּר יְהוָה אֶל־מֹשֶׁה לֵּאמֹר: שָׁמַעְתִּי אֶת־תְּלוּנֹּת בְּנֵי
יִשְׂרָאֵל דַּבֵּר אֲלֵהֶם לֵאמֹר בֵּין הָעַרְבַּיִם תֹּאכְלוּ בָשָׂר
וּבַבֹּקֶר תִּשְׂבְּעוּ־לָחֶם וִידַעְתֶּם כִּי אֲנִי יְהוָה אֱלֹהֵיכֶם:
יג וַיְהִי בָעֶרֶב וַתַּעַל הַשְּׂלָו וַתְּכַס אֶת־הַמַּחֲנֶה וּבַבֹּקֶר הָיְתָה
יד שִׁכְבַת הַטָּל סָבִיב לַמַּחֲנֶה: וַתַּעַל שִׁכְבַת הַטָּל וְהִנֵּה עַל־

VERSE 9

MEKHILTA DERABBI SHIMON

קִרְבוּ לִפְנֵי יהוה – *Come before the* Lord: Rabbi Yehoshua taught: Whenever one approaches God, it is in order to be judged. Rabbi Elazar HaModa'i taught: Israel was invited to come before God to experience revelation of the Divine Presence.

VERSE 10

MEKHILTA DERABBI SHIMON

נִרְאָה בֶּעָנָן – *Appeared in the midst of cloud:* Rabbi Yosei son of Rabbi Shimon taught: Whenever the nation tried to stone Moshe and Aharon, God revealed Himself in a cloud, saying: Better that My pillar of cloud should absorb the people's stones than that Moshe and Aharon be pelted with rocks.

VERSE 12

MEKHILTA DERABBI SHIMON

בֵּין הָעַרְבַּיִם תֹּאכְלוּ בָשָׂר – *At twilight you shall eat meat:* You asked Me for manna, and I granted your request, since human beings cannot live without bread. Then you came back and demanded meat, which was presumptuous. Nevertheless, I am prepared to serve you meat as well, lest you argue that I lack the ability to do so. I will provide you with meat, but I will also punish you for your impudence. *Then you will know that I am the* Lord *your God,* who judges and chastises.

LEKAḤ TOV

תְּלוּנֹת בְּנֵי יִשְׂרָאֵל – *The Israelites' railing:* The word *telunnot* is written defectively [without the penultimate letter *vav*] to reflect how when Israel complained they thereby reduced their merit. Another interpretation: Every time the term *telunnot* describes the nation's demands, it is written defectively to reflect how all of Israel's reproaches were accepted by God

ג וַיֹּאמְרוּ אֲלֵהֶם בְּנֵי יִשְׂרָאֵל מִי־יִתֵּן מוּתֵנוּ בְיַד־יְהֹוָה בְּאֶרֶץ מִצְרַיִם בְּשִׁבְתֵּנוּ עַל־סִיר הַבָּשָׂר בְּאׇכְלֵנוּ לֶחֶם לָשֹׂבַע כִּי־הוֹצֵאתֶם אֹתָנוּ אֶל־הַמִּדְבָּר הַזֶּה לְהָמִית אֶת־כׇּל־הַקָּהָל הַזֶּה בָּרָעָב:

ד וַיֹּאמֶר יְהֹוָה אֶל־מֹשֶׁה הִנְנִי מַמְטִיר לָכֶם לֶחֶם מִן־הַשָּׁמָיִם וְיָצָא הָעָם וְלָקְטוּ דְּבַר־יוֹם בְּיוֹמוֹ

VERSE 3

MEKHILTA DERABBI SHIMON

מִי־יִתֵּן מוּתֵנוּ – *If only we had died:* Israel complained: If only we had died during the three-day plague of darkness [when, according to tradition, the wicked among Israel were put to death]. בְּאׇכְלֵנוּ לֶחֶם לָשֹׂבַע – *And ate our fill of bread:* Rabbi Elazar HaModa'i taught: Because the Israelites were slaves to the king of Egypt, they were entitled to wander about the marketplace unhindered and to purchase there bread, meat, fish and all the victuals they wanted. Similarly, they would go out to the fields and pick figs, grapes, pomegranates, and any other produce they desired, and nobody stood in their way. לְהָמִית אֶת־כׇּל־הַקָּהָל הַזֶּה בָּרָעָב – *To kill the entire assembly by starvation:* Rabbi Yehoshua said: There is no greater torment than hunger, as the verse states: *Better to be killed by the sword than killed by hunger. The slain at least flow where they are stabbed, do not starve for the yield of meadows.* (Lamentations 4:9).

VERSE 4

MEKHILTA DERABBI SHIMON

הִנְנִי מַמְטִיר לָכֶם לֶחֶם – *I am going to rain down bread:* Rabbi Shimon taught: Because God loved Israel, He wished to give them their daily bread. To what may this be compared? To a king of flesh and blood who became angry at his son and banished him from his sight. Still, he allowed the prince to appear at the start of the year to collect his annual allowance. Now even though the son was supported by his father, the situation made him miserable, and he moaned: I would much rather be permitted to visit my father, even if that meant forfeiting my stipend. Eventually the king forgave his son and invited him to see him every day, when he would receive his sustenance. But the prince declared: "Just being allowed to call upon the king regularly is enough for me!" So it was with Israel: Because God loved them, He provided them with food daily, such that the people would yearn for the Divine Presence and go out to greet it every day.

TALMUD BAVLI

הִנְנִי מַמְטִיר לָכֶם לֶחֶם – *I am going to rain down bread:* Rav Yehuda taught in the name of Rav: Every service that Avraham provided for the ministering angels [in Genesis chapter 18], did the Holy One, blessed be He, repeat Himself for the patriarch's descendants. Whereas, each act that Avraham directed his servant to perform, the Holy One, blessed be He, also repeated using His an agent. For example, the verse states, *And Avraham ran to the herd* (Genesis 18:7), an act that finds a parallel in the verse, *And a wind went out from the* LORD *and brought quails from*

and keeping His decrees, I will not bring on you any of the sicknesses I brought on the Egyptians, for I am the LORD – your Healer." And then they arrived at Elim, where there were twelve springs and seventy date palms. They encamped there by the water. They set out from Elim, and on the fifteenth day of the second month after leaving Egypt, the congregation of Israel all arrived at the desert of Sin, between Elim and Sinai. In the desert, all the community started railing against Moshe

27

16 1

2

ḤAMISHI

LEKAḤ TOV

שְׁתֵּים עֶשְׂרֵה עֵינֹת מַיִם וְשִׁבְעִים תְּמָרִים –*Twelve springs and seventy date palms:* Rabbi Eliezer taught: When the Holy One, blessed be He, created the world, He fashioned twelve springs of water for the benefit of Israel's twelve tribes, and planted seventy palm trees to correspond to the number of elders in that nation.

CHAPTER 16, VERSE 1

MEKHILTA DERABBI SHIMON

בַּחֲמִשָּׁה עָשָׂר יוֹם לַחֹדֶשׁ הַשֵּׁנִי – *On the fifteenth day of the second month:* Why does the Torah bother to tell us the date when Israel arrived at the desert of Sin? In order to be able to subsequently identify the date that Israel first kept the Sabbath [in the continuation of this story, 16:22–27]. For since the time that the Holy One, blessed be He, created the world, the Sabbath was held in abeyance until the twenty-second of Iyar [one week after the people arrived at Elim]. Another interpretation: The text provides the date here in order to later establish that the Torah too was given on the Sabbath. Another interpretation: By informing us what the date was, the Torah tells us when the manna was first delivered. For the cakes that Israel brought with them at the exodus, as the verse states: *With the dough they had brought from Egypt, they baked cakes of unleavened bread* (12:39), lasted for thirty-one days. When the food ran out, God immediately began to serve Israel manna, saying: *I am going to rain down bread from heaven* (16:4). Rabbi Sheila taught: The food that Israel prepared before departing Egypt served them for sixty-one meals.

VERSE 2

BERESHIT RABBA

וַיִּלּוֹנוּ – *Started railing;* Rabbi Berekhya taught: When Yaakov [i.e., Israel] raises his voice in complaint, the hands of Esav triumph, for first the verse states: *All the community started railing against Moshe,* and that is followed by the report that: *Amalek came and attacked Israel* [17:8; Amalek was a descendant of Esav]. But when Yaakov speaks pleasantly, the dominion of Esav is curtailed. [The juxtaposition of "Yaakov's voice" to "Esav's hands" is based in Genesis 27:22 – *The voice is Yaakov's voice, but the hands are the hands of Esav.*] (Toledot, 65:20)

וְשָׁמַרְתָּ֙ כָּל־חֻקָּ֔יו כָּל־הַֽמַּחֲלָ֞ה אֲשֶׁר־שַׂ֤מְתִּי בְמִצְרַ֙יִם֙
לֹא־אָשִׂ֣ים עָלֶ֔יךָ כִּ֛י אֲנִ֥י יהוה רֹפְאֶֽךָ: וַיָּבֹ֣אוּ חמישי
אֵילִ֔מָה וְ֠שָׁ֠ם שְׁתֵּ֣ים עֶשְׂרֵ֞ה עֵינֹ֥ת מַ֙יִם֙ וְשִׁבְעִ֣ים תְּמָרִ֔ים
א וַיַּחֲנוּ־שָׁ֖ם עַל־הַמָּֽיִם: וַיִּסְעוּ֙ מֵֽאֵילִ֔ם וַיָּבֹ֜אוּ כָּל־עֲדַ֤ת טז
בְּנֵֽי־יִשְׂרָאֵל֙ אֶל־מִדְבַּר־סִ֔ין אֲשֶׁ֥ר בֵּין־אֵילִ֖ם וּבֵ֣ין סִינָ֑י
בַּחֲמִשָּׁ֨ה עָשָׂ֥ר יוֹם֙ לַחֹ֣דֶשׁ הַשֵּׁנִ֔י לְצֵאתָ֖ם מֵאֶ֥רֶץ מִצְרָֽיִם:
ב וַיִּלּ֜וֹנוּ כָּל־עֲדַ֧ת בְּנֵי־יִשְׂרָאֵ֛ל עַל־מֹשֶׁ֥ה וְעַֽל־אַהֲרֹ֖ן בַּמִּדְבָּֽר: וַיֹּ֨אמְר֤וּ

TALMUD BAVLI

כִּי אֲנִי יהוה רֹפְאֶךָ – *For I am the* LORD – *your Healer:* Rabbi Abba asked Rabba bar Mari: The verse that states: *I will not bring on you any of the sicknesses I brought on the Egyptians, for I am the* LORD – *your Healer,* seems contradictory. If God does not strike the Jews with any illnesses, why would He need to act as their Healer? Rabba bar Mari answered: So I learned from Rabbi Yoḥanan: The start of the verse outlines God's stipulation. First it argues: *If you listen faithfully to the voice of the* LORD *your God,* then *I will not bring on you any of the sicknesses.* But if Israel fails to heed God's commandments, He will inflict illness on the people. Still, God will then be willing to cure them, *for I am the* LORD – *your Healer.* (Sanhedrin 101a)

TANḤUMA

אִם־שָׁמוֹעַ תִּשְׁמַע – *If you listen faithfully:* If an individual shows interest in learning about a single commandment, he will end up hearing about many [this explains the doubling of the verb: *shamoa tishma*]. Rabbi Shimon ben Elazar taught: When a person makes the effort to listen, he is taught by God's voice, meaning that whenever one learns from a Torah scholar, it is as if he is listening directly to God. **וְהַיָּשָׁר בְּעֵינָיו תַּעֲשֶׂה** – *Doing what is right in His eyes:* This refers to proper conduct in business dealings. **וְהַאֲזַנְתָּ לְמִצְוֹתָיו** – *Heeding His commands:* These are the Torah's laws. **וְשָׁמַרְתָּ כָּל־חֻקָּיו** – *And keeping His decrees:* This refers to commandments that appear to have no rational basis. **כִּי אֲנִי יהוה רֹפְאֶךָ** – *For I am the* LORD – *your Healer:* Said the Holy One, blessed be He, to Israel: I have given you the Torah to serve as a curative to all of your illnesses, as the verse states: *It shall be health to your belly, and marrow to your bones* (Proverbs 3:8). (Buber, Beshalaḥ 19)

VERSE 27

MEKHILTA DERABBI SHIMON

שְׁתֵּים עֶשְׂרֵה עֵינֹת מַיִם וְשִׁבְעִים תְּמָרִים–*Twelve springs and seventy date palms:* The water at Elim was not particularly wholesome, for out of twelve springs only seventy palm trees managed to grow. But when Israel arrived with 600,000 people, the water miraculously sufficed for the entire nation. Indeed, they camped at Elim for two, even three days, and yet there was plenty of water to go around.

days, they journeyed across the desert without finding water. 23 Eventually they came to Mara, but they could not drink the water there because it was bitter; because of this it was named 24 Mara. The people railed against Moshe – "What are we to 25 drink?" Moshe cried out to the Lord. And the Lord showed him a piece of wood, which he threw into the water – and the water became sweet. It was there that the Lord gave His people decree and law; it was there that He put them to the test. 26 He said, "If you listen faithfully to the voice of the Lord your God, doing what is right in His eyes, heeding His commands

VERSE 25

MEKHILTA DERABBI SHIMON

חֹק וּמִשְׁפָּט – *Decree and law:* Rabbi Yehoshua taught: The "decree" of this verse refers to the institution of the Sabbath, while the "law" is the commandment to honor one's father and mother. But Rabbi Elazar HaModa'i said: the "decree" [*hok*] God taught Israel here refers to the laws against forbidden sexual unions, as the verse states: *Therefore shall you keep my ordinance, that you commit not any one of these abominable customs [hukkot]* (Leviticus 18:30), while the "law" refers to statutes dealing with rape, injury, and fines. נִסָּהוּ – *Put them to the test:* It was there that God performed a miracle [*nes*, evoking *nissahu*] on Israel's behalf.... It was there that God tested Israel, or alternatively, it was there that the people challenged God.

TANHUMA

עֵץ – *A piece of wood:* What exactly was this miraculous piece of wood? Rabbi Yehoshua said: It was a branch from an olive tree. Rabbi Nehemya said: It was wood from a willow tree. Other scholars suggest that Moshe cast the trunk of a fig tree or that of a pomegranate tree into the water, since there is no wood more bitter than these. The Sages argue that the wood was from the rosebay bush, which is the most bitter of all plants. Rabbi Yishmael son of Rabbi Yohanan ben Beroka taught: Witness how great the miracles are of the Holy One, blessed be He! If a person wishes to cure unpotable water, he adds something sweet to it. But the Holy One, blessed be He, mixes a bitter ingredient into the water, thus using something bitter to combat bitterness! Thus the verse states: *I will heal you of [or "by"] your wounds, says the Lord* (Jeremiah 30:17). God uses the same agents to heal as He formerly employed in wounding.

VERSE 26

MEKHILTA DERABBI SHIMON

וְהַיָּשָׁר בְּעֵינָיו – *What is right in His eyes:* This refers to honesty in business dealings, for when an individual acts properly in financial matters, and he is respected and trusted by others, the verse credits him with having fulfilled the entire Torah.

כג שְׁלֹשֶׁת־יָמִים בַּמִּדְבָּר וְלֹא־מָצְאוּ מָיִם: וַיָּבֹאוּ מָרָתָה וְלֹא
יָכְלוּ לִשְׁתֹּת מַיִם מִמָּרָה כִּי מָרִים הֵם עַל־כֵּן קָרָא־שְׁמָהּ
כד מָרָה: וַיִּלֹּנוּ הָעָם עַל־מֹשֶׁה לֵּאמֹר מַה־נִּשְׁתֶּה: וַיִּצְעַק אֶל־
כה יהוה וַיּוֹרֵהוּ יהוה עֵץ וַיַּשְׁלֵךְ אֶל־הַמַּיִם וַיִּמְתְּקוּ הַמָּיִם שָׁם
שָׂם לוֹ חֹק וּמִשְׁפָּט וְשָׁם נִסָּהוּ: וַיֹּאמֶר אִם־שָׁמוֹעַ תִּשְׁמַע
לְקוֹל ׀ יהוה אֱלֹהֶיךָ וְהַיָּשָׁר בְּעֵינָיו תַּעֲשֶׂה וְהַאֲזַנְתָּ לְמִצְוֹתָיו

MIDRASH TEHILLIM

וַיַּסַּע מֹשֶׁה — *Moshe then led:* When God performs a miracle for someone, and the recipient thanks Him with songs of praise, all of the person's sins are immediately forgiven, and he is considered a blank slate. Witness what happened to Israel when they were saved from the attacking Egyptian cavalry. As soon as the nation clambered out of the ocean, they turned to address their Savior, as the verse states: *And then, Moshe and the Israelites sang this song to the* LORD (15:1) — and we later read that *Moshe led the Israelites from the Sea of Reeds.* What did Moshe lead? He led away and disposed of the sins that Israel had committed at the seashore, as the verse states, *And they rebelled against You at the sea, the Sea of Reeds* (Psalms 106:7). (18)

LEKAH TOV

אֶל־מִדְבַּר־שׁוּר — *Into the desert of Shur:* As soon as Moshe gave the nation the order to move on from the sea they did not ask: Where exactly are we headed? How can we walk into the wilderness ahead with no food? Instead, Israel trusted in their leader and followed him into the desert. The text therefore praises the nation when it states: *Thus says the* LORD*: I remember in your favor, the devotion of your youth, your love as a bride, when you went after me in the wilderness, in a land that was not sown* (Jeremiah 2:2).

VERSE 23

PHILO

וְלֹא יָכְלוּ לִשְׁתֹּת — *But they could not drink:* At last, when they beheld some fountains, they ran up full of joy, believing that they were going to drink, but to their frustration they were deceived by ignorance of the truth, for the springs were bitter [*marim*, hence the place name "Mara"].

VERSE 24

MEKHILTA DERABBI SHIMON

וַיִּלֹּנוּ הָעָם — *The people railed:* Rabbi Yehoshua taught: What the people should have done was to consult the greatest among them [that is, Moshe] and ask him how to proceed if the water was undrinkable. Instead, they immediately attacked him with complaints. Rabbi Elazar HaModa'i taught: The Israelites were accustomed to criticizing Moshe, and indeed the people felt that it was acceptable to murmur against God Himself, hence the verse records Israel's accusation, *What are we to drink?*

they sang when Pharaoh's horses, chariots, and cavalry had gone into the sea / and the Lord had brought the waters of the sea back over them / while the Israelites had walked on dry land through the sea.

20 Then Miriam, the prophetess, sister of Aharon, took a tambourine in her hand, and all the women followed her with tam-
21 bourines and dance. And Miriam led them in song: Sing to the Lord, for He has triumphed in glory; / horse and horseman
22 He hurled into the sea.   Moshe then led the Israelites from the Sea of Reeds out into the desert of Shur. For three

---

LEKAḤ TOV (cont.)

(11:10), whereas the later success was effected through the leadership of women – specifically the prophetess Devora and Yael wife of Ḥever the Kenite.

VERSE 21

MEKHILTA DERABBI SHIMON

וַתַּעַן לָהֶם מִרְיָם – *And Miriam led them in song:* Just as Moshe had led the men in song, his sister Miriam directed the nation's women, declaring: *Sing to the Lord, for He has triumphed in glory.*

VERSE 22

TALMUD BAVLI

וְלֹא־מָצְאוּ מָיִם – *Without finding water:* Scholars who interpret the Torah metaphorically expound the verse as follows: The term "water" is an allusion to the Torah, as the verse states, *Behold! Everyone who thirsts, come to the water* (Isaiah 55:1). Our verse therefore means that after the nation had gone three days without learning Torah, they became weak. At this point the prophets among them established that the Torah should be read publicly on the Sabbath, a break should be made on the first day of the week, it should then be read on the second day [Monday], with a two-day break, followed by an additional reading on the fifth day [Thursday], and a final break on the last day of the week. This means that the people never go three days in succession without hearing the Torah being read. (Bava Kamma 82a)

TANḤUMA

אֶל־מִדְבַּר־שׁוּר – *Into the desert of Shur:* After the Holy One, blessed be He, drowned the Egyptian cavalry in the Sea of Reeds, all of the precious stones and pearls that had adorned the horses and chariots floated to the surface and washed up on the shore. Subsequently, the Israelites would go down to the beach every morning and collect the riches scattered along the sand. Once Moshe saw that the formerly impoverished slaves were reluctant to ever leave the seashore, he said to them: Do you think that the water holds an unlimited supply of jewels and wealth? He gathered the people and dragged them into the wilderness. (Buber, Beshalaḥ 16) וְלֹא־מָצְאוּ מָיִם – *Without finding water:* The water that Israel had collected from the sea had run out. When the verse states that the people could not find water, it means that even their vessels were now dry. (Beshalaḥ 19)

בָּא סוּס פַּרְעֹה בְּרִכְבּוֹ וּבְפָרָשָׁיו בַּיָּם וַיָּשֶׁב יְהוָה עֲלֵהֶם אֶת־מֵי הַיָּם וּבְנֵי יִשְׂרָאֵל הָלְכוּ בַיַּבָּשָׁה בְּתוֹךְ הַיָּם:

כ וַתִּקַּח מִרְיָם הַנְּבִיאָה אֲחוֹת אַהֲרֹן אֶת־הַתֹּף בְּיָדָהּ וַתֵּצֶאןָ
כא כָל־הַנָּשִׁים אַחֲרֶיהָ בְּתֻפִּים וּבִמְחֹלֹת: וַתַּעַן לָהֶם מִרְיָם שִׁירוּ
כב לַיהוָה כִּי־גָאֹה גָּאָה סוּס וְרֹכְבוֹ רָמָה בַיָּם: וַיַּסַּע מֹשֶׁה אֶת־יִשְׂרָאֵל מִיַּם־סוּף וַיֵּצְאוּ אֶל־מִדְבַּר־שׁוּר וַיֵּלְכוּ

VERSE 19

SEKHEL TOV

בַּיַּבָּשָׁה – *On dry land:* Not a single Israelite foot emerged dirty from the seabed, nor were anyone's shoes muddied from the experience. When the people saw this wonder, they readily accepted the kingship of God upon themselves.

VERSE 20

MEKHILTA DERABBI SHIMON

הַתֹּף – *A tambourine:* From where did Israel procure tambourines to play on the seashore following their crossing? During the exodus from Egypt the righteous among the Israelites were so sure that God would perform more miracles and wonders for them that they took musical instruments with them, to be ready to give thanks to Him.

TALMUD BAVLI

מִרְיָם הַנְּבִיאָה – *Miriam, the prophetess:* There have been seven prophetesses throughout the history of Israel. These are: Sara, Miriam, Devora, Ḥanna, Avigayil, Ḥulda, and Esther. The Torah attests to the prophetic ability of Miriam when it mentions *Miriam, the prophetess, sister of Aharon.* Was Miriam the sister of Aharon and not of Moshe? Rav Naḥman explained this verse in the name of Rav: Miriam had first prophesied when she was only the sister of Aharon [that is, before Moshe's birth], saying: "My mother is destined to give birth to a son who will redeem Israel." (Megilla 14a)

BERESHIT RABBA

אֲחוֹת אַהֲרֹן – *Sister of Aharon:* Why is Miriam referred to as the sister of Aharon and not of Moshe, if both men were her brothers? Because Aharon showed special concern for Miriam [by asking Moshe to pray for her in Numbers 12:11], the Torah labels her specifically as his sister. (Vayishlaḥ 80:10)

LEKAḤ TOV

וַתִּקַּח מִרְיָם – *Then Miriam took:* When the nation of Israel sang to God on the seashore, the men preceded the women. However, following Devora's victory [in Judges 4–5] the Israelite women sang first. This is because here the initial salvation was led by men, as the verse describes: *Moshe and Aharon had produced all these wonders before Pharaoh*

until Your people crossed, LORD, / until the people You acquired crossed over. / You will bring them, You will plant them on the mountain, Your heritage – / the place, LORD, that You made for Your dwelling, / the sanctuary, Lord, that Your hands established. / The LORD will reign for ever and all time. / This

AVOT DERABBI NATAN

כּוֹנְנוּ יָדֶיךָ – *That Your hands established:* What scriptural proof argues that God used both of His hands to create man? It is the verse that states: *Your hands have made me and fashioned me* (Psalms 119:73). And what verse shows that He constructed the Temple with both of His hands? The one that states: *The sanctuary, Lord, that Your hands established.* (1)

SHIR HASHIRIM RABBA

מָכוֹן לְשִׁבְתְּךָ פָּעַלְתָּ יהוה – *The place, LORD, that You made for Your dwelling:* When a person prays, he should focus his thoughts on the Holy of Holies in the Temple. Rabbi Ḥiyya the Great and Rabbi Shimon ben Ḥalafta disagreed as to how to interpret this dictum. Rabbi Ḥiyya the Great said this means that it refers to the celestial Holy of Holies, whereas Rabbi Shimon ben Ḥalafta insisted that one should think about the earthly chamber. Rabbi Pinḥas said: I manage to satisfy both approaches by thinking about how the heavenly Holy of Holies is situated opposite the earthly chamber, as the verse states: *The place, LORD, that You made for Your dwelling.* This refers to God's dwelling in the celestial Temple that stands above Mount Moria. (4:6)

VERSE 18

AVOT DERABBI NATAN

לְעֹלָם וָעֶד – *For ever and all time:* Everything that the Holy One, blessed be He, created in this world, He fashioned for His own glory, as the verse states: *Every one that is called by My name; for I have created him for My glory; I have formed him; I have made him* (Isaiah 43:7). Furthermore, we read, *The LORD will reign for ever and all time.* (41)

VAYIKRA RABBA

יִמְלֹךְ – *Will reign:* Said Moshe to the Holy One, blessed be He: "Master of the Universe! You have seventy principal nations in the world, and yet You have commanded me to teach just Israel, as You instruct me: *Speak to the Israelites* (Leviticus 23:2) or *Command the Israelites* (Numbers 28:2)." Answered God: "Yes, that is because Israel was the only nation to acknowledge me as their king, as they stated at the sea: *The LORD will reign for ever and all time.*" (Margaliot, Vayikra 2:4)

LEKAḤ TOV

יִמְלֹךְ – *Will reign:* Rabbi Yosei the Galilean taught: Had Israel at the sea declared: "The LORD is king over the entire world," they would have remained impervious to all attack by enemy nations. Instead they predicted only that *the LORD will reign,* meaning they anticipated that God's total authority would be established someday. The song of Moshe comprises eighteen verses. Correspondingly, our Sages composed a prayer of eighteen blessings [the *Amida*].

יַעֲבֹר עַמְּךָ יהוה עַד־יַעֲבֹר עַם־זוּ
יי קָנִיתָ: תְּבִאֵמוֹ וְתִטָּעֵמוֹ בְּהַר נַחֲלָתְךָ מָכוֹן
לְשִׁבְתְּךָ פָּעַלְתָּ יהוה מִקְּדָשׁ אֲדֹנָי כּוֹנְנוּ
יח יָדֶיךָ: יהוה ׀ יִמְלֹךְ לְעֹלָם וָעֶד: כִּי

MEKHILTA DERABBI SHIMON

תִּפֹּל עֲלֵיהֶם אֵימָתָה וָפַחַד – *Dread, terror fell upon them:* Those peoples who were near Egypt experienced "dread," while the nations situated at some distance felt "terror." Thus we read: *And it came to pass, when all the kings of the Amorites, who were on the side of the Jordan westward…heard that the* Lord *had dried up the waters of the Jordan…that their heart melted, neither was there spirit in them any more* (Joshua 5:1). **יִדְּמוּ כָּאָבֶן** – *They were stilled as stone:* After Israel crossed the sea, Amalek and all the nations of the world assembled in order to wage war against the Israelites. But Moshe prayed that the enemy be thwarted, and their voices were stilled like stone, leaving them unable to formulate a plan of attack. Thus the verse states: *By Your arm's power they were stilled as stone.*

TALMUD BAVLI

עַד־יַעֲבֹר עַמְּךָ – *Until Your people crossed:* The phrase *Until Your people crossed,* Lord, refers to the nation of Israel's first entry into the land [in the time of Yehoshua], whereas the subsequent phrase *until the people You acquired crossed over* relates to the nation's second entry [in the time of Ezra]. Based on this juxtaposition, our Sages say: During the time of Ezra the nation should have had a miracle performed for them, as occurred under the leadership of Yehoshua bin Nun [when the Jordan River was split for the people to cross], but their sins prevented such wonders. (Berakhot 4a)

VERSE 17

MEKHILTA DERABBI SHIMON

תְּבִאֵמוֹ וְתִטָּעֵמוֹ – *You will bring them, You will plant them:* The older generation prophesied, yet they were ignorant of what they were saying. For those who crossed the sea did not say: "You will bring us, You will plant us," but *You will bring them, You will plant them.* Somehow, they foretold that their children would enter the land but they would not [due to the sin of the spies; see Numbers 14:26–35]. This development is described in the verse *If you know not, O you fairest among women, go your way forth by the footsteps of the flock, and feed your kids besides the shepherds tents* (Song of Songs 1:8) — only the kids will enter the land, but the older animals will not.

TALMUD BAVLI

מִקְדָּשׁ – *Sanctuary:* Rabbi Elazar taught: The greatness of the Temple is indicated by its placement in between two instances of God's name, as the verse states: *the place,* Lord, *that You made for Your dwelling, the sanctuary, Lord, that Your hands established.* (Berakhot 33a)

13 Your right hand – / the earth swallowed them up. / In Your love, You guided out the people You redeemed. / In Your strength,
14 You led them to Your holy abode. / Nations heard and they
15 trembled; / terror seized the Philistines. / The chiefs of Edom were dismayed, then, / Moav's leaders were seized with trem-
16 bling, / the people of Canaan melted away. / Dread, terror fell upon them; / by Your arm's power they were stilled as stone – /

RUTH RABBA (cont.)

trembled; terror seized the Philistines. The chiefs of Edom were dismayed, then, Moav's leaders were seized with trembling, the people of Canaan melted away. Dread, terror fell upon them (15:14–16). But when Israel began to sin and commit wicked acts, the Holy One, blessed be He, said to them: "Do you think the rest of humanity respects you for your own greatness? Any honor that you receive is due to Me." Then the Holy One, blessed be He, turned His attention away from Israel just a bit, and that allowed Amalek to approach and attack them [in 17:8–16]. (Petiḥta 4)

MIDRASH AGGADA

חִיל אָחַז יֹשְׁבֵי פְּלָשֶׁת – *Terror seized the Philistines:* The Philistines were terrified because they had killed the people of Efrayim [who had left Egypt early; see I Chronicles 7:20–22].

VERSE 15

MEKHILTA DERABBI SHIMON

אַלּוּפֵי אֱדוֹם – *The chiefs of Edom:* Were the people of Edom [the descendants of Esav] afraid that Israel would conquer their land? Did not God state: *And command the people, saying, You are to pass through the border of your brethren the children of Esav…meddle not with them, for I will not give you their land* (Deuteronomy 2:4–5)? Rather, the Edomites were wary lest Israel attempt to take revenge, saying: Now they will seek retribution for the enmity that our father displayed toward theirs, as the verse states: *And Esav hated Yaakov because of the blessing with which his father blessed him* (Genesis 27:41).

אֵילֵי מוֹאָב – *Moav's leaders:* Were the people of Moav afraid that Israel would conquer their land? Did not God state: *Do not harass Moav, nor contend with them in battle; for I will not give you of their land for a possession* (Deuteronomy 2:9)? Rather, the Moabites were wary lest Israel attempt to take revenge, saying: Now they will seek retribution for the conflict between our father [Lot] and theirs, as the verse states: *And there was strife between the herdsmen of Avram's cattle and the herdsmen of Lot's cattle* (Genesis 13:7).

VERSE 16

MISHNA

עַד־יַעֲבֹר עַמְּךָ – *Until Your people crossed:* The Holy One, blessed be He, declared Five possessions as His own in His world: the Torah, heaven and earth, Avraham, Israel, and the Temple… How do we know this about Israel? Because it is written: *Until Your people crossed, Lord, until the people You acquired crossed over.* (Avot 6:10)

בְּחַסְדְּךָ עַם־זוּ גָּאָלְתָּ נֵהַלְתָּ בְעָזְּךָ אֶל־נְוֵה
קָדְשֶׁךָ: יד שָׁמְעוּ עַמִּים יִרְגָּזוּן חִיל
אָחַז יֹשְׁבֵי פְּלָשֶׁת: טו אָז נִבְהֲלוּ אַלּוּפֵי
אֱדוֹם אֵילֵי מוֹאָב יֹאחֲזֵמוֹ רָעַד נָמֹגוּ
כֹּל יֹשְׁבֵי כְנָעַן: טז תִּפֹּל עֲלֵיהֶם אֵימָתָה
וָפַחַד בִּגְדֹל זְרוֹעֲךָ יִדְּמוּ כָּאָבֶן עַד־

MEKHILTA DERABBI SHIMON *(cont.)*

are you from the earth, which has opened her mouth to receive your brother's blood from your hand (Genesis 4:11). How then can I receive the blood of this entire company?" Still, the Holy One, blessed be He, assured the land that it would assume no guilt for agreeing to take in the Egyptian bodies. Hence the verse states: *You reached out Your right hand* – the image of the right hand signifies an oath, as a later verse confirms: *The Lord has sworn by His right hand* (Isaiah 62:8).

VERSE 13

BEMIDBAR RABBA

נָחִיתָ – *You guided out:* The world stands on three pillars: Torah, the Temple service, and acts of righteousness. Moshe mentioned all three of these in a single verse. When he stated: *In Your love, You guided out the people You redeemed* – he referred to acts of righteousness. When he said: *In Your strength, You led them* – he referred to Torah study, as confirmed by the verse *The Lord gives strength to His people* [Psalms 29:11; the Torah is God's gift to Israel]; and when he finished with the words *To Your holy abode,* he referred to the service performed in the Tabernacle and the Temple. In addition, the phrase *In Your love, You guided out the people* refers to all the generations who lived from the time of creation to the point of the exodus. Those communities existed in an era before the Torah was given and before humanity understood how to behave properly. Yet the Holy One, blessed be He, graciously provided them with sustenance. That was the love by which He guided them. (Naso 12:12)

LEKAH TOV

בְּחַסְדְּךָ – *In Your love:* Even though Israel had performed no meritorious acts, God nevertheless redeemed the people thanks solely to His love for them. Thus the verse states, *I will mention the acts of the Lord's faithful love, and the praises of the Lord* (Isaiah 63:7). עַם־זוּ – *The people:* The term "people" refers exclusively to Israel, as the verse states: *This people have I formed for Myself; they shall relate My praise* (Isaiah 43:21).

VERSE 14

RUTH RABBA

שָׁמְעוּ עַמִּים יִרְגָּזוּן – *Nations heard and they trembled:* When Israel departed Egypt, all of the surrounding nations became terrified, as the text states: *Nations heard and they*

10 destroy them." / You blew with Your wind; the sea covered over
11 them. / They sank like lead in mighty waters. / Who is like You,
Lord, among the mighty? / Who is like You – majestic in holi-
12 ness, / awesome in glory, working wonders? / You reached out

VERSE 11

MEKHILTA DERABBI SHIMON

מִי־כָמֹכָה – *Who is like You:* When Israel saw that Pharaoh and all his cavalry had been destroyed by the sea, that the Egyptian kingdom had collapsed, and that God had made a mockery of the Egyptian gods, they began to sing praises of gratitude to God, saying: *Who is like You, Lord, among the mighty?* And it was not only Israel who reacted to the upheaval, but all the nations of the ancient world. When the gentile peoples learned what had befallen the Egyptians and their idolatry, they immediately renounced their own false religions and acknowledged the truth of God, proclaiming: *Who is like You, Lord, among the mighty?* And we can expect a similar revolution in the future, when communities around the world will abandon their idols, as the text states: *On that day a man shall cast his idols of silver, and his idols of gold, which had been made for him to worship…to go into the clefts of the rocks, and into the crevices of the ragged rocks, for fear of the Lord* (Isaiah 2:20–21). This will happen when *the idols shall utterly be abolished* (Isaiah 2:18).

TALMUD BAVLI

מִי־כָמֹכָה – *Who is like You:* Abba Ḥanan taught: When the psalmist states: *O Lord, who is like You?* (Psalms 89:9), it means: Who is like You, mighty in self-restraint? For you hear the blasphemy and the taunting of the wicked Titus and yet You are silent. The academy of Rabbi Yishmael taught: When the verse states: *Who is like You, Lord, among the mighty [ba'elim],* it should be understood: Who is like You among the mute ones [*illemim*, since You remain silent in the face of the blasphemers]. (Gittin 56b)

MIDRASH AGGADA

מִי־כָמֹכָה – *Who is like You:* Pharaoh himself recited this verse when he heard Israel singing their song on the seashore.

VERSE 12

MEKHILTA DERABBI SHIMON

תִּבְלָעֵמוֹ אָרֶץ – *The earth swallowed them up:* The verse attests to how the Creator holds in His hand the lives of every living being, as the verse states: *In whose hand is the soul of every living thing, the breath of all mankind* (Job 12:10). Why did the Egyptians merit a proper burial [in that the earth swallowed them]? They received that kindness by virtue of Pharaoh's earlier admission, *This time I have sinned. The Lord is in the right, and I and my people are guilty* (9:27). The Holy One, blessed be He, said to them: Because you confessed your wickedness, I will grant you an eternal burial, as the verse states: *The earth swallowed them up.* After drowning the cavalry, the sea cast the Egyptian bodies onto the shore, saying: "Take your children back." But the land pitched the corpses back into the sea, saying: "You killed them, you take them!" The earth explained itself: "When I agreed to absorb the blood of a single victim, Hevel, I was nevertheless cursed, as the verse states: *And now cursed*

יְ נַפְשִׁי אָרִיק חַרְבִּי תּוֹרִישֵׁמוֹ יָדִי: נָשַׁפְתָּ
בְרוּחֲךָ כִּסָּמוֹ יָם צָלֲלוּ כַּעוֹפֶרֶת בְּמַיִם
יא אַדִּירִים: מִי־כָמֹכָה בָּאֵלִם יהוה מִי
כָּמֹכָה נֶאְדָּר בַּקֹּדֶשׁ נוֹרָא תְהִלֹּת עֹשֵׂה
יב פֶלֶא: נָטִיתָ יְמִינְךָ תִּבְלָעֵמוֹ אָרֶץ: נָחִיתָ

MEKHILTA DERABBI SHIMON (cont.)

camp wanted to kill the Hebrews and plunder their wealth. Those who were only after the Israelites' possessions said: *I will divide the spoils*. Those Egyptians who were after blood said: *My desire shall gorge its fill of them*. And the third group which wanted to both murder and loot said: *I will draw my sword, and my hand destroy them*.

VAYIKRA RABBA

תּוֹרִישֵׁמוֹ יָדִי – *My hand destroy them:* Rabbi Shmuel bar Naḥman taught: Criminals are only ever dispatched from this world once they have pronounced their own sentences, as the verse states: *My hand destroy them* [torishemo yadi]. [The unusual form *torishemo* should be understood to mean:] I will bequeath [*morish*] to them my wealth and my honor as an inheritance. (Aḥarei Mot 21:1)

LEKAḤ TOV

תִּמְלָאֵמוֹ נַפְשִׁי – *My desire shall gorge its fill of them:* The wicked Pharaoh said to his army: In the past, whenever you all stole money from the Israelites, I exercised my authority to enforce its return. Now however, *I will divide the spoils*. In the past, whenever you murdered an Israelite, I took you to task for your behavior. Now however, *my desire shall gorge its fill of them*. **אָרִיק חַרְבִּי תּוֹרִישֵׁמוֹ יָדִי** – *I will draw my sword, and my hand destroy them*: This refers to the rape of the Israelites' sons and daughters.

VERSE 10

TALMUD BAVLI

בְּמַיִם אַדִּירִים – *In mighty waters:* Rabbi Ezra taught: Let the Almighty come and take vengeance upon the mighty, for the sake of the mighty, by means of the mighty. Let the Almighty come – this refers to the Holy One, blessed be He, as the verse states: *The Lord on high is mighty* (Psalms 93:4). For the sake of the mighty – this refers to Israel, as the verses states: *They are they mighty ones, in whom is all my delight* (Psalms 16:3). Upon the mighty – this refers to the Egyptians, as the verse states: *They sank like lead in mighty waters*. By means of the mighty – this refers to water, as the verse states: *The Lord on high is mightier than the noise of many waters, than the mighty waves of the sea* (Psalms 93:4). (Menaḥot 53a)

TANḤUMA

נָשַׁפְתָּ בְרוּחֲךָ – *You blew with Your wind:* The entire Egyptian army was killed with a single puff of God's breath, as the verse states: *You blew with Your wind; the sea covered over them*. (Re'eh 9)

6 them; / they sank to the depths like a stone. / Your right hand, Lord, majestic in power, / Your right hand, Lord, shatters the
7 enemy. / In the greatness of Your majesty, You overthrew those who rose against You. / You sent forth Your rage; it consumed
8 them like stubble. / By the blast of Your nostrils the waters heaped; / the surge stood upright as a wall; / the deeps con-
9 gealed at the heart of the sea. / The enemy said, "I will give chase, will overtake, / I will divide the spoils. / My desire shall gorge its fill of them. / I will draw my sword, / and my hand

---

LEKAḤ TOV

יֹאכְלֵמוֹ כַּקַּשׁ — *It consumed them like stubble:* The verb *yokhelemo* [which appears in the future tense] is actually a prophecy, as the verse states: *And the house of Yaakov shall be fire, and the house of Yosef flame, and the house of Esav stubble* (Obadiah 1:18). Burning plants make no noise, except for stubble, whose crackling sound can be heard from some distance. Such were the Egyptians, whose screams of torment traveled for miles. Burning plants leave behind charred remains, except for stubble, which is completely consumed. This comparison teaches that there was never a kingdom more despicable than ancient Egypt. They were only granted a brief moment of grandeur for the sake of Israel's honor [in defeating them].

VERSE 8

MEKHILTA DERABBI SHIMON

כְּמוֹ־נֵד — *As a wall:* Just like a full jug [*nod*] stands upright, so were the Egyptians frozen in place and overwhelmed by the smell of the sea.

LEKAḤ TOV

בְּלֶב־יָם — *At the heart of the sea:* Just like a heart is situated in a person's midst and sits high in the body toward the head, so did God collapse two sides of the sea upon the Egyptians and cover them from above.

YALKUT SHIMONI

בְּלֶב־יָם — *At the heart of the sea:* The sea had no heart until God gave it one, as the verse states: *The deeps congealed at the heart of the sea.* Declared God: Let the sea, who lacks a heart, come and punish the Egyptians who enslaved the Israelites, oppressing them with a variety of torments despite having a heart. (Beshalaḥ 248)

VERSE 9

MEKHILTA DERABBI SHIMON

אֶרְדֹּף אַשִּׂיג — *I will give chase, will overtake:* How could Israel have known what Pharaoh, sitting in Egypt, had been planning to do? The Israelites were granted divine inspiration and could divine Pharaoh's thoughts…. Now three separate Egyptian factions had attacked Israel. The first one declared: Let us merely rob them clean but not kill them. The second group was eager to slaughter the Israelites but cared nothing for their possessions. The third

¹ כְּמוֹ־אָבֶן: יְמִינְךָ יהוה נֶאְדָּרִי בַּכֹּחַ יְמִינְךָ
² יהוה תִּרְעַץ אוֹיֵב: וּבְרֹב גְּאוֹנְךָ תַּהֲרֹס
⁸ קָמֶיךָ תְּשַׁלַּח חֲרֹנְךָ יֹאכְלֵמוֹ כַּקַּשׁ: וּבְרוּחַ
אַפֶּיךָ נֶעֶרְמוּ מַיִם נִצְּבוּ כְמוֹ־נֵד
⁹ נֹזְלִים קָפְאוּ תְהֹמֹת בְּלֶב־יָם: אָמַר
אוֹיֵב אֶרְדֹּף אַשִּׂיג אֲחַלֵּק שָׁלָל תִּמְלָאֵמוֹ

YALKUT SHIMONI

תְּהֹמֹת יְכַסְיֻמוּ – *The deep waters covered them:* While the Egyptian cavalry sank into the sea, the lower water and the upper water vied with each other to torment the soldiers with all sorts of miseries. Hence the verse states: *the deep waters covered them* [using plural language]. Another interpretation: The deepest waters rose above the higher strata of water and blocked out the sky from their view, darkening the stars, as the verse states: *All the bright lights of heaven will I make dark over you, and set darkness upon your land, says the* LORD *God* (Ezekiel 32:8). (Beshalaḥ 246)

VERSE 6

MEKHILTA DERABBI SHIMON

יְמִינְךָ – *Your right hand:* As long as Israel fulfills the will of God, He will treat His left hand [generally employed to punish] as His right hand [which metes out mercies]. Thus the verse states: *Your right hand…Your right hand.* [Surely God does not have two right hands, and hence His left was working to Israel's benefit just like His right.] Conversely, when Israel ignores the will of God, He treats His right hand as His left hand, as the verse states, *He has drawn back His right hand from before the enemy* (Lamentations 2:3).

AGGADAT BERESHIT

יְמִינְךָ – *Your right hand:* Whenever you hear of God's right hand, it is indication that God is acting in Israel's defense. (24)

MIDRASH TEHILLIM

יְמִינְךָ – *Your right hand:* Rabbi Shimon ben Lakish taught: The sea swallowed up both the Egyptians and the Israelites. But the Holy One, blessed be He, reached out His right hand to rescue Israel, while simultaneously using that same hand to sink the Egyptians. Thus the verse states: *Your right hand,* LORD, *majestic in power,* referring to the salvation of the Hebrews, and *Your right hand,* LORD, *shatters the enemy,* describing the destruction of the Egyptians. (18)

VERSE 7

SIFREI BEMIDBAR

קָמֶיךָ – *Those who rose against you:* How is it possible to rise against the Creator? Rather, the verse teaches that when an enemy assaults Israel, it is as if they have attacked God Himself. (Behaalotekha 84)

strength and song – / and now my salvation. / This is my God, I will glorify Him, / my father's God, I will exalt Him. / The Lord is a Master of war; / the Lord is His name. / Pharaoh's chariots and army / He hurled into the sea; / the best of his officers / drowned in the Sea of Reeds. / The deep waters covered

---

PESIKTA RABBATI (cont.)

seemed to you like a bridegroom preparing to enter his wedding canopy. Thus the verse states: *What shall I liken to you, O daughter of Jerusalem?* [Lamentations 2:13; the first phrase can also be understood to mean "how shall I appear to you?"]. (33)

VERSE 4

BEMIDBAR RABBA

יָרָה בַיָּם – *He hurled into the sea:* The Egyptians had only been bold enough to challenge God through water, as the verse states: *Then Pharaoh commanded his entire people, saying, "Throw every boy that is born into the Nile"* (1:22). And hence God was sure to punish them with that medium, as the verse states: *Pharaoh's chariots and army He hurled into the sea.* (Naso 9:24)

SEKHEL TOV

וּמִבְחַר שָׁלִשָׁיו – *The best of his officers:* Such was the fate of the *officers over them all* (14:7). The horses, who were swift runners, were sunk like lead and mired in mud, as the verse states: *They drowned [tubbe'u] in the Sea of Reeds.* The Egyptian cavalry actually drowned in the ocean sludge, and this is what the verb *tubbe'u* implies, as the verse states: *And in the pit there was no water, but only mire, and Yirmeyahu sank [vayitba] in the mire* (Jeremiah 38:6). Similarly, we read, *I sink [tavati] in deep mire, where there is no standing* (Psalms 69:3). Now this entire episode shows God punishing Egypt measure for measure. Firstly, Pharaoh led his "officers" against Israel [as reported in 14:7], but God drowned the same "officers" [as described here]. Secondly, because the oppressors had made the Hebrews' lives miserable through clay [see 1:14], the sea water was transformed into suffocating mud which swallowed up the army.

VERSE 5

MEKHILTA DERABBI SHIMON

כְּמוֹ־אָבֶן – *Like a stone:* This refers only to the soldiers with mediocre characters. The relatively decent men within Pharaoh's army floated on the surface like "stubble" (15:7); the average individuals sunk to the bottom like "stone"; but the truly wicked Egyptians sank *like lead in mighty waters* [15:10; according to this interpretation, lead sinks faster than stone]. The common soldiers sank like stones in retribution for Pharaoh's command to the midwives, *When you help a Hebrew woman give birth, look on the birthstool* [literally, "on the stones"] (1:16). Said God: You took the moment of birth, which should be tender as water, and turned it into the harshness of stone. An additional reason why the soldiers sank like rocks is that they had turned their hearts to stone in their treatment of the Israelites.

לִישׁוּעָה׃ זֶה אֵלִי וְאַנְוֵהוּ אֱלֹהֵי
אָבִי וַאֲרֹמְמֶנְהוּ׃ יהוה אִישׁ מִלְחָמָה יהוה
שְׁמוֹ׃ מַרְכְּבֹת פַּרְעֹה וְחֵילוֹ יָרָה בַיָּם וּמִבְחַר
שָׁלִשָׁיו טֻבְּעוּ בְיַם־סוּף׃ תְּהֹמֹת יְכַסְיֻמוּ יָרְדוּ בִמְצוֹלֹת

SIFREI DEVARIM (cont.)

And He came [ata] from holy multitudes (Deuteronomy 33:2) — that is, God is the sign [*ot*] among His company [obviously more exalted than anyone in His retinue]. This was made apparent on the shores of the Sea of Reeds, as the verse states: *This is my God* [immediately identifiable]. (Vezot Haberakha 343)

TALMUD BAVLI

וְאַנְוֵהוּ – *I will glorify Him:* One does this by adorning oneself before God through fulfillment of the commandments. Construct a beautiful sukka, prepare an impressive lulav, use a sonorous shofar, wear well-woven tzitzit, write a Torah with stunning script, in rich ink, using a well-honed quill, executed by a skilled scribe, and wrapped in colorful silks. [All of the adjectives in this sentence appear as *na'eh* in Hebrew, evoking the term *ve'anvehu*.] Abba Sha'ul taught: The term *anvehu* [should be understood as a contraction of *ani vehu*, meaning "I and He."] One must imitate God: Just like God is gracious and compassionate, so should we be gracious and compassionate. (Shabbat 133b)

VERSE 3

MEKHILTA DERABBI SHIMON

יהוה שְׁמוֹ – *The Lord is His name:* The strength of a soldier may be great at the age of forty, but it wanes at age sixty or seventy; the older he gets, the lesser are his abilities. But the Creator is not like that: *The Lord is a Master of war; the Lord is His name.* His name was the Lord in the past when He defeated the Egyptians, and His name remains such forever after — He is the Lord and He does not change.

SIFREI BEMIDBAR

אִישׁ מִלְחָמָה – *A Master of war:* God does not behave like human beings. When kings go to war, they surround themselves with as many men as they can muster, and when they sue for peace their delegations are small. But when the Creator wages war, He acts alone, as the verse states: *The Lord is a Master of war,* and when He strives for peace He is accompanied by myriads, as the verse states: *The chariots of God are twice ten thousand, thousands upon thousands, the Lord is among them* (Psalms 68:18). (Behaalotekha 102)

PESIKTA RABBATI

אִישׁ מִלְחָמָה – *A Master of war:* [Says God:] In what forms have I appeared? When you stood on the seashore, I seemed like a great warrior engaging the enemy in battle, as the verse states: *The Lord is a Master of war.* At Mount Sinai I assumed the likeness of an elderly scholar, for the Torah is best received when taught by sages. At the Tabernacle I

unleashed against the Egyptians, the people were in awe of the Lord, and they believed in Him and in Moshe His servant.

15 1 And then, Moshe and the Israelites sang this song to the Lord: I will sing to the Lord, for He has triumphed in glory; / 2 horse and horseman He hurled into the sea. / The Lord is my

---

TALMUD BAVLI

אָז יָשִׁיר־מֹשֶׁה – *Then Moshe sang:* Rabbi Meir taught: An allusion to the future resurrection of the dead appears in the verse: *Moshe and the Israelites sang this song to the Lord.* The text does not actually report that Moshe "sang" [*shar*], but that he "will sing" [*yashir*]. Thus the Torah itself teaches that the dead will one day be resurrected [and Moshe will sing once more]. (Sanhedrin 92b) כִּי־גָאֹה גָּאָה – *For He has triumphed in glory:* Rabbi Shimon ben Lakish taught: Why is the word "triumph" [*ga'a*] repeated? Moshe prepared to sing a song to He who had triumphed over the triumphant. For a master taught: The lion is the king of wild animals; the ox is the king of livestock; the eagle is the king of the birds. And although man triumphs over all the animal kingdom, the Holy One, blessed be He, triumphs in glory above the entire universe. (Ḥagiga 13b)

SHEMOT RABBA

אָז יָשִׁיר־מֹשֶׁה – *Then Moshe sang:* The psalmist writes: *Your throne is established of old* [*me'az*] (Psalms 93:2). Rabbi Berekhya taught in the name of Rabbi Abbahu: Even though *You [God] are everlasting,* Your throne was not firmly established, nor was Your name thoroughly known in Your world, until Your children sang this song to You, as the verse states: *Then [az] Moshe sang.* (Beshalaḥ 23:1)

MIDRASH AGGADA

אָז יָשִׁיר־מֹשֶׁה – *Then Moshe sang:* Why does the text of Moshe's song to God begin with the word "then" [*az*]? Said Moshe: I abused the word *az* when I complained about my mission, saying: *Ever since* [*me'az*] *I came to Pharaoh to speak in Your name, he has dealt worse with this people* (5:23). So I will now atone by employing the word *az* in my praise of God. Another interpretation of *az*: The numerical value of the word *az* is eight, which teaches that Israel were rescued at the sea by virtue of circumcision which the nation was commanded to perform on a baby's eighth day. Moshe remembered that the word *az* was associated with this rite, which had saved his own life, as the verse states: *Then [az] "A bridegroom of blood," she said, "because of circumcision"* (4:26). Another allusion of the word *az* is to the Master of the world, who remains one above the seven celestial spheres [yielding a total of eight].

VERSE 2

SIFREI DEVARIM

זֶה אֵלִי – *This is my God:* A king of flesh and blood who walks among his entourage knows full well that the group comprises men who are more handsome than he is, that there are others who are more skilled than he, and even that among his servants are heroes braver than he will ever be. But the King of Kings, the Creator, is not like that, as the verse states:

הַגְּדֹלָה אֲשֶׁר עָשָׂה יהוה בְּמִצְרַיִם וַיִּירְאוּ הָעָם אֶת־יהוה וַיַּאֲמִינוּ בַּיהוָה וּבְמֹשֶׁה עַבְדּוֹ:

טו א אָז יָשִׁיר־מֹשֶׁה וּבְנֵי יִשְׂרָאֵל אֶת־הַשִּׁירָה הַזֹּאת לַיהוָה וַיֹּאמְרוּ לֵאמֹר אָשִׁירָה לַיהוָה כִּי־גָאֹה גָּאָה סוּס ב וְרֹכְבוֹ רָמָה בַיָּם: עָזִּי וְזִמְרָת יָהּ וַיְהִי־לִי

SHEMOT RABBA

הַיָּד הַגְּדֹלָה – *The wondrous power:* [Literally, "the great hand."] The Holy One, blessed be He, visited fifty plagues upon the Egyptians when they encountered Israel at the sea. For a previous verse [referring to the plague of lice] states: *"This,"* the magicians told Pharaoh, *"is the finger of God"* (8:15), whereas at the splitting of the sea, the verse mentions God's "great hand." If using just one finger God smote Egypt with ten plagues, it follows that when He employed His entire hand, He struck the villains with ten punishments for each finger, yielding a total of fifty torments at the sea. (Shemot 5:14)

SEKHEL TOV

הַיָּד הַגְּדֹלָה – *The wondrous power:* [Literally, "the great hand."] It is unclear whether God employed His right hand or His left hand. Hence a subsequent text settles the question: *Your right hand, Lord, majestic in power* (15:6). This proves that God used His right hand [i.e., the stronger one] to smash the Egyptian army.

CHAPTER 15, VERSE 1

MISHNA

אֶת־הַשִּׁירָה הַזֹּאת – *This song:* [The Hebrew phrase *vayomeru lemor* – literally, "and they said, saying" – is left untranslated here.] Rabbi Akiva taught: How should we understand the phrase *vayomeru lemor*? It means that Moshe and the people engaged in responsive singing – the leader expressed a praise of God, and Israel repeated the verse. This is similar to the way in which the Hallel is recited. (Sota 5:4)

MEKHILTA DERABBI SHIMON

רָמָה – *He hurled:* Two texts appear to contradict each other. One verse states, *He hurled into the sea* [an upward motion] while a subsequent verse claims, *they sank to the depths like a stone* (15:4). The verses imply that God both lifted the cavalry up to the heavens and cast them into the depths. The horses and their riders remained bound together during the turmoil. Usually, when one tosses two objects into the air, they fly in different directions. But in this case the water swirled the men and beasts up and down together in a whirlpool.

MIDRASH TANNA'IM DEVARIM

סוּס וְרֹכְבוֹ – *Horse and horseman He hurled into the sea:* Was there merely a single horse and a single horseman who rode it? Did not an earlier verse state: *He took six hundred elite chariots and all the other chariots of Egypt* (14:7)? What this teaches is that when Israel holds God's favor, the power of their enemies is reduced to that of a single soldier. (20:1)

29 into the sea. Not one of them remained. But the Israelites had walked through the sea on dry land, with a wall of water to their
30 right and left. That day, the LORD saved the Israelites from the Egyptians. And when the Israelites saw the Egyptians dead on
31 the seashore, and witnessed the wondrous power the LORD had

---

MEKHILTA DERABBI SHIMON *(cont.)*

were raised to the surface was to expose the axles, which had been covered with silver and gold, precious stones, and pearls. Israel was able to plunder the Egyptian wealth by combing the beach. An additional purpose for displaying the enemy corpses was to allow Israel to view them and rebuke their former tormentors for their wickedness, as the verse states: *But I will reprove you, and set the matter before your eyes* (Psalms 50:21).

TALMUD BAVLI

מֵת עַל־שְׂפַת הַיָּם – *Dead on the seashore:* Standing on the seashore, the Israelites rebelled against God and complained: "How do we know that the Egyptians will not emerge from the sea on a different beach, just as we escaped drowning by climbing ashore here?" To counter this, the Holy One, blessed be He, said to the guardian angel of the sea: "Expel the dead Egyptians upon the land." Said the angel to Him: "Master of the Universe! If a master gives his servant a gift, does he then ask for it back?" God responded: "What if I give you one-and-a-half times their number?" But the angel retorted: "Master of the Universe! Can a slave ever ensure the collection of a debt from His master?" Said God: "I hereby pledge the Kishon River as a surety." Immediately the sea spat out the Egyptian bodies, and the Israelites came down to the shore to view them, as the verse states: *The Israelites saw the Egyptians dead on the seashore.* (Pesaḥim 118b)

VERSE 31

MEKHILTA DERABBI SHIMON

וַיַּאֲמִינוּ בַּיהוה וּבְמֹשֶׁה עַבְדּוֹ – *And they believed in Him and in Moshe:* The verse seems redundant – if Israel believed in Moshe, they certainly trusted that God was fighting their battle for them. Rather, the text teaches that whenever one believes in the mission of a prophet of Israel, that individual necessarily accepts the existence of the Creator. We conversely read: *And the people spoke against God, and against Moshe* (Numbers 21:5), which again appears to state the obvious: If the nation's trust in God had been shaken, they clearly would reject the right of Moshe to lead them. Rather, the text teaches that whenever one challenges the authority of God's representatives, it is as if he has criticized his Creator.

TANḤUMA

וַיַּאֲמִינוּ בַּיהוה וּבְמֹשֶׁה עַבְדּוֹ – *And they believed in Him and in Moshe:* Why did Israel merit the privilege of singing God's praises at the sea [in the next verse]? It was a reward for the faith in God that they had gained from the experience, as the verse states: *And they believed in Him and in Moshe His servant.* (Buber, Beshalaḥ 11)

כט בַּיָּם לֹא־נִשְׁאַר בָּהֶם עַד־אֶחָד: וּבְנֵי יִשְׂרָאֵל הָלְכוּ בַיַּבָּשָׁה
ל בְּתוֹךְ הַיָּם וְהַמַּיִם לָהֶם חֹמָה מִימִינָם וּמִשְּׂמֹאלָם: וַיּוֹשַׁע
יהוה בַּיּוֹם הַהוּא אֶת־יִשְׂרָאֵל מִיַּד מִצְרָיִם וַיַּרְא יִשְׂרָאֵל
לא אֶת־מִצְרַיִם מֵת עַל־שְׂפַת הַיָּם: וַיַּרְא יִשְׂרָאֵל אֶת־הַיָּד

SEKHEL TOV *(cont.)*

purpose — to show you My power, and to have My name known throughout the land (9:16). However, other scholars believe that Pharaoh did subsequently enter the water and meet his end there, as the verse states: *[He] overthrew Pharaoh and his host in the Sea of Reeds* (Psalms 136:15). Now it is not difficult to reconcile these two interpretations. At first, the king accompanied his army into the sea, where the Holy One, blessed be He, tripped him onto his face and covered him with water. But before Pharaoh was allowed to drown, God dispatched an angel to pull him from the water and direct him to Nineveh. There Pharaoh was charged with publicizing the name of God throughout the land and singing His praises and His might before all of humanity. Hence our Sages claim that Pharaoh subsequently ruled Nineveh for five hundred years. He was the one who led the people of Nineveh to repent of their wicked ways [see Jonah 3:6–9].

VERSE 29
MEKHILTA DERABBI SHIMON

בַּיַּבָּשָׁה בְּתוֹךְ הַיָּם — *Through the sea on dry land:* The ministering angels hovered in shock and protested: How could these humans who worshipped idolatry in Egypt be permitted to cross the sea on dry land? The sea too was overcome with fury [*ḥema*] at being required to service Israel and desired to destroy them, for the verse states, *with a wall [ḥoma] of water to their right and left*.

TANḤUMA

בַּיַּבָּשָׁה בְּתוֹךְ הַיָּם — *Through the sea on dry land:* Rabbi Aḥa taught in the name of Rabbi Shmuel bar Naḥman: All of the miracles that the Holy One, blessed be He, intends to perform in the messianic age have already been demonstrated in this world on a smaller scale by the righteous. For example, the Holy One, blessed be He, plans to resurrect the dead, an act that the prophets Eliyahu, Elisha, and Yeḥezkel already practiced in a limited fashion [see I Kings 17, II Kings 4, and Ezekiel 37]. Similarly, God will eventually transform the seas into dry land, a deed that Moshe first did, as the verse states: *But the Israelites had walked through the sea on dry land*. (Emor 9)

VERSE 30
MEKHILTA DERABBI SHIMON

מֵת עַל־שְׂפַת הַיָּם — *Dead on the seashore:* God wanted to prevent the Egyptian people from claiming: Just as our cavalry was drowned in the sea, so too were the Israelites swallowed up by the water [hence he made the casualties visible to all]. Another reason the chariots

flee from the Israelites. The LORD is fighting for them against Egypt."

26 Then the LORD said to Moshe, "Stretch out your hand over the sea. The waters will flow back over the Egyptians and their
27 chariots and cavalry." Moshe stretched out his hand over the sea, and at daybreak the water came back in full force. The Egyptians fled at its approach but the LORD swept them into
28 the sea. The waters returned, covering the chariots, the cavalry, and the whole Egyptian army that had followed the Israelites

REVI'I

BERESHIT RABBA *(cont.)*
---

ben Elazar said: It was not only the seas that the Holy One, blessed be He, fashioned on such conditions. All of creation is subject to future divine manipulation. (Bereshit 5:5)

SHEMOT RABBA

נָסִים לִקְרָאתוֹ – *Fled at its approach:* [Literally, "fled toward it."] Should the text not have stated that the enemy ran away from the water, rather than toward it? Can an individual flee his fellow and approach him at the same time? Rather, what the verse implies is that the Holy One, blessed be He, discombobulated the Egyptians so they did not know which way to run. The cavalry ended up charging full force into the battering waves, until they sank in the ocean's depths, as the verse states: *But the LORD swept them into the sea.* (Bo 15:15)

SHIR HASHIRIM RABBA

וַיְנַעֵר – *Swept:* [The verb connotes the stirring of a pot.] This verse describes the swirling maelstrom to which God subjected the Egyptian cavalry. He cast the horses down and shot their riders upward. Then He drove the beasts into the depths and swept the soldiers toward the surface. Rabbi Levi taught: It was akin to a chef who mixes a soup – he scoops the bottom material to the top and stirs the upper liquid to the bottom of the pot. (1:6)

VERSE 28

PHILO

לֹא־נִשְׁאַר בָּהֶם עַד־אֶחָד – *Not one of them remained:* Not even a torchbearer survived to announce to the people of Egypt the disaster that had befallen Pharaoh's army.

TALMUD BAVLI

לֹא־נִשְׁאַר בָּהֶם עַד־אֶחָד – *Not one of them remained:* At that moment, the ministering angels wished to sing songs of praise before the Holy One, blessed be He. Said He to them: People I have created are drowning in the sea, and you wish to sing about it? (Sanhedrin 39b)

SEKHEL TOV

לֹא־נִשְׁאַר בָּהֶם עַד־אֶחָד – *Not one of them remained:* Not a single Egyptian was left standing on the beach – every soldier entered the sea, and all were enveloped by the waters and swept away. Rabbi Neḥemya taught: But not Pharaoh – he emerged unscathed from the devastation, as God explained in an earlier verse: *But I have let you survive for this*

וַיֹּאמֶר מִצְרַיִם אָנוּסָה מִפְּנֵי יִשְׂרָאֵל כִּי יהוה נִלְחָם לָהֶם בְּמִצְרָיִם:

רביעי כו וַיֹּאמֶר יהוה אֶל־מֹשֶׁה נְטֵה אֶת־יָדְךָ עַל־הַיָּם וְיָשֻׁבוּ הַמַּיִם עַל־מִצְרַיִם עַל־רִכְבּוֹ וְעַל־פָּרָשָׁיו: וַיֵּט מֹשֶׁה אֶת־יָדוֹ עַל־הַיָּם וַיָּשָׁב הַיָּם לִפְנוֹת בֹּקֶר לְאֵיתָנוֹ וּמִצְרַיִם נָסִים לִקְרָאתוֹ וַיְנַעֵר יהוה אֶת־מִצְרַיִם בְּתוֹךְ הַיָּם: וַיָּשֻׁבוּ הַמַּיִם וַיְכַסּוּ אֶת־הָרֶכֶב וְאֶת־הַפָּרָשִׁים לְכֹל חֵיל פַּרְעֹה הַבָּאִים אַחֲרֵיהֶם

VERSE 26

SHEMOT RABBA

וַיָשֻׁבוּ הַמַּיִם – *The waters will flow back:* Rabbi Elazar ben Rabbi Shimon taught: Because the Egyptians were wily, they are compared to a fox, whose scheming is punctuated by constant glances behind him. Similarly did the Egyptians slyly seek to avoid prosecution even while enslaving Israel. When the verse states: *Come, let us deal wisely with them* (1:10), it describes the oppressors' plan to subjugate the people in a manner that their God would not be able to hold them accountable. [Believing that God only punishes the wicked measure for measure,] they said: If we rule Israel by the sword, the Lord will dispatch our enemies to slaughter us on the battlefield. Should we persecute Israel with fire, He will an unleash a firestorm against us. But we know that God has vowed never to flood the world again [see Genesis 9:11]. Hence let us use the element of water to control the Hebrews. But the Holy One, blessed be He, responded: Villains! Do you not see that although I have sworn not to inundate the entire planet, I reserve the right to flood parts of the world and submerge individual nations? (Beshalaḥ 22:1)

VERSE 27

MEKHILTA DERABBI SHIMON

וַיְנַעֵר יהוה אֶת־מִצְרַיִם בְּתוֹךְ הַיָּם – *The Lord swept them into the sea:* Our early scholars taught: The lash that the nations use to whip Israel will eventually be wielded by the Jews against their enemies. Thus, the entire world would do well to learn from Pharaoh's folly. For he imposed slavery upon Israel, and the Holy One, blessed be He, subsequently drowned him in the sea, as the verse states: *The Lord swept them into the sea*. But Amalek did not appreciate the lesson and attacked Israel. And so God vowed to wipe them off the face of the earth and obliterate them from the world to come. (17:14) **וַיְנַעֵר** – *Swept:* God strengthened the Egyptians with the fortitude of youth [*naarut*, evoking *vayna'er*] to enable them to suffer the punishment He meted out [rather than immediately expiring].

BERESHIT RABBA

לְאֵיתָנוֹ – *In full force:* Rabbi Yoḥanan taught: When He created the seas of the world, the Holy One, blessed be He, included a stipulation [*tenai*] that they would agree to be divided on Israel's behalf, as hinted by the verse: *The water came back in full force [le'eitano].* Rabbi Yirmeya

23 left, the water was like a wall. The Egyptians chased after them. All Pharaoh's horses, chariots and cavalry followed them into
24 the sea. During the last watch of the night, the Lord looked down at the Egyptian army from a column of fire and cloud
25 and threw them into a panic, clogging their chariot wheels so that it was hard for them to move. The Egyptians said, "Let us

--- **MEKHILTA DERABBI SHIMON** *(cont.)* ---

no time in the new day punishing the wicked, as the verse states: *Morning by morning I will destroy all the wicked of the land* (Psalms 101:8).

--- **LEKAH TOV** ---

וַיַּשְׁקֵף – *Looked down:* Witness the wonders of the Creator! For He employs the same power for destruction that He uses to repair. On the one hand, God exercises His faculty of observation to the benefit of Israel, as the verse states: *Look down from Your holy habitation, from heaven and bless Your people Israel, and the land which You have given us, as You did swear to our fathers* (Deuteronomy 26:15). On the other hand, that same gaze was directed against the Egyptians to throw them into a panic, as the verse states: *the Lord looked down at the Egyptian army*.

VERSE 25

--- **MEKHILTA DERABBI SHIMON** ---

וַיָּסַר אֵת אֹפַן מַרְכְּבֹתָיו – *Clogging their chariot wheels:* Rabbi Yehuda taught: The heat from the pillar of fire from above burned the chariot wheels below. This resulted in the horses dragging the axles on the ground as the animals disobeyed their riders' commands to halt. For the vehicles were festooned with silver and gold, precious stones, and pearls – God had directed the Egyptians to decorate their chariots so that Israel could later collect the plunder. Rabbi Nehemya explained: It was thunder in the heavens that caused lightning to streak toward earth and snap off the chariot wheels, as the verse states: *The voice of Your thunder was in the whirlwind; the lightnings lightened the world the earth trembled and shook* (Psalms 77:19). וַיְנַהֲגֵהוּ בִּכְבֵדֻת – *So that it was hard for them to move:* The Egyptians were thus paid back in kind for the wickedness they perpetrated. For the oppressors had declared, *Make the work harder for the people* (5:9). אָנוּסָה – *Let us flee:* Foolish soldiers within the army urged: "Are we to flee from these ragged and downtrodden people?" But the intelligent Egyptians grasped what was really happening and retorted: "The Lord who fights for them against Egypt will continue to perform miracles on Israel's behalf throughout history."

--- **YALKUT SHIMONI** ---

בְּמִצְרָיִם – *Against Egypt:* [Literally, "in Egypt."] Rabbi Yosei said: The punishments unleashed against the soldiers at the sea were mirrored by sufferings the Egyptian civilians endured at home. The two groups witnessed each other's torments, as the verses state: *When the wicked, my enemies and my foes came upon me to eat up my flesh, they stumbled and fell* (Psalms 27:2), and *I would soon subdue their enemies, and turn my hand against their enemies* (Psalms 81:15). [Both of these verses employ two parallel terms for "enemy": *tzar* and *oyev*, hinting that God's wrath was directed at two fronts.] (Beshalah 235)

כג וּמִשְׂמֹאלָם: וַיִּרְדְּפוּ מִצְרַיִם וַיָּבֹאוּ אַחֲרֵיהֶם כֹּל סוּס
כד פַּרְעֹה רִכְבּוֹ וּפָרָשָׁיו אֶל־תּוֹךְ הַיָּם: וַיְהִי בְּאַשְׁמֹרֶת הַבֹּקֶר
וַיַּשְׁקֵף יהוה אֶל־מַחֲנֵה מִצְרַיִם בְּעַמּוּד אֵשׁ וְעָנָן וַיָּהָם אֵת
כה מַחֲנֵה מִצְרָיִם: וַיָּסַר אֵת אֹפַן מַרְכְּבֹתָיו וַיְנַהֲגֵהוּ בִּכְבֵדֻת

VERSE 23

MEKHILTA DERABBI SHIMON

וַיִּרְדְּפוּ מִצְרַיִם – *The Egyptians chased after them:* The Holy One, blessed be He, put the Egyptian horses and their riders on trial. Said He to the horses: "Why have you pursued My children?" "The soldiers drove us after Israel against our will," they protested, "as the verse states, *The Egyptians chased after them.*" God then turned to the humans and demanded: "Why have you hunted My children?" "It was the horses which carried us after them against our will," they answered, "as the verse states, *Pharaoh's horses, chariots and cavalry had gone into the sea* (15:19)." So the Holy One, blessed be He, put the riders on their mounts and judged them together.

SEKHEL TOV

כֹּל סוּס פַּרְעֹה – *All Pharaoh's horses:* The Holy One, blessed be He, lured the Egyptian horses into the sea by conjuring the image of a mare to appear before the cavalry's steeds. God sculpted a cloud to take this form, enticing the herd into the waves and overriding the beasts' natural inclination to avoid water. Meanwhile, their riders tried to restrain them from following the apparition despite being armed and ready to attack Israel.

VERSE 24

MEKHILTA DERABBI SHIMON

וַיְהִי בְּאַשְׁמֹרֶת הַבֹּקֶר – *During the last watch of the night:* [Literally, "the morning watch."] At first it was unclear whether Israel would be drowned in the sea along with the Egyptians or be spared that horrible fate. But thanks to the early rising of Avraham [to bind his son Yitzḥak generations earlier], the scale was tipped in his descendants' favor, as the verse states: *And Avraham rose up early in the morning* (Genesis 22:3). And the eagerness of Yitzḥak on that same day added to Israel's credit, as the verse states: *And they went both of them together* (Genesis 22:6). Furthermore, Yaakov's early-hour ardor [to give thanks to God after His revelation at Beit El] stood Israel in good stead, as the verse states, *And Yaakov rose up early in the morning* (Genesis 28:18). Indeed, morning enthusiasm would later become an admirable feature of Israelite behavior, as the Torah reports with Moshe: *So Moshe carved two stone tablets like the first. He rose early in the morning and climbed Mount Sinai* (34:4). We later see the same fervor with Moshe's disciple Yehoshua [on the day the nation crossed the Jordan River into Israel] in the verse *And Yehoshua rose early in the morning* (Joshua 3:1). Similarly, we find that *Shmuel rose early to meet Sha'ul in the morning* (I Samuel 15:12). In future times, the prophets will rise at dawn to spread the word of God, as the verse states: *They are new every morning, great is Your faithfulness* (Lamentations 3:23). So will spirituality propagate through the messianic era, as we read: *O Lord, in the morning I will direct my prayer to You, and will wait expectantly* (Psalms 5:4). Conversely, God wastes

darkness for one, but lighting the night for the other, keeping
21 the two apart all night. Then Moshe stretched out his hand over the sea, and the LORD drove the sea back by a strong east wind
22 all night, turning it to dry land and dividing the waters. So the Israelites walked through the sea on dry land. To their right and

---

BERESHIT RABBA

וַיִּבָּקְעוּ הַמַּיִם – *Dividing the waters:* Rabbi Ḥiyya bar Yosei taught in the name of Rabbi Miyasha — and some traditions attribute the teaching to Rabbi Benaya: As a reward for the splitting that Avraham performed at the binding of Yitzḥak, his descendants were rewarded in kind. For in the former episode, the verse states, *Avraham chopped up the wood for the burnt offering* (Genesis 22:3), while in the latter case the verse reads, *the LORD drove the sea back…dividing the waters.* (Vayera 55:8)

VERSE 22

MEKHILTA DERABBI SHIMON

וַיָּבֹאוּ בְנֵי־יִשְׂרָאֵל בְּתוֹךְ הַיָּם בַּיַּבָּשָׁה – *So the Israelites walked through the sea on dry land:* Rabbi Meir expounded this verse to the credit of the tribes as follows. When Israel arrived at the seashore, the tribes vied with each other for the privilege of entering the water first. While the rest were busy competing, the tribe of Binyamin got up and jumped into the waves, as the verse states: *There is Binyamin, the youngest, ruling them [rodem]* (Psalms 68:28) — read the word not as *rodem* but as *rad yam* [meaning "descended to the sea"]. In response, the tribe of Yehuda began pelting [*lirgom*] them with stones, as the verse continues: *The princes of Yehuda, their council [rigmatam]* (Psalms 68:28). Said God to them: I know that your quarrel was only intended to honor Me, and as such I will grant rewards to both of you. What compensation was afforded to Binyamin? The Divine Presence eventually dwelled in [the Temple in] their territory, as the verse states: *He shall dwell between his shoulders* (Deuteronomy 33:12). And what reward did the tribe of Yehuda receive? Its people were granted the kingship [in the Davidic dynasty].

SHEMOT RABBA

מִימִינָם וּמִשְּׂמֹאלָם – *To their right and left:* Rabbi Abbahu taught: Said God: Just like I planned to destroy the Egyptians, so I planned to destroy Israel! Why then were the Israelites spared the same fate as their pursuers? They survived on the merits of *their right and left.* The "right" is an allusion to the Torah, which Israel was destined to receive from the right hand of the Holy One, blessed be He, as the verse states: *From his right hand went a fiery law for them* (Deuteronomy 33:2). And the "left" is a reference to the *mezuza* scroll [when viewed from the inside of the house, the *mezuza* is situated on the left side of the doorframe]. (Shinan, Shemot 4:3)

כא אֶת־הַלַּיְלָה וְלֹא־קָרַב זֶה אֶל־זֶה כָּל־הַלָּיְלָה: וַיֵּט מֹשֶׁה
אֶת־יָדוֹ עַל־הַיָּם וַיּוֹלֶךְ יהוה ׀ אֶת־הַיָּם בְּרוּחַ קָדִים עַזָּה
כב כָּל־הַלַּיְלָה וַיָּשֶׂם אֶת־הַיָּם לֶחָרָבָה וַיִּבָּקְעוּ הַמָּיִם: וַיָּבֹאוּ
בְנֵי־יִשְׂרָאֵל בְּתוֹךְ הַיָּם בַּיַּבָּשָׁה וְהַמַּיִם לָהֶם חוֹמָה מִימִינָם

VAYIKRA RABBA

וַיָּאֶר אֶת־הַלָּיְלָה — *But lighting the night:* The psalmist states: *The Lord is my light and my salvation; whom shall I fear?* (Psalms 27:1). Rabbi Elazar expounded this verse as referring to the splitting of the sea, for in describing that episode the verse states: *Cloud and darkness for one, but lighting the night for the other.* The psalm also mentions salvation, which is exactly what Moshe promised Israel, as the verse states: *Stand firm and see the deliverance the Lord will bring you today* (14:13). Finally, David declares that he will not be afraid, while Moshe similarly tells Israel: *Fear not* (14:13). (Margaliot, Aḥarei Mot 21:1)

LEKAḤ TOV

וַיָּאֶר אֶת־הַלָּיְלָה — *But lighting the night:* Israel was bathed in light while the Egyptians were cloaked in darkness. Meanwhile, from their camp, the Egyptians heard their erstwhile slaves eating, drinking, and celebrating. This went on as the frustrated soldiers shot arrows and catapulted rocks in the Israelites' direction. The missiles were absorbed by the angel and the protective cloud, as the verse states: *God…is my shield, and the horn of my salvation, and my high tower* (Psalms 18:3).

VERSE 21

MEKHILTA DERABBI SHIMON

וַיִּבָּקְעוּ הַמָּיִם — *Dividing the waters:* At first, Moshe stood on the shore and uttered the holy name of God, believing this was the way to open the waters. When this failed, Moshe showed the sea the staff of God on which was inscribed the divine names, but this too had no effect. However, when the Holy One, blessed be He, revealed Himself to the ocean, the waters parted. Thus the psalmist describes the scene: *The sea saw it and fled* (Psalms 114:3). Moshe complained to the water: Did I not utter the ineffable name before you to no avail? Did I not produce the staff with the names written on it, only to be spurned by you? *What ails you, O sea, that you flee [now]?* (Psalms 114:5). But the sea answered Moshe: Why should I heed your demands, son of Amram? *I tremble in the Lord's presence* (Psalms 114:7)…. Now it was not just the Sea of Reeds that split at that hour — all the water in the world divided simultaneously. How do we know that even water sitting stagnant in wells, pits, cisterns, caves, cups, and carafes also parted? For the verse states: *The Lord drove the sea back…dividing [vayibbake'u] the waters* — had the singular term *vayibbaka* been used, that would have meant that just the Sea of Reeds was subject to God's miracle. But since the plural form *vayibbake'u* appears, it teaches that all the water around the world also split while Israel was being rescued.

EXODUS | CHAPTER 14 — THE TIME OF THE SAGES | BESHALAḤ | 17

16 Speak to the Israelites; have them move forward. Raise your staff, stretch out your hand over the sea and divide it, and the
17 Israelites will walk through the sea on dry land. I will strengthen the Egyptians' hearts and they will go after them. Then will My glory bear down hard upon Pharaoh and his entire army,
18 his chariots and cavalry. And when My glory bears down upon Pharaoh, his chariots and cavalry, the Egyptians will know that
19 I am the LORD." Then the angel of God who had been traveling ahead of the Israelite camp moved and went behind them, and the column of cloud moved from in front of them to their rear.
20 It came between the Egyptian and Israelite camps, as cloud and

--- **MEKHILTA DERABBI YISHMAEL** *(cont.)* ---

God left the country with them as well, as that verse continues: *And I will surely bring you up again.* The Divine Presence accompanied them when Israel entered the sea, as the verse states: *Then the angel of God who had been traveling ahead of the Israelite camp moved and went behind them,* and God went into the desert with them as well, as the verse states: *The LORD went ahead of them by day in a column of cloud to guide them* (13:21). (Massekhta DeShira 3)

--- **MEKHILTA DERABBI SHIMON** ---

מַלְאַךְ הָאֱלֹהִים – *The angel of God:* God would later say to Israel: *I lifted you up on eagles' wings and brought you to Me* (19:4). When other birds transport their young, they carry them by their claws, protecting them from any eagle which might swoop down from above. But an eagle fears no other bird and is therefore content to position its chicks on its shoulders. You might ask why the eagle should bother with such a habit and not simply grip the eaglets in its talons. This is because it is nevertheless wary of people who might cast stones or shoot arrows in its direction. The bird thus places itself as a barrier between its young and the dangers threatening from below. So too did God situate His ministering angels as a barricade between Israel and the encroaching Egyptians, as the verse states: *Then the angel of God who had been traveling ahead of the Israelite camp moved and went behind them.* (14:19)

--- **SEKHEL TOV** ---

מַלְאַךְ הָאֱלֹהִים – *The angel of God:* The divine attribute of Justice had been standing in front of them, intent on preventing the nation's passage and destroying them as punishment for Mikha's idolatrous statue [see Judges 17–18], which was crossing the sea with the people, as the verse states: *And he shall pass through the sea with affliction* (Zechariah 10:11).

VERSE 20

--- **SHEMOT RABBA** ---

וַיָּאֶר אֶת־הַלָּיְלָה – *But lighting the night:* [The words of the translation, "for one…for the other" are absent from the original Hebrew phrase, which literally reads: "as cloud and darkness, and lighting the night." The midrash explains the apparent contradiction:] During the splitting of the sea, the Holy One, blessed be He, sent a cloud of darkness to obscure the Egyptians' sight, while Israel's vision was unimpaired, just as happened in Egypt during the plague of darkness. (Shinan, Bo 14:3)

טז יִשְׂרָאֵל וְיִסָּעוּ: וְאַתָּה הָרֵם אֶת־מַטְּךָ וּנְטֵה אֶת־יָדְךָ עַל־
יז הַיָּם וּבְקָעֵהוּ וְיָבֹאוּ בְנֵי־יִשְׂרָאֵל בְּתוֹךְ הַיָּם בַּיַּבָּשָׁה: וַאֲנִי
הִנְנִי מְחַזֵּק אֶת־לֵב מִצְרַיִם וְיָבֹאוּ אַחֲרֵיהֶם וְאִכָּבְדָה
יח בְּפַרְעֹה וּבְכָל־חֵילוֹ בְּרִכְבּוֹ וּבְפָרָשָׁיו: וְיָדְעוּ מִצְרַיִם כִּי־
יט אֲנִי יְהֹוָה בְּהִכָּבְדִי בְּפַרְעֹה בְּרִכְבּוֹ וּבְפָרָשָׁיו: וַיִּסַּע מַלְאַךְ
הָאֱלֹהִים הַהֹלֵךְ לִפְנֵי מַחֲנֵה יִשְׂרָאֵל וַיֵּלֶךְ מֵאַחֲרֵיהֶם
כ וַיִּסַּע עַמּוּד הֶעָנָן מִפְּנֵיהֶם וַיַּעֲמֹד מֵאַחֲרֵיהֶם: וַיָּבֹא בֵּין ׀
מַחֲנֵה מִצְרַיִם וּבֵין מַחֲנֵה יִשְׂרָאֵל וַיְהִי הֶעָנָן וְהַחֹשֶׁךְ וַיָּאֶר

VERSE 16

---- SHEMOT RABBA ----

וּבְקָעֵהוּ – *And divide it:* Rabbi Elazar HaKappar taught: Moshe protested to God: Have You not declared that the sea would never become dry land, as the verse states: *God has placed the sand to bound the sea by a perpetual decree, that it cannot pass it*, while another verse claims, *Who shut up the sea with doors* (Job 38:8)? But the Holy One, blessed be He, answered him: Moshe, you would do well to read the Torah from the beginning. There the text reads: *Let the waters under the heaven be gathered together to one place, and let the dry land appear* (Genesis 1:9). When I fashioned the seas, I did so on condition that I would later divide them in two. Hence the subsequent verse states: *And at daybreak the water came back in full force [le'eitano]* (14:27) – the water thereby respected its condition [litnao] that I stipulated at its creation. (Beshalaḥ 21:7)

---- VAYIKRA RABBA ----

וּבְקָעֵהוּ – *And divide it:* Said God to Moshe: You are the only one who can divide the sea; if you do not do it, nobody will. (Vayikra 1:5)

VERSE 17

---- LEKAḤ TOV ----

וְאִכָּבְדָה בְּפַרְעֹה – *Then will My glory bear down hard upon Pharaoh:* [The word *ve'ikkaveda* can be understood as related to *kavod*, "glory," or *kaved* "heavy." According to the midrash, God is saying:] My name will become glorified [*yitkabbed*] throughout the world after what I do to Pharaoh and to his entire army. Now Israel did not enter the sea to advance their journey; they did not enter the water on one side of the sea and then emerge on the other side. The entire purpose of the miracle was to drown the Egyptian cavalry. Once that was achieved, Israel swung back and climbed ashore where they had entered, forming a sort of arc through the sea.

VERSE 19

---- MEKHILTA DERABBI YISHMAEL ----

מַלְאַךְ הָאֱלֹהִים – *The angel of God:* The Divine Presence accompanied Israel when they first descended to Egypt, as the verse states: *I will go down with you into Egypt* (Genesis 46:4), and

14 Egyptians you see today, you shall never see again. The LORD will fight for you. You stay silent."
15 The LORD said to Moshe, "Why are you crying out to Me? SHELISHI

LEKAḤ TOV (cont.)

offer extended prayers and sing God's praises. Indeed, at that hour, Moshe was engaged in prayer while Israel extolled God's virtues and glory, celebrating the Master of all wars, as the verse states: *The high praises of God are in their mouths, and a two edged sword in their hand* (Psalms 149:6).

VERSE 15
MEKHILTA DERABBI SHIMON

מַה־תִּצְעַק אֵלָי – *Why are you crying out to Me:* Rabbi Yehoshua taught: Said God to Moshe: Israel's prayers have already been accepted, all the nation has to do is move forward. Rabbi Eliezer said: Said the Holy One, blessed be He, to Moshe: My children are panicking on the beach, the sea is surrounding them, the enemy is bearing down, and you stand there praying? Why are you crying out to Me? Speak to the Israelites; have them move forward. Know Moshe, that there is a time to be brief and a time to be loquacious. And Moshe learned the lesson well: On one occasion he spoke appropriately tersely to God, as the verse states: *Heal her now, O God, I pray You* (Numbers 12:13). At another time He prayed extensively, as the verse states: *Then I abode in the mountain forty days and forty nights* (Deuteronomy 9:9). Rabbi Meir said: God reasoned: Since I was prepared to divide the waters for a single person [Adam, who required land to live on] – as the verse states: *And God said, Let the waters under the heaven be gathered together to one place, and let the dry land appear* (Genesis 1:9) – surely I am prepared to transform the sea into land for a whole community of the righteous. (Psalms 16:3).

TALMUD BAVLI

מַה־תִּצְעַק אֵלָי – *Why are you crying out to Me:* At that time, Moshe was engaged in lengthy prayers. But the Holy One, blessed be He, rebuked him, saying: My beloved creations are drowning in the sea and you stand there singing My praises? Responded Moshe: Master of the universe, what should I be doing instead? Said He: *Speak to the Israelites; have them move forward. Raise your staff, stretch out your hand over the sea and divide it* (14:15–16). (Sota 37a)

BEMIDBAR RABBA

וְיִסָּעוּ – *Have them move forward:* Rabbi Yehuda bar Ilai taught: While Israel stood on the seashore, the different tribes quarreled for the right to enter the water first – each tribe wanted the honor for itself. Suddenly, Naḥshon son of Aminadav [chief of the tribe of Yehuda] plunged into the sea, declaring: "I will go first!" Evoking Naḥshon his ancestor, King David wrote: *Save me, O God, for the waters have come up to my soul. I sink in deep mire, where there is no standing* (Psalms 69:2). Thus does the verse state, *In Yehuda is God known; His name is great in Israel* (Psalms 76:2). To reward Naḥshon for his zeal, the Holy One, blessed be He, invited him to be the first to bring his dedicatory gifts to the Tabernacle, as the verse states: *And he that offered his offering on the first day was Naḥshon the son of Aminadav, of the tribe of Yehuda* (Numbers 7:12). (Naso 13:4)

יד תֹּסִפוּ לִרְאֹתָם עוֹד עַד־עוֹלָם: יהוה יִלָּחֵם לָכֶם וְאַתֶּם תַּחֲרִשׁוּן:
טו וַיֹּאמֶר יהוה אֶל־מֹשֶׁה מַה־תִּצְעַק אֵלָי דַּבֵּר אֶל־בְּנֵי־ יא שלישי

TALMUD YERUSHALMI (cont.)

road of which I spoke to you: You shall see it no more again (Deuteronomy 28:68). (Sukka 5:1) **הִתְיַצְּבוּ** — Stand firm: At the moment of truth by the sea, the Israelites divided themselves into four camps. The first group recommended that the people cast themselves into the sea. The second group favored a return to Egypt. A third side took a combative position and advocated fighting the cavalry to the death. And the fourth party suggested that since Israel could not possibly defeat the soldiers in war, they should stand and shout at them and perhaps scare them off. In response to the first group, Moshe said: *Stand firm and see the deliverance the* L*ord* *will bring you today*. To those who demanded they all go back to slavery, Moshe retorted: *The Egyptians you see today, you shall never see again*. As for those who were ready to fight, Moshe argued: *The* L*ord* *will fight for you* (14:14). And he calmed those who would scream at the enemy, saying, *You stay silent*. (Taanit 2:5)

LEKAḤ TOV

כִּי אֲשֶׁר רְאִיתֶם — *You see:* What exactly did Israel see? The Holy One, blessed be He, opened their eyes and revealed to them myriads of ministering angels [arrayed for battle against the Egyptians]. And so we see later: *And the servant of the man of God rose early, and went out, and behold, an army surrounded the city both with horses and chariots. And his servant said to him, Alas, my master! what shall we do? And he answered, Fear not: for they that are with us are more than they that are with them* (II Kings 6:15–16).

VERSE 14

MEKHILTA DERABBI SHIMON

יהוה יִלָּחֵם לָכֶם — *The* L*ord* *will fight for you:* When the nation of Israel follows God's will, He fights on their behalf, as the verse states: *The* L*ord* *will fight for you*. On the other hand, when Israel defies God's will, God wars against them, so to speak, as a contrary verse states: *Therefore He was turned to be their enemy, and He fought against them* (Isaiah 63:10). Furthermore, God transforms from being merciful to merciless, as the verse states: *The* L*ord* *was like an enemy* (Lamentations 2:5). **וְאַתֶּם תַּחֲרִשׁוּן** — *You stay silent:* Rabbi Yehuda HaNasi taught: When Moshe assured the nation: *The* L*ord* *will fight for you* (14:14), he was telling them: "God is about to perform miracles and wonders for you while you stand by and remain silent." But the people petitioned their leader: "Is there nothing that we can do?" Said he: "Indeed, you should laud, acclaim, praise, extol, and glorify the Victor of this battle." It was at that moment that Israel opened their mouths and *sang this song to the* L*ord: I will sing to the* L*ord, for He has triumphed in glory* (15:1)

LEKAḤ TOV

יהוה יִלָּחֵם לָכֶם — *The* L*ord* *will fight for you:* Said Moshe to Israel: Even were you to be silent, the L*ord* would fight for you. How much more so can you rely on His assistance when you

Egyptians thundering after them. They were terrified and cried
11 to the Lord for help. "Were there no graves in Egypt?" they asked Moshe; "Is that why you brought us here to die in the desert? What have you done to us, bringing us out of Egypt?
12 Did we not tell you in Egypt: Leave us alone – let us serve the Egyptians. Better a life in servitude to Egypt than death in
13 the desert." But Moshe told the people, "Fear not. Stand firm and see the deliverance the Lord will bring you today. The

---

VERSE 13

PHILO

אַל־תִּירָאוּ – *Fear not*: Moshe did not criticize his people for expressing their complaints. Even in his own mind, he hedged between his conversation with the people and with his prayers to God.

MEKHILTA DERABBI SHIMON

אַל־תִּירָאוּ – *Fear not*: This statement shows how gifted Moshe was. For in the face of his nation's panic, Moshe stood his ground, calmly working to steady the people's nerves; singlehandedly allaying the fears of tens of thousands of Israelites. Of him the verse states: *Wisdom strengthens the wise more than ten rulers who are in a city* (Ecclesiastes 7:19).

הִתְיַצְּבוּ – *Stand firm*: The term *hityatzevu* signifies the presence of divine inspiration, as in the verse: *And the Lord said to Moshe... call Yehoshua and present yourselves [vehityatzevu] in the Tent of Meeting, that I may give him a charge* [Deuteronomy 31:14; this inaugurated Yehoshua's tenure as a prophet]. To what can Israel be compared at that hour? To a dove fleeing the talons of a hawk. It flies into a cave and hides in a rock crevice, but straight away a snake uncoils to attack, leaving the bird trapped – it cannot leave its refuge because of the hawk, but within the cave it is equally threatened. In desperation, the dove starts screaming and batting its wings, trying to get the attention of its owner. Now picture the Israelites: In front of them stands the impassable sea, while behind them the Egyptian enemy is closing in. They have no recourse but to lift their eyes in prayer to God. Hence one verse describes the nation: *O my dove, who is in the clefts of the rock, in the secret places of the cliff, let me see your countenance, let me hear your voice* (Song of Songs 2:14).

TALMUD YERUSHALMI

לֹא תֹסִפוּ לִרְאֹתָם עוֹד עַד־עוֹלָם – *You shall never see again*: Rabbi Shimon bar Yoḥai taught: On three occasions Israel was warned never to return to Egypt. The first was at the sea, when Moshe told the nation: *The Egyptians you see today, you shall never see again*. The second instance appears in Moshe's later speech to the people wherein he cautions that kings must not amass a large cavalry, as the verse states: *But he shall not multiply horses to himself, nor cause the people to return to Egypt, to the end that he should multiply horses; since the Lord has said to you: You shall henceforth return no more that way* [Deuteronomy 17:16; the Egyptians were renowned breeders of horses]. And finally, Israel was threatened that their misbehavior would cause God to *bring you back into Egypt with ships, by that*

עֵינֵיהֶם וְהִנֵּה מִצְרַיִם ׀ נֹסֵעַ אַחֲרֵיהֶם וַיִּירְאוּ מְאֹד וַיִּצְעֲקוּ
בְנֵי־יִשְׂרָאֵל אֶל־יְהֹוָה: וַיֹּאמְרוּ אֶל־מֹשֶׁה הֲמִבְּלִי אֵין־ יא
קְבָרִים בְּמִצְרַיִם לְקַחְתָּנוּ לָמוּת בַּמִּדְבָּר מַה־זֹּאת עָשִׂיתָ
לָּנוּ לְהוֹצִיאָנוּ מִמִּצְרָיִם: הֲלֹא־זֶה הַדָּבָר אֲשֶׁר דִּבַּרְנוּ אֵלֶיךָ יב
בְמִצְרַיִם לֵאמֹר חֲדַל מִמֶּנּוּ וְנַעַבְדָה אֶת־מִצְרָיִם כִּי טוֹב
לָנוּ עֲבֹד אֶת־מִצְרַיִם מִמֻּתֵנוּ בַּמִּדְבָּר: וַיֹּאמֶר מֹשֶׁה אֶל־ יג
הָעָם אַל־תִּירָאוּ הִתְיַצְבוּ וּרְאוּ אֶת־יְשׁוּעַת יְהֹוָה אֲשֶׁר־
יַעֲשֶׂה לָכֶם הַיּוֹם כִּי אֲשֶׁר רְאִיתֶם אֶת־מִצְרַיִם הַיּוֹם לֹא

TANHUMA

וַיִּשְׂאוּ בְנֵי־יִשְׂרָאֵל אֶת־עֵינֵיהֶם — *The Israelites looked up:* [The phrase "look up" is taken to connote prayer.] At that moment Israel adopted the behavior of their ancestors. For the Torah reports that Avraham *called on the name of the* Lord (Genesis 12:4). Regarding Yitzhak, the text states, *And Yitzhak went out to meditate in the field* (Genesis 24:63). And Yaakov is said to have *chanced [vayifga] upon a certain place* (Genesis 28:11). The verb *vayifga* implies that he prayed there to God, as seen in the verse *Therefore pray not you for this people, neither lift up cry nor prayer for them, neither make intercession [tifga] to me; for I will not hear you* (Jeremiah 7:16).

BEMIDBAR RABBA

וּפַרְעֹה הִקְרִיב — *Pharaoh drew near:* The verse that states: *Those who honor will I in turn honor* (I Samuel 2:30) refers to Pharaoh, who acted respectfully toward the Creator. For the king himself led his army to confront Israel, as the verse states: *Pharaoh drew near.* Pharaoh's servants protested to him: "Sire, it is bad form for the king to march in front of his soldiers; kings customarily follow their retinue into battle. Why then do you yourself lead the way?" Said Pharaoh to them: Am I going out to face a king of flesh and blood? Why, I am advancing against the King of Kings, the Holy One, blessed be He! As a reward for this attitude, God dealt with him directly and punished him Himself. (Naso 8:3)

VERSE 12

MEKHILTA DERABBI SHIMON

הֲלֹא־זֶה הַדָּבָר אֲשֶׁר דִּבַּרְנוּ אֵלֶיךָ — *Did we not tell you:* To what were the Israelites alluding when they reminded Moshe that they had previously asked to be left alone? They were remembering the encounter early in the tale, beginning with the verse: *Leaving Pharaoh, they met Moshe and Aharon, who stood awaiting them* (5:20). And now they said to their leaders: It is true that we suffered under the burden of the Egyptian slavery, but to die in the wilderness is a much worse end. It is true that we lamented our brethren who died during the plague of darkness, but to perish in the desert is a worse fate. For at least those who never left Egypt were buried and eulogized with some dignity. But our bones will be left to be bleached by the fierceness of the sun; our corpses will lie frozen stiff in the desert nights.

EXODUS | CHAPTER 14 — THE TIME OF THE SAGES | BESHALAḤ | 11

7 and brought out his army. He took six hundred elite chariots and all the other chariots of Egypt, with officers over them all.
8 The Lord strengthened the heart of Pharaoh King of Egypt, and he pursued the Israelites, who were leaving in defiance of
9 them. The Egyptians, with all the king's horses and chariots, sheni cavalry and infantry, chased and caught up with them as they were encamped by the sea near Pi HaḤirot, before Baal Tzefon.
10 Pharaoh drew near – the Israelites looked up: there were the

---
LEKAḤ TOV

עַל־כֻּלּוֹ – *Over them all:* It was Pharaoh's intention to obliterate "all" of Israel.

VERSE 8

MEKHILTA DERABBI SHIMON

יֹצְאִים בְּיָד רָמָה – *Were leaving in defiance of them:* [Literally, "with a high hand."] As the Egyptians chased after Israel they shook their fists skyward and cursed, and swore, and blasphemed. Meanwhile, as the Israelites were being pursued, they spread their hands toward heaven and offered praise, thanks, and blessing. Israel sang songs of glory; they extolled the magnificence of the Creator. Another interpretation: Israel's hands were raised in victory over the Egyptians.

VERSE 9

MEKHILTA DERABBI SHIMON

וַיִּרְדְּפוּ – *Chased:* Not one Egyptian stumbled during the chase lest he pause to consider that his misstep might be a bad omen. This would have led the soldier to turn back from the pursuit.

SHIR HASHIRIM RABBA

וַיַּשִּׂיגוּ אוֹתָם – *And caught up with them:* Out of fear, the Israelites began to signal to the cavalry: We belong to you, we are all yours. Said the Holy One, blessed be He, to them: Do you really think I am incapable of redeeming you? Wipe your tears and hold your tongues! Thus the verse states: *The Lord will fight for you. You stay silent* (14:14). (1:5)

LEKAḤ TOV

חֹנִים עַל־הַיָּם – *Encamped by the sea:* Israel waited for the Egyptians by the water, so that the latter would be drowned in its waves. The term *ḥonim* implies that the Hebrews were engaged in prayer and petitions [*taḥanunim*] to God.

VERSE 10

MEKHILTA DERABBI YISHMAEL

וַיִּצְעֲקוּ – *And cried for help:* Rabbi Eliezer taught: The verse that states: *Let me see your countenance* (Song of Songs 2:14) refers to Israel's longing [to see God's wonders] at the sea, for there Moshe proclaimed: *Stand firm and see the deliverance the Lord will bring you today* (14:13). And the continuation of that verse, which states: *Let me hear your voice*, also reflects Israel's emotions at that time, as the verse states: *They were terrified and cried to the Lord for help.*

ז וְאֶת־עַמּוֹ לָקַח עִמּוֹ: וַיִּקַּח שֵׁשׁ־מֵאוֹת רֶכֶב בָּחוּר וְכֹל
ח רֶכֶב מִצְרָיִם וְשָׁלִשִׁם עַל־כֻּלּוֹ: וַיְחַזֵּק יהוה אֶת־לֵב פַּרְעֹה
מֶלֶךְ מִצְרַיִם וַיִּרְדֹּף אַחֲרֵי בְּנֵי יִשְׂרָאֵל וּבְנֵי יִשְׂרָאֵל יֹצְאִים
ט בְּיָד רָמָה: וַיִּרְדְּפוּ מִצְרַיִם אַחֲרֵיהֶם וַיַּשִּׂיגוּ אוֹתָם חֹנִים   שני
עַל־הַיָּם כָּל־סוּס רֶכֶב פַּרְעֹה וּפָרָשָׁיו וְחֵילוֹ עַל־פִּי הַחִירֹת
י לִפְנֵי בַּעַל צְפֹן: וּפַרְעֹה הִקְרִיב וַיִּשְׂאוּ בְנֵי־יִשְׂרָאֵל אֶת־

BERESHIT RABBA (cont.)

servants who could have prepared his chariot for him? Rather, Yosef thereby showed how love causes people to act unusually. We see the opposite with Pharaoh about whom the verse states: *So the king harnessed his chariot.* Did Pharaoh not have numerous attendants who should have prepared his chariot for him? Rather, Pharaoh thereby showed how hatred can cause us to act abnormally. (Vayera 55:8)

MIDRASH AGGADA

וְאֶת־עַמּוֹ לָקַח עִמּוֹ – *And brought out his army:* Pharaoh bribed his people to join him in the pursuit of Israel, emptying out his treasury in the effort. [The word *lakaḥ* can connote "buying."]

YALKUT SHIMONI

וַיֶּאְסֹר אֶת־רִכְבּוֹ – *The king harnessed his chariot:* Pharaoh harnessed his own chariot himself. It is not customary for kings to do so, for usually the royals stand by and wait while their liverymen saddle their horses for them. But here Pharaoh was eager to embark on the mission and took the job upon himself. When the Egyptian nobles saw how committed their king was to the task, each of them in turn took charge of his own preparations. (Beshalaḥ 230)

VERSE 7

MEKHILTA DERABBI SHIMON

שֵׁשׁ־מֵאוֹת רֶכֶב בָּחוּר – *Six hundred elite chariots:* Pharaoh's vanity was soon humbled. For he took six hundred elite chariots to attack Israel, but not long afterward, *Pharaoh's chariots and army He hurled into the sea* (15:4). (15:1) **וְשָׁלִשִׁם עַל־כֻּלּוֹ** – *With officers over them all:* The term *shalishim* connotes champions in combat.

TANHUMA

וַיִּקַּח שֵׁשׁ־מֵאוֹת רֶכֶב בָּחוּר – *He took six hundred elite chariots:* From where did Pharaoh's cavalry procure horses for their chariots? Were not all of the country's animals killed in the cattle plague, as the verse state: *All the livestock of the Egyptians perished* (9:6)? Nonetheless, the text also reports that *those of Pharaoh's officials who feared the* Lord*'s word hurried to bring in their slaves and their livestock* [9:20, to escape the plague of hail. According to the Midrash, the same had transpired earlier with respect to the cattle plague; see commentary on Parashat Va'era 9:6]. Hence there were some horses available to pursue the Israelites.

4 land, that they are trapped in the desert. I will toughen Pharaoh's heart, and he will pursue them. I will be glorified over Pharaoh and all his force, and the Egyptians will know that I am
5 the Lord." And so they did. When the king of Egypt was told that the Israelites had escaped, he and his officials changed their minds about the people: "What have we done, releasing the
6 Israelites from serving us?" So the king harnessed his chariot

---

MEKHILTA DERABBI SHIMON *(cont.)*

the overseers, injuring some and killing others. The remaining officers fled back to Pharaoh to report what was happening, as the verse states: *when the king of Egypt was told* – it was his own men who related the situation to him. Other interpretations suggest that Pharaoh had spies along the route who relayed the information back to him. A third possibility is that Amalekite agents who were following Israel's progress were Pharaoh's source of information. כִּי בָרַח הָעָם – *That the Israelites had escaped:* Why does the text describe Israel's departure as an "escape," implying that they fled in fear and secrecy? Does the verse not state that the Israelites *were leaving in defiance of them* (14:8), i.e., with their heads held high? Rather, it was the Egyptians themselves who viewed Israel in this light, for they were behaving like runaway convicts. Once Israel started rioting and killing the Egyptian chaperones, the nation appeared like a mob with no ruler. Similarly the verse states: *The locusts have no king, yet they go forth all of them by bands* (Proverbs 30:27).

SHIR HASHIRIM RABBA

מַה־זֹּאת עָשִׂינוּ – *What have we done:* When Israel languished in Egypt they were busy working with mortar and bricks, and the Egyptians found them repulsive. Later though, when the Egyptians observed Israel encamped by the sea under their glorious banners, arranged like true subjects of a king, they gagged and whined: Why ever did we expel this people from our land? (4:12)

YALKUT SHIMONI

וַיֵּהָפֵךְ לְבַב פַּרְעֹה – *Pharaoh changed his mind:* The Egyptians suddenly realized that their state had thrived with Israel under their control. Rabbi Yosei the Galilean says: To what may this be compared? To a person who inherited a plot of land. Impulsively, the heir went and sold this land for too low a price. Subsequently, the buyer discovered springs of water in the field enabling him to plant trees and orchards there. Upon discovering this, the seller gagged in despair. Similarly, it was only after the Egyptians expelled the Israelites that they understood what they had given up, as the verse states: *What have we done, releasing the Israelites from serving us?*

VERSE 6

BERESHIT RABBA

וַיֶּאְסֹר אֶת־רִכְבּוֹ – *Harnessed his chariot:* The verse states: *And Yosef made ready his chariot,* and went up to meet Yisrael his father (Genesis 46:29). Now did Yosef not have plenty of

> הֵם בָּאָרֶץ סָגַר עֲלֵיהֶם הַמִּדְבָּר: וְחִזַּקְתִּי אֶת־לֵב־פַּרְעֹה
> וְרָדַף אַחֲרֵיהֶם וְאִכָּבְדָה בְּפַרְעֹה וּבְכָל־חֵילוֹ וְיָדְעוּ מִצְרַיִם
> כִּי־אֲנִי יְהוָה וַיַּעֲשׂוּ־כֵן: וַיֻּגַּד לְמֶלֶךְ מִצְרַיִם כִּי בָרַח הָעָם
> וַיֵּהָפֵךְ לְבַב פַּרְעֹה וַעֲבָדָיו אֶל־הָעָם וַיֹּאמְרוּ מַה־זֹּאת
> עָשִׂינוּ כִּי־שִׁלַּחְנוּ אֶת־יִשְׂרָאֵל מֵעָבְדֵנוּ: וַיֶּאְסֹר אֶת־רִכְבּוֹ

VERSE 4

SIFREI BEMIDBAR

בְּפַרְעֹה וּבְכָל־חֵילוֹ – *Over Pharaoh and all his force:* It is always the one who initiates the sin who is the first to be punished. Hence we read, *I will be glorified over Pharaoh and all his force.* Since Pharaoh introduced the oppression against Israel, the final torment at the sea began with his drowning. (Naso 18)

SEKHEL TOV

כִּי־אֲנִי יְהוָה – *That I am the Lord:* At first Pharaoh had claimed: *I do not know the Lord* (5:2). But now the Egyptians will know full well who I am. **וַיַּעֲשׂוּ־כֵן** – *And so they did:* Israel complied with Moshe's instruction and their agreement shows how wise they were. For in order not to panic the women and children, they did not protest: "What? How could we possibly go back?" Instead, they submitted to their leader, saying: Whether we want to or not, we fully trust the word of the son of Amram.

MIDRASH AGGADA

וְחִזַּקְתִּי אֶת־לֵב־פַּרְעֹה – *I will toughen Pharaoh's heart:* Initially Pharaoh had not planned on pursuing Israel following their departure. But the Holy One, blessed be He, put the idea into his head to chase after them into the wilderness. Because the Egyptians had once decreed: *Throw every boy that is born into the Nile* (1:22), therefore *the Lord swept them into the sea* (14:27). This illustrates the principle our Sages teach: With the measure that a man uses, so shall it be meted out to him (Mishna Sota 1:7).

VERSE 5

MEKHILTA DERABBI SHIMON

וַיֻּגַּד לְמֶלֶךְ מִצְרַיִם – *When the king of Egypt was told:* From Ramesses the nation traveled to Sukkot [12:37], and from Sukkot they went to Etam [13:20]. After leaving Etam, Israel arrived at Pi HaḤirot [14:2]. These journeys took place on the Sabbath eve, on the Sabbath, and on the first day of the week, which were the fifteenth, the sixteenth and the seventeenth of Nisan. On the second day of the week [Monday], which was the fourth day of their travels and the eighteenth of the month, the nation was saddling up their animals and getting ready to proceed when the army captains Pharaoh had sent to accompany Israel spoke up. "It is time," they said, "for you to start heading back to Egypt just as you promised: *Send us forth, three days' journey into the wilderness* (8:23)." But Israel responded: "As soon as we left Egypt we also left Pharaoh's jurisdiction." Said the Egyptians: "Willingly or not, you will return to Egypt and obey the king's command." This prompted the Israelites to attack

column of cloud to guide them, and at night in a column of fire to give them light, so that they might travel day and night. Neither the column of cloud by day nor that of fire by night once departed from the people.

14 ¹ Then the LORD said to Moshe, "Speak to the Israelites and tell them to turn back and camp in front of Pi HaḤirot, between Migdol and the sea, before Baal Tzefon. Encamp facing it, by ³ the sea. Pharaoh will think that the Israelites are lost across the

CHAPTER 14, VERSE 2

MEKHILTA DERABBI SHIMON

פִּי הַחִירֹת – *Pi HaḤirot:* Moshe instructed Israel to turn back slightly in the direction of Egypt. When the trumpet sounded to signal that change of course, the faithless began to tear out their hair and rip their clothing, thinking that the nation was returning to Egypt and to slavery. Said Moshe to them: I have heard from the mouth [*peh*] of God that you are to remain free people [*ḥorin* – hence the name *Pi HaḤirot*]. **מִגְדֹּל** – *Migdol:* This was the site of Egypt's greatness [*gedula*] and glory. For it was there that Yosef had once assembled the nation's wealth, as the verse states: *And Yosef gathered up all the money that was found in the land of Egypt* (Genesis 47:14).

SHEMOT RABBA

בַּעַל צְפֹן – *Baal Tzefon:* God had brought judgment against all the gods of Egypt [during the plague of the firstborn; see 12:12], and all idolatry across the world had been destroyed. The only false deity that God spared was the Egyptians' Baal Tzefon. He did this in order to deceive the people into thinking their god had outmatched Israel's. This illustrates the verse *He makes nations great and destroys them* (Job 12:23). (Bo 15:15)

VERSE 3

LEKAḤ TOV

סָגַר עֲלֵיהֶם הַמִּדְבָּר – *They are trapped in the desert:* [Literally, "the desert has shut them in."] When Israel saw the raging sea before them and the approaching enemy behind them, they turned to escape into the wilderness. But the Holy One, blessed be He, summoned wild and vicious beasts to block their way, preventing them from leaving. When Pharaoh observed the situation, he declared: Aha! It is Baal Tzefon who has sent these attack animals to hold them for us, as the verse states: *They are trapped [sagar] in the desert!* And how do we know that the term *sagar* implies a barrier of wild beasts? For the verse states [of Noah's Ark]: *And they that went in, went in male and female of all flesh, as God had commanded him; and the* LORD *shut [vayisgor] him in* (Genesis 7:16). To protect Noaḥ from his neighbors who had surrounded the ark and threatened to destroy it, God placed wild beasts around the craft.

עָנָן לַנְחֹתָם הַדֶּרֶךְ וְלַיְלָה בְּעַמּוּד אֵשׁ לְהָאִיר לָהֶם לָלֶכֶת יוֹמָם וָלָיְלָה: כב לֹא־יָמִישׁ עַמּוּד הֶעָנָן יוֹמָם וְעַמּוּד הָאֵשׁ לָיְלָה לִפְנֵי הָעָם:

יד א וַיְדַבֵּר יְהוָה אֶל־מֹשֶׁה לֵּאמֹר: ב דַּבֵּר אֶל־בְּנֵי יִשְׂרָאֵל וְיָשֻׁבוּ וְיַחֲנוּ לִפְנֵי פִּי הַחִירֹת בֵּין מִגְדֹּל וּבֵין הַיָּם לִפְנֵי בַּעַל צְפֹן נִכְחוֹ תַחֲנוּ עַל־הַיָּם: ג וְאָמַר פַּרְעֹה לִבְנֵי יִשְׂרָאֵל נְבֻכִים

SIFREI ZUTA

בְּעַמּוּד עָנָן – *A column of cloud:* God surrounded Israel with seven clouds of glory. There was one column in front of them and one behind them; one to the right and one to the left. An additional cloud hovered above them to shield them from the desert sun, while another formed a carpet to protect the Israelites' bare feet. Superior to all was the cloud of the Divine Presence which journeyed three days ahead of the camp, leveling hills and filling chasms to pave a smooth path for Israel's travels. (10:33)

VERSE 22

MEKHILTA DERABBI SHIMON

לֹא־יָמִישׁ עַמּוּד הֶעָנָן יוֹמָם – *Neither the column of cloud by day:* The brightness of the sun did not overpower the cloud. **וְעַמּוּד הָאֵשׁ לָיְלָה** – *Nor that of fire by night:* The light from the moon was negligible in comparison to the column of fire. **לֹא־יָמִישׁ** – *Neither departed:* The guiding columns maintained their presence even when Israel rebelled against God, even when they angered Him, and even when they blasphemed Him. Now why did Israel require both the pillar of cloud and the pillar of fire? They were put in place to help those with an impure discharge, menstruating women, and new mothers mark the days. [These individuals must follow detailed reckonings of the time of their impurity before being able to immerse in water for purification. The pillars of cloud and of fire identified the precise moments of evening and morning for this purpose.]

TALMUD BAVLI

לֹא־יָמִישׁ עַמּוּד הֶעָנָן יוֹמָם – *Neither the column of cloud by day:* Rav Huna said: He who regularly lights Hanukka candles will be rewarded with scholarly sons. Rav Yosef's wife used to light her Sabbath candles late in the day [close to nightfall]. Said Rav Yosef to her: The verse states: *Neither the column of cloud by day nor that of fire by night once departed from the people.* What this means is that the pillar of cloud appeared when the fire was still in the sky, and the column of cloud would not depart until the fire had arrived. [Rav Yosef was thereby reminding his wife to light the Sabbath candles while it was still daylight.] (Shabbat 23b)

19 The Israelites left Egypt armed for battle. And Moshe took with him the remains of Yosef, who had bound the Israelites by oath: "When God comes to your aid, bring my remains with you out
20 of here." They set out from Sukkot and camped at Etam, at the
21 edge of the desert. The LORD went ahead of them by day in a

---

PESIKTA DERAV KAHANA *(cont.)*

burial spot in Egypt before the exodus? Seraḥ, the daughter of Asher [mentioned in Genesis 46:17 as one who first descended to Egypt with Yaakov] was still alive at that time. Seraḥ approached Moshe and said: "Yosef's body has been submerged in the Nile river." Moshe went to the Nile and called: "Yosef! Yosef! The time has arrived for the Holy One, blessed be He, to redeem His children. The Divine Presence awaits you, Israel awaits you, the clouds of glory are waiting for you. If you reveal your location, it is well; if you do not, we are hereby absolved of the oath that you made our ancestors swear" [in Genesis 50:25, that they would bring Yosef's body out with them]. At once, Yosef's coffin floated to the surface. Other writers claim that Moshe discovered the body by writing the divine name on a piece of parchment and casting it into the river. At once, Yosef's coffin floated to the surface. (11)

VERSE 20
YALKUT SHIMONI

וַיִּסְעוּ מִסֻּכֹּת – *They set out from Sukkot:* Rabbi Eliezer taught: Israel actually built booths [*sukkot*] there, as a similar verse states, *And Yaakov journeyed to Sukkot, and built him a house, and made booths for his cattle: therefore the name of the place is called Sukkot* (Genesis 33:17). However, the Sages teach that Sukkot is merely the name of the place, as the verse states, *They set out from Sukkot and camped at Etam* – just as "Etam" is only the name of a place with no further implication, so is Sukkot. Rabbi Akiva said: Israel did not build themselves booths but were protected from the elements by clouds of glory, as the verse states: *For upon all the glory shall there be a canopy* (Isaiah 4:5). Now, this verse describes the past; why can we expect such a phenomenon in the future? For the next verse reads: *And there shall be a tabernacle for a shadow in the daytime* (Isaiah 4:6). (Bo 209)

VERSE 21
TALMUD BAVLI

הֹלֵךְ לִפְנֵיהֶם – *Went ahead of them:* Rav Yosef taught: A master is permitted to concede his honor. We learn this from God Himself, about whom the verse states: *The LORD went ahead of them by day.* [Normal etiquette would demand that a king be preceded by his retinue.] (Kiddushin 32a)

וַיהוה הֹלֵךְ לִפְנֵיהֶם יוֹמָם בְּעַמּוּד עָנָן – *The LORD went ahead of them by day in a column of cloud:* Rav Yehuda taught in the name of Rav: Whatever favors Avraham performed for the ministering angels were later repeated by the Holy One, blessed be He, for Avraham's children. For example, the verse states: *And Avraham went with them to bring them on the way* (Genesis 18:16). And later the Torah reports that *the LORD went ahead of them by day.* (Bava Metzia 86b)

יט מִצְרָיִם: וַיִּקַּח מֹשֶׁה אֶת־עַצְמוֹת יוֹסֵף עִמּוֹ כִּי הַשְׁבֵּעַ
הִשְׁבִּיעַ אֶת־בְּנֵי יִשְׂרָאֵל לֵאמֹר פָּקֹד יִפְקֹד אֱלֹהִים אֶתְכֶם
כ וְהַעֲלִיתֶם אֶת־עַצְמֹתַי מִזֶּה אִתְּכֶם: וַיִּסְעוּ מִסֻּכֹּת וַיַּחֲנוּ
כא בְאֵתָם בִּקְצֵה הַמִּדְבָּר: וַיהוָה הֹלֵךְ לִפְנֵיהֶם יוֹמָם בְּעַמּוּד

LEKAḤ TOV (cont.)

you through that great and terrible wilderness, in which were venomous serpents, and scorpions, and drought, where there was no water...that He might afflict you, and that He might prove you, to do you good at your latter end (Deuteronomy 8:15–16). יַם־סוּף – *To the Sea of Reeds:* God brought Israel to the sea in order to test them, as the verse states: *Our fathers in Egypt paid no heed to Your wonders...and they rebelled against You at the sea* (Psalms 106:7). וַחֲמֻשִׁים – *Armed for battle:* The term ḥamushim suggests that Israel was rushed out of Egypt. Similarly we find the phrase *Hurry to prepare [veḥimmesh] the land of Egypt* (Genesis 41:34).

MIDRASH AGGADA

וַיַּסֵּב – *So He led:* God let Israel recline [hissivan] as kings are accustomed to relaxing. This is the scriptural source for the practice of leaning back at the Passover Seder.

VERSE 19

MISHNA

עַצְמוֹת יוֹסֵף – *The remains of Yosef:* Yosef had had the honor of burying his father, and he had achieved the greatest success among his brothers, as the verse states: *And Yosef went up to bury his father... And there went up with him both chariots and horsemen* (Genesis 50:7, 9). And there was none greater than Yosef in that Moshe himself tended to his burial, as the verse states: *And Moshe took with him the remains of Yosef.* And there is none greater than Moshe, since God Himself tended to his burial, as the verse states: *And He buried him in the valley in the land of Moav* (Deuteronomy 34:6). (Sota 1:9)

TALMUD BAVLI

וַיִּקַּח מֹשֶׁה – *Moshe took:* Two verses seem to contradict each other: One states: *And Moshe took with him the remains of Yosef,* whereas another reads: *And the bones of Yosef, which the children of Israel brought up out of Egypt, they buried in Shekhem* (Joshua 24:32). [Was it Moshe who took Yosef's bones, or all the Israelites?] Rabbi Ḥama bar Ḥanina said: Whenever a person begins a good deed but does not complete it, and someone else steps in and finishes the work, it is the latter who receives the credit. [Since Moshe never entered the land of Israel, he was unable to bury Yosef's body despite having seen to its transport through the wilderness. This was accomplished by the people as a whole.] (Sota 13b)

PESIKTA DERAV KAHANA

וַיִּקַּח מֹשֶׁה אֶת־עַצְמוֹת יוֹסֵף עִמּוֹ – *Moshe took with him the remains of Yosef:* The verse highlights Moshe's character, for while the entire nation was busy plundering Egypt, Moshe was making preparations to transport Yosef's bones. Now who helped Moshe locate Yosef's

13 17 When Pharaoh let the people go, God did not lead them through the land of the Philistines, though it was the shorter way; "If the people face war," thought God, "they will change 18 their minds and go back to Egypt." So He led them on a roundabout course, by way of the wilderness, to the Sea of Reeds.

BERESHIT RABBA (cont.)

descendants of Avimelekh [king of the Philistines in Genesis 20–21] passed only three. [At this point seven generations had passed in Israel since Avraham's lifetime.] For why did God not lead them *through the land of the Philistines*? Because Avimelekh's grandson still lived. [Avraham had sworn to Avimelekh that he would not harm him, his son, or his grandson; see Genesis 21:23. Therefore the Israelites could not yet fight or conquer the Philistines.] (Albeck, Vayera 54)

BEMIDBAR RABBA

בְּשַׁלַּח פַּרְעֹה אֶת־הָעָם – *When Pharaoh let the people go:* What accrued merit granted the Israelites the freedom to leave Egypt? Rabbi Ḥalfai said: The nation was redeemed due to Yaakov's merit, as the verse states, *He brings out the prisoners into prosperity* [bakosharot] (Psalms 68:7), while a different text comments [regarding Yaakov]: *And he strove [vayasar] with an angel, and prevailed; [the angel] wept [bakha] and made supplication to him* [Hosea 12:5. Combining the words *bakha* and *vayasar* yields a resemblance to *bakosharot*; therefore the verse in Psalms is understood to be a veiled reference to Yaakov]. Another interpretation for the term *bakosharot*: The Israelites were redeemed thanks to the merits of noble women [*kesherot*], for the verse uses the feminine form *bakosharot* when it could have employed the masculine *bekisharon*. Another possible interpretation of *bakosharot*: God rescued Israel on the merits of the pious individuals [*kesherim*] among them. And who were these righteous people? The tribe of Levi. For while the rest of the nation was worshipping idols in Egypt, the tribe of Levi worshipped the Holy One, blessed be He, and practiced circumcision. (Bemidbar 3:6)

VERSE 18

PESIKTA DERAV KAHANA

וַחֲמֻשִׁים – *Armed for battle:* The term *ḥamushim* teaches that the Israelites wielded five [*ḥamisha*] types of weapons. Another interpretation: Only one in five Israelites actually left Egypt [while the other eighty percent perished there]. Some people put the figure at one in fifty [*ḥamishim*], while still others claim it was one in five hundred. Rabbi Nehorai said: I swear by the Temple service that the true number of escapees was even less than one five hundredth. Rabbi Yosei taught: The term *ḥamushim* implies that Israel left Egypt after five generations. (11)

LEKAḤ TOV

וַיַּסֵּב אֱלֹהִים אֶת־הָעָם – *So He led them:* God led Israel on a roundabout course to create opportunities to perform miracles and acts of salvation on their behalf. דֶּרֶךְ הַמִּדְבָּר – *By way of the wilderness:* In the wilderness Israel would be purified, as the text states: *Who led*

יג וַיְהִ֗י בְּשַׁלַּ֣ח פַּרְעֹה֮ אֶת־הָעָם֒ וְלֹא־נָחָ֣ם אֱלֹהִ֗ים דֶּ֚רֶךְ אֶ֣רֶץ פְּלִשְׁתִּ֔ים כִּ֥י קָר֖וֹב ה֑וּא כִּ֣י ׀ אָמַ֣ר אֱלֹהִ֗ים פֶּן־יִנָּחֵ֥ם הָעָ֛ם בִּרְאֹתָ֥ם מִלְחָמָ֖ה וְשָׁ֥בוּ מִצְרָֽיְמָה׃ יח וַיַּסֵּ֨ב אֱלֹהִ֧ים ׀ אֶת־הָעָ֛ם דֶּ֥רֶךְ הַמִּדְבָּ֖ר יַם־ס֑וּף וַחֲמֻשִׁ֛ים עָל֥וּ בְנֵי־יִשְׂרָאֵ֖ל מֵאֶ֥רֶץ

CHAPTER 13, VERSE 17

MEKHILTA DERABBI SHIMON

כִּי קָרוֹב הוּא – *Though it was the shorter way:* [The phrase can be understood to mean "because it was close."] The proximity that the verse refers to is the short time that Israel had to wait before they were given the Torah at Mount Sinai. [This event is what is meant by "it."] Another interpretation: What was close was the punishment that awaited Pharaoh and the Egyptians. **כִּי אָמַר אֱלֹהִים פֶּן־יִנָּחֵם הָעָם** – *Thought God, "they will change their minds":* Said the Holy One, blessed be He: If I lead Israel on a direct route through the land of the Philistines, Israel will seize their fields and vineyards and neglect their Torah study. Instead, I will guide the people through the wilderness for forty years. There they will eat manna and drink water from the [miraculous] well, while the Torah develops their souls. Based on this, Rabbi Shimon bar Yoḥai taught: Torah can only be expounded by those who eat manna or by those to whom priestly tithes are given [that is, by people who need not worry about their sustenance]. Another interpretation for God's decision is as follows: When the Canaanites heard that Israel was on its way to conquer their land, they immediately burned all of their seeds, cut down their saplings, destroyed their buildings and stopped up their springs. Said the Holy One, blessed be He: Did I promise their ancestors to bring Israel into a wasteland? No, I guaranteed them *houses full of all good things that you did not provide* (Deuteronomy 6:11). Therefore, I will detain the people in the desert and wait while the Canaanites restore what they have wrecked. **בִּרְאֹתָם מִלְחָמָה** – *If the people face war:* God wished to protect Israel from an Amalekite attack. Indeed, we later read: *Then the Amalekites came down, and the Canaanites who dwelt in that hill, and smote them* (Numbers 14:45). Alternatively, the verse refers to the fate of the tribe of Efrayim, which left Egypt ahead of the rest of the nation [for they had miscalculated the period of the exile. According to the midrash, the tribe was slaughtered by the Canaanites; see I Chronicles 7:20–22]. God feared that the nation would be faced with the bodies of their compatriots strewn across the fields and return to Egypt.

PESIKTA DERAV KAHANA

כִּי קָרוֹב הוּא – *Though it was the shorter way:* Although it had only been a short time since the Canaanites had acted righteously toward our forefather Yaakov, as the verse states: *And when the inhabitants of the land, the Canaanites, saw the mourning a the floor of Atad, they said, This is a grievous mourning to Egypt* (Genesis 50:11).

BERESHIT RABBA

אֶרֶץ פְּלִשְׁתִּים – *The land of the Philistines:* Rabbi Yosei son of Rabbi Ḥanina said: *My enemies have great vigor* (Psalms 38:20). In the time allotted to Avraham as seven generations, the

פרשת בשלח
PARASHAT BESHALAḤ

THE **TIME** OF THE **SAGES**

1ST CENTURY BCE	
1ST CENTURY CE	PHILO, 25 BCE – 50 CE
2ND CENTURY	
3RD CENTURY	HALAKHIC MIDRASHIM, 3RD CENTURY (MEKHILTA, SIFRA, SIFREI)
4TH CENTURY	TALMUD YERUSHALMI, 3RD – 5TH CENTURY
	TALMUD BAVLI, 3RD – 6TH CENTURY
5TH CENTURY	MIDRASH TANḤUMA, 5TH CENTURY
6TH CENTURY	PESIKTA DERAV KAHANA, 5TH – 6TH CENTURY
7TH CENTURY	
8TH CENTURY	AVOT DERABBI NATAN, 7TH – 9TH CENTURY
9TH CENTURY	MIDRASH RABBA, 5TH – 12TH CENTURY
	PESIKTA RABBATI, 9TH CENTURY
	AGGADAT BERESHIT, 9TH CENTURY
10TH CENTURY	MIDRASH TEHILLIM, 10TH – 11TH CENTURY
11TH CENTURY	MIDRASH LEKAḤ TOV, 11TH CENTURY
12TH CENTURY	MIDRASH SEKHEL TOV, 1139
	MIDRASH AGGADA, 12TH – 13TH CENTURY
13TH CENTURY	YALKUT SHIMONI, 13TH CENTURY

that authors make to midrashim and other commentaries. Still, we have made a supreme effort to provide citations of talmudic passages, and of course biblical verses, quoted or referred to in the material included here.

Yedidya Naveh, Managing Editor
Jerusalem, 5780 (2019)

provided citations for those works not organized sequentially, as well as for commentaries originally composed on verses other than the one under discussion. These citations can be found outside of the final punctuation at the end of the excerpt in question.

Our translation has generally relied upon the Hebrew text found in the Bar-Ilan Responsa Project and the online compendia Sefaria and AlHatorah. org, as well as the standard printed editions of commentaries not found in any of these. The Responsa Project contains more than one edition of several midrashim (Midrash Tanḥuma, Midrash Rabba, and Avot DeRabbi Natan). For these works, our citations should be understood as referring to the standard editions published in Vilna and Warsaw unless otherwise indicated. Aside from this, please note:

- Text from Mekhilta DeRabbi Shimon is understood to be from the Epstein-Melamed edition unless otherwise indicated.
- Excerpts from Ibn Ezra are almost always taken from his Long Commentary on Exodus, and we have marked those instances where we quote from his Short Commentary.
- Passages from Philo are quoted with permission from *Torah from Alexandria: Philo as a Biblical Commentator,* edited by Rabbi Michael Leo Samuel (New York: Kodesh Press, 2015).
- Selected commentaries of Rabbi Joseph B. Soloveitchik are printed with permission from *Chumash Mesoras HaRav,* edited by Dr. Arnold Lustiger (New York: OU Press and Ohr Publishing Inc., 2017).
- The commentaries of the Lubavitcher Rebbe are quoted from *The Torah, with an Interpolated Translation and Commentary Based on the Works of the Lubavitcher Rebbe,* edited by Rabbi Chaim Nochum Cunin and Rabbi Moshe Yaakov Wisnefsky (New York: Kehot Publication Society, 2017).
- The commentaries of Nehama Leibowitz are translated, with generous permission, from the Hebrew *Iyyunim Ḥadashim BeSefer Shemot* (14th edition), published by the World Zionist Organization Department for Torah Education and Culture in the Diaspora.

While we have thus done our best to aid the reader in finding and consulting the original Hebrew text of the commentaries we have translated, we emphasize that this is not a critical edition, and the scope and readership of the series do not permit us to fully cite every allusion and internal reference

often assume the reader's knowledge of other biblical episodes, midrashim, or Hebrew grammar beyond what might be expected from the English-speaking public today. To ensure clarity, we have therefore interpolated brief editor's notes where we deemed it necessary, setting them off from the original text in square brackets.

Throughout Jewish history, the text of the Tanakh has been viewed as the apogee of the Hebrew language. For many commentators, especially those of the Middle Ages, it served as a fountain of language from which they drew numerous idioms and phrases. The result is that the Hebrew text of many commentaries is shot through with snippets of biblical prose or poetry to such an extent that almost every sentence can be viewed as a quote or allusion. Marking and citing all of these would make for a cluttered translation and would hinder rather than enhance the reader's understanding. We have therefore opted to cite only those quotes which are brought by the author as explicit evidence to further the point being made, and not those that supply only a turn of phrase.

The Hebrew side of this volume contains a complete and unabridged translation of Rashi's commentary. For those who wish to follow the *parasha* on the English side of the book, we have also reprinted many of Rashi's explanations alongside those of the other classic commentators. This will allow the reader to compare Rashi's interpretation to those of Rashbam, Ibn Ezra, and others, as well as appreciate how Rashi's commentary often serves to define the issues that will be addressed by later exegetes.

The text of the commentaries is of course abridged. We have not included ellipses to mark every point where text has been omitted, to maintain a clutter-free translation. However, we have included ellipses at points where the subject of discussion would otherwise appear to have changed abruptly and inexplicably, to save the reader confusion. We have also not adhered strictly to the original heading, or s.v. (*dibbur hamat-ḥil*) of every text, changing it in instances where it would help to focus the reader on those words that are the actual subject of discussion, and adding it to texts that did not originally have it.

Most of the commentaries that we quote in this series were originally organized by chapter and verse. Therefore, anyone who wishes to consult the original Hebrew text of a given commentary can simply open to the verse in question. However, not all sources are organized this way. The midrashim in particular are often ordered loosely; an important interpretation of a verse in Exodus might be found in a midrash on Deuteronomy. For the reader's convenience in locating the original Hebrew source, we have

A NOTE ON THE TRANSLATION

The terse writing style prevalent in Jewish scholarship over most of history can be difficult for the modern reader to decipher. Since our goal in the *Koren Mikraot HaDorot* series is to make thousands of years of Torah commentary accessible to a modern, English-speaking audience, we have opted for a relatively loose translation style that accurately presents the content of the Hebrew commentary while not necessarily mirroring its exact syntax. We have also resorted occasionally to paraphrase in instances where a literal translation would be opaque in English. As any student of Torah exegesis will recognize, draconian insistence on a word-for-word translation would result in an English text that was unreadable and that preserved neither the clarity nor the majesty of the original Hebrew.

Many of the commentaries' discussions focus on the meanings of words and phrases that are ambiguous in the Hebrew text of the *parasha*. The beautiful new translation of the Torah by Rabbi Lord Jonathan Sacks that we include here often dispels these ambiguities in the interest of clarity, necessarily coming down on one side or the other of a disagreement between commentators. The reader of the commentaries should therefore view the Torah translation presented here as one possible reading of the often-cryptic Hebrew original. In a similar vein, the significance of certain interpretations may seem unclear, or their points obvious, until one encounters another commentary with a starkly different read of the same verse. These contrasts, and the realization that themes and meanings we thought to be clear are actually ambiguous and multifaceted, are the essence of *The Koren Mikraot HaDorot*.

We have, as far as possible, allowed each text to speak for itself, and have left editorial comments to a minimum. Nevertheless, the commentaries

- Economy of selection: In compiling the excerpts used in this work, we have gone through the authors' works and isolated those sections which most directly address the particular question, issue, or difficulty that confronted the scholar.
- Objectivity of presentation: This book presents ideas of the commentaries authentically, never censoring them or smoothing them over in light of our own positions or perspectives. We always strove to faithfully transmit the legal, conceptual, social, and ethical messages of the commentators.

The modern world constantly challenges us as individuals, as a society, and as communal leaders, teachers, and parents. The values and culture of the society that surrounds us force thinking Jews to seriously consider and reconsider their ideas and priorities on a regular basis as we struggle to find the correct path through life. Furthermore, we constantly must ask ourselves what teachings we wish to transmit to future generations. It is our hope that the *Koren Mikraot HaDorot* project will help guide its readers as they grapple with these very real problems. The world of Torah commentary is wide and deep beyond measure. It contains innumerable answers to the questions that face the individual, the family, the generation, and indeed all of humanity.

Rabbi Shai Finkelstein, Editor-in-Chief
Jerusalem, 5780 (2019)

interpretations. *The Koren Mikraot HaDorot* instead presents a plethora of exegetical contributions, with more than forty scholars spanning Jewish teachings from the past two thousand years represented on its pages.

Each volume of the *Koren Mikraot HaDorot* series can be opened from both the right (Hebrew) side and left (English) side. The Hebrew opening side includes the Hebrew and a new English text of the *parasha*, translated by Rabbi Lord Jonathan Sacks, with a full, new translation of Rashi and the *haftarot*. The English opening side contains the bulk of the commentaries, and is divided into four parts: The first, THE TIME OF THE SAGES, comprises commentaries from antiquity – ranging from Philo to the Yalkut Shimoni. These figures lived mainly in the land of Israel, Egypt, and Babylonia. The second, THE CLASSIC COMMENTATORS, contains interpretations from the Middle Ages – starting from Rav Se'adya Gaon and Rashi and continuing through time to the work of Rabbi Shlomo Efrayim of Luntschitz, author of the *Keli Yakar*. The authors included here represent the rich traditions of both Sephardic (Spanish and North African) and Ashkenazic (central and eastern European) schools of exegesis. The third section, CONFRONTING MODERNITY, offers the work of both Old World and New World scholars who lived between the eighteenth and twentieth centuries. Before each of these three sections we include a time line that specifies the chronological relationships between the commentators and the places they lived.

In the final section, THE BIBLICAL IMAGINATION, we provide three in-depth investigations of particular ideas through the writings of the various commentaries. There are several goals to these essays. First, we aim to reveal common threads weaving across the generations of Torah scholarship. Second, we hope to illustrate how the various authors were influenced by their lives and times, and that the lessons they transmitted to their communities reflected their environments. Finally, each essay highlights for the reader some central issues that the commentaries have grappled with. We trust that this tool will facilitate the reader's understanding of the words of the commentaries themselves.

Three principles have governed the decision making in our work on *The Koren Mikraot HaDorot*:
- Chronological order: We have striven to sketch out the historical development of Torah exegesis, an enterprise that has occupied innumerable communities of Jews in far-flung lands for centuries.

EDITOR'S INTRODUCTION

Over the course of millennia, the Jewish people have watched while the surrounding society and its values have changed unceasingly. For the Jews, the steadfast response to an evolving world has always been the study of Torah, specifically engagement with the weekly *parasha*. Devotees of Jewish learning have always looked to the weekly Torah portion for spiritual and intellectual guidance through life's challenges. And in every generation, commentaries on the Ḥumash have debated the precise interpretation of the verses therein. These scholars have continuously asked what message God is trying to convey to Israel and the world through the Torah's narratives and laws. Their explanations have struggled to identify the correct ways to apply its lessons to our daily lives.

Throughout, all these authors have approached the Torah text from their own unique perspectives, shaped in no small measure by the eras and environments they lived in. Naturally, the pantheon of commentaries present widely different styles in their writings. Occasionally the commentators will subject a particular verse to piercing scrutiny as a self-contained unit. At other times they present interpretations that seem to stray from the straightforward meaning of the text. Ultimately, all commentaries demand that a verse provide readers with theological meaning and direction for communal and social life.

Recognition of the wisdom embedded in the vast literature of commentary on the Torah spanning the various eras of Jewish history planted the seeds of the project whose fruit you now hold. We have called this publication **Mikraot HaDorot** – Readings of the Generations. This window into the world of Torah commentaries is not simply an upgrade of the classical *Mikraot Gedolot* collections, which give readers merely a handful of familiar

Our design, editing, typesetting, and proofreading staff, including Tani Bayer, Esther Be'er, Debbie Ismailoff, Estie Dishon, Tomi Mager, and Carolyn Budow Ben David, enabled an attractive, user-friendly, and accurate edition of these works.

> "One silver basin" (Numbers 7:13) was brought as a symbol of the Torah, which has been likened to wine, as the verse states: "And drink of the wine which I have mingled" (Proverbs 9:5). Because it is customary to drink wine in a basin – as we see in the verse "that drink wine in basins" (Amos 6:6) – he therefore brought a basin. "Of seventy shekels, after the shekel of the sanctuary" (Numbers 7:13). Why? Because just as the numerical value of "wine" [*yayin*] is seventy, so there are seventy modes of expounding the Torah. (Bemidbar Rabba 13:16)

Each generation produces exceptional rabbinic, intellectual leadership. It has been our purpose to enable all Jews to taste the wine of those generations, in the hope of expanding the breadth and depth of their knowledge. Torah is our greatest treasure, and we need the wisdom of those generations to better understand this bountiful gift from God. We hope that we at Koren can deepen that understanding for all who seek it.

Matthew Miller, Publisher
Jerusalem, 5780 (2019)

Opening from the English side presents four sections:
- **THE TIME OF THE SAGES** – includes commentaries from the Second Temple period and the talmudic period
- **THE CLASSIC COMMENTATORS** – quotes selected explanations by Rashi as well as most of the commentators found in traditional *Mikraot Gedolot*
- **CONFRONTING MODERNITY** – selects commentaries from the eighteenth century to the close of the twentieth century
- **THE BIBLICAL IMAGINATION** – features essays surveying some of the broader conceptual ideas as a supplement to the linear, text-based commentary

The first three of these sections each feature the relevant verses, in Hebrew and English, on the page alongside their respective commentaries, in chronological order, providing the reader with a single window onto the text without excessive page turning.

In addition to being a valuable resource in a Jewish home or synagogue library, we conceived of these volumes as a weekly accompaniment in the synagogue. There is scope for the reader to study each *parasha* on a weekly basis in preparation for the reading on Shabbat. One may select a particular group of commentators for study that week, or perhaps alternate between ancient and modern viewpoints. Some readers may choose to delve into the text through verse-by-verse interpretation, while others may prefer a conceptual perspective on the *parasha* as a whole. The broad array of options for learning means this is a series which can be returned to year after year, always presenting new insights and new approaches to understanding the text.

ACKNOWLEDGMENTS

The creation of this book was possible only thanks to the small but exceptional team here at Koren Jerusalem. We are grateful to:
- Rabbi Tzvi Hersh Weinreb, שליט״א, who conceptualized the structure of the project and provides both moral and halakhic leadership at Koren
- Rabbi Shai Finkelstein, whose encyclopedic knowledge of Torah and its interpreters is equaled only by his community leadership, formerly in Memphis and today in Jerusalem
- Rabbi Yedidya Naveh, whose knowledge, organizational skills, and superb leadership brought the disparate elements together
- Rabbi Jonathan Mishkin, translator of the commentaries, who crafted a fluent, accurate, and eloquent English translation

The text of the Torah features the exceptional new translation of Rabbi Lord Jonathan Sacks, together with the celebrated and meticulously accurate Koren Hebrew text. Of course, with the exception of Rashi – for whom we present an entirely new translation in full – the commentaries are selected. We offer this anthology not to limit our reader's exploration but rather as a gateway for further learning of Torah and its commentaries on a broader and deeper level than space here permits. We discuss below how to use this book.

We must thank **Pamela and George Rohr** of New York, who recognized the unique value of *The Koren Mikraot HaDorot* and its ability to communicate historical breadth and context to the reader. For my colleagues here at Koren, we thank you; for the many generations of users who will find this a continuing source of new learning, we are forever in your debt.

We also are indebted to **Zahava and Moshael Straus**, true leaders of this Jewish generation in so many fields, who have invested in the entire book of Shemot. Together, we were thus able to launch this innovative and unique project.

We are honored to acknowledge and thank **Debra and David Magerman**, whose support for the Koren Ḥumash with Rabbi Sacks's exemplary translation and commentary laid the foundation for the core English text of this work.

Finally, I must personally thank **Rabbi Marvin Hier**, with whom I had a special breakfast some years ago at the King David Hotel. During the meal, he raised the problem that so few people knew the writings of Rabbi Joseph B. Soloveitchik and Rabbi Aharon Kotler on the Torah; and I, who had just read some of Philo's work, had the same reaction. From that conversation came the seed for this project.

HOW TO USE *THE KOREN MIKRAOT HADOROT*

The Koren Mikraot HaDorot will be a fifty-five-volume edition of the Ḥumash (one for each *parasha* plus a companion volume). Each of the fifty-four volumes of the *parashot* can be read from right to left (Hebrew opening side), and left to right (English opening side).

Opening from the Hebrew side offers:

- the full Torah text, the translation of Rabbi Sacks, and the full commentary of Rashi in both Hebrew and the new English translation
- all *haftarot* associated with the *parasha* of the volume, including Rosh Ḥodesh and special readings, both in Hebrew and English

PUBLISHER'S PREFACE

The genius of Jewish commentary on the Torah is one of huge and critical import. Jewish life and law for millennia have been directed by our interpretations of the Torah, and each generation has looked to its rabbinic leadership for a deeper understanding of its teachings, its laws, its stories.

For centuries, *Mikraot Gedolot* have been a core part of understanding the Ḥumash; the words of Rashi, Ibn Ezra, Ramban, Rashbam, Ralbag, and other classic commentators illuminate and help us understand the Torah. But traditional editions of *Mikraot Gedolot* present only a slice in time and a small selection of the corpus of Jewish commentators. Almost every generation has produced rabbinic scholars who speak to their times, from Philo and Onkelos two thousand years ago, to Rabbi Joseph B. Soloveitchik, Rabbi Aharon Kotler, the Lubavitcher Rebbe, and Nehama Leibowitz in ours.

The Koren Mikraot HaDorot – Scriptures or Interpretations for the Generations – brings two millennia of Torah commentary into the hands and homes of Jews around the world. Readers will be able not only to encounter the classic commentators, but to gain a much broader sense of the issues that scholars grappled with in their time and the inspiration they drew from the ancient texts. We see, for example, how Philo speaks to an assimilating Greek Jewish audience in first-century Alexandria, and how similar yet different it is from Rabbi Samson Raphael Hirsch's approach to an equally assimilating nineteenth-century German readership; how the perspectives of Rabbi Soloveitchik and Rabbi Kotler differ in a post-Holocaust world; how Rav Se'adya Gaon interpreted the Torah for the Jews of Babylonia. It is an exciting journey through Jewish history via the unchanging words of the Torah.

CONTENTS

Publisher's Preface
xi

Editor's Introduction
xv

A Note on the Translation
xviii

PARASHAT BESHALAḤ WITH COMMENTARIES

THE TIME OF THE SAGES
1

THE CLASSIC COMMENTATORS
71

CONFRONTING MODERNITY
151

THE BIBLICAL IMAGINATION

The Sabbath as a Mark of Love between God and Israel
225

The Splitting of the Sea of Reeds – A Foundational Moment
230

The Prophecy of Miriam
235

FOR THE COMPLETE RASHI AND HAFTARA
TURN TO THE OTHER END OF THIS VOLUME.

Dedicated in memory of

Rabbi Dr. Norman Lamm, זצ"ל

President of Yeshiva University and Expositor of Centrist Orthodoxy
Torah Scholar, Philosopher, Leader, Orator and Rabbi
Beloved Husband, Father, Grandfather and Great Grandfather

תניא אמר רבי מאיר מניין לתחיית המתים מן התורה
שנאמר "אז ישיר משה ובני ישראל את השירה הזאת לה'"
שר לא נאמר אלא ישיר מכאן לתחיית המתים מן התורה

(Sanhedrin 91b)

Who made the words of Torah into a shira "that can heal the sick,
revive weary spirits, [and] elevate downtrodden hearts"
and taught that "Torah is eternity ensconced in music."

The Magerman Family
The Sinensky Family

The Rohr Family Edition of
The Koren Mikraot HaDorot
pays tribute to the memory of

Mr. Sami Rohr ז״ל
ר׳ שמואל ב״ר יהושע אליהו ז״ל

who served his Maker with joy
and whose far-reaching vision, warm open hand, love of Torah,
and love for every Jew were catalysts for the revival and growth of
vibrant Jewish life in the former Soviet Union
and in countless communities the world over

and to the memory of his beloved wife

Mrs. Charlotte Rohr (née Kastner) ע״ה
שרה בת ר׳ יקותיאל יהודה ע״ה

who survived the fires of the Shoah to become
the elegant and gracious matriarch,
first in Colombia and later in the United States,
of three generations of a family
nurtured by her love and unstinting devotion.
She found grace in the eyes of all those whose lives she touched.

Together they merited to see all their children
build lives enriched by faithful commitment
to the spreading of Torah and *Ahavat Yisrael*.

Dedicated with love by
The Rohr Family
NEW YORK, USA

The Koren Mikraot HaDorot, The Rohr Edition
Volume 16: Parashat Beshalaḥ
First Edition, 2020

Koren Publishers Jerusalem Ltd.
POB 4044, Jerusalem 9104001, ISRAEL
POB 8531, New Milford, CT 06776, USA

www.korenpub.com

Torah Translation © 2019, Jonathan Sacks
Koren Tanakh Font © 1962, 2020 Koren Publishers Jerusalem Ltd.

Commentary © Koren Publishers Jerusalem Ltd., except as noted:
Commentaries of Philo, used with permission of Kodesh Press
Commentaries Rabbi Joseph B. Soloveitchik, used with permission of the OU Press
Commentaries of Nehama Leibowitz, used with permission of the World Zionist Organization

Considerable research and expense have gone into the creation of this publication. Unauthorized copying may be considered *geneivat da'at* and breach of copyright law. No part of this publication (content or design, including use of the Koren fonts) may be reproduced, stored in a retrieval system or transmitted in any form or by any means electronic, mechanical, photocopying or otherwise, without the prior written permission of the publisher, except in the case of brief quotations embedded in critical articles or reviews.

The Tanakh translation is excerpted from the Magerman Edition of The Koren Tanakh.

The creation of this work was made possible with the generous support of the Jewish Book Trust Inc.

Printed in ISRAEL

ISBN 978 965 7760 71 0

KMDBS01

THE ROHR FAMILY EDITION

חומש קורן מקראות הדורות
THE KOREN MIKRAOT HADOROT

THE ZAHAVA AND MOSHAEL STRAUS EDITION OF SEFER SHEMOT
פרשת בשלח עם מפרשים
PARASHAT BESHALAḤ WITH COMMENTARIES

TORAH TRANSLATION BY
Rabbi Lord Jonathan Sacks שליט״א

COMMENTARIES COLLECTED AND ABRIDGED BY
Rabbi Shai Finkelstein, EDITOR-IN-CHIEF

COMMENTARIES TRANSLATED BY
Rabbi Jonathan Mishkin

MANAGING EDITOR
Rabbi Yedidya Naveh

•

KOREN PUBLISHERS JERUSALEM

חומש קורן מקראות הדורות
THE KOREN MIKRAOT HADOROT

פרשת בשלח
PARASHAT BESHALAḤ

KOREN